Psychology for Teaching

W9-BAO-057

changing the way the world learns

To get extra value from this book for no additional cost, go to:

http://www.thomson.com/wadsworth.html

thomson.com is the World Wide Web site for Wadsworth/ITP and is your direct source to dozens of on-line resources. *thomson.com* helps you find out about supplements, experiment with demonstration software, search for a job, and send e-mail to many of our authors. You can even preview new publications and exciting new technologies.

thomson.com: *It's where you'll find us in the future.*

A bear ~~always usually some-times rarely never always faces the front will not commit him-self just now faces the future~~ is politically correct

Psychology for Teaching

NINTH EDITION

Guy R. Lefrançois

University of Alberta

Wadsworth Publishing Company
I(T)P® An International Thomson Publishing Company

Belmont, CA ▾ Albany, NY ▾ Bonn ▾ Boston ▾
Cincinnati ▾ Detroit ▾ Johannesburg ▾ London ▾
Madrid ▾ Melbourne ▾ Mexico City ▾ New York ▾
Paris ▾ San Francisco ▾ Singapore ▾ Tokyo ▾
Toronto ▾ Washington

For my first teacher, my father,
who taught me to love books and learning,

and for my mother,
who taught me to love people and life.

Education Editor: *Sabra Horne*
Assistant Editor: *Claire Masson*
Editorial Assistant: *Kate Barrett*
Project Editor: *Angela Mann*
Text and Cover Designer: *Andrew Ogus*
Print Buyer: *Karen Hunt*
Copy Editor: *Jennifer Gordon*
Permissions Editor: *Jeanne Bosschart*
Cartoonists: *Tony Hall and Jeff Littlejohn*
Technical Illustrators: *Teresa Roberts, Natalie Hill*
Cover Illustration: *Greg Moraes*
Compositor: *Fog Press*
Printer: *Fairfield*

COPYRIGHT © 1997 by Wadsworth Publishing Company
A Division of International Thomson Publishing Inc.
I(T)P The ITP logo is a registered trademark under license.

This book is printed on
acid-free recycled paper.

Printed in the United States of America
1 2 3 4 5 6 7 8 9 10

For more information, contact Wadsworth Publishing Company, 10 Davis Drive, Belmont, CA 94002, or electronically at
http://www.thomson.com/wadsworth.html

International Thomson Publishing Europe
Berkshire House 168-173
High Holborn
London, WC1V 7AA, England

Thomas Nelson Australia
102 Dodds Street
South Melbourne 3205
Victoria, Australia

Nelson Canada
1120 Birchmount Road
Scarborough, Ontario
Canada M1K 5G4

International Thomson Publishing GmbH
Königswinterer Strasse 418
53227 Bonn, Germany

International Thomson Editores
Campos Eliseos 385, Piso 7
Col. Polanco
11560 México D.F. México

International Thomson Publishing Asia
221 Henderson Road
#05-10 Henderson Building
Singapore 0315

International Thomson Publishing Japan
Hirakawacho Kyowa Building, 3F
2-2-1 Hirakawacho
Chiyoda-ku, Tokyo 102, Japan

International Thomson Publishing Southern Africa
Building 18, Constantia Park
240 Old Pretoria Road
Halfway House, 1685 South Africa

All rights reserved. No part of this work covered by the copyright hereon may be reproduced or used in any form or by any means—graphic, electronic, or mechanical, including photocopying, recording, taping, or information storage and retrieval systems—without the written permission of the publisher.

Library of Congress Cataloging-in-Publication Data

Lefrançois, Guy R.
    Psychology for teaching: a bear is politically correct/Guy R.
  Lefrançois. — 9th ed.
        p.   cm.
    Includes bibliographical references (p.   ) and index.
    ISBN 0-534-50678-X
    1. Educational psychology   2. Teaching—Psychological aspects.
  3. Learning, Psychology of.   I. Title.
  LB1051.L568   1997
  370.15-dc20   96-8707
                                            CIP

BRIEF CONTENTS

CONTENTS

A visual guide to

Psychology for Teaching

NINTH EDITION

Dear Reader:

This is a basic text in educational psychology—a psychology for teaching. Its goal is to help you become the best teacher you can be. To this end, it presents the most useful research and theory in educational psychology clearly, accurately, and in an engaging way.

Good teaching is far more than just telling. It requires motivating, organizing, previewing, showing, illustrating, explaining, evaluating, reviewing, inspiring, perhaps even standing on one's head or dancing little jigs while singing songs in foreign languages. *Psychology for Teaching* tries to be a good teacher. It illustrates, shows and compares; it evaluates, reviews, and previews; maybe it even inspires a little. And on at least one occasion that I can think of, it almost stands on its metaphoric head.

On the following pages you will be guided through some of the features that are designed to make this ninth edition of *Psychology for Teaching* the most effective teaching/learning tool it can be—and you the best teacher you can be.

To help you organize your study,
at the beginning of every chapter . . .

◄ OUTLINES tell you at a glance where the chapter is going

PREVIEW

Of the theories that have attempted to explain human development, those that look at the growth of mind are among the most important for teachers. This chapter describes two of these theories—Piaget's and Vygotsky's—and considers their educational implications. It looks as well at the development and significance of gender roles, and at Erikson's description of personality change through childhood.

◄ CHAPTER PREVIEWS serve as advance organizers by highlighting the most important concepts in the chapter

FOCUS QUESTIONS phrase the ► chapter's objectives in the form of questions that direct your attention and focus your study

VIGNETTES lead you into the chapter ► with a brief, sometimes humorous, always relevant story

FOCUS QUESTIONS

► What are gender roles and gender typing?

► Are psychological sex differences real?

► What is psychosocial development?

► According to Piaget, how can human development be described?

► What does sensorimotor development mean? preoperational development? concrete operations? formal operations?

► What is Vygotsky's cultural/cognitive theory?

When an infant was about to be born among the Mundugumor of New Guinea, the parents would adorn themselves with their most prized clothing and jewelry. The father, should he be so lucky as to have one, would wear a skirt of brilliant parrot feathers and he would hang plumes and beetle shells around his neck; the mother would decorate herself with bracelets of wild orchids and perhaps she would wear a necklace of smoothly polished dog teeth. Through her nostrils she would run the long white leg bone of a wild guinea fowl. That others in the village looked at the parents in admiration would bode well for the child.

The Mundugumor knew that this business of dressing well for a birth is extremely important. But they also knew that other matters that they could not so easily control are even more important. For example, the Mundugumor knew without any doubt that only infants who are born with their umbilical cords wrapped around their necks have any chance of becoming great artists. And among the Mundugumor, to be a great artist is a lucky and wonderful thing. Amazingly, the Mundugumor were right: Infants not born with their umbilical cords coiled around their necks simply did not become great artists—to absolutely no one's surprise.

I and my various siblings were born at home—in a house perhaps a little more sturdy than a New Guinea hut. And while it isn't clear that the midwife and the grandmother who assisted our various births had medical training or knowledge demonstrably more advanced than that of the Mundugumor, in the end that probably made little difference. That my parents were more likely to absentmindedly crush beetles and kick them aside than to collect their carapaces and make necklaces of them may not have mattered all that much either. And that my mother was not fond of leg bones in her nostrils or dog-tooth ornaments may have been as much of a relief for my father as it surely was for our old dog, busily chewing said bones with said teeth.

When we were born, my siblings and I, our parents were not particularly concerned with the positions of our umbilical cords—unless, of course, the cord was wrapped too dangerously tightly around our scrawny necks. You see, my parents knew without any doubt whatsoever that the position of our umbilical cords at birth had absolutely nothing to do with whether or not we would become great artists. Besides, where I was born and raised, becoming a great artist was not a common ambition.

Still, my parents were very much like the Mundugumor in their attempts to foretell our futures at birth. No, they didn't look at the positions of our umbilical cords. Instead, they looked for an appendage between our legs. Why? Because based on the presence or absence of this appendage, my parents could predict with stunning accuracy a great many of our eventual characteristics.

GENDER ROLES

My parents knew that those of us with the appendage would be fast and strong and tough and just a little aggressive (it's not a bad thing in this dog-eat-dog world, you know). And those without, well, they'd be gentler and more emotional and not nearly so aggressive, and they'd want to help out in the house, but no way would they be interested in chopping wood or hunting and fishing.

My parents were heir to a vast body of beliefs dealing with the most likely characteris-

Throughout the text . . .

◄ **BOXED INSERTS** present high-interest enrichment material.

FIGURES AND ILLUSTRATIONS summarize important findings and clarify main points. ▼

◄ **CASES** describing actual classroom interactions are used to illustrate practical applications of psychology for teaching.

SORTING IT ALL OUT COGNITIVELY

The following are some common, educationally relevant terms in the new cognitive sciences:

Metacognition Knowing about knowing; our knowledge and beliefs about our own cognitive processes and our attempt to play the game of cognition well—that is, so that we learn and remember well. Meta-cognitive knowledge is what permits us to select different approaches for learning and remembering; it allows us to monitor our cognitive activities and assess the likelihood of success; it suggests alternatives when necessary.

Cognitive Strategies The tools of cognitive behavior; goal-directed sequences of actions

such as rehearsing, organizing, or elaborating; what we actually do to learn and remember.

Learning/Thinking Strategies A global term that includes both metacognition and cognitive strategies. The entire range of activities involved in learning and thinking.

Summary Learning/thinking strategies include metacognitive and cognitive strategies. Meta-cognitive skills are executive (control) skills; cognitive skills are nonexecutive (applied) skills.

Illustration of the Relationships Between Metacognition and Cognition I decide to learn the meanings of common, educationally relevant terms in the

new cognitive sciences (setting a goal of which I suspect I am capable: a metacognitive experience). I begin to read this box (cognitive activity). I stop after two lines; I have a vague feeling that I have missed something (metacognitive experience). I read the lines again (cognitive activity). I sense that I am understanding (metacognition). I continue reading. I repeat each separate definition mentally once or twice (rehearsal, a cognitive strategy). Something tells me I am learning (metacognitive experience). I finish. I look at each term and silently repeat the definition (cognitive activity). I am satisfied that I understand and will remember until tomorrow's quiz (metacognition).

---

our conceptions of intelligence have begun to change dramatically. We have begun to accept the view that among the important components of intelligent activity are cognitive functions that are largely learned, not inherited.

Haywood and Switzky (1986) make a similar point. Intelligent behavior, they assert, requires two things: native ability (what we think of as innate intelligence) and cognitive functions. The important point is that whereas native ability is, by definition, genetic and therefore unmodifiable except by extreme measures, cognitive functions are acquired. Does it not follow that if they are learned, they can also be taught?

The simple answer is yes. And there is increasing evidence that this learning need not occur only incidentally—or even accidentally—as a byproduct of school activities, the purposes

of which are far removed from teaching students how to learn. A mushrooming new field of research involves looking for ways in which students can be taught not only the cognitive skills of rehearsing, elaborating, and organizing, but also the metacognitive skills involved in monitoring their own levels of comprehension and in making other important decisions about their cognitive activities and their personal capabilities. Psychologists have been increasingly successful at discovering the rules, the strategies, and the objectives of this game of cognition that all of us are called upon to master. And, as a result, today's students may be better players tomorrow than they would otherwise have been.

Researchers who have developed and investigated programs designed specifically to

CHAPTER 5 THINKING AND REMEMBERING

FIGURE 7.6 Characteristics of children identified as high and low on measures of intelligence and of divergent thinking (creativity). Based on studies reported by Wallach and Kogan, 1965.

THE CONNECTIONS BETWEEN CREATIVITY AND INTELLIGENCE

Because measured intelligence is often used to select gifted children for special programs, it's important to determine the relationship between intelligence and creativity.

One of the classic studies in this area is that reported by Getzels and Jackson (1962), who found that creative students were not necessarily the most intelligent—although they often achieved as well in school as those who were more intelligent. Interestingly, however, the highly creative students were not as well liked by the teachers.

Unfortunately, findings from the Getzels and Jackson study cannot easily be generalized. The average IQ in the school from which the subjects were chosen was an astounding 132. The average IQ for the groups described as "high creative, low IQ" was a more-than-respectable 127. With such a limited range in intelligence test scores, it is doubtful that any relationship between creativity and intelligence would be found, even if it existed. Besides, any findings from a study such as this might well apply only to especially intelligent children.

A related study (Wallach & Kogan, 1965) also identified four groups of students classified as high or low on intelligence and creativity, respectively. The purpose of this study was to identify characteristics that might be different among the four groups. Results of the study are summarized in Figure 7.6. They indicate that

highly creative but less intelligent students are most frustrated with school and that highly intelligent but less creative students are addicted to school and well liked by their teachers. Keep in mind, however, that these four groups represent extremes of measured intelligence and creativity. The vast majority of students are not extreme. In addition, these general descriptions of school adjustment and personality characteristics are just that—general descriptions. Even with groups as highly select as these, there are numerous individual exceptions.

That there is a close relationship between intelligence and creativity seems clear, as is evident in the correlations between the two (Maker, 1993). That is, those who are highly intelligent are also more likely to be highly creative—and vice versa. But what is also clear is that intelligence tests *by themselves* are not a very good way of identifying creative children. The reason for this, as Fuchs-Beauchamp, Karnes, and Johnson (1993) found following a study of 496 children, is that although measured intelligence correlates very highly with measured creativity for the general population of schoolchildren, this is not the case for those whose measured IQ is 120 or more. At that level of intelligence, other factors such as motivation, persistence, home background, personality traits, and the individual's patterns of intellectual strengths and weaknesses become more important. One important approach to identifying these patterns is represented by Guilford's model of intellectual functioning.

262 PART FOUR DIVERSITY AND TEACHING

Disposition. For example, there may be an unfortunate change in Jenna's eagerness to participate in class activities following not only Ms. Swann's refusal to allow her to do so, but also her loud scolding for the *may I-can I* grammatical error. This change is also an example of learning, but in this case it involves changes in the learner's **disposition**—that is, in the person's inclination to do or not to do something—rather than immediately observable changes in actual behavior. Changes in disposition have to do with motivation. Such changes cannot always be observed but are no less real or important.

Capability. Learning involves not only changes in disposition but also changes in **capability**—that is, changes in the skills or knowledge required to do something. Like changes in disposition, changes in capability are not always observed directly. For instance, in Ms. Swann's class, there will probably be many other students who will also have learned to make quotation marks and to place them "around the

words that come right out of Mr. Brown's mouth." But, like Jenna, most will not be given an opportunity to demonstrate this learning immediately. To determine whether students' dispositions or capabilities have changed following instruction, teachers need to give them an opportunity to engage in the relevant behavior. The inference that dispositions or capabilities have changed—in other words, that learning has occurred—will always be based on **performance.**

Performance. If instruction affects learners in such a way that their behavior (their performance) after instruction is observably different from that before instruction, we can conclude that learning has occurred. As we saw, however, learning often involves changes in both capabilities and dispositions that will not be evident in performance until learners are placed in a situation requiring the relevant performance.

Psychologists sometimes distinguish among three kinds of learning based upon the type of performance involved. Thus, learning that involves muscular coordination and physical

---

disposition An inclination or a tendency to do (or not to do) something; an aspect of motivation.

capability A capacity to do something. To be capable is to have the necessary knowledge and skills.

performance Actual behavior. The inference that learning has occurred is typically based on observed changes in performance.

CASE: THE TALKING MARKS

THE PLACE: Lynn Swann's Second-Grade Class
THE SITUATION: A punctuation lesson on quotation marks

MS. SWANN: And what we have to do is put the talking marks around the words that come right out of Mr. Brown's mouth. (demonstrating with a cartoon character who has just said, "Here's my dog.")

TYLER: Can I do it, Ms. Swann? Can I?

MS. SWANN: May I, Tyler. It's *may* I. Yes you *may* and we'll see if you *can*. (Ms. Swann erases the quotation marks. Tyler takes the green pen

and makes a pair of recognizable opening and closing quotation marks. The children have already practiced making these "talking marks.")

MS. SWANN: Very good, Tyler. I see that you *can* do it.

JENNA: Can I do it too? Can I?

MS. SWANN: Weren't you paying any attention at all, Jenna. It's *may*! May, *not can*. No, you may not do it right now. We have to move along because it's going to be lunch time soon. (the lesson continues . . .)

Every chapter includes a number ▶ of CONCEPT SUMMARIZING TABLES that organize and simplify important ideas.

TABLE 6.1 COGNITIVE STRATEGIES RELATED TO THE FIVE PROCESSES IN GAGNÉ'S INFORMATION PROCESSING MODEL

LEARNING PROCESS	COGNITIVE STRATEGY	LEARNING PROCESS	COGNITIVE STRATEGY
Selective Perception	Highlighting	Semantic Encoding	Concept maps
	Underlining		Taxonomies
	Advance organizers		Analogies
	Adjunct questions		Rules/Productions
	Outlining		Schemas
Rehearsal	Paraphrasing	Retrieval	Mnemonics
	Note taking		Imagery
	Imagery	Executive Control	Metacognitive strategies
	Outlining		
	Chunking		

Source: Based on *Principles of Instructional Design* (4th ed.) by Robert M. Gagné, Leslie J. Briggs, and Walter W. Wager. Copyright © 1992 by Holt, Rinehart and Winston, Inc. Reproduced by permission of the publisher.

describes as being involved in learning, along with examples of specific cognitive strategies that can contribute to each of these processes. Many of these strategies are simple and straightforward (underlining and highlighting, for example), and the teacher might not need to do more than mention them. Others are more complex (the use of mnemonics or of metacognitive strategies) and might need to be systematically developed.

Table 6.2 summarizes Robert Gagné's classification of learning outcomes and of external conditions that appear to facilitate these outcomes. Clearly, knowledge of both conditions

the direction of cognitive explanations and their usefulness for instruction. "Learning," he explains, "is something that takes place inside a person's head—in the brain" (Gagné & Driscoll, 1988, p. 3).*

As a primarily cognitive approach, Gagné's theory shares a number of beliefs and assumptions with two other cognitive theories that also have tremendously important instructional implications: the theories of Jerome Bruner and David Ausubel (discussed later in this chapter). Among these common beliefs and assumptions are the following:

In your school there may well be a Beethoven or a Mozart, a Shakespeare or a Neruda—or the next world chess champion—whose special talents remain dormant and unrecognized. That not all our inherent abilities become actual may have something to do with our schooling.

he behavioristic bear believes learn- takes place *outside* the head, in in the brain?

ot readily admit to being a behav- ld be misleading to imply that hat learning takes place somewhere cognitive psychologists emphasize de the head and look there for their rast, behaviorists consider it more vents outside the head.

It may be that we still don't know very much about teaching gifted and talented children. Although current educational practice and beliefs typically insist that identifying and teaching those who have disabilities requires special training, we remain strangely ambivalent about what should be done to identify and teach those who are highly gifted. As a result, in our schools there may be many Raphaels, Da Vincis, Mozarts, and Einsteins unrecognized and undeveloped, disguised as ordinary people, totally unaware of their inherent abilities. Only in the right circumstances and with the right environmental demands will these talents become functional. Perhaps it would help if schools demanded more evaluation, implication, divergent thinking, and so on.

MAIN POINTS

At the end of each ▶ chapter MAIN POINT summaries provide a comprehensive review of the principal ideas in each chapter. These can be an excellent tool for study and review.

1. There are three basic views of intelligence: the psychometric (based on measurement concepts), the Piagetian (based on child-environment interaction), and the information processing (based on cognitive processes).

2. Psychometrically, intelligence is seen as an adaptive quality sometimes defined in terms of what intelligence tests measure, or in terms of an underlying general ability (g) that is merely potential or that might be manifested in behavior. Cattell describes fluid abilities (basic, nonverbal, and unaffected by experience) and crystallized abilities (primarily verbal, highly influenced by culture and education). Das describes an informa-

tion processing theory of intelligence (PASS, involving planning, attention, and simultaneous and successive processing).

3. Sternberg's information-processing view of intelligence includes a contextual subtheory (intelligence is defined in terms of adaptation to a specific environmental context) and a three-component subtheory: metacomponents (processes involved in selecting cognitive activities, monitoring them, and evaluating their results); performance components (activities actually used in carrying out cognitive tasks); and knowledge acquisition components (activities involved in acquiring new information).

4. Gardner describes seven unrelated, multiple intelligences: logical-mathematical, linguistic, musical, spatial, bodily kinesthetic, interpersonal, and intrapersonal.

5. A correlation coefficient is an index of relationship between variables. It is a function of covariation—not of causal relatedness. Intelligence tests typically correlate quite well with school achievement. Conventional measures of intelligence do not measure innate capacity so much as the extent to which the individual has profited from past learning experiences. In addition, they are less than perfectly valid (do not always measure only what they purport to measure) or reliable (do not always measure consistently); they typically do not tap a number of important qualities, such as interpersonal skills, creativity, and athletic ability; and many are biased against social and ethnic minorities.

6. Intelligence tests usually yield an IQ score ranging from perhaps 50 to 160 and averaging about 100 in an unselected population. They are ordinarily group or individual tests. Individual tests require trained testers, consume a great deal of time, and are consequently far more expensive, but they are more valid and reliable for important educational decisions.

7. The SOMPA (System of Multicultural Pluralistic Assessment) uses a collection of measures to assess biological and social normality and to derive an estimated learning potential (ELP) score for minority samples.

8. Common myths about the IQ is that it is fixed, constant, accurately measured by tests that are fair, and extremely important. Measured IQ does correlate highly with success.

9. Both creativity and intelligence appear to be a function of the interaction between heredity and environment. Family size and configuration also play a role, as do ethnic background and social class. None of these factors necessarily causes high or low intelligence; they are merely related to manifested intelligence. The rubber-band hypothesis is an analogy that compares innate potential for learning to a rubber band: It can be stretched by a good environment, but it will shrivel in a poorer environment.

10. Creativity is defined in various, apparently contradictory ways. Much of the contradiction disappears when the creative product, process, and person are considered separately.

11. Creative, talented, and gifted individuals are often identified in terms of performance on measures of intelligence (for example, an IQ of 130 or more), teacher, self, or peer ratings, or performance on creativity tests (for example, the Torrance Tests of Creative Ability).

12. It is likely that relatively high intelligence is required for superior creative effort. Above a certain point, however, personality and social factors are probably more important than purely intellectual ones.

13. Guilford's model describes human intellectual functioning in terms of operations (major intellectual processes such as knowing and remembering) that are applied to content (cognitive information in the form of numbers, symbols, or words, for example) to yield a product (the result of processing information, describable in terms of forms such as units, classes, relations, or implications). The model yields 120 separate abilities. Divergent and convergent thinking operations relate directly to creativity (divergent thinking) and intelligence (convergent thinking).

APPLIED QUESTIONS

▶ What are the educational implications of the views of intelligence advanced by Das, Sternberg or Gardner?

◀ APPLIED QUESTIONS rephrase each of the focus questions found at the beginning of the chapter, transforming them into actual problems, exercises, and activities closely related to your preparation for teaching.

▶ Debate the merits and the educational implications of the belief that intelligence is modifiable.

▶ Using library resources, research the proposition that measured intelligence is related to family size, birth order, and spacing of children.

▶ How might lessons be modified to encourage creativity in students?

▶ Can you think of classroom examples of divergent and convergent thinking?

STUDY TERMS

componental theory of intelligence	group tests	positive correlation
confluence model	individual tests	PREP program
content	intelligence quotient (IQ)	products
contextual theory of intelligence	knowledge acquisition components	psychometrics
convergent thinking	LPAD	reliability
creativity	metacomponents	simultaneous processsing
crystallized abilities	negative correlation	SOMPA
divergent thinking	operations	successive processing
flexibility	originality	tests of divergent thinking
fluency	PASS	theory of multiple intelligence
fluid abilities	performance components	validity
g	planning	variables

SUGGESTED READINGS

The following two-volume encyclopedia contains more than 250 current articles dealing with all aspects of intelligence and intellectual functioning, including most of the topics covered in this chapter:

STERNBERG, R. J. (ed.) (1994). *Encyclopedia of human intelligence.* New York: Macmillan.

The pros and cons of intelligence testing, and some of the myths surrounding the meaning of IQ, are presented clearly in the following three books:

LUTHER, M., & QUARTER, J. (1988). *The genie in the lamp: Intelligence testing reconsidered.* North York, Ontario: Captus Press.

MENSH, E., & MENSH, H. (1991). *The IQ mythology: Class, race, gender, and inequality.* Carbondale: Southern Illinois University.

SELIGMAN, D. (1992). *A question of intelligence: The IQ debate in America.* New York: Carol Publishing Group.

Current thinking and research in creativity are summarized in:

CROPLEY, A. J. (1992). *More ways than one: Fostering creativity.* Norwood, N.J.: Ablex.

SHAW, M. P., & RUNCO, M. A. (eds.) (1994). *Creativity and affect.* Norwood, N. J.: Ablex.

FINKE, R. A., WARD, T. B., & SMITH, S. M. (1992). *Creative cognition: Theory, research and applications.* Cambridge, Mass.: MIT Press.

A useful overview of intelligence measures, with detailed comparisons and evaluations of the Stanford-Binet and WISC-III, is:

KAMPHAUS, R. W. (1993). *Clinical assessment of children's intelligence.* Boston: Allyn & Bacon.

During hibernation, all the metabolic processes are slowed to an absolute minimum. The animal is exceedingly torpid and approaches death as closely as possible without actually dying. Bears do not truly hibernate, although they do "den-up" during severe weather (Matthews, 1969).

STUDY TERMS list ▶ all of the important terms in the chapter. Each of these is defined in the running glossary at the bottom of the page on which the term first appears, and is found again in the alphabetical glossary at the end of the text. These can be useful as a quick check of your mastery of chapter content.

◀ SUGGESTED READINGS provide quick leads on up-to-date sources of additional information, and can be useful for further study and research, or for term papers.

A Short Note About The Bear

Let me finally get to the most often-asked question about this book: "What about the Bear?" Sadly, there isn't room enough here to answer the question with the whole truth and nothing but the truth.

It all started with the first edition of this text, subtitled "A bear always faces the front." In that edition, the bear was largely whimsy—but not entirely purposeless whimsy.

A bear scrambling through the pages of a serious textbook was a bit of a jolt. It broke the tedium of uninterrupted academic content and it sometimes made readers smile—or even laugh. And it didn't really seem to detract from the serious "nuts and bolts" of the chapters. Hundreds of students and professors who read that first edition wrote letters, most of them highly positive.

Subsequent editions went from a bear always facing the front to a bear who usually, sometimes, rarely, never, and finally, once more, always faced that direction. By the seventh edition, grizzled, battle-scarred, and considerably wiser, the bear would no longer commit himself. In the eighth, he had decided that he would no longer look at the past, instead facing the future.

Over the years, the bear has become something more than whimsy, something more than a break: He has become a metaphor. A metaphor is not, of course, a real thing. It's an invention. The bear metaphor was invented as much by readers of earlier editions as by me. Some of these readers have decided that the bear is a metaphor for a teacher, or perhaps for teaching. Others reached different conclusions. All are correct. The bear, this wonderful metaphoric bear, continues in this, the ninth edition. This is a bear who has sniffed many winds of change, who has witnessed some extraordinary social and political events. Spurred by visions of a happier future, he fancies himself something of an environmental crusader. As well, he has become more sensitive to the feelings and the beliefs of others and more aware of cultural diversity. This is a more tolerant bear, a bear less likely to blunder headlong into other people's beliefs and prejudices, loudly trumpeting the correctness of his own views. This is a bear of the late nineties, a today kind of bear—in brief, he is determined to be politically correct.

A Note to the Instructor: What's New in the Ninth Edition?

Like its predecessors, this ninth edition continues to emphasize teaching and learning. Content is selected and presented always with an eye to instructional implications and actual classroom applications. This edition provides more classroom illustrations than earlier editions, many of them in the form of thought-provoking samples of classroom interaction set aside as boxed cases. Other changes in this edition include new or expanded coverage of important contemporary concerns such as:

- ▶ diversity in the classroom
- ▶ multicultural education
- ▶ gender issues and sexual stereotyping
- ▶ performance-based approaches to assessment
- ▶ new models of memory
- ▶ developing cognitive strategies
- ▶ cooperative teaching
- ▶ classroom management models
- ▶ technology in the classroom

In addition, information has been thoroughly updated throughout. There are more than 400 new references, most of them published within the last three years. The glossary has been expanded by about 60 percent (more than 200 new entries), and glossary terms are now included as study terms at the end of each chapter.

This edition continues to resist the temptation to reduce the craft of teaching to a handful of recipe-like instructions. Like its predecessors, *Psychology for Teaching*, ninth edition, believes that the best teaching decisions are based on sound psychological principles applied with enthusiasm and imagination and tempered with a love of children and of teaching—not on the application of prescriptions copied like recipes from instruction booklets. Teaching and children are too complex for simple recipes.

At the same time, however, the text is highly practical, and includes a large number of ideas and suggestions that translate directly into classroom applications. In general, this edition presents considerably more depth and detail than did earlier versions.

Earlier bears were admittedly skinny bears. The first Bear fancied himself a bit of a pioneer in his field—a leader and not a follower. He looked at his academic cousins and was saddened by their pomposity, by their pretentious academic correctness, and especially by the weightiness of their tomes. That's why he came out leaner, and in some ways a whole lot meaner, than most of his contemporaries.

Hundreds of students and professors have written over the years. The vast majority of letters have been highly encouraging. That's one of the reasons why, through succeeding generations, I've continued to resist the temptation to throw in the proverbial kitchen sink. But in recent years, more students and their professors, and a few editors, have been asking for more tools and instructions with which to understand how it works and with which to fix it when it needs fixing. So the kitchen sink isn't here yet, but there is quite a lot more REALLY USEFUL stuff—in addition to everything else that is motivating, lively, and intriguing. The Bear still wants to be a leader, not a follower.

Thank You to . . . Where to Start?

After nine editions, there are simply too many of you to name, including:

► all of the researchers, theorists, and street philosophers whose ideas are acknowledged in these pages;

► all of the above whose ideas sneaked in unrecognized;

► Richard L. Greenberg, old friend, editor for the first Bears;

► Roger Peterson, Bob Podstepny, Marshall Aronson, Joan Garbutt, Stephanie Surfus, Ken King, and Suzanna Brabant, editors for the middle Bears;

► Sabra Horne, editor for the most recent Bears;

► Tony Hall and Jeff Littlejohn, cartoonists and very funny people;

► Angela Mann, Joseph's mother, exceptionally everything one dreams of in a production editor;

► Jennifer Gordon, copy editor, who is gifted at fighting obscurity, stupidity, and long sentences;

► Andrew Ogus, designer, who keeps creating stunning designs no matter what I give him;

► Reviewers of the first eight editions whose positive influence continues still;

► Reviewers of this edition: Jo Alexander, Auburn University at Montgomery; Harold D. Beard, Central Missouri State University; Sylvan S. Beck, George Washington University; Gloria Bonner, Middle Tennessee State University; Peggy F. Harris, Tennessee State University; Eshok Jaini and Yolanda Jaini, Heritage College, for whose time, patience, and wisdom I am truly grateful;

► Marie, Laurier, Claire, Remi, Elizabeth, and Liam who make it all worth a great deal more than my while.

Guy R. Lefrançois

Photo Credits

Title page: Bob Daemmeich/Stock, Boston
Part 1: Jean-Claude Lejeune/Stock, Boston
Chapter 1: Elizabeths Crews
Part 2: Elizabeth Crews
Chapter 2: Elizabeth Crews/The Image Works
Chapter 3: Elizabeth Crews
Part 3: Jean-Claude Lejeune/Stock, Boston
Chapter 4: Akos Szilvasi/Stock, Boston
Chapter 5: Jean-Claude Lejeune/Stock, Boston
Chapter 6: Elizabeth Crews/Stock, Boston

Part 4: Judy Gelles/Stock, Boston
Chapter 7: Frank Siteman/Stock, Boston
Chapter 8: Bob Daemmerich/Stock, Boston
Chapter 9: Jeffrey Muir Hamilton/Stock, Boston
Part 5: Chapter 4: Akos Szilvasi/Stock, Boston
Chapter 10: Elizabeth Crews/Stock Boston
Chapter 11: Gail Zucker/Stock, Boston
Chapter 12: Elizabeth Crews/Stock, Boston
Chapter 13: Arthur Grace/Stock, Boston
Epilogue: John Coletti/Stock, Boston

PART ONE

"Begin at the beginning," the King said,
gravely, "and go on till you come to the end:
then stop."

LEWIS CARROLL, *Alice in Wonderland*

The Beginning

CHAPTER 1
Psychology for Teaching

THERE IS ONLY ONE *chapter in the first part—only one beginning. And when we get to the end, we will stop.*

The beginning says what educational psychology is, looks at teaching as a career, and presents an overview of each of the remaining twelve chapters. These chapters are organized into parts according to their major emphases. The second part looks at human development, at how children change through the school years. The third part examines explanations of learning and how these are related to teaching. Part IV explores diversity in the classroom, looking at individual differences in social, intellectual, and physical development and functioning. It also presents a humanistic view of teaching. And the last part looks at topics important to effective instruction: motivation, classroom management, individualized instruction and technology, and assessment.

And somewhere the subtitle of this book becomes more significant.

CHAPTER 1

Thousands . . .
Kiss the book's outside who ne'er look within.

WILLIAM COWPER, *Expostulation*

Psychology for Teaching

PREVIEW

Each chapter in this text opens with a preview *followed by a list of* focus questions. *Previews organize and summarize important concepts and increase the meaningfulness of material to be learned—sometimes by stimulating recall of important previous learning, sometimes by providing new information, and sometimes by clarifying relationships. This first chapter is a preview for the remainder of the text. Among other things, it points out that there are some important reasons for taking this course other than the fact that it might be compulsory.*

Focus questions serve as objectives for the chapter that follows. They indicate some of the things you will know and understand more clearly when you have finished the chapter. And at the end of each chapter, the chapter opening focus questions are translated into more practical applied questions and assignments.

FOCUS QUESTIONS

▶ How are psychology and education related?

▶ What are theories, laws, principles, and beliefs and how are they related?

▶ What are some different views of teaching?

▶ What is involved in the career of teaching?

▶ What are the basic elements of a useful model of teaching?

▶ What are some of the characteristics shared by expert teachers?

▶ What do bears have to do with educational psychology?

Even at age 6, John George Scott was a long-limbed, loose-walking kid whose scrawny neck seemed to stretch way too far between his shoulders and his head—a lot like a turkey's neck. So we called him Fencepost.

Fencepost was one of the last to find his desk that first day of school, after my dad had rung the morning bell.

"He can't speak no French or English," whispered Horseface, this being what we called Dennis Charpentier, which was a better name than what his brothers called him. Me, I spoke French and maybe half a dozen Cree and English words, some of which weren't the kinds of words we used in school. So both John George and I had a language problem at the beginning of first grade. I figured the best way around this problem was just to do whatever everybody else was doing—like scrunching myself into a desk and paying attention.

The rows went from first grade on the side along the blackboard, right up to eighth grade, along the wall with the windows. Fencepost sat in front of me, Noella Doré right behind. I hadn't had time to fall in love with Noella yet, but I liked the way she smelled. Which is another chapter. Across from me sat Noella's brother, Luc. We called him Barney. This had to do with *his* smell, but that, too, is another chapter.

My dad said a few things in both French and English, mostly underlining some rules that all

the older kids already knew but might have forgotten over the summer, like where's the cloak-room for boys and the one for girls and stay out of the one you're not supposed to be in and how many fingers to raise for a call of nature, depending on the nature of that call.

But he didn't mention the strap in the teacher's desk, which surprised me because I figured that was a pretty big part of school. Instead, he started to pass out the spellers. That's when Fencepost suddenly turned his head right around toward the door, like an owl facing one way and looking the other. He stared at the door for just a second or two, and then, as if he'd just made up his mind, he pulled himself out of his desk and lurched outside. "He's bolted," I thought, half wishing I had enough courage to do the same.

But John George hadn't bolted at all. He had simply felt the call of nature. So, what the hey, this being his usual custom, he trotted to the far corner of the schoolyard, squatted, and answered the call. Horseface laughed so hard he had to fight a call of nature of his own.

My father abandoned his spellers and rushed out to the corner of the yard. Through the long windows we could see him trying to explain to Fencepost, using some weird body language, the purpose of the little building in the other corner, the one with the quarter moon cut into the front, the farthest one because the closer one was for the girls. But there are some signs that are not universally understood by frightened 6-year-old boys whose pants have settled around their ankles.

So my dad came back inside and made me a teacher, which in retrospect colored a big piece of my life. "Show him where it is," he said, "and what it's for."

I took Fencepost with me and showed him.*

---

*PPC (A PPC is a prepublication critic—one of a number of people [mostly educational psychologists, but also one cantankerous grandmother] who read the manuscript prior to its publication.): It might be useful for students to know whether or not this is a true story.

AUTHOR: It is. All of the chapter opening excerpts are as true as I can remember. I swear it.

WHY STUDY
EDUCATIONAL PSYCHOLOGY?

"Showing them" *is* an important part of teaching. In fact, in Spanish the same word, *enseñar,* means both to teach and to show. Unfortunately, however, showing them is not all there is to teaching—my successful assignment with John George notwithstanding. And although this text, *Psychology for Teaching,* might not have been very useful to me that day—hey, I could scarcely read—it would have come in very handy some years later when I tried teaching other less natural things to people whose need to learn was not quite so insistent. You see, contrary to what I had hoped, teaching skills are not hereditary; we can't count on our genes to endow us with teaching ability, or with what is called the "craft knowledge" of teaching—the knowledge that expert teachers seem to have (Grimmett & Mackinnon, 1992).* Fortunately, however, we now have a large body of information that can help novice teachers become more expert, and that can contribute dramatically to the effectiveness of teachers and of schools. This textbook is your introduction to that information. Its goal is to make you a better teacher. As its title indicates, it presents a *psychology for teaching.*

TEACHING DECISIONS AND BELIEFS

Teaching is a complex sequence of ongoing actions. It may involve as many as a thousand or more teacher–student interactions in a single day. Each of these interactions requires a decision: what to do, what to say, how to react, where to go next.

Much of what the teacher is required to do in the classroom is immediate: There is often little time for careful reflection. Hence, many of the teacher's actions are based on habit and on preestablished beliefs. In fact, everything a teacher does in the classroom reflects personal beliefs. This does not mean, of course, that all of a teacher's behaviors are carefully premeditated. When teacher responses have to be immediate, as is often the case, there is little time to plan and deliberate. But even our most impulsive and habitual actions reveal our underlying convictions and implicit theories—in other words, our beliefs. It is for this reason, suggests Gallagher (1994), that getting teachers to change is a very difficult undertaking. We do not easily discard old beliefs and adopt new ones.

What Are Beliefs? Beliefs are personal convictions. Unlike knowledge, which tends to be impersonal and impartial, a **belief**[†] often has strong emotional components. Thus, beliefs are reflected in attitudes, prejudices, judgments, and opinions.

Experiences, both personal and second-hand, are closely involved in the development of our beliefs. Pajares (1992) notes that beliefs are often formed early in life, and may be maintained even in the face of strong contradiction. Such beliefs act as a sort of filter through which people view the world and interpret information.

Beliefs result not only from personal experiences, but also from information acquired through education and other sources. For example, what we believe about the effects of smoking may reflect more what we have read or heard than what we have experienced. Similarly, what we believe about human personality, or about human learning, may be based partly on our own experiences and partly on what we have learned from more formal educational experiences.

---

*References in this text are cited in the style approved by the American Psychological Association. Thus, author's names are followed by the year of the publication; the alphabetical list of references at the end of the text gives all the information necessary for locating each source.

[†]Boldfaced terms are defined in the glossary at the end of the text, as well as at the foot of the page on which they first appear.

---

belief The acceptance of an idea as being accurate or truthful. Beliefs are often highly personal and resistant to change.

How Beliefs Affect Decisions. Beliefs are what guide our thinking and our actions, says Pajares (1992). All teachers have beliefs about their work, their students, how learning occurs, the subjects they teach. A teacher who believes students learn best by memorizing assigns memory work; one who is convinced students remember only what they understand takes more pains to explain and clarify. A teacher who believes students cheat when given the opportunity supervises her examinations closely; one who thinks students are basically honest prepares her lessons while students write their tests.

As an example, see the case "Last Weekend, Tommy and I . . ." Note how Mr. Busenius believes, among other things, that:

1. Offenders must be made to stop immediately before misbehavior spreads.
2. It is better to reprimand silently and at close range without disrupting ongoing classroom activities.

Mr. Busenius might have selected other options. For example, he might simply have ignored Helena—if he believed that her behavior was designed to get attention and that it would therefore be less likely to be repeated if ignored. Or he might have used some form of punishment, such as detention, believing that Helena would subsequently behave so as to avoid punishment. Alternatively, he might have gone over to Roberta and praised her remarkable paragraphs just loudly enough to draw Helena's attention, believing that this might encourage Helena to build her own remarkable paragraphs. Also, he might have taken the time to explain how important it is to learn to express oneself in the belief that this might motivate Helena to greater efforts; or he might have explained to Helena how her hair brushing was distracting and upsetting the others, believing that her need for social approval would convince her to put her brush away.

Which of these behaviors is best? Is it always best? Which of these beliefs is most accurate and most useful?

This text is designed to help you answer these questions.

THIS TEXT AND YOUR BELIEFS

Pajares (1992) notes that beliefs about teaching and learning are already well established by the time teachers begin their training. And, as we have noted, they are resistant to change—but certainly not unchangeable. For example, Agne, Greenwood, and Miller (1994) found marked differences between the belief systems of novice teachers and those of expert teachers (in this case, teachers who had been selected as Teacher of the Year). Among other things, the expert teachers tended to be more student oriented (more humanistic) in their approaches to classroom management; novices were often more

CASE: LAST WEEKEND, TOMMY AND I . . .

THE SITUATION: Mr. Busenius' sixth-grade language class. The students are generally well behaved; most appear interested and attentive—except for Helena who, in Mr. Busenius' not-too-polite words, "is one #!!*# of a nightmare."

Today, students are asked to write two paragraphs describing the most interesting thing that happened to them over the weekend. Helena does not seem especially anxious to write about her weekend. Instead, she finds a brush and begins to brush her hair.

But before she has completed her third stroke, Mr. Busenius has quietly reached her desk, taken the brush from her, and jabbed his calloused index finger twice, quite emphatically, on the blank sheet of paper on Helena's desk.

She bends to her task. "Last weekend," she writes, "Tommy and I, I don't know if I should write this, but I will, what we did is . . ."

rigid and stricter. This suggests that the beliefs of the expert teachers might have changed from the time they were novices—but it doesn't prove it because the expert teachers might well have had different belief systems in the first place.

Additional evidence that teachers' beliefs do change is provided by Rust (1994), who conducted an in-depth investigation of the beliefs and behaviors of two beginning teachers. Both these teachers developed new beliefs about teaching and learning during their first year—beliefs that were sometimes very different from those they thought they had learned in their teacher education programs.

Beliefs that are inaccurate or prejudicial may lead to teaching behaviors that are inappropriate and ineffective. One of the important aims of this text is to encourage you to examine your beliefs—especially those that have to do with learners and with teaching—and to discard or alter them if necessary. It tries to do this in two related ways: first, by providing you with important information about learners of different ages, and about the processes involved in learning, organizing, remembering, thinking, solving problems, and being creative; and second, by describing and illustrating practical strategies for facilitating the teaching/learning process.

Among the most useful of your beliefs as a teacher are those that have to do with how students change, how they learn, what motivates, reinforces, and punishes them, and what is interesting and important to them. These topics fall within the realm of **psychology.** Hence this *psychology for teaching*.

PSYCHOLOGY

Psychology is the study of human **behavior** and experience. These are fascinating but highly complex subjects. As a result, although all psychologists are concerned with behavior in one way or another, many specialties and divisions have arisen within the field, each concentrating on specific aspects of the human experience. For example, developmental psychologists look at how behavior changes over time; clinical psychologists deal with behavioral and emotional problems; and educational psychologists are interested in the scientific study of behavior in educational settings. These are only three of the divisions in psychology; Table 1.1 labels and describes several others and provides a clearer picture of psychology's scope.

SCIENCE

The psychologist does not study or attempt to understand behavior simply by thinking about the various factors that might be involved in behaving. Rather, psychology as a **science** involves the application of scientific procedures and approaches in an attempt to understand human behavior.

Science is as much an attitude as a collection of methods. As an attitude, science insists on precision, consistency, and replicability. The methods resulting from this attitude consist of rules intended to eliminate subjectivity, bias, and the influence of random factors—in short, rules designed to maximize the extent to which we can have confidence in the conclusions of science. For most of the past century (psychology is approximately one hundred years old), the attitudes and methods that have governed the psychologist's search for greater understanding of humans and their behavior have emphasized precision, replicability, and objectivity above all else.

Unfortunately for the psychologist, human behavior is not as predictable as are events in the physical world. Using the same attitudes

---

psychology The science that examines human behavior (and that of other animals as well).

behavior The activity of an organism. Behavior may be overt (visible) or covert (invisible or internal).

science An approach and an attitude toward knowledge that emphasize objectivity, precision, and replicability.

TABLE 1.1 WHAT PSYCHOLOGISTS DO

SUBFIELD*	MAJOR CONCERNS AND ACTIVITIES
Clinical	Diagnosing and treating emotional illnesses and disturbances, frequently in a hospital or clinical setting
Counseling and guidance	Evaluating and counseling clients' behavioral, emotional, and other problems not serious enough to require hospital or clinical treatment; also, assisting with important decisions (career, marriage, and so on)
Developmental	Studying changes that define growth, maturation, and learning from birth to death; applying findings in education programs
Educational	Researching learning, thinking, remembering, instructing, and related topics in educational settings; developing and applying learning programs for students
Industrial and personnel	Applying psychology in business and industry; developing and administering tests to evaluate aptitudes; conducting workshops and programs dealing with motivation, management, interpersonal relations, and related areas
Personality	Identifying and describing important, stable characteristics of individuals; developing classification schemes for personality characteristics as well as methods for identifying and assessing these characteristics
School	Identifying individual aptitudes and skills among learners in a school setting; developing and administering tests pertinent to school-related abilities
Experimental, comparative, and physiological	Exploring psychology as an experimental science; conducting research on comparisons among species; investigating physiological functioning as it relates to psychological functioning
Psychometrics	Testing and measuring psychological characteristics and making sense of resulting measures; developing tests and measurement devices
Social	Doing research and consulting on the relationship between individuals and groups

*Not all psychologists fall neatly into one of these categories. Many would consider themselves as belonging to several areas, both by the nature of their interests and by their activities. Others would hesitate to be classified in any of these subfields.

and scientific methods as the psychologist, the chemist and the physicist have been able to discover replicable and precise laws that govern the behaviors of molecules and planets. But the psychologist has been hard-pressed to discover a single precise **law** governing the behavior of humans (more about laws shortly).

The problem for the psychologist goes beyond the observation that the behavior of humans is influenced by a tremendous variety of forces—some of which we don't understand

at all well (yet). Many aspects of human behavior cannot be measured in the way that the speed, direction, and mass of a planet or molecule can be measured. Nor are changes in human behavior as precise and predictable as are changes in the behavior of physical matter.

However, these observations should not lead you to conclude that we know little about human behavior. Nor are they meant to encourage pessimism (although a very slight skepticism might not be entirely inappropriate). Rather, what these observations emphasize is the complexity of human thought and behavior and consequently the very real difficulties of reducing these events to simple laws and principles.

---

law A statement that is accurate beyond reasonable doubt.

FACTS AND THEORIES

Science, as we have seen, is a collection of methods and attitudes that relate directly to the ways in which we discover and accumulate facts. In this context, however, the word **fact** is perhaps too strong; it implies a degree of certainty and accuracy that is not always possible in psychology or education. In these areas, our facts are simply observations of events, behaviors, or relationships. The important point is that science insists that these observations be made under controlled conditions so that the same observations can be made by anyone—that is, so that they can be replicated.

Facts (or observations), by themselves, would be of limited value to educators and psychologists if they were not organized, summarized, and simplified. That's where **theory** comes in. In a simple sense, a theory is a collection of related statements whose principal function is to summarize and explain observations. For example, when I observe that Roland Littlefork repeatedly refuses to join us for our annual fishing excursion, our regular poker games, our Christmas celebration, or our Halloween masquerade, I might develop a theory about his behavior. "I have a theory about Roland," I might say, and everybody would understand what I meant. "He doesn't like social gatherings," I might continue. That, in a nutshell, would be my theory. It summarizes and explains my observations admirably. It is a statement that might be described as a **naive theory** or, as Grippin and Peters (1984) put it,

an implicit theory. Naive or implicit theories differ from more formal theories in one important respect: Naive theories express personal convictions that need only be believed but not scientifically proved; formal theories must be tested. It isn't sufficient simply to assume that a psychological theory accounts for all the important observations and relationships; this must be demonstrably true.

There are many theories in psychology; not all are equally good. Some, for instance, do not reflect the facts very well. Let's say, for example, that Roland Littlefork plays poker regularly with George's group and that he also accepts other social invitations. If this were the case, my theory about Roland's behavior would not fit all the facts.

That it reflect all important facts is only one of the requirements of a good theory. R. M. Thomas (1992) suggests a number of others: A theory is good if it (1) accurately reflects observations, (2) is expressed clearly, (3) is useful for predicting as well as explaining, (4) is applicable in a practical sense, (5) is consistent rather than self-contradictory, and (6) is not based on numerous assumptions (unproved beliefs). A good theory should also be thought provoking and should provide satisfying explanations, says Thomas (1992).

Of these criteria, one of the most important for the educator is that of predicting. The most useful theories are those that serve not only to explain observations but also to predict events. My naive theory about Roland Littlefork, for example, allows me to predict that he will refuse all social invitations, no matter who issues them. As we saw, however, in this case the prediction is inaccurate because the theory does not account for certain important facts. Presumably, a theory that fits the facts better would lead to more accurate predictions.

A theory, then, is a statement or, more often, a collection of related statements whose main function is to summarize, simplify, organize, and explain observations and to permit predictions about events relating to this set of observations. Some of these statements may be described as laws, others as principles, and many as beliefs.

---

fact Something that observation leads us to believe is true or real. Ideally, the observations that determine our facts are sufficiently objective and repeatable that they provide us with some assurance that they accurately reflect the way things actually are.

theory A body of information pertaining to a specific topic, a method of acquiring and/or dealing with information, or a set of explanations for related phenomena.

naive theory Expression used to describe psychological theories based on intuition and folk-belief rather than on science.

LAWS, PRINCIPLES, AND BELIEFS

Laws are statements whose accuracy is generally beyond question. Physics, chemistry, astronomy, and other natural sciences have discovered numerous important laws ($E = mc^2$, for example). As we saw earlier, however, human behavior is rarely characterized by the regularity and unwavering predictability of laws.

Principles are statements that are probable rather than certain. Unlike laws, they are always open to a degree of doubt, to a certain level of improbability. Accordingly, most psychological statements about human behavior and experience take the form of principles rather than laws.

As we saw, beliefs are more private and personal than either principles or laws. Beliefs are our individual convictions, our personal attempts to explain observations. Beliefs are often based on personal experience, but can also be based on the same sorts of scientific observations that give rise to more formal theories. One of the most important goals of *Psychology for Teaching* is to provide you with a more valid basis for forming and examining important personal beliefs. After all, our beliefs are the basis for our behaviors (Pajares, 1992).

MODELS

One additional term is relevant here: **model.** A model is like a pattern or a blueprint; it's a representation of the way things are or of the way they can or should be. We could also say that a model is an organized set of beliefs about something important.

Models can be very specific and concrete, say Reese and Overton (1970), and are often included in, or derived from, theories. For example, there are models of atomic structures, models of the universe, and teaching models.

Models can also be very general. For example, they can represent all of our beliefs and assumptions about human nature. In this sense, each of us has implicit models that govern our view of the world and that guide our perceptions and our behavior.

Two general models underlie much of what psychologists think and believe about human beings. On the one hand, the mechanistic model reflects the belief that it is useful to think of humans as being like machines—predictable and highly responsive to environmental influences. On the other hand, the organismic model holds that it is more useful to view humans as dynamic, active, exploring organisms that are more responsive to internal forces than to external stimulation.

In a very real sense, psychological models are metaphors. They don't say "Humans are this or that" so much as "Humans behave as though they were like this or like that." Accordingly, models, like theories, cannot be judged in terms of their accuracy so much as in terms of their usefulness. A theory—or a model—is not right or wrong, say Wellman and Gelman (1992); it is simply more or less useful.

MODELS OF TEACHERS

There have traditionally been at least three identifiable models of teachers and their roles, claim Fenstermacher and Soltis (1992): the executive model, the therapist model, and the liberationist model.

The **executive model** sees the teacher as someone who has mastered the craft of teaching and who bears the main responsibility for arranging the teaching/learning situation so that learners acquire prescribed skills and information. This model emphasizes teaching techniques and materials preparation.

---

principle A statement relating to some uniformity or predictability. Principles are far more open to doubt than are laws but are more reliable than beliefs.

model A representation, usually abstract, of some phenomenon or system. Alternatively, a pattern for behavior that can be copied by someone.

executive model A view of the teacher as a master teacher (executive) responsible for arranging the teaching/learning situation, delivering lessons, and teaching learners prescribed skills and information.

TABLE 1.2 THREE VIEWS OF THE TEACHER

MODEL	PRINCIPAL BELIEFS	POSSIBLE TEACHER BEHAVIOR
Executive	Teacher's role is executive function of preparing best materials/lessons for learners (recipients)	Teacher-prepared lessons/activities are main source of information
Therapist	Teacher's role is that of empathetic facilitator of student growth and self-development	Cooperative group activities designed to foster positive self-concept
Liberationist	Teacher's function is to liberate students' minds, empowering them to learn on their own	Guided discovery experiences in which students are encouraged to examine their own intellectual processes and to become aware of and develop intellectual strategies

Source: Based on Fenstermacher and Soltis (1992).

The **therapist model** views the teacher not as an executive but rather as a highly sympathetic individual whose primary responsibilities are the healthy and happy development of learners. Instead of focusing on methods and content, this model is highly student centered.

Finally, the **liberationist model** regards the teacher's role as one of freeing students' minds by providing them with the tools and attitudes necessary for learning. For example, a major focus of this model is on ensuring that students become aware of the strategies they can use to do important cognitive (intellectual) things like organizing, remembering, and solving problems—in other words, that they learn how to learn. (See Table 1.2.)

Your teaching model is extremely important in determining the sorts of activities you select for your classroom and your relationship with your students. And, of course, it will affect your students' interactions with you as well as their own learning activities. Thus, teachers who see themselves as *executives* are likely to prepare well-structured lectures and lessons designed to optimize learning in their students.

In contrast, those whose models are more therapeutic will pay greater attention to the healthy development of their charges—to their happiness and their self-concepts. And those who see their roles as liberationist concentrate on encouraging students to learn how to learn.

Note that these models are simply ways of describing different emphases teachers might have; they describe various views of the teacher's role. Clearly, however, most teachers do not subscribe to only one model to the exclusion of all others. Most engage in a variety of behaviors reflecting a mixture of beliefs.*

A MODEL OF TEACHING

To simplify without unduly distorting reality, teaching may be described in terms of three stages, each characterized by different demands on the teacher: before teaching, during teaching, and after teaching (see Figure 1.1). And contrary to what we might immediately assume, the teaching stage is no more important than what occurs before or after.

---

therapist model A primarily humanistic view of the teacher's role—namely that of facilitating healthy growth and self-actualization.

liberationist model Views the teacher's role as one of freeing students' minds by providing them with the tools and the attitudes necessary for learning.

---

*PPC: My students always ask to which model I subscribe. They want to know whether they should view themselves as therapists, as teacher-executives, or as liberationists. So, what about you? With which of these models is the bear most in tune?

AUTHOR: In truth, the bear is an eclectic teacher whose behavior reflects myriad beliefs. What else would you expect of a politically correct (and totally inoffensive) bear?

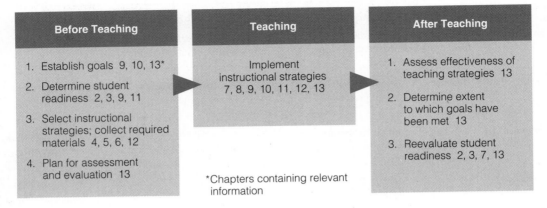

The Instructional Process

Before Teaching	Teaching	After Teaching
1. Establish goals 9, 10, 13*	Implement instructional strategies 7, 8, 9, 10, 11, 12, 13	1. Assess effectiveness of teaching strategies 13
2. Determine student readiness 2, 3, 9, 11		2. Determine extent to which goals have been met 13
3. Select instructional strategies; collect required materials 4, 5, 6, 12		3. Reevaluate student readiness 2, 3, 7, 13
4. Plan for assessment and evaluation 13	*Chapters containing relevant information	

FIGURE 1.1 A three-stage model of the teaching process.

BEFORE TEACHING

To be an effective, perhaps even exemplary, teacher, you must make a number of critical decisions before even walking into your classroom and actually engaging in the business of teaching. First, you must decide on both the long-range and short-term goals of the instructional process. To determine these goals, you need to answer some questions: What specific learning outcomes are intended and expected? How do these tie in with the broad goals of the educational process in this subject? this grade? this school? this city or county? How do these goals fit in with my values and beliefs? How important are they?

Once you have determined your instructional goals, you need to select a teaching strategy to attain these goals, and you must invent, make, or at least collect materials that are useful for teaching. What is required here is not only knowledge of the strategies themselves but also of the skills required to implement them effectively. And, perhaps most important, you must be aware of the extent to which students are ready for this specific teaching/learning experience. Student readiness involves a variety of factors, including essential prerequisite knowledge and skills, as well as appropriate motivation. Clearly, students who are eager to learn are most likely to profit from instruction; just as clearly, students who have already mas-

tered prerequisite knowledge and skills are more likely to attain advanced instructional objectives. These facts highlight the importance of knowing how students learn and develop and what motivates them.

Another critical step in the preteaching phase is that of planning for assessment: How will you determine the extent to which instructional goals have been met? By what procedures will you evaluate the instructional process itself, as well as changes that might occur among learners? How will the results of your evaluation procedures influence subsequent teaching decisions?

In summary, the preteaching phase involves at least four steps: setting appropriate goals, determining student readiness, selecting appropriate instructional strategies, and planning for assessment.

TEACHING

The instructional process—commonly called teaching—involves implementing strategies designed to lead learners to attain certain goals. In general, these strategies involve communication, leadership, motivation, and control (discipline or management).

Following a review of research on effective teaching, MacKay (1982) identifies twenty-eight behaviors that most often characterize the

teaching strategies of highly effective teachers. MacKay describes these as "suggested" or "recommended" behaviors rather than as the firm conclusions of scientific research. The behaviors are related to four aspects of the teaching process: classroom management and discipline; instructional organization, sequence, and presentation; verbal interaction (communication); and interpersonal interaction. The twenty-eight behaviors are summarized in the box entitled "Recommended Behaviors for Effective Teaching." It is worth noting that in a year-long study involving seventy-two teachers of third- and sixth-grade mathematics and language arts, researchers found a positive relationship between student achievement and each of these twenty-eight strategies, except for items 1, 4, 7, 9, 11, 13, and 14. However, these seven recommended behaviors have been found to be positively related to effective teaching in other stud-

ies, notably Evertson, Anderson, and Brophy (1978) and Brophy and Evertson (1974).

AFTER TEACHING

The third phase of the teaching process involves assessing the outcomes of instruction in relation to the goals that you set in the preteaching phase. This process of evaluation reveals the effectiveness of your teaching; it might also say a great deal about the appropriateness of your instructional goals, the readiness of your students, the appropriateness of your teaching strategies, and even the relevance and appropriateness of your evaluation procedures.

PSYCHOLOGY AND TEACHING

From the context of this simple model (preteaching, teaching, and postteaching activities), psychology's contribution to teaching is clear. It provides us with answers to some important questions: How do people learn? How can we use what we know about learning and motivation to increase the effectiveness of our instructional procedures? What do we know about people that might be of value to teachers who face student misbehavior or want to avoid being faced with such behavior? How can we motivate learners? and a thousand other related questions.

By answering these questions, psychology can make a tremendous contribution to teaching. In fact, when teachers are asked what kind of assistance they require in order to become more effective, the needs they express typically reflect these questions. For example, following a survey of 247 randomly selected elementary school teachers (22 male and 225 female), Moore and Hanley (1982) identified thirteen specific tasks with which teachers felt they could use help (see Table 1.3 on page 17). The need mentioned most often was assistance in helping students become better learners, particularly with respect to acquiring basic skills. Other needs that these teachers expressed had to do with discipline, motivating learners, identifying and developing readiness for learning,

RECOMMENDED BEHAVIORS FOR EFFECTIVE TEACHING

1. Teachers should use a system of rules dealing with personal and procedural matters.

2. Teachers should prevent misbehaviors from continuing.

3. Teachers should direct disciplinary action accurately.

4. Teachers should move around the room a lot (monitoring seat work).

5. Teachers should handle disruptive situations in a low-key manner (nonverbal messages, proximity, eye contact).

6. Teachers should ensure that assignments are interesting and worthwhile, especially when children work independently.

7. Teachers should use a system of rules that allows students to carry out learning tasks with a minimum of direction.

8. Teachers should optimize academic learning time. Students should be actively involved and productively engaged in learning tasks.

9. Teachers should use a standard signal to get students' attention.

10. Teachers should not begin speaking to the group until all students are paying attention.

11. Teachers should use a variety of instructional techniques, adapting instruction to meet learning needs.

12. Teachers should use a system of spot-checking assignments.

13. Teachers should relate mathematics (or other) games and independent activities to the concepts being taught.

14. Teachers should use techniques that provide for the gradual transition from concrete to more abstract activities.

15. Teachers should use an appropriate mixture of high- and low-order questions.

16. Teachers should be aware of what is going on in the classroom.

17. Teachers should be able to attend to more than one issue at a time.

18. Teachers should facilitate the smooth flow of the lesson or facilitate a smooth transition from one activity to another.

19. Teachers' behavior should maintain the pace of the lesson.

20. Teachers should be clear in presentations to the class.

21. Teachers should be able to motivate students.

22. Teachers should provide evidence of caring, accepting, and valuing the students.

23. Teachers should respond accurately to both obvious and subtle meanings, feelings, and experiences of the students.

24. Teachers should direct questions to many different students.

25. Teachers should use techniques such as rephrasing, giving clues, or asking a new question to help students give improved responses when their answers are incorrect or only partially correct.

26. Teachers should use praise to reward outstanding work as well as to encourage students who are not always able to do outstanding work.

27. Teachers should use mild criticism on occasion to communicate expectations to more able students.

28. Teachers should accept and integrate student-initiated interaction such as questions, comments, or other contributions.

Source: Adapted from research on effective teaching by A. MacKay, "Project Quest: Teaching Strategies and Pupil Achievement." Occasional Paper Series, Centre for Research in Teaching, Faculty of Education, University of Alberta, Edmonton, Alberta, 1982, pp. 42–44.

Educational psychology answers important questions about how people learn, what motivates them, and what instructional procedures are most effective for which students and for which teachers.

and helping students establish realistic goals. Each of these needs falls within the scope of educational psychology.

Educational psychology may be defined as the study of human behavior in educational settings. As Wittrock (1992) emphasizes, it involves not only the application of existing psychological knowledge to educational theory and practice, but also the development of new knowledge and procedures. Accordingly, educational psychology deals with learning processes, human development and motivation, social learning, human personality (especially characteristics such as intelligence and creativity), discipline and other aspects of classroom management, measuring and evaluating student development and learning, and other related questions. These broad topics, divided into five major units (thirteen chapters), are the substance of this text.

---

educational psychology A science concerned primarily with the study of human behavior in educational settings. Applies existing psychological knowledge to instructional problems and develops new knowledge and procedures.

TEACHING AS PROBLEM SOLVING

In its simplest sense, to teach is to impart skills, knowledge, attitudes, and values. It involves bringing about, or at least facilitating, changes in learners. Teaching can be accomplished by telling and persuading, by showing and demonstrating, by guiding and directing learners' efforts, or by a combination of these actions. It might involve only the teacher's own resources, knowledge, and skills; or it might rely on professionally prepared materials (films or computer software, for example), resource people, or a combination of learners' own talents, skills, and information.

Some researchers suggest that it is useful to view teaching as an exercise in problem solving. According to this model, teaching involves the ongoing solving of a series of problems. Some problems, such as those relating to specific course or lesson objectives, are obvious. For example, if one of the goals of a lesson in mathematics is for students to learn division, then the problem that requires a solution is that of arranging for student experiences that lead to the competency in question. Other related problems are not so obvious. These have to do

ELIZABETH CREWS

Teaching empowers learners not only by giving them important information and skills but also by fostering in them feelings of personal worth and confidence. Thus a reading class can empower every bit as much as a class in mathematics or in art.

with managing the classroom environment, monitoring ongoing activities, evaluating and assessing the interest and understanding of individual students, and so on.

TEACHING AS EMPOWERING STUDENTS

From the teacher's point of view, then, teaching can be viewed as a problem-solving activity—that is, as an ongoing process involving finding solutions to problems relating to communication, instruction, motivation, classroom management, evaluation, and so on.

Another way of looking at teaching is to view it in terms of its objectives, rather than its processes. The teacher must be concerned not only with the details of lesson organization and with the hundreds of routines and procedures that contribute to classroom management and effective learning, but also with the goals of the instructional process. What is it that schools ought to accomplish? What are the important objectives of education?

The answers to these questions are fundamental to the teaching/learning process. They determine not only what the content of the school curriculum will be, but also what the goals of the instructional process will be. Educational goals can be very general (for example, to develop good citizens) or very specific (to teach children to add two-digit numbers). For our purposes, a useful way of looking at educational objectives is to view them in the broadest, most general of all terms: The goal of education is to empower students.

Literally, to **empower** means to give power to—in short, to enable. At the most obvious level, education empowers students by enabling them to do things they could not otherwise do. Reading, writing, and arithmetic empower us as surely as do sight, hearing, and our other senses, for while our senses enable us to perceive the world, the three Rs empower us to deal with it at a very complex, sophisticated level. Without all

---

empower To enable; to give power to. One of the most important goals of education is to empower students by providing them with both specific information and learning/thinking strategies and by developing within them the feelings of personal power that come with the realization that one is competent and worthwhile.

TABLE 1.3 THIRTEEN TASKS WITH WHICH TEACHERS WANT HELP (RANKED FROM MOST IMPORTANT TO LEAST IMPORTANT)

1. Developing effective learners and a mastery of the basic skills

2. Guiding children to set up and achieve realistic goals

3. Locating materials and in-service support for more effective teaching

4. Establishing and maintaining discipline

5. Identifying and understanding readiness factors that affect learning

6. Motivating children to learn

7. Designing assessment devices and interpreting the resulting data

8. Supporting teaching and technological methods and materials

9. Understanding interpersonal factors that influence a child's educational goals

10. Developing a greater understanding of human behavior

11. Updating in curriculum content areas and methodologies

12. Improving multipurpose classroom grouping techniques

13. Obtaining administrative assistance with instructional planning

Source: From K. D. Moore and P. E. Hanley, "An Identification of Elementary Teacher Needs." *American Educational Research Journal*, 1982, pp. 19, 140. Copyright 1982, American Educational Research Association, Washington, D.C.

sorts of school-related knowledge, we would be hard-pressed to function easily and effectively. We need to know a great deal if we are to use banking machines, understand instruction manuals, determine how much we owe the government, read newspapers, and on and on.

Knowledge of specific things like reading and writing is only one of the sources of empowerment schools bestow. In addition, schools also foster in students both the personal power that comes with social competence and the accompanying feelings of personal confidence, of being a unique and worthwhile individual. As Kohn (1993) notes, when students are allowed to become *active* participants in their education, the resulting sense of empowerment can have a tremendous positive effect on their achievement, their behavior, and their values—not to mention their sense of well-being. It is perhaps a cliché, but no less true for it, that schools must do more than teach subjects; it is far more important that they teach individual students.

Schools provide empowerment not only through the information they impart and the feelings of confidence and personal power they foster, but also through the learning strategies they develop in students. It is becoming increasingly clear, and increasingly true, that because so much information exists in our advanced technological societies, it is impossible for students to learn more than a fraction of it. And, given the rate at which information changes or becomes obsolete, it would probably be unwise to try. As a result, it is perhaps more important to learn how to learn and how to solve problems—to learn what Mulcahy and colleagues (1990) term *learning/thinking strategies*—than it is to learn only specific items of information. These strategies are the tools of knowing. In fact, argue Husén and Tuijnman (1991), formal schooling actually increases people's measured intelligence. That's because the sorts of strategies we learn in school are what we use to think, to analyze, and to monitor and evaluate our intellectual activities. They can be applied to all sorts of situations throughout our lives. Accordingly, such strategies are a tremendous source of personal power—of empowerment.

We are a clever species, Nickerson (1986) muses. So smart are we that as a result of our "technological wizardry" we have reached a point at which we can destroy everything around us and ourselves as well. In fact, not only do we have this power, but we are in imminent danger of using it, perhaps without even wanting to. If we are to save ourselves, Nickerson cautions, we must rely not on instinct—as might another animal—but on intelligence. Hence, our ultimate survival depends on how well we can think. That, of course, is another important reason for teaching students how to learn and how to think: to encourage them to be worthwhile human beings whose concerns extend beyond the self to include the well-being of all others.

But we are in danger of moving ahead of ourselves. This chapter is simply an introduction. Later we will speak again of learning/thinking strategies, as well as of morality and ethics and of the personal power of warriors, saints, and others.

TEACHING AS A REFLECTIVE ACTIVITY

Much of what teachers do involves thinking about—hence reflecting about—what they do in the classroom and why. Similarly, much of what learners do involves reflecting about what they are learning, how they are progressing, the strategies they have been using (or should be using) to remember, to organize, to solve problems. This observation has led to the idea that teaching can usefully be described as a reflective activity. **Reflective teaching strategies** are broadly defined as strategies that lead students

to discover and learn for themselves (Freiberg & Driscoll, 1992).

Unfortunately, reflective teaching strategies themselves have not been defined very clearly, notes Calderhead (1989). In general, however, they are strategies that are based on teachers' analysis of what is happening as they teach (Korthagen, 1993). At the same time, the strategies are meant to lead learners to think about their own learning and, most important, to assume personal responsibility for that learning. In fact, research indicates that one of the most important factors in effective teaching is the extent to which students feel personally responsible for their successes and failures (Kirby & Paradise, 1992).

Reflective teaching strategies are based on a philosophy that views the learner as an active discoverer rather than as a passive recipient of information—and that sees the teacher as a facilitator of learning rather than as the source of all knowledge. Not surprisingly, then, among the strategies most often described as reflective teaching strategies are those that lead to student inquiry and guided discovery. These topics are discussed in Chapter 6.

TEACHING AS A CRAFT

But there is a great deal more to teaching than simply reflecting on the processes involved. In fact, there are a wide range of specific skills and strategies that teachers can learn and use effectively in their teaching—in much the same way as there are a wide range of very important strategies and procedures that students can learn and use in their learning. Specific teaching strategies make up what is sometimes referred to as **craft knowledge**—that is, knowledge related to the *craft* of teaching. Elements of

---

reflective teaching strategies A loosely defined collection of teaching strategies that involve both teachers and students actively and deliberately thinking (reflecting) about events in the teaching/learning process.

---

craft knowledge Knowledge of the specifics of teaching. The science of teaching, as well as a sort of practical wisdom that includes general information about teaching as well as specific information about teaching particular subjects and lessons to students with identifiable characteristics.

this craft are discussed in many places throughout this text. The specific learning and thinking strategies that students become aware of are often referred to as *metacognitive* skills. Metacognition refers to knowing about knowing, and this includes skills such as those involved in remembering, organizing information, studying, and so on. These skills are dealt with in more detail in Chapters 5 and 6, as well as elsewhere in the text.

Craft knowledge is a sort of practical wisdom, say Sykes and Bird (1992), that cannot always be verbalized completely clearly, but that can be learned through practice or perhaps by studying and analyzing cases that illustrate teaching problems and principles. Craft knowledge includes general information as well as specific information about teaching particular subjects and lessons to students with identifiable characteristics. It can also include "fragmentary, superstitious, and often inaccurate opinions," says Leinhardt (1990, p. 18). That is, craft knowledge can be based on inaccurate and inappropriate beliefs.

Knowledge of the craft of teaching is often evident in the patterns and routines that are such an important part of the classroom. These routines involve two different sets of activities: those relating to classroom management and discipline, and those having to do specifically with instructing—with giving students information and establishing learning habits. Accordingly, acquiring these patterns and routines—that is, learning the *craft* of teaching—requires a wealth of information about both learners and the process of learning. The purpose of this text is to provide you with that information. In fact, craft knowledge is one of the things that distinguishes *expert* teachers.

EXPERT VERSUS NONEXPERT TEACHERS

Expert teachers are especially adept at applying elements of the craft of teaching. This, note Sternberg and Horvath (1995), is one of the defining characteristics of teaching expertise. There are others. The expert teacher is not simply someone who has been teaching a long time. In fact, there are many nonexperts who have years of experience, and perhaps not just a few experts who have newly joined the ranks of teachers. Expert teachers are those who, by virtue of experience, training, and other intangible skills, share a number of characteristics that make them better, more effective teachers. Sternberg and Horvath (1995) suggest that the best way of arriving at a model of teaching expertise is to look at the characteristics that most clearly distinguish excellent from less excellent teachers—that is, to look at the characteristics that such teachers share, which might be used to define an ideal or prototypical category of teaching expertise.

Sternberg and Horvath's (1995) prototype model of teaching expertise identifies three areas in which experts share common characteristics: (1) knowledge, (2) efficiency of problem solving, and (3) insight with respect to solving educational problems.

Knowledge. Rich (1993) reports that expert teachers tend to be more familiar with the subjects they teach than are nonexpert (novice) teachers. That is, they have greater *content knowledge*. And, to a large extent, this greater subject-matter proficiency allows expert teachers to see relationships and connections more easily (Tochon, 1993). That is one reason why expert teachers are better teachers.

Not only do expert teachers have more content knowledge, but they also have more *pedagogical* knowledge—that is, knowledge of teaching and learning principles. Thus, expert teachers not only are better able to organize and deal with subject matter issues, but also are better classroom managers.

---

expert teachers Teachers who, by virtue of experience, training, and other intangible skills, share a number of characteristics that make them better, more effective teachers than novices. In Sternberg's prototypical model of teaching expertise, these characteristics relate to knowledge, efficiency of problem solving, and insight with respect to solving educational problems.

TABLE 1.4 SOME CHARACTERISTICS SHARED BY EXPERT TEACHERS

▶ Excel at teaching

▶ High level of content knowledge

▶ High level of pedagogical knowledge (knowledge of the craft of teaching)

▶ Perceive meaningful patterns and relationships in their teaching

▶ Highly efficient in responding to students and making teaching decisions rapidly

▶ Understand teaching problems at a deep level

▶ Devote considerable time to analyzing teaching problems

▶ Arrive at insightful solutions for pedagogical and management problems

▶ Skillful at monitoring and evaluating teaching behaviors

▶ Well-developed memories for ongoing teaching behaviors

Sources: Based in part on Chi, Glaser, and Farr (1988) and Sternberg and Horvath (1995).

Efficiency. Experts, note Sternberg and Horvath (1995), are more efficient than nonexperts. They do more in less time, and sometimes with much less apparent effort. Thus, they are better problem solvers, perhaps because they have learned how to automize certain activities. In addition, they are better planners. Expert teachers have developed sequences of routines and strategies that they can apply almost unconsciously as they teach. As a result, much of what they do in the classroom is, in a sense, on "automatic pilot" (Kagan, 1988).

As a result of relegating more of their teaching activity to well-practiced and highly effective routines, expert teachers are better able to monitor the flow of their lessons, to anticipate problems, to evaluate their teaching, and to modify their teaching activities.

Insight. Expert teachers, note Sternberg and Horvath (1995), appear to be more insightful than nonexperts. Although both groups apply knowledge and insight to their solution of problems, experts are more likely than nonexperts to arrive at creative or insightful solutions. With respect to classroom management problems, for example, experts appear to be more sensitive to the possibility of restlessness and inattention even before these occur. Not only are they skilled at recognizing potential problems, but they also are adept at applying unobtrusive solutions. Automatically—and without breaking the continuity of their ongoing activity—they bring into play new patterns of interaction that shift focus, draw students back into the flow of activity, and rechannel their attention.

Nonexpert teachers tend to view every classroom management and discipline issue as separate, and to look for an isolated and immediate solution for each problem, notes Butcher (1993). In contrast, expert teachers tend to have a hierarchical conceptualization of classroom management issues. That is, they see direct relationships between student behavior and teacher actions. Not surprisingly, when Swanson, O'Connor, and Cooney (1990) compared twenty-four novice teachers with twenty-four expert teachers, they found that the experts had better ongoing plans for identifying, defining, and solving discipline problems. As a result, they understand better than nonexperts the implications of the many preventive and corrective management strategies they have at their disposal. Thus, their classroom management is more insightful. See Table 1.4 for a summary of some of the characteristics of expert teachers.

THE ART OF TEACHING

But there is more to being an expert teacher than can be learned in one textbook—or even in a dozen texts. Not only do you need information about learners and learning, about human development, and about motivation and interests, but you need to synthesize this information—to understand it, to integrate it with your values, your goals, your personality, and your preferences. Teachers each have their own styles of teaching. No teacher training program can—or should—make us all alike.

Teaching has often been described as both an art and a science. Eisner (1982) suggests that every successful teaching performance can be analyzed not only in terms of the science involved in instruction and classroom management, but also in terms of the art involved in creating the environment—the context—in which learning occurs.

Put another way, the craft of teaching includes not only the science involved, but the art as well. Although a textbook such as this one is forced to deal with the science rather than with the art, it is worth keeping in mind that we should not resort to art only when science fails; rather, art can and should be an integral part of all classroom activity. Poetry and magic can have a place in even the most apparently mundane lesson in an ordinary classroom on a Tuesday. That is one of the things that makes teaching so exciting.

TEACHING AS A CAREER

My father was a teacher for forty-one years. Not all of those years were very easy. For some of the first years he didn't always get paid, and when he did, it was never very much. And many years he had enormous classes—as many as fifty students in an isolated, one-room school, spanning the first through the eighth grades. Nor were the teaching tasks always simple and straightforward; often his beginning students didn't even know English—only French or Cree.

But my father truly loved what he did. He knew how important teaching is, and he was proud to be a teacher. Maybe it was partly because of this that he taught as well as he did. In the end, and despite being situated in an economically depressed area, his one-room school produced several dozen university graduates, including at least two who earned doctorates and several who obtained master's degrees.

Teaching is important. It's stimulating and exciting, and it can be highly rewarding. But it isn't overwhelmingly lucrative. Nor is it exceedingly easy.

SOME PROBLEMS AND CHALLENGES FACING TODAY'S TEACHERS

Teaching in today's schools is often challenging and difficult. Consider, for example, the tremendous cultural and social diversity exemplified in the case "Surviving High School." There are obvious problems associated with teaching students who represent such a vast range of motivation, abilities, time, and energy—problems that are compounded by shrinking educational budgets that lead to overcrowded schools and classrooms and overworked teachers. In such schools, there is often tension between the need for control and learning. Social control, note Cohn and Kottkamp (1993), is a basic requirement for effective teaching. In their words, "Crowded classrooms present teachers with behavioral control problems so pressing that until they are solved, nothing else can be attempted" (p. 201).

In addition to the challenges related to overcrowding and student diversity, dramatic increases in the amount of information available to today's teachers (and students), coupled with increasingly sophisticated tools for handling that information (computers, for example), have made teaching more demanding (Downes, 1991). So too have increasing demands for teacher accountability—that is, the public's insistent call for hard evidence that teachers are effective. And, again, teachers have faced the additional challenge of changes in legislation requiring that children with special, and sometimes very complex, needs be the responsibility of teachers in ordinary classrooms (a policy labeled *mainstreaming* or *inclusive education*).*

Not surprisingly, beginning teachers typically experience more problems than experienced teachers. There are four reasons for this, says Valli (1992). First, beginning teachers have a strong tendency to imitate teachers they had as students. The result is that they fail to develop effective, personal approaches to teaching based on well-informed beliefs. Second, starting teachers tend to be isolated from other teachers; hence they have little emotional support during difficult times and little opportunity for tuition and guidance by more experienced and more expert teachers. Third, the novice teacher often finds it difficult to transfer what has been learned in teacher education

programs to the solution of actual problems in the classroom. As a result, much of what has been learned may be put aside as irrelevant theory. Finally, many new teachers become overly concerned with discovering or applying the correct teaching technique. Consequently, they fail to develop more spontaneous and creative—and often more effective—approaches.

REWARDS OF TEACHING

"As far as the money is concerned, no, I wouldn't teach. I wouldn't choose it again," says Karen, a teacher, when she is asked, "If you could choose all over again, would you choose to be a teacher?" (Cohn & Kottkamp, 1993). But my friend Nora, who has now been teaching for almost thirty years, retorts, "I think the pay's just real fine. It's one of those few things where the men don't get paid a cent more than us."

There are obviously other rewards of teaching, not the least important of which are the intrinsic rewards—like feelings of satisfaction, of accomplishment, of being and doing something worthwhile, of making a difference. Then, there are extrinsic rewards—such as the prestige and respect accorded the profession, and sometimes

---

*PPC: One of my pet peeves is that evidence of teacher competence is so often based on how well students do at the end of the year on systemwide tests or by some other standardized measure. This never takes into account how much diversity there is in different classrooms.

AUTHOR: Nor does it reflect many other subtle changes in students that aren't so easily measured—which is why teacher accountability is a difficult and controversial area. As is merit pay tied to measures of teacher competence.

CASE: SURVIVING HIGH SCHOOL

THE SITUATION: **Reporter Marina Jimenez spent a week in a local high school as an undercover student (Jimenez, 1992). She reports:**

At 2,300 students, the school is the largest in western Canada, serving people from a tremendous range of backgrounds and offering a huge variety of programs. Some students are primarily in academic programs, taking such core courses as English, social studies, and the sciences. Others study skin and nail care, learn to drive cars, or earn full course credits for grilling hamburgers in the school cafeteria. Of the students who graduated from the school last year, 34 percent earned diplomas or certificates that did not qualify them for admission to university. Many work twenty-

five or more hours a week in shops, garages, or fast-food outlets. Some of these still manage to do well in academic programs; others come to school primarily for its social opportunities. Many of these students go to bars and clubs, not only on weekends but during the week, and often don't get home until 3 or 4 in the morning. Attendance is low in many classes. Not surprisingly, some students sleep through class. Seventy-two students in this school live on their own, many because of serious problems at home.

There is racial tension in this school. Last year there were racially motivated brawls. And this year a police officer has been assigned to the school on a permanent basis.

the political and social influence associated with teaching. Also, as Kottkamp, Provenzo, and Cohn (1986) point out, there are various ancillary rewards—rewards that are byproducts of the teaching profession, but that aren't related directly to teaching itself. For example, many view the typical school schedule, with its long summer vacation, as an important reward. Similarly, many desire the common five-day work week, each day being 6 to 7 hours long, as well as the security that has traditionally been associated with a tenured (permanent) teaching contract—in terms of continued employment and in terms of stable income and eventual pension.

CAREER STABILITY AND CHANGE

A relatively large proportion of beginning teachers either do not obtain starting positions or abandon their careers after a few years. Twelve years after they first started teaching, half of all young male teachers have left the teaching profession (Murnane, Singer, & Willett, 1988); about a quarter of these male teachers later resume teaching. Not surprisingly, given that many interrupt their careers for childbearing and -rearing, half of all beginning female teachers are no longer teaching within six years. However, almost one-third of these female teachers subsequently return to teaching. Thus, although many beginning teachers abandon or switch their careers, the majority make lifelong careers out of teaching.

Many—perhaps most—love what they do.

CULTURAL AND GLOBAL DIVERSITY

Those of us reared in areas where school is universal and compulsory tend to become blasé about its role and its effects on society: We lose sight of the effect of schooling. Perhaps it would be a good thing to remind ourselves occasionally that not all of the world is an industrialized technological society like ours. Things are not everywhere as they are here. The contrast might highlight some of the differences that teaching and learning can make. (See

Figure 1.2 for an indication of how variable schooling achievement is, even in relatively advanced countries.)

GLOBAL DISPARITY

Consider, for example, that infant mortality in the United States and in Canada is now less than 9 per 1,000. In contrast, in many parts of the nonindustrialized world, more than 100 infants per 1,000 die. In fact, the United Nations reports that more than 13 million of the world's children under age 5 die each year from preventable causes, the vast majority of them in developing countries (Grant, 1993). Almost 8 million die from pneumonia, diarrheal dehydration, or vaccine-preventable diseases such as measles, tetanus, and whooping cough; about another 5 million die from starvation. That's more than 35,000 children under 5 dying every day!

What does this have to do with education? A great deal. Research makes it clear that exposure to schooling in the Third World is significantly related to a much higher probability of infant survival, as well as a reduction in birthrate. For example, mothers can be taught the simple hygiene that can prevent diarrhea, and they can be schooled in the inexpensive oral rehydration therapies that would save large numbers of lives.

It is clear that lack of schooling, illiteracy, poverty, and high mortality go hand in hand. Sadly, in most developing countries, especially in Africa, fewer than half of all children attend school (Tsang, 1988). For those who do attend school, the quality of education is extremely low, and the relative cost is very high; dropout rates are also very high. And although school enrollments in Third World countries have increased approximately fivefold since 1950, lack of funds is seriously curtailing growth of schooling and is having a significant negative impact on the quality of education (Grant, 1993).

It may be easy to imagine the impact of a high-quality, universal educational system in some remote Indian or African village; it is not so easy to see its impact closer to home. It

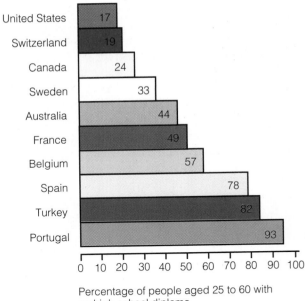

FIGURE 1.2

Percentage of persons ages 25–64 who do not have a high school diploma, by country. Based on U.S. Bureau of the Census, 1994, p. 860.

United States	17
Switzerland	19
Canada	24
Sweden	33
Australia	44
France	49
Belgium	57
Spain	78
Turkey	82
Portugal	93

Percentage of people aged 25 to 60 with no high school diploma

might be a valuable exercise to imagine the eventual effect on our society were we to abandon universal schooling and instead turn our children into the streets. (For an indication of the economic impact of schooling in North America, see Figure 1.3.)

BEING A STUDENT

When we consider the impact of schooling, notes Pallas (1993), we tend to look at the *effect* of what is taught and learned in schools. This is not surprising because the content of school learning does have a tremendous impact on what we are subsequently inclined—not to mention *able*—to do. But, says Pallas, the impact of schooling is much more than the things schools teach. Schooling is a social activity. *Being* a student is an enormously important social role closely tied to a variety of transitions that take place through the course of life. For example, the transitions from dependent preschooler to increasingly independent schoolchild, or from adolescent to adult, are often linked to the individual's status as a student. In societies characterized by prolonged compulsory schooling, much of the socialization of the

individual that might once have been shaped by family and other social institutions now occurs in school.

CULTURAL DIVERSITY

But there is enormous variation in the effects of schooling for different individuals, even within a single society. In North America, for example, educational opportunities and experiences may be profoundly affected by social class, ethnicity, language background, gender, and the special challenges and needs experienced by many individuals. As Castle (1993) notes, minority students are far more likely than majority students to fail or drop out of high school. They are also less likely to enroll in postsecondary educational institutions and significantly more likely to drop out if they do enroll. Similarly, the educational experiences of children with special needs—their relationships with teachers and other students and other aspects of their student lives—might be vastly different from those of the majority of students.

Kantor and Lowe (1995) point out that in North America educational policy has been driven by the belief that education can eliminate

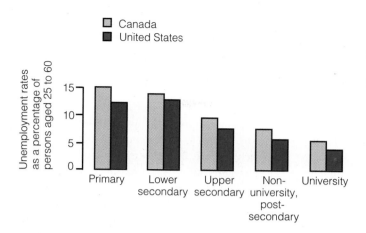

poverty, expand employment and economic opportunities for minority groups, and help those with special needs overcome their challenges. Given the enormous diversity in many North American schools, this belief in the effectiveness of education, coupled with the conviction—indeed, the legal mandate—that all students are entitled to the best education possible, presents interesting and difficult challenges for teachers.

But, notes Perez (1994), teachers should view diversity as an opportunity rather than as a problem. Classrooms characterized by the greatest variety—not only in terms of student abilities and needs, but also in terms of cultural/ethnic and social background—provide the greatest opportunities for exposing all students to diversity. One of the effects may be greater social understanding and tolerance—and perhaps ultimately less strife, hatred, bigotry, and other things the bear does not much like.*

---

*PPC: Why doesn't the author expand on this? Why doesn't the bear tell us more about injustice and intolerance and what teachers can do about them?

Author: The bear never wanted to be a preacher—just a teacher.

MAIN POINTS

1. Teaching skills are not hereditary; psychology can contribute significantly to their development. Specifically, psychological information about topics such as how students develop and learn, what motivates them, and how they think and remember can help shape our beliefs. Beliefs (personal convictions based on knowledge and experience) underlie our teaching decisions.

2. Psychology is the study of human behavior and experience. Its principal means of discovery and of knowing is science, an approach that insists on precision, consistency, objectivity, and replicability. Hence, scientific facts are observations that are objective and replicable. Facts can lead to theories, which are statements whose principal function is to summarize and explain related observations. Laws are statements whose accuracy is beyond question; principles are statements that are probable rather than certain; and beliefs are private, personal convictions.

3. Models are representations of the way things are (or should be), and are often implied in our theories and beliefs rather than explicitly stated. Three models of teachers and their roles are the executive model (teacher as master of the craft of teaching who organizes and conducts the

classroom to maximize learning), the therapist model (teacher as sympathetic individual concerned with wholesome development of learner), and the liberationist model (teacher as facilitator of learning, responsible for freeing students' minds).

4. A simple teaching model describes the teaching process in terms of activities that occur before teaching (establishing goals, determining student readiness, selecting instructional strategies and collecting necessary materials, and planning for assessment and evaluation), activities that occur during teaching (implementation of teaching strategies), and activities that occur after teaching (assessing effectiveness of teaching strategies, determining the extent to which goals have been met, and reevaluating student readiness).

5. Teaching may be viewed as an ongoing sequence of problem solving and decision making. Part of the craft knowledge of expert teachers involves developing sequences of routines and strategies that allow them to solve or avert many classroom problems almost automatically.

6. Teaching empowers students (makes them capable) by giving them important information and skills, by fostering in them the feelings of personal power that come with social competence and self-esteem, and by developing in them the learning/thinking strategies that are essential for learning how to learn.

7. Teaching is a reflective activity in the sense that both teachers and students are encouraged to reflect about their teaching and learning. The goal of reflective teaching is to develop autonomous learners. Reflective teaching strategies are often discovery oriented.

8. Teaching is a craft in that it involves the application of relevant psychological knowledge to educational theory and practice. Expert teachers share a number of characteristics that distinguish them from nonexperts: knowledge (content as well as procedural knowledge), efficiency (do more things in less time; have automized routines and are better problem solvers), and insight (find more creative solutions for pedagogical and management problems).

9. The craft of teaching requires a wealth of information about students, teaching, and learning, as well as some measure of art.

10. Teaching is not as lucrative as playing professional baseball or arranging to have wealthy parents. Teaching positions are sometimes scarce, and the demands and stresses of teaching may drive young teachers out of the profession. But many stay and love it.

11. Given that most of us live where schooling is compulsory, it is easy to lose sight of the impact of education on our lives. Conditions in Third World countries underscore the relationship between lack of schooling and poverty, high infant mortality, and other forms of misery. Cultural diversity in North American classrooms can be viewed as a source of opportunities rather than problems.

APPLIED QUESTIONS

▶ Why might it be important for teachers to study educational psychology?

▶ Define laws, principles, beliefs, and theories.

▶ What is meant by the assertions that teaching is a problem-solving activity? that teaching involves empowering students? that teaching is a reflective activity? that teaching is a craft?

▶ Outline the basic elements of a useful teaching model.

▶ List some of the characteristics that differentiate expert from nonexpert teachers.

STUDY TERMS

behavior **7**

belief **5**

craft knowledge **18**

educational psychology **15**

empower **16**

executive model **10**

expert teachers **19**

law **8**

liberationist model **11**

mainstreaming **22**

model **10**

naive theory **9**

principles **10**

psychology **7**

reflective teaching strategies **18**

science **7**

theory **9**

therapist model **11**

SUGGESTED READINGS

The following brief book provides a detailed look at teaching as a profession. Among other things, it outlines the various training programs available and provides suggestions for finding employment as a teacher:

EVANS, J. M., & BRUECKNER, M. M. (1992). *Teaching and you: Committing, preparing, and succeeding.* Boston: Allyn & Bacon.

Although there has been considerable change in the teaching profession in recent years, there is also considerable stability in the roles and expectations associated with teaching. The following book looks at stability and change from the teacher's point of view and presents an insightful look at the requirements, the challenges, and the rewards of teaching:

COHN, M. M., & KOTTKAMP, R. B. (1993). *Teachers: The missing voice in education.* New York: State University of New York.

Decisions about what to do in the classroom, the authors of the following book explain, require that teachers understand the *context* in which learning occurs, the *content* of what will be taught, and, perhaps most important, a great deal about the *learners* themselves. Theirs is a highly practical guide to various strategies and procedures for classroom use. Especially pertinent for this opening chapter is their Chapter 11, which deals with reflective teaching:

FREIBERG, H. J., & DRISCOLL, A. (1992). *Universal teaching strategies.* Boston: Allyn & Bacon.

Science is perhaps not the only way of knowing. In books that strive to crack our "cosmic eggs" (disrupt our world views) and that appeal to intuition as much as to reason, Pearce argues that science is not even the best way of knowing:

PEARCE, J. C. (1971). *The crack in the cosmic egg.* New York: Fawcett Books.

PEARCE, J. C. (1977). *Magical child.* New York: Bantam Books.

Those who have access to the Internet might want to consult the following thrice-weekly bulletin put out by the National Education Goals Panel (1850 M Street NW, Washington, D.C. 20036). It summarizes current educational news relating to grades K through 12:

http://www.utopia.com/mailings/reportcard/

A detailed analysis of teaching as a contemporary career, with attention to the goals, functions, and philosophies of schools:

RYAN, K., & COOPER, J. M. (1992). *Those who can, teach* (6th ed.). Boston: Houghton Mifflin.

Bears are rather large, bobtailed mammals. They walk on the soles of their feet; eat flesh, roots, and other vegetable matter; and have five toes on each foot (Cameron, 1956).

PART TWO

It's all that the young can do for the old, to shock them and keep them up to date.
GEORGE BERNARD SHAW, *Fanny's First Play*

Human Development and Teaching

CHAPTER 2
An Overview of Development

CHAPTER 3
Cognitive and Personality Development

Bᴜᴛ ɢᴏᴏᴅ ᴛᴇᴀᴄʜᴇʀs *cannot afford to be shocked too often by the behaviors of the young. If they are to teach them effectively, it's important that they know what to expect of them. Teachers should not be surprised at the 6-year-old's occasional bewilderment in the face of the unfamiliar; nor should they be taken aback by the sometimes startling but often impractical logic of the adolescent. Much of growing up means becoming familiar with things; and much of school learning involves learning how to use the mind well.*

The two chapters in Part Two trace the development of children through the school years. They look at the processes of human development and at the forces that shape us, and they examine the educational implications of our knowledge of how children develop.

The childhood shews the man,
As morning shews the day.
JOHN MILTON, *Paradise Lost*

As for being a General, well, at the age of
four with paper hats and wooden swords
we're all Generals. Only some of us never
grow out of it.

PETER USTINOV, *Romanoff and Juliet*

An Overview of Development

PREVIEW

It seems clear to teach children effectively it is useful to understand them. We don't expect our 6-year-olds to understand Boolean logic, nor do we expect our teenagers to become excited at the prospect of being allowed to play on the swings if they color their drawing of mommy nicely, staying inside the lines. But what can 6-year-olds understand? And what excites teenagers? This chapter presents the beginnings of answers for questions such as these in its summary of some of the important findings in the study of child development. It is important to keep in mind, however, that our discussion is necessarily limited to that mythical but convenient invention, the "average child." Your children are not likely to be average; they will need to be understood as individuals. Nevertheless, knowledge of the average may prove valuable in understanding the individual.

Focus Questions

▶ What is a cohort? Why are cohorts important in studying human development?

▶ How are development, growth, learning, and maturation related?

▶ What are some important principles that characterize human development with respect to genetics and environment? differential growth rates? the importance of the timing of environmental influences? the sequence of development? the stages of development? sex (and other) differences?

▶ How do children learn language?

▶ What is multicultural education?

▶ What is morality? How does it develop?

That year, I dreamed often of bears. "Bears," Fencepost's grandmother whispered to me, "have power. They have power to kill. And power to heal, too."

One night I dreamed a huge black bear reared on his hind legs in front of me down by the creek where I had gone to see if I could snare a sucker. His breath made me gag and I thought I might throw up, but I couldn't move. Later in my dream, Fencepost's grandmother whispered to Chief Papiwin that I, the white coureur-de-bois, should be named Faces the Bear. And then I woke up and found that I *had* thrown up and my mother said, "Poor thing, he's got the grippe again," refusing to believe that the smell of a dream bear could have made me sick. I was anxious for morning so I could tell Fencepost's grandmother about the dream.

But the next day my father dragged me off to my first fair, and, sitting in the big tent smelling the sawdust and cotton candy and elephant dung, I watched the "freaks" and forgot all about the dream. A guy strutted onto the stage, threw back his head, and swallowed a sword about as long as my leg. Then they brought out a woman and stuffed her into a box and sawed her in half, which almost made me throw up

again except there was no blood and when they opened the box, the two halves were glued back. After that came a midget who stuffed flaming balls into his mouth and spit out fire—which would have been a neat trick for Father Paradis to use in his Sunday sermons.

As soon as I got home, I ran to tell Fencepost about the fair but I forgot to tell his grandmother about my dream.

Concepts in Human Development

I am still fascinated by fairs, freaks, and fools.* When the fair came to our town one summer, I quickly offered to take my youngest, who was then 7. He was not overly enthusiastic, Saturday being cartoon day. Besides, he didn't yet know how wonderful fairs are.

So we went to the fair. And, to paraphrase an old song, all the wonderful things were there.

But my son didn't see them! When we stood in front of the sideshow tent, listening to a man with a voice like a bullhorn urging us to come in and see the two-headed calf, the woman with the skin of an elephant, the largest man in the whole world, and the one-handed midget concert pianist, my son didn't even look skeptical. He just looked bored. But I dragged him in anyway.

Later that night, when we talked about the fair, I learned that my son had seen neither the calf with the two heads nor the woman with the skin of an elephant. All he had seen was an unfortunate one-headed calf with a hint of a

---

*PPC: I don't think you should make fun of those less fortunate. One of them might be offended. Besides, for a bear who now professes to be politically correct, this seems to me a little unwise.

AUTHOR: I mean fools in the sense of clowns. I used the term because of the alliteration. Besides, few of the other kinds of fools would actually read a book like this. Also, the bear would not be so bold as to use this kind of language when describing a contemporary scene. This is history, this event having occurred in the olden days when it was not yet politically incorrect to notice freaks and fools and call them just that.

second head where its right ear should have been and a pathetic woman with a revolting skin disease. Nor had he seen a giant with a great rumbling voice. Instead, he had watched an unhappy, grotesquely obese man walk painfully across a barren stage, making plaintive breathing noises as he moved. And he had not heard heart-rending sonatas played by the one-handed midget; all he had heard was a handful of sad notes played on a tinny miniature piano.

I had always thought there was magic in the fair—perhaps because the world in which I was raised had fewer wonders. My son's world is far less naive than mine was. Television, among other things, has seen to that. And, at least partly because of our dramatically different contexts, we have developed into people who respond very differently to the same things.

Developmental psychology tries to understand and explain how people develop and change, and how they come to respond differently—or similarly—to the same things. Among other things, it looks at how **contexts** influence the changes that occur between conception and death, and at how contexts interact with genes to influence and determine these changes. It provides teachers with descriptions of human characteristics at different ages, as well as with explanations of the processes that account for developmental changes. Thus, developmental psychology describes what it's like to be a 7-year-old, how 7-year-olds might be different from 14-year-olds, how 7-year-olds got to be the way they are, and how and why they will continue to change. This information is important to teachers, who must always be concerned with students' readiness, interests, and capabilities.

Different Contexts. One factor especially important to the developmental psychologist is the place and time in which individuals are born

and raised. My son and I are clearly a case in point. We are of different worlds—of different contexts. As developmental psychologists would say, we are of different cohorts.

A **cohort** can be described as a group of individuals who were all born within the same period of time—say, the 1940s or the 1970s. Thus, a cohort is initially of a fixed size and composition, and it cannot grow in size after the time period that defines it has elapsed. Not only does it become smaller with the passage of time as members die but other predictable changes occur. For example, the proportion of males to females changes because males tend to die sooner than females throughout the world. Thus, although there are 105 males born for every 100 females, the numbers of each still alive by early adulthood are approximately equal. But by age 85, only 53 males are still alive for every 100 females (U.S. Bureau of the Census, 1994). These predictable changes have implications for understanding the lives of men and women.

From developmental psychology's point of view, the most important thing about a cohort is that its members have had a similar sequence of historical influences in their lives, particularly if their geographic, social, and other circumstances are also similar. In interpreting the conclusions of developmental psychology, we must keep in mind that many of these conclusions are based on research conducted with a small number of cohorts—often only one—and that they might not be valid for other cohorts. In our increasingly multicultural societies, differences among individuals are magnified, and the need for teachers to take these differences into account becomes more important.

This chapter gives a brief overview of some important findings about human development. The next chapter deals more specifically with cognitive and social development.

---

context Refers to all of the developmentally important characteristics of the environment in which development occurs—for example, culture, cohort influences, the family, historical events, educational experiences, and so on.

cohort A group of individuals born within the same specified period of time. For example, the cohort of the 1950s includes those born between January 1, 1950, and December 31, 1959, inclusive.

SOME DEFINITIONS

Development is the process whereby individuals adapt to their environments. It involves growth, maturation, and learning.

Growth refers to physical changes such as increases in height and weight. These changes are quantitative rather than qualitative; that is, they are changes in quantity or amount rather than transformations that result in different qualities.

Maturation, a somewhat less precise term than *growth,* describes changes that are relatively independent of the environment. Maturational changes are assumed to be closely related to the influences of heredity. In most areas of development, however, there is a very close interaction between heredity and environment. For example, learning to walk depends on the maturation of certain muscle groups and on increasing control over their movements (maturational developments), as well as on the opportunity to practice the various skills involved (environment, learning). Maturation is clearly illustrated by the changes in early adolescence that lead to sexual maturity (puberty)—changes collectively labeled "pubescence." Although their onset seems to be affected by environmental conditions (menarche—the onset of menstruation—occurred progressively earlier between 1850 and 1970, apparently because of nutritional factors; see Frisch & Revelle, 1970), the changes of pubescence are largely genetically programmed.

Learning is defined in terms of actual or potential changes in behavior as a result of experience. Thus, all relatively permanent changes

in behavior that are not the result of maturation or of external factors, the effects of which are unrelated to environment (such as the temporary effects of drugs or fatigue), are examples of learning.

PRINCIPLES OF HUMAN DEVELOPMENT

The most important information in developmental psychology can be summarized as principles of development. The nine principles that follow are not an exhaustive summary of developmental psychology; rather, they have been selected mainly for their relevance to the teaching/learning process.

INFLUENCES ON DEVELOPMENT: NATURE AND NURTURE

Development is influenced by both heredity (nature) and environment (nurture). We know, for example, that our genes are responsible for many of our physical characteristics, such as hair and eye color, facial features, and to some extent height and weight. But even here, the influences of heredity are not entirely simple and straightforward. Although some characteristics (for instance, hair and eye color) do appear to be entirely under the control of our genes, other characteristics (for instance, height and weight) clearly are also influenced by environmental factors.

Twin Studies. The situation is far less clear for personality and intellectual characteristics than for physical characteristics. In fact, it has been extremely difficult to determine how qualities such as intelligence and creativity are influenced by heredity and the extent to which they can be modified by the environment (see Rose, 1995). In attempting to clarify this question, many studies have focused on identical twins because, as Gould (1981) notes, they are "the only really adequate natural experiment for separating genetic from environmental effects in humans" (p. 234). This is because **identical**

---

development The growth, maturational, and learning processes from birth to maturity.

growth The quantitative, physical aspects of development.

maturation The process of normal physical and psychological development. Maturation is defined as occurring independently of particular experiences.

learning Changes in behavior due to experience; does not include changes due to motivation, fatigue, or drugs.

(**monozygotic**) **twins** are genetically identical, a condition that is not true for any other pair of humans, including fraternal (**dizygotic**) twins. Therefore, if intelligence is genetically determined, identical twins should have almost identical intelligence test scores (almost but not exactly identical because we cannot measure intelligence completely accurately). But if intelligence is largely a function of the environment, ordinary siblings and **fraternal twins** should resemble each other about as closely as identical twins—and far more closely than identical twins who are brought up in separate homes.

Figure 2.1 presents a summary of studies of the relationship between intelligence and genetic relatedness. What does this figure reveal?

---

identical twins Twins whose genetic origin is one egg. Such twins are genetically identical.

monozygotic Twins resulting from the division of a single fertilized egg. The process results in identical twins.

dizygotic Resulting from two separate eggs and forming fraternal (nonidentical) twins.

fraternal twins Twins whose genetic origins are two different eggs. Such twins are as genetically dissimilar as nontwin siblings.

First, note that the correlation coefficient (a measure of relationship that ranges from –1 to +1) for intelligence test scores is lowest for those who are least alike genetically (unrelated persons) and becomes progressively higher as the degree of genetic similarity increases. Intelligence is clearly influenced by heredity.

Note too, however, that the correlations are higher when environments are more similar. Thus, the intelligence test scores of identical twins reared together are more alike than those of twins reared apart. Also, fraternal twins, who are no more alike genetically than are other pairs of **siblings,** nevertheless manifest higher correlations—presumably because their environments are more alike than are those of most siblings. After all, fraternal twins are of exactly the same age and are often exposed to the same experiences at about the same time.

Adopted Children Studies. Studies of adopted children also provide a rich source of information for disentangling the interactions of heredity and environment. When it's possible

---

siblings Offspring whose parents are the same. In other words, brothers and sisters.

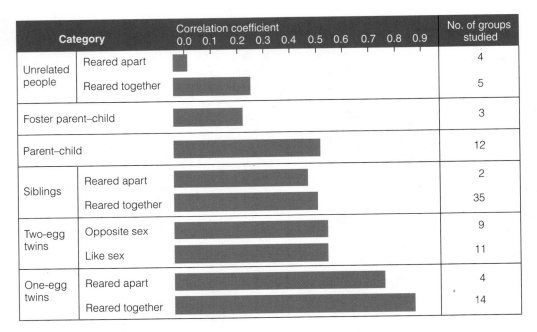

Category		Correlation coefficient (0.0–0.9)	No. of groups studied
Unrelated people	Reared apart		4
	Reared together		5
Foster parent–child			3
Parent–child			12
Siblings	Reared apart		2
	Reared together		35
Two-egg twins	Opposite sex		9
	Like sex		11
One-egg twins	Reared apart		4
	Reared together		14

FIGURE 2.1 Correlation coefficients for intelligence test scores from fifty-two studies. The high correlation for identical twins shows the strong genetic basis of measured intelligence. The greater correlation for siblings or twins reared together, compared with those reared apart, supports the view that environmental forces are also important in determining similarity of intelligence test scores. Adapted from L. Erlenmeyer-Kimling and L. F. Jarvik (1963), "Genetics and Intelligence: A Review," *Science, 142,* 1478. Copyright 1963 by the American Association for the Advancement of Science. Used by permission.

to obtain information about adopted children, about their biological and adoptive parents, and about other natural children these parents might have had, we can make comparisons among individuals who have common environments or common genes, or both. For example, adopted children and their adoptive parents are not biologically related but share a common environment. On the other hand, adopted children and their biological mothers have common genes but separate environments. And the natural children of adoptive parents share both genes and environment.

As Figure 2.2 shows, the highest correlations for intelligence test scores are for those who share both genes and environment; the lowest are for those who share environments but are not biologically related—clear evidence of the importance of genes in determining measured intelligence. Note, for example, that the correlation between adopted children and their biological mothers is *higher* than that between adopted children and adoptive mothers, a finding that has been corroborated in a variety of adoption studies (for example, DeFries, Plomin, & Fulker, 1994).

To conclude, as we stated at the beginning of this section, development is influenced by both heredity and environment. The two interact in complex ways that are not clearly understood to determine what you and I become. What is most important about this principle, from a teacher's point of view, is that many of our characteristics can be influenced by the environment. And although there is relatively little that we can do about heredity at this

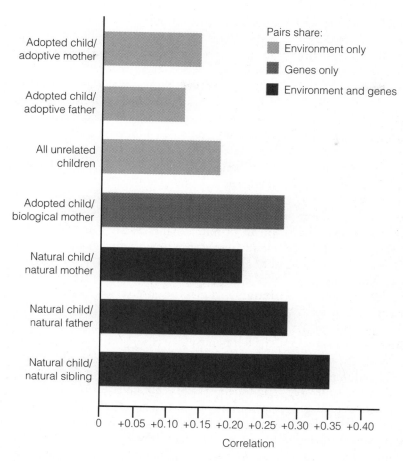

FIGURE 2.2 IQ correlations from the Texas Adoption Project.

Source: Data from J. M. Horn, The Texas Adoption Project. *Child Development*, 1983, 54, 268–275. Reprinted by permission of The Society for Research in Child Development, Inc.

point, much of the environment still remains under our control. (See Chapter 7 for further discussion of the roles of heredity and environment relative to intelligence.)

VARYING GROWTH RATES

Development occurs at different rates for different parts of the organism. This does not mean that the left foot grows rapidly for a short while, then the right foot, and then one arm. What it means is that various parts of the body, as well as some aspects of personality and intellectual and perceptual ability, grow at different rates and reach their maximum development at different times. For example, Bloom (1964) found that by the age of 2½, humans have reached half their future height. He suggests that in the same way about half of a male's tendency to be aggressive toward others is established by age 3, and much of our intellectual potential has already been developed by age 6, a fact that may be partly related to how and when the brain grows.*

---

*Statements such as these are hypothetical approximations at best and refer to variation rather than to absolute amount. The important point is simply that major personality and intellectual characteristics appear to be strongly influenced (and perhaps partly determined) by early experiences.

Investigations of brain development reveal several interesting and important facts. First, most of the *neurons* (nerve cells) that make up the human brain are formed during the prenatal period, although some additional neurons may form in the first few months after birth (DeLong, 1993). At birth, the infant's brain weighs approximately one-quarter of what it will weigh at its maximum, which is reached at about age twenty-five. Most of the increase in brain weight between birth and adulthood seems to be caused by the growth of *axons* and *dendrites* (the elongated portions of the nerve cell that permit neural transmission) and by *myelination* (the growth of a protective covering around the axon), and not by the growth of new cells.

Second, brain growth also seems to be subject to varying rates. The brain does not grow at a uniform rate between conception and birth nor between birth and adulthood. Instead, it appears to grow in spurts. These growth spurts are reflected by increases in cranial (head) circumference. Examinations of head measurements suggest that there is a dramatic spurt in brain growth during the later stages of fetal development. This time of rapid brain development appears to be a critical period during which the effects of maternal malnutrition can be especially severe (Crawford et al., 1993). In fact, note Crawford and colleagues, the most vulnerable period for neural development is prenatal. Not surprisingly, maternal nutrition is closely related to the birthweight of newborns, as well as to the circumference of their heads. In the majority of the world's undeveloped nations, where malnutrition is most prevalent, scientists have noted smaller than average head circumference among children (Winick, 1976).

Another observation related to the principle of varying growth rates is **lateralization,** a term that refers to the fact that the two halves (hemispheres) of the brain do not exactly duplicate each other's functions. In newborns, the hemispheres do not seem to be highly specialized, but in early infancy, the **principle of opposite control** becomes evident. This principle is manifested in the fact that the right hemisphere is typically involved in sensations and movements of the left side of the body, and vice versa. Hemisphere asymmetry is also evident in the fact that about 90 percent of all people are right-handed and only 10 percent left-handed (Halpern & Coren, 1990). This seems to have been true of our ancestral cave dwellers as well, as deduced from the fact that about 90 percent of all primitive hand tracings are of the left hand (hence, presumably drawn by the right hand) (Springer & Deutsch, 1989).

Additional evidence of hemisphere specialization includes the observation that in the majority of individuals (95 percent of right-handed people and 70 percent of left-handed) the left hemisphere is somewhat more involved in language production functions (Bradshaw, 1989). However, this does not mean that the right hemisphere is not involved in language. In fact, when the left hemisphere suffers damage early in life, the right hemisphere frequently takes over language functions with little apparent subsequent difficulty. When damage is suffered later, however, recovery may not occur or may be more limited (Bradshaw, 1989).

Findings such as these have led some to speculate that in the majority of people the right hemisphere is more concerned with emotions and with the spatial and the temporal (for example, art and music) and that the left hemisphere is concerned more with logic, math, science, and language. Thus, individuals who are logical are sometimes described as "left-brain oriented," those who are more intuitive and artistic as "right brained." Some, such as Sonnier (1991) for example, believe that *hemisphericity*—that is, a predominance of one hemi-

---

lateralization A term that refers to the division of functions and capabilities between the two hemispheres of the brain.

principle of opposite control Describes the tendency for sensations and movements on either side of the body to be controlled by the opposite cerebral hemisphere.

sphere over the other—may be one of the important contributors to individual differences. A number of researchers and theorists point out that our current educational practices emphasize left-brain functions, as is reflected in our preoccupation with verbal learning, mathematics, science, and logic (see, for example, Sonnier, 1985; Hooper, 1992; Sonnier & Sonnier, 1992). Our schools neglect right-brain functions, they claim. Hence we should change our educational fare and philosophy to educate both halves of our students' brains. The phrase **holistic education** has been coined to represent this point of view. One advocate of holistic education describes it as a radically new approach that is person-centered, ecological, global, and spiritual (Miller, 1990).

Unfortunately, investigating the dual function of the brain has proved difficult, and much of what passes for information is speculation rather than fact (Hellige, 1990). Hines (1991), for example, following a review of the evidence that links creativity with the right hemisphere, concludes that there is little such evidence, and that the topic is characterized by naive, uncritical, and pseudoscientific beliefs. Similarly, Brown and Kosslyn (1993) emphasize that the brain does not function in terms of simple dichotomies. That is, it is simplistic and misleading to insist that the left hemisphere is logical and analytical whereas the right hemisphere is "artistic." They suggest that the dichotomy is more a matter of degree—that the right and left hemisphere might be *relatively* better for some tasks than for others, but that there is considerable overlap in their functions. However, this does not lessen the importance of holistic education's emphasis on some of the often-neglected aspects of education—specifically

---

holistic education A comprehensive term for educational approaches that attempt to remedy what is seen as traditional education's failure to educate the whole brain. Advocates of holistic education believe that the right hemisphere, which speculation links with art, music, and emotion, is neglected by curricula that stress reason, logic, language, science, and mathematics.

those having to do with the more affective and artistic aspects of the human experience.*

TIMING OF ENVIRONMENTAL INFLUENCES

The observation that growth and development occur at different times and at different rates for different human features leads directly to a third, important developmental principle described by Bloom (1964, p. vii): Variations in environment have the greatest quantitative effect on a characteristic at its period of most rapid change and least effect on the characteristic at its period of least rapid change. This principle is clearly illustrated with respect to physical growth. Twenty-four-year-old Rudolph, who was malnourished through much of his childhood and who is now 5 feet tall, is not likely to grow an additional foot as a result of a sudden change in his diet. In contrast, the eventual height of 24-week-old Christianne is clearly more susceptible to the effects of dietary changes.

This principle also holds for intellectual development. As we saw, for example, brain growth is highly vulnerable to malnutrition during growth spurts, especially during prenatal and early postnatal development (Crawford et al., 1993). Similarly, there is evidence that cognitive development may be most sensitive to

---

*PPC: This whole business has become pretty controversial in our district where they brought some lady in to do a workshop on right- and left-brain functions, and she convinced a lot of teachers they should do some pretty wild things with how they place student desks, how they should use different colors, and on and on. Does the bear have any further thoughts on this?

AUTHOR: Yes and no. But other than to express some uncertainty about what might be involved in the "on and on" part of your workshop recommendations, the bear can only, in fine, politically correct fashion, repeat that what is most important about the so-called holistic education movement is its emphasis on worthwhile areas of development that might otherwise be neglected. But to say that the bear is a creative and intuitive thinker because he is right brained—or to say that he is a right-brained individual because he is creative and intuitive—is really not to say anything at all. Labels name and categorize; they don't explain.

JIM WHITMER/STOCK, BOSTON

ARTHUR GRACE/STOCK, BOSTON

Certain environments appear to be more conducive than others to optimal intellectual, social, and physical development. But it would be a mistake to assume that those from less-advantaged backgrounds are always at a disadvantage, or that those from the richest of backgrounds will always fare better.

environmental influences earlier rather than later in life. For example, Lee (1951) examined intelligence test scores of three groups of African Americans living in Philadelphia, one of which included individuals who had been born in the South; the other two comprised individuals who had moved to Philadelphia either before first grade or at fourth grade. The greatest increases in intelligence test scores were for children who had moved from impoverished backgrounds to better school environments before first grade. In addition, the greatest changes occurred during the first few years. Not surprisingly, those born and raised in Philadelphia scored higher than the other two groups at all grades (see Figure 2.3).

Additional evidence suggesting that the timing of environmental influences can be very important is found in language acquisition: Infants and young preschoolers can easily learn two or more languages simultaneously and well, whereas adults experience more difficulty and less success.

Educational Implications. The fact that environmental influences may be most influential during periods of rapid growth has important edu-

cational implications. It suggests, for example, that educators need to know about periods of greatest and least rapid change, and need to arrange for relevant experiences during these periods. This line of thinking is illustrated in preschool programs such as Project Head Start, in which disadvantaged children are given experiences designed to allow them to catch up with more advantaged children. Although initial evaluations of these programs were not always positive (see, for instance, Bronfenbrenner, 1977), much of the research suffered from the extreme difficulty of measuring many of the important positive changes that can result from these programs. Typically, for example, research looks at obvious things, such as achievement on standardized tests, but fails to take into account important social and emotional events, such as changes in self-concept, motivation, and so on. Also, much of this research compared disadvantaged children who had been exposed to Head Start programs with other children from more advantaged backgrounds. Not surprisingly, the research typically failed to find that the Head Start children were performing at the same level as the more advantaged children. However, when Head

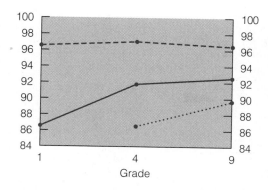

FIGURE 2.3 Changes in intelligence test scores on measures obtained in first, fourth, and ninth grades for African-American students born and raised in Philadelphia (dashed line), those born in the South who moved to Philadelphia in the first grade (solid line), and those who did not move to Philadelphia until the fourth grade (dotted line). Adapted from E. S. Lee, *American Sociological Review*, 1951, p. 231. Copyright 1951 by the American Sociological Association. Used by permission of the author.

Start children are compared to other disadvantaged children not exposed to any programs of this kind, the results are far more positive. For example, after reviewing a number of such programs, Haskins (1989) concludes that they have an immediate, positive impact on children. In addition, they also appear to have long-term benefits. Barnett (1993) looked at individuals from disadvantaged backgrounds twenty-five years after the termination of their Head Start programs and found that the apparent economic benefits to the participants (and the community) far exceeded the costs of the program. Some of these long-term benefits are evident in "life success measures" like reductions in teenage pregnancy, lower delinquency rates, lower unemployment, and less reliance on welfare assistance (Barnett, 1993).

SEQUENTIAL DEVELOPMENT

Development follows an orderly sequence. In fetal development, the heart appears and begins to function before the limbs reach their final form; the lips and gums form before the nasal passages do, the tail regresses before the permanent tooth buds form, and so on.

In motor development, children can lift their chins from a prone position before they can raise their chests, they can sit before they can stand, they can stand before they can crawl, and they can crawl before they can walk.

In intellectual development, the same principle seems to apply, although the sequences are less obvious and the stages less distinct. Piaget's theory (see Chapter 3) is based on the assumption that human development is characterized by distinct sequential stages. For example, an analysis of changes in children's play behavior reveals two distinct developmental sequences—one dealing with the child's actual behavior in game situations and the other with the child's verbalized notions of rules. Specifically, until about age 3, children do not understand the concept of rules, and they play as though there were none. Their play is "free play" in the sense that it is unencumbered by notions of what is permitted and what isn't.

During a second stage, lasting until age 5 or so, children have begun to imitate aspects of the rule-regulated play of adults, but the rules by which they play are idiosyncratic and constantly changing. They make rules up as they go along. But if asked about rules, they describe them as being external and unchangeable.

In the third stage (until age 11 or 12), children realize that rules are inventions that can be changed. But their play behavior is again a contradiction of their beliefs in that they now follow rules rigidly, seldom (if ever) changing them. It isn't until the fourth stage (beyond age 11 or 12) that their play behavior finally reflects their understanding of the function of rules. Now, although they play according to rules, they occasionally change them by mutual consent. (See Table 2.1.)

The understanding of rules is only one small aspect of development that follows an orderly and predictable sequence. Piaget's investigations suggest that notions of reality, logical reasoning, understanding of time and space, and a wealth of important cognitive and perceptual events are sequential and predictable.

TABLE 2.1 PIAGET'S DESCRIPTION OF CHILDREN'S UNDERSTANDING AND USE OF RULES

APPROXIMATE AGE	DEGREE OF UNDERSTANDING	PLAY BEHAVIOR
Before 3	No understanding of rules	Do not play according to any rules
To 5 or so	Believe rules come from God (or some other high authority) and cannot be changed	Break and change rules constantly
To 11 or 12	Understand social nature of rules and that they can be changed	Do not change rules; adhere to them rigidly
After 11 or 12	Complete understanding of rules	Change rules by mutual consent

The observation that much of development follows an orderly and predictable sequence is especially valuable for teachers, who need to be concerned with the readiness of students. Teachers need to know when specific skills and abilities develop if they are to present children with tasks that are not impossible for them but are challenging enough to be interesting and to promote growth. As is made clear in the next chapter, it may also be extremely important to understand the factors that enhance—or that retard—development.

DEVELOPMENTAL STAGES

Many developmental theories are *stage theories;* that is, they describe important developmental events in terms of age-defined stages. Stage theories are based on the belief that although development is a relatively smooth, ongoing process, distinct and important changes nevertheless occur in a predictable sequence.

Stages are useful. They give us convenient places to "hang" our facts; they simplify our understanding, help our organization, and facilitate recall. They have been used extensively by theorists such as Freud, Erikson, and Piaget. Like theories, stages are invented by theorists to clarify and organize their observations. They are best evaluated in terms of their usefulness rather than their accuracy.

Given that stages are inventions, it is not surprising that the stages described by different theorists are usually different; they are all expressions of different points of view, and they all describe different features of child development.

Stage theories are important for teachers because they provide information about the sequence of human development, about the most likely behaviors of children in different stages, and perhaps about the factors that facilitate transition from one stage to the next. We consider these matters again in the next chapter.

CORRELATION VERSUS COMPENSATION

Correlation, not compensation, is the rule in development—although a popular stereotype contradicts this principle. This stereotype assumes that those who are gifted in one area must not be nearly as well endowed in others. The egghead, the stereotype informs us, is a blundering social idiot, unattractive and frail, weak sighted, and completely useless at any kind of task requiring even the smallest degree of dexterity. The same stereotype insists that the athlete may be stunningly attractive but is remarkably stupid, spells with difficulty, cannot write a check without a lawyer to correct it, reads only simple comic books, and laughs uproariously at unfunny events.

Not so. In fact, the person who excels in one realm is more likely to excel in others. The corollary, which is also true, is that people who are below average in one area tend to be below

BIZARRO By DAN PIRARO

SO — AS A "COWBOY", DO YOU EXPECT TO GROW UP TO BE A COW?

Reprinted courtesy of Chronicle Features, San Francisco, California. All rights reserved.

average in other areas as well. Although there are clearly many exceptions to this principle, it nevertheless serves as a useful guide in understanding the overall development of children.

RATE OF DEVELOPMENT

Development usually proceeds at the rate at which it started. A child who learns to walk and talk at an early age is more likely to be advanced later than is a child who begins developing more slowly. Bloom (1964) surveyed a large number of studies that, taken as a whole, suggest that human characteristics are remarkably stable. In other words, there is relatively little change in the rate of development after the initial period of rapid development that characterizes most physical and intellectual qualities.

SEX DIFFERENCES

There are systematic, predictable differences in the development of boys and girls. From birth until early adolescence, boys are both taller and heavier than girls. But by about age 11, girls' average weight surpasses that of boys, and by age 11½, the average girl is taller than the average boy. At about age 14, boys catch up and surpass girls—and remain taller and heavier for the rest of their lives (on average).

Girls have a temporary height and weight advantage over boys in early adolescence because girls mature sexually (reach **puberty**) earlier than boys. On average, they undergo the dramatic growth spurt of early adolescence, one of the first of the changes of **pubescence** (changes that lead to sexual maturity), about two years earlier than boys. These changes are accompanied by important hormonal changes that are evident not only in physical developments but also in changing interests and awakening sexuality.

The average adolescent girl has her first menstrual period—usually taken as a signal of puberty (sexual maturity)—at about age 12; the average boy reaches puberty at about age 14. But individuals are not averages; they are unique. For some girls, the changes of pubescence can begin as young as age 7—or quite a bit later.

Evidence suggests that early or late maturation can be a disadvantage when it puts the adolescent dramatically out of step with peers, especially if the changes (or lack of change) are seen as undesirable (Petersen, 1988) (see the case "I Just Want to Be Average"). Early maturation is generally more positive for boys than girls, perhaps because the precocious boy's greater social maturity is seen as something to be admired and because male sexuality is still more acceptable than female sexuality. By the same token, boys who mature significantly later than average are sometimes more restless, more attention seeking, less confident, and less well adjusted than early maturers (Crockett & Petersen, 1987).

---

puberty Sexual maturity.

pubescence Changes of adolescence leading to sexual maturity.

On average, the adolescent growth spurt occurs two years earlier for girls than for boys. But within sexes, it can also occur at widely different ages, as is evident in the different physical sizes of these sixth graders. Age of sexual maturation can have important implications for the well being and happiness of the adolescent.

In addition to predictable sex differences in average age of maturation, there are other gender differences in interests and abilities. However, unlike maturational timetables, which are largely genetically controlled, differences in interests and abilities—where they exist—are mainly a function of different experiences and different expectations. These gender differences are discussed in Chapter 3.

INDIVIDUAL DIFFERENCES

Each of us is different from every other. This has to do with the fact that we are profoundly influenced by our different environments and the fact that, excepting identical twins, each of us inherits different genetic characteristics. But no matter how different and unique each of us is, we can still make valid generalizations about human behavior and development. But—and this is extremely important—these generalizations apply to children as a group and not to any specific individual child. There is no normal, average child; the average child is a myth invented by grandmothers and investigated by psychologists.

The preceding developmental principles constitute an overview and summary of some educationally relevant statements that can be made about developmental processes. Even though they do not suggest highly specific instructional implications, they can nevertheless provide teachers with general concepts that might be useful for understanding students better.

There is, of course, far more to human development than can be summarized in nine principles. From the teacher's point of view, cognitive (intellectual) development is absolutely central to the teaching/learning process; it is dealt with in Chapter 3. Two other important topics for teachers are language development and moral development. We turn to these next.

LANGUAGE DEVELOPMENT

Our ability to communicate through **language** is one of the things that clearly separates us from other beasts—and not simply because language makes it possible for us to communicate with one another at levels of abstraction that we suspect are beyond the imaginations and the capacities of these other beasts. Language separates us from wild and domestic beasts in at least two other related ways: It provides us with a means for storing our knowledge and wisdom; and it allows us to transform that knowledge. More than this, language is what makes possible the universality of meanings and the sharing of human experience. And because it is the chief medium of instruction in schools, its importance can hardly be overestimated.

---

language The use of arbitrary sounds in the transmission of messages from one individual or organism to another. Language should not be confused with communication.

LANGUAGE AND COMMUNICATION

Language is not synonymous with **communication.** Animals communicate, but they do not have language. A dog who gets its master's attention, walks to its dish and barks, looks its master in the eyes, and then begins to growl is not using language but is nevertheless communicating very effectively. Animals that are not domesticated also communicate. Pronghorn antelope convey alarm by bristling their rump patches, white-tailed deer by flagging their long tails. Pheasants threaten rivals by crowing, elk by bugling, and moose by grunting. Much of this communication, notes Hebb (1966), is purely reflexive. The behavior of the dog, however, is an example of *purposive* communication, but it is still not language.

To communicate is to transmit a message; it requires a sender and a receiver. To communicate through language is to make use of arbitrary sounds or symbols in a purposeful manner to convey meaning. Further, the use of language involves sounds or other signs that can be combined or transformed to produce different meanings. A parrot, for example, can mimic a word or even a phrase and can be taught to make the sequential noises of a phrase so that its utterance will appear purposive. A parrot

that says "You bore me" after a guest has been talking incessantly for 2 hours may appear to be using language in a purposeful manner. But the parrot is not using the phrase with the intention of communicating meaning and cannot deliberately transform the phrase to change its meaning. That would be the use of language as opposed to simple imitation.

THE EARLY DEVELOPMENT OF LANGUAGE

In the course of babbling, infants may emit most of the sounds used in all the world's languages. How these sounds become organized into meaningful patterns of language is still a matter of some speculation.

One account of early language learning is based on what we know about the effects of reinforcement on behavior (described in Chapter 4). This explanation maintains that while babbling, the infant emits wordlike sounds, which tend to be reinforced by adults. In addition, parents or siblings may repeat the infant's vocalizations, thus serving as models. Eventually, through reinforcement, children learn to imitate the speech of those around them. Were it not for this imitation and reinforcement, frequency and variety of speech sounds would probably decrease. This is borne out by the observation that deaf children make sounds much like those made by hearing children until about the age of 6 months; after that they utter few sounds, and not many of these are repetitive (Eilers & Oller, 1988).

---

communication The transmission of a message from one organism to another. Communication does not necessarily involve language because some nonhuman animals can communicate, usually through reflexive behaviors.

C A S E : I JUST WANT TO BE AVERAGE

When she was in fourth grade, Sandra often spent hours in front of her mirror trying on different bulky sweaters and loose-fitting shirts, trying to make herself look normal. That's all she wanted. Just to look normal. But no! Only 9, and she already had to let out her breath to fasten her bra—which was, in fact, her mother's bra. But

she refused to get her own, a bigger one, because it seemed to her that maybe if she could hold them in tight in her mother's little bra, they wouldn't be so noticeable. She was, after all, only in fourth grade, and it didn't seem right that she should already have such big ones, almost like an infirmity, when all her friends were still nice and flat.

Note that even though reinforcement may be a relatively good explanation for the early learning of speech sounds (**phonology**) and simple meanings (**semantics**), it is not an adequate explanation for either the rapidity with which children learn language or for the acquisition of complex **syntax** (sentence formation rules), **grammar** (rules of word classes and functions), and **pragmatics** (implicit rules governing conversation—for example, who should speak and when, and the meanings of pauses, intonations, gestures, and so on). These—phonology, semantics, syntax, grammar, and pragmatics—are the elements of language.

Researchers who have looked at the origins of language have been particularly interested in infants' first sounds and gestures and the interactions of infants and their caregivers. It seems clear that the ability to use and understand words develops through a complex series of such interactions, which Bruner (1983) labels the "language acquisition support system" (LASS). Among other things, this system involves learning how to make eye contact, how to direct attention through eye movements, and how to emphasize and communicate meaning through facial and other bodily gestures.

For convenience and simplicity, the learning of language can be divided into a series of stages. Wood (1981) describes six stages, summarized in Table 2.2.

Six Stages. The prespeech stage spans most of the first year of life. It is marked by two critical achievements, notes Masur (1993). The first is the appearance of the infant's intention to communicate, which is evident in the signals and gestures that the infant uses—like pointing or grunting or crying to obtain something. The second is the infant's discovery that things and actions have their own names, reflected in the appearance of words at about age 1.

The second stage begins with the appearance of the **holophrase,** or sentencelike word. This usually occurs by the age of 12 months. Holophrases are so called because, in the beginning, many of the infant's newly discovered words contain a great variety of meanings—meanings that an adult could not easily express in less than an entire sentence. For example, the holophrase "up," uttered in an unmistakably imperious tone by 1-year-old Elizabeth, means very clearly, "Pick me up right now and tell me a story or I may yell and think of some forbidden thing to do."

Two-word sentences (the third stage), made up primarily of modifiers joined to nouns or pronouns, appear by the age of 18 months. At this stage, speech is still highly telegraphic; that is, complex meanings are squeezed into simple, and sometimes grammatically incorrect, two-word utterances. For example, the sentence "Mummy gone" may mean something as complex as "My dear mother is currently on a business trip in Chicago." During this third stage, beginning at around 18 months, there is ordinarily a tremendous spurt in the acquisition of vocabulary (Masur, 1993).

The fourth stage, multiple-word sentences, is reached between ages 2 and 2½. Sentences may now be five or more words long. Although they continue to be telegraphic, they make use of more grammatical variations to express different meanings, and they typically consist of appropriate subjects and predicates.

---

phonology The structure of speech sounds of a language.

semantics The meanings of the words of a language.

syntax The arrangement of words to form sentences.

grammar Rules of word classes and functions; characteristic system of word forms and syntax of a language.

pragmatics The implicit language rules that govern practical things such as when to speak and how to take turns in conversation.

---

holophrase A sentencelike word uttered by young children early in the course of learning a language. A holophrase is a single word by which the child conveys as much meaning as an adult would convey with a much longer phrase.

TABLE 2.2 STAGES OF GRAMMATICAL DEVELOPMENT IN CHILDREN

STAGE OF DEVELOPMENT	NATURE OF DEVELOPMENT	SAMPLE UTTERANCES
1. Prespeech (before age 1)	Crying, cooing, babbling.	Waaah, Dadadada
2. Sentencelike word or holophrase (by 12 months)	The word is combined with nonverbal cues (gestures and inflections).	Mommy (meaning: "Would you please come here, Mother?")
3. Two-word sentences (by 18 months)	Modifiers are joined to topic words to form declarative, interrogative, negative, and imperative structures.	Pretty baby (declarative) Where Daddy? (question) No play. (negative) More milk! (imperative)
4. Multiple-word sentences (by 2 to 2½ years)	Sentence includes a subject and a predicate. Grammatical morphemes are used to change meanings (-*ing* or -*ed,* for example).	She's a pretty baby. (declarative) Where Daddy is? (question) I no can play. (negative) I want more milk! (imperative) I running. I runned.
5. More complex grammatical changes and word categories (between 2½ and 4 years)	Elements are added, embedded, and permuted within sentences. Word classes (nouns, verbs, and prepositions) are subdivided. Clauses are put together.	Read it, my book. (conjunction) Where is Daddy? (embedding) I can't play. (permutation) I would like some milk. (use of *some* with mass noun) Take me to the store. (use of preposition of place)
6. Adultlike structures (after 4 years)	Complex structural distinctions are made, as with *ask-tell* and *promise.*	Ask what time it is. He promised to help her.

Source: Based in part on B. S. Wood, *Children and Communication: Verbal and Nonverbal Language Development* (2nd ed.), 1981, p. 142. Reprinted by permission of Prentice-Hall, Inc., Englewood Cliffs, New Jersey.

Between ages 2½ and 4, children learn to use progressively more complex grammatical structures (the fifth stage), culminating in adultlike structures in the late preschool years.

Note that although ages are assigned to each of these stages, these are simply approximations based on the average performance of large groups. Here, as in all areas of human development, it is normal for some to display a behavior earlier and others later. An average is not an expression of normality in the sense that those who deviate from it are abnormal; it is simply a mathematical indication of a point around which observations are distributed.

LANGUAGE AND INTELLIGENCE

The **correlation** between verbal ability and measured intelligence is high. This means that if one ability is highly developed, the other is also likely to be highly developed—and vice versa (see Chapter 7 for a more complete explanation of correlation). In other words, those who score high on measures of intelligence will also tend to score high on measures of verbal ability.

The close relationship between intelligence and language may be partly due to the fact that most measures of intelligence are highly verbal. They usually require not only that children understand verbal directions but also that they make oral or written responses to questions. In addition, many tests measure the extent and sophistication of vocabulary directly. The fact

correlation A statistical relationship between variables.

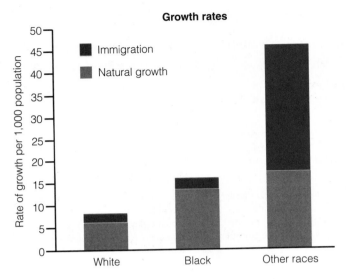

Growth rates

Rate of growth per 1,000 population

Immigration
Natural growth

White   Black   Other races

F I G U R E 2 . 4 **Rate of annual population growth from natural increases and immigration for three U.S. groups, 1989. Based on U.S. Bureau of the Census, 1992, p. 14.**

that verbal ability is given such an important role in measures of intelligence is an indication of its importance in our definitions of intelligence (see Chapter 7).

MULTILINGUALISM AND MULTICULTURALISM

In 1982, almost 75 percent of the school-age population in the United States was white; Hispanic children accounted for only 10 percent of school-age children. Now, in some states like California, the "minority" has become the "majority," reports Garcia (1993): 52 percent of students currently belong to "minority" categories. Projections are that, by 2020, 50 percent of elementary school children in the United States will belong to nonwhite groups. At that time, Hispanics will make up about one-quarter of all elementary school children; just under 20 percent will be African Americans (Pallas, Natriello, & McDill, 1989). These changing demographics are due partly to lower birthrates

and consequently smaller average family size among white families (3.18) than among blacks (3.62) and Hispanics (4.02) (U.S. Bureau of the Census, 1994). In addition, immigration rates are much higher for nonwhites (see Figure 2.4).

These projections are tremendously important for American education because if they are accurate, they will in all likelihood be reflected in dramatic changes in the school. Whereas in 1982 the majority of American schoolchildren spoke English—the dominant, standard, majority language—by 2020, 70 percent of all beginning first-grade students will belong to a nonwhite group. What are the implications of these changes? Even today, more than 15 percent of all Americans speak a language other than English at home. And in more than half of all cases, that language is Spanish (U.S. Bureau of the Census, 1994).

NONSTANDARD LANGUAGES

The languages that most majority-group people understand, speak, and read are referred to as

Striking evidence of the increasingly multilingual and multicultural nature of North American societies. Chances are that within our lifetimes the majority of beginning first-grade students in the United States will belong to nonwhite groups.

standard languages. Standard languages are viewed as correct, acceptable language forms against which other forms of the same language can be compared. The varieties of English spoken by many African Americans, by Hispanic Americans, by French Canadians, and by Native Americans and Canadians are cases in point. We generally assume that these forms of language are inferior and that they are responsible for the frequent schooling problems experienced by those less proficient in standard English. In fact, however, the most plausible explanation for the poorer performance of those who speak a nonstandard English may not be that their language is inferior (less complex, less sophisticated, and less grammatical) but simply that it is different. Because instruction in schools typically occurs in standard English and because evidence of achievement requires understanding of and expression in standard English, these children are clearly at a disadvantage.

---

standard language The socially prestigious form of a society's dominant language; the form that is taught in schools and against which other dialects are judged for correctness.

What, if anything, can—or should—be done to enhance the child's sophistication in the use of standard language? The first part of the question is simple; the second isn't. Several things *can* be done. One obvious solution is to emphasize standard English, both in the home and in the school. Those who favor this approach argue that most commerce, both outside and inside school, is carried out in standard English and that those children who do not learn standard forms of the dominant language therefore will be at the same disadvantage outside school as they are in school. Another solution is to allow minority-language children to use their nonstandard dialects, at least part of the time, in schools.

What *should* be done is another matter. Such issues cannot always be resolved through either research or reason alone.

MULTICULTURAL EDUCATION

As we saw, because of differential birth and immigration rates, the demographic characteristics of North American societies are changing rapidly. As a result, increasing numbers of students come to school with limited English language proficiency. And, as has repeatedly been shown, such students are at serious risk of not doing very well in school (Jiménez, García, & Pearson, 1995). Brisk (1991) notes that in the United States this was traditionally viewed as the students' problem—a problem for which schools need not accept any special responsibility. In some instances, the problem would rectify itself with exposure to traditional schooling, but in many cases students would simply fail. In fact, there is evidence that the number of Hispanic students in the United States not completing high school is actually growing (Waggoner, 1991). Similarly, Edwards and Redfern (1992) report significant, and often unrecognized, underperformance among children from nondominant cultures in both Canada and England. These authors explain that although multiculturalism has long been a fact of life in these countries, through much of their history they have encouraged a sort of linguistic homogeneity. The clearest signs of this myth of homogeneity was found in schools in which all instruction typically occurred in English and minority cultures and languages tended to remain largely invisible.

The second half of this century has seen rapid demographic changes and increasing recognition and appreciation of the multicultural aspects of North American society. As a result, many school jurisdictions have begun to assume increasing responsibility for the growth and performance of all their students, an increasing number of whom represent different cultures and languages. The result is what is loosely termed **multicultural education.**

The Goals of Multicultural Education. Multicultural education is a loosely defined concept that reflects the attempts of educators to take into consideration the cultural diversity of their classrooms and communities. And because it is very difficult to separate culture from language, in the majority of cases, multicultural education is also *multilingual*—that is, it involves instruction in more than one language.

Banks (1993a) describes several important goals of multicultural education. One of its major goals, he notes, is to reform educational systems so that all children, regardless of their cultural and language background, are treated equally by the schools. A second related goal is to rid school systems of unequal treatment of boys and girls. Meeting these goals, notes Banks, requires major changes not only in curriculum and teaching methods, but also in teachers' and administrators' attitudes.

Aspects of Multicultural Education. Multicultural education requires accommodating cultural diversity—which is not a simple matter. One problem is that many teachers have not been sufficiently exposed to different cultures and languages to appreciate the subtle but important differences that distinguish cultural groups (see, for example, the case "Adapting to Cultural Diversity"). As a result, note Pérez and Torres-Guzmán (1992), a number of misconceptions about cultures and cultural groups often characterize teachers' and curriculum builders' approaches to multicultural education. Among them is the simplistic view that cultures are static and unchanging, easily described in terms of things like folk art, clothing, dances, and music. Perhaps even more misleading and simplistic is the assumption that minority cultures are highly homogeneous, and that all individuals of a culture are therefore pretty much the same. Finally, our ethnocentrism leads us to the assumption that one culture—usually the dominant, majority culture (to which most of you belong)—is really better than the others and should be held up as a model for members of other cultures.

Ideally, says Banks (1993a), multicultural education accomplishes several tasks. First, it integrates information and examples from a variety of different cultures, making all students, in a sense, *culture literate*. Second, it helps students understand how knowledge and beliefs are influenced by cultures (as well as by social class and language). Third, and extremely important in an increasingly tribalistic world, it reduces racial prejudice through increasing understanding and, consequently, tolerance of other people and other belief systems. Fourth, it reduces racial, social-class, and gender inequities. And fifth, it empowers all students so that even those from disadvantaged backgrounds or very different cultural groups acquire the information and skills, as well as the confidence and sense of personal power, to succeed.

SECOND LANGUAGE PROGRAMS

Multicultural education, given that it usually deals with different cultures and languages, is typically also multilingual—or, more precisely, *bilingual,* because in many North American schools there is a clearly identifiable main sec-

---

multicultural education Educational procedures and curricula that are responsive to the different cultures and languages of students with the goal of ensuring that all children experience high-quality education.

ond language. As a result, numerous bilingual or English as a Second Language (ESL) programs have been established. And although the main purpose of these programs, notes Brisk (1991), has been to prepare students to fit into the traditional, English-only school curriculum, this is no longer always the case. Brisk argues strongly that as students become increasingly multilingual and multicultural, schools need to become more responsive to their needs. This does not mean preparing students to fit into a traditional English-only curriculum as much as developing a curriculum that truly integrates the diversity of students whose language and cultural backgrounds are different. What schools should focus on, say Collett and Serrano (1992), is becoming truly inclusive—that is, schools that are truly multicultural rather than schools that simply admit students from diverse backgrounds and then try to make them all the same. Multicultural education, notes Banks (1993b), is education de-signed to allow all students to function well in a pluralistic and democratic society. As such, it is indispensable.

The Other Side. The multicultural education movement is one response to cultural diversity; there is another, notes Ogbu (1994). Sometimes labeled the "core curriculum movement," it advocates that the most important offerings of schools are certain basic "core" subjects like arithmetic, reading, and writing—all in the dominant language. In the United States, powerful, well-funded, and highly vocal groups of English-only advocates argue that English should be designated the official language, as it has now been in at least eighteen states (Padilla, 1991). Many members of these groups—English Only, English First, and U.S. English, to name three—are firmly opposed to the use of public resources for bilingual education.

The argument against multicultural education, notes Banks (1993b), is made not only by

CASE: ADAPTING TO CULTURAL DIVERSITY

THE SITUATION: Eric Johnson, white, Anglo-Saxon, male, age 24, B.Ed., beginning teacher

Eric had always figured he'd be a good teacher: He'd gotten good marks, he liked kids, and he was well organized and hard working. So when they offered him one of the inner-city schools, one with a lot of immigrant children, he didn't even hesitate. He knew about multicultural education, about developing respect for other cultures, about molding his curriculum and his lessons to accommodate the richness of the cultures he would have in his class. He would welcome his fourth-grade minority-culture students with open arms; they would love it.

Or so he thought. But it didn't work that way at all. In fact, many of his immigrant students seemed lost and confused through much of that first school year. And it wasn't until much later that Eric began to understand why. For example:

- The East Indian students were taken aback by the free-wheeling interchanges between the native-born students and the teacher; in their culture, teachers speak and students listen.

- The Japanese students were shocked at the possibility of disagreeing with the teacher—and even more at the possibility of disobeying and scarcely being punished.

- The Vietnamese children felt humiliated at having their heads touched affectionately by the teacher.

- The Moslem girls were profoundly embarrassed at having to change into shorts for physical education.

- The boys from Afghanistan found it very difficult to take directions from the female principal.

Source: Based in part on Stewart (1993).

the *traditionalists* who want to maintain and defend the dominance of Western civilization, but also by various ethnic groups who believe that *their* culture (rather than multiple cultures) should be at the center of the curriculum.

Other groups, notably English Plus, advocate expanding bilingual programs both for adults and for children. There is considerable tension surrounding the debate, notes McGroarty (1992). In fact, in the United States, bilingual education has been mandated by law following court decisions that found that putting all children in English-speaking classes, regardless of their language and cultural background, does not amount to treating all children equally. However, Los Angeles county is now revising its bilingual policy, apparently because of declining English fluency (Daily Report Card, 1995). The emphasis will now be on English proficiency and on academic results. As a consequence, children who are not fluent in English will be assigned to special classes for a much shorter period of time. In Canada, the right to instruction in both official languages (English and French) is guaranteed in some provinces but not others. Most notably, Quebec's Bill 101 tends to entrench the use of only French in all public sectors in the province of Quebec (Padilla, 1991).

Immersion Programs. Research suggests that one of the best ways to learn a second language is not to take occasional lessons, private instruction, expensive audio- or videotape courses, or concentrated study but to become immersed in the language. In essence, **language immersion** involves entering an environment in which only the language that is to be learned is spoken. Immersion programs might be used for speakers of the dominant language who want to learn a second language (for example,

English-speaking children in western Canada entering a French immersion program). They are also used to help children who speak a minority language learn the dominant language (for example, Spanish-speaking children being placed in an English immersion program).

Stewart (1993) describes three different types of English immersion programs currently in use. *Sheltered immersion* is commonly used at the high school level and is designed for students who speak some English but who would profit from a higher level of proficiency. In a sheltered immersion class, students are taught subjects in English, but teachers attempt to keep the vocabulary and grammar at a level that is understood by all students. When students have progressed sufficiently in their knowledge of English, they return to the regular program.

Structured immersion typically begins in the first grade, although it can also begin later. It involves providing all instruction in the immersion language. And *pull-out immersion* is an immersion program typically used when the school enrollment is too low for a structured immersion program. In such cases, students are pulled out of their regular classes for special instruction in the second language, very often given by teachers specifically trained in teaching English as a second language (ESL).

There is ample evidence to suggest that when immersion occurs early enough (soon after the first language is firmly established), children can painlessly learn a second language and perhaps even a third and a fourth.

French and Spanish immersion programs for English-speaking students are a mushrooming phenomenon in North America. Most of these are structured immersion programs that begin in preschool settings and continue through the elementary grades. In a typical program, teachers and teacher assistants speak only the immersion language in the first year; that is, the second language is not taught as a separate subject but is simply the language through which the regular curriculum is taught. In the second year, English is introduced for perhaps 10 percent of the school day.

---

language immersion An approach to teaching a second language that involves placing the learner in an environment in which only the second language is used.

The percentage increases each year, until by sixth grade half the school day is conducted in English and half in the second language.

Research indicates that immersion programs can be extremely effective in teaching a second language (for example, Ambert, 1991). Participants quickly reach high levels of proficiency in understanding and speaking the second language, as well as in reading and writing, although the majority do not reach as high a level of proficiency as native speakers. In addition, perhaps only a small number will ever become what Diaz (1983) calls "balanced bilinguals" (individuals who are equally proficient in both languages). However, as Genesee (1985) points out, the language deficiencies of immersion students do not appear to interfere with their functional use of the second language. In addition, these students typically perform as well as students in conventional English programs in academic subjects such as mathematics, science, and social studies, as well as on measures of social and cognitive development. If the immersion program is entirely in the second language and students have not yet received instruction in English language arts, they do not, of course, do as well on measures of English literacy. But Genesee (1985) reports that within one year of receiving English instruction, they perform as well as children in monolingual English programs. In fact, research summarized by Lindholm and Aclan (1991) indicates that bilingual proficiency relates positively to high academic achievement.

Bilingual Programs. Language immersion programs teach a second language by immersing students in the language to be learned. However, many bilingual programs use other approaches. For example, Lam (1992) describes six distinct types of bilingual programs used in schools. These include programs designed primarily to establish English-language competency, programs intended to develop a high level of competency in a second language as well as in English, and various other programs for students with special needs.

Which Approach? There has been a staggering amount of research on the effects of different approaches to teaching a second language, says Cziko (1992). But the conclusions are neither clear nor simple. One of the problems, as Lam (1992) notes, is that some programs are exemplary and others not; some students learn quickly, and others slowly. Also, sadly, some teachers are less competent than others. In fact, following a major evaluation of different approaches to bilingual education, Meyer and Fienberg (1992) conclude that it is unreasonable to expect that any one method might be highly effective given "the unexceptional nature of the instruction" (p. 102). This evaluation, commissioned by the American National Research Council, compared three strategies for second language learning: immersion programs, in which teachers understand and speak both languages but use only the immersion language in school; early exit programs, in which children who begin school with limited proficiency in English are placed in English classes as soon as possible; and late exit programs, which attempt to develop proficiency in English over time while maintaining a high level of proficiency in the native language. Among their conclusions was the observation that although these programs are theoretically distinct, in practice they are often indistinguishable.

Effects of Bilingualism. Learning a second language may not always be an entirely positive experience. Lambert (1975) coined the expression **subtractive bilingualism** to describe the situation in which learning a second language has a negative influence on the first. **Additive bilingualism** describes the opposite situation. And

---

subtractive bilingualism Phrase used to describe a situation in which learning a second language has a generally negative effect often evident in lower proficiency in both languages.

additive bilingualism Phrase used to describe situations in which learning a second language has a positive effect on the first, as well as on general psychological functioning.

Behaving morally requires four things: recognizing a moral problem; evaluating it in terms of personal values; deciding what should be done; and acting. Role-playing situations, such as this mock trial in a real courtroom with an actual judge supervising, might do much to sensitize children to moral issues.

ELIZABETH CREWS/STOCK, BOSTON

transitional bilingualism describes a very common situation in which the native language is completely replaced by the dominant language within a few generations.

Research indicates that the circumstances under which learning a second language is most likely to be a negative experience involve minority-group children whose first language is a minority language. In such instances, the second language—the dominant, majority language—is extensively reinforced in the mass media and in society, whereas the minority language is not. Thus, learning the second language is a subtractive experience in the sense that as children become more proficient in the dominant language, they become less functional and less fluent in the first (Pease-Alvarez & Hakuta, 1992). This may be the case, for example, for French-speaking children in Canada or Hispanics in the United States who learn English as a second language in school. Because television and other media (and perhaps most

community transactions) use English, the first language receives little support and reinforcement outside the home—and perhaps not even in the home. As a result, the first language tends to be seen as less valuable and is used at a less advanced level (Landry, 1987). Moreover, speakers of the minority language in the home are often poor models of that language. Thus, the Spanish or the French spoken at home might be more colloquial—less developed in terms of vocabulary, liberally sprinkled with English expressions, grammatically incorrect, and characterized by idiosyncratic pronunciation (Carey, 1987). And if the minority language is not part of children's schooling, they are unlikely to learn to read and write it. Ultimately, their first-language proficiency may be largely oral.

Learning a second language most often has a positive effect on children when the language learned is a minority language. This would be the case, for example, for English-speaking American or Canadian children enrolled in Spanish or French immersion programs. Growing evidence suggests that such programs are successful in developing a high level of proficiency in the second language and that they contribute to general academic achievement

---

transitional bilingualism Describes a situation in which a minority language is gradually replaced by the dominant language, essentially disappearing within a few generations.

(Garcia, 1993). In addition, they frequently strengthen the first language.

There are, of course, numerous exceptions to these simple generalizations; real life is rarely as simple as our interpretations of research might suggest. But given the probability that our conclusions are more often correct than incorrect, there may be merit in Cummins' (1986) recommendation that the primary language of instruction for minority-group children be the minority language—and that the majority language be presented as a second language. And if our demographic projections are accurate, these issues may be far more pressing by the year 2020.*

MORAL DEVELOPMENT

Many decades ago, Piaget (1932) questioned children to find out what they knew about rules and laws, right and wrong, good and evil. He found that very young children do not behave according to abstract concepts of right and wrong but respond instead in terms of the immediate personal consequences of their behavior. In effect, the **morality** of young children is governed by the principles of pain and pleasure. Children consider good those behaviors that

---

*PPC: After all this stuff on language and language programs, it isn't entirely clear which side the bear is on. I'm sure my students will want to know.

AUTHOR: We are talking, here, of a politically correct bear—a bear no longer so foolish as to take sides. It's partly the wisdom of advancing age, says he, quick to take offense at the suggestion that he has simply become chicken—with age. There was a time, he confesses, when, inflamed with the idealism of his bear-youth, he would have stepped over on the side of his convictions and made noises as loud as anyone's on the other side. "Maintenant, je ne dis rien," he says, with that sardonic twinkle in his eye. "Nada. En boca cerrada no entran moscas."

---

morality The ethical aspect of human behavior. Morality is intimately bound to the development of an awareness of acceptable and unacceptable behaviors. It is therefore linked to what is often called conscience.

---

have pleasant consequences (or at least do not have unpleasant consequences); bad behaviors are those that have unpleasant consequences.

Piaget's label for this initial stage of moral development is **heteronomy.** During this stage, the child responds primarily to outside authority, which is the main source of rewards and punishments. This initial stage is followed by the appearance of more autonomous moral judgments. During the stage of **autonomy,** behavior is guided more and more by internalized principles and ideals.

KOHLBERG'S STAGES

Some three decades after Piaget's pioneering studies, Kohlberg (1964) began to study moral beliefs and behaviors by telling stories involving moral dilemmas to his participants. Subjects were asked how they would behave under similar circumstances and the reasons for their choice. Analysis of responses led Kohlberg to a description of three sequential levels of moral orientation, each of which is divided into two stages (see Table 2.3). In principle, these stages are similar to Piaget's description of a progression from heteronomy (control by others) to autonomy (self-control). Each of the levels and stages is described briefly here.

Level I: Preconventional. At the earliest level, children respond mainly in terms of the immediate hedonistic consequences of their behaviors and in terms of the power of those who have authority over them. Thus in Stage 1 (punishment and obedience orientation), the child believes that obedience is good in and of itself. Evaluation of the morality of an action is totally divorced from its more objective consequences but

---

heteronomy Piaget's label for the first stage of moral development, marked by reliance on outside authority.

autonomy Piaget's label for the second stage of moral development, characterized by a reliance on internal standards of right and wrong as guides for action and for judging the morality of an action.

TABLE 2.3 KOHLBERG'S LEVELS OF MORALITY

Kohlberg identified levels of moral judgment in children by describing to them situations involving a moral dilemma. One example is the story of Heinz, whose wife is dying. One special drug, discovered by a local druggist, might save her, but the druggist is selling it at an exorbitant price. So Heinz, after failing to borrow the money he needs, pleads with the druggist to sell the drug cheaper or let him pay later. But the druggist refuses. Should Heinz steal the drug for his wife? Why? (Kohlberg, 1969, p. 379)

LEVEL I: PRECONVENTIONAL	Stage 1: punishment and obedience orientation	"If he steals the drug, he might go to jail." (Punishment.)
	Stage 2: naive instrumental hedonism	"He can steal the drug and save his wife, and he'll be with her when he gets out of jail." (Act motivated by its hedonistic consequences for the actor.)
LEVEL II: CONVENTIONAL	Stage 3: "good boy, nice girl" morality	"People will understand if you steal the drug to save your wife, but they'll think you're cruel and a coward if you don't." (Reactions of others and the effects of the act on social relationships become important.)
	Stage 4: law-and-order orientation	"It is the husband's duty to save his wife even if he feels guilty afterward for stealing the drug." (Institutions, law, duty, honor, and guilt motivate behavior.)
LEVEL III: POSTCONVENTIONAL	Stage 5: morality of social contract	"The husband has a right to the drug even if he can't pay now. If the druggist won't charge it, the government should look after it." (Democratic laws guarantee individual rights; contracts are mutually beneficial.)
	Stage 6: universal ethical principles*	"Although it is legally wrong to steal, the husband would be morally wrong not to steal to save his wife. A life is more precious than financial gain." (Conscience is individual. Laws are socially useful but not sacrosanct.)

Source: Based on Kohlberg (1971, 1980).

*None of Kohlberg's subjects ever reached Stage 6. However, it is still described as a "potential" stage. Kohlberg suggests that moral martyrs like Jesus or Martin Luther King, Jr., exemplify this level.

instead rests solely on its consequences to the actor. Behavior for which one is punished is bad; that for which one is rewarded must necessarily be good.

In Stage 2 (naive instrumental hedonism), there is the beginning of reciprocity ("Do for me and I will do for you"). The reciprocity characteristic of this stage is strikingly practical. Children will do something good for others only if they expect it to result in someone's doing something good for them in return. Their moral orientation remains largely hedonistic (pain and pleasure oriented).

Level II: Conventional. Conventional morality is a morality of conformity: Behaviors that are good are those that maintain established social order. This level reflects the increasing importance of peers and of social relations and is expressed in two stages. In the first substage at this level (Stage 3: "good boy, nice girl" morality), children judge their actions largely in terms of their role in establishing and maintaining good relations with authority and with peers. Approval is all-important and is assumed to be the result of "being nice." And in the next stage (law and order), morality is characterized by blind obedience. What is legal is, by definition, good. The good person is the one who is aware of rules and obeys them unquestioningly.

Level III: Postconventional. At the highest level of moral reasoning, the individual makes a deliberate effort to clarify moral rules and principles and to arrive at self-defined notions of good and evil. In Stage 5 (morality of social contract), for example, although there is still an element of conformity to laws and legal systems, the important difference is that legal systems are interpreted as being good to the extent that they guarantee and protect individual rights. The individual can now evaluate laws in terms of social order and individual justice and is capable of reinterpreting and changing them.

The sixth and final stage of moral development (universal ethical principles) is characterized by individually chosen ethical principles that serve as major unifying guides to behavior. Individual moral principles are highly abstract rather than concrete. They are not illustrated in rules like the Ten Commandments but are implicit in deep-seated convictions that guide behavior—for example, beliefs in justice or equality.

KOHLBERG'S MODEL EVALUATED

Kohlberg's early research (1971) suggested that a child's progression through these stages is sequential and universal; that is, all children were assumed to progress through all stages in the same sequence. This did not mean, however, that all individuals eventually reached the sixth stage (self-determined principles) and that adults operated only on that level. In fact, a reanalysis of Kohlberg's original data using more careful criteria found that only one-eighth of subjects (in their 20s) seemed capable of fifth-stage judgments. The same analysis found no evidence whatsoever of sixth-stage judgments (Colby & Kohlberg, 1984; Lapsley, 1990). In fact, the stage is more potential than actual.

There have been criticisms of Kohlberg's stages. For example, Holstein (1976) found that many subjects skipped stages, reverted apparently randomly to earlier stages, or otherwise responded in ways that provided little evidence of stages. In addition, Holstein's female subjects often expressed moral judgments that appeared to be systematically different from those of male subjects. Furthermore, there is often so much inconsistency among responses given by the same subject for different moral dilemmas that subjects cannot be described as operating at one level rather than another (Fishkin, Keniston, & MacKinnon, 1973).

What this evidence suggests is that moral judgments depend not only on the ages of subjects but also on a host of other variables, including the intentions of the transgressor, previous experiences in similar situations, and the social, material, or personal consequences of the behavior (Darley & Shultz, 1990; Tisak, 1993).

Apart from the observation that progression through stages of moral development might not be as predictable and as systematic as Kohlberg suggested, Gilligan (1982) suggests that this research has at least two other important weaknesses. One is that Kohlberg's subjects were all males—and, as noted earlier, there is evidence of some gender differences in morality. The other is that the moral dilemmas that Kohlberg used may not always be immediately meaningful in the lives of children. It may be that our responses to hypothetical moral dilemmas ("What would you do if you were at war and you had the opportunity to shoot an enemy soldier who hasn't seen you and is unlikely to?") will be quite different from our actual behaviors, if we ever must in fact make a choice. It might also be that the dilemmas Kohlberg described are too complex for young children—and perhaps even for adolescents and adults. They require that a great deal of information be kept in mind, and they demand an analysis of complex situations involving a number of actors and circumstances. In fact, when moral dilemmas are made simpler, or when children and adolescents are observed in their normal, daily activities, investigators sometimes find evidence of surprisingly sophisticated moral reasoning even at young ages (Darley & Shultz, 1990).

In an attempt to examine morality in women by means of meaningful moral dilemmas, Gilligan interviewed a sample of pregnant women struggling with a decision about abortion. All twenty-nine women in the sample had been referred by a counseling clinic for pregnant women. Twenty-one of these women subsequently had an abortion, four had their babies, one miscarried, and three remained undecided throughout the duration of the study. The study found that it is not so much the decision itself (to have or not to have the baby) that reflects the person's level of moral development as the person's reasons for the decision.

Gilligan identified three stages in the women's moral development. In the first stage, the woman is moved by selfish concerns ("This is what I need . . . what I want . . . what is important for my physical/psychological survival"). In the second stage, there is a transition from selfishness to greater responsibility toward others. This change is reflected in reasoning that is based not on simple, selfish survival but on a more objective morality (notions of what is right and wrong; specifically, a growing realization that caring for others rather than just for self is a form of "goodness"). The third stage reflects what Gilligan labels a "morality of nonviolence" toward self and others. This level of morality is reflected in the fact that the woman will now accept sole responsibility for her decision and that she bases this decision on the greatest good to self and others. The best moral decision at this level is the one that does the least harm to the greatest number of those for whom the woman is responsible.

In summary, Gilligan describes adult female moral development in terms of three stages, beginning with a selfish orientation, progressing through a period of increasing recognition of responsibility to others, and culminating at a level at which moral decisions reflect a desire to treat the self and others equally—that is, to do the greatest good (or the least harm) for the greatest number. At each of these three levels, what women respond to most when initially considering their moral dilemmas are the emotional and social implications of their decision for the self and subsequently the implications for others as well as for self. In contrast with Kohlberg's description of a male moral progression that moves from initial hedonistic selfishness toward a greater recognition of social and legal rights, Gilligan describes a female progression from selfishness toward greater recognition of responsibility to self and others.

Put another way, one of the important differences between male and female morality (as described by Kohlberg and Gilligan) is that moral progression in males tends toward the recognition and use of "universal ethical principles"; in contrast, women respond more to considerations of fairness and equality for self and others. As Stander and Jensen (1993) put it, women's is a morality of "*caring*" rather than of "*abstract justice.*"

Additional corroboration of these sex differences is implicit in a number of studies that have found that girls frequently reach Kohlberg's third stage, morality of good relations, earlier than boys and remain at that level long after boys have gone on to the fourth stage, morality of law and order (see, for example, Eisenberg et al., 1991). One plausible explanation for this observation is that girls are more responsive to social relationships, more concerned with empathy and compassion, and more in touch with real life and less concerned with the hypothetical. In contrast, boys are more concerned with law and order, social justice, and the abstract as opposed to the personally meaningful dimensions of morality.

EDUCATIONAL IMPLICATIONS OF MORAL DEVELOPMENT

Knowing how children develop morally can be valuable to the teacher in several ways. First, knowing how and why children judge things to be morally right or wrong relates directly to the types of rationalizations a teacher might use when trying to convince students to "behave" and/or not to "misbehave." There is evidence, for example, that rationalizations that stress the object—"The toy might break"—are more effective for younger children than rationalizations that are more abstract—"You should not play with toys that belong to other children" (see Chapter 11). By the same token, the types of rationalizations that might be given to adolescents would be quite different from those offered younger children. Also, the most meaningful rationalizations for girls might stress social relationships, empathy, and responsibility; the most meaningful rationalizations for boys might stress legal rights and social order.

Knowledge of moral development might also be useful for actually teaching morality—an important undertaking given that there does appear to be a close relationship between level of moral development and actual behavior (Kohlberg & Candee, 1984). Various techniques have been used successfully in schools to accomplish this. For example, simply discussing moral dilemmas and evaluating the ethical implications of behavior sometimes increases moral sensitivity and behavior (Damon & Colby, 1987). Similarly, Stoll and Beller (1993) report that a variety of approaches including role-playing situations involving moral dilemmas, modeling procedures, and direct teaching were successful in bringing about significant behavior change in a group of student athletes over a three-year period (evident in a decline in fighting, improved classroom behavior, and even an improvement in grades.)

Teachers, says Giroux (1992), have played three different types of roles in the moral development of their students. The teacher as master is an advocate of good behavior and strong consciences. This role emphasizes teaching values and principles. The teacher as facilitator tries to help students develop and understand their own values, sometimes using discussion or other approaches such as values clarification programs. This role views the student rather than the teacher as the source of values. The teacher as mentor is a guide and a friend, an enlightened leader, a source of vision and wisdom. In this role the teacher as mentor is an example rather than a tutor.

Each role underlines the importance of the teacher's personal morality.

MAIN POINTS

1. A cohort is a group of individuals who were born during the same time period and who therefore are subject to the same historical influences.

2. Development can be viewed as comprising all changes attributable to maturation (natural unfolding), growth (physical changes), and learning (the effects of experience). Development results from the interaction of heredity and environment.

3. Development takes place at different rates for different features of the organism. For example, the brain seems to grow in spurts, with a major spurt occurring just before and just after birth (during which nutrition is critical).

4. Environmental changes are most effective during the period of fastest growth and least effective during slowest growth. In practice, this principle favors early intervention, particularly with respect to such things as language development.

5. Development follows an orderly sequence, although the age at which various events occur can vary considerably from one child to another.

6. Development may be described in terms of arbitrary stages. Stages are useful inventions for organizing our observations about children.

7. Correlation, not compensation, is the rule in development.

8. Development usually proceeds at approximately the rate at which it started.

9. There are systematic, predictable differences in the development of boys and girls. But in spite of the generality of our developmental principles, individuals vary considerably.

10. The ability to use language for purposive communication is one of the things that most clearly separates us from other animals. The elements of language are phonology (speech sounds), semantics (meanings of sounds), syntax (sentence formation rules), grammar (word classes and functions), and pragmatics (implicit rules governing conversation).

11. The early development of language is facilitated by a complex network of caregiver–infant interaction, which includes learning how to make eye contact, how to direct attention through eye and body movements, the meanings of expressions and gestures, and so on.

12. Wood's six stages of language development are prespeech (before age 1, cooing and babbling), sentencelike word, or holophrase (by age 1), two-word sentence (by 18 months), multiple-word sentences containing subject and predicate (ages 2 to 2½), more complex sentences and grammatical changes (by age 4), and adultlike structures (age 4 onward).

13. Multicultural education seeks to look after the needs of all children no matter what their cultural background. Accommodating cultural diversity is not a simple task. Nor is it without controversy.

14. Language immersion programs appear to be among the most effective means of learning a second language. Bilingual school programs are a controversial and highly researched phenomenon. Learning a second language sometimes has a negative effect on the first language (subtractive bilingualism), especially for minority-group children who learn the dominant language as a second language. For native speakers of the dominant language, learning a second language is most often an additive experience that results in a relatively high level of proficiency in both languages.

15. Moral development in boys seems to proceed from a preconventional level (hedonistic and obedience oriented) to a conventional level (conformity; desire to maintain good relationships). The postconventional level (individual principles of conduct) is seldom, if ever, reached by anyone. Moral development in girls may be tied more to social responsibility, empathy, and social relationships than to law and social order.

16. Knowledge of moral development might help teachers select the most effective rationalizations for different children. Also, it might be possible to foster moral growth through systematic educational programs.

APPLIED QUESTIONS

▶ How might age and grade cohorts be of very different cultural contexts?

▶ Give an example of each: development, growth, learning, and maturation.

▶ Explain the educational relevance of at least one developmental principle relating to genetics and environment, differential growth rates for different aspects of development, why timing of experiences may be important, how development follows an orderly sequence, gender differences.

▶ Observe and do a brief diary description of a toddler's language development.

▶ How has multicultural education been a part of your schooling?

▶ In what ways are preconventional, conventional, and postconventional moral reasoning evident in the classroom? Provide examples of each type of reasoning.

STUDY TERMS

additive bilingualism **53**	holistic education **39**	pragmatics **46**
autonomy **55**	holophrase **46**	principle of opposite control **38**
cohort **33**	language **44**	puberty **43**
communication **45**	language immersion **52**	pubescence **43**
contexts **33**	lateralization **38**	semantics **46**
correlation **47**	learning **34**	siblings **35**
development **34**	maturation **34**	standard languages **49**
dizygotic **35**	monozygotic **35**	subtractive bilingualism **53**
grammar **46**	morality **55**	syntax **46**
growth **34**	multicultural education **50**	transitional bilingualism **54**
heteronomy **55**	phonology **46**	

SUGGESTED READINGS

For elaboration on and greater clarification of the developmental principles outlined in this chapter, you might consult the following textbooks:

LEFRANÇOIS, G. R. (1995). *Of children: An introduction to child development* (8th ed.). Belmont, Calif.: Wadsworth.

—. (1996). *The lifespan* (5th ed.). Belmont, Calif.: Wadsworth.

Plomin describes his little book as an exploration of the hyphen in nature-nurture. It is a clearly written look at the evidence we have concerning the relationship between heredity and environment. Among other things, it explores the thesis that genes and environment are not entirely independent but that, in particular, genes affect the environment:

PLOMIN, R. (1994). *Genetics and experience: The interplay between nature and nurture.* Thousand Oaks, Calif.: Sage.

Language development is described in considerably more detail in:

WOOD, B. S. (1981). *Children and communication: Verbal and nonverbal language development* (2nd ed.). Englewood Cliffs, N.J.: Prentice-Hall.

The first of the following three books presents a clear look at many of the issues involved in Spanish/English "biliteracy"; the second is a more detailed look at the methods and the politics of multicultural education; and the third explores the implications of multiculturalism for schools:

PÉREZ, B., & TORRES-GUZMÁN, M. E. (1992). *Learning in two worlds: An integrated Spanish/English biliteracy approach.* New York: Longman.

STEWART, D. W. (1993). *Immigration and education: The crisis and the opportunities.* New York: Lexington.

LABELLE, T. J., & WARD, C. R. (1994). *Multiculturalism and education: Diversity and its impact on schools and society.* Albany: State University of New York Press.

An excellent collection of chapters dealing with bilingual education is:

PADILLA, A. M., FAIRCHILD, H. H., & VALADEZ, C. (Eds.). (1990). *Bilingual education: Issues and strategies.* Beverly Hills, Calif.: Sage.

The following is an excellent introduction to Kohlberg's theory:

KUHMERKER, L. (ED.). (1991). *The Kohlberg legacy for the helping professions.* Birmingham, Ala.: Religious Education Press.

A useful collection of articles that describes various approaches and programs for fostering moral development is:

KURTINES, W. M., & GEWIRTZ, J. L. (Eds.). (1991). *Handbook of moral behavior and development: Vol. 3: Application.* Hillsdale, N.J.: Erlbaum.

Folklore has it that many years ago in Switzerland, bears were worshipped because the faithful believed that they were descended— not from Adam and Eve—but from the bear (Engel, 1976).

The parent who could see his boy as he really
is would shake his head and say: "Willie is no
good: I'll sell him."

STEPHEN LEACOCK, *The Lot of the
Schoolmaster*

Youth will be served, every dog has his day,
and mine has been a fine one.

GEORGE BORROW, *Lavengro*

Cognitive and Personality Development

PREVIEW

Of the theories that have attempted to explain human development, those that look at the growth of mind are among the most important for teachers. This chapter describes two of these theories—Piaget's and Vygotsky's—and considers their educational implications. It looks as well at the development and significance of gender roles, and at Erikson's description of personality change through childhood.

- What are gender roles and gender typing?

- Are psychological sex differences real?

- What is psychosocial development?

- According to Piaget, how can human development be described?

- What does sensorimotor development mean? preoperational development? concrete operations? formal operations?

- What is Vygotsky's cultural/cognitive theory?

When an infant was about to be born among the Mundugumor of New Guinea, the parents would adorn themselves with their most prized clothing and jewelry. The father, should he or she be so lucky as to have one, would wear a skirt of brilliant parrot feathers and he would hang plumes and beetle shells around his neck; the mother would decorate herself with bracelets of wild orchids and perhaps she would wear a necklace of smoothly polished dog teeth. Through her nostrils she would run the long white leg bone of a wild guinea fowl. That others in the village looked at the parents in admiration would bode well for the child.

The Mundugumor knew that this business of dressing well for a birth is extremely important. But they also knew that other matters that they could not so easily control are even more important. For example, the Mundugumor knew without any doubt that only infants who are born with their umbilical cords wrapped around their necks have any chance of becoming great artists. And among the Mundugumor, to be a great artist is a lucky and wonderful thing. Amazingly, the Mundugumor were right: Infants not born with their umbilical cords coiled around their necks simply did not become great artists—to absolutely no one's surprise.

I and my various siblings were born at home—in a house perhaps a little more sturdy than a New Guinea hut. And while it isn't clear that the midwife and the grandmother who assisted our various births had medical training or knowledge demonstrably more advanced than that of the Mundugumor, in the end that probably made little difference. That my parents were more likely to absentmindedly crush beetles and kick them aside than to collect their carapaces and make necklaces of them may not have mattered all that much either. And that my mother was not fond of leg bones in her nostrils or dog-tooth ornaments may have been as much of a relief for my father as it surely was for our old dog, busily chewing said bones with said teeth.

When we were born, my siblings and I, our parents were not particularly concerned with the positions of our umbilical cords—unless, of course, the cord was wrapped too dangerously tightly around our scrawny necks. You see, my parents knew without any doubt whatsoever that the position of our umbilical cords at birth had absolutely nothing to do with whether or not we would become great artists. Besides, where I was born and raised, becoming a great artist was not a common ambition.

Still, my parents were very much like the Mundugumor in their attempts to foretell our futures at birth. No, they didn't look at the positions of our umbilical cords. Instead, they looked for an appendage between our legs. Why? Because based on the presence or absence of this appendage, my parents could predict with stunning accuracy a great many of our eventual characteristics.

GENDER ROLES

My parents knew that those of us with the appendage would be fast and strong and tough and just a little aggressive (it's not a bad thing in this dog-eat-dog world, you know). And those without, well, they'd be gentler and more emotional and not nearly so aggressive, and they'd want to help out in the house, but no way would they be interested in chopping wood or hunting and fishing.

My parents were heir to a vast body of beliefs dealing with the most likely characteristics associated with gender. These characteristics define **gender role** (also called sex role). Thus, there are masculine roles and feminine roles. These roles are defined in terms of the behaviors, personality characteristics, and attitudes that cultures find appropriate for each sex. The learning of behaviors according to one's gender is called **sex typing**.

SEX TYPING AND SEXUAL STEREOTYPES

Sex typing begins very early in life. In fact, claim Serbin, Powlishta, and Gulko (1993), one of the first social dimensions that children notice is sex. And even within the first year of life, they have begun to develop what researchers label **gender schemas**—notions about what male and female are and about what the characteristics of each are (or should be). Much of this knowledge consists of our common **stereotypes** of masculinity/femininity, which are highly culture-specific notions of the ways in which males and females should think, act, and feel (Levy, 1993). Thus, not only can children correctly label people as "man" or "woman," "boy" or "girl" almost as soon as they can talk, but they can also predict the sorts of activities in which each is most likely to engage. And once they have begun to develop gender schemas, these act as powerful constraints on behavior. Bussey and Bandura (1992) found that even at the age of 2 children have already begun to approve of sex-typed behavior and, by the same token, to disapprove of cross-sex behavior. As a result, notions of gender act not only as guides for children's behavior, but also as constraints. Because boys aren't supposed to cry, Robert bites his lip and tries hard to hold back the tears; because girls aren't supposed to like playing with boys' things, Elizabeth tries to ignore her brother's gleaming red fire truck.

Development of Gender Roles. As for all aspects of human development, there are two main influences on the development of gender roles: genetics and environment.

Although the evidence is not entirely complete, there are strong indications that some male–female differences are, to a large extent, biological (Maccoby & Jacklin, 1980; Jacklin, 1989). This is most obvious in the greater aggressiveness of males relative to females. Evidence that at least some of the males' greater aggressiveness is biological is found in the observation that males tend to be more aggressive not only in most human societies, but also among most nonhuman animal species. Indications are that male aggressiveness may be linked to the presence of male hormones. In fact, when females are given testosterone injections, they too tend to become more aggressive.

But even with respect to the greater aggressiveness of males, the influence of social roles and expectations cannot be ignored. In North American societies, for example, most occupations and many sports requiring **aggression** have traditionally been restricted to males; those requiring nonaggressive, more nurturant behavior have typically been considered appropriate for females. As a result, society provides children with clear models. Children see them everywhere: at home, on television, on the playground, and, of course, at school. The message is unmistakable that there are behaviors, occupations, interests, and attitudes that are clearly appropriate; and others that, just as clearly, are not.

---

gender roles Attitudes, personality characteristics, behavior, and other qualities associated with being male or female. Gender roles define masculinity and femininity. Also termed *sex roles.*

sex typing The learning of behaviors according to the gender of an individual in a given society; the acquisition of masculine and feminine gender roles.

gender schemas Notions about the characteristics associated with being male or female.

stereotype A strong, relatively unexamined belief typically generalized to a class of superficially similar situations or individuals.

---

aggression In human beings, a much-studied characteristic that is generally defined as the conscious and willful inflicting of pain on others.

Gender Role Stereotypes and Preferences.

When young North American children are asked which personality characteristics are masculine and which are feminine, they typically have no problem in agreeing on the characteristics for each gender. And when they are asked about boys' and girls' toys and preferences, they again show marked agreement. Interestingly, however, both boys and girls are far more likely to think that girls might like boys' toys and activities than the opposite. When Henshaw, Kelly, and Gratton (1992) questioned groups of 8- and 9-year-old boys and girls, they found that only 7 percent of the children thought "John" might like girls' toys; in contrast, half agreed that "Sally" might like boys' toys.

In this study, there were many indications that masculine roles are more constraining than feminine roles. While it is often acceptable for girls to show masculine interests and to engage in masculine activities, it is far less acceptable for boys to be feminine. "Girls in trousers are acceptable in a way that boys in dresses will probably never be," note Henshaw and colleagues (1992, p. 230). Or, as one of the boys in this study put it, "Skipping's for girls— I wouldn't skip and my friends wouldn't skip" (p. 234).

Although boys might be more constrained by their roles, both boys and girls generally agree that the masculine role is the preferable role, as is shown dramatically in the "sex-change" study conducted by Tavris and Baumgartner (1983). The study is simple and straightforward: Boys and girls were asked, "If you woke up tomorrow and discovered that you were a girl (boy), how would your life be different?" "Terrible," the boys answered. "That would be a catastrophe." "A disaster." "I would immediately commit suicide." "I would be very depressed." But the girls responded very differently. "Great," they said. "Now I can do what I want." "Now I can play sports." "Now I can be happy."

When, half a decade later, Intons-Peterson (1988) replicated this study using the same sex-change question, she reported no major changes and no surprises. Boys still responded negatively to the thought of becoming female. They

North American gender stereotypes have traditionally reflected strong agreement about the appropriateness and likelihood of certain behaviors for girls and boys. But there are growing indications of change.

saw girls as more passive, weaker, more restricted in their activities, more emotional, and burdened by menstruation. And although most girls were content with their gender, the majority nevertheless responded to the sex-change question by describing what they saw as the highly positive aspects of being male. They viewed males as more active, less concerned with appearance, more aggressive, more athletic, and better able to travel and develop a career.

Parents, too, agree on proper behavior for boys and girls. In general, they feel that boys should be more aggressive, more boisterous, more adventurous, and less emotional and that girls should be more passive, more tender, more emotional, and less boisterous (Holland, Magoon, & Spokane, 1981).

One Example of Gender Inequity. In recent decades, there has been a strong reaction against the basic inequities of gender roles and the stereotypes they foster, as well as against the injustices of traditionally male-dominated societies. And although there have been tremendous strides in reducing gender inequities, much remains to be done. For example, although the number of women working outside the home has increased significantly—in the

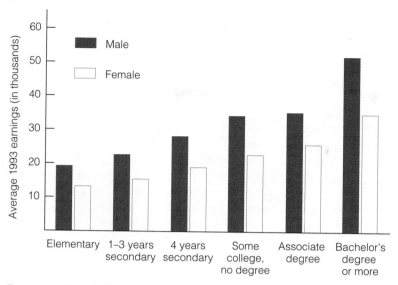

FIGURE 3.1 U.S. male and female earnings by educational attainment in 1993. Based on U.S. Bureau of the Census, 1994, p. 474.

United States, 58 percent of all women above age 16 in 1993, compared with 38 percent in 1960 (U.S. Bureau of the Census, 1994)—jobs held by women are still not on a par with jobs held by men in terms of status, prestige, or income. In Canada, the average income for women is approximately 65 percent that of men (Statistics Canada, 1992); in the United States, it's about 67 percent (U.S. Bureau of the Census, 1994). In 1993, women with a bachelor's degree or more could expect to earn about as much as men with one or two years of college—and less than two-thirds as much as men who also had college degrees (see Figure 3.1).

THE REALITY OF GENDER DIFFERENCES

Parents, children, and society in general assume that there are important differences between males and females and that these should be reflected in their different attitudes, interests, and behaviors—in other words, in their different *gender roles*. Most of us can even agree on the nature of these differences with little difficulty. But just because our naïve psychologies agree does not mean that they are always correct.

Following an early review of research on gender differences, Maccoby and Jacklin (1974) suggested four areas in which there are significant gender differences: (1) verbal ability, particularly in the early grades, favoring females; (2) mathematical ability, favoring males; (3) spatial-visual ability (evident in geographic orientation, for example), favoring males; and (4) aggression (lower among females).

But these differences no longer seem as clear in the 1990s as they did in 1974. In fact, sex differences among adolescents, especially in academic areas, have declined dramatically in recent decades (Feingold, 1993). There is mounting evidence that when early experiences are similar, many of these male–female differences are nonexistent. Furthermore, even when differences are found, they tend to be modest and far from universal (Deaux, 1985). Marsh (1989) reports that research now finds only trivial male–female differences in verbal performance, except among underprivileged populations. And Kaiser-Messmer (1993) points out that differences in mathematics and science achievement are more closely related to culturally determined interests and motivation. In fact, a number of studies done in Hawaii report results that are directly opposed to those most often reported in North America. In those studies, girls typically perform better than boys on standardized mathematics tests (Brandon, Newton, & Hammond, 1987).

Still, contemporary research continues to find that on average males score higher than females on tests of general knowledge and mechanical reasoning; females score higher than males on tests of language usage (grammar and spelling). Significantly, there are no differences in measures of verbal ability, arithmetic, abstract reasoning, or memory span (Feingold, 1992; Hedges & Friedman, 1993). But, on the whole, males are more variable than females on most tests. That is, more are at the highest and at the lowest levels.

IMPLICATIONS OF GENDER ROLES FOR TEACHERS

Teachers need to take gender roles and differences into consideration—keeping in mind that many of these differences are increasingly trivial (or even nonexistent) and quite unjust. Although teachers need to treat all children equally and fairly, this does not mean that all children need to be treated in exactly the same manner. If girls are less interested than boys in violent contact sports, it might be more than a little foolish to insist that they don shoulder pads and participate in the school's football games. And if their interest in the opposite sex manifests itself earlier, and if it sometimes expresses itself in different ways, that too needs to be taken into consideration. At the same time, however, there is a sometimes desperate need for teachers to be aware of and to eliminate the many flagrant and subtle instances of sex bias that still permeate our attitudes, our books, our schools, and our society.

See the case "And for Noon Detention, Here Is the List . . ." for snippets of gender inequities that persist in today's schools. These inequities are found in three areas, note Sadker, Sadker, and Klein (1991):

1. There is still sexism in school administration. At Wes Horman, the principal and vice principal are both male; the majority of teachers are female. In the United States in 1988, fewer than one-third of elementary school principals and 11 percent of high school principals were female (and about

---

CASE: AND FOR NOON DETENTION, HERE IS THE LIST . . .

THE TIME: Early morning at Wes Horman School

THE PLACE: Ms. Fenna's fifth-grade class

Morning messages are just ending on the intercom. "And," says Mr. Sawchuk, school principal, "for noon detention in Mr. Klein's office, the list is Ronald West, Frank Twolips, Eddie Mio, and Eddie Nyberg . . . and I hope there won't be any more by noon."

Ms. FENNA: You heard that, Ronald?
  Ronald nods.
  "Also," continues Mr. Sawchuk, "grade sixers who aren't going on the field trip: the boys will spend the day in Mr. Klein's phys ed classes, and the girls will go to the art room. . . . That's all."

Ms. FENNA: Now, class, I want you to open your math workbooks to page 34, which we started yesterday, and finish the assignment on that page before we go on.

TOM LARSEN: I finished mine. What can I do now?

Ms. FENNA: I'll come check it in a minute.

ROSA DONNER: Me too.

Ms. FENNA: In this class, we raise our hand, Rosa.

TEDDY LANGEVIN: Can we read our *Tom Sawyers* if we're finished?

Ms. FENNA: How many are finished with page 34?

4 percent of superintendents (Jones & Montenegro, 1988). Yet most teachers are female. And in recent years, female graduate students in education have outnumbered male graduate students (National Center for Education Statistics, 1989).

2. There is inequity in the treatment of students. Note that when Tom and Teddy called out, Ms. Fenna responded to them directly. But when Rosa echoed Tom, Ms. Fenna reprimanded her: "In this class, we raise our hand," said she.

   Unusual? No. At virtually all educational levels, teachers interact more with male than with female students (Sadker & Sadker, 1986). On average, boys receive more instructional time and attention from their teachers. They also receive more praise and more encouragement. And, like the detainees at Wes Horman School, they are also more often the subject of reprimands and punishment.

3. Sexual stereotypes are still found in books, in the curriculum, in classroom examples, and elsewhere. At Wes Horman school, boys who need looking after because they did not go on a field trip are sent to gym classes; girls are sent to the art room. And for those who have finished their arithmetic, the reading assignment is *Tom Sawyer*. Although "male hero" books are no longer as pervasive in schools as they once were, boys are often portrayed as more dominant, girls as more helpless (Sadker, Sadker, & Klein, 1991).

It isn't sufficient simply to know that schools reflect much of the racism, the sexism, and other prejudices of society. Teachers (and principals) need to be on guard constantly, lest they unconsciously propagate the same old stereotypes and inequities. It is worth noting, too, that in the United States, gender equity is mandated by laws that prohibit discrimination by sex in any federally funded educational program. But this doesn't mean, as Klein and Ortman (1994) point out, that all equities have now been wiped out. There is still much to be done.

PERSONALITY DEVELOPMENT: ERIK ERIKSON

Gender is one very important aspect of our **personality.** But personality is much more than our notions of being male or female together with related attitudes and interests. It includes all of the abilities, predispositions, habits, and other qualities that make each of us different from every other.

Precisely how personality develops—for example, the extent to which personality characteristics are innate and the extent to which they result from experiences—is not entirely certain. But one highly useful theory of personality development for teachers is that of Erik Erikson. Much of Erikson's theory was inspired by Sigmund Freud. Unlike Freud, however, Erikson downplays the importance of sexuality and of psychosexual conflicts in human development. Instead, he emphasizes the importance of the child's social environment. The result is a theory of **psychosocial** rather than **psychosexual** development. The major emphasis in Erikson's theory is on the development of a healthy self-concept or, in his words, on the development of **identity.**

---

personality The set of characteristics that we typically manifest in our interactions with others. It includes all the abilities, predispositions, habits, and other qualities that make each of us different.

psychosocial Pertaining to events or behaviors that relate to the social aspects of development. Erikson's theory is psychosocial in that it deals with the resolution of social crises and the development of social competencies (independence or identity, for example).

psychosexual A term used to describe psychological phenomena based on sexuality. Freud's theories are psychosexual in that they attribute development to sexually based forces and motives.

identity In Erikson's theory, a term closely related to *self*. Identity refers to the individual's self-definition, a sort of personal sense of who and what one is. To achieve identity is to arrive at a clear notion of who one is. One of the important tasks of adolescence is to select and develop a strong sense of identity.

PSYCHOSOCIAL STAGES

Human development, explains Erikson, can be described in terms of eight stages. The first five span infancy, childhood, and adolescence; the last three describe adulthood. Each stage involves a conflict, brought about primarily by the person's need to adapt to the social environment. And because the demands of a given environment tend to be much the same for all individuals within that culture, we tend to go through the same stages at about the same ages—hence the notion of stages.

Trust Versus Mistrust. For example, for infants to adapt to an initially complex and largely bewildering world, they have to develop a sense of trust in this world—a world about which they are initially mistrustful because it is strange and unfamiliar. Hence, the basic psychosocial conflict, *trust versus mistrust.* Resolving the conflict results in a sense of competence and enables the infant to continue to develop and grow. The most important person in the child's life during this first stage, says Erikson, is the mother or some other primary caregiver. That is because successful resolution of the conflict between trust and mistrust depends largely on the infant's relationship with this caregiver and on the gradual realization that the world is predictable, safe, and loving. According to Erikson, if the world is unpredictable and the caregiver rejecting, the infant may grow up to be mistrustful and anxious.

Autonomy Versus Shame and Doubt. Initially, infants do not deliberately act upon the world but, instead, they *react* to it. Sucking, for example, is something that happens when the stimulation is appropriate; it isn't something that the infant deliberately decides to do. But during the second year of life, children gradually begin to realize that they are the authors of their own actions, and as a result, they begin to develop a sense of autonomy. Now, it's important for parents to encourage attempts to explore and to provide opportunities for independence. Overprotectiveness can lead to doubt and uncertainty in dealing with the world.

Initiative Versus Guilt. By the age of 4 or 5, children have begun to develop a sense of autonomy—a sense that they are somebody. Now they must discover who it is that they are. This discovery, Erikson (1959) explains, comes about largely as a result of children identifying with their parents. That is, true to his Freudian orientation, Erikson assumed that children seek to discover who they are—and, in fact, become what they will be—largely by trying to be like their parents.

During this stage, children's worlds expand dramatically, not only in a physical sense, but also through their use of language. With their increasing ability to explore and know the world, children need to develop a sense of initiative with respect to their own behaviors. They are autonomous as well as responsible for initiating behavior. Because the central process involved in resolving the initiative versus guilt conflict is one of identification, parents and the family continue to be the most important influences in children's development—although preschool teachers may now begin to assume an increasingly important role. It is important for parents and teachers to encourage the young child's sense of initiative and to nurture a sense of responsibility, claims Erikson.

Industry Versus Inferiority. The fourth developmental phase spans the elementary school years. Keeping in mind that each of Erikson's stages reflects the principal social/cultural demands in the child's life, it is not surprising that this stage is marked by children's increasing need to interact with and be accepted by peers. It now becomes extremely important for children to receive assurance that their selves, their identities, are significant, important, worthwhile. During this stage, children often take advantage of opportunities to learn things they think are important in their culture. It is as though by so doing, they hope they will become someone important. And successful resolution of this stage's conflict depends largely on how significant agencies—especially schools and teachers—respond to children's efforts. Recognition and praise are especially important in developing a positive self-concept. If children's work is continually demeaned, seldom praised, rarely rewarded, the outcome may well be a lasting sense of inferiority.

Identity Versus Identity Diffusion. Adolescence brings with it an extremely critical, and sometimes very difficult, task: that of developing a strong sense of identity. The crisis implicit in this stage concerns a conflict between a strong sense of self and a vague, uncertain **self-concept.**

The formation of an identity, notes Erikson, involves arriving at a notion not so much of who one *is* but rather of who one *can be.* The source of conflict is the almost overwhelming number of possibilities open to children. The conflict is made worse by the variety of models and the opposing values evident in society. In the absence of clear commitment to values, and perhaps to vocational goals as well, adolescents are in a state of **identity diffusion.** Later in adolescence, children may experiment with a variety of identities. In this sense, Erikson explains, adolescence serves as a sort of "moratorium"—a period during which adolescents can try out different roles without a final commitment. The crisis of adolescence is simply the conflict between the need to achieve an identity and the difficulties involved in doing so. And resolution of the crisis is implicit in the achievement of a relatively mature identity—which is not something that happens to all adolescents by the time they are out of their teens.

Stages of Adulthood. Erikson describes three additional psychosocial conflicts that occur during adulthood and old age. Each of these reflects the most common social realities in North American cultures. And each requires new competencies and adjustments.

The first of the adult stages, *intimacy and solidarity versus isolation,* reflects most adults' need for intimate relationships with others (as opposed to being isolated). Such relationships are especially important for those who want marital and parental roles. For others, developmental tasks might be quite different.

The second adult stage, *generativity versus self-absorption,* describes individuals' need to take on social, work, and community responsibilities that will be beneficial to others (that will be generative). The basic conflict here is between a tendency to remain preoccupied with the self (as are adolescents, for example) and cultural demands that individuals contribute to society in various ways.

The final adult stage in the human lifespan, *integrity versus despair,* has to do with facing the inevitability of our own death and realizing that life has meaning—that we should not despair because the end of life is imminent. (Erikson's stages are summarized in Table 3.1.)

RELEVANCE FOR TEACHERS

Among other things, Erikson's theory is especially important for teachers because of the insights it provides concerning normal, healthy development. In addition, it emphasizes the role of teachers and parents in helping children develop the competencies that underly the successful resolution of developmental conflicts.

It's important to note that according to Erikson, although developmental progress involves resolving major conflicts by acquiring new competencies, the resolution is never quite complete. That is, aspects of each of the central conflicts that describe a developmental stage may be present throughout life. As Baltes and Silverberg (1994) note, for example, the conflict between the need to be autonomous and the urge to remain dependent continues after infancy. In the same way, the need to trust and the opposing tendency to mistrust also continues through life.

---

self-concept The concept that an individual has of him- or herself. Notions of the self are often closely allied with individuals' beliefs about how others perceive them.

identity diffusion An expression for a stage in early adolescence during which the adolescent has a vague and changing sense of identity with no firm vocational commitment and ambiguous belief systems.

TABLE 3.1 ERIKSON'S EIGHT PSYCHOSOCIAL STAGES

ERIKSON'S PSYCHOSOCIAL STAGES	FREUD'S CORRESPONDING PSYCHOSEXUAL STAGES	PRINCIPAL DEVELOPMENTAL TASK	IMPORTANT INFLUENCES FOR POSITIVE DEVELOPMENTAL OUTCOME
Trust vs. mistrust	Oral (0–18 months)	Developing sufficient trust in the world to explore it	Mother; warm, loving interaction
Autonomy vs. shame and doubt	Anal (18 months–2 or 3 years)	Developing feeling of control over behavior; realizing that intentions can be acted out	Supportive parents; imitation
Initiative vs. guilt	Phallic (2 or 3–6 years)	Developing a sense of self through identification with parents and a sense of responsibility for own actions	Supportive parents; identification
Industry vs. inferiority	Latency (6–11 years)	Developing a sense of self-worth through interaction with peers	Schools, teachers; learning and education; encouragement
Identity vs. identity diffusion	Genital (11 years and older)	Developing a strong sense of identity—of ego (self); selecting among various potential selves	Peers and role models; social pressure
Intimacy vs. isolation	Genital (young adulthood)	Developing close relationships with others; achieving the intimacy required for marriage	Spouse, colleagues, partners, society
Generativity vs. self-absorption	Genital (adulthood)	Assuming responsible adult roles in the community; contributing; being worthwhile	Spouse, children, friends, colleagues, community
Integrity vs. despair	Genital (older adulthood)	Facing death; overcoming potential despair; coming to terms with the meaningfulness of life	Friends, relatives, children, spouse, community and religious support

Source: Derived from *Identity and the Life Cycle* by Erik H. Erikson, by permission of W. W. Norton & Company, Inc. Copyright © 1980 by W. W. Norton & Company, Inc. Copyright © 1959 by International Universities Press, Inc.

To the extent that each of Erikson's stages reflects some truth about human nature, perhaps about our most basic tendencies and conflicts, it can be important in helping teachers better understand children. And in the same way as parents are the most important source of influence in the lives of infants, so too are teachers a fundamentally important source of influence in the lives of schoolchildren. One of the things that Erikson's theory emphasizes is the importance of the child's self-concept. As we noted, teachers can do a great deal to enhance self-concept. They can also do a great deal to facilitate the adolescent's occasional struggles with issues of identity.

COGNITIVE DEVELOPMENT

Cognition, says my dictionary, is "the art or faculty of knowing." Hence, cognitive theorists are concerned with how we obtain, process, and use information. *Cognitive development* refers to the stages and processes involved in the child's intellectual development.

The remainder of this chapter looks at cognitive development, paying particular attention to Jean Piaget's theory, which is the most influential child development theory of this century. Piaget's approach looks at how the child's interaction with the environment leads to cognitive development. The chapter also looks at Lev Vygotsky's theory, which is concerned mainly with how culture and language affect development.

BASIC PIAGETIAN IDEAS

Piaget's early training was in biology rather than psychology. As a result, he approached the study of children as would a biologist, asking the two fundamental questions of the evolutionary biologist:

1. Which characteristics of the organisms under study enabled them to adapt to their environments?

2. What is the simplest, most accurate, and most useful way to classify living organisms?

Translated to a study of children, these questions become:

1. What are the characteristics of children that enable them to adapt to their environment?

2. What is the simplest, most accurate, and most useful way to classify or order child development?

Piaget's answers to these questions, which are found in more than thirty books and several hundred articles, form the basis of his theory.* Many of these answers result from the application of a special technique for studying children developed by Piaget: the **méthode clinique.** This is an interview approach in which the experimenter has a relatively clear idea of the questions to ask and of how to phrase them. However, using this approach, the investigator occasionally allows the child's answers to determine the next series of questions. Hence, the technique provides for the possibility that the child will give unexpected answers and that further questioning will lead to new discoveries about thinking.

Piaget's answers to the two questions of biology (briefly, what permits adaptation, and how can development be classified?) are complex and detailed but can be simplified—as they are here:

ASSIMILATION AND ACCOMMODATION
PERMIT ADAPTATION

"Babies are very competent," says Bower (1989). "They are set to use whatever information we give them" (p. ix). Even the newborn is a remarkable little sensing machine. Almost from birth, it can detect sounds, odors, sights, tastes, and touches; it can respond by squirming and wriggling, by crying, by flinging its limbs about and grasping things, and by sucking.

*Throughout a large part of his long career (he was active and prolific until his death in 1980, at the age of 84), Piaget's closest associate and collaborator was Barbel Inhelder, who co-authored a large number of their publications and was sole author of many other books and articles.

méthode clinique Piaget's experimental method. It involves an interview technique in which questions are determined largely by the subject's responses. Its flexibility distinguishes it from ordinary interview techniques.

cognition To cognize is to know. Hence, cognition deals with knowing, understanding, problem solving, and related intellectual processes.

Characteristics of the Newborn. But can it think? Does it have a store of little ideas? Of budding concepts? We can't answer these questions easily; the **neonate** (newborn) doesn't communicate well enough to tell us. But Piaget tells us that the child probably does not have ideas or concepts—does not think—in the sense that we ordinarily define these terms. The newborn does not have a store of memories or hopes or dreams—does not have a fund of information about which, and with which, to think.

But what this little sensing machine does have are the characteristics necessary for acquiring information. Flavell (1985) describes these characteristics somewhat like this: First, in order for the human system to acquire as much information as quickly as it does, it must be predisposed to process an extraordinary amount of information, even when there is no tangible reward (such as food) for doing so; that is, the system must be primarily intrinsically (internally) motivated—it must derive satisfaction from its own functioning and from its gradual acquisition of information.

Second, the human information processing system must be preset to focus on the most informative—and therefore the most cognitively useful—aspects of the environment. Accordingly, the system must respond most strongly to novelty, surprise, and incongruity. It should search out the unexpected, because it is in the unexpected that the greatest amount of new information can be found. Similarly, it should be pretuned to attend to speech sounds and to make the hundreds of subtle distinctions that are so important in learning a language.

The human newborn that Jean Piaget describes is exactly such a system. It continually seeks out and responds to stimulation, and by so doing it gradually builds up a repertoire of behaviors and capabilities. The system is initially limited to a number of simple reflexive behaviors, such as sucking and grasping. Rapidly, however, these behaviors become more complex, more coordinated, and eventually purposeful. The process by which this occurs is **adaptation.** And, to answer the first question posed just before this section began, adaptation is made possible through the twin processes of **assimilation** and **accommodation.**

Assimilation and Accommodation. In its simplest sense, assimilation involves making a response that has already been acquired; to accommodate is to change a response. Or, to put it another way, to assimilate is to respond in terms of preexisting information using previously learned behaviors. It often involves ignoring some aspects of the situation in order to make the response fit. In contrast, to accommodate is to change a behavior in response to external characteristics. As a result, explains Piaget, assimilation involves little change in the child's cognitive system because old learning and old behaviors are being used and practiced. But accommodation involves changes in the mental system because old behaviors and old learning are now being modified.

As an illustration, imagine an infant lying idly in her crib, not doing anything in particular. Now she waves her little hands seemingly haphazardly in the air, and one of them comes in contact with a pacifier that is fastened to her shirt by means of a safety pin and a length of purple ribbon. Her hand closes immediately around the familiar object, raises it into the air, and brings it unerringly to her mouth, which has already opened in anticipation and which

neonate A newborn infant. The neonatal period terminates when the infant regains birth weight (about two weeks after birth).

adaptation Changes in an organism in response to the environment. Such changes are assumed to facilitate interaction with that environment. Adaptation plays a central role in Piaget's theory.

assimilation The act of incorporating objects or aspects of objects into previously learned activities. To assimilate is, in a sense, to ingest or to use something that was learned previously.

accommodation Modification of an activity or ability in the face of environmental demands. In Piaget's description of development, assimilation and accommodation are the means by which individuals interact with and adapt to their world.

closes greedily around the rubber end of the pacifier. Suck! Suck! Suck!

In Piaget's terms, there are **schemata** (singular: *schema*) involved here—mental representations of the infant's knowledge of pacifiers, including information concerning their suitability as objects to be grasped, to be transported toward the mouth, and to be sucked. The pacifier is being *assimilated* to these schemata; it is being understood and dealt with in terms of previous learning.

Imagine, now, that a generous grandmother replaces the infant's familiar old pacifier with a brand new one—one of those with the patented Easy Suck bulb on one end and the patented Easy Grab plastic knob on the other. The infant swings her tiny arms around again, until one pudgy little hand accidentally strikes the new object. Her hand closes on it at once; that's what hands are for. And again, her mouth begins to open; that's one of the important ways of exploring the world. Besides, in the very beginning, what can't be sucked isn't all that valuable.

But the Easy Grab knob is too large, the little girl's grip inadequate, and the new pacifier squirts away.

"Here, sweetie," grandmother purrs, shoving the object back into the child's hand. Now the infant's grip is rounder, more secure; subtle changes have occurred in the positioning of the fingers and in the pressure of the palm. In Piaget's terms, she has begun to *accommodate* to the characteristics of this new object. She has *adapted*. As a result, the mental system—the arrangement of schemata—has changed in subtle ways.

Assimilation and accommodation are the processes that make adaptation possible throughout life. Note, however, that they are not separate and independent processes. All activity, Piaget maintains, involves both assimilation and accommodation. We cannot begin to make changes in schemata (to accommodate) without first having some basis for responding—that is, without having relevant previous learning to which we can assimilate new situations. Thus, all accommodation requires assimilation. At the same time, all instances of assimilation involve some degree of change to schemata, no matter how familiar the situation or how well learned the response—even if the change is no more significant than that the response will be a tiny fraction better learned and more readily available in the future. As Flavell (1985) puts it, assimilation and accommodation are simply two sides of the same cognitive coin; both always occur together.

Equilibration. One of the governing principles of mental activity, explains Piaget, is a tendency to maintain a balance between assimilation and accommodation (he labels the process of maintaining this balance **equilibration**). At one extreme, if the infant always assimilated stimulation to previous learning and responses, there would be no new learning. Everything would simply be sucked or looked at or grasped in the same way as always—a state of disequilibrium that would lead to little cognitive change (hence, little learning). On the other hand, if everything were always accommodated to, behavior would be in a constant state of flux, forever changing—again an extreme state of disequilibrium resulting in little new learning.

As a further illustration, using a school-related example, if Matthew always calculates area by multiplying two dimensions of a figure, he can be said to be assimilating all area problems to what he has already learned about the area of squares and rectangles. This state of disequilibrium will not only lead to an incorrect

---

schemata (singular: *schema*) The label used by Piaget to describe a unit in cognitive structure. A schema is, in one sense, an activity together with whatever structural connotations that activity has. In another sense, a schema may be thought of as an idea or a concept.

equilibration A Piagetian term for the process by which we maintain a balance between assimilation (using old learning) and accommodation (changing behavior, learning new things). Equilibration is essential for adaptation and cognitive growth.

TABLE 3.2 PIAGET'S FOUR FACTORS THAT SHAPE DEVELOPMENT

The development of progressively more advanced ways of representing the world and of interacting with it (that is, the construction of knowledge) depends on:

EQUILIBRATION	The tendency to balance assimilation (responding in terms of previous learning) and accommodation (changing behavior in response to the environment)
MATURATION	Genetic forces that do not determine behavior but are related to its sequential unfolding
ACTIVE EXPERIENCE	Interaction with real objects and events allows individual to discover things and to invent (construct) mental representations of the world
SOCIAL INTERACTION	Interaction with people leads to the elaboration of ideas about things, people, and self

answer every time an area problem involves some other geometric figure (such as a circle or a triangle), but will also result in little new learning about calculating area. However, if Matthew insists on using a new and different method of calculating area each time he is faced with a different problem, he will be accommodating (modifying responses) excessively and inappropriately. Again, this state of disequilibrium may lead to few correct answers and little stable new learning.

Factors that Shape Development. The tendency toward equilibration, says Piaget (1961), is one of the four great forces that shape the child's development, accounting for the *construction* of knowledge. A second is *maturation,* a biologically based process closely related to the gradual unfolding of potential. According to Piaget's system, maturation does not actually determine development, but simply makes certain kinds of learning possible and even probable. Thus, physical maturation makes it possible for infants to learn to control tongue, lip, and mouth movements, enabling them to learn to speak. But without the right experiences, of course, physical maturation alone would not result in a child who speaks. Hence, the need for *active experience,* another of the four factors that shape development. It is through active interaction with the real world, claims Piaget, that the child develops important notions about objects and their properties. Similarly, through *social interaction*—that is, interaction

with other people—children elaborate their ideas about things and about others as well as about the self (see Table 3.2).

HUMAN DEVELOPMENT CONSISTS OF STAGES

The answer to the second of Piaget's questions (What is the simplest, most accurate, and most useful way to classify or order child development?) is found in Piaget's description of a series of stages through which children progress as they develop. Each of these stages is characterized by certain kinds of behaviors and certain ways of thinking and solving problems. Piaget's descriptions of these ways of solving problems, of behaving, and of thinking can be valuable in helping teachers understand their students. Essentially, it's a description of how cognitive structure develops and changes.

PIAGETIAN COGNITIVE STRUCTURE

One of the principal tasks of theories of intellectual development (also called cognitive theories) is to describe both how we process perceptual (sensory) information to derive meaning from it and how we organize resulting meanings into long-term memory. In effect, the organization of our long-term memories defines what is meant by cognitive structure.

Piaget is a cognitive theorist. His principal interests have to do with the origins of cognitive structure—specifically, with its development from birth to adulthood. For Piaget, as for other cognitive theorists, **cognitive structure** can be thought of as the contents of the intellect—that is, as those properties of intellect that underly knowledge and behavior. These properties are inferred rather than real—that is, a cognitive structure can neither be isolated and looked at nor described in concrete terms. It is, after all, only a metaphor.

In newborns, cognitive structure consists of **reflexes**—the simple, unlearned behaviors (like sucking or grasping) of which the neonate is capable. Piaget labels each reflex a "schema." Schemata become more firmly established as children assimilate objects to them; and they change as children accommodate to objects. A schema is usually named for the activity it represents. For example, there is a sucking schema, a looking schema, a reaching schema, a grasping schema, even a crying schema. Structure in later stages of development, usually after age 7 or 8, is defined less in terms of overt acts than in terms of mental activity. By this age, children have *internalized* activities; that is, they can represent activities in thought. In addition, thought is subject to certain rules of logic. These rules define the term **operation.** In its simplest sense, an operation is a logical thought process. In Piaget's system, operations, or mental activities, are an outgrowth of real activities with concrete objects.

Piaget's description of development is really a description of changes in cognitive structure that occur at certain ages. The details of these developmental changes are discussed next (see Table 3.3).

SENSORIMOTOR INTELLIGENCE: BIRTH TO 2 YEARS

During the first two years of life, Piaget explains, infants understand the world only in terms of the actions they perform and the sensations that result—hence his label **sensorimotor intelligence.** It seemed to him that until the child develops some way of representing the world mentally, intelligent activity must be confined mainly to sensorimotor functions.

The Object Concept. The child's world at birth is a world of the here and now, says Piaget. Objects exist when they can be seen, heard, touched, tasted, or smelled; when they are removed from the infant's immediate sensory experience, they cease to be. One of the child's major achievements during the sensorimotor stage is the acquisition of what Piaget calls the **object concept**—the notion that objects have a permanence and identity of their own and that they continue to exist even when they are outside the child's immediate frame of reference.

To investigate infants' understanding of the permanence of objects, Piaget (1954) devised a simple experiment. It involves showing an attractive object to an infant and then hiding it. At the earliest level, children will not even look for the object, evidence that it does not exist when they can no longer see or touch it. Later, they will begin to search for the object if they have seen it being hidden. It is usually

cognitive structure The organized totality of an individual's knowledge. Also termed *mental structure*.

reflexes Simple, unlearned stimulus–response links such as salivating in response to food in one's mouth or blinking in response to air blowing in one's eye. For Piaget, behavioral reflexes such as looking, reaching, grasping, and sucking are especially important for early intellectual development.

operation A Piagetian term that remains relatively nebulous but refers essentially to a thought process. An operation is an action that has been internalized in the sense that it can be "thought" and is reversible in the sense that it can be "unthought."

sensorimotor intelligence The first stage of development in Piaget's classification. It lasts from birth to approximately age 2 and is so called because children understand their world during that period primarily in terms of their activities in it and sensations of it.

object concept Piaget's expression for the child's understanding that the world is composed of objects that continue to exist apart from his or her perception of them.

TABLE 3.3 PIAGET'S STAGES OF COGNITIVE DEVELOPMENT

STAGE	APPROXIMATE AGE	SOME MAJOR CHARACTERISTICS
SENSORIMOTOR	0–2 years	Motoric intelligence
		World of the here and now
		No language, no thought in early stages
		No notion of objective reality
PREOPERATIONAL	2–7 years	Egocentric thought
PRECONCEPTUAL	2–4 years	Reason dominated by perception
INTUITIVE	4–7 years	Intuitive rather than logical solutions
		Inability to conserve
CONCRETE OPERATIONS	7–11 or 12 years	Ability to conserve
		Logic of classes and relations
		Understanding of number
		Thinking bound to concrete
		Development of reversibility in thought
FORMAL OPERATIONS	11 or 12–14 or 15 years	Complete generality of thought
		Propositional thinking
		Ability to deal with the hypothetical
		Development of strong idealism

not until around age 1 that children will search for an object they have not just seen.

The processes by which infants discover that the world is real and permanent depend on experiencing and interacting with real objects and events. Nor is this a trivial achievement; our understanding of the world and our reasoning about it absolutely depends on our belief that things are real and permanent, and that they continue to exist even when we're not looking at them or touching them. It also depends on our belief that the physical world is subject to certain laws that allow us to predict the effects of different events. We are not born with this understanding, says Piaget; we develop it later.

Imitation. One of the very important means by which young infants begin to develop understanding and learn things revolves around the process of **imitation** or of what Piaget calls *internal representation*. Among other things, imitation is closely involved in the early acquisition of language.

Early in the sensorimotor period, there is no language but there is the beginning of symbolization—that is, the beginning of the internal representation of objects and events. This, says Piaget, is what makes thinking possible. In fact, for Piaget thought is simply the internalization of activity; it begins when children can represent to themselves (in a sense, imitate) a real activity. The first step in this process of internalization involves activities relating to objects or events that are in children's immedi-

---

imitation Copying behavior. To imitate a person's behavior is simply to use that person's behavior as a pattern.

ate presence. At a later stage, that of **deferred imitation,** children can imitate in the absence of the object or event. This internal imitation is a symbolic representation of aspects of the environment. It is also the beginning of language because eventually words will come to replace more concrete actions or images as representatives. Imitation in infancy makes at least three different kinds of learning possible, claim Hay, Stimson, and Castle (1991): (1) Children learn about *places* by imitating the movements of other people, following them around; (2) by copying the behaviors of peers and adults, they learn *familiar social behaviors* such as sharing toys; and (3) by observing them in others, they learn *new social behaviors* such as those involved in speaking a language.

Accomplishments of the Sensorimotor Period. Among important accomplishments of the sensorimotor period is the establishment of early internal representations of the world—the acquisition of internally controlled schemata. In other words, by age 2, children have made the transition from a purely perceptual and motor representation of the world to a more symbolic representation. They have begun to distinguish between perceiving and thinking.

A second major accomplishment is the development of a concept of objective reality. Much of children's development can be viewed in terms of how they organize information about the world. Clearly, this information will largely be a function of what children think the world is. As long as children don't know that the world continues to exist by itself, they are not likely to have a stable representation of it. Thus, the development of a notion of object constancy is absolutely essential for children's further cognitive development.

A third accomplishment of this period is the development of some recognition of cause and effect. This is an essential prerequisite for intention because intentional behavior is engaged in deliberately for its effect. Piaget sees intention as being inseparably linked with intelligence; for him, intelligent activity is activity that is, in fact, intentional.

Although these accomplishments describe children at the end of the period of sensorimotor intelligence, they are not the general characteristics of that period. Those are implicit in the label given to the stage—"sensorimotor." In general, the first two years of life are characterized by a motor representation of the world. The next stage progresses from the sensory and motor realm to the conceptual.

THE PREOPERATIONAL PERIOD: 2 TO 7 YEARS

The preoperational period is so called because, according to Piaget, children do not acquire operational (logical) thinking until around age 7. Before that, their fumbling attempts at logic abound with contradictions and errors.

The period of **preoperational thinking** is often described in terms of two substages: the period of preconceptual thought and the period of intuitive thought.

PRECONCEPTUAL THOUGHT: 2 TO 4 YEARS

The period of **preconceptual thinking** is preconceptual not in the sense that children don't use concepts but in that the concepts they use are incomplete and sometimes illogical.

Preconcepts. Piaget illustrates this by describing his son's reaction to a snail they had seen while

---

deferred imitation The ability to imitate people or events in their absence. Deferred imitation is assumed to be crucial in the development of language abilities.

preoperational thinking The second of Piaget's four major stages, lasting from around age 2 to age 7 or 8. It consists of two substages: intuitive thinking and preconceptual thinking.

preconceptual thinking The first substage in the period of preoperational thought, beginning around age 2 and lasting until age 4. It is so called because the child has not yet developed the ability to classify.

walking one morning. The boy's reaction, para-phrased, went something like this:

"Papa! Cher Papa! Mon cher Papa!" (Swiss children like their fathers.) "Papa! Papa! Papa!" he repeated. "Voici un escargot."

To which Piaget probably replied, "Mon fils, mon fils, mon cher fils! Oui, mon fils, c'est un escargot!" All of which is an interesting enough, but not especially remarkable, conversation. It happened, however, that a short while later they came across another snail, where-upon the boy again turned to his father and said, "Papa! Cher Papa! Mon cher Papa! Mon Papa! Voici encore l'escargot! Regardez! Regardez!"*

This, Piaget says, is an example of precon-ceptual thinking. The child does not yet under-stand that similar objects define classes (all snails are snails) but are not identical (snail A is not snail B). In the same way, a child who is shown four different Santa Clauses in four dif-ferent stores, all on the same day, and who still thinks there is one Santa Claus, is illustrating

preconceptual thinking. She evidently knows something about the concept "Santa Claus," because she can recognize one; but she doesn't know that objects with similar characteristics can all belong to the same class, yet each have an identity of its own. A young child who sees another child with a toy identical to one he has at home can hardly be blamed for insisting that he be given back his toy.

Transduction. Another feature of thinking in the preconceptual stage is labeled **transductive reasoning.** Whereas inductive reasoning pro-ceeds from particular instances to a generaliza-tion (these 20,000 horses have manes; therefore, all horses have manes) and deductive reasoning begins with the generalization and proceeds toward the particulars (all horses have manes; therefore, this new racehorse should have a

---

transductive reasoning The type of reasoning that proceeds from particular to particular rather than from particular to general or from general to partic-ular. One example of transductive reasoning is the following:

Cows give milk.

Goats give milk.

Therefore goats are cows.

---

*PPC: Should this be translated?

AUTHOR: Dad! Dear Dad! My dear Dad! Dad! Dad! Dad! Here is a snail.

My son, my son, my dear son! Yes, my son, it is a snail! Dad! Dear Dad! My dear Dad! My Dad! Here is the snail again! Look! Look!

mane), transductive reasoning goes from particular instances to other particular instances. It is not a logical reasoning process, but it does occasionally lead to the correct answer. Consider, for example, the following transductive process:

A gives milk.

B gives milk.

Therefore, B is an A.

If A is a cow, and B is also a cow, then B is an A. However, if A is a cow but B is a goat, B is not an A. Surprising as it might sound, children do appear to reason in this way, as is evident when a child calls a dog "kitty" or a stranger "Daddy."

INTUITIVE THOUGHT: 4 TO 7 YEARS

After age 4, children's thinking becomes somewhat more logical, although it is still largely dominated by **perception** rather than by reason. Thinking at this stage is characterized by egocentricity, improper classification, and intuition—hence, it is **intuitive thinking**.

Egocentric. As an example of **egocentrism,** Piaget describes the answers given by children for this simple problem: Two dolls are placed side by side on a string. One is a girl doll, the other a boy. A screen is placed between the child and the experimenter, who are facing each other. The experimenter holds one end of the string in each hand so that the dolls are hidden behind the screen. The child is asked to predict which doll will come out first if the string is moved toward the right. Whether the child is correct or not, the boy doll is moved out and hidden again. The question is repeated; again the boy doll will come out on the same side. This time, or perhaps next time, but almost certainly before many more trials, the child will predict that the other doll will come out. Why? "Because it's her turn. It isn't fair." The child interprets the problem only from a personal point of view, from an egocentric view.

Perception Dominated. A child is asked to take a bead and place it in one of two containers. As she does so, the experimenter places a bead in another container. They repeat this procedure until one of the containers is almost full. To confuse the child, the experimenter has used a low, flat dish, whereas the child's container is tall and narrow. The experimenter now asks, "Who has more beads, or do we both have the same number?" "I have more," the child says, "because they're higher." Or she might say, "You have more 'cause they're bigger around." In either case, she will be answering in relation to the appearance of the containers. This reliance on perception, even when it conflicts with thought, is one of the major differences between children and adults.

Inability to Classify. Another striking characteristic of children's thinking during the intuitive period relates to the problems they experience with classification. A 5-year-old child is shown a collection of wooden beads, of which ten are brown and five are yellow. He acknowledges that all the beads are wooden but when asked whether there are more, fewer, or the same number of brown beads as wooden beads, he says there are more. Piaget's explanation of this phenomenon is simply that asking children to consider the subclass (brown colored beads in this case) destroys the larger class for them (all brown and yellow beads). In other words, children at this level understand that classes may contain many different but similar members (they would not make the preconceptual

---

perception The translation of physical energies into neurological impulses—that is, stimuli into sensations—that can be interpreted by the individual.

intuitive thinking One of the substages of Piaget's preoperational thought, beginning around age 4 and lasting until age 7 or 8, marked by the child's ability to solve many problems intuitively and by the inability to respond correctly in the face of misleading perceptual features of problems.

egocentrism A way of functioning characterized by an inability to assume the point of view of others. A child's early thinking is largely egocentric.

"escargot" error), but they do not yet understand that classes can be "nested," one inside the other, in hierarchies (as the class of brown beads is nested within that of wooden beads, each being separate but related).

Intuitive. Children's problem solving in this period is largely intuitive rather than logical. Whenever possible, mental images rather than rules or principles are used in arriving at answers, as is strikingly illustrated by Piaget's rotated-bead problem: Three different-colored beads are placed on a wire, and the wire is then inserted into a tube so that the child can no longer see the beads. She knows, however, that the red one is on the left, the yellow in the middle, and the blue on the right. She is then asked what the order of the beads will be if the tube is rotated through a half turn, a full turn, one-and-a-half turns, two turns, and so on. Young, preoperational children are likely to be thoroughly confused by the question; older children will solve it correctly as long as they can imagine the actual rotations—but they will not apply any rule to the solution of the problem (odd versus even number of turns, for example).

The thinking of the 6- and 7-year-old, says Piaget, is more magical than ours. It does not draw as fine a line between reality and imagination; the logic that governs it is less compelling, more easily swayed.

The dinosaur case (see "Aren't Dinosaurs Real?") shows how it can be with magical thinking. Dinosaurs can be completely extinct, yet there remains the chilling possibility that there might still be a real one somewhere, maybe even in this classroom, today. When, later that day, the teacher asked this same class, apropos of something entirely different, "How many of you have ever seen a real dinosaur?" fully a third of those little grade 2 hands shot instantly in the air.

A Summary of Preconceptual Thinking. In summary, the thought processes of the intuitive period are not always entirely logical. Often, they are egocentric and dominated by perception. In addition, children have not yet acquired the ability to classify or apply formal rules of logic for problem solving. And a final significant difference between thought at this period and thought during the subsequent period of concrete operations is that preconceptual children have not yet acquired the ability to conserve.

Some of the general characteristics of pre-operational thought are well illustrated by an experiment in which Fabricius and Wellman (1993) asked 4- to 6-year-olds to judge the distances covered by different routes going to the same destination. Some of the routes went directly, some were indirect, and some were segmented by different objects. Strikingly, many of the participants insisted that the indirect and the segmented routes were shorter than the most direct routes. Why? Perhaps, suggest Fabricius and Wellman, because the children could only focus on one aspect of the route at a time, and were misled by appearances, as Piaget had suggested. And perhaps, too, because they had difficulty representing the routes mentally, and comparing them mentally, hence making it

CASE: AREN'T DINOSAURS REAL?

THE PLACE: Marie's second-grade classroom

THE SETTING: A dinosaur expert from the Provincial Museum is visiting the class. He has brought a large stuffed tyrannosaurus rex with him.

EXPERT: Dinosaurs are extinct. Does anyone know what that means?

ROSEANNE: Means there's no more.

BILLY: Means they stink bad. (burst of laughter)

RONALD: Means they're all gone and all dead and there's no more, and . . . and I don't know.

EXPERT: That's right. It means there's no more. They're all gone. They're extinct.

ROSEANNE (very seriously, pointing to the stuffed tyrannosaurus rex): Is that a real dinosaur?

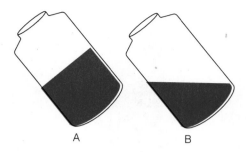

FIGURE 3.2 When asked to draw the fluid level in a tilted jar, young children typically draw the figure shown in A rather than B—not because they have ever seen anything like A in the real world, but because the logic they use in their attempts to make meaning out of their experiences is not always appropriate.

very difficult for them to solve the problem intuitively.

One of the great advances of preoperational thinking over the sensorimotor period is that children begin to apply logic in solving problems, explains Smith (1993). But their trying to use logic does not mean that they will always answer correctly. In fact, the incomplete logic that preschoolers often use sometimes dooms them to error. Consider, for example, the following simple problem: A child is shown a drawing of a jar partly filled with liquid, with the horizontal water level clearly shown, and is then asked to draw what the water level would look like in a tilted jar. When a 3- or 4-year-old is presented with this problem, the typical response, say Thomas and Lohaus (1993) is "a scribbling or the like" (p. 9). But when 5- to 7-year-olds are given the same problem, they immediately apply a clever but inappropriate logic, as is shown in A of Figure 3.2. Kuhn (1984) points out that the children have never seen anything like this drawing; hence, the response does not reflect actual experience with the real world. But what it does reflect is an understanding that water level is ordinarily parallel to the bottom of its container, and a logical application of that understanding. (See Figure 3.3 for a summary of preoperational thought.)

It would probably be wise for the reader who is not already familiar with Piaget to stop at this point. If you have available an electroencephalograph, a cardiograph, a thermometer, and a pupillometer (or any other graph or meter), these should be connected and read at once. Alpha waves, together with decelerated heart rate, abnormal temperature, and reduced pupil size, are symptoms of imminent **jargon shock.** This condition in advanced stages can be extremely detrimental to concentration and learning. Several hours of sleep or some other amusement may bring about a significant improvement.

If you don't have any of this sophisticated electronic gadgetry readily available, you can substitute a hand mirror. Hold the mirror up to your face, and look at your eyes. If they are closed, you are probably in the terminal stage of jargon shock.

CONCRETE OPERATIONS: 7 TO 11 OR 12 YEARS

An operation is a mental activity—a thought, in other words—that is subject to certain rules of logic. Before the stage of concrete operations, children are described as preoperational not because they are incapable of thinking but because of their thinking's limitations. As we saw, these limitations are related to their reliance on perception, intuition, and egocentric tendencies rather than on reason.

But with the advent of **concrete operations,** children make a fundamentally important transition from a prelogical form of thought to thinking characterized by rules of logic. The operations—or thought processes—of this stage apply to real, concrete objects and events; hence, the label. The period of concrete operations is distinguished most clearly from

---

jargon shock See glossary entry on page 546.

concrete operations The third of Piaget's four major stages, lasting from age 7 or 8 to approximately age 11 or 12, and characterized largely by the child's ability to deal with concrete problems and objects or objects and problems easily imagined.

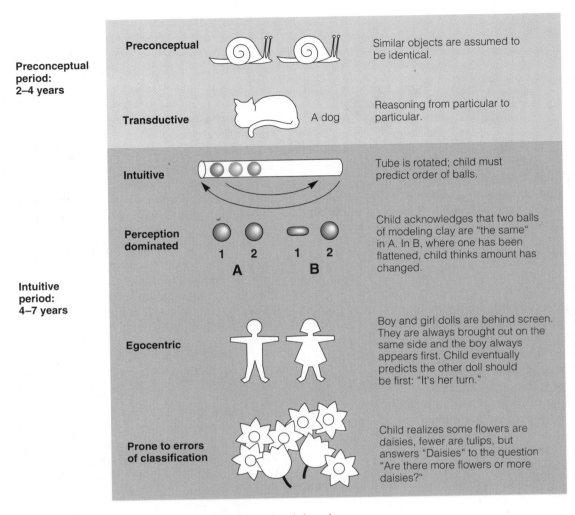

Preconceptual period: 2–4 years

Preconceptual — Similar objects are assumed to be identical.

Transductive — A dog — Reasoning from particular to particular.

Intuitive period: 4–7 years

Intuitive — Tube is rotated; child must predict order of balls.

Perception dominated — 1 2 1 2 — A B — Child acknowledges that two balls of modeling clay are "the same" in A. In B, where one has been flattened, child thinks amount has changed.

Egocentric — Boy and girl dolls are behind screen. They are always brought out on the same side and the boy always appears first. Child eventually predicts the other doll should be first: "It's her turn."

Prone to errors of classification — Child realizes some flowers are daisies, fewer are tulips, but answers "Daisies" to the question "Are there more flowers or more daisies?"

FIGURE 3.3 **Some characteristics of preoperational thought.**

the preoperational period by the appearance of one group of capabilities: the ability to conserve.

The Conservations. Recall the experiment in which an equal number of wooden beads are put into two containers of very different shape, leading the preoperational child to conclude that one container has more beads than the other because it's taller or wider. This illustrates not only the preoperational child's reliance on perception, but also lack of conservation.

Simply put, **conservation** is the realization that quantity or amount does not change unless something is taken away from or added to an object or a collection of objects, despite changes in appearance.

---

conservation A Piagetian term for the realization that certain quantitative attributes of objects remain unchanged unless something is added to or taken away from them. Such characteristics of objects as mass, number, area, and volume are capable of being conserved.

A correct response to a conservation problem is evidence of one or more rules of logic that now govern and limit children's thinking. Among these rules are **reversibility** and **identity.** The rule of reversibility specifies that for every operation (internalized action or thought) there is an inverse operation that cancels it. Identity is the rule stating that for every operation there is another that leaves it unchanged. Both can easily be illustrated with number operations. For example, the operation of addition can be reversed (and nullified) by subtraction ($2 + 4 = 6$; $6 - 4 = 2$). The identity operator for addition is zero (that is, $2 + 0 + 0 + 0 = 2$); for multiplication it is 1 ($2 \times 1 \times 1 \times 1 = 2$).

The importance of these rules to children at the concrete operations level of thinking is evident in the conservation problems. The child who has placed one bead in a tall container for every bead placed by the experimenter in a flat container—and who now maintains that there is the same number in each despite their appearances—may be reasoning as follows: (1) If the beads were taken out of the containers and placed again on the table, they would be as they were before (reversibility), or (2) nothing has been added to or taken away from either container, so there must still be the same number in each (identity).

There are as many conservations as there are measurable characteristics of objects. Thus, there is conservation of number, length, distance, area, volume, continuous substance, discontinuous substance, liquid substance, and so on. None of these conservations is achieved before the period of concrete operations; even then, some (volume, for example) will not be acquired until quite late in that period. Several experimental procedures for conservation are described in Figure 3.4, together with the approximate ages of attainment. The experiments are interesting and easily replicated, and the results are often striking.

One of the intriguing things about conservation is that preoperational children can be made to contradict themselves many times without ever changing their minds. After the experiment on conservation of liquid quantity, for example, the experimenter can pour the water back into the original containers and repeat the question. The subject now acknowledges that they have the same amount; but as soon as the water is again poured into the tall and flat containers, the decision may be reversed.

In addition to conservation, children acquire three other abilities as they come into the stage of concrete operations: the abilities to classify, to seriate, and to deal with numbers.

Classification. To classify is to group objects according to their similarities and differences. The **classification** process involves incorporating subclasses into more general classes, while maintaining the identity of the subclasses. This process leads to the formation of what Piaget calls **hierarchies of classes** (Piaget, 1954). An example is given in Figure 3.5. Preoperational children's incomplete understanding of classes was illustrated in the experiment involving the ten brown and five yellow wooden beads. Recall that at that stage the child thought there were more brown than wooden beads, even while

---

reversibility A logical property manifested in the ability to reverse or undo activity in either an empirical or a conceptual sense. An idea is said to be reversible when a child realizes the logical consequences of an opposite action.

identity In Piaget's theory, a logical rule that specifies that certain activities leave objects or situations unchanged.

classification The act of grouping in terms of common properties. Classification involves abstracting the properties of objects or events and making judgments concerning how they are similar to or different from other objects or events.

hierarchy of classes An arrangement of concepts or classes in terms of their inclusiveness. At the top of the hierarchy is the concept (class) that is most inclusive (for example, writing instruments); below this highly inclusive concept are those that are included in it (for example, pens, typewriters, pencils, and so on).

1. Conservation of substance (6–7 years)

A

The experimenter presents two identical modeling clay balls. The subject admits that they have equal amounts of clay.

B

One of the balls is deformed. The subject is asked whether thay still contain equal amounts.

2. Conservation of length (6–7 years)

A

Two sticks are aligned in front of the subject. The subject admits their equality.

B

One of the sticks is moved to the right. The subject is asked whether they are still the same length.

3. Conservation of number (6–7 years)

A

Two rows of counters are placed in one-to-one correspondence. Subject admits their equality.

B

One of the rows is elongated (or contracted). Subject is asked whether each row still contains the same number.

4. Conservation of liquids (6–7 years)

A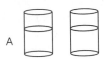

Two beakers are filled to the same level with water. The subject sees that they are equal.

B

The liquid of one container is poured into a tall tube (or a flat dish). The subject is asked whether each still contains the same amount.

5. Conservation of area (9–10 years)

A

The subject and the experimenter each have identical sheets of cardboard. Wooden blocks are placed on these in identical positions. The subject agrees that each cardboard has the same amount of space remaining.

B

The experimenter scatters the blocks on one of the cardboards. The subject is asked whether each cardboard still has the same amount of space remaining.

FIGURE 3.4 Some simple tests for conservation, with approximate ages of attainment.

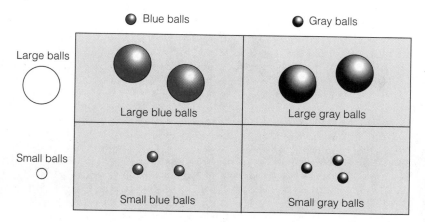

FIGURE 3.5 The use of multiplication to answer the question "If there are blue balls and gray balls, and some are large whereas others are small, how many different kinds of balls are there?" illustrates the classification abilities of children during the period of concrete operations.

acknowledging that all the beads were wooden. Concrete operations children no longer make this error.

Seriating. Understanding **seriation**—that is, understanding how to order objects in terms of some attribute—is essential for understanding number. One experiment that Piaget conducted to investigate the understanding of seriation involves presenting children with a series of different size dolls. The problem is simply to arrange these dolls in order, a task that preoperational children find very difficult. Typically, they compare only two dolls at a time and fail to make an inference that is almost essential for the solution of the problem: If A is greater than B, and B is greater than C, A must be greater than C. Preoperational children do not hesitate to put C before A if they have just been comparing B and C (see Figure 3.6).

Numbers. Understanding numbers depends on classification and seriation. A number involves classes in the sense that it represents a collec-

---

seriation The ordering of objects in terms of one or more properties. To seriate is to place in order.

Children's understanding of number and of classes, says Piaget, grows out of actual experiences they have with real objects. School experiences, too, are real-life experiences.

FIGURE 3.6 A test of children's understanding of seriation. The elements of the series are presented in random order, and children are asked to arrange them in sequence of height. The top row was arranged by a 3½-year-old; the bottom, by an 8-year-old.

tion of objects (cardinal property of numbers); it involves seriation in the sense that it is ordered in relation to larger and smaller numbers (ordinal property of numbers). And because it isn't until the period of concrete operations that children develop a relatively complete understanding of classification and seriation, Piaget suggests that their understanding of number would also develop at about the same time. However, as is shown shortly, we know that many preschoolers have a very advanced *intuitive* knowledge of numbers—a knowledge that allows many of them to count, to add, and to subtract unerringly in real-life situations (like when they're buying candy). As Piaget suggests, these ideas about adding and subtracting grow out of children's experiences in combining and separating real objects (Voss, Wiley, & Carretero, 1995).

To summarize, children at the stage of concrete operations can apply rules of logic to classes, to relations (series), and to numbers. In addition, their thinking has become relatively decentered in that it is no longer so egocentric or perception bound. However, they are still incapable of applying rules of logic to objects or events that are not concrete. In other words, they deal only with the real or with that which they are capable of imagining. Their ready answer to the question "What if Johnny West had a short nose?" is "Johnny West does not have a short nose!"

FORMAL OPERATIONS:

11 OR 12 TO 14 OR 15 YEARS

The final stage in the development of thought structures is labeled **formal operations**—formal because the subject matter with which chil-

formal operations The last of Piaget's four major stages. It begins around age 11 or 12 and lasts until age 14 or 15. It is characterized by the child's increasing ability to use logical thought processes.

dren can now deal may be completely hypothetical, and their thinking may involve a formal set of rules of logic.

An example of the difference between the thinking of children at the formal operations level and at the concrete level is provided by an item from Binet's reasoning test (forerunner to the well-known Stanford-Binet test). The item deals with abstract relations: Edith is fairer than Susan; Edith is darker than Lilly; who is the darkest of the three? This problem is difficult not because it involves seriation (seriation has already been mastered in the stage of concrete operations) but because of the abstract nature of the events that are to be ordered. If Edith, Susan, and Lilly were all standing in front of a 10-year-old subject, the subject could easily say, "Oh! Edith is fairer than Susan, and she is darker than Lilly—and Susan is the darkest." However, when the problem is not concrete but verbal, it requires thinking that is more formal (more abstract).

In a second experiment that illustrates a distinction between formal and concrete thinking, participants are presented with four different test tubes, certain combinations of which, when combined with the contents of a fifth tube, will yield a yellow liquid. The object is to discover which combination(s) yield the yellow liquid.

When presented with this problem, typical 10-year-olds might begin by combining two of the liquids, then perhaps two more, and so on, continuing, almost haphazardly, to try to guess what the correct combination might be. And if, by chance, they stumble across one of the two possible correct solutions, they will have no way of knowing whether there might be yet another. Because their approach is unsystematic, it will seldom exhaust all possibilities.

In contrast, bright 14-year-olds might well approach the problem highly systematically, combining all tubes by twos, then threes, then finally all four, thus testing every possible combination (as shown in Figure 3.7).

What this problem demonstrates most clearly is: (1) the concrete nature of younger children's thinking—every combination is an actual hypothesis translated into an immediate real test, an actual behavior; (2) the hypothetical and deductive capacities of older children's thinking. Thus, formal operations children begin by imagining all the possible solutions and then trying them out. The logic involved is described by Piaget as a form of "combinatorial thinking." It is a far more powerful logic than the concrete thinking of younger children. Among other things, it allows children to begin to understand abstract concepts such as proportion and heat, as well as to deal in the hypothetical world rather than merely the immediately real. As a result, an important feature of formal operations thinking is an increasing concern with the ideal. Once children are able to reason from the hypothetical to the real or from the actual to the hypothetical, they can conceive of worlds and societies that, hypothetically, have no ills.

BEYOND FORMAL OPERATIONS

For a long time, developmental psychologists believed that the primary intellectual changes of human development take place between birth and the end of adolescence. This model held that after adolescence there is a long period of relatively little change, a sort of plateau, that is eventually followed by gradual decline in old age.

Piaget's description of intellectual development reflects this long-prevalent model. Thus, he describes intellectual growth in terms of changes reflected in identifiable stages. The last of these stages, formal operations, is a stage descriptive of adolescents; beyond that—nothing.

But what of adults? Is adulthood merely a plateau followed by inevitable decline? Are no more positive changes possible?

The simple answer is no; there is good evidence that important positive changes come in adulthood—although these changes are not characteristic of everyone. In fact, even formal operations thinking is not characteristic of all adolescents or even of all adults. For some, thinking remains at a concrete stage throughout life; for others, thinking never even

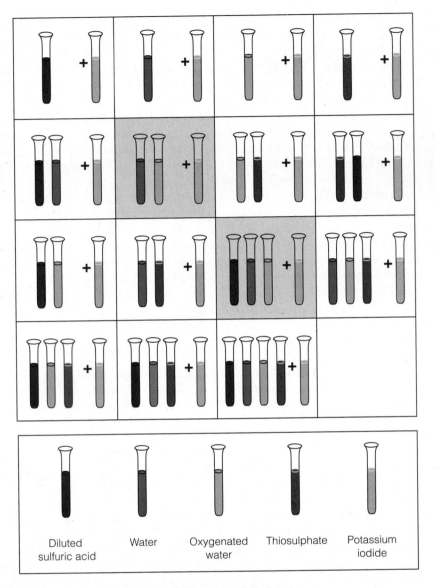

FIGURE 3.7 All possible combinations of the four test tubes to which the fifth can be added. The experiment requires the subject to discover the combination(s) that yields a yellow liquid when potassium iodide is added. The correct solutions have a light gray background.

progresses beyond the intuitions of the preconceptual level.

But the truly adult thinker, Basseches (1984) informs us, does not think like the schoolchild or the adolescent. Cognitive development, Basseches insists, continues after adolescence. But instead of becoming more logical—more unwaveringly rational—thinking becomes more relative, more attuned to conflict, and more sensitive to moral, ethical, social, and political realities. It is a form of thinking that Basseches terms **dialectical thinking.** Dialectical thinking struggles to create meaning and order by resolving conflict. The dialectical thinker is always aware of other possibilities and recognizes that no solution is necessarily absolute and final.

Labouvie-Vief (1980) agrees. Formal logic, she informs us, might be entirely appropriate for some of the problems that children face, especially in schools. But it might be inadequate and perhaps even largely irrelevant for many of the problems that adults face. The most logical solution may well be entirely wrong, entirely inappropriate. Mature reasoning requires "concrete pragmatics"; that is, it must take into account what will work and what is acceptable—what is, in other words, pragmatic (Labouvie-Vief, 1986). The thinking of the truly wise person is not bound simply by logic—which is not to say that it is illogical. Instead, it is sensitive to a wide range of possibilities; it considers implications; it factors in social and moral realities.

In summary, Basseches, Labouvie-Vief, and others concerned with the intellectual growth of adults claim that Piaget's model is not adequate for describing adult thought processes. According to these theorists, adult cognitive growth may take the form of learning new ways to resolve a wide range of personal problems that could involve relationships, artistic activities, business transactions, religion—indeed, all of life. They argue that adult thinking is more sensitive to and tolerant of ambiguity and contradiction and that it is more likely to bring into play a variety of factors (for example, morality, social and political implications, economic considerations, and so on) in addition to simple logic.

---

dialectical thinking Thinking that recognizes, accepts, and attempts to resolve conflicts. Dialectical thinking is thought to be more characteristic of adults than of children or adolescents.

PIAGET EVALUATED

Although Piaget's stature in developmental psychology is unequaled, he has a number of critics. Among the standard criticisms are that he has not used sufficiently large samples, sophisticated analyses, or adequate controls. The validity of these criticisms can be assessed by determining whether replications support his findings.

Replications. Of the many hundreds (or thousands) of studies that have attempted to replicate Piaget's findings, a majority provide at least some evidence that the sequence of intellectual stages is much as Piaget described, especially the sensorimotor period. However, many of these studies have found that North American and European children often reach Piaget's stages earlier than he had thought—although less privileged groups might reach them later.

There is somewhat less agreement with respect to sequencing and descriptions of major stages in later childhood and adolescence than there is for earlier stages. Here, there are two major criticisms: The first is that Piaget has drastically underestimated the cognitive achievements of preschoolers; the second is that he has overestimated the formal operations capabilities of adolescents (and even of adults).

Achievements of Preschoolers. With respect to the first criticism, current research suggests that it is inappropriate and misleading to refer to the preschooler's mind as "preconceptual," "preoperational," or "prelogical" (see, for example, Flavell, 1985; Campbell, 1993). This research indicates that a number of significant cognitive achievements of this period were underemphasized or simply overlooked by Piaget. Among these are monumental advances in preschoolers' ability to represent symbolically and to discover relationships among ideas. And perhaps the most dramatic illustration of children's impressive abilities with respect to discovering and working with relationships is their understanding of numbers. It's clear that children's knowledge of concepts like big and small, or few and many, as well as their understanding of the effects of adding or subtracting, are often highly developed by the time they start school. What they appear to have, explains Aubrey (1993), is an intuitive knowledge of mathematics very similar to the *street mathematics* that unschooled street vendors might develop. Street mathematics is the type of knowledge required for calculating, say, the price of two or more things given the price of one. It allows the street vendor or the street urchin (or the preschooler) to buy or sell and to make change. And, in some instances, it demands very sophisticated intuitive knowledge of number operations. But, as Nunes, Carraher, and Schliemann (1993) found when they reviewed Brazilian studies of the mathematics knowledge of street vendors, it is not the same as the more formal kind of mathematics knowledge that is learned and required in school.

Gelman (1982) and colleagues (Gelman, Meck, & Merkin, 1986) describe two kinds of knowledge about numbers that appear during the preschool period. The first kind is number abstraction skills. They give the child an understanding of number, or quantity—how many things there are in a collection of, for example, baby mice in one's pockets. A number of principles underlie number abstraction skills. These include the one-on-one principle (if you're going to count mice, you must assign one, and only one, number to every mouse that is to be counted), the stable order principle (the correct order for counting is one, two, three, four . . . and not one, three, four, two . . .), the cardinal order principle (the last number assigned is the one that indicates the quantity of the collection), the abstraction principle (absolutely anything and everything can be counted), and the order irrelevance principle (the order of counting is irrelevant to the final outcome of the counting operation).

These five number abstraction principles have to do with how to count, what to count, and what it means to count. Children as young as 2 or 3 often behave as though they understand these principles clearly, even though they might still make mistakes (often systematic errors) in their counting. The second kind of knowledge about numbers that appears during the preschool period relates to numerical reasoning principles. This is the knowledge that permits the child to reason about or predict the outcome of simple numerical operations such as adding to or taking from.

Number abstraction and numerical reasoning are important and complex cognitive activities. They serve as dramatic illustrations of the cognitive achievements of the preschooler, in sharp contrast to Piaget's description of the intuitive, egocentric, perception-dominated, prelogical, preoperational child.

Limits of Formal Operations. Some criticism of Piaget's stage of formal operations has been based on the observation that many people aren't capable of formal operations thinking during adolescence or even beyond (Papalia, 1972; Rubin, et al., 1973). Piaget (1972) has conceded that this stage may be less general than he originally had thought.

In addition, Piaget is sometimes criticized for using difficult, unclear, and often unnecessary terms and concepts in describing formal operations, as well as for making errors in his use of models of logic to describe adolescent thought (Ennis, 1976, 1978).

Summary. In evaluating the importance and seriousness of these criticisms, it's important to keep in mind that Piaget's theory, like other theories, is simply a metaphor. Specifically, Piaget's theory is a philosophical/biological metaphor intended to explain intellectual adaptation through the growth of intellectual capabilities and functions. Some of the criticisms of the theory stem from a misunderstanding of the basic metaphor and intentions of the theory and from too narrow an application of its principles. In the final analysis, it may not be fundamentally important to the basic metaphor that some of the observations upon which it is based are inaccurate or that there are errors of logic, interpretation, or emphases in its description. Its explanatory strength and its practical usefulness may be far more important.

EDUCATIONAL IMPLICATIONS OF PIAGET'S THEORY

Piaget's cognitive theory is monumental in child development and has had (and continues to have) a profound impact on educational practices. Its most useful instructional applications relate to three topics: instructional theory, the acceleration of development, and the derivation of specific principles for teaching.

INSTRUCTIONAL THEORY

Robert Gagné (1985) describes an instructional model based on the notion that learning is hierarchical in that higher order skills and concepts depend on subordinate capabilities (described in Chapter 4). Hence, instruction based on this model always begins by analyzing what is to be learned and arranging content into a hierarchy of tasks—a process called **task analysis.** Case (1975) suggests that Piaget's developmental theory can be combined with Gagné's instructional theory. Specifically, Piaget's theory can be used to assess the learner's developmental level and cognitive capabilities. Careful task analysis can reveal why certain tasks are too difficult—for example, for preoperational children—and might also suggest ways in which tasks can be structured to be more compatible with students' developmental level.

CAN DEVELOPMENT BE ACCELERATED?

Although this question was of little direct concern to Piaget, the theory at least suggests the possibility that certain carefully structured experiences might be useful for speeding up

---

task analysis The process of analyzing what is to be learned in terms of a sequential series of related tasks. Task analysis provides the teacher with information about important skills and knowledge that might be prerequisite for what is to be taught.

development. Not surprisingly, a large number of researchers have looked at ways to accelerate the appearance of developmentally important concepts such as conservation, for example. But the results have generally been mixed, with many researchers failing to bring about any significant change. What appears to be one of the easiest teaching tasks possible—simply convincing a 5-year-old that an amount of modeling clay does not change unless something is added to or taken away from it—is next to impossible. And although several systematic training procedures have succeeded in accelerating the appearance of conservation behavior in young children, no evidence has yet been provided that this has a generally beneficial effect on other aspects of intellectual functioning (see, for example, Campbell & Ramey, 1990; Perry, Pasnak, & Holt, 1992). As Nagy and Griffiths (1982) conclude, "attempts to prescribe instructional strategies that accelerate intellectual development have borne little fruit" (p. 513). What is not clear is whether the general failure of these attempts is due to the fact that intellectual development cannot easily be accelerated or to the fact that we simply don't understand enough about the nature of intellectual development to devise more appropriate strategies.

INSTRUCTIONAL PRINCIPLES

Development, insists Piaget (1961), does not occur independently of children's surroundings and activities. To the contrary, as we saw, it depends on four important factors: equilibration, maturation, active experience, and social interaction. These four factors are the cornerstones of Piaget's system. Not surprisingly, they also suggest important instructional implications. Some of these implications are summarized here. They are not intended as recipes for classroom practice but rather as guiding principles for developing your own teaching style.

Providing Activity. To the extent that concepts arise from sensing and acting upon the environment (active experience), children should be involved in numerous real and meaningful activities. For example, Piaget argues that the ability to deal with classes, relations, and numbers results from the activities of combining, separating, and setting up correspondences among real objects during the preoperational stage. Because children's natural methods of learning and of stabilizing what they know involve activity, much classroom learning should also involve activity. For Piaget, activity is not only physical activity but internalized mental activity. The point of this principle is twofold:

1. Provision should be made for a relatively large amount of physical activity in school, but obviously mental activity should be provided as well.
2. Provision should be made for relating learning to real objects and events, especially before the formal operations stage.

As an illustration, consider the case, "The B Store." In many ways, this little classroom store mirrors real life, giving the learning of mathematics a degree of realism, practicality, and meaningfulness not often found in cold numbers on workbook pages. Not only does it provide for actual activity in meaningful circumstances, but it also gives the teacher a simple way of administering or of withholding reinforcement. And it permits teaching an extremely wide range of mathematical concepts in addition to simple addition and subtraction. For example, multiplication concepts can be introduced easily by doubling (or tripling) all prices; division might involve selling a fraction of something and then calculating what the price of the fraction should be, and so on.

Providing Optimal Difficulty. To the extent that cognitive growth is facilitated by equilibration, schools should provide activities that encourage a balance between assimilation and accommodation. Recall that assimilation and accommodation are children's two ways of interacting with the world; all activity involves both. Assimilation occurs when children can react to new objects or events largely in terms of previous learning; accommodation involves modification

CASE: THE B STORE

THE PLACE: Miss Moskal's third-grade classroom

THE MATHEMATICS LEARNING CENTER: In the corner of the room, the children have set up a small store. Items for sale vary from week to week. These are sometimes made by the students, donated by parents, or purchased through school funds. Among the various items for sale this week are a number of tiny potted plants Miss Moskal has started from seeds. Also, there are "privilege" cards. Some of these cards allow children to erase the whiteboards; others provide access to special books; still others allow their purchaser to be captain of one of the play teams, leader of one of the cooperative learning teams, storekeeper for a day, bank teller, or payroll clerk. Price tags, attached to each item, are printed in bold, colorful numbers.

In this class, each student receives a basic weekly "salary," with the possibility of bonuses for various behaviors—and sometimes fines as well. The payroll clerk is responsible for keeping track of everybody's salary, adding in bonuses and subtracting fines, and writing "paycheques." Student auditors are charged with verifying the pay clerk's calculations. Cheques are "cashed" at a bank adjoining the store, or are sometimes used at the store when making large purchases (like lunch with Miss Moskal). During specified periods, sales clerks sell items from the store, taking responsibility for making change.

Students were responsible for naming the store. The name was Sandra's idea.

"Let's call it the B store," she said.

"Why?"

"Because that's a little better than a C store."

or change. Assimilation requires that a situation be somewhat familiar; accommodation will take place only if the situation is, at the same time, somewhat different. Therefore, what is required is an optimal discrepancy between new material and old learning. (This point is also made by other theorists—for example, Ausubel [1963] and Bruner [1966]; see Chapter 6.) By knowing a student's level of functioning, a teacher can more effectively and realistically determine which learning experiences are best.

Understanding How Children Think. Although it has always been recognized that there are some important differences between children and adults, Piaget, more than anyone, has demonstrated precisely what some of these differences are. When a child says that there is more water in a tall container than in a short, flat one, she truly believes what she is saying. When a row of disks is made shorter than a corresponding row, and the child changes his mind and says that now there are fewer disks in that row, he is not really contradicting himself because he sees no error and therefore no contradiction. When a second-grade student becomes completely confused by a verbal seriation problem—for example, "Frank Twolips has a shorter nose than Johnny West, and Johnny West has a longer nose than John George. Who has the longest nose?"—she is not being unintelligent.

These and other discoveries about the world of young children should help teachers both to accept more easily the limitations of children's thought and to communicate more effectively with children.

Knowing Children's Limitations. A teacher needs to be aware of the limitations of children at different ages. Concepts of proportion cannot easily be taught to 7-year-olds. Nor can conservation of volume be taught to 5-year-olds. And even if this statement were proved false, it would probably still be true that the amount of time required to teach 5-year-olds conservation of volume might be better spent teaching them to read. This is especially true because they would probably acquire conservation of volume

by themselves, but they would be less likely to learn to read without instruction.

Providing Social Interaction. One of the chief factors in making thought more objective, claims Piaget, is social interaction. The egocentric point of view of the young child is essentially one that does not recognize the views of others. It is largely through social interaction that children become aware of the ideas and opinions of peers and adults. Piaget contends that the socialization of thought, the development of moral rules as well as game rules, and even the development of logical thought processes are highly dependent on verbal interaction. One implication for teaching is that instructional methods should provide for learner–learner as well as teacher–learner interaction.

Assessing Students' Readiness. Detailed accounts of Piaget's experimental procedures and findings provide the classroom teacher with many informal and easily applied suggestions for assessing students' thought processes. It is not particularly difficult or time-consuming, for example, to ascertain whether a child has acquired conservation of numbers or the ability to seriate. Both abilities are important for early instruction in mathematics.

Researchers have developed several scales to assess Piagetian concepts in children (for example, Pinard & Laurendeau, 1964; Goldschmid & Bentler, 1968; Uzgiris & Hunt, 1975). Unfortunately, none of these scales has been widely used or standardized. Still, a general knowledge of Piaget's theory and of some of the related research can do a great deal to improve teacher knowledge of students' cognitive processes. Consequently, such knowledge can also do much to suggest more optimal ways of teaching.

VYGOTSKY'S CULTURAL/ COGNITIVE THEORY

Theories such as Piaget's emphasize the role of interactions between the individual and others, as well as the role of innate tendencies and predispositions. In a sense, they attempt to account for both our biological and our social aspects. Another approach that places even more emphasis on social/cultural influences is that of Lev Vygotsky, the Russian psychologist.

THE MAN AND HIS IDEAS

A quick look at current writings in education and psychology might make one think that Lev Vygotsky is a contemporary theorist. Almost all major textbooks have at least one or two references to him, and many of his major works have just recently been translated into English (for example Vygotsky, 1992, 1993; Vygotsky & Luria, 1993). In fact, what might be an important book for teachers has not yet been translated from the Russian (Vygotsky, 1991; see Davydov, 1995).

But Vygotsky is not contemporary in a literal sense; he has been dead for more than half a century (he died of tuberculosis in 1934 at the age of 38). And although he was already a major intellectual force in the Soviet Union by the time he was 28, his work was not well known outside that country until much later. In fact, because he worked in the field that was labeled **pedology** in the former Soviet Union, for several decades after his death it was forbidden to reprint or even to discuss his work. Soviet authorities had determined that pedology, a science of child development that used Western tests for assessing development and diagnosing developmental disorders, was a "bourgeois pseudoscience" and, in effect, wiped out the discipline, closing down all pedology centers and repressing all related research and publica-

tions. Imagine what Vygotsky's contributions and his stature might have been had his work not been repressed—and had he lived as long as Piaget.

Vygotsky has been described as "the Mozart of Psychology," its child genius, notes Davydov (1995). By age 28, he had assimilated all of the major theories and findings of the psychology of the day, and he had begun to map out a new theory with ideas that still seem fresh even today. Unfortunately, however, many of these ideas are complex and not entirely clear. As Nicolopoulou (1993) puts it, "Despite the fact that his writings are full of intuitions and illuminations, they are often sketchy and at times incomplete" (p. 7).

Three underlying themes unify Vygotsky's complex and far-reaching theory. The first theme is the importance of culture; the second is the central role of language; the third is what Vygotsky labels the "zone of proximal growth." We look at each of these briefly.

THE IMPORTANCE OF CULTURE

Human development, says Vygotsky, is fundamentally different from that of animals. Why? Because humans use tools and symbols and, as a result, create **cultures.** And cultures are powerful things; they have a life of their own. They grow and change, and they exert tremendously powerful influences on each of us. Cultures specify what the end product of successful development is. They determine what we have to learn, the sorts of competencies we need to develop. Hence, during different historical periods, psychological development might be very different—in the same way as it might be very different from one culture to another. We are not only culture producing, notes Bronfenbrenner (1989), but also culture produced, giving voice to one of the most fundamental contem-

---

pedology A Soviet discipline of child development, very popular in the Soviet Union in the 1930s, that used Western tests for psychoassessment. Vygotsky and Luria were pedologists. In the mid-1930s, the Soviet government decreed that pedology was a "bourgeois pseudoscience" and ordered that it no longer be written about, researched, or even discussed, wiping out all pedology centers and putting all pedologists out of work.

---

culture The pattern of socially acceptable behaviors that characterizes a people or a social group. It includes all the attitudes and beliefs that the group has about the things it considers important.

porary themes that underlies the study and understanding of human development. Amazingly, Vygotsky had already adopted this theme as the very basis of his theory more than six decades ago.

Vygotsky makes an important distinction between what he calls *elementary mental functions* and *higher mental functions*. Elementary functions are our natural, and therefore unlearned, capacities, such as attending and sensing. In the course of development, these elementary capacities are gradually transformed into higher mental functions such as problem solving and thinking, largely through the influence of culture. It is culture, after all, that makes language possible, and it is social processes that bring about the learning of language (referred to as *signs*). Language, or signs, ultimately make thought possible. Thus, during the preverbal stage of development, infants' intelligence is a purely practical, purely natural capacity that is closely comparable to that of apes.*

THE ROLE OF LANGUAGE

Language makes thought possible and regulates behavior, explains Vygotsky. Language, which is the basis of human culture, is also the basis of consciousness, and consciousness was one of Vygotsky's central concerns. Without language, we would be limited to elementary mental functions—animalistic activities such as sensing and perceiving. But with language, we can interact socially. And with social interaction comes what Vygotsky describes as "upbringing† and teaching," which is essential for development.

Vygotsky (1962) describes three stages in the development of the functions of speech: social, egocentric, and inner.

Social speech (or external speech) emerges first. Its function is largely to control the behavior of others (as in "I want juice!") or to express simple and sometimes poorly understood concepts.

Egocentric speech predominates from ages 3 to 7. It serves as a bridge between the primitive and highly public social speech of the first stage and the more sophisticated and highly private inner speech of the third stage. During this stage, children often talk to themselves in an apparent attempt to guide their own behavior. For example, they might speak about what they are doing as they do it. Unlike older children, however, they are likely to say things out loud (externalize) rather than silently, as though they believe that if language is to direct behavior, it must be spoken.

Inner speech is silent self-talk. It is characteristic of older children as well as adults. It is what William James (1890) called the "stream of consciousness." Our self-talk—our inner speech—is what tells us that we are alive and conscious. It permits us to direct our thinking and our behavior. More than this, it makes all higher mental functioning possible (see Table 3.4).

---

*PPC: How about bears? What is their intelligence like?
Author: They are possessed of a great wisdom, tempered by a savage cunning. They are accomplished dialectical thinkers, both pragmatic and poetic. They are pensive and somber, jovial and—in truth, Vygotsky does not say.
†Davydov (1995) explains that the translation of the Russian word *vospitateli* to "upbringing" is inexact—that the term *nurture* might be closer but less comfortable. He notes, as well, that the Russian expression that we translate to mean "teaching" would be better translated as "teaching/ learning," showing how close these two processes are in the minds of Russian educators and theorists.

social speech In Vygotsky's theorizing, the most primitive stage of language development, evident before age 3, during which the child expresses simple thoughts and emotions out loud. The function of social speech is to control the behavior of others.

egocentric speech Vygotsky's intermediate stage of language development, common between ages 3 and 7, during which children often talk to themselves in an apparent effort to control their own behavior.

inner speech Vygotsky's final stage in the development of speech, attained at around age 7, and characterized by silent "self-talk," the stream-of-consciousness flow of verbalizations that give direction and substance to our thinking and behavior. Inner speech is involved in all higher mental functioning.

TABLE 3.4 VYGOTSKY'S THEORY OF THE ROLE OF LANGUAGE

STAGE	FUNCTION
Social (external) (to age 3)	Controls the behavior of others; expresses simple thoughts and emotions
Egocentric (3 to 7)	Bridge between external and inner speech; serves to control own behavior but spoken out loud
Inner (7 onward)	Self-talk; makes possible the direction of our thinking and our behavior; involved in all higher mental functioning

JEFFRY MYERS/STOCK, BOSTON

Vygotsky's theory suggests that the most useful educational experiences are those that lie within the child's zone of proximal growth—specifically activities that at first the child can understand and accomplish only with the help of adults or more competent peers, but that the child can later accomplish alone. Effective tutoring, as illustrated here, reflects this principle.

THE CONCEPT OF A ZONE OF PROXIMAL GROWTH

Higher mental functioning involves activities such as thinking, perceiving, organizing, and remembering. These functions originate in social activity and are inseparably linked with language, which is also a social phenomenon. In a very real sense, these higher mental functions define intelligence.

One of Vygotsky's strong interests was in maximizing intellectual development. He was far less interested in measuring past accomplishments or in assessing current levels of functioning than in arriving at some notion of potential for future development. Every child, he maintained, has a sphere or a zone of current capabilities—in Vygotsky's words, a **zone of proximal growth,** a sort of potential for

---

zone of proximal growth Vygotsky's phrase for the individual's current potential for further intellectual development. Conventional measures of intelligence assess current intellectual development rather than potential for future development. Vygotsky believed that the zone of proximal growth (future potential) might be assessed by further questioning and the use of hints and prompts while administering a conventional intelligence test.

developing (Belmont, 1989). Take, for example, two 5-year-olds, who can both, under normal circumstances, answer questions that other average 5-year-olds can also answer. Their mental ages might be said to correspond to their chronological ages, and their intelligence would be described as average. But if, when prompted, one of these children could successfully answer questions corresponding to a mental age of 7 but the other could not, it would be accurate to say that the first child's zone of proximal growth is greater than the other's (that is, it spans a wider range of higher functions).

Davydov (1995) explains what is meant by zone of proximal growth as follows: "What the child is initially able to do only together with adults and peers, and then can do independently, lies exactly in the zone of proximal psychological development" (p. 18). As we see later when we look more closely at the educational implications of Vygotsky's theory, the task of educators, parents, and others charged with the "upbringing/teaching" of children is to arrange for children to engage in activities that lie within this zone—activities that, by definition, are neither too difficult nor too simple, and that therefore lead to continued growth. In Davydov's (1995) words, "Teaching must lead development forward and not lag behind" (p. 18).

EDUCATIONAL IMPLICATIONS OF VYGOTSKY'S THEORY

Russian education is currently in a state of reform, claims Davydov (1995). And much of this reform is based on the ideas of Lev Vygotsky, many of which also have important applications in education in other parts of the world. He summarizes five of these ideas as they apply to education (p. 13):

1. Education, which includes teaching/learning and upbringing (nurturing), is intended to develop children's personalities.

2. Because the development of personality is linked with the development of creative potential, one of the important tasks of schools is to provide opportunites for the development of this creative potential.

3. Teaching/learning and upbringing require actual *activity* on the part of students; hence, students must be true participants in the teaching/learning process.

4. Teachers should be guides and directors of student activity without forcing their will on them. Hence, teaching should be a *collaborative* process.

5. The most effective teaching methods are those that take into consideration individual differences among learners. Hence, the best teaching methods cannot be uniform in a class.

It's interesting to note that many of these ideas, which are based on Vygotsky's decades-old theory, reflect almost exactly recent theories and beliefs. In fact, most of these ideas are discussed in some detail in various parts of this text. For example, Vygotsky's belief that teaching/learning (and upbringing) are intended to develop personality is reflected in the humanistic insistence on the importance of self-development discussed in Chapter 9; his attention to the development of creative potential is reflected in detailed sections on intelligence and creativity in Chapters 7 and 8; his view of learning as requiring active involvement finds expression in Piaget's theory as well as in many theories of learning; his belief that learning should be collaborative is reflected in the recent proliferation of cooperative approaches to learning that are discussed in Chapter 9; and his admonition that the best teaching methods have to be sensitive to individual differences are at the center of the multicultural and inclusive education movements.

SCAFFOLDING

One of the most important educational implications that can be derived from Vygotsky's theory is termed **scaffolding.** Essentially, scaffolding is defined by the large number of different methods by which teachers provide support for students as they learn—in much the same way that a scaffold might be used by a pair of energetic farmhands building an especially tall, multilevel doghouse.* To elaborate the analogy, in the early stages of the construction, the

---

*PPC: Why a doghouse? Wouldn't the bear have preferred a . . . what? . . . a bearhouse?
Author: It's just an analogy to explain a metaphor. They didn't actually build a doghouse at all. Besides, the bear is a wild and poetic creature whose soul cringes at the thought of being domesticated—like a dog—and made to sleep in a house, for crying out loud!

---

scaffolding A Vygotskian concept to describe the various types of support that teachers/upbringers need to provide for children if they are to learn. Scaffolding often takes the form of directions, suggestions, and other forms of verbal assistance, and is most effective if it involves tasks within the child's zone of proximal growth.

scaffold has to be very close to the ground, and very sturdy, because there is nothing else to stand on or even to lean against. As the construction progresses, the scaffold must also rise or it would soon become useless. But now the farmhands can hang onto the wall studs of the new construction; they can sometimes even stand on the first rafters of the lower levels. And eventually, the doghouse will have been built and they will no longer need any scaffolding at all. In fact, if they want to, they'll be able to walk on the very highest roof.

Learning, too, requires scaffolding, claims Vygotsky. In the early stages, scaffolding—that is, guidance and support—is often essential. For example, a preschooler who knows nothing about the significance of the letters of the alphabet can hardly be expected to discover or invent accurately the various sounds they represent. By telling, demonstrating, pointing, correcting, the teacher/upbringer *builds scaffolds* for the child. And as the child begins to learn, the nature of the scaffolding required changes. Often there is less need for scaffolding as the learner begins to build on previous learning, gradually learning how to learn.

There are a tremendous variety of specific types of scaffolding—in other words, of support—that teachers and parents can build for children. These include:

▶ Demonstrating how to do things

▶ Explaining procedures

▶ Providing written or actual models

▶ Systematically developing all the prerequisite skills required for more demanding tasks

▶ Asking questions that lead to certain important realizations

▶ Correcting on-task errors

▶ Identifying and correcting misconceptions

▶ Motivating students

▶ Providing clear and realistic objectives

Hey, you say, so what's new? Seems to me that most of what good teachers do involves what you're calling *scaffolding*. Yes, but what is new is the relationship between Vygotsky's concept of scaffolding and his notion of the zone of proximal growth. Recall that the zone of proximal growth is defined in terms of those tasks of which learners are capable *with the help of adults or peers*. Put another way, the zone of proximal growth describes tasks with which learners require support (that is, scaffolding). The implication for teachers and other upbringers is very clear: It is simply to arrange for children to engage in activities that lie within this zone—activities that are challenging enough that they initially require assistance, but that are not so challenging that they will never be accomplished. Specifically, to the extent that the environment requires that children perform at a level slightly in advance of the current developmental level, progress will be enhanced. Vygotsky suggests that the level at which instructions and questions are phrased is extremely important. These, he argues, should be sufficiently ahead of the student's developmental level that they present a genuine intellectual challenge—but they must not be so far ahead of the child's current biological maturation and developmental level that they present too great a challenge (Valsiner, 1987).

Vygotsky's social/cognitive developmental theory underscores the role of culture (and its most important invention, language) in the development of higher mental functions. Without culture, he argues, our intelligence would be comparable to that of apes*—hence, the fundamental role of education is cultural transmission.

We knew that. But we were perhaps not entirely aware of the theoretical underpinnings of this belief.

Do bears have a culture?

---

*PPC: And bears?
AUTHOR: And perhaps to bears, too.

MAIN POINTS

1. Gender roles are learned patterns of culturally approved masculine and feminine behaviors; they are a combined function of genetic, family-based, and cultural forces. Traditional gender roles, which are changing slowly, reflect males as more aggressive, more boisterous, and more adventurous than females. Both boys and girls tend to prefer male to female roles.

2. Sex differences, which typically have both genetic and environmental roots, are sometimes evident in the greater aggressiveness of males. In addition, there is a declining tendency for males to score slightly higher on tests of general knowledge and mechanical reasoning, and females, on tests of language usage. On a number of measures, male scores reflect more variability.

3. Sex differences in abilities are too trivial and too inconsistent to be important to teachers. What is important is that teachers be sensitive to both the interests of boys and girls and to the many instances of sexual bias that still permeate society.

4. Erik Erikson describes personality development in terms of a series of psychosocial stages through which children pass. Each stage involves a major conflict, the resolution of which leads to greater social competence. In order, the stages are trust versus mistrust, autonomy versus shame and doubt, initiative versus guilt, industry versus inferiority, identity versus identity diffusion, intimacy versus isolation, generativity versus self-absorption, and integrity versus despair.

5. Piaget's theory stems partly from his biological orientation and focuses on cognitive (intellectual) development as it results from equlibration (the tendency to balance using previous responses [assimilation] with modifying behavior [accommodation]), maturation, active experience, and social interaction. It describes the characteristics of human behavior that permit adaptation, and it classifies important intellectual events in terms of sequential developmental stages.

6. The sensorimotor period (birth to 2 years, the first of Piaget's four major developmental stages) is characterized by a sensory and motor representation of the world. Among the sensorimotor child's achievements are the learning of language, the acquisition of the object concept, the development of internally controlled representational schemes, and the recognition of cause-and-effect relationships.

7. The preoperational stage (ages 2 to 7) includes the preconceptual period (ages 2 to 4; reasoning is characteristically transductive—it proceeds from particular to particular)—and the intuitive period (ages 4 to 7; reasoning is egocentric, perception dominated, and intuitive).

8. The stage of concrete operations (ages 7 to 11 or 12) is marked by new skills relating to classifying, ordering, and dealing with numbers, as well as by the appearance of thought processes that are subject to some logical rules (identity and reversibility, for example) evident in the development of concepts of conservation (the realization that certain qualities of objects, such as weight or volume, do not change unless matter is added or subtracted).

9. During the formal operations stage (ages 11 or 12 to 14 or 15), the child becomes freed from concrete objects and events and can deal with the hypothetical.

10. Researchers such as Basseches (dialectical thinking) and Labouvie-Vief (pragmatic reasoning) argue that although formal operations may be appropriate for problems requiring nothing but logic, mature adult reasoning is more sensitive to and tolerant of ambiguity and contradiction and is more likely to consider the practical, social, ethical, and personal implications of decisions.

11. Replications of many of Piaget's experiments have tended to confirm the general sequence of stages up to formal operations, although Piaget may sometimes have underestimated children's capacities and the ages of some developmental accomplishments.

12. Piaget's description of the four factors involved in development (equilibration, maturation, active experience, and social interaction) suggest some important instructional principles, including the need to provide opportunities for student activity, to recognize that there is an optimal level of difficulty for new learning, and to be aware of the characteristics and limits of children's abilities.

13. Vygotsky's social/cognitive theory stresses the importance of culture and of its principal invention, language. Without culture, our intellectual functioning is limited to apelike, elementary mental functions; given culture and language, we become capable of higher mental functions involved in thinking, reasoning, remembering, and so on.

14. The child progresses through three stages in developing language functions: social (external) speech, predominant before age 3 or 4, used largely to control others or to express simple concepts; egocentric speech (ages 3 to 7 or so), which is self-talk that is spoken out loud and that has a role in controlling and directing the child's own behavior; and inner speech, marked by unspoken verbalizations that control thought and behavior.

15. Vygotsky's zone of proximal growth is the child's potential for development and is defined in terms of what the child can do with the help of adults and competent peers. Vygotsky emphasizes the importance of assessing potential rather than simply measuring past accomplishments. His theory presents a strong argument for language-related activities in schools and for instruction at the upper edge of the student's zone of proximal growth—that is, for challenging instructional materials and methods.

APPLIED QUESTIONS

▶ Read Margaret Mead's *Growing Up in New Guinea* or *Sex and Temperament in Three Primitive Societies.* Can you find similar examples of gender typing in your world?

▶ Debate the proposition that gender differences are more fanciful than real.

▶ What are the main characteristics of each of Erikson's stages of psychosocial development?

▶ Describe Piaget's answers for the primary biological questions he asked: How do children adapt? How can development be classified?

▶ What are the most important features of children's behavior at each of Piaget's developmental stages?

▶ Give an example of what is meant by zone of proximal growth. What are the educational implications of this concept?

Study Terms

Suggested Readings

Theorists such as Erikson, Piaget, and Vygotsky were prolific and sometimes difficult writers. It is generally easier and perhaps more valuable to begin with secondary sources for information about their theories. The following are useful starting points:

MILLER, P. H. (1993). *Theories of developmental psychology* (3rd ed.). New York: Freeman.

THOMAS, R. M. (1992). *Comparing theories of child development* (3rd ed.). Belmont, Calif.: Wadsworth.

WADSWORTH, B. J. (1989). *Piaget's theory of cognitive and affective development* (4th ed.). New York: Longman.

The following is of particular value in understanding the logical thought processes of children in the concrete operations and formal operations stages:

INHELDER, B., & PIAGET, J. (1958). *The growth of logical thinking from childhood to adolescence*. New York: Basic Books.

The following is a comprehensive collection of articles that deal with many important aspects of gender and with its implications:

BEALL, A. E., & STERNBERG, R. J. (eds.) (1993). *The psychology of gender*. New York: Guilford.

For a clear account of Vygotsky's life and theories, see:

KOZULIN, A. (1990). *Vygotsky's psychology: A biography of ideas*. New York: Harvester Wheatsheaf.

Delayed implantation is one of the common features of brown and polar bears, badgers, mink, and a small number of other animals. The fertilized egg does not become implanted in the uterine wall shortly after conception, but may remain dormant for weeks and sometimes months. Although delayed implantation clearly has survival value, ensuring that the young will be born at the optimal time of the year, the mechanisms that delay embryonic development and later serve to trigger it are not understood (Matthews, 1969).

PART THREE

Learning and Teaching

We know that you are mad with much learning.
PETRONIUS, *Satyricon*

CHAPTER 4
Behaviorism and Social Cognitive Theory

CHAPTER 5
Thinking and Remembering

CHAPTER 6
Cognitive Instructional Models

LEARNING IS MOSTLY *what the educational process is all about—although it does not ordinarily make us mad. The three chapters in Part III deal with learning and thinking, and especially with the instructional implications of what we know about these topics. The first chapter presents a behavioristic look at learning, and the next two chapters look more closely at thinking, problem solving, decision making, and remembering. Perhaps most important, we look at the strategies that make us better at doing these things, and at what teachers and schools can do to improve these strategies.*

CHAPTER 4

When I carefully consider the curious habits
   of dogs
I am compelled to conclude
That man is the superior animal.
When I consider the curious habits of man
I confess, my friend, I am puzzled.

EZRA POUND, *Meditatio*

Let such teach others who themselves excel.
ALEXANDER POPE, *Essay on Criticism*

A little learning is a dangerous thing
Drink deep or taste not the Pierian spring
ALEXANDER POPE, *Essay on Criticism*

Behaviorism and Social Cognitive Theory

PREVIEW

For teachers, one of the most important questions about learning is which conditions lead most effectively to desirable changes in behavior. In other words, how can what we know about learning be applied to instruction? But before we can begin to answer this question, we must look at psychology's explanations of learning. This chapter presents two kinds of explanations: the behavioristic (which looks at how behavior is controlled by its consequences) and the social cognitive (which also takes into consideration our ability to think and anticipate).

Focus Questions

▶ What is learning?

▶ Why are theories like those of Pavlov, Watson, and Skinner labeled "behaviorism"?

▶ What are classical and operant conditioning?

▶ What is the difference between negative reinforcement and punishment?

▶ Why might schedules of reinforcement be important in the classroom?

▶ What are the processes and effects of learning through imitation?

About halfway through eighth grade, Horseface stopped coming to school, which I didn't notice right away because Gloria Switalo had just moved into the district. She was in grade 6, a honey-blonde contrast to the dark hair and skin that most of us had. I had fallen quite miserably in love and had no idea what to do, television not yet having made it as far north as we lived. So I spent a lot of time staring at her, and didn't realize that Horseface wasn't there until we began to choose sides for the Friday afternoon hockey game. It was my turn to be captain, and when I got to choose first I said "Horseface" because we always chose him first.

"He's not here no more," said John George in his new English.

"Where is he?" I asked.

"Jail," said Barney.

"They don't send kids to jail," said his sister, Noella, glaring at Gloria, although Gloria hadn't said anything.

"It's the same thing," explained Barney. "They put him in reform school, which is where Roland Boutin was, and it's just exactly like jail."

Horseface had stolen that little rabbit .22 from Pelletier's store and they had caught him this time. And because it wasn't the first time, the judge figured they'd better straighten him out while they still could, before he became a real criminal.

"The way I see it," the judge explained, "my theory is you take these kids when they're young enough and you can reform them. That's why we have reform schools."

Theory

As we saw in Chapter 1, a theory is a collection of related statements, the principal function of which is to summarize and explain observations. It is, in a sense, an invention designed to explain what we know or suspect. Theories are especially useful in giving us a basis for making predictions. For example, a portion of the judge's theory was based on the belief that certain experiences, presumably of the kind available in a so-called reform school, can lead to significant positive changes among aspiring delinquents. Such a theory allows the judge to predict that those, like Horseface, who are sentenced to a term in reform school have a good chance of becoming fine, upstanding citizens like His Honor. That Horseface eventually did end up in a real jail simply indicates that our theory-based predictions are not always completely accurate—especially when these theories are intuitive, homegrown theories based more on anecdotes and wishful thinking than on scientific methods applied to clear, replicable observations.

One of the big differences between the observations of the armchair theorist and those of scientists is that we can have more faith in scientific observations because science demands that observations be made with precision and objectivity that are beyond the patience of naïve theorists. As a result, the conclusions and generalizations of social scientists are likely to apply to a greater number of individuals. Whereas the judge could, with profound conviction, base his conclusions about human nature on a handful of isolated instances, science insists on samples that are large enough and representative enough to justify making generalizations.

Another important difference between naïve theories and those of science is that theo-

Learning, psychology informs us, is the acquisition of information and knowledge, of skills and habits, and of attitudes and beliefs. It always involves a change in one of these areas—a change that is brought about by the learner's experiences. Take tying shoes, for example. This complex skill requires knowledge about how laces can be twisted and looped and pulled, hours of practice and experience, and maybe just a little luck as well.

rists like the judge do not habitually take random (chance) factors into account. Science, on the other hand, is guided by a mathematically precise model of probability. Accordingly, science is far more likely than the judge to detect when certain outcomes and observations are due to chance (or at least to unknown factors) rather than to specific things like the experiences of a reform school.

Although our psychological theories improve our explanations and allow us to make useful predictions, they are far from absolutely precise. Hence, they cannot be judged in terms of absolute standards of rightness or wrongness. Instead, we judge theories on the basis of how well they reflect the facts, how consistent and logical they are, how useful they are for explaining and for predicting, and how practical they are in suggesting how to solve problems or simply how to behave in certain situations.

In this chapter, we take a brief look at several theories that attempt to explain learning. And because learning is the inescapable other side of the teaching/learning coin, these theories have tremendously important educational implications.

WHAT IS LEARNING?

Learning is the acquisition of information and knowledge, of skills and habits, and of attitudes and beliefs. It always involves a change in one of these areas—a change that is brought about by the learner's experiences. Accordingly, psychologists define *learning* as all changes in behavior that result from experience, providing these changes are relatively permanent, do not result simply from growth or maturation, and are not the temporary effects of factors such as fatigue or drugs.

DIMENSIONS OF LEARNING

Not all changes involved in learning are obvious and observable. In the case "The Talking Marks," for example, there may be some immediately apparent changes in the students' actual behavior—as, for example, when Tyler makes a pair of "talking marks" and places them appropriately, a behavior of which he was incapable earlier. There also may be other important changes that are not apparent but that are a fundamental part of learning.

Disposition. For example, there may be an unfortunate change in Jenna's eagerness to participate in class activities following not only Ms. Swann's refusal to allow her to do so, but also her loud scolding for the *may I-can I* grammatical error. This change is also an example of learning, but in this case it involves changes in the learner's **disposition**—that is, in the person's inclination to do or not to do something—rather than immediately observable changes in actual behavior. Changes in disposition have to do with motivation. Such changes cannot always be observed but are no less real or important.

Capability. Learning involves not only changes in disposition but also changes in **capability**—that is, changes in the skills or knowledge required to do something. Like changes in disposition, changes in capability are not always observed directly. For instance, in Ms. Swann's class, there will probably be many other students who will also have learned to make quotation marks and to place them "around the

words that come right out of Mr. Brown's mouth." But, like Jenna, most will not be given an opportunity to demonstrate this learning immediately. To determine whether students' dispositions or capabilities have changed following instruction, teachers need to give them an opportunity to engage in the relevant behavior. The inference that dispositions or capabilities have changed—in other words, that learning has occurred—will always be based on **performance**.

Performance. If instruction affects learners in such a way that their behavior (their performance) after instruction is observably different from that before instruction, we can conclude that learning has occurred. As we saw, however, learning often involves changes in both capabilities and dispositions that will not be evident in performance until learners are placed in a situation requiring the relevant performance.

Psychologists sometimes distinguish among three kinds of learning based upon the type of performance involved. Thus, learning that involves muscular coordination and physical

---

disposition An inclination or a tendency to do (or not to do) something; an aspect of motivation.

capability A capacity to do something. To be capable is to have the necessary knowledge and skills.

---

performance Actual behavior. The inference that learning has occurred is typically based on observed changes in performance.

CASE: THE TALKING MARKS

THE PLACE: Lynn Swann's Second-Grade Class

THE SITUATION: A punctuation lesson on quotation marks

MS. SWANN: And what we have to do is put the talking marks around the words that come right out of Mr. Brown's mouth. (demonstrating with a cartoon character who has just said, "Here's my dog.")

TYLER: Can I do it, Ms. Swann? Can I?

MS. SWANN: *May* I, Tyler. It's *may* I. Yes you *may* and we'll see if you *can*. (Ms. Swann erases the

quotation marks. Tyler takes the green pen and makes a pair of recognizable opening and closing quotation marks. The children have already practiced making these "talking marks.")

MS. SWANN: Very good, Tyler. I see that you *can* do it.

JENNA: Can I do it too? Can I?

MS. SWANN: Weren't you paying any attention at all, Jenna? It's *may*! *May, not can.* No, you may not do it right now. We have to move along because it's going to be lunch time soon. (and the lesson continues . . .)

skills (**motor learning**) appears to be different from learning involving emotions (**affective learning**) or that involving information or ideas (**cognitive learning**). These three distinctions are based on fairly obvious differences among the responses involved. Learning may also be classified by reference to the conditions that lead to it—an approach adopted by R. Gagné (1977a) and described in Chapter 6.

THREE APPROACHES TO HUMAN LEARNING

Learning, as we saw, is defined as changes in *behavior* as a function of experience. Not surprisingly, therefore, one of the oldest scientific approaches to understanding learning looks at actual behavior. This approach, labeled **behaviorism,** begins by trying to explain simple behaviors—observable and predictable responses. Accordingly, it is concerned mainly with conditions (called **stimuli**) that affect organisms and that may lead to behavior, as well as with simple behaviors themselves (**responses**). Behavior-oriented (or behavioristic) researchers attempt to discover the rules that govern the formation of relationships between stimuli and responses (the rules of **conditioning**). For this reason, these theories are often referred to as **stimulus–response (S–R) theories** or as **behavioristic theories.**

In contrast to behaviorism, a second approach termed **cognitivism** tries to look at the more intellectual or mental aspects of learning. Cognitive approaches deal mainly with questions relating to cognition, or knowing. Cognitive theorists are concerned with how we develop a fund of knowledge and how we eventually arrive at notions of ourselves as learners and rememberers and problem solvers. Children's gradual development of an awareness of themselves as knowers, their growing awareness of the strategies they can use to acquire and process information, and their ability to direct their efforts and to evaluate their cognitive activities are aspects of **metacognition.** Put another way, cognition refers to knowing; *metacognition* refers to knowing about knowing. Cognition-oriented researchers attempt to understand the nature of information—how it is acquired and organized by learners; how it can be recalled, modified, applied, and analyzed; and how the learner understands, evaluates, and controls the activities involved in cognition. Piaget, whose theory is described in Chapter 3, is a good example of a cognitive theorist.

---

motor learning Learning that involves muscular coordination and physical skills. Such common activities as walking and driving a car involve motor learning.

affective learning Changes in attitudes or emotions (affect) as a function of experience.

cognitive learning Learning concerned primarily with acquiring information, developing strategies for processing information, decision-making processes, and logical thought processes.

behaviorism A general term for theories of learning concerned primarily with the observable components of behavior (stimuli and responses).

stimulus (stimuli) Any change in the physical environment capable of exciting a sense organ.

response Any organic, muscular, glandular, or psychic process that results from stimulation.

---

conditioning A type of learning describable in terms of changing relationships between stimuli, between responses, or between both stimuli and responses.

stimulus–response (S–R) theories Learning theories with primary emphasis on stimuli and responses and the relationships between them. These theories are also termed *behavioristic theories.*

cognitivism Theories of learning concerned primarily with such topics as perception, problem solving, information processing, and understanding.

metacognition Knowledge about knowing. As we grow and learn, we develop notions of ourselves as learners. Accordingly, we develop strategies that recognize our limitations and that allow us to monitor our progress and to take advantage of our efforts.

A third approach to understanding human behavior is **humanism.** Humanistic psychologists are concerned more with human individuality and uniqueness than with discovering general rules to explain human responses. They focus on emotional development more than on information processing or on stimuli and responses.

This chapter deals with some of the behaviorists' explanations of learning and their implications for teaching. Chapters 5 and 6 look at cognitive explanations. Chapter 9 discusses humanism (see Table 4.1).

PAVLOV'S AND WATSON'S BEHAVIORISM

Some simple forms of learning require little information processing or understanding. They can occur unconsciously, and they apply to some kinds of animal learning as well as to human learning.

Consider, as an example, the case "Of Pig Grunting and Flinching." Prior to Robert's telling lies and being punished, he would not have flinched to hear Mrs. Grundy squeal. That he subsequently did so is an example of a simple, unconscious, and sometimes very powerful type of learning called **classical conditioning.** The qualifier *classical* is used simply to differentiate this specific form of learning from other forms of learning loosely referred to as *conditioning* in ordinary speech.

---

humanism A philosophical and psychological orientation that is primarily concerned with our humanity—that is, with our worth as individuals and with those processes that are considered to make us more human.

classical conditioning Also called "learning-through-stimulus substitution" because it involves the repeated pairing of two stimuli so that eventually a previously neutral (conditioned) stimulus comes to elicit the same response (conditioned response) that was previously elicited by the first stimulus (unconditioned stimulus). This was the type of conditioning first described by Pavlov.

PAVLOV'S CLASSICAL CONDITIONING

Ivan Pavlov, a Russian physiologist, was one of the first to draw attention to classical conditioning. He had noticed that the dogs in his laboratory began to salivate when they were about to be fed, even before they could see or smell the food. Strangely, they seemed to be salivating at the mere sight of their keeper or even when they simply heard his footsteps.

This simple observation led Pavlov to a series of well-known experiments. These experiments involved ringing a bell or sounding a buzzer—neither of which ordinarily leads to salivation—and then immediately presenting the dogs with food, a stimulus that does lead to salivation. Pavlov soon found that if the procedure was repeated often enough, the bell or buzzer alone began to elicit salivation.

In Pavlov's experiments, the bell is referred to as a **conditioned stimulus (CS)**; the food is an **unconditioned stimulus (US)**; and salivation in response to the food is an **unconditioned response (UR)**, whereas salivation in response to the bell or buzzer is a **conditioned response (CR)**.

The Mrs. Grundy/Robert case is a simple illustration of classical conditioning, as is shown in Figure 4.1. In this example, the sound

---

conditioned stimulus (CS) A stimulus that initially does not elicit any response or that elicits a global, orienting response but that, as a function of being paired with an unconditioned stimulus and its response, acquires the capability of eliciting that same response. For example, a stimulus that is always present at the time of a fear reaction may become a conditioned stimulus for fear.

unconditioned stimulus (US) A stimulus that elicits a response before learning. All stimuli that are capable of eliciting reflexive behaviors are examples of unconditioned stimuli. For example, food is an unconditioned stimulus for the response of salivation.

unconditioned response (UR) A response that is elicited by an unconditioned stimulus.

conditioned response (CR) A response elicited by a conditioned stimulus. In some obvious ways, a conditioned response resembles, but is not identical to, its corresponding unconditioned response.

TABLE 4.1 THREE APPROACHES TO LEARNING

THEORY	MAJOR FOCUS	KEY VARIABLES/ CONCEPTS	REPRESENTATIVE THEORISTS	PRINCIPAL USEFULNESS FOR TEACHERS
BEHAVIORISM	Behavior	Stimuli Responses Reinforcement Punishment Behavior modification	Watson Guthrie Thorndike Skinner	Explains learning of skills and attitudes Emphasizes reinforcement
COGNITIVISM	Knowing	Decision making Understanding Cognitive structure Perception Information processes Memory	Ausubel Bruner Gagné, R. Piaget Sternberg	Explains development of understanding (meaning) Emphasizes importance of meaningfulness and organization
HUMANISM	The person	Self-concept Self-actualization Self-worth	Maslow Rogers	Focuses on affective development Emphasizes adjustment and well-being

of the grunt serves as a conditioned stimulus. The fear reaction (flinch) is the initial unconditioned response; the pain of the cane serves as an unconditioned stimulus.

In general terms, a stimulus or situation that readily leads to a response can be paired with a **neutral stimulus** (one that does not lead to a response) to bring about classical conditioning. Note that this learning typically is unconscious; that is, learners do not respond to the conditioned stimulus because they become aware of the relationship between it and an unconditioned stimulus. In fact, classical conditioning can occur even for responses over which the subject ordinarily has no control. For example, the application of cold or hot packs directly to the skin can bring about constric-

tion or dilation of blood vessels. If these stimuli are paired with a neutral stimulus such as a tone, the tone by itself will eventually lead to vascular constriction or dilation.

WATSON'S ENVIRONMENTALISM

According to J. B. Watson (1913, 1916), who was greatly influenced by the work of Pavlov, people are born with a limited number of reflexes. Learning, explained Watson, is just a matter of classical conditioning involving these reflexes. Hence, differences among people are entirely a function of their experiences. (This point of view, referred to as **environmentalism,** is discussed in more detail in Chapter 7.)

Watson's view was extremely influential in the early development of psychology in the United States. His insistence on precision, rigor, and objectivity—and his rejection of such

---

neutral stimulus A stimulus that does not initially lead reliably to a predictable response. For example, neutral stimuli are not associated with emotional responses until learning has occurred, at which point they are referred to as conditioned (rather than neutral) stimuli.

---

environmentalism The belief that whatever a child becomes is determined by experience (the environment) rather than by genetic makeup.

previously popular but difficult to define (and measure) terms as *mind, feeling,* and *sensation*—was very much in line with the scientific spirit of the times. In addition, the belief that what we become is a function of our experiences presents a just and egalitarian view of humans. If what we become is truly a function of the experiences to which we are subjected, we are in fact born equal. As Watson declared, any child can become a doctor or a judge. In fact, however, things are not quite that simple: Not everybody can become a doctor or a judge (see Chapter 7).

EDUCATIONAL IMPLICATIONS OF PAVLOV'S AND WATSON'S BEHAVIORISM

Classical conditioning, especially of emotional reactions, occurs in all schools, virtually at all times, regardless of the other kinds of learning going on at the same time. And it is largely through these unconscious processes that students come to dislike schools, subjects, teachers, and related stimuli—or to like them.

To illustrate, a school subject, assuming that it is new to the student, is a neutral stimulus that evokes little emotional response in the beginning. But the teacher, the classroom, or some other distinctive stimulus in the student's immediate environment that is repeatedly associated with the subject may serve as an unconditioned stimulus. This unconditioned stimulus might be associated with pleasant responses (a comfortable desk, a friendly teacher) or with more negative reactions (a cold, hard desk; a cold, hard teacher with a grating voice and squeaking chalk). Following successive pairings of the subject (mathematics) with this distinctive unconditioned stimulus (teacher's unpleasant voice, and so on), the emotions (attitudes) associated with the unconditioned stimulus may become classically conditioned to the subject. Mathematics will now be associated with the negative responses previously linked with the unconditioned stimulus (see Figure 4.2). Put another way, students learn attitudes toward subjects, learning, school, and so on largely as a function of classical conditioning. Thus, it is entirely possible to teach students mathematics while at the same time teaching them to dislike mathematics. Whereas learning mathematics is likely to involve cognitive processes (and perhaps some form of conditioning as well, particularly if repetitive skills are involved), learning to dislike mathematics may involve mainly classical conditioning.

CASE: OF PIG GRUNTING AND FLINCHING

THE TIME: 1848

THE PLACE: Mrs. Evelyn Grundy's classroom in Raleigh, North Carolina

THE SITUATION: 6-year-old Robert has been Misbehaving to Girls and Telling Lyes

In this Raleigh school system in 1848, the prescribed punishment for Misbehaving to Girls and Telling Lyes totals eleven lashes.* But because there are two separate infractions involved, Mrs. Grundy deems it wise and judicious to double the punishment to twenty-two lashes. She administers the lashes herself. And every time she raises the cane to strike Robert, the effort makes her squeal hoarsely, a little like pig grunting. By the tenth lash, Robert has begun to flinch a little just before the cane hits. He cries out quite loudly when it lands.

Later that day, when Mrs. Grundy is passing out the spellers, her back turned to Edward, his ruler-propelled spitball catches her just behind the left ear. She squeals loudly. And Robert flinches.

---

*PPC: The punishment sounds a little extreme. Readers will think you're making this up. Are you?

AUTHOR: Nope. See Table 4.3 if you don't believe me.

Before Conditioning

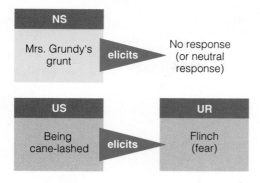

An unconditioned stimulus elicits an
unconditioned fear response

Conditioning Process

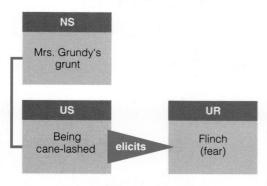

A neutral stimulus is repeatedly
paired with the US

After Conditioning

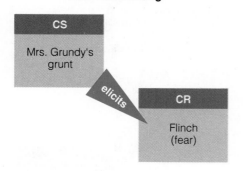

The previously neutral stimulus becomes
a conditioned stimulus eliciting the
conditioned response of fear

FIGURE 4.1 Classical conditioning. An initially neutral or pleasant stimulus (NS) is paired with an unconditioned, fear-producing stimulus (US) so that the subject is eventually *conditioned* to fear the previously neutral stimulus. Fear is now a conditioned response (CR) to a conditioned stimulus (CS).

The most important instructional implications of classical conditioning may be expressed as follows:

▶ Teachers need to do whatever they can to maximize the number, the distinctiveness, and the potency of pleasant unconditioned stimuli in their classrooms.

▶ Teachers should try to minimize the unpleasant aspects of being a student, thus reducing the number and potency of negative unconditioned stimuli in their classrooms.

▶ Teachers need to know what is being paired with what in their classrooms

The old adage that learning should be fun is more than a schoolchild's frivolous plea; it follows directly from classical conditioning theory. A teacher who makes students smile and laugh while she has them repeat the 6-times table may, because of the variety of stimuli and responses being paired, succeed in teaching students (1) how to smile and laugh—a worthwhile undertaking in its own right, (2) to associate stimuli such as 6 × 7 with responses such as "42"—a valuable piece of information, and (3) to like arithmetic—and the teacher, the school, the smell of chalk, the feel of a book's pages, and on and on.

What does a teacher who makes students suffer grimly through their multiplication tables teach?

THORNDIKE'S CONNECTIONISM

People are always trying to show how intelligent their pet animals are, claimed psychologist Edward L. Thorndike (1898). If a dog gets lost and then finds its way home, newspapers run stories about how smart dogs are. Stories about

FIGURE 4.2 Classical conditioning of math phobia.

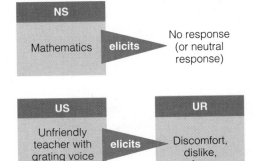

Before Conditioning

Mathematics elicits no strong emotional response; the unconditioned stimulus elicits negative reactions

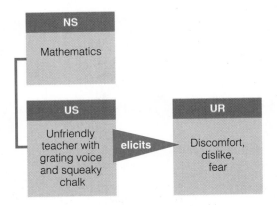

Conditioning Process

Mathematics is paired repeatedly with the unconditioned stimulus (teacher)

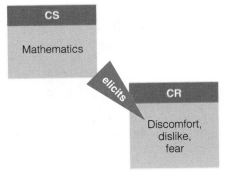

After Conditioning

Mathematics has become a conditioned stimulus associated with negative reactions

the hundreds of dogs who go out for an evening stroll and stupidly get lost, never to find their way home again, are much less interesting and seldom get published—except in the lost pets column.

Trial-and-Error Learning. But are animals really intelligent, asked Thorndike, reasoning that anecdotes make very poor scientific evidence. And so he devised a series of tasks that, in a sense, serve as crude measures of animal intelligence. The most famous of these are the so-called puzzle *boxes,* the most common of which is illustrated in Figure 4.3. It's designed so that a cat locked in the box can only get out if it does three things: pull a string to release one lock, step on a lever to release a second, and flip a latch upright so that the door will open. To make sure that the cat will be highly motivated to get out, Thorndike typically placed some juicy morsel, like a dead fish, just far enough away that the cat couldn't quite reach it through the bars.

So what does a hungry cat do in this situation? It uses up all of its ready-made solutions like trying to squeeze between the bars, scratching and clawing at the door, and meowing for help. And when none of these work, it doesn't sit back and contemplate the situation, trying to figure out a solution. No, says Thorndike. What the cat does instead is continue to try out dozens of different actions until, by chance, really, it stumbles upon the right combination of actions and escapes from the puzzle box. The remarkable thing, however, is that the next time the cat is placed in the same situation, it escapes quicker—and even quicker the third time, and the next. As Figure 4.4 shows, one typical Thorndikean cat took almost 3 minutes to escape the first time—which is really not very long at all. But after that, it typically took far less than a minute.

"*That is the correct answer, Billy, but I'm afraid you don't win anything for it.*"

Drawing by Lorenz; © 1986 The New Yorker Magazine, Inc.

It seems clear, Thorndike explained, that this is **trial-and-error learning** and certainly not learning through what might be called insight or other similar mental processes. And people, Thorndike insisted, learn in exactly the same way: "These simple semi-mechanical phenomena . . . which animal learning discloses are the fundamentals of human learning also" (Thorndike, 1913b, p. 16).

The essence of Thorndike's explanation of human learning, then, can be summarized as follows: In a given situation, a person makes a number of different responses until a response is made that leads to a solution (or, in Thorn-dike's words, "a satisfying state of affairs"). That response is then learned or, again to use Thorndike's words, "stamped in." Thus, learning involves the "stamping in" of connections between stimuli and responses: Hence the label **connectionism** for the theory.

Contiguity or Reinforcement. In attempting to explain the formation of relationships between stimuli, between responses, or between stimuli and responses, behaviorists can make one of two choices. They can maintain, as did Watson and Pavlov, that the simultaneous occurrence of events is sufficient to bring about learning. Thus, it is sufficient to pair the buzzer and the food X number of times (that is, to present them

trial-and-error learning Thorndikean explanation for learning based on the idea that when placed in a problem situation, an individual will emit a number of responses but will eventually learn the correct one as a result of reinforcement. Trial-and-error explanations for learning are sometimes contrasted with insight explanations.

connectionism A theory that explains learning as the formation of bonds (connections) between stimuli and responses. The term is attributed to E. L. Thorndike.

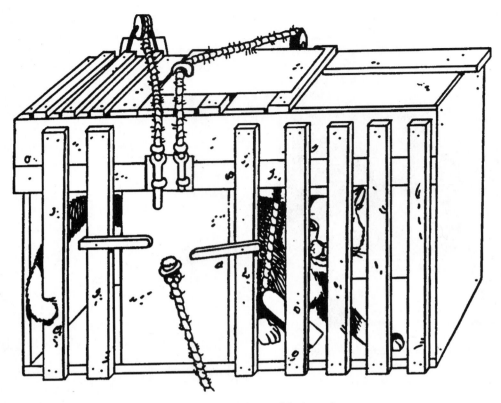

FIGURE 4.3 Thorndike's puzzle box. To get out of the box, the cat had to pull a string to release one of the door locks, step on the lever to release the second, and then flick one of the door latches down. From E. L. Thorndike, "Animal Intelligence: An Experimental Study of the Associative Processes in Animals." *Psychological Review Monograph Supplement*, 1898, 2(8).

in *contiguity*) for learning to occur. This reasoning is referred to as a **contiguity** explanation.

A second option is to explain the formation of S–R bonds by reference to the effects of the behavior. This explanation, introduced by Edward L. Thorndike and popularized by B. F. Skinner, is labeled a "reinforcement approach."

contiguity The occurrence of things both simultaneously and in the same space. Contiguity is frequently used to explain the occurrence of classical conditioning. It is assumed that the simultaneity of the unconditioned and the conditioned stimulus is sufficient to explain the formation of the link between the two.

What this explanation maintains is that it is the consequences of a response that lead to it being learned (or not learned).

Much of Thorndike's theory deals specifically with the conditions that lead to the stamping in or stamping out of "bonds," which is his word for connections. Details of these conditions are expressed in a series of laws of learning, most of which were derived directly from experiments with animals. Interestingly, later in his career (after 1930) Thorndike made important changes in several of the most important of these laws. These laws form the basis of his theory of human learning.

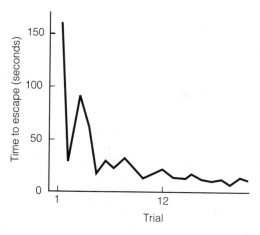

FIGURE 4.4 The behavior of one cat in Thorndike's puzzle box. The cat took almost 3 minutes to escape the first time, but almost always less than 1 minute after the first successful escape. From E. L. Thorndike, "Animal Intelligence: An Experimental Study of the Associative Processes in Animals." *Psychological Review Monograph Supplement,* 1898, 2(8).

The Law of Effect. Perhaps the most important of Thorndike's laws is the **law of effect.** It states that responses that occur just before a satisfying state of affairs tend to be stamped in (learned); those that occur before an annoying state of affairs tend to be stamped out. Thus, the law of effect expresses Thorndike's belief that learning is a function of the consequences of behavior rather than simply of contiguity.

It's important to note that after 1930, Thorndike (1931) modified the law of effect. He had previously believed that satisfying states of affairs lead to stimulus response connections being stamped in (learned) and unsatisfying or annoying states of affairs lead to connections being stamped out (forgotten or not learned). But further experimentation led him to the view that whereas *satisfiers* lead to learning,

---

law of effect A Thorndikean law of learning that states that it is the effect of a response that leads to its being learned (stamped in) or not learned (stamped out).

annoyers do not lead to forgetting but simply lead the learner to do something else.

The Law of Exercise. The **law of exercise** expresses Thorndike's initially very strong belief that bonds become strengthened the more often they are repeated (or exercised). This psychological finding had a tremendous influence on education in North America throughout several decades of this century because it lent scientific credibility to the belief that practice and repetition were among the most important of all instructional techniques. Ironically, however, this was the one law of learning that Thorndike rejected most emphatically after 1930. He had determined through experimentation—with human subjects this time—that repetition alone does not cause learning. In his words, "The repetition of a situation may change a man as little as the repetition of a message over a wire changes the wire" (Thorndike, 1931, p. 14).

The Law of Readiness. A third law, the **law of readiness,** recognizes that certain responses are more or less likely than others to be learned (stamped in), depending on the learner's readiness. Such factors as maturation and previous learning are clearly involved in determining whether learning is easy, difficult, or impossible. This important law provides the basis for Thorndike's definitions of **reward** and

---

law of exercise Thorndikean law of learning that states that bonds (connections) become strengthened the more often they are repeated (exercised). Thorndike rejected this law late in his career.

law of readiness A Thorndikean law of learning that takes into account the fact that certain types of learning are impossible or difficult unless the learner is ready. In this context, readiness refers to maturational level, previous learning, motivational factors, and other characteristics of the individual that relate to learning.

reward An object, stimulus, event, or outcome that is perceived as being pleasant and that may therefore be reinforcing.

punishment. Specifically, it is the learner's readiness that determines whether a state of affairs is pleasant or not. Thorndike maintained that a pleasant state of affairs—a reward—results when a person is ready to do something and is allowed to do it. By the same token, not being allowed to do something when one is ready, or being forced to do something when one is not ready, results in an annoying state of affairs—punishment.

Subsidiary Laws. A number of subsidiary laws also form an important part of Thorndike's theory. These can be summarized briefly as follows:

▶ The **law of multiple responses** is based on Thorndike's observation that when faced with a difficult problem for which they have no ready solution, individuals will engage in a variety of different responses until one response produces a satisfying effect. In other words, it is through trial and error that problems are solved. As a result of this law, Thorndike's theory came to be known as the theory of trial-and-error learning.

▶ The **law of set or attitude** recognizes that learning is partly a function of predeter-

mined attitudes or tendencies to react in given ways (a tendency to react is defined as a *set*). Attitudes are strongly influenced by culture. For example, in some cultures people are more likely to react aggressively than in others—and hence more likely to be reinforced for and to learn aggressive responses.

▶ The **law of prepotency of elements** suggests that organisms typically react to the most significant (or *prepotent*) elements of a situation. Thus, the cat in the puzzle box doesn't spend much time scratching at the ceiling, but is more likely to try different responses with the lever and the string, both of which are more salient (more striking) features of the situation.

▶ The **law of response by analogy** points out that when placed in a new situation, we tend to react in ways that would be appropriate in similar (analogous) situations. That is, we transfer responses from one situation to another, an ability that is extremely important to our adaptation. For example, it is because of transfer (or, in Thorndike's terms, response by analogy) that we are able to apply laws of addition and subtraction when buying new items in stores where we have never shopped before.

---

punishment Involves either the presentation of an unpleasant stimulus or the withdrawal of a pleasant stimulus as a consequence of behavior. Punishment should not be confused with *negative reinforcement*.

law of multiple responses One of Thorndike's laws based on his observation that learning involves the emission of a variety of responses (multiple responses) until one (presumably an appropriate one) is reinforced. It is because of this law that Thorndike's theory is often referred to as a theory of trial-and-error learning.

law of set or attitude A Thorndikean law of learning that recognizes the fact that we are often predisposed to respond in certain ways as a result of our experiences and previously learned attitudes. This subsidiary law acknowledges the influence of culture and experience in determining our attitudes and, therefore our most likely responses in a given situation.

INSTRUCTIONAL APPLICATIONS

Much of Thorndike's research and writing was directed specifically toward applying his findings to education; not surprisingly, his theories are rich with instructional implications.

---

law of prepotency of elements A Thorndikean law of learning that states that people tend to respond to the most striking (prepotent) of the various elements that make up a stimulus situation.

law of response by analogy A Thorndikean law to explain transfer. An analogy is typically an explanation, comparison, or illustration based on similarity. In Thorndike's system, response by analogy refers to responses that occur because of similarities between two situations.

Rewarding Correct Trials. Perhaps most obvious are the implications of his belief that learning occurs through trial and error and results from the fact that the eventual correct response is rewarded—and therefore learned (stamped in). This belief leads directly to the principle that teachers and schools need to provide opportunity for students to emit a variety of responses and that correct responses need to be rewarded. The theory also stresses that rewards and punishments need to be tailored to the situation and to the child and that, among other things, the child's readiness needs to be taken into consideration.

Establishing Attitudes. Many of the instructional implications of Thorndike's theory are to be found in his subsidiary laws. The law of set or attitude, for example, recognizes that people often respond to novel situations in terms of the sets, or attitudes, that they bring with them. Teachers often exercise considerable influence in determining student attitudes. For example, they can encourage students to develop attitudes that place high value on creativity. Subsequently students will be more likely to prize creative behavior and perhaps even to respond creatively.

This law also implies that cultural background and immediate environment not only affect how a person responds but also determine what will be satisfying or annoying. For example, the student's environment may determine that academic success will be satisfying— or that popularity will be more satisfying than academic success.

Readiness. The importance of the law of readiness for teaching is clearly apparent. A child who is ready for a specific type of learning is far more likely to profit from such learning experiences than another who is not ready. What is not so obvious is precisely what is involved in being ready. There are various types of readiness, some relating to physical maturation, some to the development of intellectual skills and the acquisition of important background information, and some to motivation. Hence,

to assess as well as to enhance readiness, teachers need knowledge of children's emotional and intellectual development—topics covered in Chapters 2 and 3. They also need to know something about how students learn and about their motivation, topics covered in the chapters that make up Part III of this text, as well as in Chapter 10.

Attracting Attention. The law of prepotency of elements recognizes that people respond to the most significant or the most striking aspects of a stimulus situation and not necessarily to the entire situation. Obviously, students cannot and probably should not respond to all the sights and sounds that surround them at any given moment. Hence, teachers must be careful to stress (make prepotent) important aspects of the learning situation (for example, by underlining or boldfacing, through the use of color, through the use of voice and gestures, through repetition, and so on).

Generalizing. Generalization (sometimes referred to as **transfer** or response by analogy) is one of the important goals of education. Generalization occurs whenever a previously learned response is used in a new situation—or when a new stimulus is reacted to as though it were familiar. When Tamy uses a multiplication rule she learned in school to determine how many packs of bubble gum two quarters will buy, she is generalizing. Thorndike believed that the transference of a response to a new stimulus is a function of the similarity between the two stimuli—hence the law of response by analogy.

Thorndike suggested that teachers can facilitate transfer by pointing out a variety of

---

generalization The transference of a response from one stimulus to a similar stimulus (stimulus generalization) or the transference of a similar response for another response in the face of a single stimulus (response generalization). A child who responds with fear in a new situation that resembles an old, fear-producing situation is showing evidence of stimulus generalization. Also termed *transfer*.

situations in which a single response (or rule) is applicable. He also emphasized the importance of pointing out connections among ideas. These connections, Thorndike insisted, are the basis of knowledge.

SKINNER'S OPERANT CONDITIONING

By definition, behaviorists are concerned with behavior. They define learning in terms of changes in behavior and look to the environment for explanations of these changes. Their theories are **associationistic;** they deal with connections or associations that are formed among stimuli and responses. And, as we have seen, these theories make use of one or both of two principal classes of explanations for learning: those based on contiguity (simultaneity of stimulus and response events) and those based on the effects of behavior (reinforcement and punishment). Pavlov and Watson are contiguity theorists; Thorndike is a reinforcement theorist. And so is Burrhus Frederic Skinner, one of the most influential psychologists of the twentieth century and the originator and chief spokesman for the theory of **operant conditioning.**

RESPONDENTS AND OPERANTS

Skinner accepted the existence and validity of classical conditioning. He claimed that many responses, called **elicited responses,** can be brought about by a stimulus and can become conditioned to other stimuli in the manner described by Pavlov and Watson. He labeled this behavior **respondent** because it occurs in response to a stimulus.

But there is a second, much larger and more important class of behaviors, said Skinner. It consists of behaviors that are not elicited by any known stimuli but are simply **emitted responses.** These are labeled **operants** because, in a sense, they are operations performed by the organism. Another way of making this distinction is to say that in the case of respondent behavior the organism is *reacting to* the environment, whereas in the case of operant behavior the organism *acts upon* the environment. Still another way of distinguishing between respondents and operants is to note that respondents appear largely involuntary whereas operants are more voluntary (Skinner would not have used these terms, however, believing them to involve unnecessary speculation). (See Table 4.2.)

The distinction between respondent and operant behavior can be clarified further by examining some simple behaviors. Sneezing, blinking, being angry, afraid, or excited—these may all be respondents. What they have in common is that they are largely automatic, involuntary, and almost inevitable responses to specific situations. Put another way, they are responses that can reliably be elicited by specific stimuli. Such responses are learned through processes of classical conditioning.

In contrast, driving a car, writing a letter, singing, reading a book, and kissing a baby are generally operants (although these, too, may

---

associationistic Theories that are associationistic are concerned with behavior and the connections or associations that are formed among stimuli and responses.

operant conditioning A type of learning that involves an increase in the probability that a response will occur as a function of reinforcement. Most of Skinner's experimental work investigates the principles of operant conditioning.

elicited response A response brought about by a stimulus. The expression is synonymous with the term *respondent*.

respondent A term used by Skinner in contrast to the term *operant*. A respondent is a response that is elicited by a known, specific stimulus. Unconditioned responses are examples of respondents.

emitted response A response not elicited by a stimulus but simply emitted by the organism. An emitted response is, in fact, an operant.

operant Skinner's term for a response not elicited by any known or obvious stimulus. Most significant human behaviors appear to be operants (for example, writing a letter or going for a walk).

TABLE 4.2 CLASSICAL AND OPERANT CONDITIONING

CLASSICAL (PAVLOVIAN)	OPERANT (SKINNERIAN)
Deals with respondents, which are elicited by stimuli and appear involuntary	Deals with operants, which are emitted as instrumental acts
Reactions to the environment	Actions upon the environment
Type S conditioning (S for stimuli)	Type R conditioning (R for reinforcement)

involve respondents, as when a red light leads me automatically to slam on the brakes). Their common characteristics are that they are deliberate and intentional. They occur not as inevitable responses to specific stimulation but as personally controlled actions (rather than reactions). And they are subject to the laws of operant conditioning.

Because it does not involve obvious stimuli, operant conditioning is somewhat different from Thorndike's conception of learning and his law of effect. Whereas Thorndike believed that the effect of reinforcement is to strengthen the bond that exists between the stimulus and the response, Skinner declared that not only is the stimulus usually unknown but, in any case, it is irrelevant to the learning. The link is formed between response and reinforcement rather than between stimulus and response. Essentially, all that happens in operant learning is that when an emitted response is reinforced, the probability increases that it will be repeated.

WHAT IS OPERANT CONDITIONING?

Operant conditioning is most simply illustrated by reference to a typical Skinnerian experiment with a rat. In this experiment, a rat is placed in a **Skinner box,** a small, controlled environment (see Figure 4.5). The Skinner box

Skinner box Various experimental environments used by Skinner in his investigations of operant conditioning. The typical Skinner box is a cagelike structure equipped with a lever and a food tray attached to a food mechanism. It allows the investigator to study operants (for example, bar pressing) and the relationship between an operant and reinforcement.

is constructed to make certain responses highly probable and to make it possible for the experimenter to measure these responses and to punish or reward them. For our typical experiment, the box contains a lever, a light, an electric grid on the floor, and a food tray, all arranged in such a way that when the rat depresses the lever, the light goes on and a food pellet is released into the tray. Under these circumstances, most rats will quickly learn to depress the lever, and they will continue to do so for long periods of time even if they do not receive a food pellet each time they work the lever. Similarly, rats can quickly be trained to avoid the lever if depressing it activates a mild electric current in the floor grid. However, if the electric current is constant and ceases only when the lever is depressed, rats will learn to depress it.

Most of the basic elements of Skinner's theory are evident in this situation. The rat's act of depressing the lever is an operant—an almost random behavior that is simply emitted rather than being elicited by a specific stimulus. The food pellets serve as reinforcement. Their availability increases the probability that whenever the rat finds itself in this situation, it will saunter over to the lever and depress it.

In general terms, operant conditioning is an increase in the probability that a response will occur again, this increase being a result of reinforcement (about which more is said shortly). Furthermore, Skinner's model of operant conditioning states that the reward, together with whatever **discriminated stimuli**

discriminated stimulus(S^D) A stimulus that is perceived by the organism. In operant conditioning, the discriminated stimulus elicits the response.

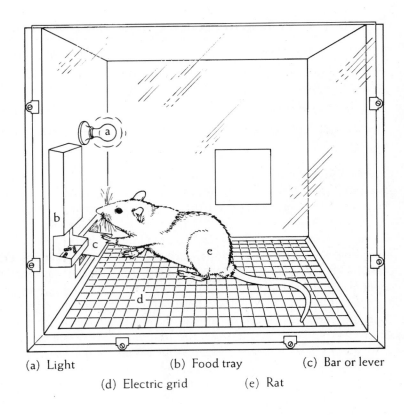

FIGURE 4.5 A Skinner box. From G. R. Lefrançois, *Theories of Human Learning: Kro's Report* (3rd ed.). Copyright © 1995 by Wadsworth, Inc. Reprinted by permission of Brooks/Cole Publishing Company, Pacific Grove, California.

(a) Light (b) Food tray (c) Bar or lever

(d) Electric grid (e) Rat

($\mathbf{S^D}$)* were present at the time of reinforcement, are stimuli that, after learning, may bring about the operant. For example, the rat's view (and smell) of the inside of the Skinner box may eventually serve as stimuli for lever-pressing behavior. But, cautions Skinner, they are not stimuli in the sense that a puff of air in the eye is a stimulus that elicits a blink. Rather these discriminated stimuli simply serve as signals that a certain behavior may lead to reinforcement (See Figure 4.6 for a model of operant learning in the classroom and Figure 4.7 for additional classroom examples.)

PRINCIPLES OF OPERANT CONDITIONING

One of Skinner's main concerns was to discover the relationship between reinforcement and behavior and to clarify how behavior is affected by its consequences.

Reinforcement. Skinner made an important distinction between two related terms: **reinforcer** and **reinforcement**. A reinforcer is a thing, or, in Skinnerian terms, a stimulus; reinforcement is the effect of this stimulus. For example, candy may be a reinforcer because it can be reinforcing and because it is a stimulus. A piece of candy, however, is not a reinforcement, although

---

*Also referred to as discriminative stimuli; refers to those aspects of a situation (stimuli) that differentiate it from other situations.

---

reinforcer A stimulus that causes reinforcement.

reinforcement The effect of a reinforcer; specifically, to increase the probability that a response will occur.

Before Conditioning

Stimulus Context: Classroom

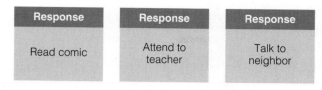

Response	Response	Response
Read comic	Attend to teacher	Talk to neighbor

Various responses are emitted
in a certain stimulus context

FIGURE 4.6 Operant conditioning in the classroom. Note that in operant conditioning, unlike classical conditioning, the original response is emitted rather than elicited by a stimulus. In this example, a variety of off-task and on-task behaviors are emitted. Reinforcement leads to the more frequent occurrence of on-task behaviors.

Conditioning Process

Stimulus Context: Classroom

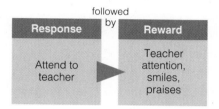

One response is systematically reinforced

After Conditioning

Stimulus Context: Classroom

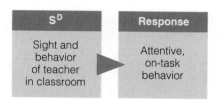

The reinforced response becomes more frequent.
Stimuli accompanying the reward (discriminated
stimuli, or S^D) acquire control over the response

its effect on a person may be an example of reinforcement.

Although reinforcers may be defined in different ways, the most widely accepted definition is any stimulus that increases the probability that a response will occur. This definition makes it clear that it is the effect of a stimulus that determines whether it will be reinforcing. Thus, any given situation may be highly reinforcing for one person and highly unpleasant

Stimulus Context: Classroom

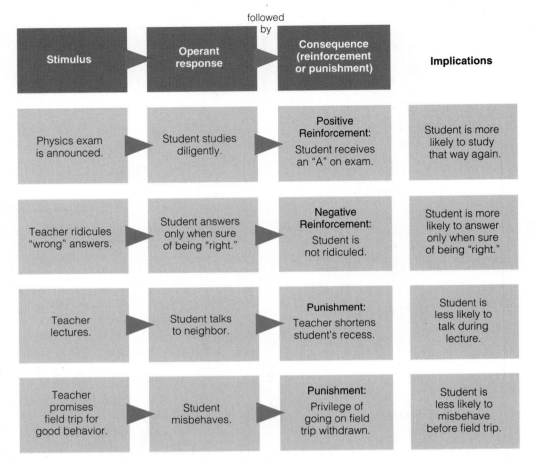

Stimulus	Operant response	Consequence (reinforcement or punishment)	Implications
Physics exam is announced.	Student studies diligently.	**Positive Reinforcement:** Student receives an "A" on exam.	Student is more likely to study that way again.
Teacher ridicules "wrong" answers.	Student answers only when sure of being "right."	**Negative Reinforcement:** Student is not ridiculed.	Student is more likely to answer only when sure of being "right."
Teacher lectures.	Student talks to neighbor.	**Punishment:** Teacher shortens student's recess.	Student is less likely to talk during lecture.
Teacher promises field trip for good behavior.	Student misbehaves.	**Punishment:** Privilege of going on field trip withdrawn.	Student is less likely to misbehave before field trip.

FIGURE 4.7 Classroom examples of operant conditioning. Note that the first two examples (positive and negative reinforcement, respectively) lead to an *increase* in the likelihood of the response. The last two examples (both forms of punishment) lead to a *decrease* in the likelihood of the response. Note also that teachers may inadvertently reinforce maladaptive behaviors (second example).

for another. First-grade students may react positively when they are presented with little gold stars in recognition of their work. College students whose professor offered them little stars might think, with some justification, that the professor was a little strange.

Reinforcers may be primary or generalized. A **primary reinforcer** is a stimulus that is naturally reinforcing—that is, that the organism does not have to learn is reinforcing. Primary reinforcers are ordinarily related to an unlearned need or drive: food, drink, sex. Presumably, people do not have to learn that these can feel good.

primary reinforcer A stimulus that is reinforcing in the absence of any learning. Such stimuli as food and drink are primary reinforcers because, presumably, an organism does not have to learn that they are pleasant.

A **generalized reinforcer** is a previously neutral stimulus that, through repeated pairings with a number of other reinforcers in various situations, has become generally reinforcing for many behaviors. Prestige, money, and success are examples of extremely powerful generalized reinforcers.

Primary and generalized reinforcers can be positive or negative. A **positive reinforcer** is a stimulus that increases the probability of a response occurring when it is added to a situation. A **negative reinforcer** has the same effect as a result of being removed from the situation.

In the Skinner box example, food pellets are a positive reinforcer—as is the light. If, however, a mild current were turned on in the electric grid that runs through the floor of the box, and if this current were turned off only when the rat depressed the lever, turning off the current would be an example of a negative reinforcer.

REINFORCEMENT AND PUNISHMENT IN THE CLASSROOM

In summary, there are two types of reinforcement. One involves presenting a pleasant stimulus (positive reinforcement; *reward*); the other involves removing an unpleasant stimulus (negative reinforcement; **relief**). In the same way, there are two types of punishment, each the converse of one type of reinforcement. On the one hand is the punishment that occurs when a pleasant stimulus is removed (**penalty**); on the other is the more familiar situation in which a noxious (unpleasant) stimulus is presented. Figure 4.8 summarizes these four possibilities; the sections that follow illustrate each in the classroom.

Positive Reinforcement (Reward). Examples of positive reinforcement in the classroom are so numerous and obvious as to make citing any one appear platitudinous. Whenever a teacher smiles at students, says something pleasant to them, commends them for their work, assigns high grades, selects someone for a special project, or tells a mother how clever her child is, the teacher is using positive reinforcement. (See Chapter 11 for a more detailed discussion of various kinds of classroom reinforcement.)

Negative Reinforcement (Relief). Implicit or explicit threats of punishment, failure, detention, ridicule, parental anger, humiliation, and sundry other unpleasant eventualities make up the bulk of the modern, well-equipped teacher's arsenal of negative reinforcers. When these follow unruly, nonstudious, or otherwise unacceptable behaviors, they may be interpreted as punishment (the presentation of an unpleasant stimulus following undesirable behavior). When the threat of these possibilities is removed following acceptable behavior, they provide a clear example of negative reinforcement (the removal of an unpleasant stimulus following desirable behavior). Negative and sometimes maladaptive behaviors, such as the tendency to escape or

---

generalized reinforcer A stimulus that is not reinforcing before being paired with a primary reinforcer. Generalized reinforcers are stimuli that are present so often at the time of reinforcement that they come to be reinforcing for a wide variety of unrelated activities. Stimuli such as social prestige, praise, and money are generalized reinforcers for human behavior.

positive reinforcer A stimulus that increases the probability that a response will recur as a result of being added to a situation after the response has occurred once. Usually takes the form of a pleasant stimulus (reward) that results from a specific response.

negative reinforcer A stimulus that has the effect of increasing the probability of occurrence of the response that precedes it. Negative reinforcement ordinarily takes the form of an unpleasant or noxious stimulus that is removed as a result of a specific response.

---

relief A common expression for negative reinforcement—the type of reinforcement that results when an unpleasant stimulus is removed as a consequence of behavior.

penalty The type of punishment that involves losing or giving up something pleasant.

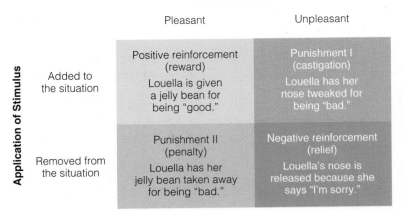

Nature of Stimulus Effect

	Pleasant	Unpleasant
Added to the situation	Positive reinforcement (reward) Louella is given a jelly bean for being "good."	Punishment I (castigation) Louella has her nose tweaked for being "bad."
Removed from the situation	Punishment II (penalty) Louella has her jelly bean taken away for being "bad."	Negative reinforcement (relief) Louella's nose is released because she says "I'm sorry."

(vertical axis label: Application of Stimulus)

FIGURE 4.8 Reinforcement and punishment.

avoid situations, often result from the overzealous administration of negative reinforcement.

Punishment I. The first type of punishment involves presenting a noxious stimulus, usually in an attempt to eliminate some undesirable behavior. A classic example is the use of the lash in one North Carolina school in the year 1848 (see Table 4.3, opposite, and Mrs. Grundy's case, earlier in this chapter)—a practice that is no longer widely accepted.

Punishment II (Penalty). The second type of punishment involves the removal of a pleasant stimulus. The fairly common practice of detaining students after regular class hours, insofar as it removes the apparently pleasant privilege of going home, is an example of this type of punishment.

EFFECTS OF REINFORCEMENT
AND PUNISHMENT

The simple fact is that reinforcement often leads to changes in behavior that define learning, as can easily be demonstrated in the behavior of both animals and people. That punishment has an equal, if opposite, effect is not nearly so obvious. As Thorndike conceded in 1931, pleasure is much more potent in stamping in responses than pain is in stamping them out.

Other than ethical or humanitarian considerations, there are several reasons why the use of punishment is not an entirely satisfactory means of behavior control:

▶ Punishment does not ordinarily illustrate or emphasize desirable behavior but simply draws attention to undesirable responses, so it is not very useful in a learning situation.

▶ Punishment is often accompanied by highly undesirable emotional side effects that may be associated with the punisher rather than with the punished behavior.

▶ Punishment does not always lead to the elimination of a response but sometimes only to its suppression. That is, a behavior is seldom forgotten as a result of punishment, although it may be avoided—sometimes only temporarily.

▶ Punishment often simply does not work. Sears, Maccoby, and Lewin (1957) report that parents who punish their children severely for being aggressive are more likely than other parents to have aggressive children. And mothers who are unduly punitive when attempting to toilet train their chil-

TABLE 4.3 EXCERPT FROM A LIST OF PUNISHMENTS IN A NORTH CAROLINA SCHOOL, 1848

NO.	RULES OF SCHOOL	LASHES
1	Boys and Girls Playing Together	4
3	Fighting	5
7	Playing at Cards at School	4
8	Climbing for Every Foot Over Three Feet Up a Tree	1
9	Telling Lyes	7
11	Nick Naming Each Other	4
16	For Misbehaving to Girls	10
19	For Drinking Spirituous Liquors at School	8
22	For Waring Long Finger Nails	2
27	Girls Going to Boy's Play Places	2
33	Wrestling at School	4
41	For Throwing Anything Harder than Your Trab Ball	4
42	For Every Word You Miss in Your Heart Lesson Without Good Excuse	1
47	For Going about the Barn or Doing Any Mischief about the Place	7

Source: From C. L. Coon. (1915). *North Carolina schools and academies*. Raleigh, N.C.: Edwards and Broughton.

dren are more likely to have children who wet their beds.

All of which might indeed lead to valuable advice, whether it be interpreted by sages or by fools.*

AVERSIVE CONTROLS

It should be stressed again that negative reinforcement and punishment describe two very different situations. The two are often confused because each usually involves unpleasant (nox-

---

*PPC: Perhaps Lefrançois should point out that the use of punishment is sometimes highly effective and highly appropriate. Or was it punishment that made a fool out of the bear who always used to face the front so sagely?
AUTHOR: I do in Chapter 11. And the bear is too smart to be a fool, although he is not yet a sage.

ious) stimuli. But whereas punishment results in a reduction in behavior, negative reinforcement, like positive reinforcement, increases the probability that a response will occur. Thus, a child can be encouraged to speak politely to teachers by being smiled at for saying "please" and "thank you" (positive reinforcement). Another child can be beaten with a cane (or threatened therewith) when pleases and thank yous are forgotten (punishment)—with the clear understanding that the cane will be put away only when behavior conforms to the teacher's standards of politeness (negative reinforcement). In the end, both children may be wonderfully polite. But which child, do you suppose, will like teachers and schools more?

Strange as it might seem, the use of negative reinforcement as a means of control is highly prevalent in today's schools, homes, and churches, as is the use of punishment. These methods of **aversive control** (in contrast to **positive control**) are evident in the use of low grades and verbal rebukes, in threats of punishment, in detention in schools, and in the unpleasant fates that await transgressors in most major religions. They are evident as well in our legal and judicial systems, which are extraordinarily punitive rather than rewarding. Material rewards for being good are seldom obvious, but criminality is clearly punished. In fact, the reward for being good frequently takes the form of not being punished. That, in a nutshell, is negative reinforcement.

It is difficult to determine which is more important in our daily lives—positive reinforcement or negative reinforcement. Nor is it always easy to separate the two in practice, daily life being considerably more tolerant of ambiguity than is psychological theory. Consider, for example, that I work to obtain the "good" things in life: food, prestige, power, and a soft, wet kiss. It seems obvious that I am controlled by positive reinforcement. Or is it true, as my grandmother suggested, that I am really working to prevent hunger, to escape from anonymity and helplessness, and to avoid loneliness?

The issue cannot easily be resolved, but it is worth noting that I am much more likely to be happy if positive rather than negative contingencies (response consequences) control my behavior. Indeed, **avoidance learning** and/or **escape learning** are among the most important consequences of aversive control. A child who performs well in school because of parental and teacher rewards probably likes school; another who performs well in order to escape parental wrath and school punishments will probably have quite different emotional reactions to school and may avoid further non-compulsory schooling or might even consider escaping from the situation.

Aversive control of behavior may have one additional, highly undesirable effect. When Ulrich and Azrin (1962) placed two rats in a situation in which they had to turn a wheel to avoid an electric shock, the rodents fell, tooth and nail, upon each other. Although each understood (in a primitive rat way, to be sure) that the source of their pain was the wheel and not the other rat, they insisted on behaving in a most unfriendly fashion.

It should be noted that the most dedicated proponents of applied behavioral techniques and principles strongly advocate the use of positive rather than aversive control methods. This was especially true of B. F. Skinner.

TYPES AND EFFECTS OF REINFORCEMENT SCHEDULES

Through experiments with pigeons and rats, Skinner attempted to discover (1) the relationship between the type and amount of reinforcement used and the quality of learning achieved and (2) the relationship between the way reinforcement is administered and learning.

The first relationship cannot easily be determined because type and amount of reinforcement appear to affect individuals in unpredictable ways. It is clear from numerous

---

aversive control The control of human behavior, usually through the presentation of noxious (unpleasant) stimuli. This is in contrast to techniques of positive control, which generally use positive reinforcement.

positive control The control of human behavior, usually through the presentation of pleasant stimuli. This is in contrast to techniques of aversive control, which generally use negative reinforcement.

avoidance learning A conditioning phenomenon usually involving aversive (unpleasant) stimulation, wherein the organism learns to avoid situations associated with specific unpleasant circumstances.

escape learning A conditioning phenomenon whereby the organism learns means of escaping from a situation, usually following the presentation of aversive (unpleasant) stimulation.

experiments that even a very small reward will lead to effective learning and will maintain behavior over a long period. It is also clear that too much reward (satiation) may lead to a cessation of behavior. Several guidelines for the use of reinforcement are presented in Chapter 11. However, these should be interpreted cautiously.

The relationship between how reinforcement is administered (referred to as the **schedule of reinforcement**) and the resulting behavior can be investigated directly. Schedules invariably use either **continuous reinforcement** or **intermittent reinforcement** (also called partial reinforcement). In the first case, a reward is provided for every correct response (referred to as every trial). In the second case, only some of the trials are reinforced, in which case the experimenters have two options. They may choose to reinforce a certain proportion of trials (a **ratio schedule**), or they may base their schedule on the passage of time (an **interval schedule**). They might, for example, decide to reinforce one out of five correct responses, or they might reinforce one correct response for every 15-second lapse. In either case, they have two more options. They might choose to assign reinforcement in a predetermined fashion (**fixed schedule**) or in a more haphazard manner (**random** or **variable schedule**). Or, to really confuse things in proper psychological fashion, they might combine a number of these schedules and gleefully claim that they are using a mixed or **combined schedule.**

They have no more choices, fortunately . . . except maybe one. It is referred to as a **superstitious schedule.**

A superstitious schedule provides regular reinforcement no matter what the learner is doing. In fact, it's a fixed interval schedule without the provision that there has to be a correct response before reinforcement occurs. When Skinner (1948) left six pigeons on a superstitious schedule overnight (they received reinforcement at regular intervals no matter what they did), he found that by morning one bird had learned to turn clockwise just before each reinforcement, another pointed its head toward the corner, and several had learned to sway back and forth. Skinner suggests that we too learn superstitious behaviors as a result of reinforcement that occurs independently of what we do. For example, some of us frown when we're thinking or chew our hair or scratch our heads. Do we do these things because they actually help us think? Or do we do them because we happened to be doing them when we were reinforced (perhaps with a good idea) in the past?

---

schedule of reinforcement The time and frequency of presentation of reinforcement to organisms.

continuous reinforcement A reinforcement schedule in which every correct response is followed by a reinforcer.

intermittent reinforcement A schedule of reinforcement that does not present a reinforcer for all correct responses. Also termed *partial reinforcement*.

ratio schedule An intermittent schedule of reinforcement that is based on a proportion of correct responses.

interval schedule An intermittent schedule of reinforcement that is based on the passage of time.

fixed schedule A type of intermittent schedule of reinforcement in which the reinforcement occurs at fixed intervals of time (an interval schedule) or after a specified number of trials (a ratio schedule).

random schedule A type of intermittent schedule of reinforcement. It may be of either the interval or the ratio variety and is characterized by the presentation of rewards at random intervals or on random trials. Although both fixed and random schedules may be based on the same intervals or on the same ratios, one can predict when reward will occur under a fixed schedule, whereas it is impossible to do so under a random schedule. Also termed *variable schedule*.

combined schedule A combination of various types of schedules of reinforcement.

superstitious schedule A fixed-interval schedule of reinforcement in which the reward is not given after every correct response but rather after the passage of a specified period of time. It is so called because it leads to the learning of behaviors that are only accidentally related to the reinforcement.

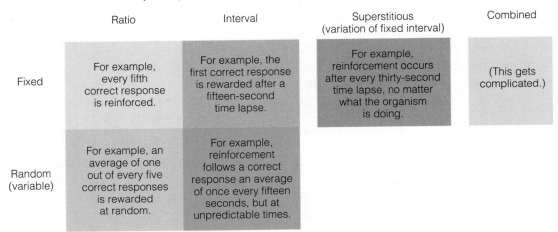

A. Continuous

> Every correct response is reinforced.

B. Intermittent (Partial)

	Ratio	Interval	Superstitious (variation of fixed interval)	Combined
Fixed	For example, every fifth correct response is reinforced.	For example, the first correct response is rewarded after a fifteen-second time lapse.	For example, reinforcement occurs after every thirty-second time lapse, no matter what the organism is doing.	(This gets complicated.)
Random (variable)	For example, an average of one out of every five correct responses is rewarded at random.	For example, reinforcement follows a correct response an average of once every fifteen seconds, but at unpredictable times.		

FIGURE 4.9 Schedules of reinforcement. Each type of reinforcement tends to generate its own characteristic pattern of response.

The section on schedule of reinforcement may, at first glance, appear somewhat confusing. You are advised to read it again slowly and consult Figure 4.9. It is really quite simple. Experimenters have two choices: If they choose A, they have no more choices, but if they choose B, they have two new options. Each of these, in turn, offers two further options. And finally, the last four options may be combined, or the experimenter might throw in a superstitious schedule.

Much of Skinner's work was directed toward discovering the relationship between various schedules of reinforcement and one of three measures of learning: **rate of learning,** **response rate,** and **extinction rate.** Some of these results have important implications for teaching.

The Effects of Schedules on Rate of Learning. In the early stages of learning, it appears that continuous reinforcement is most effective. When learning simple responses such as lever pressing, the rat might become confused and would almost certainly learn much more slowly if only some of its initial correct responses were reinforced. In terms of classroom practice, this

---

rate of learning A measure of the amount of time required to learn a correct response, or, alternatively, a measure of the number of trials required before the correct response occurs.

response rate The number of responses emitted by an organism in a given period of time. Response rates for operant behaviors appear to be largely a function of the schedules of reinforcement used.

extinction rate Time lapse between the withdrawal of reinforcement and the cessation of a response.

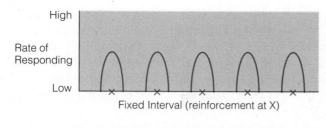

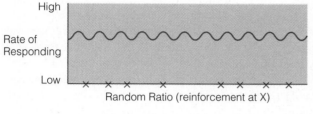

FIGURE 4.10 Idealized curve showing pigeon pecking under two reinforcement schedules.

means that initial learning, particularly for very young children, requires far more reinforcement than does later learning.

The Effects of Schedules on Rate of Extinction.
Interestingly, although continuous reinforcement often leads to more rapid learning, it does not usually result in longer **retention** of what is learned. In fact, the rate of **extinction** for behavior that has been reinforced continuously is considerably faster than for behavior that has been reinforced intermittently. Extinction means the cessation of a response as a function of withholding reinforcement. The extinction rate is simply the time that elapses between the beginning of the nonreinforced period and the cessation of behavior.

The use of extinction in schools, often in the form of the withdrawal of attention in the case of unruly, attention-seeking behavior, is widespread and effective. Several illustrations are provided in Chapter 11.

In general, therefore, the best schedule would appear to consist initially of continuous reinforcement, followed later by intermittent reinforcement. Among the intermittent sched-

---

retention A term often used as a synonym for *memory*.

extinction The cessation of a response as a function of the withdrawal of reinforcement.

ules, a random ratio arrangement ordinarily results in the slowest rate of extinction.

The Effects of Schedules on Rate of Responding.
The rate of responding can also be brought under the control of the schedule used. Interestingly, the behavior of pigeons and rats often suggests that they have developed expectations about reward. A pigeon that has been taught to peck a disk and is reinforced for the first peck after a lapse of 15 seconds (fixed interval) often completely ceases pecking immediately after being reinforced and resumes again just before the end of the 15-second interval. If, on the other hand, the pigeon is reinforced on a random ratio basis, its response rate will be uniformly high and constant, often as high as 2,000 or more pecks an hour. (See Figure 4.10.)

Schedules and People. So! One can reinforce the behavior of rats and pigeons in a variety of clever ways and can note a number of consistent effects that this has on their ridiculously simple behaviors. From this, many graduate dissertations and great quantities of published research can be derived for the erudition of the scholars and the amazement of the people.

But what of human beings? How are they affected by schedules of reinforcement?

The answer seems to be: in much the same way as animals. Marquis (1941), for example, investigated the behavior of babies who were fed regularly (fixed interval schedule) and of others who were fed on demand. Not surprisingly, infants on fixed schedules showed a marked increase in activity just before feeding time. And Bandura and Walters (1963) note that behaviors engaged in by young children who want their parents' attention tend to be randomly reinforced—and, as a result, are highly persistent. In the same way, the observation that extinction is more rapid in rats following continuous reinforcement appears to be valid for humans as well.

There are many examples of the effects of schedules on people's behaviors. The fisherman who goes to the same stream time after time, although he rarely (but occasionally) catches fish, is demonstrating the persistence that results from an intermittent schedule of reinforcement. The small-town student who was at the top of her classes for eight years—but now finds herself being outdone in the fierce competition of a new school—ceases to study; she may be demonstrating the rapid extinction that follows continuous reinforcement.

Knowing how schedules of reinforcement affect people's behaviors can be useful in a variety of practical situations—as the wife who occasionally but not too frequently praises her husband's appearance or his cooking will attest. He may continue to cook and to look good despite long sequences without reinforcement.

SHAPING

It is relatively simple to train a rat to press a lever, a pigeon to peck a disk, or a 2-year-old to pronounce "Wazoo." Why? Because these are some of the things rats, pigeons, and children do. But as Guthrie (1935) observes, "We can not teach cows to retrieve a stick because this is one of the things that cows do not do," (1935, p. 45).

Yet it might well be possible to train a cow to retrieve a stick. The psychologist charged with that task could stand there, leaning on the fence, day after day, watching for the operant in question to appear. And when it did, when the cow finally decided in her cowlike way to pick up the stick, it would be a simple matter (theoretically, to be sure) to reinforce her—say with a nice new bale of timothy hay—thus increasing the probability that the behavior would occur again. Unfortunately, both the psychologist and the cow likely would die of old age before the desired operant appeared.

Another, much better way of teaching animals complex behaviors using operant conditioning is called **shaping.** Shaping involves reinforcing the animal for every behavior that brings it slightly closer to the desired behavior. For example, if the objective is to teach the cow to pick up the stick, the experimenter might initially reinforce it every time it turned toward the stick. Later, once the cow had learned to turn reliably and predictably toward the stick, it would no longer be reinforced until it moved slightly closer to it. And if the reinforcements were accompanied by a distinctive stimulus such as the sound of a cowbell (a discriminated stimulus), eventually the cow might walk directly to the stick every time it heard the bell. And, following the systematic reinforcement of behaviors successively closer to the desired operant, it might in the end have learned to pick up and retrieve the stick, placing it in the psychologist's hand. Which would surely have amazed and confounded my grandmother!

For obvious reasons, shaping is also called the **differential reinforcement of successive approximations.** It is one of the most common techniques used in training performing animals. Does it have any relevance to the lives of humans?

---

shaping A technique whereby animals and people are taught to perform complex behaviors that were not previously in their repertoires. The technique involves reinforcing responses that become increasingly closer approximations of the desired behavior. Also termed the *method of successive approximations* or the *method of differential reinforcement of successive approximations*.

differential reinforcement of successive approximations The procedure of reinforcing only some responses and not others. Differential reinforcement is used in the shaping of complex behaviors.

Shaping and People. Yes. A great deal of human behavior is shaped through reinforcement. For example, as previously reinforcing activities become habitual and less rewarding, they tend to be modified. A motorcyclist may initially derive considerable reinforcement from the sensation of turning a sharp corner at high speed, but in time the sensation diminishes and the excitement decreases. And as the reinforcement begins to decrease, speed increases, imperceptibly but progressively. The motorcyclist's behavior has gradually been shaped as a consequence of its outcomes.

There are many examples of shaping in the classroom. Peer approval or disapproval, sometimes communicated in subtle, nonverbal ways, can significantly affect a student's behavior. The classroom clown would probably not continue to be a clown if no one paid any attention to her. Indeed, she might never have been shaped into a clown had her audience not reinforced her in the first place.

GENERALIZATION AND DISCRIMINATION

It isn't possible for schools and teachers to expose their students to all the situations in which the behaviors they learn will be appropri-ate. Nor is it possible to give them experience with all situations in which a specific learned behavior will *not* be appropriate. Yet one of the most important tasks of schools is to prepare their charges to respond appropriately in novel situations. And reassuringly often, children do respond appropriately when faced with completely new situations; also, they often discriminate between situations in which a behavior is appropriate and others in which it isn't. The first process, that of *transferring* a response from one situation to another similar situation, is labeled *generalization*. **Discrimination** involves refraining from making the response in question because of some difference between this situation and other situations for which the response was clearly more appropriate.

As an example, many children learn very early in life that they will receive their mother's attention if they cry. And they soon learn to generalize this behavior from specific situations in which they have obtained their mother's attention to new situations in which they desire

---

discrimination Processes involved in learning that certain responses are appropriate in specific situations but inappropriate in other similar situations. Generalization is an opposite process.

her attention. And often, a wise mother can bring about discrimination learning simply by not paying attention to her child in those situations in which she does not want to be disturbed. While on the phone, she might completely ignore her child's crying; soon the child will learn to discriminate between situations in which attention-getting behavior is not reinforced and other situations in which it is more likely to be reinforced.

EDUCATIONAL IMPLICATIONS OF OPERANT PRINCIPLES

It is difficult to overestimate the relevance of the principles of operant learning to teaching. As Sparzo (1992) points out, Skinner has made major contributions with his analysis of the role of behavior's consequences, as well as in the areas of understanding verbal behavior, programmed instruction, social behavior, and so on.

A classroom is in many ways like a gigantic Skinner box. It is so engineered that certain responses are more probable than others. For example, it is easier to sit at a desk than to lie on one; and it is easier to remain awake when sitting than when lying. And at the front of a million classrooms stand those who are among the powerful dispensers of childhood reinforcement—the teachers. They smile or frown; they say "Great" or "Rubbish"; they give high grades or low grades; occasionally they grant special favors; at other times they withhold or cancel privileges. By means of their use of reinforcement and punishment, sometimes deliberate and planned and sometimes quite unconscious, they shape the behavior of their students.

Drawing an analogy of a classroom, a teacher, and a student on the one hand and a Skinner box, a psychologist, and a rat on the other is somewhat unappealing and perhaps a little frightening (shades of Orwell's *1984*). Yet the analogy is relevant and potentially useful. As Table 4.4 illustrates, classroom teachers can often profit immensely from the discoveries of experimental psychologists. See also Chapter 11 for a detailed discussion of the systematic use of rewards and punishments in the classroom, and for a description of the various kinds of reinforcers available to teachers.

One of the first direct results of the application of Skinner's theory to teaching involved using operant conditioning techniques in the systematic delivery of information by means of written programs (Deutsch, 1992). These programs were a form of *programmed instruction*—a topic discussed in some detail in Chapter 12.

Another application of the theory to **instruction** has taken the form of a strong emphasis on methods of *positive* control (positive reinforcement, for example) rather than *aversive* control (negative reinforcement and punishment). In a 1965 article entitled "Why Teachers Fail," Skinner claimed that efforts to improve education seldom involve attempts to improve teaching as such and that teachers therefore continue to teach the way they themselves were taught. Unfortunately, chief among their methods are the techniques of aversive control. Skinner is a strong advocate of positive reinforcement, together with "attractive and attention compelling" approaches to teaching. In addition, he presents numerous suggestions for the development of a **technology of teaching** in a book by that title (Skinner, 1968). Interestingly, some ten years later another behaviorist, Fred Keller (1978, p. 53), was to assert: "Never before in the history of mankind have we known so much about the learning process and the conditions under which an individual human being can be efficiently and happily trained." And others, such as Greer (1983), argue strongly that the effectiveness of behavioristic principles for teaching is not equaled by any other approach.

---

instruction The arrangement of external events in a learning situation in order to facilitate learning, retention, and transfer.

technology of teaching A Skinnerian phrase for the systematic application of the principles of behaviorism (especially of operant conditioning) to classroom practice.

The specific and systematic application of operant conditioning principles to education requires that teachers become behavior analysts—that they dedicate themselves both to identifying and establishing environments that will lead to desirable behaviors and to providing reinforcement contingencies that will serve to maintain these behaviors. The success of such an approach has been demonstrated experimentally numerous times, perhaps most dramatically with mentally retarded, autistic, and other learning-disadvantaged children. A collective label for the application of these principles in education and in therapy is **behavior modification.** Specific behavior modification techniques are discussed in Chapter 11.

A SUMMARY OF BEHAVIORISTIC CONTRIBUTIONS TO INSTRUCTION

"To satisfy the practical demands of education, theories of learning must be 'stood on their heads' so as to yield theories of teaching" (Gage, 1964, p. 269). Presumably, the same result would be obtained if students were asked to stand on their heads while the theories remained upright. Unfortunately, however, even as extreme a measure as standing these behavioristic theories on their heads would be unlikely to yield theories of teaching. On the other hand, they need be tilted only very slightly to produce a variety of principles of practical value—many of which are mentioned and illustrated earlier in the chapter. The most important of these can be summarized as follows:

▶ Reinforcement is critically important in determining learning and behavior. This belief forms the cornerstone of both the Skinnerian and Thorndikean systems.

▶ Punishment is not very effective for eliminating undesirable behavior (Thorndike, 1932).

---

behavior modification Changes in the behavior of an individual; also refers to psychological theory and research concerned with the application of psychological principles in attempts to change behavior.

▶ Interest in work and in improvement is conducive to learning (Thorndike, 1935).

▶ Significance of subject matter and the attitude of the learner are important variables in school (Thorndike, 1935).

▶ Repetition without reinforcement does not enhance learning (Thorndike, 1931).

ANOTHER POINT OF VIEW

There are many others, however, who are quick to point out that behaviorism is not a universal cure for all our educational ills. Even if we were to agree that behavioristic principles should be applied whenever possible, we would soon discover that there are countless instances in which they cannot be applied very effectively at all. As H. Walker (1979) points out, teachers seldom control some of the most powerful reinforcers that affect student behavior—for example, peer acceptance and praise, parental approval, and so on. What this means is that teachers are often relegated to using what are, at least for some students, the relatively weaker reinforcers—teacher approval and grades.

A second problem in the universal application of behavioristic principles in teaching is, as Brophy (1983) argues, that most of our instructional problems do not involve establishing a reinforcement schedule so as to maintain a desirable response but instead involve bringing about the response in the first place. This is quite unlike the Skinner box situation, in which the major problem has been to control and maintain a specific response through the manipulation of reinforcement and in which eliciting the response is often a minor problem.

A third problem is that although operant principles can be used to control maladaptive behavior, its application sometimes has serious limitations. Palardy (1991) points out that behavior modification techniques applied to behavior problems ignore the causes of misbehavior, place insufficient emphasis on prevention, and often do not have long-term benefits. However, he notes that these techniques are effective and that all teachers should be familiar

TABLE 4.4 SOME OPERANT CONDITIONING CONCEPTS APPLIED TO INSTRUCTION

CONCEPT	EXPLANATION/EFFECT	ILLUSTRATION	PROBABLE CONSEQUENCES
POSITIVE REINFORCEMENT (REWARD)	Probability of behavior increases following the presentation of a consequence usually perceived as positive or pleasant.	Ellen writes an original poem, reads it in class, and receives high praise.	An increase in the likelihood of Ellen's writing more poems and reading them in class.
NEGATIVE REINFORCEMENT (RELIEF)	Probability of a behavior increases following the removal of a consequence usually perceived as negative or unpleasant.	Leonard is terribly afraid of making a fool of himself when he presents his science experiment to the class; he stays home on the day of the science fair; his fear disappears.	An increase in the likelihood that Leonard will subsequently try to avoid stressful situations.
PUNISHMENT I (CASTIGATION)	Probability of a behavior decreases following a consequence usually perceived as noxious or unpleasant.	Leonard's father reprimands him severely for having stayed home from school.	Leonard may be more likely to go to school in the future, even when faced with fearsome tasks.
PUNISHMENT II (PENALTY)	Probability of a behavior decreases when it leads to the loss of a stimulus ordinarily perceived as pleasant.	Sammy bullies the smaller children on the playground; as a consequence, his teacher slashes his playtime in half for a week.	Sammy is less likely to bully the playground children again.
SHAPING	A complex behavior is brought about or modified through reinforcement of successively closer approximations.	Early in her Spanish class, Sylvia is praised for saying "Hey meee, nah me emportay," and other similar phrases, no matter what her pronunciation. But later in the class, she receives praise only for phrases that no longer contain her most elementary errors. Finally, there is praise only for correctly pronounced phrases.	Sylvia's pronunciation improves dramatically from the beginning to the end of her class.
GENERALIZATION	Responses learned in one situation are transferred to another similar situation.	The grade 2 teacher sets up a "store" in her multicultural ESL class where children can use play money to buy various objects.	Juan, who is newly learning English, can subsequently shop in his neighborhood store with far more confidence, applying addition and subtraction rules learned and practiced in school.

TABLE 4.4
CONTINUED

CONCEPT	EXPLANATION/EFFECT	ILLUSTRATION	PROBABLE CONSEQUENCES
DISCRIMINATION	Responses learned in one situation are judged inappropriate in another similar but not identical situation.	In early September, all the children yell and shout at each other on the playground during recess; many of the first-grade children continue to do so when they go back into their classrooms after the buzzer sounds; teachers in the different classrooms use various combinations of reinforcement and punishment to suppress some of the noise.	By October most of the first-grade children have learned to discriminate more readily between situations where loud noise is appropriate and situations where it is less appropriate.
EXTINCTION	Responses that are not reinforced become less frequent.	Cheryl delights in making her classmates laugh, usually by contorting her face or making rude noises with her palms and her armpits, often disrupting the flow of classroom activities; she pays no attention to the teacher's request that she stop these behaviors, and appears unfazed by the various punishments organized by the teacher and principal. In the end, the teacher asks the students to ignore Cheryl as much as they possibly can; they comply.	Cheryl's acting out becomes more and more infrequent, finally disappearing altogether.*

with them; they simply are not sufficient by themselves. (More about specific behavior modification techniques in Chapter 11.)

That there are problems in applying behavioristic principles and that these principles are not easy solutions for all teaching problems should not blind us to their potential. Some of

that potential is discussed in greater detail in Chapters 11 and 12.

BEYOND FREEDOM: A PHILOSOPHICAL ARGUMENT

If most significant human behaviors are controlled by reinforcement or the lack of it, it follows that we are controlled by our environments—that the freedom of which we are so proud is merely an illusion. If I awaken in the morning and decide to brush my teeth, am I

---

*PPC: I think the author should point out that this is just theory. I know it doesn't always work in practice.

AUTHOR: This is theory, but not *just* theory. It's theory that leads to application, much of which does work remarkably well—as is shown in Chapter 11.

really free to make the choice? Can I either brush or not brush according to the whim of the moment? Or am I bound by the dictates of past reinforcement (and/or punishment), real or imagined? In his book dealing with freedom and dignity, Skinner asserts that the autonomous person is a myth. "Autonomous man," he explains "is a device used to explain what we cannot explain in any other way. He has been constructed from our ignorance, and as our understanding increases, the very stuff of which he is composed vanishes" (Skinner, 1971, p. 200). We are controlled by our environment, says Skinner, but he reassures us that it is an environment of which we are almost totally in control—or at least an environment that is almost wholly of our own making. There is a fundamental difference between the two. An environment over which we have control implies an environment in which we are free, because we can change the reinforcement contingencies of that environment. An environment of our own making, but over which we have no immediate control, implies an environment in which we are not free. It may be that as a species we have controlled our own destiny, but as individuals we do not control our own actions.

Skinner discusses at length the possibility of applying a science of human behavior for the benefit of humanity, an undertaking that would involve a degree of control over human behavior (Skinner, 1953, 1961). It is this aspect of his work that has met with the greatest resistance and has led some to speculate that Skinnerian behaviorism can as easily be made a weapon as a tool. The question is an ethical and moral one. The science exists, imperfect and incomplete as it is—and is sometimes used deliberately and systematically. Skinner (1961) describes, for example, how advertising uses emotional reinforcement by presenting alluring women in commercials and how motivational control is achieved by creating generalized reinforcers—as when a car becomes a powerful reinforcer by being equated with sex. He describes a society that controls through positive reinforcement in the form of wages, bribes, or tips—or that controls through drugs, such as "fear-reducers" for soldiers and steroids and cocaine for athletes.

But all of this began happening before Skinner, and, as he notes, "No theory changes what it is a theory about; man remains what he has always been" (1971, p. 215).

Nevertheless, this description of the human condition has come under severe attack from a wide variety of critics—as Skinner predicted it would. In essence, he has questioned the control exercised by the "autonomous" person and has demonstrated the control exercised by the environment in an attempt to create a science of behavior. The approach itself brings into question the worth and dignity of people. "These are sweeping changes," Skinner said, "and those who are committed to traditional theories and practices naturally resist them" (1971, p. 21).

The dispute is essentially between humanistic psychologists (those concerned more with humanity, ideals, values, and emotions; see Chapter 9) and experiment-oriented psychologists (those more concerned with developing a relatively rigorous science of behavior). But the two positions are not really incompatible. "Man is much more than a dog," Skinner tells us, "but like a dog he is within range of scientific analysis" (1971, p. 21).

BANDURA'S SOCIAL COGNITIVE THEORY

One of the things that makes humans more than dogs, the cognitive psychologists suggest, is that they *understand* something of the consequences of their behaviors. That is, they can anticipate and reason and decide to act or not to act. The fact that behaviorists such as Skinner did not deal with mentalistic concepts such as these does not mean that they denied that these events take place. What it means, instead, is that they believed that it was unnecessary and wasteful to include such poorly defined, imprecise, and often unobservable activities in a science of human learning and behavior. However, some psychologists, such as Albert Bandura (1977; Bandura & Walters, 1963), have attempted to recognize and understand these mentalistic activities while still remaining faithful to the behaviorist's emphasis on observable events. Thus, Bandura makes extensive use of the concepts of operant conditioning in a theory that looks at some of the more cognitive aspects of social learning and behavior. Conceptually, the theory serves as an important transition between behavioristic and cognitive approaches, and is often labeled a **social cognitive theory.**

SOCIAL LEARNING

In psychology, the phrase **social learning** is often used without precise definition, as though everybody intuitively knows exactly what it means and all agree about that meaning.

Not so. In fact, the term is used in two ways. For some writers, it means all learning that occurs as a result of, or involves, social interaction. Others use the term to signify the type of learning that is involved in finding out what sorts of behaviors society accepts and expects, as well as those that are unacceptable. This difference in meanings is essentially a distinction between process and product. In other words, *social learning* might refer to the way in which learning occurs (that is, through social

interaction) or to what is learned (the product: acceptable behaviors).

Socially Accepted Behaviors: The Product.
Socially acceptable behavior varies both from culture to culture and from group to group within a single culture. For example, it is socially acceptable for students in some Asian countries to bow to their teachers and to offer them gifts. In most Western countries, a student who habitually bows to teachers and offers gifts might embarrass both self and teacher.

Similarly, socially acceptable behavior is often a function of age and of sex. Young children are not expected to address teachers and other adults by their first names; they are expected to learn and obey an assortment of unwritten rules of respect and of social distance. In much the same way, some behaviors are socially expected—hence, culturally appropriate—for males but not for females and vice versa.

Probably one of the most important tasks of the home in the early years of a child's life, and later of the school, is to foster the development of appropriate behaviors—a process called **socialization.** This process involves transmitting the culture of a society to children and teaching them behaviors appropriate for their sex and social circumstance—or, in a more ideal world, teaching them that appropriateness of behaviors does not depend on sex.

Learning Social Behaviors: The Process.
A central question from the teacher's point of view is how the child learns socially acceptable behaviors. Bandura's answer is that social learning occurs largely through *imitation*, a process that is also called **observational learning.**

social cognitive theory Label for Bandura's theory that attempts to explain human social learning through imitation using principles of operant conditioning while recognizing the importance of intellectual activities, such as imagining and anticipating. Hence, the theory serves as a transition between purely behavioristic and more cognitive approaches.

social learning The acquisition of patterns of behavior that conform to social expectations; learning what is acceptable and what is not acceptable in a given culture.

socialization The complex process of learning both those behaviors that are appropriate within a given culture and those that are less appropriate. The primary agents of socialization are home, school, and peer groups.

observational learning A term used synonymously with the expression "learning through imitation."

Learning through imitation, or observational learning, involves acquiring new responses or modifying old ones as a result of seeing a model do something. According to Bandura (1969), the processes involved in imitation are "one of the fundamental means by which new modes of behavior are acquired and existing patterns are modified" (p. 118).

It is largely through the processes of social learning and imitation that fads and expressions sweep through countries: Overnight (almost), men begin to wear their hair long or short; short skirts are in, then out, then in; everyone is saying "yeah" or "outasight"; things are "cool" or "neat" and people are "beautiful."*

But these are trivial matters in the grand scheme of more cosmic events—although how to dress and what to say are by no means trivial in our more private, less cosmic, worlds. Social learning theory explains much more than our fads and expressions.

OVERVIEW OF BANDURA'S
SOCIAL COGNITIVE THEORY

The theory proposed by Bandura is based partly on a model of operant conditioning. As such, it can be summarized as follows:

▶ Much human learning is a function of observing and imitating the behavior of others or of such symbolic models as fictional characters in books or television programs. Using Skinner's terms, imitative behaviors may be considered operants.

▶ We learn to imitate by being reinforced for doing so; continued reinforcement maintains imitative behavior.

---

*PPC: Your faddish words are now a bit outdated. How about "totally" or one of the other valley girl expressions to add to the list?

Author: This is no longer a real young bear. He has almost stopped trying to keep up with fads. But he still thinks valley girl talk is like awesome, vertical, and totally tubular. Ya know? He has humongous appreciation for valleys, fer sure. But now he's told that valley girl talk is totally passé, which, since he had learned some of it, he finds just a little distressing.

▶ Some aspects of imitation (or observational learning) can therefore be explained in terms of operant conditioning principles.

In addition to being based on operant conditioning principles, and perhaps even more important, Bandura's theory recognizes the fundamental importance of our ability to symbolize, to imagine, to ferret out cause-and-effect relationships, and to anticipate the outcomes of our behaviors. The environment clearly affects our behavior, Bandura informs us; there is little doubt that we engage in many behaviors because of the reinforcing consequences of so doing. But reinforcement does not control us blindly; its effects depend largely on our awareness of the relationship between our behavior and its outcomes. As Grusec (1992) points out, the main emphasis of Bandura's theory is on the information capacities that guide the individual's behavior. It isn't reinforcement that leads to or affects behavior directly, notes Bruner (1985), because reinforcement occurs after the behavior (sometimes considerably after). Rather, it is the individual's *anticipation* of consequences that immediately affects learning and behaving.

Our ability to symbolize and to anticipate is reflected not only in our ability to imagine the consequences of our behavior and therefore govern ourselves accordingly but also in our habit of deliberately arranging our environments so as to control some of the consequences of our actions. As Bandura (1977) puts it, "By arranging environmental inducements, generating cognitive supports, and producing consequences for their own actions, people are able to exercise some measure of control over their own behavior." Accordingly, one of Bandura's labels for his theory is **reciprocal determinism.**

---

reciprocal determinism Bandura's label for the recognition that even though environments affect individuals in important ways, individuals also affect environments by selecting and shaping them. Thus, the influence (determinism) is two-way (reciprocal).

Calvin and Hobbes

by Bill Watterson

WHAT'S THE TEACHER HANDING OUT?

OUR REPORT CARDS.

OUR REPORT CARDS?

YOU KNOW, OUR GRADES.

GRADES? WE'RE BEING GRADED?

OF COURSE, DUMMY. WHAT DID YOU THINK?

DON'T WE EVEN GET A FEW PRACTICE SEMESTERS?

Calvin and Hobbes © Watterson. Distributed by Universal Press Syndicate. Reprinted with permission. All rights reserved.

THE PROCESSES

OF OBSERVATIONAL LEARNING

Although reinforcement is important in learning through imitation, Bandura (1977) makes it clear that the effects of models are largely a result of what he refers to as their "informative function." In other words, from observing models we learn *cognitively* not only how to do certain things but also what the consequences of our actions are likely to be.

According to Bandura (1977), four distinct processes are involved in observational learning: attentional processes, retention processes, motor reproduction processes, and motivational processes (see Figure 4.11).

Attentional Processes. It is clear that we are not likely to learn much from models unless we pay attention to the significant features of the behaviors we want to learn. Many of the behaviors in which our models engage have no value for us; therefore, we pay little attention to them and do not learn them. For example, when I lived with my grandmother as a young adolescent, I was quite passionately interested in, among other things, trapping and snaring wild things for food and money. And when I had the opportunity to go out into the woods with the renowned trapper George Ahenikue, I watched his every move like a hawk—how he walked, how he looked around, how and where he stopped, how he fashioned his sets and arranged his snares. These behaviors had high value for me.

But when I caught a rabbit who stupidly blundered into my snare, I paid little attention to the way my grandmother disjointed, sautéed, and stewed the beast; I just sat at the table and licked my chops in anticipation. The culinary preparation of the rabbit held no interest for me, although I relished the final result.

It wasn't until many years later, when I had a rabbit to prepare in my own kitchen, that I realized how little I had learned from my grandmother of the mysteries of the kitchen. Although I had watched her prepare dozens of rabbits, the behavior had not been sufficiently valuable for me to pay attention.

So I called my grandmother and I asked her about the stewing of snowshoe hares and jackrabbits, and she explained. Her explanation was every bit as much a model as her behavior might have been years earlier (had I been paying attention), but it was now a symbolic rather than a real-life model.

In addition to the affective and functional value of the behavior being modeled, a number of other factors affect attentional processes. These include the distinctiveness, the complexity, and the prevalence of the stimuli. Also, a number of characteristics of the learner are

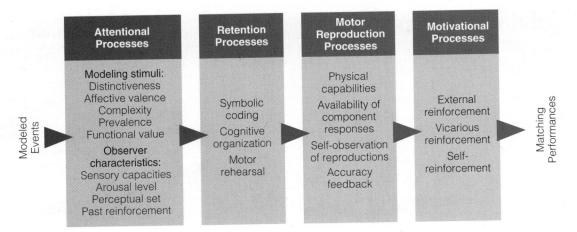

FIGURE 4.11 Component processes governing observational learning in social learning theory. From A. Bandura, *Social Learning Theory,* © 1977, p. 23. Reprinted by permission of Prentice-Hall, Inc., Englewood Cliffs, New Jersey.

important, including arousal (motivation), perceptual set (readiness to observe), and history of previous reinforcement.

Retention Processes. Just as we must pay attention if we are to learn, so too must we remember what we have observed. Because the effects of imitation are usually delayed rather than immediate, we need some way of symbolizing, understanding, and organizing our observations.

According to Bandura (1977), observational learning involves two types of representation systems: visual (his term is *imaginal*) and verbal. For example, to learn a complex motor skill, it is sometimes useful to observe a model closely and store a visual sequence of the behavior. It is then possible to rehearse the desired behavior mentally. Bandura (1977) cites research indicating that mentally rehearsing a complex motor sequence (as in high jumping, diving, or gymnastics, for example) can significantly improve performance. He suggests that the best way to learn from a model is to organize and rehearse the observed behavior cognitively and then act it out.

Motor Reproduction Processes. Acting out a modeled behavior involves transforming sym-

bolically represented (mentally visualized or imagined) actions into actual physical movements. Being able to do so successfully, of course, depends on essential physical capabilities: Clearly, some of us will never be able to jump very high no matter how many models we observe. Accurate motor reproduction of an observed behavior depends also on the individual's ability both to monitor attempted reproductions and to use motor feedback to make corrections. Imitations of motor behavior are seldom perfect the first time—they have to be refined. A coach might demonstrate repeatedly how a batter should stand, how she should hold the bat, how she should distribute and shift her weight, what her eyes and toes should do. But in the end, the truly good batter will have refined and perfected her batting through a long succession of trials (motor reproductions). These, however, are not blind trial-and-error reproductions repeated until the right one is accidentally found. Rather, they are carefully modeled trials that are evaluated and slowly modified as a function of feedback, involving, among other things, how often contact is made with the ball, how far the ball goes when it is hit, and whether the coach smiles or frowns while watching the batter.

Motivational Processes. Much of what people observe and could learn is never manifested in their behavior. George Ahenikue, for example, was an important model for me with respect to trapping snowshoe hares; he knew a dozen clever little tricks for ensnaring them. I emulated as many of these tricks as I could. But he also knew a fantastic trick for blowing his nose. I have little doubt that I learned it; I remember it very clearly. But I don't do it. Ever. Put another way, I have acquired the behavior but do not perform it.

The distinction between acquisition and performance is important in social learning theory because, as we have noted, much of what is observed and presumably acquired is never performed. Whether the modeled behavior will ever be performed is a function of reinforcement or, perhaps more precisely, of anticipated reinforcement.

In summary, observational learning begins with a modeled event (perhaps a real-life model doing something, a verbal or symbolic model, or a combination of these) and culminates in some sort of matching performance on the part of the observer. Four processes intervene between the presentation of the model and the appearance of the modeled behavior. First, the observer must pay attention; second, the observer must represent the observed behavior cognitively, store it, and perhaps rehearse it; third, if the observer has the required capabilities, he or she reproduces and refines the observed behavior; and fourth, given appropriate motivational conditions (defined primarily in terms of anticipated reinforcement), the observer performs the learned behavior.

THE PREVALENCE OF IMITATION

Copying the behavior of others is a widespread phenomenon that is perhaps more obvious among nontechnological societies such as the Canadian Ojibwa. Until the turn of this century, the Ojibwa depended almost exclusively upon trapping, hunting, and fishing for their living. In Ojibwa tribes, young boys followed their fathers around trap lines as soon as they were physically able. For the first few years, they simply observed. Later, they would fashion their own weapons and traps and set their own snares as they had seen their fathers do. Whatever they bagged would be brought back to the father's lodge. If a boy had a sister, she would learn how to prepare hides, meat, and fish, how to make clothing, how to erect shelters, and how to do the many other things she had seen her mother doing. When old enough, she would take care of her brother's catch, prepare his meals, and make his clothing.

In more technological societies such as ours, it is usually not possible to provide children with miniature working replicas of the tools used by their parents—nor is it possible for children to observe their parents at work. Still, knowledge of observational learning can be of tremendous practical value for teachers. We may not learn to set traps or prepare furs from our parents, but we learn many other things from them—and from the wealth of other models that surround us.

Models. The term *model* may refer to an actual person whose behavior serves as a stimulus for an observer's response, or, as is more often the case in our society, it may refer to a **symbolic model.** Symbolic models include such things as oral or written instructions, pictures, mental images, cartoon or film characters, religious figures, and, not least important, the content and characters in books and television. For some children, symbolic models may be as important as real-life models. This is not to deny that peers, siblings, and parents serve as models or that teachers and other well-behaved people are held up as **exemplary models.** ("Why don't you

---

symbolic model A model other than a real-life person. Any pattern for behavior may be termed a symbolic model if it is not a person. For example, books, television, and written instructions can provide symbolic models.

exemplary model A good example. A teacher, for example.

behave like Dr. Lefrançois? See how nicely he sits in church with his eyes closed. He's praying for us, dear man.")*

SOURCES OF REINFORCEMENT IN IMITATION

Imitation may be reinforced in three ways. **Direct reinforcement** of the learner by the model is most evident in the early learning of children, as when parents praise an infant for repeating a word correctly, or a toddler for rolling a ball back to mother.

A second source of reinforcement is the *consequences of behavior,* particularly if it is socially acceptable behavior that is effective in attaining a goal. Even though a child may learn to say "milk" partly as a function of imitation and partly as a function of her model's reinforcing her, she is not likely to go on saying "milk" unless someone occasionally gives her milk when she says the word.

A third type of reinforcement is termed **vicarious reinforcement.** It involves deriving a kind of secondhand—hence, vicarious—reinforcement from observing someone else behave in a certain way. It is as though the observer assumes that the model does something because he or she derives reinforcement from that behavior. Therefore, in the observer's logic, anyone else engaged in the same behavior would receive the same reinforcement.

Interestingly, vicarious reinforcement can lead an observer to engage in ineffective behavior over a prolonged period of time. The fact that the behavior is maintained despite an apparent lack of direct reinforcement is evidence that some sort of vicarious reinforcement is involved. In fact, studies have shown that the administration of reward or punishment to a model has an effect on the behavior of observers similar to that which the direct administration of the reward or punishment would have. One such study (Bandura, 1962) involved exposing three groups of children to three different models. All models behaved aggressively toward an inflated plastic doll. The first model was rewarded for doing so, the second was punished, and the third received neither positive nor negative consequences. Subsequently, the model-rewarded group behaved significantly more aggressively than the model-punished group. The effect of reward and punishment on the models was transferred vicariously to the subjects.

THE EFFECTS OF IMITATION

An examination of the responses involved in observational learning suggests that there are three different categories of imitative behavior. Bandura (Bandura & Walters, 1963) describes these as the *effects* of imitation: the modeling effect, the inhibitory-disinhibitory effect, and the eliciting effect.

The **modeling effect** involves the acquisition of new responses. The **inhibitory-disinhibitory effect** involves the **inhibition** or the **disinhibition** of deviant responses, usually as a result of seeing a model punished or rewarded

---

*PPC: I trust you are careful not to snore. . . .
AUTHOR: How cynical.

---

direct reinforcement The type of reinforcement that affects the individual in question directly rather than vicariously.

vicarious reinforcement Reinforcement that results from observing someone else being reinforced. In imitative behavior, observers frequently act as though they are being reinforced when in fact they are not being reinforced; rather, they are aware, or simply assume, that the model is being reinforced.

modeling effect The type of imitative behavior that involves learning a novel response.

inhibitory-disinhibitory effect The type of imitative behavior that results either in the suppression (inhibition) or appearance (disinhibition) of previously acquired deviant behavior.

inhibition In imitative learning, the suppression of a previously acquired behavior. This sometimes occurs when a learner observes a model being punished for the behavior.

disinhibition The appearance of a suppressed behavior.

TABLE 4.5 THREE EFFECTS OF IMITATION

LABEL	DEFINITION	ILLUSTRATION
MODELING EFFECT	Acquiring new behavior as a result of observing a model.	After watching a television program, Kristina begins to use the word *not* in the sense of "no," as in, "Is she smart? *Not.*"
INHIBITORY-DISINHIBITORY EFFECT	Ceasing or starting some deviant behavior as a result of seeing a model punished or rewarded for similar behavior.	Ralph burns all his cigarette papers and flushes his grass down the toilet after his brother is caught and punished by their parents.
ELICITING EFFECT	Engaging in behavior related to that of a model.	Robin starts piano lessons after her cousin plays a trumpet solo at the family reunion.

for the behavior. The **eliciting effect** involves behavior that is neither novel for the observer nor deviant; it is manifested when the observer engages in behavior related (but not identical) to that of the model. Because of their importance in teaching, each of these effects will be illustrated and explained in more detail (see Table 4.5).

The Modeling Effect. The modeling effect involves the acquisition of a new behavior as a result of seeing a model emit that behavior. This effect is well illustrated in the acquisition of aggressive behaviors, which have been extensively studied in laboratory situations, usually with nursery school children (Bandura, 1962; Bandura, Ross, & Ross, 1963). The typical experiment involves exposing the subjects to a real-life model or a cartoon or filmed model doing something aggressive to a large inflated plastic doll—like punching it, striking it with a hammer, kicking it, or sitting on it. Control groups are exposed to the same model sitting quietly with the doll. The results of experiments such as this almost invariably illustrate the modeling effect. That is, when left alone with the dolls, children exposed to aggressive models are more aggressive than control groups. Furthermore, their aggressive responses are usually precisely imitative. That is, if the model punched the doll, that is what subjects are most likely to do; and if the model kicked the doll instead, then that, too, is what observers do.

Studies such as this have been widely used to support the belief that much aggression is learned through imitation, and that television, because of its predominantly violent content, is highly influential in fostering aggressive behavior. Others point out that these studies involve laboratory situations that are somewhat unrealistic, and that aggression directed at an inanimate object is a far cry from aggression against real people in real life. Ethical considerations, however, prevent the use of babies instead of dolls in these experiments. It is therefore difficult to illustrate the acquisition of meaningful aggressive responses experimentally. Still, general summaries of the television research suggests that television violence does increase the violence of viewers (Rosenkoetter, Huston, & Wright, 1990). It isn't clear, however, that television violence has significant *long-term* impact (Evra, 1990).

Many other behaviors are also transmitted through imitation and are examples of modeling. The initial learning of socially appropriate behavior in primitive cultures such as that of the Ojibwa provides one illustration; learning a language is another. This is especially obvious in the case of adults learning to speak a foreign language by imitating a teacher or an audiotape.

eliciting effect Imitative behavior in which the observer does not copy the model's responses but simply behaves in a related manner.

The Inhibitory-Disinhibitory Effect. The inhibitory effect is the suppression of deviant behavior in an observer, usually as a result of seeing a model punished for engaging in the same behavior. The disinhibitory effect is the opposite; it occurs when an observer engages in previously learned deviant behavior, usually as a result of seeing a model rewarded (or at least not punished) for the same behavior. The inhibitory-disinhibitory effect of imitation is especially important for teachers when dealing with deviant behavior.

As experimental evidence of disinhibition, Bandura and Walters (1963) cite studies in which viewing films led to aggression in children; the aggressive responses were not novel but were previously learned behaviors that the children had suppressed. Evidence from this research indicates that exposure to aggressive models may have a disinhibitory effect on young observers. Typically, the number of aggressive responses manifested by members of experimental groups is significantly higher than the number engaged in by the control groups. Also, the Bandura (1962) study that looked at the effects on observers of punishment or reward of the model showed that punishing a model inhibited similar behavior in observers and that rewards had an opposite, disinhibiting effect.

A related finding from the Bandura (1962) study is especially striking: When observers were offered rewards for behaving aggressively, all differences between the groups were wiped out! Now those who had been exposed to models who were punished for being aggressive nevertheless behaved as aggressively as those whose models had been rewarded for being aggressive. This observation is especially important in explaining why punishing those who misbehave often fails to discourage other transgressors. One of the reasons for punishing criminals is the hope that others will take heed and cease committing crimes. In other words, the intention is to *inhibit* criminal behavior by punishing a model. It follows from the Bandura experiment, however, that as long as subjects have their own incentives for criminal behavior,

Children who are shown films of models kicking and punching inflated plastic dolls often imitate these aggressive behaviors later. But it isn't clear that these findings can be generalized to more realistic settings—or that they say very much about the effects of television violence.

the model may just as well be rewarded as punished, as far as deterrence is concerned.

A series of sobering experiments illustrates that socially unacceptable behavior in adults can be disinhibited through the use of models (Walters, Llewellyn, & Acker, 1962; Walters & Llewellyn, 1963). These studies were modeled after the famous obedience studies by Milgram (1963), in which college students willingly administered what they thought were extremely dangerous, high-voltage electrical shocks to other students, simply because they had been told to do so by an experimenter.

In the studies conducted by Walters and his associates, adult subjects were asked to participate in an experiment dealing with memory. Subjects were first shown one of two films: The first group saw a scene from the film *Rebel Without a Cause* in which two youths engage in a fight with knives; the second group saw adolescents engaged in artwork. All subjects were then asked to help with another experiment. This one involved administering a series of shocks to students in order to study the effects of punishment on learning. The student subjects involved in this learning experiment were actually confederates of the experimenters. The adults, who were the actual subjects, were made to sit in the confederate's chair and were administered one or two mild shocks so that they would know what the punishment was like. They were then seated at a control panel that consisted of two signal lights (one red and one green), a dial for selecting shock intensities, and a toggle switch for administering the shock. Instructions were simply to administer a shock whenever the red light went on, because it indicated that the subject had made an error.

These studies indicated that exposure to films with aggressive content significantly increases aggressive behavior, as revealed in the number and intensity of shocks the subjects were willing to give. (The students did not actually receive any shocks because one electrode was always disconnected before the experiment.)

The results of these studies have been used to explain various wartime atrocities perpetrated by apparently normal people who claimed they were simply obeying some powerful authority. They may also be important for interpreting and predicting the possible effects of television violence.

The Eliciting Effect. The eliciting effect of imitation involves a model's behavior bringing about responses that do not necessarily precisely match those of the model (although they might) but that belong to the same class of behavior. For example, a man might serve as a model of generosity if he works hard for civic organizations, church activities, and school functions. A number of his neighbors might be moved by his example to be generous in differ-

ent ways. One might give money to local charities, a second might donate a prize for a church raffle, a third might give freely of advice. None of these observers imitates the model's behavior precisely, but each of them emits a response that is related to it in that it involves being generous.

Another illustration of the eliciting effect is the herd behaviors that are sometimes apparent in crowds at sporting events. One person's applause might elicit applause from the entire crowd, or one person's booing and hissing might elicit similar behavior from others. Similarly, when people begin to rise for the national anthem, the same behavior may be elicited in a great many who are not immediately aware of why they are standing. In each of these illustrations of the eliciting effect, no new behavior is involved (as is the case in the modeling effect), and the behavior in question is not deviant (as it is in the inhibitory-disinhibitory effect).

INSTRUCTIONAL IMPLICATIONS OF SOCIAL COGNITIVE THEORY

The greatest advantage that learning by imitation has over other forms of learning is that it provides a complete behavioral sequence for the learner. There is no need for successive approximations, for trial and error, or for association by contiguity. Nobody would put a person behind the wheel of a car and allow the person to learn to drive by trial and error alone. One might, on the other hand, teach driving to someone by presenting one or more models: exposure to a person driving, a driving manual, or a series of oral instructions. In this, as in many other types of learning, it would be foolhardy to permit people to learn only by doing.

A careful analysis of the processes involved in social learning suggests a number of considerations that might be important for teaching. For example, many of the factors associated with attentional processes (such as distinctiveness of stimuli, the learner's arousal level, history of past reinforcement, and so on) are at least partly under the teacher's control. Similarly, teachers can provide direction and opportunity for the activities involved in retention and in reproduction. And because the effects of reinforcement depend on our awareness of the connection between our behavior and its consequences, teachers can also exercise considerable influence on motivational processes. The deliberate use of social learning theory for changing and controlling behavior (sometimes included under the general term **behavior management,** or behavior modification) presents yet another important educational implication, considered in Chapter 11.

More recently, Bandura's social cognitive theory has taken a new twist, one that is even more clearly cognitive (Bandura, 1986; Evans, 1989). It has to do with what is termed **self-referent thought**—that is, thought that has to do with our own mental processes and, perhaps most important for teachers, with our estimates of our personal effectiveness, or what is labeled **self-efficacy.** "Efficacy beliefs," says Bandura (1993), "influence how people feel, think, motivate themselves, and behave" (p. 118). Hence the importance of how we feel about our personal competence can hardly be overestimated. That aspect of Bandura's theory is covered in detail in Chapter 10, which deals with human motivation.

---

behavior management See *behavior modification*, p. 137.

self-referent thought Thought that pertains to the self. Self-referent thought is thought that concerns our own mental processes (for example, thoughts that evaluate our abilities or that monitor our progress in solving problems).

self-efficacy A term that refers to judgments we make about how efficacious (effective) we are in given situations. Judgments of self-efficacy are important in determining our choices of activities and in influencing the amount of interest and effort we expend.

MAIN POINTS

1. Science demands that its theories be based on objective, replicable observations, that chance factors be taken into account, and that they be generalizable.

2. Learning involves all changes in behavior that result from experience, providing that these changes are relatively permanent, do not result simply from growth or maturation, and are not the temporary effects of factors such as fatigue or drugs. Changes in disposition or capability are not always manifested in performance.

3. Behavioristic theories of learning are concerned with stimulus-response events and with the effects of repetition, contiguity, and reinforcement. Cognitive theories address problems relating to the organization of memory, information processing, problem solving, and metacognition (knowing about knowing). Humanistic approaches are more concerned with human worth and individuality.

4. Classical conditioning (Pavlov and Watson) involves the repeated pairing of a previously neutral stimulus (conditioned stimulus, or CS) with an effective stimulus (unconditioned stimulus, or US) so that the CS eventually brings about a response (conditioned response, or CR) similar to that for the unconditioned stimulus.

5. Classical conditioning is sometimes useful in explaining the learning of emotional responses. Hence, it is important for teachers to know what is being paired with what in schools and to maximize situations associated with positive emotions while minimizing those associated with negative feelings.

6. Thorndike introduced the notion of reinforcement in learning theory through the law of effect, which asserts that responses followed by satisfaction tend to become linked to the stimuli that preceded them (S–R bonds are "stamped in"). In the

absence of previous learning, behavior will take the form of trial and error. Choice of responses attempted may be affected by set, by identical elements in stimulus situations, by classical conditioning, or by prepotent elements.

7. Thorndike's theory suggests that one of the important goals of education is to teach for transfer (generalization) by stressing connections among ideas, and emphasizes the importance of students' readiness and of reinforcement, while recognizing the limited effectiveness of punishment.

8. Respondents result from a known stimulus (respondents are reactions to); operants are simply emitted (operants are actions upon). The Skinner box is a cagelike device used by Skinner to study the relationship between operants and reinforcement—ordinarily in rats or pigeons.

9. The model of operant conditioning maintains that when an operant is reinforced, the probability of its recurrence increases. A reinforcer is any stimulus that has the effect of increasing the probability that a response will occur. It may do so by being added to a situation (positive reinforcement; reward) or by being removed (negative reinforcement; relief).

10. Negative reinforcement is not punishment. The effect of punishment is to decrease, not increase, the probability that a response will occur. Punishment occurs when a pleasant stimulus is removed or an unpleasant one is introduced following behavior. Aversive control involves the use of negative reinforcement (often in the form of removal of threats) and of punishment. The emotional consequences of positive control are usually more desirable.

11. Reinforcement may be administered continuously (for every correct response) or in a random or fixed manner relative to a ratio or interval basis (that is, it can be continuous, random ratio, random interval, fixed ratio, or fixed interval). In general continuous schedules lead to faster learning, whereas intermittent schedules result in longer extinction periods.

12. Shaping, the differential reinforcement of successive approximations, may be used to teach animals novel behaviors or to subtly alter human behavior. To generalize is to respond to similarities (make the same response in similar situations); to discriminate is to respond to differences (distinguish among situations in which identical responses are not appropriate).

13. Among the instructional implications that may be derived from these behavioristic theories are suggestions relating to the value of repetition, reinforcement, and punishment, as well as some practical suggestions for managing misbehavior.

14. There are those who believe that behavioristic principles can provide us with a technology of teaching that is more effective than any other approach and who lament the apparent reluctance of many educators to apply this technology. Others emphasize that the effectiveness of behavioristic approaches is limited, that teachers often control only the weaker reinforcers, and that many problems of instructing (organizing, sequencing, explaining, illustrating) cannot easily make use of behavioristic principles.

15. It is possible that we are not free, that we are controlled by our environment, and that we have only the illusion of freedom.

16. Bandura's social cognitive theory assumes that imitation is a central process in determining behavior. Social learning reflects the effects of reinforcement, the observer's awareness of the connections between behavior and outcomes, and the observer's ability to symbolize. Learning through imitation requires paying attention, remembering, reproducing, and being motivated to do so.

17. The term *model* refers to a person who serves as an example for another or to more symbolic models. Sources of reinforcement in observational learning include direct reinforcement by the model, reinforcement as a consequence of behavior, and vicarious reinforcement (when the punishment or reward an observer thinks a model has received affects the observer's behavior).

18. Three effects of imitation include the modeling effect (the learning of novel responses), the inhibitory-disinhibitory effect (deviant behavior is disinhibited or suppressed, usually as a function of response consequences to the models), and the eliciting effect (the emission of responses that are related to those made by the model but that are neither novel nor deviant). These three effects of imitation have important instructional implications.

APPLIED QUESTIONS

▸ Can you give school-based examples of changes that define learning?

▸ List a number of key terms most closely related to the theories of Pavlov, Watson, Skinner, and Bandura.

▸ Can you think of classroom-related examples of classical and operant conditioning?

▸ Illustrate the difference between negative reinforcement and punishment using examples from a hypothetical instructional sequence.

▸ Explain how schedules of reinforcement might be important in the classroom.

▸ What is an example of how one of the effects of imitation might be applied in the classroom?

STUDY TERMS

affective learning **111**
associationistic **122**
aversive control **130**
avoidance learning **130**
behavior management **150**
behavior modification **137**
behaviorism **111**
behavioristic theories **111**
capability **110**
classical conditioning **112**
cognitive learning **111**
cognitivism **111**
combined schedule **131**
conditioned response (CR) **112**
conditioned stimulus (CS) **112**
conditioning **111**
connectionism **117**
contiguity **118**
continuous reinforcement **131**
differential reinforcement of successive approximations **134**
direct reinforcement **146**
discriminated stimuli (S^D) **123**
discrimination **135**
disinhibition **146**

disposition **110**
elicited response **122**
eliciting effect **147**
emitted responses **122**
environmentalism **113**
escape learning **130**
exemplary models **145**
extinction **133**
extinction rate **132**
fixed schedule **131**
generalization **121**
generalized reinforcer **127**
humanism **112**
inhibition **146**
inhibitory-disinhibitory effect **146**
instruction **136**
intermittent reinforcement **131**
interval schedule **131**
law of effect **119**
law of exercise **119**
law of multiple responses **120**
law of prepotency of elements **120**
law of readiness **119**
law of response by analogy **120**

law of set or attitude **120**
learning **109**
metacognition **111**
modeling effect **146**
motor learning **111**
negative reinforcer **127**
neutral stimulus **113**
observational learning **141**
operant conditioning **122**
operants **122**
penalty **127**
performance **110**
positive control **130**
positive reinforcer **127**
primary reinforcer **126**
punishment **120**
random schedule **131**
rate of learning **132**
ratio schedule **131**
reciprocal determinism **142**
reinforcement **124**
reinforcer **124**
relief **127**
respondent **122**
response rate **132**

SUGGESTED READINGS

Among the many attempts to apply learning theories to educational practice, the following three sources have been selected as the most representative and the most practical. Skinner's book is a collection of his papers on teaching, Lefrançois provides a simple explanation of early theories of learning, and Joyce, Weil, and Showers present a useful look at instructional models based on a variety of psychological theories:

SKINNER, B. F. (1968). *The technology of teaching.* New York: Appleton-Century-Crofts.

LEFRANÇOIS, G. R. (1995). *Theories of human learning: Kro's report* (3rd ed.). Monterey, Calif.: Brooks/ Cole.

JOYCE, B., WEIL, M., & SHOWERS, B. (1992). *Models of teaching* (4th ed.). Boston: Allyn & Bacon.

Skinner provides a highly readable and important behavioristic estimation of the human condition:

SKINNER, B. F. (1971). *Beyond freedom and dignity.* New York: Knopf.

The social development theory of Bandura and Walters is presented in the following:

BANDURA, A. (1977). *Social learning theory.* Morristown, N.J.: General Learning.

BANDURA, A., & WALTERS, R. (1963). *Social learning and personality development.* New York: Holt, Rinehart & Winston.

Hall and Kelson (1959) list exactly 130 subspecies and types of bears, ranging alphabetically from *Ursus absarokus,* found in 1914 at the head of the Little Bighorn River in Montana, to *Ursus yesoensis.*

CHAPTER 5

I've a grand mind for forgetting, David.
ROBERT LOUIS STEVENSON, *Kidnapped*

The Right Honorable gentleman is indebted
to his memory for his jests and to his imagination for his facts.

RICHARD BRINSLEY SHERIDAN, SPEECH IN REPLY
TO MR. DUNDAS

Thinking and Remembering

PREVIEW

Conditioning theories explain how stimuli, responses, and the consequences of behavior can become associated under certain circumstances. Accordingly, these theories are useful in explaining many relatively simple behaviors—and perhaps some complex behaviors as well. But how well do they explain the processes by which you and I can recognize, or at least contemplate, the role of, say, metaphoric bears, in the grand scheme of things?

Focus Questions

▶ What is meant by cognitivism?

▶ What is the most basic current information processing model?

▶ What are the types and characteristics of long-term memory?

▶ What are common theories of forgetting?

▶ How can memory be improved?

▶ What is meant by metacognition?

▶ How can students be taught to think?

"It hides in clothes closets and under beds," said my cousin, Claude. "Really dark places. It'll get you when you sleep mostly."

"What . . ."

"It'll bite your neck and suck your blood. Or it'll just take you away somewhere."

"You can't scare me," said my older brother, Maurice. "I heard that story before. Papooses aren't real."

But that night when we lay in the darkness beneath the old green comforter, everybody else sleeping, a sudden creaking of the house's ancient frame jolted Maurice bolt upright.

"Did you hear that?" he whispered hoarsely.

"Yeah."

"It might be a papoose."

"Nah," I answered bravely, but I couldn't still the beating of my heart.

"Go check the clothes closet."

"No, you go."

"You go first."

In the end, more because I was younger rather than braver, I checked the black recesses of the corner clothes closet, sticking my hand in behind the shirts like Maurice insisted. Then I got down on my hands and knees and peered under the bed.

From that night on, we took turns, Maurice and I, looking into each of the four corners of the room, then the closet, finally under the bed. Only then could we sleep.

Cognitivism

We're grown up, now, Maurice and I. We have become totally familiar with our closets; we know there's nothing under our beds.

But, as I discovered again last week when I spent the night alone in a little wilderness cabin not far from where I live, there are still things that go bump in the night. The bump woke me in the middle of a moonless night, setting my heart racing. I could see nothing in the gloom inside the cabin, but when I listened to hear what had awoken me, I heard the mournful crying of a great horned owl. For a moment, a jumble of emotions and images threatened to overwhelm me. I had just finished reading *Bendécime Ultima*, by Rudolfo Anaya, a book in which an old lady's *lechuza* (an owl) has strange and frightening powers. And only the week before, I had been told by my Colombian language instructor the stories of *La Llorona* and *El Silbón*.* And for one desperate moment, straining my eyes to see through the murky darkness of my little cabin, I saw again the papoose I thought I had left behind forever.

It's very difficult to understand mental processes such as these using the language and the explanations of behaviorism. That's because, as we saw in Chapter 4, behaviorism is essentially the study of actual behaviors and of the effects of the consequences of behavior. In a behavioristic analysis of learning, the primary emphasis is on the *external* conditions that affect behavior and not on *internal* conditions like imagining and remembering and associating. The unspoken assumption is that all learners are initially equal but the conditions to which they are exposed vary. This variance is what accounts for subsequent differences in behavior.

---

*These are stories like that of the papoose, often told to young children to frighten them into being good. "Come la sopa o te va a llevar La Llorona." ("Eat your soup or the Llorona [the lady who is doomed to cry eternally because she has drowned her children] will come and get you.") Or "Callete o te va a secuestrar El Silbón." ("Be quiet or the Silbón [the ghost you can hear whistling in the darkness—and the farther away the whistle, the more dangerous] will kidnap you.")

In contrast to behaviorism, cognitivism involves study of mental events rather than of actual behaviors. These mental events have to do with acquiring, processing, storing, and retrieving information. Accordingly, the main emphasis in a cognitive analysis of learning is on the learner's **mental structure,** a **concept** that includes not only the learner's previous related knowledge but also the strategies that the learner might bring to bear on the current situation. In this view, the implicit assumption is that learners are far from equal. It is the individual's preexisting network of concepts, strategies, and understanding that makes experience meaningful. Thus, it is because of images and ideas left over from things I have recently heard and read, combined with leftover terrors of childhood, that the cry of an owl might make my heart race. And for you, who have not learned to fear, or perhaps even to respect, the *lechuza,* the same sound might make you smile as you snuggle beneath your dreams.

Because cognitivism deals with mental events rather than simply with observable behavior, it represents a dramatic departure from behaviorism, a departure that has led to considerable conflict and disagreement over the years. Amsel (1989), for example, uses a parliamentary metaphor to describe the confrontation between behaviorism and cognitivism: "I like to point out," says he, "that the S–R psychologists, who at one time formed the government, are now in the loyal opposition, the cognitivists being the new government" (p. 1). And the rapidity and thoroughness with which the cognitivists appear to have become "the new government" has led many writers to refer to a *cognitive revolution* (for example, Bruner, 1992). This cognitive revolution, as is made clear in this and in other chapters in this text, is having a profound effect on educational theory and practice.

---

mental structure see *cognitive structure* on page 536.

concept A collection of perceptual experiences or ideas that are related by virtue of their possessing common properties.

*"I've been a cow all my life, honey.
Don't ask me to change now."*
Drawing by Ziegler; © 1992 The New Yorker Magazine, Inc.

Cognitivism, E. Hunt (1989) asserts, is a perspective rather than a discipline. It is a way of looking at things rather than a readily identifiable collection of findings. This way of looking at things is characterized by basic underlying beliefs that are apparent in the metaphors of cognitivism.

THE METAPHORS OF COGNITIVISM

Cognitivism abounds with metaphors, claims Bruner (1990b). That, of course, is because much of what it deals with cannot be described very precisely, cannot be pointed to or photographed, and, in short, has to be inferred rather than actually seen. Hence the need for metaphors, which are simply a comparison. Metaphors don't say, "This is that"; instead, they say, "It is interesting, or amusing, or useful, to look at this as though it were *like* that." Hence, a metaphor cannot be judged in terms of whether it is accurate but only in terms of whether it is useful—or interesting and amusing.

A Definition of Cognitivism. *Cognitivism* is defined in terms of cognition or of "mental events"—and cognitive psychology, as Gagné, Yekovich, and Yekovich (1993) put it, "is the scientific study of mental events" (p. 4) (while behavioristic psychology is the study of *behavioral* events).

Cognition is not a simple concept. Literally, to cognize is to know; hence, cognition is knowing. As Neisser (1976, p. 1) puts it: "Cognition is the activity of knowing: the acquisition, organization, and use of knowledge." Or, in Glass, Holyoak, and Santa's (1979, p. 2) words: "All our mental abilities—perceiving, remembering, reasoning—are organized into a complex system, the overall function of which is termed cognition." What is common to these and other definitions of cognition is that they emphasize the role of mental structure, or organization, in the processes of knowing. In other words, they deal with how mental representations are manipulated (Hunt, 1989). Not surprisingly, then, a major emphasis of cognitive approaches concerns the ways information is processed and stored. Note how dramatically this departs from the major emphasis of a behavioristic approach, which concentrates on behavior and its consequences.

A Computer Metaphor. The dominant metaphor in cognitive psychology, note Massaro and Cowan (1993), is an **information processing (IP)** metaphor. This metaphor arose with the development of information processing machines, more commonly called computers. The metaphor is closely related to the branch of computer science concerned with **artificial intelligence (AI).** This is the branch of computer science that attempts to understand the ways in which brains are like computers, and that tries to simulate intelligent behavior using computers. It is also the branch of computer science that tries to make computers smarter, says Raphael (1976). One of the benefits of developing a truly smart computer is that

doing so might clarify how our own information processing systems—our minds—work. Scientists concerned with this potential benefit typically use computers in one of two ways: to mimic the functioning of the human mind or to generate models of human functioning. In these models, the brain, with its neurons and their networks of interconnections, might be compared to the chips and the storage and relay systems of computers. Or the processes involved in receiving, organizing, storing, and retrieving information might be compared to the programmed functions of the computer. In that case, it is the program rather than the computer itself that serves as a model for human functioning. (See Figure 5.1.)

Other Metaphors. The computer and its information processing capabilities is a central metaphor of the cognitive sciences. This metaphor says, in effect, "It is useful to look at human cognitive functioning as though it functioned like a computer." But there are also several other approaches that invent their own metaphors—that look at cognitive functioning not in terms of something known, such as a computer, but in terms of something that is initially unknown and that requires that its characteristics be described. They use labels such as "knowledge base," "cognitive strategy," or "schema" for their metaphors. No one has seen a knowledge base, a cognitive strategy, or a schema; these are abstractions, inventions of cognitive theory. But each of these inventions can be described. And, once described, it is possible to say, "Learners behave as though they have a knowledge base and cognitive strategies."

Our current model of cognitive functioning, as we noted, is essentially an information processing model. This model looks at three things. First, it looks at what Chi and Glaser (1980) call the **knowledge base**—the store-

---

information processing (IP) Relates to how information is modified (or processed), resulting in knowledge, perception, or behavior. A dominant model of the cognitive approaches, it makes extensive use of computer metaphors.

artificial intelligence (AI) Describes models, procedures, devices, or mechanisms intended to simulate or duplicate some of the intelligent functions of human mental activity.

---

knowledge base The storehouse of concepts, information, associations, and procedures that we accumulate over time.

		Human			
S	Cognitive acts (thinking, problem solving, creating, and other mental processes)	R	Senses	Nervous system (sometimes called *wetware*)	Response systems

		Computer			
Input	Software (programmed operations)	Output	Sensors (keyboard)	Hardware (chips, relays, wiring)	Printers, screens

FIGURE 5.1 Analogies between computer and human structures and functions. Cognitive science's basic computer metaphor compares input to stimuli, output to responses, and the cognitive functioning of the nervous system to the computer's software-driven operations. From G. R. Lefrançois, *Theories of Human Learning: Kro's Report* (3rd ed.). Copyright © 1995 by Wadsworth, Inc. Reprinted by permission of Brooks/Cole Publishing Company, Pacific Grove, California.

house of information, concepts, and associations that we build up as we develop from children into adults. Second, it looks at **cognitive strategies**—the processes by which information becomes part of the knowledge base, is retrieved from it, or is used. And third, it deals with the individual's awareness of self as a knower and processor of information—with what is termed *metacognition*. We look at each of these aspects of cognitive functioning in this chapter. In Chapter 6 we look at the tremendous potential contribution of the cognitive sciences to education, especially in developing ways to teach and improve cognitive strategies.

A BASIC INFORMATION PROCESSING MODEL

The most basic model of information processing currently used as a metaphor in cognitive science is essentially a model of human **memory** (our knowledge base, after all, is composed of all we have in memory; and cognitive strategies are the means by which material becomes part of the knowledge base, is retrieved from it, or is used). This model is based largely on the work of Atkinson and Shiffrin (1968). It makes an important distinction between two types of information storage: **short-term memory** (also

cognitive strategies The processes involved in learning and remembering. Cognitive strategies include identifying problems, selecting approaches to their solutions, monitoring progress in solving problems, and using feedback. Cognitive strategies are closely related to metacognition and metamemory.

memory The effects that experiences are assumed to have on the human mind. Refers to the storage of these effects.

short-term memory A type of memory in which material is available for recall for a matter of seconds. Short-term memory involves primarily rehearsal rather than more in-depth processing. It defines our immediate consciousness. Also termed *primary memory* or *working memory*.

called **working memory**), and **long-term memory.** In some versions of the model, such as that depicted in Figure 5.2, a third memory component is included: **short-term sensory storage** (sometimes called **sensory memory**).

Each type of storage is distinct primarily in terms of the nature and extent of the processing that information undergoes. **Processing** refers to activities such as organizing, analyzing, synthesizing, rehearsing, and so on. In addition, the three types of storage differ in capacity and in the extent to which their contents are accessible. Bear in mind, however, that what we are discussing is a model—a metaphor. It is not intended to be a literal description of the way things actually are stored in our brains. In other words, there isn't actually a box or some other type of container in our brains into which short-term memory items are placed, and another for longer-term storage. In fact, the metaphor says far more about how psychologists choose to investigate and talk about memory than it does about the physical and neurological characteristics of remembering.

This basic information processing model of cognitive psychology does two related things: First, it provides us with an overall model of human memory. Second, it addresses a number of learning-related questions that are critically important for teachers—questions such as how information is organized and sorted, which teaching and learning methods can facilitate information processing, and how memory can be improved.

SENSORY MEMORY

The information processing model shown in Figure 5.2 is, in effect, a model of human learning and memory. And it begins with the raw material of all learning experiences: sensory sensation.

Our sensory systems (vision, hearing, taste, touch, smell) are sensitive to an overwhelmingly wide range of stimulation. Clearly, however, they respond to only a fraction of all available stimulation at any given time; the bulk of the information available in this stimulation is never actually processed—that is, it never actually becomes part of our cognitive structure. "Sensory memory" is the label used to describe the immediate, unconscious effects of stimulation. Research indicates that much of the stimulation to which we aren't actually paying attention is nevertheless available for processing for perhaps a fraction of a second. Thus, if you are engaged in a conversation with someone in a crowded room, you might be totally unaware of what is being said in any other conversation. But if the topic in one of these other conversations turns to something that passionately interests you (for example, you hear your own name), suddenly you become aware of what you would otherwise not have heard. This occurrence is labeled the **cocktail party phenomenon** (Cherry, 1953). It describes a type of memory that is unconscious, fleeting, and very much like an echo—so much so, in fact, that Neisser labels it **echoic memory** (for auditory stimuli) or **iconic memory** (for visual stimuli).

---

long-term memory A type of memory whereby, with continued rehearsal and recoding of sensory information (processing in terms of meaning, for example), material will be available for recall over a long period of time.

short-term sensory storage The phrase refers to the simple sensory recognition of such stimuli as a sound, a taste, or a sight. Also termed *sensory memory.*

processing The intellectual or cognitive activities that occur as stimulus information is reacted to, analyzed, sorted, organized, and stored in memory or forgotten.

cocktail party phenomenon An expression to describe sensory memory. The fleeting and unconscious availability for processing stimuli to which the individual is not paying attention.

echoic memory Neisser's term for sensory memory involving auditory stimulation—the fleeting availability for processing of auditory stimuli to which the individual is not paying attention.

iconic memory Neisser's term for sensory memory involving visual stimulation—the fleeting availability for processing of visual stimuli to which the individual is not attending.

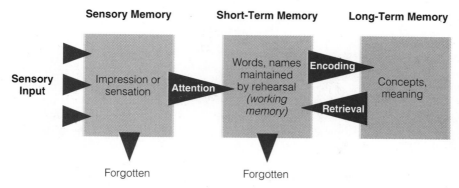

Sensory Memory   **Short-Term Memory**   **Long-Term Memory**

Sensory Input → Impression or sensation — **Attention** → Words, names maintained by rehearsal *(working memory)* — **Encoding** → Concepts, meaning

← **Retrieval**

Forgotten   Forgotten

F I G U R E 5 . 2 The three components of memory. The top row depicts three types of memory; the boxed items depict the content of the memory process. Sensory information first enters sensory memory (iconic or echoic memory). From there it may go into short-term memory (also called primary memory), where it is available as a name or word, for example, as long as it is rehearsed. Some of the material in short-term memory may then be coded for long-term storage, where it might take the form of meanings and concepts. Note that these three components of memory do not refer to three different locations in the brain or other parts of the nervous system, but to how we remember—to how we study memory.

Note that sensory memory is highly limited, both in terms of the length of time during which stimulus information is available for processing and in terms of the absolute amount of information available—except, perhaps, for some rare cases such as are described in the box "Eidetic Images." Put another way, sensory memory is no more than the immediate sensory effect of a stimulus. If, without giving any prior instructions, I read you a list of numbers in a dry, professorial monotone and then ask you to repeat the numbers some 10 seconds later, you are not likely to remember many of the numbers. But if I interrupt my reading and ask immediately, "What was the last number I read?" you will, in all likelihood, respond correctly. In fact, each of the numbers is stored in sensory memory for a very short period of time, but if it is not attended to or processed within a fraction of a second, it will no longer be available.

SHORT-TERM MEMORY

Sensory memory precedes attention; when the individual attends to a stimulus (in other words, becomes conscious of it), it passes into short-term memory. In essence, then, short-term memory consists of what is in our immediate consciousness at any given time. As Calfee (1981) notes, it is a sort of scratch pad for thinking; it contains all that is in our immediate awareness. For this reason, short-term memory is often called *working memory*. The label draws attention to the function of this level of memory rather than simply to its duration.

One of the important characteristics of short-term memory is that it is highly limited in capacity. Following various memory experiments, Miller (1956) concluded that its average capacity is about seven separate items (plus or minus two); that is, our immediate conscious awareness is limited to this capacity, and as

EIDETIC IMAGES

Sometimes when we remember something, we say, "I can picture it in my mind." But what, exactly, is it that we can "picture"? Most often, psychologists inform us, we see a sort of mental image—an imperfect representation from memory, subject to all the distortions and inaccuracies to which memory is prone. But there are those rare individuals whose mental images are more accurate: They possess **eidetic imagery.**

In effect, an eidetic image is a photographlike recollection of some stimulus—hence, the popular expression "photographic memory." People who have eidetic imagery are sometimes able to remember with amazing accuracy and detail. For example, in a typical investigation of eidetic imagery, subjects might be shown a picture, such as that reproduced here, for a brief period and then asked questions such as "How many oranges are there in the tree?" "How many stripes are there in the flute player's skirt?" "How many flowers can you see?" Investigations such as these reveal that some degree of eidetic imagery is not uncommon among young school-age children, but that it is far less common after adolescence (Ahsen, 1977a,b). These investigations also indicate that recall based on eidetic imagery is very much like looking at the actual picture. Those so gifted continue to "see" the picture after it is removed. When they are asked how many flowers they can see, their eye movements are similar to the eye movements of someone actually looking at the picture.

Contrary to popular opinion, eidetic imagery does not usually present any advantage in learning school-related tasks because it rarely involves any transference to long-term memory. In fact, the eidetic image is seldom available for recall even an hour later; typically, it fades within minutes. However, there are some recorded cases of remarkable, eideticlike memories that are not subject to the ravages of time. Among these, Luria's (1968) description of a young Russian known to us only as S is perhaps the best known. S went to Luria, a psychologist, because he was bewildered and confused. His mind was such a jumble of sights, sounds, and colors that he had difficulty following ordinary conversations. S's problem, quite simply, was an absolutely remarkable memory. On one occasion, Luria presented S with the array of numbers shown here. After spending 3 minutes examining the table, S was able to reproduce the numbers flawlessly in

additional items of information come in, they push out some that are already there.

Short-term memory lasts a matter of seconds (not minutes, hours, or days) and appears to be highly dependent on rehearsal. That is, for items to be maintained in short-term storage, they must be repeated (consciously thought about). In the absence of repetition, they quickly fade—usually before 20 seconds have elapsed.

The apparent limitations of short-term memory are not nearly as serious as they might at first seem. Although we cannot easily attend to more than seven discrete items, a process called **chunking** dramatically increases the capacity of short-term memory. In effect, a chunk is simply a group of related items of information. Thus, a single letter might be one of the seven items held in short-term memory,

---

eidetic imagery A particularly vivid type of visual image in memory. In many ways, it is almost as though the individual were actually able to look at what is being remembered—hence the synonym *photographic memory*.

---

chunking A memory process whereby related items are grouped together into more easily remembered chunks (for example, a prefix and four digits for a phone number rather than seven unrelated numbers).

6	6	8	0
5	4	3	2
1	6	8	4
7	9	3	5
4	2	3	7
3	8	9	1
1	0	0	2
3	4	5	1
2	7	6	8
1	9	2	6
2	9	6	7
5	5	2	0
x	0	1	x

The Dream by Henri Rousseau. 1910. Oil on canvas, 6′8½″ x 9′9½″. Collection, The Museum of Modern Art, New York. Gift of Nelson A. Rockefeller. Reprinted by permission.
Table from *The Mind of a Mnemonist: A Little Book About a Vast Memory* by A. R. Luria, translated from the Russian by Lynn Solotaroff. Copyright 1968 by Basic Books, Inc., Publishers. Reprinted by permission of Michael Cole and Jonathan Cape Ltd.

40 seconds. Within 50 seconds, he read off each of the four-digit numbers forming the first twelve horizontal rows, as well as the two-digit number in the last row. But what is even more remarkable is that even after several months had elapsed, during which time the table was never again presented, S could reproduce it flawlessly (although he took somewhat longer to "reimagine" the array).

But memories such as S's are exceptionally rare. Most of the memories with which teachers deal are more ordinary.

or it might be chunked with other letters to form a single word—which can, in turn, be one of seven items in short-term memory. To illustrate this phenomenon, Miller (1956) uses the analogy of a change purse that can hold only seven coins. If the purse holds seven pennies, its capacity is only seven cents. But if it holds seven quarters, seven fifty-cent pieces, or even seven gold coins, its capacity increases dramatically.

In summary, short-term memory is the ongoing availability of a small number of items, or chunks, of information in conscious awareness. Without continued rehearsal, these items are generally lost from memory within 20 seconds. The great usefulness of short-term mem-ory is that it enables us to keep information in mind long enough to make sense of sequences of words and directions, to solve problems, and to make decisions.

Some Educational Implications of Short-Term Memory. The most common measure of short-term memory is to have subjects repeat a sequence of unrelated single-digit numbers they have just heard, a task that is used in many intelligence tests. Under these circumstances, adults and adolescents typically remember six or seven items (or sometimes nine or more). In contrast, 6-year-olds are not likely to remember more than two or three.

These differences may be highly important for teachers. It may well be, as Siegler (1989) suggests, that certain problems are difficult or impossible for younger learners simply because they cannot keep in mind enough relevant information at one time—as might be the case, for example, if a young child were asked to add several numbers at once. Case (1991) argues that one of the most serious limitations on the young child's ability to understand and solve problems is simply a limitation in the number of items that the child can retain in working memory for immediate availability.

Teachers have two courses of action in such cases. If many of the young child's cognitive limitations result from limited short-term memory capacity, teachers can either wait for appropriate changes in memory before progressing to more demanding tasks. Or they can take steps to improve the child's memory.

In practice, teachers most often resort to the first alternative; they simply wait for the child to mature. Recently, however, growing evidence suggests that it might be possible to teach certain aspects of cognitive strategies—such as rehearsal—that are important for short-term memory. (More about this later.)

JERRY HOWARD/STOCK, BOSTON

Recollections that make up our long-term memories are highly stable and not easily disrupted. In a week these people are not likely to remember what they had for dinner tonight; but they are highly unlikely to have forgotten the names of any of the people whose photographs they now recognize. The objective of schools is to teach for long-term memory.

LONG-TERM MEMORY

The type of memory that is clearly of greatest concern to educators is long-term memory. Long-term memory includes all our relatively stable information about the world—all that we know but that is not in our immediate consciousness. In fact, one important distinction between short-term and long-term memory is that short-term memory is an active, ongoing, conscious process, whereas long-term memory is a more passive, unconscious process. Accordingly, short-term memory is easily disrupted by external events—as we demonstrate every time we lose our train of thought because of some distraction. In contrast, long-term memory cannot easily be disrupted. If you know the capital of Finland today, you are likely to know it tomorrow, next month, and even next year.

As noted earlier, we transfer information from sensory storage to short-term storage through the process of attending, and we maintain it in short-term memory largely through rehearsal. But the transference of material from short-term to long-term memory involves more than simple rehearsal: It involves **encoding,** a process whereby meaning is derived from experience. To encode information is to transform or abstract it—to represent it in another form.

Encoding clearly involves information processing, an event that can occur at different levels. Craik and Lockhart (1972; Cermak & Craik,

---

encoding A process whereby we derive meaning from the environment. To encode is to represent in another form. At a mental level, encoding involves the process of abstracting—representing as a concept or a meaning.

TABLE 5.1 THREE LEVELS OF MEMORY

	SENSORY	SHORT-TERM	LONG-TERM
ALTERNATE LABELS	Echoic or iconic	Primary or working	Secondary
DURATION	Less than 1 second	Less than 20 seconds	Indefinite
STABILITY	Fleeting	Easily disrupted	Not easily disrupted
CAPACITY	Limited	Limited (7±2 items)	Unlimited
GENERAL CHARACTERISTICS	Momentary, unconscious impression	Working memory; immediate consciousness; active, maintained by rehearsal	Knowledge base; associationistic; passive; the result of encoding

1979), originators of the **levels of processing** model, suggest that memory results specifically from the level to which information is processed. Information that is not processed leaves only a momentary sensory impression (sensory memory), information that is merely rehearsed is available for seconds (short-term memory), and information that is processed to a greater degree finds its way into long-term memory. But not all material in long-term memory is processed to the same level. If, for example, subjects are asked to learn and remember a word, they can process it at a highly superficial level, paying attention only to its physical appearance. At a somewhat deeper level, they might pay attention to the word's pronunciation. And at the deepest level, they would take into account the word's meaning—a process called *semantic encoding*. (Table 5.1 summarizes the characteristics of all three levels of memory.)

It's important to note that our long-term memories are not always exact reproductions of what we have experienced. In fact, memories change considerably over time, often in pre-

dictable ways. As Loftus (1979) notes, they tend to be *generative* rather than purely reproductive. As an illustration, she had subjects view a film in which a sports car was involved in an accident and later asked them different questions about the accident. For example, some subjects were asked, "How fast was the sports car going when it passed the barn while traveling along the country road?" Other subjects were asked instead, "How fast was the sports car going while traveling along the country road?" When subjects were later asked whether they had seen the barn, 17 percent of those who had earlier been asked the first question claimed to remember seeing one; fewer than 3 percent of the others actually remembered a barn. In fact, there was no barn in the film.

As a result of this and a host of related studies, Loftus argues that much of what we remember has been modified by intervening events and dulled by the passage of time. In the end, perhaps fewer than half of us will be able to identify the thief; even fewer will remember the color of his hair or eyes. And some of us will remember things that we have never even experienced.

---

levels of processing An information processing theory, attributed to Craik and Lockhart, maintaining that memory is a function of the level to which information is processed. At the lowest level, a stimulus is simply recognized as a physical event (and is available momentarily in short-term sensory memory); at a much deeper level, a stimulus is interpreted in terms of its meaning (and is available in long-term memory).

TYPES OF LONG-TERM MEMORY

When a meddling philospher asked the centipede how it managed to walk with its many legs, the poor thing was totally bewildered. You see, it had never really thought about the problem; it just darn well knew how. Sadly, after it had been asked the question, it began to try to understand the process, tried to figure out which leg went where, when, which next, and on and on, until, finally, completely perplexed and befuddled, it had wrapped its hundred legs in the world's biggest headache of a knot.*

Declarative and Nondeclarative Long-Term Memory.

Much of our knowledge, too, is like the centipede's knowing how to walk. It isn't information that we know consciously and can put into clear, understandable words and instructions. Instead, it's knowledge that we have in our muscles or maybe in some unconscious part of our nervous systems. It includes information relating to things like riding bicycles, hitting long drives in golf, or even our thoughtless responses to things that frighten or excite us. These kinds of memories are labeled **nondeclarative memory** (or *implicit memory*) simply because they can't be put into words.

But we also have many stable memories that we can put into words—memories having to do with our names, our addresses, the meanings of words, the colors of our cars, and on and on. These memories make up what is termed **declarative memory** (also called *explicit memory*). As Squire, Knowlton, and Musen (1993) explain, the principal difference between declarative and nondeclarative memory is that declarative memory is *conscious* memory for facts and events; nondeclarative memory is *unconscious* memory.

Semantic Versus Episodic Memory. Declarative memory consists of at least two distinct types of memories, explains Tulving (1991). Abstract, general knowledge about the world, such as what children learn in school, for example, makes up what is called **semantic memory.** In addition, each of us has a large store of very personal recollections about the things we have done and thought, the experiences we have had, and so on. This autobiographical knowledge consists of all of the little episodes of our lives and defines what is meant by **episodic memory.**

To summarize, there are two different kinds of long-term memory: those that are implicit, unconscious, and not easily verbalized (nondeclarative) and those that are explicit, conscious, and that can be put into words (declarative). Memories that are declarative might be abstract and general (semantic) or more personal and autobiographical (episodic). Figure 5.3 summarizes these distinctions.

PROCESSES IN LONG-TERM MEMORY

The functioning of the information processing system (memory model) that we have been describing has a simple goal: make sense of significant sensation while ignoring or discarding more trivial matters. To achieve this goal, the system uses a number of processes. And, in fact, one of the important distinctions among the three levels of memory relates to the type and amount of processing that information undergoes. As we have seen, a great deal of sensory data that is not attended to (not processed)

---

*PPC: This doesn't sound like that good an example for humans. We're far from having as many legs as a centipede. Or does the bear often trip over his four?

AUTHOR: The bear, old as he might be, walks with the sprightly step of those much younger. The point, however, is not how many legs we have or how elegantly we walk. Rather, it has to do with the fact that there are things that we know—hence *remember*—that we cannot readily put into words. Read on.

---

nondeclarative memory Refers to unconscious, nonverbalizable effects of experience such as might be manifested in acquired motor skills or in classical conditioning. Also termed *implicit* or *procedural memory*.

declarative memory Explicit, conscious long-term memory, in contrast with implicit (or nondeclarative) memory. Declarative memory may be either semantic or episodic. Also termed *explicit memory*.

semantic memory A type of declarative (conscious, long-term) memory consisting of stable knowledge about the world, principles, rules, and procedures, and other verbalizable aspects of knowledge, including language.

episodic memory A type of declarative, autobiographical (conscious, long-term) memory consisting of knowlege about personal experiences, tied to specific times and places.

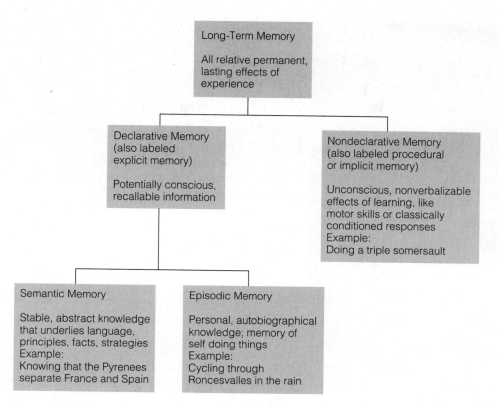

Long-Term Memory

All relative permanent, lasting effects of experience

Declarative Memory (also labeled explicit memory)

Potentially conscious, recallable information

Nondeclarative Memory (also labeled procedural or implicit memory)

Unconscious, nonverbalizable effects of learning, like motor skills or classically conditioned responses
Example:
Doing a triple somersault

Semantic Memory

Stable, abstract knowledge that underlies language, principles, facts, strategies
Example:
Knowing that the Pyrenees separate France and Spain

Episodic Memory

Personal, autobiographical knowledge; memory of self doing things
Example:
Cycling through Roncesvalles in the rain

FIGURE 5.3 **Types of long-term memory. Memories that are implicit, unconscious, and not easily verbalized are nondeclarative. Those memories that are explicit, conscious, and able to be put into words are declarative. Declarative memories can be either abstract and general (semantic memories) or personal and autobiographical (episodic memories).**

does not go beyond immediate sensory memory. Paying attention is one of the important activities, or processes, of our information processing system. It is the means by which information is transferred from sensory to short-term storage. Three other basic processes that are involved in remembering include rehearsal, elaboration, and organization.

REHEARSAL

Rehearsal involves repeating, the simplest rehearsal strategy being to name the material ("five, five, five, one, two, one, two") over and over again until it seems unlikely that it will escape. Rehearsal serves not only to maintain information in short-term memory but also to transfer material from short- to long-term storage. Most children younger than 5 do not

rehearse spontaneously and cannot easily be taught to do so (Wellman, 1990).

ELABORATION

Elaboration is a cognitive process whereby material is extended or added to (elaborated) in order to make it more memorable. One way of elaborating material is to associate mental images with items to be remembered. Higbee (1977) suggests that because our memories are highly visual (photographs are more easily

---

rehearsal A memory process involving repetition, important in maintaining information in short-term memory and in transferring it to long-term memory.

elaboration A long-term memory process involving changing or adding to material, or making associations to make remembering easier. .

Organization refers to grouping and relating material. Assume, for example, that you need to memorize the following list: man, dog, green, cayenne, woman, cat, child, canary, jalapeño. Some of you will immediately notice that the list can easily be organized into three groups of related items (pets, persons, and peppers) and will use this organization to help remember the items—which, again, is not something younger children will spontaneously do.

The organizational strategies that are so important to long-term memory can be either extremely complex or quite simple. What most of them have in common, however, is that they are based on our recognition of similarities and differences. Humans (and perhaps other animals as well, although it is difficult to be certain) seem to have a tendency to see similarities and differences (as well as other relations) and to generalize from them. Put another way, we seem to be information processing organisms whose function it is to make sense of all the data that surround us. One of the important methods we use for making sense of the world is to extract common elements from various experiences, thereby arriving at concepts or ideas that we can remember (Hintzman & Ludham, 1980).

In addition to this apparently natural tendency to look for relationships, there is evidence that many of our organizations of related concepts or ideas result from the application of strategies we have learned. More than this, as we become aware of various strategies that we can use to make sense of the world (and to learn and remember), we also become aware of ourselves as organisms capable of learning and remembering. We learn things, and we learn about learning. Put another way, we develop *metacognitive* skills, about which more is said later in this chapter.

A map might reveal where we are, where we want to go, and how we can get there. But each of these revelations is totally dependent on the individual's being able to retrieve from memory all sorts of complex things about maps, space, movement, and direction. Even knowing that we know how to read maps is no small accomplishment.

remembered than paragraphs), the use of mental images is an important aspect of most mnemonic systems (systems for remembering). Some of these systems are described later in this chapter.

Sometimes, elaboration involves forming associations between new material and material that is already well known. Research suggests that elaborations that relate to meaning are highly memorable. For example, when Bradshaw and Anderson (1982) asked subjects to recall sentences such as "The fat man read the sign," those who had elaborated the sentence to something like "The fat man read the sign warning of thin ice" performed significantly better than those who had not elaborated. Children younger than 12 do not deliberately elaborate to improve recall (Justice, 1985).

organization A memory strategy involving grouping and relating material to maintain it in long-term memory.

EDUCATIONAL APPLICATIONS: TEACHING FOR RETRIEVAL

There is a common belief, note Semb and Ellis (1994), that students begin to forget much of what they have learned very soon after they have written their examinations. And, in fact, research on long-term memory seems to indicate that most of what is forgotten is lost very soon after it is learned and that, by the same token, things that we succeed in remembering days or weeks later may well continue to be available even years afterward. To the extent that this is true, it presents an important challenge for teachers. After all, one of the important functions of schools is to impart skills and knowledge that will be available to learners not specifically for examinations but rather for the rest of their lives. In short, the function of schools is to teach for long-term memory.

Fortunately, the belief that there is little long-term retention of material learned in school does not appear to be entirely true, claim Semb and Ellis (1994). They point out that the studies upon which this conclusion is based are mainly laboratory studies rather than school-based studies. In laboratory studies, the material to be learned is usually presented and learned in a single session. In contrast, schools typically provide learners with a tremendous number and variety of opportunities in which to learn, and they make use of a far greater assortment of presentation modes (like films, lectures, CDs, demonstrations, books, and so on). Hence, it isn't particularly surprising that when Semb and Ellis analyzed sixty-two studies that looked specifically at long-term retention of school-taught material, they found evidence of considerable long-term retention. Perhaps even more important for teachers, they also found clear evidence that long-term retention reflects how well students learn in the first place, a factor that is dependent in part on how they are taught as well as on individual student abilities.

The challenge for teachers is to find ways in which to improve learning—and, consequently, long-term retention. Consider, for example, the case "Boring with the Cost of Borrowing." Here is a lesson that has little chance, especially with

C A S E : BORING WITH THE COST OF BORROWING

THE PLACE: **Medicine Hat High School**

THE TIME: **3:00 P.M. Friday**

THE SETTING: **The beginning of Orville Radcliffe's class, Life and Career Skills 10, taught to a tenth-grade class of low achievers—administratively labeled an "opportunity class"**

THE LESSON: **Personal banking**

There is much noise and shuffling, much talking and restlessness. Little attentiveness. Mr. Radcliffe glances at his lesson notes. He reads the main heads:

▶ The purposes of banks

▶ Alternatives

▶ Fluctuating interest rates

▶ The cost of borrowing . . .

"Borrrrrrring!" Mr. Radcliffe acknowledges to himself. He clears his throat:

"Ahem," says he, by way of getting their attention. It doesn't work.

"Today we're going to talk about personal banking," he mumbles uncertainly—soon, he knows, he will have lost them all until the bell rescues him.

But that's the lesson he prepared, and so he forges onward: "Take out your notebooks 'cause you should make notes, 'cause there'll be questions about this on the exam, especially about the effects of interest rates and all that . . ." He is wishing he had prepared a different lesson. . . .

this class on a Friday afternoon. But the lesson in the corresponding case, "I've Won the Bejiggered Lottery!" might work wonderfully well—and might be remembered.* Why? It begins with material that is striking, it presents a situation that is meaningful, it provides opportunities for relating items of information and for emphasizing concepts (perhaps with stacks of money), and it uses visual (and memorable) teaching aids. Nor will it be difficult to find opportunities for rehearsal and repetition. This is one lesson students might remember.

WHY WE FORGET

If teachers are to teach for long-term retention, then it might also be useful to know why it is that students forget. Knowing why forgetting

---

*PPC: (Note to the Editor) I don't know what your policy is, but the bear borders on profanity. I don't really know exactly what *bejiggered* means, but I don't like the sound of it, and I think some of my younger students might be . . . well "shocked" is probably too strong, but certainly, "taken aback."

AUTHOR: *Bejiggered* is an ancient Mayan word that means, literally, "hit on the nose by a long stick thrown by a left-handed beggar with one eye looking the other way." Hence, to be truly bejiggered is a rare thing. As, of course, is winning the lottery. The bear is *not* the least bit profane!

occurs might suggest a variety of methods to impede the process.

Although no one knows precisely what the physiology of memory is or what happens when **forgetting** takes place, a number of theories have been advanced to explain these processes.

Fading. Fading theory holds that material that is not brought to mind frequently enough (that is not used) tends to fade from memory. I know at this moment that the oldest recorded age at which a woman has given birth to a live infant is 57. This fact was brought to my attention as I perused *The Guinness Book of World Records* in search of a record that I might break. Unless I review this information again, or have it brought to mind by someone or something, I probably won't remember it next year. It will have faded.

Many psychologists don't consider fading theory (also called *decay theory*) very useful or informative. They argue that time, by itself,

---

forgetting The cessation of a response as a function of the passage of time, not to be confused with *extinction*.

fading theory The belief that inability to recall in long-term memory increases with the passage of time as memory traces fade. Also termed *decay theory*.

CASE: I'VE WON THE BEJIGGERED LOTTERY!

THE PLACE: Medicine Hat High School

THE TIME: 3:00 P.M. Friday

THE SETTING: The beginning of Orville Radcliffe's class, Life and Career Skills 10, taught to a tenth-grade class of low achievers— administratively labeled an "opportunity class"

THE LESSON: Personal banking

Orville struts to the front of the class, opens his briefcase flat on his desk so none of the students can see its contents—and then exclaims, "Now

that's more like it!" And then he takes great stacks of money from the briefcase and begins to pile them on his desk (well, maybe not exactly money, but great stacks of newspaper cut just so, bound with elastics, with real bills on top).

"We don't get paid this much in a lifetime of teaching," says he. "But I've won the bejiggered lottery!"

And together, Mr. Radcliffe and his class examine the various banking alternatives open to a lottery winner, the implications of each, and on and on. . . .

does not cause forgetting any more than it causes metal to rust or mountains to erode. It's other events that occur during the passage of time that account for these phenomena.

Distortion. Those memories that do not fade entirely are often distorted. It is now difficult for me to remember a specific sunset accurately; I have seen so many that even the most striking have become distorted until, in my memory of sunsets, there isn't a single one that looks very different from any other. It's sad but true. My sunrises fare better (probably because I haven't seen as many). The notable unreliability of eyewitnesses (Loftus, 1979) is another illustration of memory distortion.

Repression. It appears that people tend to forget events that are particularly unpleasant. One explanation for this phenomenon is Freud's belief that unpleasant memories filter into the subconscious mind, where the individual is not aware of them even though they may continue to have a profound effect on the person's emotional life.

Interference. The most popular theory of forgetting, and one that has direct relevance for teachers, says that interference from previous or subsequent learning is an important cause of forgetting. When previous learning interferes with current recall, **proactive inhibition** is said to occur; **retroactive inhibition** takes place when subsequent learning interferes with recall of previous learning. Teachers often have difficulty remembering the names of new students, especially if they have been teaching for a long time and have known many students with similar names. They confuse old names with new but similar faces. By the same token, once teachers have learned the names of all their current students, they sometimes find it difficult to remember the names of students from years past. The first case illustrates proactive inhibition; the second, retroactive inhibition.

Fortunately for us, as Banaji and Crowder (1989) note, not all laboratory findings concerning memory can be generalized to real life. Thus, although interference appears to describe what happens in the laboratory when learning relatively meaningless lists of words or syllables, it does not describe well what happens in real life. If it did, the more we learned, the more susceptible we would be to the effects of interference. Yet evidence suggests that although old and new learning might occasionally conflict, most of us can spend our lifetimes learning new things without becoming totally confused.

Retrieval Cue Failure. Some psychologists maintain that forgetting can be accounted for by the inability to retrieve from memory, rather than by simple memory loss, distortion, suppression, or interference. In other words, individuals appear not to remember simply because of what is termed **retrieval cue failure**—the inability to find a way to recall an item of information from memory.

EDUCATIONAL IMPLICATIONS OF THEORIES OF FORGETTING

There are several general characteristics of long-term memory that have clear educational implications. Among them are the observation that material that is meaningful and well organized is learned more easily and remembered for longer periods of time than insignificant material; events that are particularly striking tend to be recalled more easily and more clearly; frequent rehearsal improves long-term recall; and visual material has a greater impact on memory than verbal material. One of the reasons why each of these statements is true relates to the five theories of forgetting we have reviewed.

---

proactive inhibition The interference of earlier learning with the retention of subsequent learning.

retroactive inhibition The interference of subsequently learned material with the retention of previously learned material.

---

retrieval cue failure Inability to remember due to the unavailability of appropriate cues—as opposed to forgetting due to changes in memory traces.

Fading theory, for example, suggests that information may be forgotten because it has faded or decayed through disuse. If students forget because of disuse, teachers can provide repetition and review to remind them of important items. In fact, one of the reasons why long-term memory for school-learned items seems better than memory for material learned in laboratory situations, suggest Semb and Ellis (1994), is precisely because schools do provide students with a variety of opportunities to practice and rehearse what they have learned.

In addition, good teachers are careful to emphasize the most important and distinct (the most memorable) aspects of a situation. Doing so may be highly effective in countering subsequent *distortion.* So, too, might presenting material in a variety of forms.

Repression theory holds that memories of highly unpleasant (traumatic) events may be unconsciously repressed. Ideally, schools and teachers seldom provide students with experiences so horrendous that they end up being buried in some unconscious place.

Among the most important suggestions for countering the effects of *interference* and increasing the ability to recall information are those relating to the use of similarities and differences among items of information, a topic touched upon in the section on generalization and discrimination in Chapter 4. These topics are frequently treated under the heading of "transfer" (or "generalization"). The terms refer to the effects of old learning on new learning. Transfer can be either positive or negative. Positive transfer occurs when previous learning facilitates new learning and is sometimes evident in learning second languages. For example, it is easier to learn Spanish if you know French than if you know only English; the similarities between French and Spanish facilitate positive transfer. Negative transfer occurs when previous learning interferes with current learning; it is similar to proactive interference. Negative transfer occurs, for example, when I go to Bermuda, rent a motor scooter, and discover that all the traffic is on the wrong side of the street.

One way to teach for positive transfer while at the same time eliminating negative transfer is, as suggested previously, to relate new material to old material, emphasizing similarities and differences. The similarities should facilitate positive transfer; knowledge of differences should minimize negative transfer.

Retrieval cue failure is a general term for the inability to find ways of remembering material. The assumption is that the material has not actually been forgotten (in the sense that it might have decayed or been interfered with), but that the learner simply lacks the cues—the specific retrieval tools—that would permit remembering.

There is evidence that for declarative (semantic) information—the explicit, conscious sorts of learning with which schools are most concerned—certain types of retrieval cues are most effective. For example, Tulving (1989) reports that the most effective retrieval cues are those that closely match the type of recall in question. Thus, if students are to be asked to remember the meanings of words, then cues that emphasize meanings are best. In contrast, if they are to remember the spellings of words, cues that draw attention to letters are most effective. In addition, there are a variety of other specific retrieval cues and techniques that can be taught and learned and that are potentially very valuable in schools. We look at some of these next. (See Table 5.2 for a summary of theories of forgetting and some of their educational implications.)

SPECIFIC MEMORY AIDS

A large number of specific memory aids, or **mnemonic devices,** make use of specific retrieval cues.

Rhymes and Other Sayings. Rhymes, patterns, acronyms, and acrostics are common mnemonic devices. "Thirty days hath September . . ." is a simple rhyme without which many of us would

---

mnemonic devices Systematic aids to remembering, like rhymes, acrostics, or visual imagery systems.

TABLE 5.2 THEORIES OF FORGETTING AND SOME EDUCATIONAL APPLICATIONS

THEORY	EXPLANATION	POSSIBLE INSTRUCTIONAL COUNTERMEASURES
FADING	Memory traces decay from disuse.	Provide opportunities for repetition and rehearsal; teach in a variety of settings using different approaches.
DISTORTION	Memory is generative rather than reconstructive; what is recalled changes over time.	Emphasize the most important, the most salient, features of what is to be learned.
REPRESSION	Traumatic experiences are unconsciously buried and no longer consciously accessible.	Avoid traumatizing students.*
INTERFERENCE	Old memories interfere with learning new material (proactive); or new learning interferes with recall of old learning.	Teach for transfer; highlight similarities and differences.
RETRIEVAL CUE FAILURE	Learner lacks cues that enable specific recall.	Point out relationships and associations that can serve as retrieval cues; teach specific retrieval cues; teach learners some of the memory aids described in this chapter.

*PPC: Is the bear serious? Was he traumatized as a cub?

Author: Yes, of course the bear is serious. Always. After all, teachers aren't like horror films, meant to be memorable because they are frightening. And no, neither the bear, nor the author, were traumatized as youngsters—that is, neither of them remembers being traumatized. But . . . shoot, come to think of it, repression being what it is, there is no way of remembering such things!

not know how many days hath November. Similarly, the year in which Columbus sailed the ocean blue is nicely recalled by its little rhyme. The number "five million, five hundred fifty-one thousand, two hundred twelve" is considerably more difficult to remember than the number 555-1212; "triple five, double twelve" may be even easier. The mnemonic aid of chunking makes use of patterns.

Acronyms are letter cues that help to recall relatively complex material. *NATO, U.N.,* and *UNESCO* are popular acronyms. *Roy G. Biv* is another acronym, made up of the first letters of the words for the ordered colors of the visible light spectrum. Acrostics are similar to acronyms, except that they generally make use of sentences in which the first letter of each word represents an item of information to be remembered. Without the bizarre sentence "Men very easily make jugs serve useful nocturnal pur-

poses," I would have considerable difficulty recalling the planets in order from the sun. "Every good boy does fine" is meaningful to beginning music students.

A number of more complex mnemonic techniques are described in detail by Higbee (1977) and are reviewed briefly here. All have one thing in common: They make extensive use of visual imagery. Recall that visual material appears to have a greater impact on memory and can be retrieved much more easily than most nonvisual material.

The Link System. The simplest of these techniques is the **link system.** It requires the subject to visualize the item to be remembered and to

---

link system A mnemonic system wherein items to be remembered are linked to one another using visual images.

form a strong visual association (link) between it and other items to be remembered. It is easily illustrated with reference to a grocery list. (Once you have mastered this system, you need never write a grocery list again.) Suppose the list contains the following items: bread, salt, ketchup, dog food, and bananas. Visualize the first item. Concentrate on the picture that comes to mind first because it is likely to come to mind again when you think of bread. It might be bizarre, or it might be a simple image of a loaf or slice of bread. Now visualize the second item, salt, and form a visual link between the first image and the second. For example, you might see a slice of bread perched delicately on a large silver salt shaker. The salt shaker is dripping with ketchup being poured from a bottle held by a hungry dog with a banana in its ear. In most cases, you need not spend more than a few seconds with each image, nor should you rehearse them while you are learning the list.

The link system works amazingly well, although it has disadvantages. One is that it is sometimes difficult to remember the first item on the list. In that case, it might also be impossible to remember any of the other items because they are linked one to the other. This problem can be overcome by forming a visual association between the first item and a setting that is likely to remind you of the item. You might, for example, see the loaf of bread reclining in a grocery cart.

A second disadvantage of the link system is that if you cannot recall one of the items, it is unlikely that you will recall any of the subsequent items.

The Loci System. A variation of the link system, the **loci system,** overcomes this second disadvantage. In effect, in the loci system you simply form associations between items you need to remember and places that are familiar to you and that you therefore can visualize clearly. Rooms in a familiar house make good loci

"You simply associate each number with a word, such as 'Table' and 3,476,029."

© 1996 Sidney Harris.

(locus is Latin for "place"). You can quite easily "place" a grocery list in the rooms of a house simply by forming strong visual images of the objects, one in each of the rooms. The advantage of this system is that if you cannot remember what you placed in the hallway, you can always go to the bathroom.

The Phonetic System. A third mnemonic system, the **phonetic system,** is by far the most powerful, although it requires considerably more effort. Indeed, if you master this system, you could become a professional mnemonist. At the very least, you will impress your grandmother. The phonetic system allows you to recall items in order, backward, by twos, threes, fours, or—perhaps even more impressive—to recall any specific item (for example, the fourteenth item listed).

The first step in learning the system is to make an association between numbers and consonants. (Vowels do not count in the system.) Traditionally, the number 1 is represented by a letter such as *t* or *l*, because each has a single

---

loci system A mnemonic system wherein items to be remembered are associated with visual images of specific places.

phonetic system A particularly powerful mnemonic system that makes use of associations between numbers and letters combined to form words; visual images associated with these words are then linked with items to be remembered. Professional memorizers often use some variation of a phonetic system.

downstroke; the number 2 might be represented by an *n* because it has two downstrokes; 3 is *m* and 9 is *p* because each member of the pairs resembles the other. Once you have associated a letter with each digit, you can form words that represent numbers. Thus, the number 13 might be *tam, tome,* or *team* (remember, vowels don't count); the number 21 might be *nut* or *net;* and so on. The next step is simply to form a strong visual image of each of the words that correspond to numbers (1 through 25, for example). Having done so, you can stand on stage and have your audience describe or show you twenty-five items, which are recorded in order by your assistant, on a large chalkboard that remains out of your sight. By forming strong visual associations between each of these items and your number-linked words, you can recall all twenty-five items in any order or any specific item by its number of appearance. For example, if the twenty-first item the audience displays is a shoe, you visualize a shoe caught in a *net* (net representing 21).

This must have some classroom implication. Surely.

METACOGNITION

Young children do not learn these memory strategies as readily as do older children and adults; and they are also far less able to organize material. More than this, they are less aware of the importance of doing so. One of the very important differences between them and older learners is that they are not yet reflective about themselves as knowers; they have not yet recognized the special skills that allow them to extract information, to organize, to learn, and, of course, to remember. Put another way, they know far less about knowing; they understand less about understanding (Flavell, 1985). In the current jargon, they have not yet developed the skills of *metacognition* or **metamemory.**

---

metamemory The knowledge we develop about our own memory processes—our knowledge about how to remember, rather than simply our memories.

Metacognition is our knowledge and beliefs about knowing. Similarly, metamemory involves knowing about remembering. Because knowing necessarily involves remembering, metacognition includes metamemory. As an example, your belief that you can learn and remember better by underlining important parts of this text illustrates metacognition.

It's useful to distinguish between two different aspects of metacognition: personal knowledge and beliefs about cognition itself and the individual's attempts to regulate or control cognitive activity (Baker & Brown, 1984). Thus, your belief about the effectiveness of underlining represents the first aspect of metacognition: knowledge about cognition itself. Your attempt to estimate the difficulty of a chapter or a passage, and your decision about whether it would be best to make notes, to underline, or simply to read illustrates the second aspect of metacognition: your attempt to control your cognitive activity.

The skills of metacognition allow us to monitor our progress when we try to understand and learn something. They provide us with ways of estimating the effects of our efforts, and they allow us to predict the likelihood of being able to remember the material later. Metacognitive knowledge tells us that there are ways to organize material to make it easier to learn and remember, that some rehearsal and review strategies are more effective for one kind of material than another, and that some forms of learning require the deliberate application of specific strategies whereas others do not.

THE DEVELOPMENT OF METACOGNITION

As we noted earlier, metacognitive skills seem to be largely absent in very young children. This does not mean that they make no use of cognitive strategies; it simply means that they are not aware of them and do not apply them consciously. By the same token, they are far less able to monitor, evaluate, and direct their own learning. In most instances, they do not realize that there are strategies that might make it easier to learn and remember. When Moynahan

(1973) asked young children whether it would be easier to learn a categorized list of words or a randomly ordered list, children below third grade chose either list with approximately equal frequency. In contrast, older children almost invariably chose the categorized list; they knew more about knowing.

Among young children, there seems to be a greater spread between memory behavior and memory knowledge, note Borkowski, Milstead, and Hale (1988). For example, when questioned, children may reveal that they know specific learning (memory) strategies—for example, that grouping items makes it easier to remember them. However, when these same children are asked to learn lists of items, they make no use of the grouping strategy.

Specific strategies such as this can be taught to young children (Lawson, 1993, Mayo, 1993). But children also need to be taught when they need to use the strategy. Unfortunately, as Borkowski and associates note, teachers are not often systematic about teaching the strategies of cognition. Instead, children are left to discover them on their own.

THE STRATEGIES OF COGNITION

We appear to have a natural tendency to extract generalities from experience, as well as to learn how to learn and remember. As we learn how to learn, we begin to see ourselves as players of what Flavell (1985) calls the *game of cognition,* and we become aware of an increasing number and variety of strategies that can make us better players of this game. The object of the game of cognition is not to beat someone at something. Winners of this game are those who are successful in making sense of information and who can recall and use it effectively.

Some people play the game of cognition very badly. They learn and remember with difficulty; much that they encounter is bewildering and frustrating. Others play the game extraordinarily well. They learn rapidly and with apparent ease; their understanding is often startling.

One difference between those who play the game of cognition well and those who play it less well may have to do with how clearly each understands the process of learning and remembering—in other words, it has to do with the strategies of cognition. It may be that those who play the game best are those who have learned more about learning and who are better able to apply what they have learned.

Cognitive Strategies Defined. Among other things, the best players of the game of cognition are those who have learned the best strategies and know when to use them. Simply defined, cognitive strategies are the tools of intellectual activity. With respect to school learning, E. Gagné (1985, p. 33) defines cognitive strategies as "goal-directed sequences of cognitive operations that lead from the student's comprehension of a question or instructions to the answer or other requested performance."

Cognitive strategies are what allow us to learn, to solve problems, to study, and to understand. Strategies themselves have little to do with the content of what we learn. They are general, relatively abstract, "contentless" series of tactics or procedures (Gagné & Briggs, 1983).

Historically, most of the teaching (and learning) of cognitive strategies has occurred incidentally, in the course of teaching other things. Recently, however, a number of concerted attempts have been made to develop programs designed specifically to teach cognitive strategies. Several of these programs are reviewed in some detail later in this chapter.

LEARNING/THINKING
STRATEGIES IN EDUCATION

The teaching/learning process has two broad classes of goals, note Weinstein and Mayer (1986): those relating to the *products* of learning and those relating to the *process* of learning. Goals that relate to the products of learning are the *what* of the instructional process—the information being taught. Goals that have to do with the process of learning are the *how* of learning—the skills and strategies that can be used in acquiring and processing content; that is, they deal with learning to learn.

Cognitive psychology's most important current contribution to educational psychology is a renewed emphasis on the second of these major goals: learning to learn. This emphasis is especially evident in education's current attention to cognitive strategies or to what are often labeled **learning/thinking strategies.** The phrase "learning/thinking strategy" is preferred to the "cognitive strategy" for two reasons: It is broader, including specific strategies such as rehearsing or elaborating as well as metacognition; and it emphasizes that the strategies and processes involved in learning to learn are the very same processes that we use in what we ordinarily define as thinking. Put another way, learning/thinking strategies are the learner's information processing/thinking tools.

Classes of Learning/Thinking Strategies. And what, you may ask, are these learning/thinking strategies? Recall from earlier in this chapter that our basic information processing model (the memory model) describes three main processes or activities involved in maintaining material in short-term memory and encoding and transferring it to long-term memory: rehearsal, elaboration, and organization. There are learning strategies, Weinstein and Mayer (1986) tell us, for each of these processes. Some are basic; others are more complex. Accordingly, there are basic rehearsal strategies, complex rehearsal strategies, basic elaboration strategies, complex elaboration strategies, basic organizational strategies, and complex organizational strategies.* And, in addition to these six classes of learning strategies, there are comprehension-monitoring strategies, which are essentially identical to what we have described as metacognitive skills, and affective and motivational strategies, which direct our attention, maintain our interest, and help us to relax and control impediments to learning and thinking (such as test anxiety).

Table 5.3 summarizes these eight classes of learning/thinking strategies and gives a simple example of each.

EDUCATIONAL APPLICATIONS:
TEACHING LEARNERS HOW TO THINK

We saw in Chapter 4 that behavioristic approaches to learning lead to a number of instructional recommendations. Among other things, these approaches emphasize the importance of reinforcement and attempt to sort out the particular kinds and schedules of rewards and punishments that are most effective in the classroom. Later (in Chapter 11, for example), we will see that behaviorism has also led to specific techniques for behavior modification.

At first glance, the educational implications of the cognitive perspective seem quite different from those of behaviorism. After all, cognitivism is concerned much less with behavior, stimuli, rewards, and punishments than with thinking. It asks how children become thinkers and how we can make better, more critical, more creative thinkers of them.

The cognitive perspective suggests a two-pronged answer to these important questions. First, learners must develop an awareness of themselves as thinkers/learners/information processors; second, they must develop and practice the approaches and strategies involved in critical, creative, and effective thinking and problem solving. Put another way, the cognitive perspective argues that learners must develop metacognitive skills as well as appropriate cognitive strategies. These are the skills involved in learning to learn.

---

learning/thinking strategies Processes involved in learning and thinking; another expression for "cognitive strategy," introduced to emphasize that the strategies involved in cognition (knowing) are also involved in learning and thinking.

---

*PPC: Terms such as *cognitive strategies, metacognition, learning/thinking strategies,* and *metacognitive strategies* are used in different ways in the literature. This can be very confusing. Maybe the bear could straighten things out, once and for all.

AUTHOR: Perhaps not once and for all, but for the time being, see the box entitled, "Sorting It All Out Cognitively."

TABLE 5.3 CATEGORIES OF LEARNING/THINKING STRATEGIES

BASIC REHEARSAL STRATEGIES	Simple repetition: "hablo, hablas, habla, hablamos, hablais, hablan"
COMPLEX REHEARSAL STRATEGIES	Highlighting all the important points in a text
BASIC ELABORATION STRATEGIES	Forming mental images or other associations such as "*men very easily make jugs serve useful nocturnal purposes*" (the first letter of each word stands for a planet in the solar system)
COMPLEX ELABORATION STRATEGIES	Forming analogies, paraphrasing, summarizing, relating
BASIC ORGANIZATIONAL STRATEGIES	Grouping, classifying, ordering
COMPLEX ORGANIZATIONAL STRATEGIES	Identifying main ideas; developing concept-summarizing tables such as this one
COMPREHENSION-MONITORING STRATEGIES	Self-questioning; reciting main points; setting goals and checking progress toward those goals
AFFECTIVE AND MOTIVATIONAL STRATEGIES	Anticipating consequences of academic success (for example, a scholarship); deep breathing and other relaxation activities; positive thinking

Source: Based on C. E. Weinstein and R. E. Mayer, "The Teaching of Learning Strategies." In M. C. Wittrock (ed.), *Handbook of Research on Teaching* (3rd ed.). New York: Macmillan, 1986, 315–327.

As we noted earlier, schools have traditionally devoted the bulk of their formal efforts to teaching specific curriculum content; the learning of cognitive strategies and the development of metacognitive awareness have been largely incidental—and sometimes accidental. But the best learners, argue Alexander and Judy (1988), are those who possess *strategic* as well as domain-specific (content) knowledge. Strategic knowledge deals with how to do things: how to solve problems, how to learn and memorize, how to understand, and perhaps most important, how to monitor, evaluate, and direct these activities as they occur. In other words, strategic knowledge is *metacognitive* knowledge.

Recently, an increasing number of researchers have developed programs designed specifically to develop cognitive skills in learners. Many of these programs are designed both to make students aware of the existence of cognitive strategies and to teach them to monitor and evaluate their use of these strategies. Such programs advocate a variety of approaches to teaching, including group learning (for example, cooperative learning), individual instruction (for example, teachers' questions designed to foster specific thinking skills), modeling procedures (in which, for example, a cognitive strategy is verbalized as it is being executed), and various programs in which learners are trained in the use of specific strategies (see, for example, Mulcahy et al., 1990). The main objective that these programs share is to develop in learners metacognitive knowledge—knowledge that allows children to learn how to learn.

LEARNING HOW TO LEARN: CHANGING VIEWS

Learning how to learn in schools is not entirely new. What is new is our attitude toward what it is that makes learning difficult or easy. Traditionally, we have simply assumed that the most important factor in learning is inherited or natural intelligence—recognizing, of course, that motivation, persistence, and other similar factors are important as well. Recently, however,

SORTING IT ALL OUT COGNITIVELY

The following are some common, educationally relevant terms in the new cognitive sciences:

Metacognition Knowing about knowing; our knowledge and beliefs about our own cognitive processes and our attempt to play the game of cognition well—that is, so that we learn and remember well. Metacognitive knowledge is what permits us to select different approaches for learning and remembering; it allows us to monitor our cognitive activities and assess the likelihood of success; it suggests alternatives when necessary.

Cognitive Strategies The tools of cognitive behavior; goal-directed sequences of actions such as rehearsing, organizing, or elaborating; what we actually do to learn and remember.

Learning/Thinking Strategies A global term that includes both metacognition and cognitive strategies. The entire range of activities involved in learning and thinking.

Summary Learning/thinking strategies include metacognitive and cognitive strategies. Metacognitive skills are executive (control) skills; cognitive skills are nonexecutive (applied) skills.

Illustration of the Relationships Between Metacognition and Cognition I decide to learn the meanings of common, educationally relevant terms in the new cognitive sciences (setting a goal of which I suspect I am capable: a metacognitive experience). I begin to read this box (cognitive activity). I stop after two lines; I have a vague feeling that I have missed something (metacognitive experience). I read the lines again (cognitive activity). I sense that I am understanding (metacognition). I continue reading. I repeat each separate definition mentally once or twice (rehearsal, a cognitive strategy). Something tells me I am learning (metacognitive experience). I finish. I look at each term and silently repeat the definition (cognitive activity). I am satisfied that I understand and will remember until tomorrow's quiz (metacognition).

---

our conceptions of intelligence have begun to change dramatically. We have begun to accept the view that among the important components of intelligent activity are cognitive functions that are largely learned, not inherited.

Haywood and Switzky (1986) make a similar point. Intelligent behavior, they assert, requires two things: native ability (what we think of as innate intelligence) and cognitive functions. The important point is that whereas native ability is, by definition, genetic and therefore unmodifiable except by extreme measures, cognitive functions are acquired. Does it not follow that if they are learned, they can also be taught?

The simple answer is yes. And there is increasing evidence that this learning need not occur only incidentally—or even accidentally—as a byproduct of school activities, the purposes of which are far removed from teaching students how to learn. A mushrooming new field of research involves looking for ways in which students can be taught not only the cognitive skills of rehearsing, elaborating, and organizing but also the metacognitive skills involved in monitoring their own levels of comprehension and in making other important decisions about their cognitive activities and their personal capabilities. Psychologists have been increasingly successful at discovering the rules, the strategies, and the objectives of this game of cognition that all of us are called upon to play. And, as a result, today's students may be far better players tomorrow than they would otherwise have been.

Researchers who have developed and investigated programs designed specifically to teach students how to learn and think have emphasized a variety of skills. Nickerson's (1988) review suggests that there have been at least seven identifiable emphases:

1. Basic operations such as classifying or generalizing

2. Domain-specific knowledge (for example, mathematical functions or history)

3. Knowledge about reasoning principles (for example, logic)

4. Knowledge about informal principles of thinking that might be used in problem solving

5. Metacognitive knowledge—that is, learners' beliefs about their own learning, as well as their attempts to monitor and control their cognitive activities

6. Values such as fairness and objectivity

7. Personal beliefs (for example, about problems, about the world, about causes, and about the role of luck and effort)

These different emphases have led to the development of a variety of programs for teaching thinking. These programs typically take one of two forms: *stand-alone,* in which cognitive skills are taught as a separate subject, and *embedded,* in which cognitive skills are taught within the context of subject matter. A third approach described by Prawat (1991), *immersion,* places more emphasis on ideas than on skills and processes but is much like an embedded approach. Several illustrative programs are described in the sections that follow; there are others. Note that these are complex and highly developed programs that cannot be explained thoroughly in a few paragraphs so that they can then be used by a beginning teacher. Their implementation generally requires a more detailed study of the approaches and often involves in-service training and workshops. At the same time, however, these summaries suggest a number of specific teaching strategies that can be useful by themselves.

Dansereau's Metastrategies. For example, Dansereau and his associates have developed a stand-alone program designed to teach some general cognitive strategies to college students (Dansereau, 1985). These strategies apply mainly to verbal learning and are divided into two groups: primary and support strategies.

Primary strategies are information processing skills for learning, storing and retrieving, and deriving meaning from textual material. They consist of such activities as using visual imagery, summarizing, paraphrasing, analyzing questions, and using context to facilitate recall. Support strategies are involved in maintaining an appropriate mind-set for learning and remembering. They include such metacognitive activities as setting goals, arranging schedules, monitoring comprehension, and self-evaluation.

A general program for studying devised by Dansereau and his associates is based directly on their analysis of what they term *metastrategies* (strategies of metacognition). It is called MURDER, an acronym for the following sequential procedure: set your *m*ood, read for *u*nderstanding, *r*ecall, *d*igest information (a procedure that involves recalling correctly, rehearsing, organizing, and storing), *e*xpand knowledge (involves elaboration through a process of self-inquiry), and *r*eview mistakes. MURDER is a somewhat more complex process than this brief description might imply. For example, a number of specific tactics are taught and practiced in connection with each of the major steps in the program (relaxation techniques associated with mood-setting and imaging strategies associated with recall, for example). Studies of this program at the college level have generally shown increases in measures of cognitive functioning.

Feuerstein's Instrumental Enrichment. In practice, intelligence is most often assessed in terms of performance on tests that reveal how much a person has benefited from past experience. According to Reuven Feuerstein (1979), whose work is primarily on the topic of mental retardation, such tests represent a static rather than a dynamic view of intelligence: They reveal what the child has done rather than what the child can do in the future. They do not assess learning potential.

More useful measures of intelligence, Feuerstein argues, would do more than reflect what the child has done in the past; they would provide some estimate of capacity for benefiting from future experience. To this end, he has developed the **Learning Potential Assessment Device (LPAD),** which focuses on intellectual functioning—on cognitive processes—rather than simply on whether the child can answer correctly within a given time limit. The test allows the examiner to actually teach the child, to offer hints and clues, and to direct and help. Described as a dynamic rather than a static measure, it makes it possible both to identify strengths and detect absent or deficient cognitive functions. In Feuerstein's (1980) terms, it permits the construction of a "cognitive map" of the learner, which can serve as the basis for analyzing the cognitive functioning of what he calls "retarded performers" and as a blueprint for remediation.

Among Feuerstein's greatest contributions is the development of a complex and far-reaching series of activities and exercises designed to improve cognitive functioning. This program, **Feuerstein's Instrumental Enrichment (FIE),** is based squarely on the assumption that motivates all the learning-to-learn research: a strong belief in cognitive modifiability.

A logical outgrowth of the LPAD, the FIE program is largely content-free; that is, it attempts to teach cognitive functioning rather than academic content. It is a clear example of a stand-alone program.

Learning Potential Assessment Device (LPAD)
Feuerstein's measure of intelligence, developed to provide a *dynamic* rather than passive measure of intelligence—a measure of how the child can profit from experience rather than simply a measure of the effects of past experiences. Assessment procedures allow the examiner to coach, to provide hints and clues, to direct, and to help.

Feuerstein's Instrumental Enrichment (FIE) A detailed and comprehensive program designed to teach cognitive strategies and to make learners more aware of their own strategies.

The FIE program uses a series of progressively more abstract paper-and-pencil exercises designed to help students identify strategies used in thinking and to encourage them to become aware of their use of those strategies. In all, there are more than five hundred pages of exercises—enough for a 1-hour daily lesson over the course of several years.

Even though the FIE program was initially developed for use with "retarded performers" (Feuerstein deliberately avoids the term *mental retardation*), he argues that its principles are applicable to a wide range of ages and subjects. Use of the FIE program requires that teachers be specially trained.

Initial evaluation of the FIE materials involved a longitudinal experiment in which performance-retarded adolescents exposed to the FIE program were compared with similar adolescents in a more conventional, content-oriented enrichment program. Results were highly positive (Feuerstein, 1980).

Subsequent research in a number of countries, including Canada, the United States, Venezuela, and Israel, has been summarized by Savell, Twohig, and Rachford (1986). Although many of the studies they reviewed do not report clearly positive results—usually because of experiment-design inadequacies (such as lack of a control group) or shortcomings in applying the program—they nevertheless conclude that FIE has generally positive results. The most commonly reported cognitive gains are on non-verbal measures of intelligence and involve students between 12 and 18 years old. Teachers in the most successful FIE programs had typically been given at least one week of training before the program, and students who were most likely to gain had been exposed to a minimum of eighty hours of FIE instruction. Gains were most likely to occur when FIE had been taught in conjunction with subjects of significant interest and importance to students.

One of the major contributions of the LPAD and of Instrumental Enrichment, notes Feuerstein (1994), is reflected in the view that intelligence is the propensity to change and to adapt—in contrast to the view that intelligence is a relatively fixed and largely inherited quality. Hence the emphasis on assessment procedures that require adaptation and that attempt to facilitate it. Hence, too, the development of instructional methods designed specifically to enhance cognitive functioning and, by definition, intelligence.

SPELT. Another large-scale cognitive program is Mulcahy and associates' Strategies Program for Effective Learning/Thinking (SPELT) (Mulcahy et al., 1986; Marfo et al., 1991). Described as a learning/thinking instructional program, SPELT is designed for use with all children—from learning disabled to gifted. Like the Dansereau program, it focuses on cognitive processes rather than content; and unlike Dansereau's metastrategies, it is aimed at elementary and junior high school students rather than adolescents or college students. A second important difference between SPELT and the Dansereau program is that SPELT is an embedded rather than a stand-alone program. Embedded programs have the advantage of being more relevant to students and are more easily applied because they are part of the regular curriculum. In addition, because they don't require a separate classroom period, they are less expensive and easier to schedule than stand-alone programs (Derry & Murphy, 1986).

SPELT has three major characteristics. First, its overriding goal is to involve students actively in the learning process. It attempts to make students increasingly aware of their own cognitive processes and is geared toward discovery rather than reception learning.

Second, SPELT requires active teacher participation in identifying and discovering strategies as well as in devising methods for teaching them. Initially, teachers are presented with tested strategies and methods; after continuing in-service training, they are encouraged to develop their own.

Third, SPELT is designed to encourage students to recognize and generate their own cognitive strategies; that is, students are expected to become increasingly aware of their own intellectual processes and to become actively involved in developing and improving these processes. In short, they are encouraged to recognize and develop the tools they use in playing the game of cognition. The main objective of SPELT, says Mulcahy (1991), is to develop autonomous learners—learners who have truly learned how to learn, who are in control of their own "cognitive as well as affective resources and activities" (p. 385).

The learning/thinking strategies developed and emphasized in SPELT cover a vast range—for example, general problem solving, math and reading strategies, memory strategies, study skills, test-taking strategies, mood-setting strategies, and general metacognitive strategies such as comprehension monitoring. In addition, special effort is made to develop social problem-solving strategies.

Implementation of SPELT occurs in three overlapping phases. In the first phase, students are taught a number of learning/thinking strategies by teachers trained in using and teaching these strategies. Instructional procedures in this phase are direct and teacher controlled. Their basic elements include motivating students, modeling the strategies, providing memorization and practice drills with feedback, and evaluating students' learning. The goal of this phase, as expressed by Peat, Mulcahy, and Darko-Yeboah (1989), is "metacognitive empowerment"—a condition that comes about as students become increasingly aware of the existence of cognitive strategies and of the contribution their systematic use can make to learning and problem solving.

The objectives of the second phase are to maintain the use of strategies learned in the first phase, to begin to evaluate the effectiveness of these strategies, and to modify and extend them to different content areas. The principal instructional method is no longer one of direct tuition but rather one of facilitating the application of previously learned strategies to new situations (teaching for transfer). The instructional method is now Socratic rather than direct; that is, students are encouraged to extend and apply strategies through an interactive question-and-answer process. Among the teacher's guidelines for questioning are the following (with illustrations) (Mulcahy et al., 1990):

- *Start with what is known.* (What strategy did you find useful when you read the material in the box? [student response has to do with underlining material and reviewing it])
- *Ask for more than one reason.* (Why? . . . Can you think of any other reasons why underlining and reviewing are useful?)
- *Ask students to describe steps in their reasoning processes.* (What were you doing that made this strategy useful? What did you do next? What did you think as you tried to review?)
- *Formulate general rules from specific cases.* (Could you use underlining and reviewing for reading other things? With what sorts of material do you think it would help you?)
- *Provide counterexamples when student overgeneralizes.* (Do you think underlining and reviewing would be useful when you're watching a video?)
- *Probe for differences among cases.* (Underlining and reviewing is a useful strategy for some written material; how is it different from, say, highlighting and rehearsing a multiplication table?)
- *Ask students to make predictions.* (Do you think you understand the box better after underlining and reviewing? Do you think you'll do better on the test?)

In the third phase of the SPELT program, the learner is encouraged to generate new cognitive strategies and to monitor and evaluate them. The principal instructional method continues to be that of Socratic dialogue. In contrast with the first phase, learning at this level is largely student rather than teacher controlled.

The SPELT program was evaluated during a three-year project involving some nine hundred gifted, average, and learning-disabled students in grades 4, 5, 7, and 8. Results were positive, especially for learning-disabled students and most notably at the fourth-grade level, at which reading comprehension and comprehension-monitoring skills improved most dramatically. Gifted students also benefited significantly. Use and awareness of cognitive strategies improved at all grade levels and for all groups. In addition, parents, teachers, and administrators responded favorably to the program. A year after termination of the experimental project, more than 85 percent of the teachers reported that they continued to use aspects of the program in their teaching.

Reciprocal Teaching. Palincsar and Brown (1984) describe an instructional technique designed to teach students how to think and understand specifically with respect to what they read. In **reciprocal teaching,** students are taught four cognitive strategies for increasing reading comprehension: generating questions, summarizing, attempting to clarify word meanings and confusing text, and predicting what will happen next. In the early stages, teachers help students with each of these strategies, modeling and illustrating them with various examples of written text. As students systematically practice the strategies, teachers help them with hints, feedback, additional modeling, and explanations. In the course of this guided practice, students are encouraged to ask questions, comment on each other's predictions, ask for clarification, and help clear up misunderstandings. Gradually, teachers do less and less of the work as students do more. Eventually, the procedure becomes a little like a cooperative instructional approach as one student asks questions, a second answers, a third comments on the answer, another elaborates, and so on. Note, however, that reciprocal teaching does not involve work in groups, as do other cooperative approaches (see Chapter 9 for a description of cooperative teaching). Rather, it is a cognitive strategies instructional program, specifically designed for developing strategies useful for increasing reading comprehension.

---

reciprocal teaching Instructional technique that involves teaching four cognitive strategies for increasing reading comprehension: generating questions, summarizing, clarifying word meanings and confusing text, predicting what will happen next.

A number of studies have reported highly positive results following experimental applications of reciprocal teaching, both with normal children (for example, Garner, 1992) and with children who have reading disabilities (Bruer, 1993). Rosenshine and Meister (1994) reviewed sixteen studies on reciprocal teaching. They concluded, "When experimenter-developed comprehension tests were used, students in the reciprocal teaching treatment had scores that were significantly superior to those of the control group in 8 of 10 studies" (p. 505).

A CONCLUSION

Dansereau's metastrategies, Feuerstein's FIE, Mulcahy and associates' SPELT, and Palincsar and Brown's reciprocal teaching are only a few of a large number of learning/thinking programs being developed, modified, and evaluated (see, for example, Nickerson, 1988).* Two things seem clear at this point: First, our attempts to teach students how to think and how to learn are not always as deliberate and as focused as they might be; and second, systematic programs can significantly improve learning and thinking for a variety of individuals and in many different contexts (Turner, 1993; Ashman, Wright, & Conway, 1994).

The foregoing should not be taken to suggest that teachers who do not use systematic programs for teaching their students thinking/ learning skills are failing to meet their responsibilities. As Marzano (1993) points out, many classroom teachers use a variety of strategies and techniques to promote cognitive skills, even if these aren't always entirely systematic— strategies that include various sorts of questioning as well as a variety of exercises designed to encourage learners to analyze, match, encode, and otherwise become aware of and improve their information processing.

Although it would clearly be premature to suggest that teachers should now begin using this or that program for this or that purpose, it is not at all premature to repeat many education critics' claim that the schools have not always done much to teach thinking and learning skills. The contemporary cognitive sciences are based on the assumption that much more can be done. They have also begun showing us how.

---

*PPC: I don't think the author provides enough information for students to actually be able to go out and use any of these programs with their classes.

AUTHOR: True. In fact, using most of these approaches requires systematic training, often by way of workshops and other in-service programs. Knowing *about* them is nevertheless very important for teachers who, otherwise, would not likely make the effort to study them in more detail. In addition, there may be a significant benefit simply in accepting that teaching students *how to learn* is an important function of schools, and in knowing that there are systematic ways in which this can be accomplished.

MAIN POINTS

1. The main emphasis of cognitive psychology is on the mental events involved in knowing, acquiring information, solving problems, and remembering. Cognitive psychology looks at three things: knowledge base (the learner's storehouse of information), cognitive strategies (processes used in learning and thinking), and metacognition (awareness of the self as a knower and capacity to understand and monitor cognitive processes).

2. Computers, especially the branch dealing with artificial intelligence, present a useful model (metaphor) for human cognitive functioning. A second model describes the learner as a three-level information processing and storage system in which the levels are labeled "sensory memory," "short-term memory," and "long-term memory."

3. Sensory storage is the immediate, unconscious, momentary availability of sensory data for processing, lasting only a fraction of a second.

4. Material to which we pay attention is processed into short-term (working) memory, where it is maintained for perhaps as long as 20 seconds, providing it is rehearsed. Short-term memory capacity is seven (plus or minus two) items, some of which might include chunks of related material. Young children's sensory memories are limited to two or three items before age 6.

5. Material is transferred from short-term to long-term memory through encoding (transforming or changing to abstract generalities and deriving meaning). Encoding involves three processes: rehearsal (repetition), elaboration (extending), and organization (relating, sorting). Long-term memory might be declarative (conscious; explicit) or nondeclarative (implicit; unconscious). Declarative memory might be semantic (general, verbalizable knowledge) or episodic (personal, autobiographical knowledge).

6. Theories of forgetting maintain that information is forgotten because it is unused, distorted, repressed, or interfered with or because the individual has a poor retrieval system. These theories suggest that teachers should both emphasize distinct and important aspects of situations and stress similarities and differences in order to minimize interference and maximize transfer.

7. Mnemonic devices include rhymes, patterns, acrostics, and acronyms. More complex mnemonic techniques are the link system, the loci system, and the phonetic system. Each of these is based on the principle that visual imagery is an extremely powerful aid to memory. Useful strategies for teaching for retrieval emphasize meaningfulness, organization, visual imagery, and rehearsal.

8. As we learn about things (facts, problem-solving techniques, and so on), we also learn about learning. Knowledge about our own cognitive processes is metacognition. The skills of metacognition allow us to direct, monitor, evaluate, and modify our ongoing learning and thinking.

9. Cognitive (learning/thinking) strategies are the tools of cognitive behavior. Weinstein and Mayer describe eight classes of learning/thinking strategies: the first six are rehearsal, elaboration, and organizational strategies for either basic or complex problems; the last two are comprehension-monitoring strategies (strategies of metacognition) and affective (motivational) strategies.

10. Cognitivism asks how children become thinkers and how we can make better, more critical, more creative thinkers of them. Part of its answer is by making them aware of themselves as knowers and information processors (metacognitive skills) and by teaching them specific cognitive strategies (for example, how to rehearse, organize, monitor, and so on).

11. Dansereau's metastrategies program for teaching thinking is a stand-alone approach (separate from ordinary curriculum content) that attempts to teach primary strategies (those used for learning, storing, and retrieving) and support strategies (those involved in maintaining mindset for learning) to college populations. MURDER (*m*ood, *u*nderstand, *r*ecall, *d*igest, *e*xpand, *r*eview) is a Dansereau metastrategy.

12. Feuerstein's Instrumental Enrichment (FIE) program is based on the Learning Potential Assessment Device (LPAD), which attempts to assess the retarded performer's highest potential for achievement. It consists of paper-and-pencil exercises to develop cognitive strategies and was

developed primarily for adolescents with performance deficits (below-average intelligence or normal intelligence with learning disabilities or cognitive deficiencies).

13. The Strategies Program for Effective Learning/Thinking (SPELT), developed by Mulcahy and associates, is an embedded program (designed for use within the context of ordinary curriculum) for elementary and junior high school students. It encourages teachers and students to identify and generate cognitive strategies in a variety of areas (general problem solving, social problem solving, math, reading, studying, test-taking, mood-setting, and general metacognitive strategies).

14. Palincsar and Brown's reciprocal teaching attempts to develop strategies for increasing reading comprehension by having students eventually assume responsibility for helping one another.

APPLIED QUESTIONS

▶ What are some of the most important metaphors of cognitive theory?

▶ Compare and contrast sensory memory, short-term memory, and long-term memory using school-based examples.

▶ Can you outline an educational implication related to each of the characteristics of short-term and long-term memory?

▶ Describe one educational implication for each of the common theories of forgetting.

▶ Describe and illustrate one or more mnemonic system.

▶ What would you include in a basic program designed to teach students how to think?

STUDY TERMS

artificial intelligence (AI) **158**
chunking **162**
cocktail party phenomenon **160**
cognitive strategies **159**
cognitivism **157**
concept **157**
declarative memory **166**
echoic memory **160**
eidetic imagery **162**
elaboration **167**
encoding **164**
episodic memory **166**
explicit memory **166**
fading theory **170**
Feuerstein's Instrumental Enrichment (FIE) **181**

forgetting **170**
iconic memory **160**
implicit memory **166**
information processing (IP) **158**
knowledge base **158**
Learning Potential Assessment Device (LPAD) **181**
learning/thinking strategy **177**
levels of processing **165**
link system **173**
loci system **174**
long-term memory **160**
memory **159**
mental structure **157**
metamemory **175**

mnemonic devices **172**
nondeclarative memory **166**
organization **168**
phonetic system **174**
proactive inhibition **171**
processing **160**
reciprocal teaching **183**
rehearsal **167**
retrieval cue failure **171**
retroactive inhibition **171**
semantic memory **166**
sensory memory **160**
short-term memory **159**
short-term sensory storage **160**
working memory **160**

SUGGESTED READINGS

The following book is a clear and detailed description of contemporary cognitive psychology and its implications for education. The authors look not only at human information processing and knowledge acquisition, but also at the application of cognitive science in specific subject areas like reading, writing, mathematics, and science:

GAGNÉ, E. D., YEKOVICH, C. W., & YEKOVICH, F. R. (1993). *The cognitive psychology of school learning.* New York: HarperCollins.

A very practical, classroom-oriented book that looks at how teachers can help students become more thoughtful is

BARELL, J. (1991). *Teaching for thoughtfulness: Classroom strategies to enhance intellectual development.* New York: Longman.

The following two books present useful descriptions of how children learn science and how schools and teachers can make use of cognitive psychology in teaching science:

FENSHAM, P. J., GUNSTONE, R. F., & WHITE, R. T. (eds.) (1994). *The content of science: A constructivist approach to its teaching and learning.* Washington, D.C.: Falmer.

BLACK, P. J., & LUCAS, A. M. (eds.) (1993). *Children's informal ideas in science.* New York: Routledge.

A highly readable, informative, and practical discussion of memory and mnemonic aids is provided in

HIGBEE, K. L. (1977). *Your memory: How it works and how to improve it.* Englewood Cliffs, N.J.: Prentice-Hall.

The Eskimo believe that the soul of a wounded bear tarries near the spot where it leaves its body. Many taboos and propitiatory ceremonies are observed with regard to the slaughtering of the carcass and the consumption of the flesh (Engel, 1976, p. 69).

CHAPTER 6

Some folks are wise, and some are otherwise.
TOBIAS SMOLLETT, *Roderick Random*

If a little knowledge is dangerous, where is the man who has so much as to be out of danger?

THOMAS HENRY HUXLEY, *Science and Culture*

Cognitive Instructional Models

PREVIEW

Decision making, problem solving, analyzing, synthesizing, evaluating, remembering—these are all cognitive or intellectual functions. Understanding them is the goal of cognitive theories. And a number of these theories are especially important for education because they lead to clear and highly explicit instructional recommendations and models. This chapter looks at three such theories: Robert Gagné's theory, which advocates the deliberate arrangement of events in order to facilitate and support learning; Jerome Bruner's theory, which argues for discovery-oriented learning; and David Ausubel's strong case for a more didactic approach to teaching. The merits of each are examined.

▶ What are the processes or events that define what Gagné terms an "act of learning"?

▶ What are some of the conditions that facilitate learning through discovery?

▶ What are some conditions that foster reception learning?

▶ What is cognitive apprenticeship?

▶ What does research say are the best ways of teaching?

They never did call me *"Faces the Bear"* when I was growing up. But then, they didn't call me *"Horseface"* either.

Still, I continue to dream of bears—or, more often, of *the* bear, the one who rears up in front of me in my dream, his paws clawing uncertainly at the air as though fending off some unseen enemy. He still smells as he did in the dreams of my childhood, and his power is unmistakable—the power of which John George's grandmother spoke. But I cannot tell whether he is angry. It is not clear whether he will kill, or whether he will heal. Sometimes I think he is just sad, that he is perhaps a little overwhelmed.

I let the bear into the first edition of this book more as a distraction than as an inspiration. I had thought he might make your reading and studying easier and that, perhaps, he might bring some wisdom with him. I thought, too, that he might go away after the first edition, and that I could then rest from that dream.

But he has not gone away. And sometimes the dream of the bear comes not in the stillness of the night, but instead in the stillness of the woods when I am wide awake. It has become a waking dream.

There was a time in my early childhood when I began to fear the bear. Although even then I think I knew that he would not hurt me, I could not still the hammering of my heart when I found his tracks on the edge of the river, or when I saw where he had clawed through a fallen log, drawn to the acid smell of the ants.

My fear was at least partly the magic of behaviorism, a conditioning phenomenon.

But now when I see the bear in a waking dream, when, fully awake, I let him walk through my mind, I can change the direction of his travels at my whim. With only the slightest twisting of my thoughts, I can make of myself a man so cunning and so brave that none dare call me anything but *"Faces the Bear."* And in the same instant, using the same magic, I can now send the bear chasing after wild cows at *my* whim, not his. And that is a cognitive magic, no longer a behavioristic one.*

THE CONDITIONS OF LEARNING AND INSTRUCTION: GAGNÉ'S THEORY

Robert Gagné presents a theory of learning that is both behavioristic and cognitive. It's a theory that incorporates many of the principles of behavioristic learning theories. But it is also fundamentally a cognitive theory based squarely on the basic information processing/memory model described in the last chapter. That is, it looks at how learners process and store information in long-term memory, and at how information can then be retrieved.

THE UNDERLYING COGNITIVE THEORY

The learning sequence described by contemporary cognitive theory may be summarized as follows, says Gagné (Gagné, Briggs, & Wager, 1992): Stimulation affects the learner's sense receptors and, in the absence of further processing, is available only for fractions of seconds—sort of like an echo on the sensory register. But with the learner's focused attention, a process Gagné labels **selective perception,** information

---

*PPC: Does the author want us to believe all this about dreams?
AUTHOR: Yes, the author does, thank you.

---

selective perception Gagné's term for the process of paying attention to sensory stimulation so that it becomes available in sensory (working) memory for immediate use (like a phone number) or for further processing and long-term storage.

is stored briefly in short-term memory where it remains in consciousness as long as it is rehearsed. In a succeeding stage, material might be changed again through a process of **semantic encoding**—that is, through a process of according the material *meaning*—following which it is then stored in long-term memory. Various search and retrieval procedures may then allow the learner to recall this information from long-term storage when it is relevant for behavior. And another process, termed *response organization* by Gagné, may serve to combine and modify retrieved information and use it in guiding behavior.

To summarize, Gagné describes nine distinct processes or events that occur during what he refers to as *an act of learning* (Gagné, Briggs, & Wager, 1992, p. 11):

► Reception of stimuli
► Registration of information by sensory registers
► Selective perception or attending and momentary storage in short-term memory (STM)
► Rehearsal that maintains information in STM
► Semantic encoding that transfers information to long-term memory (LTM)
► Retrieval from LTM
► Response generation
► Actual performance by the learner
► Use of strategies to control all of these processes

This information processing/memory model is illustrated in Figure 6.1. As we noted, it's essentially identical to the general information processing model described in the preceding chapter and closely associated with the development of cognitive psychology. But Gagné's use of the model is far more practical, far more instructionally oriented, than that of most other cognitive theorists. His goal is not

so much to describe human learning in an abstract sense, but rather to describe very specifically the conditions under which learning occurs and the most effective instructional procedures for it to occur. In effect, explains Gagné, instruction is simply the manipulation of the *conditions of learning*.

THE CONDITIONS OF LEARNING

Learning, notes Gagné, is a multifaceted phenomenon. Very often it involves reinforcement, repetition, contiguity, and other *external* conditions that have been extensively investigated by behavioristic psychologists. But it can also involve a variety of other *internal* conditions. These conditions are evident in the learner's state of mind (Gagné, Briggs, & Wager, 1992). They are defined by such things as the learner's motivation and goals, as well as in terms of previous learning. If instruction is to be as effective as it can be, teachers need to take into consideration all of the internal as well as the external **conditions of learning.** Instruction can then be tailored specifically for given subjects and

---

semantic encoding The process of assigning or discovering meaningfulness. A largely verbal process involved in transferring information from short-term to long-term memory.

conditions of learning Robert Gagné's expression for the internal and external circumstances that affect behavior as well as information processing and retrieval. External conditions of learning might include factors such as repetition, reinforcement, stimulus intensity, and so on; internal conditions include motivation, goals, and previously learned capabilities.

Structure	Process

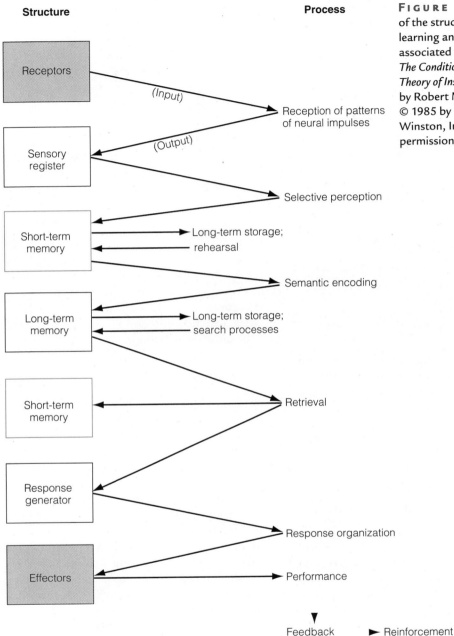

FIGURE 6.1 Gagné's theory of the structures of cognitive learning and the processes associated with them. From *The Conditions of Learning and Theory of Instruction,* (4th ed.) by Robert M. Gagné. Copyright © 1985 by Holt, Rinehart & Winston, Inc. Reproduced with permission of the publisher.

learners. Psychology's responsibility is to clarify for the teacher what the various possible outcomes of the learning process are (that is, what sorts of things can be learned) and to describe the external and internal conditions that are associated with effective learning with respect to each of these outcomes.

THE EVENTS OF INSTRUCTION

To simplify somewhat, a careful examination of the learning model summarized in Figure 6.1 leads Gagné to suggest that there are nine distinct instructional activities or events that teachers need to employ:

- Stimulating to gain attention—given that stimulation to which the learner is not attending will not be available beyond a fraction of a second
- Informing learners of the objectives of instruction so that they develop appropriate expectations
- Reminding learners of relevant previously learned material
- Presenting material clearly and distinctly
- Guiding learning by guiding semantic encoding
- Eliciting learner performance that uses new learning
- Providing feedback about learning
- Assessing the learner's performance (and the effectiveness of instruction)
- Arranging for future practice to aid retention and generalization

THE OUTCOMES OF LEARNING

The goals of the instructional process are to bring about new learning, new capabilities. There are five major domains of such learned capabilities, says Gagné (1985): intellectual skills, verbal information, attitudes, motor skills, and cognitive strategies. These five domains represent, in effect, all the possible outcomes of the learning process. The practical usefulness of Gagné's instructional theory derives largely from his analysis of the conditions most conducive to learning the capabilities represented by each of the five domains. Knowledge of these conditions can be valuable in suggesting appropriate instructional strategies. Accordingly, each of these categories is described in the sections that follow, together with the conditions believed to be conducive to their learning.

intellectual skills Robert Gagné's term for the outcomes of the learning process. He describes seven such skills ranging from simple conditioned responses to abstract problem solving.

Intellectual Skills. Intellectual skills correspond to the *how* of learning; the other four major domains (verbal information, cognitive strategies, attitudes, and motor skills) are more closely related to the *what* of learning. In one sense, intellectual skills are the outcomes of the simple learning processes described earlier (classical and operant conditioning, for example); they also include more complex outcomes, such as the learning of discriminations, rules, and concepts. They include all of the skills that are involved in acquiring information, solving problems, discovering rules, and learning how to learn, among other things. As such, intellectual skills cannot be learned simply by being looked up, studied, and memorized. Instead they have to be learned, remembered, and applied in appropriate situations.

Gagné distinguishes among eight different types of intellectual skills, the first four of which are lumped together as *simple types of learning*. In order from simplest to most complex, the other four categories are *discriminations, concepts, rules,* and *higher-order rules* (Gagné & Dick, 1983). Definitions and examples of each of these types of intellectual skills follow, along with a description of the conditions most clearly associated with their acquisition:

Simple Types of Learning. These include outcomes such as classical or operant conditioning, as well as the linking of sequences of verbal or motor responses in what are termed **chains.** One example is that of a child learning to count, "one, two, three, four . . ." The counting sequence is a verbal chain in which each response serves as a stimulus for the next

chains A term used by Robert Gagné to signify the learning of related sequences of responses. A chain is a series of stimulus–response bonds in that each response in the sequence serves as a stimulus for the next response. Motor chains are involved in my keyboarding of this material. In a sense, it's as though when I type Y-O-U, the stimulus Y leads to the response of depressing the "Y" key, which is now a signal (stimulus) that leads to the next response (pressing "O"), and so on.

response in the chain. The conditions most clearly associated with these simple types of learning relate to the manipulation of stimuli as well as to the consequences of behavior (rewards and punishment).

Discrimination Learning: This is learning to discriminate among highly similar stimulus input. Discrimination learning is "essentially a matter of establishing numbers of different chains," says Gagné (1965, p. 115). For example, when learning a second language, the learner acquires a large number of verbal chains that must then be differentiated from chains in the first language that have the same meaning.

As a second example of discrimination learning in schools, consider the task of teaching students to discriminate between the letters *p* and *b*. One of the conditions necessary for discrimination learning is the presence of the related individual sequences of responses (chains). In this case, these consist of the students' being able to say "pee" or "bee." Also, the individual chains must be repeated and reinforced, and distinctions among them must be highlighted. For example, the teacher might draw attention to the most obvious differences between the two letters and might also invent certain mnemonics that highlight these differences (for example, *b* looks like a boot and is also the first letter of that word).

Discrimination learning is prevalent in much school learning. Among other things, it is involved in learning to make different responses to printed letters, numbers, or words, in learning to differentiate among classes of things, and in learning to identify similar objects.

Concept Learning. Although discrimination learning and concept learning both involve responding to similarities and differences, discrimination is concerned more with differences, whereas concept learning is concerned mainly with detecting similarities. At a simple level, a concept is a notion or an idea that reflects the common characteristics of related events or objects. R. Gagné suggests that repeated experience with situations and events that present exam-

ples of the concept in question is one of the important external conditions that facilitate the learning of concepts. As an illustration, he describes a simple procedure whereby a child can be taught the meaning of the concept *odd.* The procedure involves presenting the child with a series of three objects; two are identical, the other is odd. The procedure continues with a variety of groups of objects and might involve placing a tangible reward (candy, for example) under the odd object or simply reinforcing the child verbally for selecting correctly. Subsequently, the teacher verifies the child's grasp of the concept by asking for additional examples.

The importance of concept learning can hardly be overemphasized. Concepts are essential elements of our thought processes; they are the substance of our views of the world; they enable us to make sense of both the world and our own behaviors. They reduce the complexity of the environment and make it possible to generalize, to make decisions, and to behave appropriately.

Rule Learning. Although concepts are fundamentally important, they are not sufficient. Clearly, students cannot be presented with all the different instances for which they will need a response. For example, if one of the instructional goals of a mathematics program is that students should be able to subtract 1,978 from 2,134, from 7,461, from 1,979, and so on, each of these instances need not (and probably cannot) be taught separately. Instead, a concept or a combination of concepts is used. This combination of concepts takes the form of a rule. Rules reflect that which is systematic and predictable, thereby enabling us to respond to different situations in similar, rule-regulated ways. Rules, explains Gagné, enable us to actually do things, as opposed to simply being able to state the rule.

Spoken language offers numerous illustrations of rules. A child who says, "He jumps, cats jump, men jump, and rabbits jump" is obviously applying the rule that a verb preceded by a plural subject does not ordinarily end in *s*.

One of the important external conditions that facilitate the learning of rules is verbal

ELIZABETH CREWS

Much of our learning, says R. Gagné, consists of hierarchies of information and skills. One of the tasks of teachers is to sequence instruction so that learners acquire essential subordinate concepts and skills first. There is much that this lad must already know if he is to understand the mysteries that now confront him.

instruction, note Gagné and Briggs (1983). In this case, the purpose of the instruction is usually to remind the learner of relevant concepts as well as to highlight important relationships among these concepts. As an illustration, Gagné and Briggs (1983) describe a situation in which a teacher presents students with a list of words, such as *made, fate, pale,* has them pronounce these words, and points out to them that the first vowel in each has a "long" sound. Following this, students are asked to pronounce *mad, fat,* and *pal;* then the instructor points out that the vowel has a "short" sound and also verbalizes the relevant rule. Alternatively, the teacher might simply present a variety of examples and encourage students, perhaps through appropriate questioning, to discover the rule for themselves.

Higher-Order Rules. Rules are what permit us to solve problems. In fact, Gagné refers to problem solving as a category of higher-order rules. Problem solving refers to the thinking out of a solution to a problem by combining old rules

to form new ones. It is the main reason for learning rules in the first place.

Numerous examples of problem solving through the use of higher-order rules can be drawn from people's daily activities. Whenever no previously learned rule is appropriate for the solution of a problem, problem solving may be said to take place (providing, of course, that the problem is in fact solved). A child who is learning to tie a shoe may combine several rules in order to succeed. The idea that laces go into holes and the notion that intertwined laces tend to cling together are rules that may be combined to form the higher-order rule: "Laced shoes with intertwined laces may be considered tied."

A condition clearly necessary for problem solving is the presence of the appropriate rules in the learner's repertoire. Gagné (1985) also describes some external conditions that appear to be useful for problem solving:

▶ Verbal instructions or questions may be used to elicit the recall of relevant rules.

▶ The direction of thought processes may also be guided by verbal instructions.

The Hierarchical Nature of Intellectual Skills.
Gagné (1977b) points out that many school subjects consist of a hierarchy of information or skills such that in order to understand higher levels, it is necessary to have mastered a number of subordinate capabilities. It follows that instruction must proceed from the subordinate to the final task. The validity of this observation is perhaps clearest in subjects such as mathematics, in which solving higher-level problems requires mastery of a variety of subordinate skills. Similarly, Ranzijn (1991–92) describes two experiments that illustrate the importance of sequencing information so that prerequisite subordinate knowledge is acquired prior to exposure to higher-level concepts.

Just as knowledge within a given content area may be described in terms of a hierarchical arrangement of subordinate capabilities, so may classes of learning skills. The learner must master lower levels before progressing to higher ones. In a nutshell, problem solving depends upon rules, which are derived from concepts, which require as prerequisites the learning of discriminations. Discriminations depend on either verbal associations or motor chains, both of which are derived from stimulus–response connections.

The instructional implications of this position can be summarized as follows:

▶ Content in a given area should be arranged in hierarchical fashion so that simpler abilities and concepts necessary for later learning are mastered first.

▶ Instructional goals should be analyzed in terms of the types of learning involved in their attainment. Instructional procedures should then be premised on knowledge of the conditions required for those types of learning.

Verbal Information. Intellectual skills, as we saw, are concerned mainly with how learning occurs; the other four categories of learning outcomes deal more specifically with what it is that is learned. For example, a great deal of the school learning that is of most direct concern to teachers takes the form of verbal information. In effect, verbal information is nothing more or less complicated than what is generally described as knowledge. An identifying characteristic of verbal information is that it can be expressed as a sentence or that it implies a sentence. Thus, the statement "Individuals of *Ursus arctos* are the true bears" and the single word *bear* are both expressions of verbal information; both presumably have meaning for whoever expresses them. This does not mean that verbal information is always learned and stored verbally. Much of our verbal information is derived from pictures and illustrations, perhaps from visions and dreams, but surely from our own behavior and that of others, as well as from the countless observations that we make in the course of our daily activities.

Quite apart from whatever practical value it might have, verbal information, says Gagné, is essential for acquiring further information. In addition, verbal information makes thinking possible. It's little wonder that schools devote so much time and energy to deciding which bodies of knowledge (verbal information) should be transmitted to students and how they can best be transmitted.

Many of the conditions that Robert Gagné describes as desirable external conditions for the acquisition of verbal information are similar to those described by Ausubel (discussed later in this chapter). Thus, Gagné mentions the importance of advance organizers and meaningful context. In addition, verbal information can often be made more meaningful by using photos, charts, illustrations, and other pictorial representations. Other useful instructional strategies are intended to ensure that learners pay attention and to facilitate recall and generalization. Thus, varying tone and emphasis in oral presentations and using attention-compelling instructional aids such as slides and films and a variety of other stimuli can be important attention-directing and motivating features of teaching. (See Chapter 10 for a more complete discussion of motivation in the classroom.)

Attitudes. Educators throughout the world have a number of grand goals: We want to develop students who love life and learning, who respect the people, institutions, and ideas that we respect, and who want to be good citizens. In short, we want to develop students with positive attitudes. In fact, however, our educational systems teach attitudes only incidentally; they are aimed more toward teaching motor skills, verbal information, intellectual skills, and to some extent cognitive strategies. Why? Because an attitude is a personal affective (emotional) reaction; as such, it is not an easy thing to teach. In brief, an **attitude** is a positive or negative predisposition that has important motivational components. A positive attitude toward school, for example, implies not only liking school but trying to do well in school, to be liked by teachers, and to conform to the explicit and implicit goals of the school.

---

attitude A prevailing and consistent tendency to react in a certain way. Attitudes can be positive or negative and are important motivational forces.

Attitudes are clearly affected by reinforcement. Students who have been most successful in school usually have more positive attitudes toward school than those who have not been successful (that is, have not been reinforced). And although this observation is obvious, teachers do not always behave as though they are fully aware of it. If you want your students to have positive attitudes toward whatever it is you are trying to teach them, it is imperative that they meet with success (reinforcement) rather than failure, particularly in their initial encounters with you and the subject you are teaching.

R. Gagné (1974) refers to Bandura's description of imitative learning as one of the principal indirect methods for teaching attitudes (see Chapter 4). Steps in the instructional sequence include selecting an appropriate model, preferably one with whom the student identifies (teachers are powerful models), arranging for the model to display personal choices reflecting the attitudes to be established, and drawing attention to the model's consequent reinforcement. If, for example, a teacher describes some small act of honesty that she engaged in and for which she was subsequently reinforced, either directly or simply through feeling good about her behavior, she has gone some distance toward developing positive attitudes toward honesty in her charges. Lest this sound too simplistic, let me hasten to point out that attitudes are subtle, pervasive, and powerful predispositions to think, act, and feel in certain ways; they are established in many ways and places (out of school as well as in it), and they are not nearly as easy to modify as the preceding discussion might imply.

Motor Skills. Motor skills are the many skills in our repertoires involving the execution of sequences of controlled muscular movements. Writing, typing, driving, walking, talking, dancing, and digging holes for outdoor toilets are motor skills. Some of these are important for school; others aren't. They can be taught through appropriate verbal instructions and demonstration (for example, "This is how you should sit in front of your computer . . . address the ball . . . grasp the shovel . . . hold the pencil . . . point your nose."), and they are perfected primarily through practice. Like other skills, motor skills are highly susceptible to reinforcement. Not only is reinforcement involved in determining whether a learner is likely to want to acquire a skill (in other words, whether the learner's attitude will be positive), but it is intimately involved in determining how well and how rapidly the skill will be learned and perfected. A word processor would learn very slowly if he could not see the results of his work. He would not correct his mistakes and would receive little reinforcement for a good performance.

Cognitive Strategies. Our intellectual functioning is guided by complex, highly personal strategies. These strategies govern how we pay attention, how we go about studying and organizing, and how we analyze, synthesize, and recall. In a sense, they result from the development of the elusive capabilities involved in learning how to think, to create, to discover, and to remember. In Chapter 5 we looked at a number of programs designed specifically to teach cognitive strategies such as those involved in rehearsing, organizing, and elaborating. Unfortunately, however, as Gagné notes, cognitive strategies tend to be largely self-learned rather than deliberately taught. As a consequence, they are not always learned well by everybody; nor are they always applied well.

One of the important conditions for the development of cognitive strategies is that the learner be exposed to novel and challenging problems—problems that require the deliberate application of cognitive strategies. Also, as has been demonstrated in various programs designed specifically to develop such strategies, there is much that teachers can do to make students aware of their cognitive strategies, and to make them aware of the usefulness of developing, practicing, and monitoring their use of these strategies.

Table 6.1 presents a highly useful description of the five major processes that Gagné

TABLE 6.1 COGNITIVE STRATEGIES RELATED TO THE FIVE PROCESSES IN GAGNÉ'S INFORMATION PROCESSING MODEL

LEARNING PROCESS	COGNITIVE STRATEGY	LEARNING PROCESS	COGNITIVE STRATEGY
Selective Perception	Highlighting	Semantic Encoding	Concept maps
	Underlining		Taxonomies
	Advance organizers		Analogies
	Adjunct questions		Rules/Productions
	Outlining		Schemas
Rehearsal	Paraphrasing	Retrieval	Mnemonics
	Note taking		Imagery
	Imagery	Executive Control	Metacognitive strategies
	Outlining		
	Chunking		

Source: Based on *Principles of Instructional Design* (4th ed.) by Robert M. Gagné, Leslie J. Briggs, and Walter W. Wager. Copyright © 1992 by Holt, Rinehart and Winston, Inc. Reproduced by permission of the publisher.

describes as being involved in learning, along with examples of specific cognitive strategies that can contribute to each of these processes. Many of these strategies are simple and straightforward (underlining and highlighting, for example), and the teacher might not need to do more than mention them. Others are more complex (the use of mnemonics or of metacognitive strategies) and might need to be systematically developed.

Table 6.2 summarizes Robert Gagné's classification of learning outcomes and of external conditions that appear to facilitate these outcomes. Clearly, knowledge of both conditions and outcomes can be of considerable value in helping teachers develop appropriate and effective instructional strategies.

COGNITIVISM: SOME COMMON BELIEFS

Although R. Gagné's theory recognizes and includes behavioristic kinds of learning—for example, in his inclusion of simple types of learning among the class of "Intellectual Skills"—his most recent emphases are clearly in the direction of cognitive explanations and their usefulness for instruction. "Learning," he explains, "is something that takes place inside a person's head—in the brain" (Gagné & Driscoll, 1988, p. 3).*

As a primarily cognitive approach, Gagné's theory shares a number of beliefs and assumptions with two other cognitive theories that also have tremendously important instructional implications: the theories of Jerome Bruner and David Ausubel (discussed later in this chapter). Among these common beliefs and assumptions are the following:

---

*PPC: Does this mean the behavioristic bear believes learning is something that takes place *outside* the head, somewhere other than in the brain?

AUTHOR: The bear does not readily admit to being a behaviorist. But no, it would be misleading to imply that behaviorists believe that learning takes place somewhere else. The point is that cognitive psychologists emphasize events that occur inside the head and look there for their explanations. In contrast, behaviorists consider it more fruitful to deal with events outside the head.

TABLE 6.2 GAGNÉ'S MAJOR LEARNING OUTCOMES, ILLUSTRATED, AND WITH SUGGESTIONS RELEVANT FOR INSTRUCTION

OUTCOMES OF LEARNING	EXAMPLES	CONDITIONS THAT FACILITATE OUTCOMES
1. INTELLECTUAL SKILLS		
Higher-order rules	Learner determines how to calculate the area of a trapezoid.	Review of relevant rules; verbal instruction to aid in recall of rules; verbal instructions to direct thinking.
Rules	Learner discovers characteristics that are common to all mammals.	Learner is made aware of desired learning outcome; relevant concepts are reviewed; concrete examples are provided.
Concepts	Learner classifies objects in terms of size and color.	Examples presented; learner engaged in finding examples; reinforcement.
Discriminations	Learner distinguishes among different printed letters.	Simultaneous presentation of stimuli to be discriminated; reinforcement (confirmation); repetition.
Simple types of learning (signal learning; stimulus–response learning; chaining)	Learner is conditioned to respond favorably to school.	Reinforcement; models; positive experiences in various school contexts.
2. VERBAL INFORMATION	Learner writes down Gagné's five major learning domains.	Information that organizes content (advance organizers); meaningful context; instructional aids for retention and motivation.
3. COGNITIVE STRATEGIES	Learner devises personal strategy for remembering components of the basic information processing model.	Frequent presentation of novel and challenging problems; discussion and direct teaching of cognitive strategies.
4. ATTITUDES	Learner chooses to read an educational psychology text rather than a novel.	Models; reinforcement; verbal guidance.
5. MOTOR SKILLS	Learner types a summary of this chapter.	Models; verbal directions; reinforcement (knowledge of results); practice.

Current Learning Builds on Previous Learning.
As we saw in Chapter 5, cognitive approaches to human behavior stress the importance of the learner's previous knowledge and skills—of what R. Gagné terms *previously acquired capabilities*. Unlike behaviorism, which tends to view all learners as initially equal—as equally susceptible to the effects of the consequences of behavior—cognitivism emphasizes that we often derive different meanings from experience, largely because we *construct* rather than simply discover meaning. Consequently, we often learn different things.

Learning Involves Information Processing.
Common to most cognitive theories is the basic assumption that the learner is a processor of information. Accordingly, these theories attempt to analyze learning in terms of what is often labeled "cognitive structure." At a simple

level, cognitive structure is the content of the mind. It includes concepts, relationships that the learner establishes among concepts, and strategies used in abstracting concepts and in organizing them in long-term memory. Terms such as *schema* or *script* are often used to describe cognitive structure.

Meaning Depends on Relationships. Cognitive theorists maintain that knowledge does not exist in a vacuum, but that it depends on relationships. As E. D. Gagné (1985) puts it: "All of a person's declarative knowledge can be conceptualized as a large network of interrelated propositions." In this context, **declarative knowledge** is the same as declarative memory. It consists of all the facts we have learned and all the experiences we have had. In short, declarative knowledge involves knowing that something is the case. Declarative knowledge is contrasted with **procedural knowledge,** (also called *procedural memory*), which involves knowing how to do something (that is, knowing a procedure for doing something). Procedural knowledge, too, derives its meaningfulness from interrelationships (Anderson, 1983).

The idea that knowledge consists of networks of relationships is not new. Recall from Chapter 5 that our contemporary models of long-term memory are invariably associationistic; that is, they are models of relationships. What is new, however, is the recent upsurge of interest in exploring this idea in an effort to understand how we learn and know things and how we think. Thinking, according to this approach, involves the manipulation of what is represented mentally. In other words, it involves forming and manipulating relationships among items of information (Hunt, 1989).

___

declarative knowledge All the facts, information, and experiences that are part of what we know. Also termed *declarative memory*.

procedural knowledge Knowing how to do something; knowing procedures as well as facts (declarative knowledge). Also termed *procedural memory*.

An Illustration. First, to simplify. Why do we say that knowledge and understanding depend on interrelationships among items of information? What does this concept mean?

Consider the following passage:

> If the balloons popped, the sound wouldn't be able to carry since everything would be too far away from the correct floor. A closed window would also prevent the sound from carrying, since most buildings tend to be well insulated. Since the whole operation depends on a steady flow of electricity, a break in the middle of the wire would also cause problems. Of course, the fellow could shout, but the human voice is not loud enough to carry that far. An additional problem is that a string could break on the instrument. Then there would be no accompaniment to the message. It is clear that the best situation would involve less distance. Then there would be fewer potential problems. With face to face contact, the least number of things could go wrong. (Bransford & Johnson, 1973, pp. 392–393)

If you find this passage confusing and unclear, don't despair; so does almost everyone else. It's a frustrating experience because the language is clear and simple, the sentences are short and straightforward, none of the concepts is very difficult—yet the whole thing makes no sense.

Turn now to Figure 6.2 and glance at the illustration.

Now the passage makes sense. Why? Simply because the illustration provides a framework within which to understand; it activates what a number of cognitive psychologists refer to as a *schema* (plural, *schemas* or *schemata*).

Schemata are metaphors for cognitive structure and functioning. They are like clusters of related items of knowledge that define concepts. They are what we know about things. For example, schemata relevant to understanding the balloon passage include, among other things, our knowledge that balloons filled with lighter-than-air substances will rise, our recognition of the musical equipment involved, and certain assumptions about the intentions and motives of the serenader and the serenadee. Note that each of these concepts is defined by one or more relationships (for example, the relationship between weight and falling or rising, the relationship between musical sounds and a guitar, the presumed relationship between the individuals involved, and so on).

One aspect of schemata that is important for learning and remembering real-life things is called a **script.** Schank and Abelson (1977) describe a script as that part of cognitive structure that deals with routines and sequences. We all know countless routines, countless scripts. We know, for example, that a sensible way to dress is to put on undergarments, socks, shirts, pants, and shoes, more or less in that order. This is a verbal description of a common script. For dressing on a day like today in this somewhat harsh climate, I added putting on a heavy coat and gloves to my script—in that order. Had I wanted to be creative this morning and altered my script—say, by reversing it—I might have found dressing considerably more difficult and time-consuming. And I would have had to wear my socks over my shoes and my shorts over my jeans, in which case I would probably not have been courageous or foolish enough to come in to the university.

Scripts, like schemata, deal with relationships. A script is, in a sense, an expression of sequential relationships. Scripts and schemata clearly have their uses. Nevertheless, they are still only metaphors that need to be made more concrete for our purposes.

Instructional Applications Should Stress Relationships and Strategies.

Cognitive approaches are concerned with how information is processed. Accordingly, these approaches look at how we derive information from the environment; how we organize and interpret this information, teasing out relationships in order to abstract meaning from our experiences; how we organize and store meaning; and how our thought processes make use of what we have stored.

From the educator's point of view, these concerns translate directly into a renewed emphasis on cognitive strategies and a recognition of the importance of relationships among items of information. Specifically, they suggest two things: First, the school's curriculum (and the teacher's presentation of that curriculum) needs to be organized to reveal and underline important relationships, and second, the school should pay systematic and deliberate attention to developing strategies that are involved in perceiving, interpreting, organizing, analyzing, evaluating, storing, and retrieving information.

A number of cognitively based theories reflect these two educational applications especially clearly. Among them are the theories of Jerome Bruner and David Ausubel. In many important ways these theories are similar, although they use different terms to describe the units and processes of cognitive organization.* There is, however, one important respect in which the theories are dramatically different from each other. Bruner advocates that learners be guided toward organizing material for themselves, once they have been provided with opportunities to discover relationships. In contrast, Ausubel argues that in most cases the teacher can organize the material and present it to the student in relatively final form. In other words,

---

script Term describing our knowledge of what goes with what and in what sequence. Scripts are a part of cognitive structure that deals with the routine and the predictable.

---

*PPC: Wouldn't the bear find life a lot easier if all cognitive theorists agreed to use the same clearly defined vocabulary, rather than so many insisting on inventing their own meanings or, perhaps worse, their own terms? Weren't *schema* and *schemata* and *script* and *cognitive structure* enough?

AUTHOR: Yes and no. No, those terms aren't enough; and yes, we need a variety of terms. Besides, the bear is an old bear; he's seen much jargon come and go. "The meaning is in the meaning, not in the jargon," he says. "Do you get my meaning?" he adds slyly.

Bruner is a strong advocate of **discovery learning**; Ausubel argues for **reception learning.**

DISCOVERY LEARNING: BRUNER'S THEORY

Cognitive psychology assumes that the learner is an active information processor. It asks how the learner derives information from the environment, how information is organized and interpreted, and how it is used. Jerome Bruner's theory provides one set of answers for these questions—and for many other questions as well.

Bruner's cognitive theory describes learning and perception as information processing activities that reflect our need to simplify and make sense of the environment (Bruner, Goodnow, & Austin, 1956; Bruner, 1973). These activities involve the formation of concepts (Bruner's term is **category**) that result from the abstraction of common elements among events and experiences. From these abstractions, we derive implicit rules that allow us to categorize (conceptualize) the world and discover a wealth of relationships among concepts. Bruner's metaphor for these relationships is called a **coding system**—a hierarchical arrangement of con-

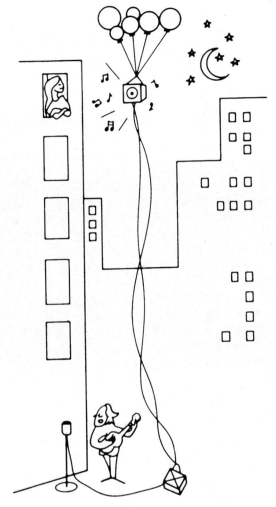

FIGURE 6.2 From J. D. Bransford and M. K. Johnson, "Consideration of Some Problems in Comprehension" (p. 394). In W. G. Chase (ed.), *Visual Information Processing.* Copyright 1973 by Academic Press. Reprinted by permission of Academic Press, New York and J. D. Bransford.

---

discovery learning The acquisition of new information or knowledge largely as a result of the learner's own efforts. Discovery learning is contrasted with expository or reception learning and is generally associated with Bruner, among others.

reception learning The type of learning that involves primarily instruction or tuition rather than the learner's own efforts. Teaching for reception learning, often associated with Ausubel, usually takes the form of expository or didactic methods; that is, the teacher structures the material and presents it to learners in relatively final form rather than asking them to discover that form.

category A term used by Bruner to describe a grouping of related objects or events. In this sense, a category is both a concept and a percept. Bruner also defines it as a rule for classifying things as equal.

coding system A Brunerian concept; refers to a hierarchical arrangement of related categories.

cepts of increasing (or decreasing) generality. Thus, our long-term memories—our relatively permanent store of knowledge, strategies, impressions, and so on—can be seen as a complex, highly associationistic arrangement of categories (concepts) and coding systems. And all school subjects, as well as topics within these subjects, can also be seen as having a similar sort of structure. The structure of a subject,

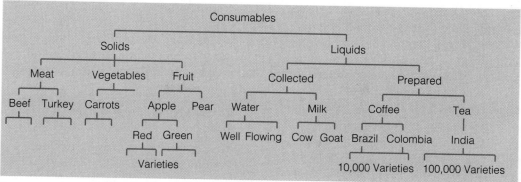

FIGURE 6.3 A coding system.

argues Bruner, reflects the most fundamental relationships and ideas in the field. Thus to truly learn a subject and to be able to think about it, learners need to develop their own coding systems—their own mental representations of these important ideas and relationships. And the best way of developing a coding system is to *discover* it rather than to have it presented in final form by a teacher. (See Figure 6.3 for a graphical illustration of a coding system.)*

---

*PPC: There's no getting around the fact that this chapter is heavy going. (I just put the kettle on for more coffee.) How about some bears or cases?

AUTHOR: Okay. I have a cow warning I've been wanting to pass on in any case. So here's a clipping from the local newspaper. (This is true, I swear it.)

A 77-year-old farmer is in serious condition in a Graymont, Ill. hospital after being attacked by a gang of cows. Martin Duffy suffered a concussion and broken ribs after he was attacked, butted about and knocked unconscious by his own herd. Rescuers said Duffy had gone into his pasture to check on a cow due to deliver a calf when the attack occurred. "Apparently, Martin wanted the cow to move into the barn so she could have the calf in an enclosed area, but she did not want to move, and he approached her, she kicked him and he must have fallen down," said Mary Jo McSherry, one of the first on the scene. Other cows got excited too. "The cows were butting him with their heads. They had their heads down, pushing him, and when they would roll him, they would throw him up about three feet in the air." ("Cowed by Cows," 1992)

You've been warned.

DISCOVERY LEARNING IN SCHOOLS

As we saw in Chapter 3, one way to describe cognitive development is Piaget's notion that as a function of interacting with the environment (through assimilation and accommodation), the child gradually builds up a store of knowledge. In a very real sense, it is as though the learner *constructs* knowledge—in contrast with a situation in which the learner would be given that knowledge by someone else (parents or teachers, for example).

Bruner's theory is based on the same fundamental belief. We make up our own versions of reality, says Bruner (1986); we discover our own meanings (Bruner, 1990). And the functions of schools, he insists emphatically, should be to provide conditions that will foster the discovery of relationships; hence, his strong arguments for discovery learning in schools.

Discovery learning can be defined as the learning that takes place when students are not presented with subject matter in its final form but rather are required to organize it themselves. This requires learners to discover for themselves relationships that exist among items of information. In Bruner's theory, discovery is the formation of categories or, more often, the formation of coding systems, which are defined in terms of relationships (similarities and differences) that exist among objects and events.

The most important and most obvious characteristic of a discovery approach to teaching is that it requires far less teacher involvement and direction than most other methods. Note, however, that this does not imply that the teacher ceases to give any guidance once the initial problem has been presented. As Corno and Snow (1986) point out, teachers can offer a continuum of guidance (their phrase is "teacher mediation") by adapting their teaching to different students and different purposes. At one extreme, too little or no mediation can leave students without the means for discovery; at the other extreme, constant direction and guidance from the teacher may remove all opportunity for self-direction and discovery by students.

The advantages of a discovery approach, claims Bruner, are that such learning facilitates transfer and retention, increases problem-solving ability, and increases motivation (Bruner, 1961a).

DISCOVERY AS A REFLECTIVE TEACHING STRATEGY

Recall from Chapter 1 that reflective teaching strategies are broadly defined as strategies that lead students to discover and learn for themselves (Freiberg & Driscoll, 1992). In general, these strategies require not only that teachers think about and analyze what is happening as they teach, but also that learners be encouraged to think about their learning. Perhaps even more important, learners are encouraged to assume responsibility for their own learning and thinking (Korthagen, 1993). Thus, reflective teaching mirrors a philosophy that emphasizes the active, discovery-oriented role of the learner, and that views teaching as largely a question of facilitating learning and discovery rather than being the final source of all information. Not surprisingly, the most important reflective teaching strategies are those that lead to student inquiry and guided discovery.

Very often, discovery in the classroom takes the form of systematically following a number of logical steps that guide the search for gener-alizable conclusions, as in scientific investigation. And an important part of the guidance that the "teacher as learning facilitator" provides revolves around the deliberate and systematic application of these steps. Summarized briefly, these involve:

- ▶ Formulating and clarifying a question or problem
- ▶ Collecting examples; making relevant observations
- ▶ Arriving at hypotheses (intelligent, observation-based guesses)
- ▶ Devising and conducting tests, experiments, and other observations to confirm or refute hypotheses
- ▶ Applying, extending, generalizing, "going beyond" the new information

The case "Making Dew" provides one example of the application of this method of scientific inquiry in a discovery-oriented science unit. Keep in mind that although the most obvious illustrations are often in science, these methods can also be used in a variety of other subjects.

CONDITIONS THAT FACILITATE DISCOVERY LEARNING

According to Bruner, four sets of conditions contribute to discovery learning: set, need state, mastery of specifics, and diversity of training. Awareness of each of these is important for teachers.

Set. Set refers to a predisposition to react in certain ways. A discovery-oriented person is one whose customary approach to a problem is to look for relationships among items of information. One way to affect set, says Bruner, is through instructions. For example, a student can be encouraged to memorize subject matter

---

set A predisposition to react to stimulation in a given manner.

as though it consisted of isolated bits of information simply by being told to do so—or by being tested only for knowledge of isolated items of information. This is what Marton and Saljo (1984) call the "surface approach" to teaching and learning. It focuses on memorizing facts, completing tasks, and passing tests.

As an alternative to "surface" teaching, students can be encouraged to look for relationships among items of information, either by being instructed to do so or by being told that they will be examined on their understanding of these relationships. This is Marton and Saljo's "deep approach." It focuses on relationships and on understanding.

Need State. Need state is the level of arousal, excitation, or alertness of the learner (see Chapter 10). Bruner suggests that a moderate level of arousal is more conducive to discovery learning than is either an excessively high or low level. That is, students need to be alert rather than sleepy. They also need to be excited and interested rather than frightened or panicked.

Mastery of Specifics. The degree of **mastery of specifics** refers to the extent of the learner's knowledge of specific, relevant information. Bruner argues that discovery (which is really the formation of coding systems) is not accidental. Clearly, it is far more likely to occur when the individual is well prepared—and highly unlikely if the individual is not prepared. Herbert Gaudry, my childhood buddy who knew absolutely nothing about machinery, was not very likely to invent the round-bale hay-baler. In the same way, a student who knows little of geography, history, and commerce is unlikely to discover that the locations of most major cities is not entirely accidental. As Bruner

---

need state Bruner's expression describing the arousal level of an organism.

mastery of specifics A Brunerian term for the learning of details. Mastery of relevant specifics is necessary for acquiring concepts and discovering relationships among them.

CASE: MAKING DEW

THE PLACE: Tremont Elementary School

THE SITUATION: Mr. Creasy's eighth-grade science class

THE TOPIC: The formation of dew

Mr. Creasy: So the question is: What causes dew?
Paul: I know. It's just rain.
Jackie: It's not. Cause there's dew when there's no rain.
Mr. Creasy: What's our method? How do we find out?
Chorus of answers: Scientific inquiry.
Patiently, then, Bob Creasy leads his class through what they have previously established as the steps of the scientific method. Next, they clarify what is meant by "dew," and students are charged with collecting relevant real-life observations and facts.

In a later class, they pool their observations and they develop intelligent guesses, or hypotheses, based on these facts (dew falls from the sky; dew comes out of the air; dew comes out of objects themselves). Creasy guides the students so that they make pertinent observations, sometimes devising experiments to do so (dew forms on comparatively cool objects; there is dew on cloudless nights; dew forms even on objects that are initially completely dry).

Eventually students begin to agree on a conclusion (the cooling of moist air by a relatively cool object "squeezes" out water droplets that collect on the object's surface). Students devise various experiments to determine whether this conclusion is always correct.

points out, the wider the range of information learners possess, the more likely they are to find relationships within that information.

Diversity of Training. Bruner's fourth variable, **diversity of training,** is related to this. Bruner argues that a learner who is exposed to information in a wide variety of circumstances is more likely to develop coding systems to organize that information. Partly for this reason, he recommends that the same subjects be taught to learners more than once—say, at different grade levels—but with different amounts of detail and at different levels of abstraction depending on the changing interests, capabilities, and background knowledge of the learners.

SPECIFIC EDUCATIONAL RECOMMENDATIONS

Bruner's plea for the use of discovery-oriented techniques in schools is advanced in several articles and books (for example, *The Process of Education,* 1961b). In addition, renewed interest in discovery approaches to education can be seen in what is termed the **constructivist approach** to teaching (for example, Brown, Collins, & Duguid, 1989). This is a general term for approaches based on the assumption that students should build (construct) knowledge for themselves. Hence, constructivist approaches are basically discovery oriented.

Related to the constructivist approach is the **conceptual change movement,** which is

---

diversity of training Bruner's expression relating to his belief that exposure to information under a wide range of circumstances is conducive to discovering relationships among concepts.

constructivist approach A general term for discovery-oriented approaches to teaching, so-called because of their assumption that learners should build (construct) knowledge for themselves.

conceptual change movement Literally, cognitive changes such as might be evident in great understanding, knowledge, and awareness. More specifically, the expression refers to instructional approaches designed to foster mental reorganization rather than simply to increase the number of facts learned.

---

also discovery oriented (see Vosniadou & Saljo, 1994). Conceptual change curricula present ideas that challenge the learner, that contain problems and puzzles, and that ultimately result in a reorganization of knowledge (hence, conceptual change). Research on conceptual change approaches to teaching indicate that these approaches are especially suitable for science (Bar et al., 1994), but that they can also be used in other subjects like social studies (Wade, 1994). Not surprisingly, teachers who were trained with courses using a conceptual change orientation are more likely to incorporate such methods in their own teaching, and to be more successful at doing so (Stofflett & Stoddart, 1994).

Bruner advances a number of specific recommendations and observations that are especially important for discovery-oriented classrooms such as those that make use of conceptual change curricula. Among them are the following:

1. ". . . the curriculum of a subject should be determined by the most fundamental understanding that can be achieved of the underlying principles that give structure to that subject" (1961b, p. 31).

   Bruner argues that knowledge of underlying principles and of the structure of a subject facilitates discovery because constructing knowledge requires knowledge of organizing principles. For example, it is much easier to arrive at a concept that relates aspen, birch, and alder once it has been discovered that they are all deciduous hardwoods. Indeed, it is the "peopleness" of individuals, the "treeness" of trees, and the "birdness" of birds that allows them to be reacted to in similar ways and that permits the learner to make inferences about specific people, trees, or birds—in Bruner's terms, that allows "going beyond the information given" (1957a). Bruner argues that unless the organization of the curriculum is such that it facilitates the formation of structure (coding systems), it will be learned with difficulty, it will not lend itself to transfer, and it will be remembered poorly.

2. ". . . any subject can be taught to any child in some honest form" (1961b, p. 52).

Bruner's critics have been quick to point out that not every concept can be taught to children of any age. For example, proportion probably cannot be understood by a 4-year-old. Bruner's reply to this is that we should look at the possibility of teaching aspects of any subject at any age level. Perhaps some aspects of proportion can be taught to a 4-year-old. The important question is how teaching can be made effective for very young children. Bruner's (1966) answer is that the form can be simplified and the mode of presentation geared to the simplest representational systems available. Because children progress from motor or sensory (**enactive**) representation to relatively concrete images (**iconic**), and finally to abstract (**symbolic**) representation, it follows that the sequence in teaching should be the same. In other words, if it is possible to present a subject so that a child can first experience it, then react to a concrete presentation of it, and finally symbolize it, that is the best instructional sequence.

3. A **spiral curriculum** that develops and redevelops topics at different grades is ideal for acquiring generic codes.

---

enactive A term used by Bruner to describe young children's representation of their world. It refers specifically to the belief that children represent the world in terms of their personal actions.

iconic A term that refers to a developmental stage in children's representation of their world. The term is used by Bruner to describe an intermediate stage of development characterized by a representation of the world in terms of relatively concrete mental images.

symbolic The final stage in the development of children's representations of their world. The term is used by Bruner and describes the representation of the world in terms of arbitrary symbols. Symbolic representation includes representation in terms of language as well as in terms of theoretical or hypothetical systems.

Bruner argues in several places (1961b, 1966) that spiral curricula are ideally suited to discovery. First, such a curriculum organizes subject matter according to principles, and it usually presents them systematically, from simplest to most complex. This progression parallels the development of coding systems. Second, a spiral curriculum involves the sort of repetition that is useful for constructing knowledge. To begin with, learners are exposed to the most general, most inclusive idea and then to a series of specific simple instances of concepts. As they discover relationships among these concepts, they build knowledge (coding systems) that is highly conducive to transfer, recall, and discovery.

4. ". . . a student should be given some training in recognizing the plausibility of guesses" (1961b, p. 64).

In this connection, Bruner speaks of the usefulness of the *intuitive leap*—the educated guess that is something more than a blind attempt but something less than simply making inferences or predictions on the basis of what is known about similar instances. An intuitive leap is less certain than that. Bruner argues persuasively that to discourage guessing is to stifle the process of discovery.

5. Aids to teaching (audiovisual, concrete, and so on) should be used.

One reason advanced to support this recommendation is that audiovisual aids provide students with direct or vicarious experiences and thus facilitate the formation of concepts. This relates directly to Bruner's suggestion that the best instructional sequence is often one that progresses in the same direction as the child's representation of the world—that is, from enactive to iconic to symbolic (see the box, "Guided Discovery").

---

spiral curriculum Bruner's term for a curriculum that revisits the same topics repeatedly, often at different grade levels, but at different levels of abstraction and generality depending on the interests and background knowledge of learners.

GUIDED DISCOVERY

Some school subjects lend themselves more readily to discovery-oriented techniques than do others. For example, some (though by no means all) scientific principles can be discovered by students in guided discovery situations that provide them with sufficient background information and the appropriate experimental equipment. Similarly, children on field trips can discover a variety of phenomena, although understanding and interpreting these phenomena (and even noticing them in the first place) often require considerable guidance.

The beginning teacher should not make the mistake of assuming that teaching through discovery implies letting students go out on their own with no more than the simple instruction to "discover." Not only must the processes of discovery be taught—through experience as well as through more didactic procedures—but the student must frequently be given guidance while in the process of discovering. Hence the expression **guided discovery.** The guidance need not ruin the discovery or destroy its magic.

As an example of guided discovery learning, Bruner (1961a) describes how a class of elementary school children is led to discover important relationships between human settlements and geographic features. Among other things, they are asked where they would establish a settlement if they were exploring an area for the first time. Their reasons for settling in certain areas rather than others gradually lead them to "discover" that major settlements should be at the confluence of rivers and near natural harbors. Thus, studying geography becomes an activity of discovering relationships between the environment and humans rather than simply of memorizing maps and related data.

Can the principle of the combustion engine be discovered by an eighth-grade class? Yes, it can. What might be the major features of a guided discovery lesson that you could design for this purpose?

RECEPTION LEARNING: AUSUBEL'S THEORY

Not all educators agree that discovery is the best approach. Perhaps most outspoken among those who advocate a different approach is David Ausubel (1963, 1977). Most people learn primarily through *reception learning* and not through discovery, claims Ausubel. That is, most of what students learn they receive in relatively final form rather than having to discover it for themselves. In the vast majority of school situations, he insists, discovery is ineffective and largely a waste of time.

---

guided discovery A reflective teaching technique in which students are given much of the responsibility for finding relationships and organizing knowledge, but in which teachers are careful to provide necessary guidance to ensure that discovery and learning occur.

AUSUBEL'S COGNITIVE THEORY

Ausubel's cognitive theory of learning is specifically intended to deal almost exclusively with what he calls "meaningful verbal learning." More important from the point of view of educational psychology, Ausubel's work is explicitly a search for the "laws of meaningful classroom learning."

Meaning. According to Ausubel, an object has meaning when it elicits an image in the "content of consciousness" as a result of being related to something already known. Similarly, a concept acquires meaning when it is related to an idea that is already present in the mind. In other words, for a stimulus or concept to have meaning, there must be something in the learner's cognitive structure (preexisting ideas and knowledge) to which it can be related. For example, the word *car* has meaning for an indi-

ZEBRAS AND ASSES

As part of a science lesson, a teacher wishes to familiarize her students with the many breeds of cows. Her students already know what cows are; they also know colors. But they do not know that an Aberdeen Angus is a sleek-looking black cow. She tells them so. Is this likely to be meaningful learning? What type of subsumption is involved?

This same teacher now wishes to teach her class what a zebra is. She tells them what it is; she compares it with horses, donkeys, mules, and—being

resourceful—asses; she then shows them a picture of a zebra. What type of subsumption is involved here?

Why would the simple statement that a zebra is an herbivorous, black-and-white African animal be almost meaningless for urban, North American children if they have never seen a zebra in books or on television?

vidual only when it can be related to a mental representation of what cars are.

Meaningful Learning. Meaningful learning, says Ausubel, requires that the learner have already learned associated concepts to which new material can be related—or, in Ausubel's terms, concepts that can "subsume" new learning. Learning therefore involves **subsumption,** of which there are two kinds. **Derivative subsumption** occurs when new material is so similar to what is already known that it could have been derived from it; **correlative subsumption**

---

subsumption Ausubel's term for the integration of new material or information with existing information. The term implies a process in which a new stimulus becomes part of what is already in cognitive structure.

derivative subsumption The type of subsumption (or learning) that takes place when new material can be derived directly from what is already known.

correlative subsumption The type of learning that takes place when new information requires an extension of what was previously known and could not, therefore, have been derived directly from it.

involves material that is sufficiently novel that it requires some change in existing cognitive structure. (See the box "Zebras and Asses" for an illustration of these kinds of subsumption in the classroom.)

Cognitive Structure. *Cognitive structure* consists of more or less organized and stable concepts (or ideas) in a learner's consciousness. Much like Bruner's, Ausubel's metaphor for cognitive structure assumes that this organization is hierarchical, with the most inclusive concept at the apex and increasingly specific concepts toward the base. Therefore, argues Ausubel, instruction should proceed from the most general and inclusive idea toward details of specific instances. This is somewhat like Bruner's notion that teaching should follow a sort of spiral curriculum in which the big idea (the most general concept) is presented first and then systematically revisited, perhaps over a period of years, at increasingly more complex levels of abstraction. The fundamental difference between Bruner and Ausubel, with respect to their instructional theories, is that Ausubel argues that learners should be provided with

Table 6.3 Summary of Ausubel's Theory of Meaningful Verbal Learning

1. Subsumption may be derivative or correlative.	Learning (subsumption) involves either (a) relating new material to previously learned, highly similar material (derivative subsumption), or (b) extending previous knowledge to similar but new material (correlative subsumption).
2. Subsumption leads to a hierarchical arrangement of knowledge, from most general to most specific.	Learning is evident in new information and in changes in the learner's awareness of relationships among items of information.
3. Remembering is dissociative subsumption.	Remembering requires being able to separate new learning from old.
4. Forgetting involves zero dissociability, or obliterative subsumption.	Forgetting occurs when material can no longer be differentiated from what is already in the mind.

organized information. Bruner, as we saw, maintains that students should be presented with specifics and allowed to discover their own organization (their own coding systems). For a summary of Ausubel's theory, see Table 6.3.

EXPOSITORY TEACHING

If reception learning accounts for most of what students learn, then **expository teaching** is the instructional technique of choice. Expository teaching is an instructional technique in which the teacher, who bears the major responsibility for finding and organizing information for learners, presents that information in relatively final form. Accordingly, the learner is not called on to discover relationships but rather to learn them.

Ausubel argues not only that expository teaching can lead to a high level of understanding and generality but also that discovery approaches are extremely time-consuming

without being demonstrably superior. In a review of the literature on discovery learning, Ausubel and Robinson (1969) conclude that research supporting such learning is virtually nonexistent. "Moreover," they state, "it appears that enthusiasts of discovery methods have been supporting each other by citing one another's opinions and assertions as evidence and by generalizing extravagantly from questionable findings" (1969, p. 494).

Ausubel's emphasis on expository teaching and its outcome, reception learning, stems in part from the fact that most classroom learning seems to be of that type. In addition, meaningful verbal learning, with which his theory deals, occurs mainly in the course of expository teaching. He argues that this type of learning is not passive and does not stifle creativity or encourage rote learning. Indeed, meaningful verbal learning is anything but rote, says Ausubel, because it involves relating new material to existing structure. In contrast, rote learning involves ingesting isolated bits of information.

Ausubel advances some general recommendations for the planning and presentation of subject matter in expository teaching. These take the form of a discussion of the most important variables involved in subsumption: advance organizers, discriminability, and meaningfulness.

---

expository teaching An instructional technique, strongly advocated by Ausubel, wherein the teacher bears the responsibility of organizing and presenting information in relatively final form. This is associated with reception learning rather than with discovery-oriented approaches.

Advance Organizers. Advance organizers are complex sets of ideas or concepts given to the learner before the material to be learned is presented. Organizers are meant to provide cognitive structure to which the new learning can be anchored (subsumed). Another function of organizers is to increase recall (prevent loss of what Ausubel calls **dissociability**—the ability to separate concepts from one another). (Ausubel's phrase for forgetting is **obliterative subsumption.**) The use of advance organizers is called for, then, under two circumstances: when students have no relevant information to which they can relate the new learning and when relevant subsuming information is already present but is not likely to be recognized as relevant by the learner (Ausubel & Robinson, 1969).

Grippin and Peters (1984) describe four characteristics of advance organizers. First, advance organizers are presented before the lesson. Second, they are designed to bring to mind prior knowledge that is relevant to the lesson (to activate related **subsumers**). Third, advance organizers are presented at a higher level of abstraction than the material presented later. Put another way, advance organizers ordinarily consist of subsuming concepts, which are, by definition, more generic than subsumed concepts. Finally, advance organizers make explicit the connection between prior knowledge and the lesson to be presented.

Ausubel describes two different types of organizers—one to be used when the material is completely new and the other when it is somewhat familiar. The first is termed an **expository organizer** because it presents a description or exposition of relevant concepts. The second is called a **comparative organizer** because it is likely to make use of similarities and differences in new material and existing cognitive structure.

An expository organizer in a lesson on gold, for example, might describe the general, defining characteristics of metals before the lesson on the specific qualities of gold. The organizer is intended to provide concepts (subsumers) to which the new material can be related.

There are a number of examples of comparative organizers in this text. Many take the form of brief introductory sections that compare material about to be presented with material previously discussed. Some of the chapter previews are organizers of this kind. Recall that at the beginning of this chapter we associated Bruner with discovery learning and Ausubel with reception learning before actually discussing their theories—another advance organizer. Of necessity, a textbook is primarily expository (although parts of it may lead to a type of guided discovery)—hence, the frequent use of organizers in most textbooks.

In the classroom, teachers sometimes unconsciously make use of something very much like advance organizers when they summarize earlier lessons before beginning a new presentation. However, these summaries often

---

advance organizers Introductory information that is given to learners to help them understand, learn, and remember new material.

dissociability A term used by Ausubel to indicate the ease with which material that is to be recalled can be separated (dissociated) from other related material that is also in memory.

obliterative subsumption Ausubel's term for forgetting. The incorporation of new material into pre-existing cognitive structure so that the new material eventually becomes indistinguishable—in other words, becomes obliterated (reaches zero dissociability, in Ausubel's terms).

subsumer The term used by Ausubel to describe a concept, an idea, or a combination of concepts or ideas that can serve to organize new information. Cognitive structure is therefore composed of subsumers.

expository organizer An idea or concept that serves as a description (exposition) of concepts that are relevant to new learning.

comparative organizer A concept or idea that serves to facilitate the learning of new material by making use of the similarities and differences between the new material and previous learning.

fail to make the connection between new and old learning sufficiently explicit, nor are they abstract enough to qualify as advance organizers in the sense in which Ausubel uses the expression. A summary is often simply a summary—an accounting of the things that have been taught before. An advance organizer is more abstract; it draws a concept from previous learning, an idea that is general enough to subsume the new material to be taught. (See, for example, the case "Why Turbo-Charged WZ 222As Cost So Much.")

Notice how Eddie Lemming's lesson is preceded by a single, very abstract concept: the principle of supply and demand. Notice, too, that there is a promise to relate this concept to the question that constitutes the substance of today's lesson: Why is gold so expensive? The students have been reminded of a single, abstract, highly generic, stable concept upon which to anchor their new learning.

Research that has examined the effectiveness of advance organizers has often used organizers much like this one, sometimes presented in the form of a written paragraph, sometimes described by the teacher, sometimes elicited from students. Typically, the subsequent performance of a group of students that was given advance organizers is compared with that of a control group given the lesson without the advance organizer.

The results of much of this research are not entirely clear. Some researchers have found that advance organizers provide no measurable advantage (for example, Clawson & Barnes, 1973); others report significant positive effects (for example, Gabel, Kogan, & Sherwood, 1980). White and Tisher (1986) note evidence suggesting that students who lack relevant prior knowledge are most likely to benefit from the use of advance organizers and that this may well explain the contradictions among studies. In addition, the fact that teaching strategies such as these do not always lead to immediately measurable effects should not be taken as clear evidence that they are a waste of time. Many good things that teachers do are never measured—and perhaps they should not be.

Perhaps, just perhaps, the long-term effects of a single propitiously presented advance organizer might become apparent years later when the student, now an adult, correctly answers the $20 million question on a television game show. Or maybe the long-term effects will become evident in the bankrupt investor's recollection that gold is not really a useful metal, that the demand for it is rather artificial, and that the supply is quite abundant after all.

CASE: Why Turbo-Charged WZ 222As Cost So Much

THE PLACE: Carmel Mid-Valley School

THE SETTING: Introduction to Mr. Eddie Lemming's seventh-grade unit on gold and other precious metals

Mr. Lemming: So can anyone tell me why turbo-charged WZ 222As are so expensive?

Bruce: Is it 'cause they cost more to make?

Mr. Lemming: Well, no, Bruce, not really. That'd be a good reason, though, if they did cost more.

Jack: 'Cause everybody wants one?

Sally: 'Cause there's not enough for everyone who wants one?

Mr. Lemming: Right. Right. You're both right.

Jack: It's like you said before, about workers and their pay. Too much demand.

Sally: And too little supply.

Mr. Lemming: Supply and demand. Keep that in mind. If nobody wants a thing, or if there's a lot of it, it won't cost very much. Like your textbook. Everybody wants it, so it costs an arm and a leg! Heh, heh. Supply and demand. Now, today we're going to talk about gold! Pretty exciting stuff, gold! And pretty expensive. Is that because of supply? demand? something else? Let's see what we can find out. . . .

Discriminability. In Ausubel's theory, a major variable in determining the stability of what is learned is the ease with which new material can be discriminated from previous learning. Ausubel notes that information closely resembling previous knowledge (derivative subsumption) is quickly forgotten, whereas dissimilar material (correlative subsumption) tends to be retained longer. It follows from this that teaching techniques that highlight the differences between new material and old learning will lead to longer retention. At the same time, it is still necessary to relate the new to the old in order to facilitate subsumption (learning). Hence, comparing information in terms of similarities and differences should help both learning and retention. Also, the stability and clarity of the subsuming idea directly relate to the ease with which new material can be both incorporated with it and dissociated from it.

Making Learning Meaningful. Ausubel's emphasis on reception learning as opposed to discovery learning is partly based on his belief that the most desirable kind of learning is meaningful, as opposed to rote. This does not mean that discovery techniques do not lead to meaningful learning. However, Ausubel believes that expository approaches have some advantages, especially in terms of the efficient use of the learner's time, as well as in terms of the meaningfulness of what is learned.

Learning is meaningful, says Ausubel, when there is a clear relationship between new material and existing cognitive structure (knowledge). Thus, meaning derives directly from associations that exist among ideas, events, or objects. However, there will be no meaning unless the learner is aware of these associations. For example, students can quite easily learn to pronounce and spell words that do not relate to any of their existing ideas and thus are meaningless to them. It seems clear that a new concept will have meaning if it relates to both the learner's past experiences and other ideas being learned.

It's important to note that meaning is not a property of objects or concepts themselves.

No idea, concept, or object is meaningful in and of itself; it is meaningful only in relation to a learner and in relation to other ideas in the learner's cognitive structure. One clear implication for teaching, therefore, is that the teacher should present no new material until the learner is ready to understand it. And understanding requires appropriate cognitive structure. Consequently, much of the teacher's effort should be directed at providing the student with background information, frequently through the use of advance organizers (see the box "Meaningless Learning").

DISCOVERY OR RECEPTION?

It is not especially difficult to reconcile the two apparently opposing views presented by Bruner and Ausubel; they are not nearly so different as their juxtaposition here might make them seem. In fact, in many ways they are simply different emphases. Neither is necessarily superior to the other, and neither needs to be used to the exclusion of the other. Clearly, both have their uses. Even Ausubel suggests that discovery learning can be useful (Ausubel & Robinson, 1969). For example, it can be used with younger learners who do not yet have a large store of information to which new learning can be related. When this is the case, expository approaches are not always highly meaningful.

Discovery can also be used to test the meaningfulness of new learning. For example, learners might be asked to generate (that is, discover) instances in which some new learning might be applicable—for example, a new principle in arithmetic. In fact, Ausubel argues that discovery learning is essential in problem solving if students are to demonstrate that they understand what they have learned. Furthermore, says Ausubel, there are indications that students more readily apply to new situations information that they discover, as opposed to material that is presented to them in final form. In addition, discovery approaches might be more motivating than expository approaches, and self-learning might be more intrinsically satisfying.

MEANINGLESS LEARNING

"Learning involves the derivative or correlative subsumption of meaningful material to existing cognitive structure in such a way as to permit subsequent dissociability rather than obliterative subsumption."

This particular pearl of psychological wisdom is undoubtedly meaningful to you but only because you know through previous learning what derivative and correlative subsumption are, what meaningful material is, and what type of beasts cognitive structure and obliterative subsumption are.* For anyone who did not already know these terms, the sentence would be meaningless.

It is remarkably easy for teachers to fall into the trap of asking students to learn material that is meaningless for them because they do not have the required background information. One widely cited example of this is the use of white, middle-class-oriented readers for children from nonwhite, poor neighborhoods, or, as was the case in the Arctic until recently, for Eskimo children. The Eskimo children, who had never seen a city, an automobile, a telephone,

or an indoor toilet, were asked to learn to read sentences similar to "John goes for a drive," "Fire fighters, police officers, and college professors are our friends." (Now, of course, many Eskimos have satellite dishes and access to hundreds of television channels, so their cultural isolation has been much reduced.)

Do you remember learning that a demagogue is "an unprincipled politician who panders to the emotions and prejudices of the populace"? That the center

of the earth is "in a stage of igneous fusion"? That the closest star is "several billion light-years away"? How meaningful was this information?

---

*PPC: It ain't all that clear to me. Man, that's a lot of jargon in one sentence. Is that the way the bear actually talks?

AUTHOR: No (although that might be the way he thinks). But it makes the point: Even jargon can be clear if it's well anchored among other meaningful ideas.

Although Ausubel accepts the usefulness of a discovery approach in some instances, he remains a strong advocate of expository teaching. He argues that most learning is of the reception variety and that any alternative would be highly inefficient in terms of the time involved, the cost incurred, and the benefits to the learner. Relatively little school learning can be discovered by a student, says Ausubel, not only because it would take too long but also because students are not always capable of discovering much that is significant. Even subjects that apparently lend themselves to discovery approaches can often be mastered as well and faster if the information is given to the learner in relatively final form. Ausubel believes that after the age of 11 or 12, the learner possesses enough background information to understand many new concepts clearly if they are explained simply. After this age, says Ausubel, asking a student to "discover" is largely a waste of time.

SCIENTIFIC COMPARISONS

Because a number of studies have attempted to compare discovery-oriented and reception-oriented approaches to teaching and learning, it should be possible to evaluate the two without relying solely on opinion, conjecture, or theoretical speculation. However, that is not really the case because the research does not consistently support one approach over the other and is often confusing and contradictory. Why? Partly because different studies often use different criteria for assessing the effectiveness of different approaches. For example, some studies look at speed of learning, others are concerned with retention, some attempt to assess transfer, and others look at affective or motivational changes in learners.

Another reason that the conclusions of teaching-outcome studies are sometimes contradictory is that it is often impossible to control (and therefore to equate or compare) the approaches used in different studies—or sometimes even within a single study. Not only are students and classes dramatically different from one another but so are teachers. A well-prepared expository lesson might be extremely effective when presented by Mr. Joneskowski, but Ms. Rudifesk might present the same lesson poorly. By the same token, one fifth-grade class might respond exceptionally well to a discovery lesson, whereas another might be totally confused by the same lesson presented by the same teacher.

Some Studies. Studies that have attempted to evaluate the effectiveness of a single approach (rather than comparing two different approaches) have not led to clear conclusions, either. Among these are a large number of studies that have looked at the contribution of advance organizers to learning, retention, and transfer. Grippin and Peters (1984) point out

that about half these studies indicate that the use of organizers makes a significant difference; the other half find that learning is just as effective without the use of organizers. The most important conclusion from their survey, however, is that *good* organizers are effective more often than not.

Mayer (1979) suggests that the most effective organizers are those that (1) allow the student to generate all or most of the logical relationships in the material to be learned, (2) point out clear relationships between familiar and less familiar material, (3) are relatively simple to learn and use, and (4) are used in situations in which the learner would not spontaneously use an organizer, perhaps because of inexperience or inability to recall relevant information.

The effectiveness of discovery approaches has also been researched. Here, too, there is often confusion and contradiction, resulting in part from inconsistent definition, inappropriate measurement, and uncontrolled (and often uncontrollable) differences among teachers and students. However, even strong advocates of other approaches generally concede that discovery approaches can be highly effective in a variety of circumstances, particularly given the right sort of learner guidance. (See, for example, Corno & Snow, 1986; Leutner, 1993).

Some Conclusions. What, then, should the teacher conclude? Should teachers use mostly discovery or mostly expository approaches? The simple answer is that the question is not as simple as it sounds, nor are the choices as clear. A good teacher will, of course, use both.

Disturbing as it might be for those who prefer the uncomplicated comfort of a black or white position, in a great many instances it is impossible to use only one instructional approach to the complete exclusion of others. Johnny, intensely motivated to discover the mating habits of that noble barnyard fowl, the turkey, runs to the local library and finds a learned exposition on the turkey. From this exposition he learns a bewildering amount. Discovery learning? In contrast, Frank's teacher, a recent reception-learning convert,

In discovery-oriented instruction, students are given much of the responsibility for discovering concepts, principles, and relationships; in reception-oriented learning, teachers present the material in relatively final form, pointing out important relationships among new and old learning. Discovery learning, which is sometimes especially suitable in some science lessons,

ELIZABETH CREWS

presents a brilliant exposition of the mating habits of turkeys to his bench-bound students. During the course of this exposition, it occurs to Frank that turkeys have been unnecessarily and unjustly demeaned in recent times, as is evident in the popular expression, "You turkey!" In the course of his inspired musings, he discovers that there is little reason not to rank turkeys with eagles as birds worthy of our respect and admiration. Reception learning?

The confusion arising from these illustrations may be lessened by the realization that learning is what students do and teaching is what teachers do. A teacher who emphasizes discovery will try to arrange the teaching/learning situation so that students are encouraged to experiment, to think, to gather information, and, most important, to arrive at their own organization of that information. Teachers who emphasize expository teaching will be more concerned with organizing information so that it is immediately meaningful for students and therefore becomes a stable part of their existing cognitive structure. In the end, however, it is the student who learns. And, in spite of a teacher's emphases to the contrary, students may discover new information and new relationships for themselves, or they may discover no more than a structured exposition ready to be learned and assimilated as is.

OTHER COGNITIVE INSTRUCTIONAL MODELS AND EMPHASES

The juxtaposition of apparently opposing points of view is sometimes a useful teaching device. It highlights differences and, if Ausubel is correct, makes the points of view more memorable—more easily dissociated from each other.

But there is also a disadvantage to this approach: It exaggerates differences and masks similarities. It leaves the impression that the points of view are more different and the theorists more adamant in their beliefs than is actually the case.

This chapter is a case in point. Juxtaposing the theories of Bruner and Ausubel has underlined the differences between them—especially the discovery-versus-expository debate. At the same time, this approach has perhaps glossed over important points of agreement between them—especially the conviction of each that the

RICHARD PASLEY/STOCK, BOSTON

may have some advantages in terms of motivation of students and meaningfulness of the material learned. Reception learning, which lends itself well to large-group presentations, may offer advantages in terms of efficient and effective use of time.

key to successful cognitive processing is to be found in the learner's organization of knowledge. Both positions are, after all, unwaveringly cognitive. Both present a view of the learner as an active, information processing organism for whom the environment is meaningful to the extent that new material can be related to existing cognitive structure. Furthermore, the descriptions that each theory provides of the formation of cognitive structure are similar, even though their language is different (categories and coding systems on the one hand; subsumers and subsumption on the other). And, as we have seen, in the final analysis discovery and reception learning are not totally incompatible approaches to teaching and learning. As described by Bruner and Ausubel, each is intended to lead to the acquisition of meaningful concepts, to maximize transfer, retention, and motivation, and to reduce the extent to which school learning is a passive exercise in rote learning.

COGNITIVE APPRENTICESHIP

An educational model that attempts to pull together these different emphases is termed **cognitive apprenticeship** (Collins, Brown, &

Newman, 1989). This model views the learner as an apprentice in much the same sense as novices who are apprenticed to experts to learn new trades and skills. In the cognitive sphere, the experts are parents, siblings, other peers, or adults, and, most important, teachers. Within this model, the role of the teacher is less to fill the learner's mind with information, facts, figures, procedures, and so on, than to present examples, to invite the student to explore, to provide guidance and encouragement. The model suggests that teachers need to be concerned with developing a variety of cognitive strategies so that students are equipped to explore, organize, discover, and learn on their own.

Cognitive apprenticeship approaches are not restricted to adult teachers as experts and normal ability or above-average younger students as apprentices. Evidence suggest that these approaches can be highly effective for special-needs learners (for example, Rojewski &

cognitive apprenticeship An instructional model wherein parents, siblings, other adults, and especially teachers serve as a combination of model, guide, tutor, mentor, and coach to foster intellectual growth among learners.

Modeling is an instructional technique in which learners are shown how something is done. It is highly evident in physical education, for example, where learners can easily be shown actual examples of desired behaviors. It can also be an important part of learning how to perform cognitive tasks, where it requires that teachers make cognitive procedures highly explicit and evident.

Schell, 1994), as well as for adult learners. For example, LeGrand-Brandt, Framer, and Buckmaster (1993) report that cognitive apprenticeship can be highly effective in developing both practical and theoretical knowledge in adults. Similarly, De Bruijn (1993) notes that many of the methods, as well as the sequencing and the content of adult education, are very similar to the methods and sequences often advocated by proponents of cognitive apprenticeship.

The Methods of Cognitive Apprenticeship.

Cognitive apprenticeship advocates the use of a number of specific techniques designed to clarify the role of the teacher (expert) and the learner (apprentice) (Farnham-Diggory, 1992). These include the following:

Modeling. In its simplest sense, this technique involves having teachers *show* learners how something is done. The object, notes Farnham-

Diggory (1992), is not so much that learners will then simply copy the expert's performance, but rather that they will develop conceptual models of a task. Modeling is therefore as appropriate for cognitive as for motor tasks (this is, after all cognitive apprenticeship). But if an expert is to show a novice how to perform some cognitive task, it's necessary that the steps and procedures involved in the task be made explicit and evident—among other things, by describing how specific cognitive strategies such as rehearsal or organization are being used, and using other forms of thinking out loud.

Coaching. **Coaching** involves guiding specific aspects of the student's performance. Note that in the same way as a cognitive apprenticeship

---

coaching A technique sometimes used in cognitive apprenticeship approaches to instruction, in which the learner's cognitive behavior is guided by an expert.

TABLE 6.4 SOME SCAFFOLDING TECHNIQUES

TECHNIQUE	DESCRIPTION	EXAMPLE
RECRUITMENT	Gaining the child's attention and focusing it on the requirements of the task	Okay, what we want to do is calculate the area of this right-angle triangle when we know the length of all its sides. How many square inches (cm) does it contain?
REDUCTION IN DEGREES OF FREEDOM	Reducing the tasks to manageable subtasks	Remember how to find the area of a rectangle? Can you make this triangle into a rectangle?
DIRECTION MAINTENANCE	Keeping the learner on track and motivated	Why don't you draw out the triangle, make it into a rectangle, and measure each of the sides? Maybe try another triangle and see if it's the same.
MARKING CRITICAL FEATURES	Drawing attention to the most relevant aspects of the task	How many identical right-angle triangles do you need to make a rectangle? Why don't you draw a triangle on the corner of this piece of paper and cut three or four out and make squares with them? Do you always need the same number of triangles?
FRUSTRATION CONTROL	Easing frustration associated with difficulties the child might experience	This is sometimes a hard problem even for eighth graders. You're doing really well.
DEMONSTRATION	Imitating the child's attempts, but modifying them slightly so that they are more appropriate and can then be imitated in turn by the child	Here, let me cut out two triangles exactly the same and, here, let me make a square. Now what's the area of this square. And . . . that's it . . . exactly half. And . . . right! That is the formula, you genius!

Source: Based on Bruner, Wood, & Ross (1976).

approach uses modeling to demonstrate the performance of cognitive tasks, coaching, too, is aimed at guiding the learner's cognitive behavior. Teachers might use any of a variety of techniques designed to teach thinking (to develop cognitive and metacognitive strategies), discussed in Chapter 5.

Scaffolding. Scaffolding involves providing support so that students can accomplish tasks that would otherwise be too difficult for them. The concept is discussed in Chapter 3 in connection with Vygotsky's zone of proximal growth. Recall that scaffolding is defined in terms of the various types of support that teachers need to provide for children if they are to learn. Scaffolding often takes the form of directions, suggestions, and other forms of verbal assistance, and is most effective if it involves tasks within the child's zone of proximal growth—that is, if it deals with tasks of which the child is initially incapable but that can be accomplished with the support and guidance of others.

Wood, Bruner, and Ross (1976) describe six procedures or techniques that might be used in scaffolding. These are summarized and illustrated in Table 6.4.

Fading. In a sense, **fading** is the complement of scaffolding. Scaffolding involves providing support and guidance so that the learner can perform tasks within the zone of proximal growth (by definition, tasks that require the support and assistance of others). In contrast, fading involves removing supports as the learner becomes capable of performing a given task without assistance—in other words, as the task moves from Vygotsky's zone of proximal growth to within the sphere of the learner's acquired competence. Fading assures that students eventually assume responsibility for solving problems and learning.

Articulation. **Articulation** involves verbalizing or putting into words. As a cognitive apprenticeship technique, articulation encourages learners to put their conclusions, their descriptions, the principles they have discovered, into words. Deliberate verbalization forces students to think more clearly about their cognitive processes, and is frequently an important technique in programs designed to foster the development of cognitive strategies. One example of articulation is Mulcahy's (1991) use of the Socratic dialogue, a series of questions and answers designed specifically to lead learners to become aware of their own thought processes and cognitive strategies.

Reflection. Closely related to articulation, **reflection** also requires that the learner think and verbalize the execution and results of cognitive tasks. But when reflecting, learners are encouraged to think more abstractly, and perhaps to compare their cognitive activity with a conceptual model, or sometimes with an actual physical model.

Exploration. **Exploration** is the final step in the cognitive apprenticeship instructional process—as it is in most instructional approaches. It involves generalizing what has been learned or accomplished, and is analogous to what the behaviorists refer to as transfer or generalization.

The Sequence in Cognitive Apprenticeship. Three principles guide the sequencing of material in Collins, Brown, and Newman's (1989) model of cognitive apprenticeship. The first, **global before local,** refers to the belief that learners should be provided with an overall view of what is to be learned or performed before they begin to work on specifics. In practice, the global aspect of the instruction might take the form of a summary, an overview, a completed activity, a final rendition. In this sense, the global-before-local principle is similar to Ausubel's use of advance organizers.

Second, the model suggests that material should be presented in order of increasing complexity—that is, from simplest to most complex. This is very much in line with Bruner's notion that learners should begin with the simplest examples of concepts and proceed to more general, more inclusive concepts.

---

fading A technique used in cognitive apprenticeship programs. Involves the gradual withdrawal of supports (scaffolds) for the learner as these become progressively less necessary.

articulation A cognitive apprenticeship technique in which learners are encouraged to put their conclusions, descriptions, and principles into words.

reflection In cognitive apprenticeship, a procedure in which learners are asked to think about their cognitive activities and to compare them with that of others or with abstract models.

exploration A cognitive apprenticeship procedure that requires that learners apply or generalize what they have learned in order to investigate and test the potential applications of their learning.

global before local A phrase used to describe a sequencing principle in cognitive apprenticeship. Refers to the recommendation that learners should be given some notion of what the final performance, the final task, the final global rendition will be before being asked to work on the individual subtasks that make up the whole.

Third, to increase transfer and meaningfulness of learning, the model suggests that once acquired, knowledge and skills should be applied in an ever-increasing diversity of situations. Collins, Brown, and Newman (1989) note that much that we learn from textbooks, lectures, and labs is never applied outside these situations, often because we don't know when or how to make applications. In this sense our knowledge is "inert" rather than active. Hence, the importance of exploration described earlier—the cognitive apprenticeship technique of applying and generalizing learning.

Cognitive Apprenticeship and Reflective Teaching. Earlier in this chapter we reviewed what is meant by reflective teaching strategies and described their relationship to discovery-oriented approaches to instruction. Reflective teaching strategies, we noted, are strategies designed to lead students to discover and learn for themselves, and designed as well to encourage them to think about their learning and thinking. More than this, they also require that teachers think about and analyze (reflect on) what is happening as they teach (Freiberg & Driscoll, 1992). Thus, reflective teaching is based on a philosophy that emphasizes the learner's active role in learning and that views teaching as largely a question of facilitating learning and discovery.

Cognitive apprenticeship is based on exactly the same philosophy. The learner is the apprentice; the teacher is a guide and mentor. The role of the teacher is essentially to serve as a master, an expert, who shows the novice apprentice how different cognitive tasks can be accomplished. More than this, the expert guides the apprentice's progression, selecting and arranging tasks, providing support (scaffolding) and then gently withdrawing it (fading) as it is no longer required.

An instructional model of cognitive apprenticeship, notes Roth (1993), can serve as a useful guide not only by structuring the instructor's activities (as well as those of the learner), but also by providing a metaphor for reflecting about teaching. This metaphor of "teacher as master guide" and "student as apprentice learner" lends itself especially well to teachers analyzing their instructional behaviors and evaluating the cognitive progress of their apprentices.

EMPOWERMENT

If you leave a door unlocked, says Wiske (1994), it is as though everyone has been given a key to it. The function of schools, she argues, is to unlock the doors to understanding. Hence, it is imperative that schools that have not already done so abandon the philosophy that considers intellectual matters as private and in the hands of masters who dole them out as they see fit. Instead, schools need to view their purpose as one of sharing and collaborating with learners with a view to empowering them intellectually.

It is worth repeating again the one-sentence summary of one of the most important of education's objectives, first presented in Chapter 1: The goal of education is to *empower* students. This goal, notes Mann (1994), should be the goal of all education—for the gifted as well as the less gifted. Empowering students, says Shannon (1994), is fundamental to the management of today's school.

As we saw, to empower is to enable, to give power. At a simple level, education empowers students by providing them with skills and knowledge that enable them to do important things they could not otherwise do (for example, read newspapers, write love poems, add up the money in their pocket or purse, and so on). At a deeper level, education empowers by contributing to the development of cognitive content and intellectual processes; that is, it empowers by teaching people actual things (content) as well as by teaching them how to think (process). And finally, education empowers by developing in students the sort of power that comes with feelings of social, intellectual, and personal competence.

MISCONCEPTIONS AND THEIR EFFECTS ON LEARNING

Cognitive psychology's attention to how the student learns and understands has led to some important discoveries about the ways students think. For example, it seems that many students (and many teachers as well) sometimes find it difficult to understand what might otherwise be relatively simple concepts and principles, simply because they have learned, and incorporated into their cognitive structures, certain stubborn misconceptions that interfere with learning. These are sometimes referred to as *alternative conceptions* or as *children's science*, which are less negative expressions (Soloman, 1993). Evidence suggests that more than three-quarters of fifth-grade students believe that eyes actually see objects—rather than responding to reflected light that travels in straight lines and bounces off various objects (Anderson & Smith, 1984). Similarly, elementary school children who readily state that the earth is round often have a conception different from what you or I might have of what a round earth means (Nussbaum, 1979). Some see it as a flat round thing, something like a cookie, perhaps surrounded by water; others conceive of the earth as a huge globular object with the ground near the bottom of the globe, the sky at the top, and air in between. Others, report Vosniadou and Brewer (1992), see it as a flattened sphere or perhaps as a hollow sphere like a basketball. In much the same way, some teacher trainees report that the insulating coating on electrical wires is designed to keep electrons from escaping from their pathway (West, 1988). And Lockhead (1985) found that more than three-quarters of college students don't really understand ninth-grade algebra, even if they can correctly manipulate algebraic symbols and equations.

These and a large number of related studies have been concerned primarily with what students don't know—or, more precisely, with what they think they know that is not only fundamentally incorrect but is also such a basic part of cognitive structure in specific subjects like physics or mathematics that it interferes with learning (Aron, 1994). Voss, Wiley, and Carretero (1995) summarize a number of studies that indicate how persistent these misconceptions can be.

Among the implications of these studies is the need for teachers to be aware of their students' naïve and misleading beliefs and to take pains to correct them (see, for example, Amir & Tamir, 1994; Watson, 1994). Advance organizers, questioning, verbalizing solutions to problems, and related activities might be used for this purpose. Ramsden (1988b) suggests that today's teacher needs to adopt a relational view of teaching. This view emphasizes that learning is about changing conceptions rather than simply about the addition of more facts. Accordingly, teachers need to be concerned as much with the processes of learning—with learning how to learn—as with its content. They also need to focus on the relationship between the subject matter and the learner rather than simply on the relationship between teaching methods and test performance. In Nickerson's words, "it should be the goal of education to help people become competent knowers, thinkers, and learners" (1988, p. 34). Or in Bruner's words: "The salvation is in learning how to go about learning. . . ." (1985, p. 8).

EFFECTIVE TEACHING

"A school," write Mac Iver, Reuman, and Main (1995), "is an organization that exists to provide students with opportunities to learn" (p. 377). And the challenge for educators is to find the most effective means of providing students with these opportunities.

What is the most effective of all teaching methods? The one-to-one tutorial, claims Benjamin Bloom (1984), following an extensive review of the literature. In fact, if given good tutoring, the average student can be expected to achieve at somewhere around the ninety-eighth percentile in a group of comparable students taught in a conventional classroom setting. In other words, in a tutorial situation, an average student will outperform 98 percent of students in ordinary classrooms! Hence one of the most important current challenges for educational research is to discover or devise instructional procedures that are as effective with entire classes as one-to-one tutorials are with single students. The potential for higher achievement is apparently there; only the method is lacking. Finding that method (or those methods) is the challenge.

Research on Effective Teaching. Educational literature abounds with research that has looked at the effectiveness of different instructional models and methods. This research spans a wide variety of age and grade levels and involves many subjects and instructional procedures. As a result, it is not easily described or summarized. For our purposes, however, the most important research is that which has looked at the effects of specific, theory-derived instructional procedures on the performance of learners. Often, the research has involved elaborate, relatively long-term experimental, school-based programs (see Rosenshine & Stevens, 1986, or Glaser & Bassok, 1989, for summaries and reviews).

More important, what does the research tell us?

Two Undisputed Facts. Alexander and Judy (1988) claim the research tells us many things, among which are two findings they describe as "undisputed facts." The first of these is that the more the learner knows about a specific subject (that is, the more domain-specific knowledge there is in the individual's cognitive structure), the better the learner will understand and remember. And the second is that learners who are most adept at monitoring and controlling their cognitive activities typically do better than other learners who are less adept.

These two undisputed findings have profound implications for teachers' behavior. That those with the greatest amount of domain-specific prior learning (as opposed to more general information) are better learners highlights the importance of advance preparation for learning. It also emphasizes the cumulative and hierarchical nature of much of our learning, and it lends support to the contention that both lessons and curricula need to present material so that new understanding builds on a firm base of knowledge and skills. It makes no difference whether we use the language of a Bruner (numerous, varied instances of concepts need to be presented so that the learner can discover coding systems that will permit going beyond the information given); of an Ausubel (learners need to be given—and reminded of—stable, relevant subsuming concepts so that there will be something in cognitive structure to give meaning to new learning and to which new learning can be firmly anchored); or of a Robert Gagné (the content in any given subject area needs to be presented hierarchically so that essential subordinate skills and understanding are available). In the final analysis, the instructional implications of each of these differently worded and somewhat jargon-laden statements are much the same: Understanding depends very much on what we already know. It isn't a particularly startling revelation, but it is a fundamentally important one.

The second of Alexander and Judy's (1988) undisputed facts—that learners who are best at monitoring and controlling their cognitive strategies perform better—also has clear instructional implications: Specifically, teachers must devote more time and energy to teaching the skills and strategies of thinking and learning; they must adopt methods and philosophies that reflect not only their fundamentally important role as guides and mentors but also learners' responsibility for their own learning. Approaches such as cognitive apprenticeship, various programs designed to teach cognitive and metacognitive strategies, inquiry-based instruction, reflective teaching, and the school's recognition of its need to empower students are all logical outgrowths of this second undisputed finding.

Other Findings. In addition to these two findings (which relate to the role of previous learning in achieving understanding and to the role of self-monitored cognitive strategies), cognitive research on learning presents several other findings that are relevant to instruction. Among these, Shuell (1986) includes cognitive psychology's emphasis on the active nature of learning (in contrast to a more passive view that stresses the importance of response consequences) and its concern with comprehension (rather than simply with performance). Another important line of cognitive research, mentioned earlier, deals with the role of the learner's preconceived and often incorrect notions. As Nickerson notes, "an approach to instruction that ignores [learner misconceptions] is likely to fail" (1988, p. 35).

Rosenshine and Stevens (1986) summarize a number of experimental studies that have looked at the effectiveness of theory-generated instructional programs in schools. In general, these studies show that it is possible to train teachers to follow specific instructional procedures and that students exposed to experimental programs often outperform comparable control groups on a variety of measures.

The studies reviewed by Rosenshine and Stevens (1986, p. 377) suggest that effective teaching is characterized by a number of behaviors that can be taught and encouraged in teachers. Specifically, the most effective teachers, with respect to teaching well-structured subjects, are those who

- Start their lessons with a brief review of prerequisite learning

- Begin by stating the lesson's goals
- Present material in small steps, allowing students to practice between steps
- Give explicit and detailed instructions and explanations
- Allow all students to practice lessons actively
- Ask many questions to check students' understanding and obtain responses from all students
- Provide students with immediate guidance for initial practice
- Provide systematic feedback and correct students' errors as they occur
- Provide clear and explicit instructions for seat work and monitor students' performance as necessary

Rosenshine and Stevens caution that these teaching procedures do not apply to all students at all times. As noted, they are most applicable to well-structured content that can be presented in small steps and for which the teacher can provide detailed and explicit instructions while allowing for students to practice with immediate corrective feedback. But when the lesson deals with more abstract, less-structured content (such as morality and ethics, creative writing, politics, and so on), different teaching approaches are necessary.

MAIN POINTS

1. R. Gagné's cognitive theory is based on the standard information processing (sensory memory, short-term memory, long-term memory) model. It looks for the internal and external conditions that facilitate learning—knowledge of which can improve instruction. The theory classifies learning outcomes in five major domains: intellectual skills, verbal information, cognitive strategies, attitudes, and motor skills.

2. Intellectual skills (learning discriminations, rules, and concepts) are hierarchical in that higher-level skills depend upon lower-level skills. Discriminations result from the ability to respond differentially to similar stimuli. Concepts involve responding to similarities and are best explained by reference to cognitive theories. Rules, which are statements of relationships among concepts, enable us to predict and organize and may be combined to solve complex problems.

3. Verbal information (knowledge) can be expressed in sentence form and is indispensable to conversation and other ordinary daily activities, as well as to acquiring information and to thinking.

4. Attitudes are affective predispositions to make certain choices or to behave in certain ways, given a choice of behaviors. They therefore have important motivational properties.

5. Motor skills, such as keyboarding and writing, involve the execution of controlled sequences of muscular movements.

6. R. Gagné defines cognitive strategies as including both metacognitive and cognitive skills. Metacognitive skills such as comprehension monitoring relate to knowing about knowing; cognitive skills are what we actually do when we learn, think, and remember—highlighting, underlining, note taking, outlining, making concept maps, for example.

7. Cognitive theories stress the importance of the individual learner's cognitive structure and look at how information is processed, organized, and recalled. Cognitive theories view knowledge as consisting of vast networks of relationships in which learning is built on previous knowledge and involves information processing. Declarative knowledge consists of all the facts we have learned (things that are or have been); procedural knowledge involves knowing how to do something. Schemata are metaphors for cognitive structure and functioning. Scripts are the aspects of schemata that deal with routines and sequences.

8. Cognitive psychology's principal tenets suggest that (a) the curriculum needs to be organized to reveal and emphasize relationships, and (b) schools should pay deliberate attention to developing strategies for organizing and using knowledge.

9. Bruner's cognitive theory describes learning and perception as information processing activities that involve the formation of concepts (categories) that result from abstracting commonalities among events and experiences. Hierarchical arrangements of related categories are referred to as coding systems. Coding systems are important for retention, discovery, and transfer.

10. Bruner is a strong proponent of discovery approaches to instruction, which require the learner to structure information by discovering the relationships that exist among concepts or principles. Discovery learning is affected by set (predisposition to learn in a given way), need state (degree of arousal), mastery of specifics (amount and detail of learning), and diversity of training (variety of conditions under which learning takes place).

11. Renewed interest in discovery approaches are found in constructivist approaches (based on the assumption that students construct knowledge), in the conceptual change movement (based on the recognition that teachers should be more concerned with the learners' concepts and cognitive strategies that lead to conceptual change than simply with factual information), and in reflective teaching strategies (designed to lead students to discover and learn for themselves).

12. Ausubel's theory is a cognitive attempt to explain meaningful verbal learning, especially in the classroom. He defines meaning as involving a relationship between new material and old material (cognitive structure). Cognitive structure consists of hierarchically organized concepts (subsumers) arranged much as categories are arranged in Bruner's coding systems.

13. To learn is to subsume material to existing cognitive structure. This may take the form of deriving material from preexisting structure (derivative subsumption), or it may involve material that is an extension of what is already known (correlative subsumption). Loss of ability to recall (to dissociate new material from old) is obliterative subsumption.

14. Ausubel argues that discovery learning is highly time-consuming and often impossible. His most important instructional technique involves the use of advance organizers—highly generic concepts presented before the lesson, designed to bring to mind relevant prior knowledge, and intended to clarify the relationships between new and old learning.

15. Discovery methods and expository teaching are not mutually exclusive. Both are useful. Ausubel suggests that discovery may have advantages for teaching in the early grades, for testing meaningfulness and problem solving, for ensuring transferability, and for establishing intrinsic motivation. In the end, teaching is what teachers do, and learning is what students do. Discovery teaching does not always lead to discovery learning—and vice versa.

16. Although Bruner and Ausubel present points of view that are opposite in many respects, both present a fundamentally cognitive view of the learner as an active, information processing organism whose efforts to derive meaning from the environment are closely related to the development of associated networks of concepts. Their recommendations for instruction are intended to lead to the acquisition of meaningful concepts, to maximize transfer, retention, and motivation, and to reduce passive rote learning.

17. The cognitive apprenticeship model suggests a relatively complex role for today's teacher—one that recognizes a wide diversity of desired learning outcomes (procedural as well as declarative knowledge, for example), a range of different instructional approaches (including modeling, coaching, scaffolding, fading, articulation, and reflection), and some important sequencing principles (global before local, from simplest to most complex, and toward increasing diversity).

18. An important objective of education is to empower students by providing them with knowledge, skills, and confidence.

19. Occasionally, what students don't know, or the inaccurate and misleading things they are convinced they do know, interfere with learning and understanding, hence the importance of advance organizers, questioning, and other approaches in ensuring that all learners have appropriate prerequisite knowledge and skills for new learning.

20. Two findings from cognitive research have important implications for effective teaching: (a) The more background knowledge a learner has about a subject, the more effective the learning (domain-specific knowledge), and (b) learners who are most skilled at monitoring and controlling their use of cognitive strategies learn and solve problems (use strategic knowledge) most effectively.

21. The most effective teachers for well-structured material are those who (a) begin by reviewing (often using advance organizers), (b) state goals clearly at the beginning, and (c) present material in small, detailed, and explicit steps with both ample opportunity for practice and systematic feedback during the lesson and during seat work.

APPLIED QUESTIONS

▶ Illustrate each of what Gagné describes as the nine events of instruction.

▶ Design a guided discovery lesson.

▶ What would you include in an expository lesson making use of various kinds of advance organizers?

▶ Describe and illustrate several of the techniques of scaffolding.

▶ If you were to develop a mnemonic device for learning some of the behaviors and characteristics of the most effective teachers, what would you create?

STUDY TERMS

advance organizers **211**
articulation **220**
attitude **196**
category **202**
chains **193**
coaching **218**
coding system **202**
cognitive apprenticeship **217**
comparative organizer **211**
conceptual change
  movement **206**
conditions of learning **191**
constructivist approach **206**
correlative subsumption **209**

declarative knowledge **200**
derivative subsumption **209**
discovery learning **202**
dissociability **211**
diversity of training **206**
enactive **207**
exploration **220**
expository organizer **211**
expository teaching **210**
fading **220**
global before local **220**
guided discovery **208**
iconic **207**
intellectual skills **193**

mastery of specifics **205**
need state **205**
obliterative subsumption **211**
procedural knowledge **200**
reception learning **202**
reflection **220**
script **201**
selective perception **190**
semantic encoding **191**
set **204**
spiral curriculum **207**
subsumers **211**
subsumption **209**
symbolic **207**

SUGGESTED READINGS

Original sources are among the best references for approaches to learning theory such as Gagné's, Bruner's, and Ausubel's. The following references are clear presentations of their theories and educational recommendations:

GAGNÉ, R. M., BRIGGS, L. J., & WAGER, W. W. (1992). *Principles of instructional design* (4th ed.), Fort Worth: Harcourt Brace Jovanovich.

BRUNER, J. S. (1961). *The process of education*. Cambridge, Mass.: Harvard University Press.

BRUNER, J. S. (1990). *Acts of meaning*. Cambridge, Mass.: Harvard University Press.

BRUNER, J. S., GOODNOW, J. J., & AUSTIN, G. A. (1956). *A study of thinking*. New York: Wiley.

AUSUBEL, D. P. (1968). *Educational psychology: A cognitive view*. New York: Holt, Rinehart & Winston.

An excellent collection of articles dealing with the implications of children's ideas about science for teachers is:

BLACK, P. J., & LUCAS, A. M. (eds.) (1993). *Children's informal ideas in science*. New York: Routledge.

Farnham-Diggory's book is highly recommended for the contemporary teacher concerned about the intellectual development of learners. The Hamilton and Ghatala book presents a practical attempt to link theories of learning with instructional strategies:

FARNHAM-DIGGORY, S. (1992). *Cognitive processes in education* (2nd ed.). New York: HarperCollins.

HAMILTON, R., & GHATALA, E. (1994). *Learning and instruction*. New York: McGraw-Hill.

The much feared grizzly bear (*Ursus horribilis*) weighs about 900 pounds at maturity. Many "experts" consider the grizzly to be a species of the brown bear (*Ursus arctos*). The grizzly's prodigal strength is attested to by one bear that moved an 850-pound trap one-quarter of a mile and then escaped (Soper, 1964).

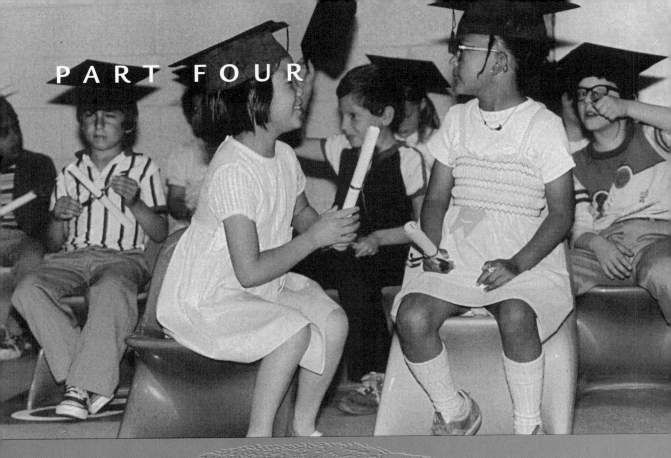

PART FOUR

I will not Reason and Compare: my business
is to Create.
WILLIAM BLAKE, *Jerusalem*

*Diversity
and Teaching*

IN EDUCATION, THERE IS *clearly a need for reason and comparison, a need for analysis, contemplation, reflection, and other calculated and calculating processes. But are these incompatible with creativity? Does reason leave no room for intuition and insight, no time or inclination for inspiration? The first two chapters in Part IV look at these questions and suggest ways in which teachers can enhance creativity in students. They look, as well, at other human characteristics that sometimes make us dramatically different from one another; this, too, has tremendous implications for teaching. And the last chapter in this section presents an antidote to the accusation that our sciences tend to mechanize and to dehumanize; it presents some humanistic approaches to teaching.*

CHAPTER 7

Since when was genius found respectable?
ELIZABETH BARRETT BROWNING,
   Aurora Leigh

Intelligence and Creativity

PREVIEW

Intelligence and creativity, those nebulous and ill-defined characteristics, are among the most prized of our "possessions"—and perhaps among the most useful as well. This chapter examines the meanings of these terms, the forces that shape the qualities they represent, and some of the methods that have been devised to assess them. In addition, the chapter looks at the relationship between creativity and intelligence. Is it possible to be creative but stupid? to be intelligent but totally devoid of creative talent?

- What is intelligence, as defined by Das, Sternberg, and Gardner?

- How are group and individual intelligence tests alike? Different?

- What are the most common myths concerning intelligence?

- How are family and educational variables related to intelligence?

- What is creativity?

- What is the relationship between creativity and intelligence?

When I was in tenth grade, Sister Sainte Mélanie, our teacher, announced that someone would be sent from the Shell Lake School Unit office to give us an intelligence test. "You'll have to do very well on this test," she warned. "Or else."

"Or else what?" asked Barney, who never did well on any test. As my grandpa put it, wit rather than kindness being his main strength, "The only test Barney'll ever do good on is his urine test . . . but only if he stays up all night to study for it." (Maybe his wit was not that much of a strength either.)

"Well," explained the good sister, "those who don't do well on this test, it means they got a poor IQ. An those that got a poor IQ are going to fail lots of things in life, they'll never get very far, maybe they'll just have to stay right here in Victoire and milk cows and fork hay for someone else until they die."

"And those that got good IQs," she continued, "they're the ones who'll get to go places and do things and make money and buy cows and be important. That's the way it is with IQ."

So for about a week we worried about this IQ test until finally the day came and the guy arrived with a box of tests and another one of pencils and he laid a pencil and a test, face down don't-you-dare-touch-it-until-I-give-you-the-signal, one on each desk and then, bang he smashed his fist down on the stopclock to start it and yelled, "Go!" and we turned our papers over and started to read questions and write answers like mad until, bang, he smashed down again on the clock and yelled "Stop!" which we did.

Then the guy placed the intelligence tests in a box, very carefully, and took them away with him. For a long time after that we wondered what our IQs were, would he write us a letter and let us know. But he didn't do that. Instead, he stuffed all our IQs inside an envelope and brought them to school one day, and he and Sister Sainte Mélanie huddled over them speaking in hushed whispers while we labored over our desk assignments. At recess they called Barney in and asked him what chores were his favorite. "I told them feeding the pigs," he explained to us, "and they said, 'with your IQ that kind of job would be just about perfect'."

Later they called in Priest, which is what we called Louis Boutin on account of how he was an altar boy and he'd been studying Latin since fourth grade. "What'd they tell you?" we asked Priest. "Told me I could be a brain doctor," he bragged, "or a science wizard."

Me, they never called me in and so I never did find out for sure whether I had a high or a low IQ—because I never actually believed Horse-face when he said he'd gotten into the school and copied out all the IQ numbers for everybody from where they were kept in Sister Sainte Mélanie's desk. But some of those who had big numbers thought he was telling the truth.

WESTERN VIEWS OF INTELLIGENCE

We in the Western world, notes Lund (1994), think that IQ is an extremely important concept. To a large extent, its importance represents an outgrowth of our preoccupation with the individual rather than with the group. IQ, we think, is a measure of one of the most important differences among individuals. One reason we consider IQ so important is that we naively believe it to be a mysterious something that each of us has just so much of. And we think too, that those who have the most are the fortunate ones who will succeed at just about anything they try; and those who have the least are doomed to sadness and failure.

As we see later in this chapter, these are just two of the myths that cloud our understanding of intelligence and of measured IQ. Belief in these myths explains our surprise at the fact that Priest did not become a brain surgeon or a scientist, that he became a drunk and panhandled for his living until a train finally ran over him. That Barney founded an oil company and is making tons of money also seems surprising—and says little for my grandfather's wisdom.

Is measured IQ of no consequence? Or is it sometimes simply measured very badly? These are some of the questions this chapter addresses.

Not all cultures give the same significance to intelligence. As a case in point, consider the case "Hiroki's About Average; Like Everybody Else." Note how the teacher, Fukui-sensei, perceives and responds to individual talents—or, more precisely, how she *fails* to perceive individual differences. This culturally linked tendency might, in fact, be one of the important differences between Japanese and North American schools.

In contrast, North American teachers and parents are alert and highly responsive to individual differences. In fact, most school jurisdictions allocate a high percentage of their resources to identifying individual strengths and weaknesses, and responding to them. And of all the different measures of individual talent and capability, the one to which we attribute the greatest significance is clearly intelligence. Unfortunately, it is also one of the most global, the most poorly defined, and the most misunderstood of human characteristics.

Wagner and Sternberg (1984) suggest that there are basically three different views of intelligence. They label the first the "psychometric view." Historically, it has been the most common approach to understanding intelligence. **Psychometrics** refers to the measurement of psychological functions; hence, the psychometric view of intelligence is that which is based on a measurement approach.

The second view is Piaget's. This perspective sees intelligence as an active process involving progressive adaptation through the interplay of assimilation and accommodation. The results of intelligent activity are manifested in cognitive structure. The principal characteristics of cognitive structure change with age; the

---

psychometrics Refers to the measurement of psychological functions and characteristics.

CASE: HIROKI'S ABOUT AVERAGE; LIKE EVERYBODY ELSE

THE PLACE: Komatsudani preschool, east side, Tokyo.

THE SITUATION: Fukui-sensei, the preschool teacher, has been putting the children through their paces while a group of American observers watches and takes notes. When the class ends for the day, the observers meet with Fukui-sensei.

Observer 1: That little boy, what's his name, the one with the yellow shirt, over on that side . . .

Fukui-sensei: That's Hiroki.

Observer 1: Yes, Hiroki. How intelligent he is. Compared to the others, I mean.

Observer 2: Yes, superintelligent . . .

Fukui-sensei: No, no. Hiroki's intelligence is about average, the same as everybody else's.

Observer 1: But he seems so gifted.

Observer 2: Yeah, he always finished his work before all the others. And then he sang those wonderful songs so well to entertain the others.

Fukui-sensei: But surely you don't think speed is the same thing as intelligence. And his entertaining the other children is a reflection not so much of intelligence as it is of his great need for attention.

Source: Based in part on Tobin, Wu, & Davidson, 1989, p. 24.

changes are the essential features of Piaget's developmental theory.

The third view of intelligence is the information processing view. Like Piaget's approach, it is more qualitative than quantitative. That is, it seeks to describe the important characteristics of intelligence in terms of processes rather than to measure its products.

We looked at Piaget's theory in Chapter 3; in this chapter, we discuss the psychometric approach, and we look at two approaches related to the information processing view: Gardner's "multiple intelligences" and Sternberg's "componential theory."

PSYCHOMETRIC DEFINITIONS
OF INTELLIGENCE

There are a tremendous variety of measurement-based (psychometric) definitions of intelligence; here are four of them:

▸ "Intelligence is what the tests test" (Boring, 1923, p. 35).

▸ "The global and aggregate capacity of an individual to think rationally, to act purposefully, and to deal effectively with his environment" (Wechsler, 1958, p. 7).

▸ "Intelligence A: The innate potential for cognitive development." . . . "Intelligence B: A general or average level of development of ability to perceive, to learn, to solve problems, to think, to adapt" (Hebb, 1966, p. 332).

▸ To Hebb's definition, West and MacArthur added another dimension, labeled Intelligence A[1]: "The present potential of an individual for future development of intelligent behavior, assuming optimum future treatment adapted to bring out that potential" (1964, p. 18).

The first definition ("intelligence is what the tests test") is not meant to be facetious. It is at once an admission that intelligence is a difficult concept to define and an assertion that intelligence tests are useful if the scores they provide are related to success on tasks we think require intelligence. Whatever they measure can then be called "intelligence," even if its exact nature is unknown. But, argues Gallagher (1994), this definition is not especially productive or useful compared with more recent definitions that look more specifically at the actual processes involved in intelligent behavior.

The second definition ("global and aggregate capacity") defines intelligence in terms of clear thinking, purposeful activity, and effective interaction with the environment. Wechsler sees intelligence as a "global" capacity, in contrast to the view advanced by Spearman (1927) and Thurstone (1938), among others, that intelligence is not a single characteristic but instead consists of a number of separate abilities or factors. Guilford (1959), whose work is reviewed later in this chapter in the section on creativity, also suggests that it's useful to view intelligence as consisting of separate abilities.

The third and fourth definitions make useful distinctions among different types of intelligence. As Vygotsky (1986) points out, people are born with different potentials for development—what Hebb calls "Intelligence A." However, conventional measures of intelligence assess "Intelligence B"—current level of development—rather than Intelligence A. Inferences about potential are then based on measures of current performance. In contrast, Vygotsky's approach to measuring intelligence (as well as Feuerstein's, 1980), gives test subjects hints and suggestions in an effort to arrive at a better estimate of potential performance.

In another psychometric approach, Cattell (1971) makes an important distinction between two kinds of intelligence. On the one hand, certain capabilities seem to underlie much of our intelligent behavior. These capabilities are essentially nonverbal and are relatively unaffected by culture or experience; Cattell labels them **fluid abilities.** Measures such as general

---

fluid abilities Cattell's term for intellectual abilities that seem to underlie much of our intelligent behavior and that are not highly affected by experience (for example, general reasoning, attention span, and memory for numbers). Fluid abilities are more likely to decline in old age.

reasoning, memory, attention span, and analysis of figures reflect fluid abilities. And although these fluid abilities are less affected by culture and schooling, various programs designed to teach learning/thinking strategies can have a measurable effect on them. So, too, does general schooling, which is clearly associated with gains or losses in measured intelligence (Lohman, 1993).

In contrast with fluid abilities is a grouping of intellectual abilities that are primarily verbal and that are highly influenced by culture, experience, and education. These **crystallized abilities** are reflected in vocabulary tests, tests of general information, and arithmetic skills. Not surprisingly, performance on crystallized measures tends to increase with age, sometimes into very old age (Horn & Donaldson, 1980). In contrast, fluid abilities seem to be more dependent on physiological structures and more susceptible to the ravages of age; they typically show declines in old age (Horn, 1976).

A Synthesis. How, then, should we define intelligence? Is it what the tests test? a global and aggregate sort of thing? a two-sided thing involving what is potential as well as what is actual? a different two-sided thing involving relatively pure capabilities on the one hand and capabilities that are highly affected by experience on the other? Or should we use a combination of all these definitions?

As Vernon (1969) observes, when we speak of intelligence, we often mean any one of three things or a combination thereof: a genetic capacity (presumably reflected in fluid intelligence or in Hebb's Intelligence A), a test score (derived from any of a large number of different intelligence tests), or observed behavior (reflected in Hebb's Intelligence B).

Or should we, as Das (1992) argues, abandon the search for this elusive, almost immea-surable thing called "general intelligence" (commonly abbreviated **g**)? "If I were a young psychologist," says Das, "I wouldn't waste my life looking for g . . ." (p. 137). Not only does trying to rank people on a single scale of merit like general intelligence fail to take into consideration the tremendous variation of interests, skills, and capabilities of different individuals but it is politically dangerous. It leads too easily to the conclusion that such and such a race is intellectually inferior, especially if we assume that intelligence is largely genetically determined—as do Jensen (1980) and Rushton (1988).*

Instead, says Das, we have to look at three aspects of intelligence: the processes and components of intelligent behavior, the individual's competence in relation to the person's culture and age, and the possibility of improving competence through training and experience.

DAS' PASS THEORY OF INTELLIGENCE

Das' description of the processes and components of intelligent behavior takes the form of an information processing theory of intelligence (Das, Naglieri, & Kirby, 1994). Simplified, the theory recognizes three separate units involved in intellectual functioning. The first is basic to all mental processes, and is simply attention or arousal. Without the proper level of arousal of the brain, and without attention, the individual would be largely unresponsive to the environment.

---

*PPC: Perhaps the author should point out how controversial and inflammatory this issue is. I think the bear should be careful to divorce himself from statements such as those of Jensen and Rushton.

AUTHOR: This is a controversial and inflammatory issue, as is illustrated later in this chapter (see, for example, the box "Experience and Intelligence: A Debate"). A politically correct bear would never align himself on *that* side. No way.

---

crystallized abilities Cattell's term for intellectual abilities that are highly dependent on experience (verbal and numerical abilities, for example). These abilities do not appear to decline significantly with advancing age.

g Abbreviation for general intelligence—a basic intellectual capability sometimes assumed to underlie all manifestations of intelligence.

The second unit involved in intelligence, says Das, is actual cognitive processing—the processes by which the individual recognizes, organizes, interprets, or otherwise responds to stimulation. Hence, it is this second unit that is responsible for receiving, processing, and retaining information.

Cognitive processing, explain Das, Naglieri, and Kirby (1994), involves two distinct types of processes. **Simultaneous processsing** occurs when at least some of the elements of a situation can be responded to at the same time (are simultaneously "surveyable" in the authors' terms). As an example, a child's recognizing a geometric figure involves primarily simultaneous scanning because the recognition depends on recognizing interrelationships among elements, and these interrelationships can be perceived immediately or simultaneously.

Successive processing, in contrast, involves a sequential processing of information. It is required when elements of a problem or activity form a series; moving to the final element in the chain is impossible until preceding elements have been processed in the appropriate sequence. For example, solving a complex problem in mathematics may require successive processing if it requires that an ordered series of subordinate tasks be sequentially accomplished to reach the final solution. Similarly, most motor tasks (such as writing or pitching a baseball, for example) involve successive processing.

The third unit in the Das model of intelligence is that which allows the individual to

One widely accepted western view of intelligence maintains that it is evident in the ability to adapt and to solve problems—sometimes very practical problems like where do these big round things go and in what order? When psychologists speak of intelligence they might also mean an innate, largely genetic capacity, some of the characterisatics of which are evident in the individual's performance on a test of intelligence.

form plans, to put them into effect, and to evaluate their effectiveness. It is, in a sense, the intentional or conscious aspect of intelligence. Put another way, **planning** in this model corresponds to metacognitive strategies—the strategies that allow the individual to control cognitive activity, to monitor and evaluate it, and to modify it as necessary.

To summarize, the three units of intelligent functioning described by Das and associates are *p*lanning, *a*ttention, and *s*uccessive and *s*imultaneous processing: Hence the acronym

simultaneous processing One of four major components of the PASS model of intelligence. Involves cognitive processing wherein important elements of the stimulus situation are reacted to simultaneously—as in perceptual recognition, for example.

successive processing Cognitive processing where elements of a stimulus situation need to be responded to sequentially—as in solving some logical problems or executing motor tasks. An important element in the PASS model of intelligence.

planning In the Das model of intelligence, this is the intentional or conscious aspect; in other terms, *metacognitive strategies*.

PASS. Not only does this model provide a useful cognitive processing view of intelligence, but there are indications that it might be especially useful in suggesting ways of remedying cognitive deficits in some children with learning problems. In the **PREP program** (PASS remedial program) developed by Das and associates, children are first assessed for deficits in simultaneous or successive processing. They are then given a series of eight to ten tasks designed specifically to provide strategies to remedy deficits. These tasks typically involve procedures related to cognitive processes such as rehearsing, categorizing, predicting, monitoring performance, and so on. In one study using PREP, a group of fifty-one children who had been experiencing reading problems showed significant improvement following training (Das, Mishra, & Pool, 1995).

STERNBERG'S VIEW

Robert Sternberg's theory (1984a, 1984b, 1986) is also an information processing view of intelligence—one that stresses the importance of the strategies and processes involved in knowing. Accordingly, it is a cognitive perspective; it maintains that one of the main components of intelligent activity is cognitive functions. And, most important from the teacher's point of view, it suggests that these functions are largely acquired and can therefore be taught. That, in a

nutshell, is the rationale underlying the cognitive strategies programs currently being developed and tested.

Contextual Intelligence. Sternberg's view of intelligence is sometimes labeled a **contextual theory of intelligence** and a **componential theory of intelligence.** The theory is contextual in that it defines intelligence in terms of adaptation to a particular environment. In Sternberg's words, intelligence is the "purposive selection and shaping of and adaptation to real-world environments relevant to one's life" (1984a, p. 312). One important feature of this definition is that it emphasizes the individual's control over the environment. It says, in effect, that intelligent individuals exercise control over their environments not only by changing and molding significant aspects of them but also by selecting them in the first place. Thus, it would be quite stupid (or at least moderately unintelligent) for someone who is tone deaf to select a career in music or for someone who suffers from severe vertigo to buy a home high on a cliff.

How can we measure contextual intelligence? Sternberg says that one way is simply to ask people what is considered intelligent and stupid in their culture. After all, contextual intelligence is a highly practical kind of intelligence—a kind of intelligence in which adaptation to the day-to-day tasks of living is far more important than abstract notions of what is rational and what isn't (Sternberg, 1993). Because intelligence is simply an indication of how well a person adapts in a specific environment, people who live in that environment may

---

PASS The Das model of intellectual functioning, based on a three-unit model of information processing: attending (involving arousal and paying attention); processing (successive or simultaneous processing); and planning (metacognitive components, that is, involved in monitoring and controlling cognitive activity).

PREP program A cognitive strategies training program based on the PASS model of intellectual functioning. It seeks to identify specific deficiencies and problems in cognitive processing and to remedy them by providing learners with tasks designed to develop processing skills.

---

contextual theory of intelligence Robert Sternberg's view that intelligence involves adaptation in the real world—that is, adaptation in the individual's context.

componential theory of intelligence Sternberg's view that intelligence can usefully be viewed as consisting of three sets of components, each of which relates to how the individual processes information: metacomponents (metastrategies), performance components, and knowledge acquisition components.

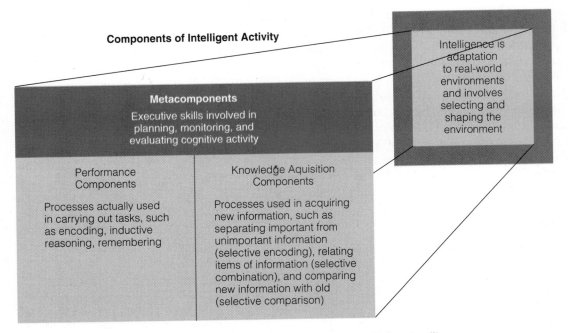

Components of Intelligent Activity

Metacomponents
Executive skills involved in planning, monitoring, and evaluating cognitive activity

Performance Components	Knowledge Aquisition Components
Processes actually used in carrying out tasks, such as encoding, inductive reasoning, remembering	Processes used in acquiring new information, such as separating important from unimportant information (selective encoding), relating items of information (selective combination), and comparing new information with old (selective comparison)

Intelligence is adaptation to real-world environments and involves selecting and shaping the environment

F I G U R E 7 . 1 Sternberg's information processing view of intelligence defines intelligence as adaptation to the real world (a contextual view). Adaptation is made possible through cognitive processes such as planning and monitoring intellectual activity (metacomponents), actually carrying out cognitive activity (performance components), and learning (knowledge acquisition components).

be expected to be the best sources of information about what is required for effective adaptation. Not surprisingly, an analysis of the responses of people in North American cultures to the question of what makes up intelligent behavior reveals three broad groupings of abilities that best describe intelligent people: practical problem-solving ability, verbal ability, and social competence. In other cultures, responses might be different.

One advantage of a contextual view of intelligence is that it highlights the importance of the individual's success in coping with the ordinary demands of life in the social and physical context; that is, it removes intelligence from the realm of the abstract and theoretical and brings it to a more concrete, more easily understood level. But this view also has a number of disadvantages. First, it is too inclusive. Because all adaptive behaviors are intelligent, almost all behaviors are potentially intelligent (even if they are perhaps somewhat stupid in one con-

text, they may be adaptive in some other context). Second, the contextualist view does not adequately describe the processes and structures that underlie intelligence; instead, it describes intelligence in terms of the characteristics and effects of behavior.

A Componential View. As a response to these weaknesses, Sternberg (1986) has proposed a componential theory of human intelligence. This theory identifies three separate components of intelligence (see Figure 7.1). First are the components involved in metacognition—that is, in planning, monitoring, and evaluating cognitive performance. These are labeled **metacomponents.** They also include what Sternberg

metacomponents One of Sternberg's three components of human intelligence. Metacomponents include the skills involved in planning, monitoring, and evaluating cognitive performance—in other words, the skills of metacognition.

calls "executive skills"—those used in making decisions about which cognitive activities to use in monitoring and evaluating the results of these ongoing activities. Conventional measures of intelligence typically do not measure metacomponents.

Second, there are **performance components.** These are processes that are actually used in carrying out tasks. They include inductive reasoning, encoding, analyzing, remembering, paying attention, and so on. Note that these processes are what Cattell defines as *fluid abilities*. They appear to be relatively independent of experience and more dependent on innate factors. Sternberg suggests that a number of conventional intelligence tests that measure fluid intelligence can also serve as good measures of performance components.

The third of Sternberg's three components of intelligence are the **knowledge acquisition components.** Sternberg (1984c) identifies three processes that are important for acquiring new information: selective encoding (separating relevant from irrelevant information), selective combination (combining selected information with other information so as to make it meaningful), and selective comparison (deriving meaning from new information by relating it to previous learning).

GARDNER'S MULTIPLE INTELLIGENCES

Sternberg's componential theory of intelligence and Das' PASS model are especially useful for teachers for one principal reason: They emphasize the extent to which intelligence is an activity—an information processing activity. This view presents a sharp contrast to earlier views that tended to view intelligence as a mysterious quality or characteristic that some people were lucky enough to have a great deal of; others, less fortunate, had to get by with much less. A cognitive processing view suggests that intelligence is a little like a box of tools that we use to play the game of cognition. We may not all have the same tools in our kits, but we can certainly improve how we use them, and we can learn a great deal from how others use theirs.

From the teacher's point of view, it's also important to recognize not only that intelligence involves different cognitive processes, but also that high competence and talent may be manifested in some but not necessarily all areas of human functioning. This underlines the need to encourage the development of competencies in those areas where the individual might be especially gifted and to provide support and assistance in other areas.

Gardner (1983) suggests that we have not one but seven largely unrelated kinds of intelligences. This **theory of multiple intelligence** describes competence in seven distinct areas— that is, it describes seven kinds of intelligence: logical-mathematical, linguistic, musical, spatial, bodily kinesthetic, interpersonal, and intrapersonal (see Table 7.1).

There are problems with attempts to assess each of these seven capabilities, note Gardner and Hatch (1989). First, most of our experience in measuring intelligence involves mathematical, linguistic, and logical tasks. That is because in Western cultures, these are the sorts of tasks that we assume are most closely related to intelligent behavior. But the Gardner view of multiple intelligence requires the development of a

---

performance components One of Sternberg's three components of human intelligence. Performance components are the skills and processes actually used in carrying out intellectual tasks (reasoning, encoding, analyzing, remembering, and so on).

knowledge acquisition components One of Sternberg's three facets of human intelligence, related to procedures used for learning new information (separating the important from the unimportant, associating items of information, comparing the new with the old).

theory of multiple intelligence Howard Gardner's belief that human intelligence consists of seven distinct and largely unrelated areas of talent or capability: logical-mathematical, linguistic, musical, spatial, bodily kinesthetic, interpersonal, and intrapersonal.

TABLE 7.1 GARDNER'S SEVEN INTELLIGENCES

INTELLIGENCE	POSSIBLE OCCUPATION	CORE COMPONENTS
Logical-mathematical	Scientist Mathematician	Sensitivity to and capacity to discern logical or numerical patterns; ability to handle long chains of reasoning
Linguistic	Poet Journalist	Sensitivity to the sounds, rhythms, and meanings of words; sensitivity to the different functions of language
Musical	Composer Violinist	Abilities to produce and appreciate rhythm, pitch, and timbre; appreciation of the forms of musical expressiveness
Spatial	Navigator Sculptor	Capacities to perceive the visual-spatial world accurately and to manipulate the mental representations that result
Bodily kinesthetic	Dancer Athlete	Abilities to control one's body movements and to handle objects skillfully
Interpersonal	Therapist Salesperson	Capacities to discern and respond appropriately to the moods, temperaments, motivations, and desires of other people
Intrapersonal	Person with detailed accurate self-knowledge	Access to one's own feelings and the ability to discriminate among them and draw upon them to guide behavior; knowledge of one's own strengths, weaknesses, desires, and intelligences

Source: From Gardner & Hatch (1989). "Multiple Intelligences Go to School: Educational Implications of the Theory of Multiple Intelligences." *Educational Researcher*, 18(8): 4–10.

range of new tasks to tap previously neglected competencies such as bodily kinesthetic, intra-personal, and interpersonal.

Second, it now seems clear that intelligence cannot easily be separated from culture and background. As a result, assessing these multiple intelligences requires taking into consideration the extent to which social background influences the child's competence, interest, and even willingness in the testing situation. "The goal of detecting distinctive human strengths, and using them as a basis for engagement and learning may prove to be worthwhile . . ." conclude Gardner and Hatch, (1989, p. 9). Gardner (1993) argues that schools need to pay far more attention to what and how they teach. In particularly, many schools fail in their most important mission: teaching so that children truly understand (Kieran & Gardner, 1992).

SUMMARY OF VIEWS OF INTELLIGENCE

In summary, there are three separate views of intelligence. The psychometric view looks at intelligence as a phenomenon that is evident in the individual's performance on tasks assumed to require intelligent behavior and that can therefore be measured by a carefully selected assortment of these tasks. Piaget's view describes what he terms "intelligence in action." He sees intelligence as an ongoing adaptive process involving the interplay of assimilation and accommodation and resulting in the gradual development of cognitive structure. And the information processing view is concerned with the cognitive processes that underlie intelligent behavior.

Current approaches to intelligence have two things in common: They stress processes more than products, and they recognize the diversity of skills and capabilities that compose

INTELLIGENCE AND SIZE OF BRAIN

We somewhat arrogantly assume that of all animals on earth, we are by far the most intelligent and the most inventive. Thus have we named ourselves *homo sapiens*, the wise one. As evidence, of our wisdom, we point proudly to our increasing domination of nature, and we scoff at the perennial struggle for survival of those less gifted than we.* So viewed, we appear to be the creature that has adapted best to the environment—and this, the ability to adapt, is a useful definition of intelligence.

Ironically, we, the self-designated wise ones, do not have the largest brain of the earthly species. In fact, the adult male brain weighs a mere 3¼ pounds, and the female brain weighs about 10 percent less— not even 3 pounds. This, compared with the 13-pound elephant brain or the brain of a whale, which in some cases weighs 19 pounds, is relatively

unimpressive. However, given the strong likelihood that the absolute weight of the brain is less related to intelligent behavior than is the ratio of brain to body weight, we still retain the advantage. Our brain-to-body-weight ratio is approximately 1 to 50; that of the whale and elephant approaches 1 to 1,000. And among those few small monkeys that have even better brain-to-body-weight ratios than we have—as high as 1 to 18—the absolute size of the brain is so small that it probably cannot do much more than handle simple physiological functioning.

But the dolphin, on the other hand, is not inordinately small or large. In fact, it often weighs no more than an adult man. Yet its average brain weight is a full 3¾ pounds. This fact has led to a great deal of speculation and research on the dolphin's intelligence—research that has not yet succeeded in determining how intelligent the dolphin really is.

Although a fairly accurate ranking of species in terms of intelligence may be based on their brain-to-body-weight ratios, such a crude indicator of intelligence does not appear to be of any real value in gauging the subtle but significant differences that exist between geniuses and less-gifted individuals within the human species. For this, instruments labeled "intelligence tests" are commonly used. Not only are these tests generally unsuitable for nonhumans, but they are often suitable only for very specific groups within the human species.

---

*And we turn a blind eye to our dwindling supply of irreplaceable resources, our idiotic penchant for polluting the environment, our unreasoning failure to control our numbers, and the increasing risk of nuclear self-annihilation.

---

intelligence. Thus, Das describes three functional units that are involved in human cognitive processing and that make up intelligence. Gardner outlines seven separate and presumably relatively independent intelligences. And Sternberg presents a contextualist definition of intelligence (intelligent behavior is behavior that is adaptive in a particular context) and argues that intelligence consists of three components: Metacomponents have to do with metacognition (planning, organizing, monitoring, and selecting processing strategies), performance components are processes that are actually used in carrying out a task (encoding, inductive reasoning, and so on), and knowledge

acquisition components have to do with acquiring new information (separating the important from the unimportant, relating items of new information, and comparing new information with old knowledge).

From an instructional point of view, intelligence is an important concept, both to the extent that it relates to school achievement and to the extent that it may sometimes require teachers to modify their instructional strategies. And from a practical point of view, teachers will most often obtain evidence of intelligence from the actual performance of their students and somewhat less often from more formal measures of intelligence.

THE CONCEPT OF CORRELATION

In fact, good teachers are sometimes remarkably good at estimating the IQs of their students without measuring them—and so are mothers, report Delgado-Hachey and Miller (1993). The correlation between teachers' estimates and actual measures is on the order of 0.55, notes Follman (1991). What does that mean?

Correlation is a frequently used term that is not always clearly understood. Two or more **variables** (properties that can vary) correlate if there is some correspondence between them. Size of shoe correlates with size of sock, income correlates with standard of living, size of house correlates with number of windows, and drunkenness correlates with alcohol consumption. These are all examples of **positive correlation:** As one variable increases, so does its correlate. The inverse relationship, labeled **negative correlation,** can also hold: Number of wild animals correlates with number of people, amount of pollutants in water correlates with number of fish, and sobriety correlates with alcohol consumption. In each of these cases, as one variable increases, the other decreases; therefore, each is an example of negative correlation.

The measure (called an *index* or *coefficient*) of correlation most often used ranges in value from –1.00 to +1.00. (The symbol used for a correlation coefficient is usually *r.*) Each extreme (plus or minus 1) indicates perfect correlation, whereas zero indicates complete lack of relatedness (see Figure 7.2). A correlation of 0.55, which

---

variable A property, measurement, or characteristic that is susceptible to variation. In psychological experimentation, qualities of human beings such as intelligence and creativity are considered variables.

positive correlation The type of relationship that exists between two variables so that high or low scores on one are associated with correspondingly high or low scores on the other.

negative correlation The type of relationship that exists between two variables when high values in one are associated with correspondingly low values in the other.

"If his IQ is based on guessing the right answers, perhaps we could assume he'll go through life being a remarkably successful guesser."

© 1996 Sidney Harris.

Follman (1991) found between IQ scores and teachers' estimates of intelligence, means that there is a relatively high probability that if a teacher estimates a student's IQ as being high (or low), testing will reveal that it is high (or low).

It's important not to make an inference of causality solely on the basis of correlation. Even though any two variables that vary together correlate, variation in one does not necessarily cause the other to vary. It's true, for example, that there is a high positive correlation between the number of liquor outlets in urban areas and the number of churches in those same areas. However, some people would prefer to think that one does not cause the other.

INTELLIGENCE AND ACHIEVEMENT

One assumption underlying the development and use of most intelligence tests is that intelligence is related to successful performance of school tasks. It is not surprising, therefore, that these tests correlate relatively highly with measures of school achievement. In fact, intelligence tests and achievement tests both measure much

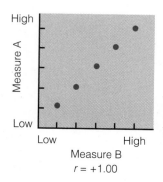 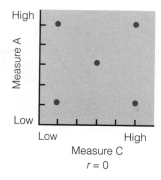 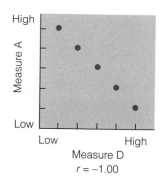

FIGURE 7.2 Representations of correlation (*r*), which indicate the extent to which two measures tend to vary together. The *direction* of the relationship (positive or negative) is shown by the *sign* of the correlation coefficient (plus or minus). The *strength* of the relationship is indicated by the *magnitude* of the correlation coefficient: The closer *r* is to ±1, the stronger the observed relationship; the closer it is to 0, the weaker the relationship. In this example, scores on Measure A correlate perfectly with scores on Measures B and D and not at all with scores on Measure C.

the same sorts of things—that is, both measure the effects of previous learning (achievement), and both typically are highly verbal. The principal differences between the two are that intelligence tests sample from a wider range of behaviors and (to some degree) emphasize the ability to apply knowledge and skills to new problems; in contrast, achievement tests tend to be limited to specific content areas or subjects.

Conventional intelligence tests, particularly the kinds of paper-and-pencil (or computer-administered) group tests that are most commonly used in classrooms, do not measure innate capacity directly, but rather by inference. That is, psychologists sometimes make the inference that those who do well on these tests have higher innate capacity for learning than those who do less well. And a marked discrepancy between expected and actual performance is often interpreted as evidence of a specific learning disability or some other problem (Fletcher, 1992).

In fact, however, what the tests actually provide is a measure of the learning experiences that subjects have had, as well as a crude measure of how much they have profited from these experiences. Vygotsky (1986) and Feuerstein (1979) both argue that in order to measure learning *potential,* subjects must be placed in sit-

uations in which they must *learn* rather than in situations in which their past learning is tapped—hence, the use of hints and clues in Feuerstein's measurement of aptitude—the **Learning Aptitude Potential Device (LAPD).**

In view of the close relationship between what achievement and intelligence tests measure, it is not surprising that the correlation between the two ranges from 0.30 to 0.80 over a large number of studies (Barrett & Depinet, 1991). It would appear, then, that knowledge of a student's score on an intelligence test may be of considerable value to a teacher. Unfortunately, as is pointed out later in this chapter, intelligence test scores are not usually very valuable in predicting how a *specific* individual will perform. That is because their results are not completely reliable. Scores sometimes fluctuate widely for the same individual from one test to another, and for any given individual they may not accurately reflect past performance or

---

Learning Aptitude Potential Device (LAPD) A measure of aptitude devised by Feuerstein in which the tester is encouraged to actually teach the child, to offer hints and clues, to direct and help, in order to arrive at a more accurate measure of actual potential for further learning rather than simply at a measure of how much the child has profited from past experience.

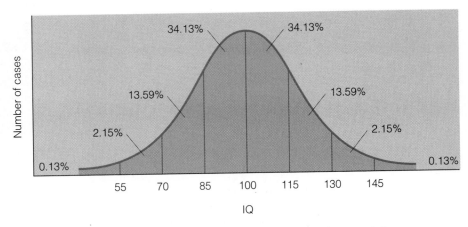

FIGURE 7.3 A normal curve depicting the theoretical distribution of IQ scores among humans. (Average score is 100; 68.26 percent of the population score between 85 and 115; only 2.28 percent score either above 130 or below 70.) Actual scores for a population may vary somewhat from this theoretical distribution.

predict future performance very well either. However, they can be of considerable value in predicting how well *groups* of students are likely to do. Accordingly, they are widely used for grouping students for instruction and counseling purposes. Keep in mind, however, that intelligence is only one factor that correlates with school success. Previous success is an even better predictor of future success.

INTELLIGENCE TESTS

Given the relationship between performance and measures of intelligence, the main use of intelligence tests is for prediction. In a sense, an intelligence test is simply a prediction that an individual will do well (or less well) on tasks that require intelligence.

A wide variety of intelligence tests are available, most of which yield a score referred to as the **intelligence quotient (IQ).** The average IQ of a randomly selected group of people on most tests is about 100. Approximately two-thirds of the population score between 85 and 115. About 11 percent score above 120, and 1.6 percent score above 140. Figure 7.3 depicts the distribution of measured intelligence in a normal population.

There are two general types of intelligence tests: group and individual. The former are administered simultaneously to a group of test subjects; the latter require individual administration. Typically, **group tests** are paper-and-pencil tests or are computer-administered (and often computer-scored as well). There are many more group than individual tests, probably because group tests are inexpensive and more widely used. Unfortunately, their validity and reliability are often poor. **Individual tests,** in contrast, are much more expensive in terms of equipment and administration time. The scores they yield are often more valid and more reli-

intelligence quotient (IQ) A simple way to describe intelligence by assigning it a number that represents the ratio of mental to chronological age, multiplied by 100. Average IQ is therefore 100 and is based on a comparison between an individual's performance and that of comparable others.

group tests A type of test, usually used to measure intelligence, that may be given to large groups of subjects at one time. It is typically of the pencil-and-paper variety.

individual tests Tests, usually used to measure intelligence, that can be given to only one individual at a time.

able, however. Hence they can provide greater insight into intellectual processes. They are especially valuable in diagnosing specific learning problems in children. It is relatively rare, for example, to find school systems that base decisions to put students in special classrooms or programs simply on the basis of a group assessment. Typically, an individual assessment is required after initial screening with a group measure, partly to determine whether the test has been fair to the student.

Group tests can usually be administered and scored by any reasonably competent classroom teacher. However, with few exceptions the administration of individual tests requires a great deal of training and skill. Brief descriptions of some of the most commonly used individual and group tests are given here.

INDIVIDUAL INTELLIGENCE TESTS

Individual intelligence tests, as we saw, are administered to a single student at one time, usually by a trained examiner.

Peabody Picture Vocabulary Test–Revised (PPVT–R). This is among the most easily administered and scored individual intelligence tests. It is an untimed test, usually requiring 15 minutes or less per subject. It consists simply of having the subject point to the one picture out of four that represents a word that has been read by the examiner. There are two forms of the test (L and M), each consisting of 175 words (plates) arranged from easiest to most difficult. After six consecutive incorrect answers, the test is discontinued. An intelligence score can then be computed on the basis of the subject's age and the level of the last correct response. Because of this simple format, the Peabody is sometimes used with individuals who have severe communication problems or motor dysfunctions (Wagner, 1994).

Revised Stanford-Binet. The Stanford-Binet is among the best-known and most widely used individual measures of intelligence. A high degree of training and competence is required to administer it. It consists of a wide variety of different tests graded in difficulty so as to correspond to various age levels. It yields a score that can be converted to an IQ. A recent revision of the Stanford-Binet (4th edition, Thorndike, Hagen, & Sattler, 1985) yields scores in four separate areas: verbal reasoning, quantitative reasoning, abstract/visual reasoning, and short-term memory. It also provides a composite score that is described as a measure of "adaptive ability" and is generally interpreted as an IQ.

The Stanford-Binet is widely used to assess children with normal abilities as well as those who have learning and developmental problems. It is also highly useful in identifying giftedness (Ellzey & Karnes, 1993) and can also be used as a preliminary screening test for children with autism (Carpentieri & Morgan, 1994). And, because of the wide age range it covers, it can also be used with college students and older adults (Nagle & Bell, 1993).

Wechsler Intelligence Scale for Children (3rd. ed.) (WISC-III). This individual test is similar to the Stanford-Binet, but it is somewhat easier to administer. It also yields scores on a number of specific tests (for example, vocabulary, block design, digit span, comprehension) and two major "intelligence" scores—one verbal and one performance. These can be combined to yield what is referred to as a "full-scale IQ score." There is an adult version of this test as well as a preschool version. Various subtests of the WISC-III are described in Table 7.2.

System of Multicultural Pluralistic Assessment (SOMPA). In several instances in this chapter, the point is made that many intelligence tests are unfair to those from ethnic and social groups outside the white middle-class majority. Indeed, several court decisions in the United States have recognized this fact. For example, in *Diana v. California State Board of Education,* twelve Mexican American children claimed that they had been improperly placed in classes for the mentally retarded on the basis of testing that was conducted in a language other than their

TABLE 7.2 THE WECHSLER INTELLIGENCE SCALE FOR CHILDREN, REVISED (WISC-III)

VERBAL SCALE	PERFORMANCE SCALE

VERBAL SCALE

1. *General information.* Questions relating to information most children have the opportunity to acquire (M)*

2. *General comprehension.* Questions designed to assess child's understanding of why certain things are done as they are (M)

3. *Arithmetic.* Oral arithmetic problems (M)

4. *Similarities.* Child indicates how certain things are alike (M)

5. *Vocabulary.* Child gives meanings of words of increasing difficulty (M)

6. *Digit span.* Child repeats orally presented sequence of numbers in order and reversed (S)*

PERFORMANCE SCALE

1. *Picture completion.* Child indicates what is missing in pictures (M)

2. *Picture arrangement.* Child arranges series of pictures to tell a story (M)

3. *Block design.* Child is required to copy exactly a design with colored blocks (M)

4. *Object assembly.* Child assembles puzzles (M)

5. *Coding.* Child pairs symbols with digits following a key (M)

6. *Mazes.* Child traces way out of mazes with pencil (S)

7. *Symbol search.* Child performs symbol location task that measures mental processing speed and visual search skills (S)

*(M) mandatory; (S) supplementary

---

native one. Specifically, these children had been administered standard English versions of the Wechsler scales and of the Stanford-Binet. The judgment—in favor of the plaintiffs—ordered that the children be retested by someone fluent in Spanish, that greater emphasis be placed on nonverbal parts of the tests, and that new tests be developed for Spanish-speaking children.

This and a number of related court cases have had several effects on testing in schools. One not entirely beneficial effect has been to discourage the use of tests. It is probably a lot better to rely on tests, however biased they might be, than to rely on the judgments of teachers and other professionals who are not allowed the assistance of test results. Biases in tests are fixed and therefore perhaps detectable and measurable; human biases are no less real, but they are more subtle—and therefore harder to detect and control. As Seligman (1992) puts it in his argument against banning intelligence tests: "With or without IQ tests, somebody will still have to decide which kids need help and which are candidates for scholarships. It is hard

to argue that those decisions will be better and fairer if made without the unique, often surprising insights flowing from test scores" (p. xi).

Another effect of these court cases has been to stimulate the development of new tests and new approaches to testing. Among these is Mercer's **SOMPA** (System of Multicultural Pluralistic Assessment: Mercer, 1979; Mercer & Lewis, 1978, 1979). The SOMPA consists of a battery of ten separate individual measures. These measures reflect assessments in three areas, which Mercer refers to as models: the medical model, the social system model, and the pluralistic model. Measures relating to the medical model attempt to determine whether the child is biologically normal. These measures include

---

SOMPA Mercer's procedure for assessing the learning potential of culturally different children, the system of multicultural pluralistic assessment. It combines assessments in three areas: medical, social, and pluralistic. Pluralistic assessment involves the use of measures of intelligence standardized on culturally different groups.

tests of visual and auditory acuity, measures of physical dexterity and motor coordination, and indexes of health and physical development. Measures relating to the social system model are intended to determine whether the child is socially "normal"—that is, whether the child behaves in expected ways in social situations. The WISC-III and a test called the Adaptive Behavior Inventory for Children (ABIC) are used to measure functioning in the social system. Mercer's assumption is that children who fall in the bottom 3 percent of the WISC-III will not behave as expected in school. In her terms, their school functioning levels will be abnormally low.

The pluralistic model is of particular interest because it considers the child's cultural and social background in attempting to determine the probability of his or her success in school. The principal measure used here is the WISC-III, administered in the usual fashion but with different standards. Specifically, Mercer administered the WISC-III to a California standardization sample consisting of 456 African Americans, 520 Hispanic Americans, and 604 whites. As expected, Hispanics and African Americans scored significantly lower than the white groups—91.9 and 88.4 were the average full-scale IQs for Hispanics and blacks, respectively, compared with 103.1 for the whites. Combining these norms with information relating to the child's family (family size, family income, family structure, and socioeconomic status), Mercer developed a formula for predicting the likelihood of the child's success in school. This prediction, labeled an "estimated learning potential (ELP) score," is pluralistic in that it attempts to take into account social and ethnic background as well as measured potential.

Sattler (1982) has criticized the SOMPA on the grounds that the California sample is not nationally representative, there is insufficient evidence that predictions based on the SOMPA are more valid than those based solely on the WISC-III, and there is some question about the wisdom of using a medical model in making educational decisions.

There is evidence, however, that the SOMPA may be effective for some important purposes.

For example, Matthew and colleagues (1992) used the SOMPA to identify a group of African American children as gifted; none of these children had been so identified using the usual unadjusted measures. Yet on various measures of cognitive processes, they performed as well as groups of gifted children identified in the usual manner. And after they had been in a gifted program for seven months, there were no significant differences between the group identified using the SOMPA approach and other students.

GROUP INTELLIGENCE TESTS

Group tests of intelligence are usually paper-and-pencil or computer-administered tests that can be given to a large group at one time. Only a few examples of the hundreds of tests available are described briefly here.

Draw a Person Test. This interesting measure of intelligence, developed by Goodenough (1926) and later revised by Harris (1963) and Naglieri (1988), is based on the assumption that children's drawings reflect their conceptual sophistication. The child is simply asked to draw the best person possible; no time limit is imposed (see Figure 7.4). Drawings are scored primarily on the basis of detail and accuracy, according to a well-defined set of criteria. Tables for converting raw scores to IQ scores are provided.

Cognitive Abilities Test (CogAT). This is a widely used, multilevel, paper-and-pencil test suitable for grades 3 through 13. It yields three scores—verbal, quantitative, and nonverbal—as well as a composite IQ score. The test includes tables for converting individual scores to percentile scores based on the performance of other children at the same grade level. (A percentile indicates the percentage of cases that fall at or below a given point. For example, a student who scores at the seventy-fifth percentile has performed as well or better than 75 percent of students in the same grade.)

Otis-Lennon School Ability Test. A test designed to assess school-related ability, the Otis-Lennon consists of five levels of items suitable for

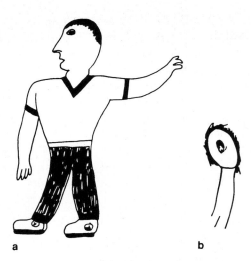

a   b

FIGURE 7.4 Two examples of the Goodenough-Harris Drawing Test. Both subjects were boys aged 10 ¾ years. The raw scores and IQ equivalents, respectively, for the drawings are **a** 41 and 110; **b** 4 and 54. The child who drew **b** also had a low Stanford-Binet IQ score. From the Goodenough-Harris Drawing Test. Copyright © 1963 by The Psychological Corporation. Reproduced by permission. All rights reserved.

grades 1 through 12. Items are intermingled (for example, vocabulary, reasoning, numerical, and other items are in mixed order) and are presented in order of increasing difficulty. The test yields a single standardized score labeled a "school ability index" (SAI).

MYTHS CONCERNING IQ

Teachers who make use of intelligence tests should be aware of their limitations and of the myths that frequently surround the concept of intelligence quotient or IQ.

Misconception 1. IQ is a mysterious something, synonymous with intelligence, possessed in greater or lesser amounts by everyone. This myth is evident in the question "What's your IQ?" or the expression "My IQ is . . ." In fact, the numerical index of intelligence known as the IQ is simply a score obtained by an individual in a specific testing situation and on a specific "intelligence" test. And the intelligence tests on

which estimates of IQ are based have less than perfect **validity.** A test is valid to the extent that it measures what it claims to measure; hence, an intelligence test is valid if it measures intelligence and nothing else. But, as we saw, intelligence tests tend to measure the effects of past experience rather than intelligence itself. In addition, many also reflect (measure) the effects of other variables such as fatigue or motivation. Hence, IQ and intelligence are not synonymous although, as Mensh and Mensh (1991) note, the terms have been used synonymously "longer than almost anyone can remember" (p. 1).

In addition to their imperfect validity, intelligece tests do not have perfect **reliability.** Reliability is defined as the accuracy with which intelligence tests measure whatever it is that they do in fact measure. Measures of intelligence can vary considerably from one testing time to another for the same individual. This variation, technically known as the *error of measurement,* is such that any teacher looking at a specific intelligence quotient should reason: "This score of 130 means that this student probably has a measured IQ that ranges somewhere between 120 and 140." (See Chapter 13 for a more detailed discussion of reliability and validity.)

Misconception 2. IQ is a constant. I have X, you have Y, and that's that. Not so. Research increasingly points to the fact that measured IQ is not fixed. True, there is a substantial correlation between measures of intelligence taken after early childhood and those obtained later (Bloom, 1964). And Gustafsson and Undheim

---

validity The extent to which a test measures what it says it measures. For example, an intelligence test is valid to the extent that it measures intelligence and nothing else. Educational and psychological tests are limited by their frequently low validity.

reliability The consistency with which a test measures whatever it measures. A perfectly reliable test should yield the same scores on different occasions (for the same individual), providing what it measures has not changed. Most educational and psychological tests are severely limited in terms of reliability.

Most intelligence tests are highly verbal and tend to measure abilities related to working with abstract ideas and symbols. Very few tap the communication and group interaction skills at play in situations such as that depicted here. Yet these skills are a fundamental part of intelligent adaptation.

(1992) found high stability of factors that underly measured intelligence. But there is mounting evidence that interaction with new technologies (such as computers or even calculators) is increasing measured intelligence (Salomon, Perkins, & Globerson, 1991). And there is also striking evidence that schooling increases intelligence. In Husén and Tuijnman's words, "Child IQ has an effect on schooling outcomes [and] also schooling per se has a substantial effect on IQ test scores" (1991, p. 22). The effect may be even more evident with the implementation of new cognitive strategies curricula that aim to develop cognitive competence (see Chapter 5).

Misconception 3. Intelligence tests measure all the important things. In fact, most intelligence

tests measure relatively limited kinds of abilities—typically, the ability to work with abstract ideas and symbols. They seldom tap interpersonal skills, athletic ability, creativity, and a variety of other desirable human attributes. As Weinberg (1989) notes, they do not reveal many important things about human cognition. For example, most measures of intelligence do not tell us anything about social intelligence, motivation, adaptive skills, or emotion.

Misconception 4. Intelligence tests are impersonal, impartial, and fair. The fact is that many intelligence tests are culturally biased; that is, they tend to favor children whose backgrounds are similar to that of the sample that was used as the norm for the test. In North America that sample has often consisted of white, middle-class children, which explains why many intelligence tests have been unfair for a variety of minority groups. However, the most recent revisions of such tests as the Stanford-Binet and the Wechsler have expanded their standardization samples to include minority groups in a representative way. Accordingly, they are now fairer to minorities.

A number of other tests—none of them widely used in practice, though some are used more extensively in research—attempt to minimize cultural bias. Such tests, sometimes labeled "culture-fair," or, more accurately, "culture-reduced," are typically nonverbal. They attempt to tap intellectual functions through problems involving pictures or abstract designs (for example, the Ravens Progressive Matrices Test). One important approach to overcoming some of the cultural biases in testing is Mercer's System of Multicultural Pluralistic Assessment (Mercer & Lewis, 1978; Mercer, 1979).

Fact. IQ is related to success, both in school and in life. This, however, might not mean that IQ is the most important predictor of future success. For example, Thorndike and Hagen (1977) and Cohen (1972) point out that although the correlation between intelligence test scores and school achievement is substantial, previous achievement correlates even more highly with future achievement than does IQ. And McClelland (1973) argues strongly that intelligence test scores bear little relationship to success in life or in careers. But, following a detailed review of the research, Barrett and Depinet conclude, "The evidence from these varied scientific studies leads again and again to the same conclusion: Intelligence and aptitude tests are positively related to job performance" (1991, p. 1016).

USES OF INTELLIGENCE TESTS

Although still used in many school systems, intelligence tests are no longer routinely administered to all students everywhere. This is partly because of a strong antitest movement among parents and others and partly because of a growing recognition of the potential weaknesses and abuses of testing.

Chief among the purposes for which intelligence tests are used are counseling, career guidance, class placement, and diagnosis for remedial or enrichment purposes. There is little doubt that when skillfully administered and intelligently interpreted, they can be of considerable value for any and all of these purposes. Unfortunately, they are not always skillfully administered and intelligently interpreted.

A number of important cautions should be kept in mind when interpreting the results of intelligence tests, most of them related to the misconceptions described earlier. For example, teachers need to remember that the validity and reliability of all measures of intelligence are less than perfect. If Johnny's measured IQ today is 120 and Frank's is 115, it would be foolish in the extreme to conclude that Johnny is more intelligent than Frank and that he should therefore be granted the privilege of studying with the group called the "Orioles" rather than with the "White-Breasted Kites." It might well be that Johnny's measured IQ next month would be 110 or that Frank's measured IQ on another test today would be 130. It is, in fact, precisely the relative imprecision of measured IQ that has served to justify the secrecy that

"We realize you do better on your IQ tests than you do anything else, but you just cannot major in IQ."

© 1996 Sidney Harris.

sometimes surrounds the IQ. Unfortunately, the concept of IQ is not at all well understood by parents; perhaps even more unfortunate, it is often not well understood by educators.

Teachers need to keep in mind, too, that intelligence is not a fixed and unchanging characteristic. As we saw, formal schooling and continued interaction with things like televisions and computers increase intelligence.

What these cautions mean is that a teacher's decisions based on test results should be tentative and subject to continual review, that students should not be labeled on the basis of limited and changing samplings of their behavior, and that, in short, good sense should prevail here as it should elsewhere.

DETERMINANTS OF INTELLIGENCE

Intelligence doesn't just happen; it has a cause. And the causes of intelligence are also the causes of stupidity because one is the absence of the other. The assumption that human characteristics result from the interplay of heredity and environment is discussed in Chapter 2 (also see the box "Experience and Intelligence: A

Debate"). As we see there, the debate has by no means ended, although a great deal of evidence has been gathered on both sides. Heredity versus environment is clearly no longer an important question. More important questions have to do with how individuals and environments interact during development, with the processes that account for intellectual change, and with how deficits can be remedied and gifts fostered (see Rose, 1995).

THE RUBBER-BAND HYPOTHESIS

One of the better analogies advanced to describe the interaction of heredity and environment is Stern's rubber-band hypothesis. It compares innate potential for intellectual development to a rubber band. Intelligence at any time is reflected by the length of the band. Obviously, a short piece (poorer genetic background) can be stretched; with a great deal of effort it can be stretched a long way. The forces that exert the pull on the band, or that fail to, are environmental. Hence, genetic and environmental forces interact in such a way that less environmental stimulation may be required for average development if genetic endowment is high. The reverse is also true. One of the functions of schools is to stretch rubber bands (see Figure 7.5).

BIRTH ORDER, FAMILY SIZE, AND SPACING OF CHILDREN

Some evidence suggests that family size, birth order, and spacing of children may influence manifested intelligence of children.

Birth Order. More than a century ago, for example, Galton (1869) observed a much higher than expected number of firstborn children among the greatest scientists that Britain had produced. Since then, many studies have shown that firstborn and only children (who are necessarily also firstborn) speak more articulately and at a younger age than later-born children, score higher on measures of intellectual perfor-

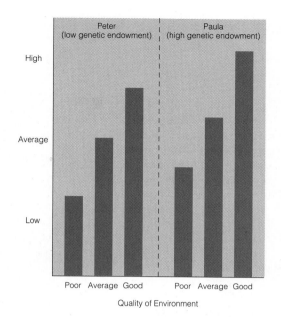

FIGURE 7.5 The Stern hypothesis: Individuals with different inherited potentials for intellectual development (genetic endowment) can manifest below-average, average, or above-average intelligence as a function of environmental forces.

mance, have a higher need for achievement, perform better academically, are more likely to attend college and to achieve eminence, and, of course, are more likely to become kings and queens (see, for example, Gaynor and Runco, 1992).

A closer examination of birth-order data suggests, however, that the contribution of birth order to such things as academic achievement or intelligence is negligible at best; at worst, birth order may make no contribution whatsoever. Following a massive investigation of 9,000 high school graduates and their brothers and sisters (more than 30,000 subjects), Hauser and Sewell (1985) found that birth order made absolutely no difference. They did find, however, that size of "sibship" (number of brothers and sisters) has a negative effect on schooling. In other words, the larger the family, the more likely that academic achievement will be lower.

EXPERIENCE AND INTELLIGENCE: A DEBATE

The most important question from an educator's point of view is whether the child's experiences can increase intelligence. A sample of the research relevant to this question, and relevant to the general nature–nurture question, is summarized here in the form of an imaginary debate between John Watson (a champion of environmentalism) and Francis Galton (who believed that intelligence is entirely inherited). The debate is replete with glaring anachronisms.* In order to know all that they claim to know, Galton and Watson would both have to be older than 100.

GALTON: My dear Watson, if you will simply open your mind to the problem, I can demonstrate for you beyond any doubt that heredity is the most powerful factor in development. As I said in 1869, "I have no patience with the hypothesis occasionally expressed, and often implied, especially in tales written to teach children to be good, that

babies are born pretty much alike. . . ."

WATSON: Give me a dozen healthy kids . . .

GALTON: You've said that before. But just look at all twins studies that have been done. As you know, identical twins are genetically exactly alike, but fraternal twins are as dissimilar as any two siblings.

WATSON: I know that.

GALTON: Sorry, I didn't mean to talk down to you. Anyway, Burt's famous 1958 study shows that the IQ scores of identical twins, whether you raise 'em together or apart, are more highly correlated than the scores of fraternal twins. And I have no doubt that if we had more reliable measures of intelligence, the correlations would be even higher. Bloom summarized this study—on page 69 in his 1954 book—along with four others. They all show the same thing.

WATSON: Whoa now! That is a highly prejudiced interpretation. If you look at the 1937 Newman, Freeman, and Holzinger study—and that one too is in Bloom's summary—if you look at that study, you'll see just where environment comes in. Why do you suppose it is that the correlation for twins reared together is always higher than for twins reared apart? Ha! What do you say to that?

GALTON: I say that studies involving the measurement of intelligence in people are highly suspect. Now, take rats, for example.

WATSON: That's irrelevant!

GALTON: It is not! Now you just hold on and listen here for a minute. In 1940, R. C. Tryon did a fascinating study, and it proves you wrong. Do you know it?

WATSON: You mean Tryon's study?

GALTON: Yes.

WATSON: No.

GALTON: I thought not. You don't read much, do you? You're just a popularizer. What Tryon did was take 142 rats and run them through a 17-unit maze 19 times. The brightest rat made, I forget . . . about 20 errors [author's note: actually, he made 14] and the dullest made 200 errors. [Again Galton is wrong. The dullest rat made 174 errors.] The brightest rats were then bred with each other, and the dull males were given dull females. That usually happens to people, too. Heh! Heh! Well, after repeating the same procedure for only eight generations, a remarkable thing began to happen. The dullest rats in the bright group consistently made fewer errors than the brightest rats in the dull group. In other words, the brightest

---

*PPC: "Replete with glaring anachronisms . . ." Even some of our brighter students won't know what this means. Isn't there a simpler way of saying this?

AUTHOR: Yes. I could have said: "Filled with instances that are out of temporal synchrony." Or, "Filled with descriptions of events that did not or could not have happened when they are alleged to have happened." A watch on Robin Hood's arm would be an anachronism.

rats in the dull group were duller than the dullest rats in the bright group—or the dullest rats in the bright group were . . . you know. Imagine what we could do with people. John Humphrey Noyes would have done it if the American government hadn't outlawed polygamy. [Noyes set up a religious, communal, free-love group in Oneida, New York, in the late nineteenth century. He practiced selective breeding with the aim of producing a superhuman race but had to disband the group when polygamy was outlawed in the 1880s.]

WATSON: So that's the kind of ridiculous evidence you base your eugenic movement on. [*Eugenics* is the term for the practice of selective breeding.] Let me tell you about a rat study, seeing as you're the one who brought it up. Hebb in 1947 and Krech, Rosenzweig, and Bennett—in 1960, '62, and '66—provide evidence that randomly selected rats can be significantly affected by environment. In the first case, Hebb showed in 1947 that rats raised as pets did better than laboratory rats on maze tests. Krech, Rosenzweig, and Bennett, in 1962, even changed the brain chemistry of rats by enriching their environments. And if you don't

think that's enough evidence, consider Heyns' 1967 work in South Africa. He's been affecting the intelligence of babies by using vacuum cleaners.

GALTON: Whoa, there, whoa up a little! Vacuum cleaners! You're going too far now.

WATSON: That's what you think. It was reported in *Woman's Own* on February 4th, 1967.

GALTON: You read *Woman's Own*?

WATSON: My wife does. Anyway, what Heyns did was set up a decompression unit using a vacuum cleaner motor. He put this plastic bubblelike thing over the woman's abdomen and sucked the air out. It relieves all kinds of aches and pains and makes babies brighter, too.

GALTON: It sounds like a gimmick to me. Jensen reviewed the research in 1968, and he concluded genes determine intelligence. And Scarr did the same thing in 1987 and she clearly concludes that the geneticists have won the nature–nurture battle. And she re-emphasizes that conclusion in a 1992 article. And the monograph by Rowe in 1994—well, it provides pretty strong evidence that even families don't make that much difference—that genes are really the important thing.

WATSON: Well, that's just one side of the debate. And if you look at Baumrind or

Jackson's 1993 articles, you'll see the other side, which is not only the most accurate side, but also the most optimistic one. And the optimistic point of view is the one that teachers should have. It's my view. It's the view that says, you bet your sweet donkey, the family and the school and television and everything else that's important in the environment makes one whack of a difference. That's the optimistic view because you can do something about the environment, but you can't do a dang thing about genetics. Changing the environment, that's what acceleration is and television for kids and books and programs for gifted kids . . .

GALTON: Don't get carried away, Watson. Your point of view might be more optimistic, but it's less accurate. I'm a scientist, not a philosopher or a salesman.

The argument ends with Watson's wife calling him in to wash dishes.

But the debate continues, although most scientists now believe that both heredity and environment are important, that their relative influences cannot easily be separated. As Rose (1995) puts it, "The questions are not whether genes matter, but, rather, how they matter and how genetic effects are modulated across lifespans of environmental interactions" (p. 627).

Family Size. The negative relationship between family size and academic achievement, as well as that between family size and performance on intelligence tests, has been corroborated in a number of studies. In an attempt to explain this finding, Zajonc (1975, 1976, 1986) and Zajonc and Markus (1975) suggest that one important influence on intellectual development is the intellectual climate of the home. Furthermore, they provide a simple formula, based on the **confluence model,** for determining the approximate intellectual climate of a home.

According to this model, each family member is assigned a value related to age: Parents are worth 30 points each; newborn infants, 0; and all other children, values that range from 0 to 30. The index of intellectual climate is then calculated by averaging values assigned to each individual in the family. For example, a first-born child is born into an intellectual climate valued at 30 plus 30 (when there are two parents) plus 0 (for the infant), divided by 3 (this equals 20, for those whose calculators are not functioning). A child born later or born into a large family in which there are many young children would be born into a family with a lower index of intellectual climate. The Zajonc–Markus model predicts, simply, that measured intelligence for large groups will be related to the intellectual climate index. And there is, in fact, some evidence that this is the case (see, for example, Grotevant, Scarr, & Weinberg, 1977).

Do these observations support the notion that family size and birth order are among the important influences on intelligence? Zajonc and Markus argue yes. And, in fact, most of the evidence does not question the conclusion that family size correlates inversely with measured intelligence (larger families equal lower intelligence), although this correlation is not always very high or very general. What is often questioned, however, is whether the most important variable is family size. In one of several large-scale and systematic investigations of this type, Page and Grandon (1979) found pretty much the same correlations that Zajonc and Markus and others had previously reported. But they also found that when the variables of social class and race were included, correlations of these factors with manifested intelligence were even more significant than that of family size. Put more simply, in most studies that found a high correlation of family size, birth order, and intelligence, researchers did not consider the fact that large families tend to be more common in lower social classes, in certain ethnic minorities, among rural rather than urban families, and among those who are less well educated. And perhaps the "intellectual climate" in large families is more a function of ethnic, social, and educational variables than of family size.

Spacing of Children. Taken together, family size, birth order, and social class are important predictors of performance and achievement as well as of measured intelligence and even creativity. And the prediction becomes even more powerful if age intervals, or spacing of children, are factored into the equation. For example, Gaynor and Runco (1992) examined the correlation between the creative abilities of 116 children and the age intervals between these children and their closest sibling. They corroborated an often-reported finding: The larger the age interval between a child and the closest sibling, the greater the probability that this child will score high on measures of achievement and intelligence. As Wagner, Schubert, and Schubert (1985) conclude: "The findings on spacing effects are astonishingly consistent. Close spac-

---

confluence model Zajonc's term for the hypothesis that the intellectual climate of the home, determined principally in terms of the numbers and ages of family members, contributes in important ways to the development of children's intelligence. According to this model, children born into a relatively adult environment (first born and only children, for example) should, on average, have an intellectual advantage over those born in a less-adult environment (later-born children, children in large families, children in single-parent homes).

ing . . . seems deleterious to intelligence and achievement [and] to good relations between children and parents" (p. 196).

Note that where there are very small intervals between children, family size is typically greater—and the probability that the family will be characterized by social and economic variables associated with developmental disadvantages is also higher. Hence the influence of age intervals, like that of birth order and family size, is probably best explained in terms of the interaction of a number of related variables (like social and economic variables) as well as in terms of the sorts of family relationships and interactions that are most likely to result. A child whose siblings are much older or much younger, Gaynor and Runco (1992) explain, is more likely than other children to be perceived by parents as special—and is also more likely to be born into an economically and socially advantaged family.

A Conclusion. The most reasonable conclusion at this point is that many variables are influential in determining intellectual development. Among the important variables are genetic forces (over which we have relatively little control) and such environmental variables as formal schooling and interactions among children and their parents and siblings, as well as between children and technological aspects of society.

All of which is far from simple.

Finally, it should always be kept in mind that the grand conclusions of social science are most often based on the average performance of large groups of individuals. Invariably, within these groups are many individuals whose behavior contradicts the conclusion at every turn. In other words, there are geniuses among families whose members number into the dozens, and among all social and ethnic groups; and there are fools, dullards, and simpletons who are born first into tiny little families.*

---

*PPC: Is the bear a cynic? Does he mean this?
AUTHOR: Older bears are often cynical.

CREATIVITY

A great deal of attention has been devoted to the subject of **creativity** in the past several decades, particularly following the work of J. P. Guilford (1950, 1959, 1962). However, the central question in creativity research and speculation—what is creativity?—remains largely unsolved. Few people agree on an answer, and the definition of creativity remains one of the major problems in the area (Hoge, 1988).

While conversing with George Bernard Shaw, his biographer, Stephen Winsten, alluded to the proverbial hairsbreadth that separates genius from madness: "The matter-of-fact man prefers to think of the creative man as defective, or at least akin to madness," he said. And Shaw replied, "Most of them are. I am probably the only sane exception" (1949, p. 103).

Although we no longer fear the creative person as openly as we might once have, uneasiness and uncertainty remain. As Cross, Coleman, and Terhaar-Yonkers (1991) put it, creativity is still stigmatized in our society, and those who are exceptional are often subjected to tremendous pressure to conform—to behave like those who are more ordinary.

Are creative people nonconformists, eccentrics, radicals, and fools, or are they ordinary people? The answer is probably that there are some of both, but that there really is no mystical or magical quality about creativity—although there is some limited evidence that a number of highly creative people are somewhat more prone to emotional disorders (Bowden, 1994; Richards, 1994). In general, however, like intelligence, creativity is a quality of humans and of human behavior that everybody possesses to some degree. Just as low intelligence is stupidity, so low creativity is ordinariness. There are few geniuses as identified by tests of intelligence; there are also few very highly creative people.

---

creativity Generally refers to the capacity of individuals to produce novel or original answers or products. The term *creative* is an adjective that may be used to describe people, products, or processes.

SOME DEFINITIONS OF CREATIVITY

Creativity is not easily defined. For example, here are three of many possible definitions:

1. Creativity involves fluency, flexibility, and originality (Guilford, 1959).

2. Creativity is "the forming of associative elements into new combinations which either meet specified requirements or are in some ways useful. The more mutually remote the elements of the new combination, the more creative the process of solution" (Mednick, 1962, p. 221).

3. Creativity results in "a novel work that is accepted as tenable or useful or satisfying by a significant group of others at some point in time" (Stein, in Parnes & Harding, 1962, p. 86).

Consider the three examples presented in the cases of Réné Choumard, Joseph Lalonde, and Rollie Wozny below. Each of these people is creative by one definition but not the others. Réné is creative according to Guilford: His behavior is original, and he shows remarkable verbal fluency and flexibility. However, he is not creative according to Mednick and Stein. Joseph, in contrast, meets Mednick's criteria for creativity—highly remote associations satisfying his own specifications. We might even assume that he is original, fluent, and flexible. But he does not produce anything "tenable or useful or satisfying." But Rollie Wozny, the scientist, does. Yet his behavior is not original, but simply clumsy. And he makes no remote associations whatsoever.

This discussion highlights the confusion that makes defining and assessing creativity so difficult. The problem is partly resolved by accepting that *creativity* is a global term and that it does not necessarily represent only one event or quality. If we distinguish among the creative *process*, the creative *product*, and the creative *person*, many of the contradictions implicit in earlier formulations disappear. Réné is a creative person who doesn't produce anything; Joseph uses a creative process but also produces nothing creative; the scientist neither is creative

CASE: DIFFERENT COLORS OF CREATIVITY

THE NAME: Réné Choumard

THE PLACE: Pascal, Saskatchewan

For the past three years, Réné has been sitting on an inverted washtub on the porch of his seen-a-better-day shack, knitting himself purple mittens that have no thumbs and dreaming about what cows were really like when he was young. He talks to himself incessantly about everything he has ever seen or done.

THE NAME: Joseph Lalonde

THE PLACE: Pascal, Saskatchewan

Joseph is Réné's neighbor. He's the local wit; his humor is also local humor. His jokes are associations between extremely remote ideas—but they're not always funny. "Here's one I just made up," he said to his wife this very morning. "Did you hear about the teacher who went to church to take his pills. Knelt on the pew, he did, and took his pills. You know why? Huhn? You figure it out yet? It's his pewpill—his pupil! Get it?"

THE NAME: Rollie Wozny

THE PLACE: Biomiracle Technologies

While carrying a cup of coffee, black, no sugar thanks, from the vending machine to his desk in the corner of the Biomiracle Technology main lab, Rollie stumbles over a pile of discarded computer innards. He manages to hang onto the coffee cup but loses his grip on the test tube in his other hand, accidentally spilling a small amount of newly recombined DNA into a vat containing 1055.4 U.S. gallons (4,000 liters) of sweet cream. The cream immediately turns into four cows (a reversal phenomenon).

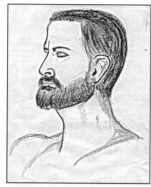

Which is the most creative of these six renditions of the same person, each drawn by a different artist? There is no easy answer, judgments of artistic creativity being a highly subjective matter. Not surprisingly, psychologists have been hard-pressed to reach agreement on what creativity involves and what it means. Part of the problem lies in the observation that creativity is evident not only in products (as illustrated in these six drawings, for example), but also in characteristic ways of doing things or processes, as well as in a unique combination of personality characteristics. Drawings (clockwise from top left to bottom right) courtesy of David Mors, C. Stinson, Peter Sentkowski, David Rose, Tim Gallagher, and Andrew Ogus.

nor uses a creative process, but he produces something valuable.

Distinctions among the creative person, product, and process, although useful, solve only part of the problem because they are seldom reflected in current attempts to measure creativity. The inference continues to be made, at least implicitly, that creative personalities and processes can be identified and assessed on the basis of products that are judged to be creative. As Csikszentmihalyi (1994) argues, creativity is perhaps best viewed as a complex interaction among personality and creative processes and products.

IDENTIFYING CREATIVITY AND GIFTEDNESS

From an educational point of view, it's important to be able to define *creativity* and *giftedness* so that we can identify and select students for special programs. Accordingly, many school systems lump together various categories such as "creative," "talented," and "gifted" under a single label (such as "talented and gifted" or simply "gifted") and provide specific criteria for identifying students who belong to this group. The most often used criterion is, not surprisingly, measured intelligence expressed in the form of an IQ—and the most common cutoff is 130; that is, all students whose measured IQ is 130 or more would qualify as gifted (Humphreys, 1985). (Programs for the gifted are reviewed in the next chapter.)

A number of problems are associated with defining creativity or giftedness solely (or even primarily) in terms of intelligence. In the first place, as is shown in a later section, independent measures of creativity do not always correlate well with measured intelligence. For example, Tyler-Wood and Carri (1991) looked at the scores that a group of gifted children had obtained on four different measures of intelligence and found that those who would have been identified as gifted varied widely depending on the test used. A second problem is that given the rather unimpressive validity and reliability of our intelligence tests, their use for selecting students for special programs is often unfair. And third, defining giftedness solely on the basis of intelligence means overlooking a number of other important characteristics that appear to be related to creative functioning. For example, Sternberg and Lubart (1993) argue that creativity depends on the interaction of qualities such as intelligence and background knowledge, styles of thinking, motivation, personality, and the person's context.

One interesting approach to defining creativity and giftedness is taken by Gardner (1983), who, as we saw earlier in this chapter, speaks of seven largely unrelated kinds of intelligence. He believes that creativity (or giftedness) can occur in any one of these domains and that it represents the highest level of functioning in each. Thus, it is possible to be highly gifted in one aspect but not in any other—as may be evident among the musically or the scientifically gifted. Wallach (1985) has a similar point of view, arguing that creativity can be manifested in excellence in any specific domain.

The argument that creativity is largely domain specific is not shared by all researchers. Many believe that although giftedness is often manifested in one domain rather than another, certain general underlying qualities make it possible for the creative person to be described as generally creative. And perhaps it is possible to measure these qualities.

APPROACHES TO IDENTIFYING CREATIVITY

One of the simplest (and most unreliable) ways of identifying creative talent is to have teachers rate students. Gallagher (1960) cites research indicating that teachers miss approximately 20 percent of the most highly creative students. As Shaklee (1992) points out, teachers often don't recognize giftedness in students who are not the higher-achieving school or class leaders. Furthermore, says Shaklee, most schools confine children to a lock-step curriculum that is not likely to foster the development of giftedness or to permit its recognition.

Heinzen (1991) describes three approaches to measuring creativity: personality inventories, biographical inventories, and behavioral measures. Personality inventories focus on what are thought to be the characteristics of creative people (for example, flexibility, curiosity, openness). Biographical inventories look at past production and behavior, assuming that these are the best predictor of future creativity. And behavioral measures try to predict future creativity on the basis of behaviors in schools or on tests. Some researchers, like Osborne and Byrnes (1990), advocate that a combination of these approaches be used when attempting to identify gifted and talented children.

Creativity Tests. Another method for identifying creativity is to use one of several tests designed specifically for that purpose. Among the most common of these are **tests of divergent thinking**, first proposed by Guilford (1950) and developed by Torrance (1966, 1974: Torrance

---

tests of divergent thinking Creativity tests. Usually open-ended, *production* tests designed to measure factors such as fluency, flexibility, and originality.

TABLE 7.3 SAMPLE ANSWERS AND SCORING PROCEDURE FOR ONE ITEM FROM A CREATIVITY TEST

Item How many uses can you think of for a nylon stocking?

Answers

☆ Wear on feet	❂✳☆ Make upholstery	✳☆ Tie up robbers
❂☆ Wear over face	✳☆ Hang flower pots	❂✳☆ Cover broken window panes
☆ Wear on hands when it's cold	☆ Hang mobiles	❂✳☆ Use as ballast in a dirigible
✳☆ Make rugs	❂✳☆ Make Christmas decorations	✳☆ Make a fishing net
☆ Make clothes	✳☆ Use as a sling	

Scoring

☆ Fluency: 14 (total number of different responses)

✳ Flexibility: 9 (number of shifts from one class to another)

❂ Originality: 5 (number of unusual responses—responses that occurred less than 5 percent of the time in the entire sample)

Tests of Creative Thinking). These tests are based on the assumption that creative ability comprises several separate factors, among which are **fluency, flexibility,** and **originality.** Tasks have been designed that encourage the production of a variety of responses, which can then be scored in terms of these and other factors. One such test is the Unusual Uses Test, in which subjects are asked to think of as many uses as they can for an ordinary object, such as a brick or a nylon stocking. Responses are counted to arrive at an index of fluency. Flexibility is measured by counting the number of shifts among classes of response. For example, a brick might be used for building a house, a planter, a road, and so on. Each response

---

fluency A factor thought to be involved in creativity, evident in the production of a large number of responses or solutions in a problem situation.

flexibility A factor tapped by production measures of divergent thinking (of creativity). Evident in the ability or propensity to switch from one class of responses or solutions to another.

originality A measure of creativity evident in the production of novel (unexpected or statistically rare) responses or solutions in a problem situation.

scores for fluency but not for flexibility. A shift from this category of uses to one involving throwing the brick would illustrate flexibility. Originality is scored on the basis of the number of responses that are either statistically rare or are judged unusual by the experimenter. A statistically rare response might be one that occurs less than 5 percent of the time. (See Table 7.3.)

Some tests of creativity try to assess cognitive processes thought to be involved in creative behavior (for example, Urban & Jellen, 1986). These approaches typically reflect the observation that gifted children manifest higher metacognitive skills (Swanson, 1992; Cheng, 1993). However, these are used mainly in research and in the development of theory where, notes Baer (1993-94), the validity of divergent thinking tests has been called into question. In practice, however, creativity tests are seldom used in school settings where teachers and administrators need to identify the gifted and the talented. As is pointed out in the next chapter, gifted children are most often identified solely on the basis of academic achievement and measured intelligence—although the official criteria for giftedness typically include high aptitude in other areas such as creativity, leadership, psychomotor ability, and visual or performing arts.

Measured Intelligence

	High	Low
High Divergent Thinking (Creativity)	high control over their own behavior; capable of adultlike and childlike behavior	high internal conflict, frustration with school, feelings of inadequacy; can perform well in stress-free environment
Low	addicted to school, strive desperately for academic success; well liked by teachers	somewhat bewildered by environment; defense mechanisms include intensive social or athletic activity; occasional maladjustment

THE CONNECTIONS BETWEEN CREATIVITY AND INTELLIGENCE

Because measured intelligence is often used to select gifted children for special programs, it's important to determine the relationship between intelligence and creativity.

One of the classic studies in this area is that reported by Getzels and Jackson (1962), who found that creative students were not necessarily the most intelligent—although they often achieved as well in school as those who were more intelligent. Interestingly, however, the highly creative students were not as well liked by the teachers.

Unfortunately, findings from the Getzels and Jackson study cannot easily be generalized. The average IQ in the school from which the subjects were chosen was an astounding 132. The average IQ for the groups described as "high creative, low IQ" was a more-than-respectable 127. With such a limited range in intelligence test scores, it is doubtful that any relationship between creativity and intelligence would be found, even if it existed. Besides, any findings from a study such as this might well apply only to especially intelligent children.

A related study (Wallach & Kogan, 1965) also identified four groups of students classified as high or low on intelligence and creativity, respectively. The purpose of this study was to identify characteristics that might be different among the four groups. Results of the study are summarized in Figure 7.6. They indicate that

highly creative but less-intelligent students are most frustrated with school and that highly intelligent but less-creative students are addicted to school and well-liked by their teachers. Keep in mind, however, that these four groups represent extremes of measured intelligence and creativity. The vast majority of students are not extreme. In addition, these general descriptions of school adjustment and personality characteristics are just that—general descriptions. Even with groups as highly select as these, there are numerous individual exceptions.

That there is a close relationship between intelligence and creativity seems clear, as is evident in the correlations between the two (Maker, 1993). That is, those who are highly intelligent are also more likely to be highly creative—and vice versa. But what is also clear is that intelligence tests *by themselves* are not a very good way of identifying creative children. The reason for this, as Fuchs-Beauchamp, Karnes, and Johnson (1993) found following a study of 496 children, is that although measured intelligence correlates very highly with measured creativity for the general population of schoolchildren, this is not the case for those whose measured IQ is 120 or more. At that level of intelligence, other factors such as motivation, persistence, home background, personality traits, and the individual's patterns of intellectual strengths and weaknesses become more important. One important approach to identifying these patterns is represented by Guilford's model of intellectual functioning.

GUILFORD'S MODEL OF INTELLECT

It seems clear that talents and gifts can manifest themselves in a variety of different areas. So, too, can deficits. Yet many of our theories of intelligence, and our models of mental functioning, fail to take this into account.

One exception is J. P. Guilford's (1959, 1967) model of the intellect. This unusual representation is relevant both to intelligence and creativity. The model is organized around three main aspects of intellectual functioning: operations, products, and content. All abilities, says Guilford, involve a combination of these three aspects of functioning. Because there are 4 different kinds of content, 5 different operations, and 6 different types of products, there are at least 120 distinct human abilities (see Figure 7.7).

The Three Faces of Intellect. Guilford's multifactor theory of intelligence is most easily understood by looking at the three aspects of intellectual functioning:

1. **Operations.** An operation is a major intellectual process. The term includes such activities as knowing, discovering, or being aware (cognition), retrieving from storage (memory), generating multiple responses (divergent thinking), arriving at a single, accepted solution (convergent thinking), and judging the appropriateness of information or decisions (evaluation).

   The two operations that have stimulated the most research and interest are **convergent** and **divergent thinking.** These are also the two operations most closely related to creativity and intelligence. Because convergent thinking involves pro-ducing one correct solution to a problem, it is a crucial factor in intelligence testing. Divergent thinking, which involves producing multiple solutions or hypotheses, is central in the creative process. In fact, the phrase "divergent thinking" is often used as a synonym for creative thinking. And, as we saw, *production* tests of creativity are often referred to as tests of divergent thinking.

2. **Content.** An operation is performed upon certain kinds of information. This information, or content, may be figural, symbolic, semantic, or behavioral. Figural content is concrete information, such as images. Symbolic content is information in the form of arbitrary signs, such as numbers or codes. Semantic content is information in the form of word meanings. And behavioral content is nonverbal information involved in human interaction—for example, emotion.

3. **Product.** Applying an operation to content yields a product—the form that information takes once it is processed. Products include single, segregated items of information (units), sets of items grouped by virtue of their common properties (classes), connections between items of information (relations), organizations of information (systems), changes of information (transformations), and extrapolations or predictions from information (implications).

   Guilford's model, like Gardner's theory of multiple intelligences, is based on the assump-

operation A term used by Guilford to describe major kinds of intellectual activity, such as remembering, evaluating, and divergent and convergent thinking.

convergent thinking A term used by Guilford to describe the type of thinking that results in a single, correct solution for a problem. Most conventional tests of intelligence measure convergent rather than divergent thinking.

divergent thinking An expression used by Guilford to describe the type of thinking that results in the production of several different solutions for one problem. Divergent thinking is assumed to be closely related to creative behavior, and the term is used interchangeably with the term *creativity*.

content A term used by Guilford to describe the content of a person's intellect. Intellectual activity (operations) involves content and results in products.

product A term used by Guilford to describe the result of applying an operation to content. A product may take the form of a response.

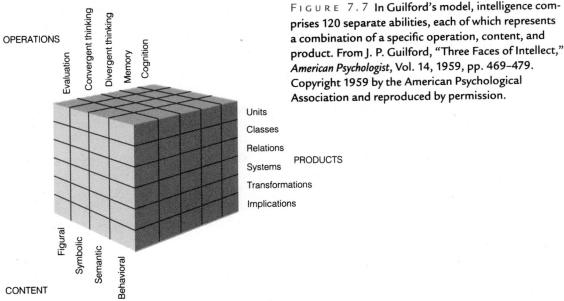

OPERATIONS

Evaluation
Convergent thinking
Divergent thinking
Memory
Cognition

Units
Classes
Relations
Systems
Transformations
Implications

PRODUCTS

Figural
Symbolic
Semantic
Behavioral

CONTENT

FIGURE 7.7 In Guilford's model, intelligence comprises 120 separate abilities, each of which represents a combination of a specific operation, content, and product. From J. P. Guilford, "Three Faces of Intellect," *American Psychologist*, Vol. 14, 1959, pp. 469–479. Copyright 1959 by the American Psychological Association and reproduced by permission.

tion that intelligence is not a single trait but a collection of separate abilities. This viewpoint resolves the apparent contradiction among some of the studies that have examined the relationship between creativity and intelligence. If intelligence is defined in terms of the entire structure, and if creativity involves only some of the 120 abilities described in the model, it is likely that there will be some correlation between the two. At the same time, the correlation may range from very low to very high according to the individual's pattern of abilities.

Instructional Implications. Guilford's model of the intellect has a number of important implications for the teaching/learning process. To begin with, the model draws attention to both the complexity of intellectual processes and the variety of forms in which these processes can be expressed. By so doing, it highlights the crucial role that the instructional process can play in intellectual development. If, for example, teachers always require that students remember content as presented, only memory operations are being emphasized. And if, as is often the case, only semantic content is involved, figural, symbolic, and behavioral content are being overlooked.

In short, consideration of this model makes it apparent that the intellectual development of students may well be shortchanged if only the traditional, highly limited operations, products, and content are attended to. Although schools have traditionally fostered the development of a variety of abilities in children—providing repeated practice in psychomotor skills, mathematics, verbal skills, social skills, and so on—teachers have not always systematically attended to the development of some of the more complex abilities, such as those involved in creative thinking (divergent thinking), evaluating, arriving at implications, and so on. Programs designed to foster learning/thinking strategies are an attempt to correct this failure.

It is alarming to note that the school dropout rate for gifted adolescents is often higher than that of the general population (McMann & Oliver, 1988). There are a number of possible reasons for this, including the frustration that may result when school programs do not permit adequate expression and development of special abilities. In addition, Kanchier (1988) suggests that the expectations that gifted adolescents have of themselves—and that others have for them—may affect some of them negatively.

In your school there may well be a Beethoven or a Mozart, a Shakespeare or a Neruda—or the next world chess champion—whose special talents remain dormant and unrecognized. That not all our inherent abilities become actual may have something to do with our schooling.

It may be that we still don't know very much about teaching gifted and talented children. Although current educational practice and beliefs typically insist that identifying and teaching those who have disabilities requires special training, we remain strangely ambivalent about what should be done to identify and teach those who are highly gifted. As a result, in our schools there may be many Raphaels, Da Vincis, Mozarts, and Einsteins unrecognized and undeveloped, disguised as ordinary people, totally unaware of their inherent abilities. Only in the right circumstances and with the right environmental demands will these talents become functional. Perhaps it would help if schools demanded more evaluation, implication, divergent thinking, and so on.

MAIN POINTS

1. There are three basic views of intelligence: the psychometric (based on measurement concepts), the Piagetian (based on child–environment interaction), and the information processing (based on cognitive processes).

2. Psychometrically, intelligence is seen as an adaptive quality sometimes defined in terms of what intelligence tests measure, or in terms of an underlying general ability (g) that is merely potential or that might be manifested in behavior. Cattell describes fluid abilities (basic, nonverbal, and unaffected by experience) and crystallized abilities (primarily verbal, highly influenced by culture and education). Das describes an information processing theory of intelligence (PASS, involving planning, attention, and simultaneous and successive processing).

3. Sternberg's information processing view of intelligence includes a contextual subtheory (intelligence is defined in terms of adaptation to a specific environmental context) and a three-component subtheory: metacomponents (processes involved in selecting cognitive activities, monitoring them, and evaluating their results); performance components (activities actually used in carrying out cognitive tasks); and knowledge acquisition components (activities involved in acquiring new information).

4. Gardner describes seven unrelated, multiple intelligences: logical-mathematical, linguistic, musical, spatial, bodily kinesthetic, interpersonal, and intrapersonal.

5. A correlation coefficient is an index of relationship between variables. It is a function of covariation—not of causal relatedness. Intelligence tests typically correlate quite well with school achievement. Conventional measures of intelligence do not measure innate capacity so much as the extent to which the individual has profited from past learning experiences. In addition, they are less than perfectly valid (do not always measure only what they purport to measure) or reliable (do not always measure consistently); they typically do not tap a number of important qualities, such as interpersonal skills, creativity, and athletic ability; and many are biased against social and ethnic minorities.

6. Intelligence tests usually yield an IQ score ranging from perhaps 50 to 160 and averaging about 100 in an unselected population. They are ordinarily group or individual tests. Individual tests require trained testers, consume a great deal of time, and are consequently far more expensive, but they are more valid and reliable for important educational decisions.

7. The SOMPA (System of Multicultural Pluralistic Assessment) uses a collection of measures to assess biological and social normality and to derive an estimated learning potential (ELP) score for minority samples.

8. Common myths about the IQ is that it is fixed, constant, accurately measured by tests that are fair, and extremely important. Measured IQ does correlate highly with success.

9. Both creativity and intelligence appear to be a function of the interaction between heredity and environment. Family size and configuration also play a role, as do ethnic background and social class. None of these factors necessarily causes high or low intelligence; they are merely related to manifested intelligence. The rubber-band hypothesis is an analogy that compares innate potential for learning to a rubber band: It can be stretched by a good environment, but it will shrivel in a poorer environment.

10. Creativity is defined in various, apparently contradictory ways. Much of the contradiction disappears when the creative product, process, and person are considered separately.

11. Creative, talented, and gifted individuals are often identified in terms of performance on measures of intelligence (for example, an IQ of 130 or more), teacher, self, or peer ratings, or performance on creativity tests (for example, the Torrance Tests of Creative Ability).

12. It is likely that relatively high intelligence is required for superior creative effort. Above a certain point, however, personality and social factors are probably more important than purely intellectual ones.

13. Guilford's model describes human intellectual functioning in terms of operations (major intellectual processes such as knowing and remembering) that are applied to content (cognitive information in the form of numbers, symbols, or words, for example) to yield a product (the result of processing information, describable in terms of forms such as units, classes, relations, or implications). The model yields 120 separate abilities. Divergent and convergent thinking operations relate directly to creativity (divergent thinking) and intelligence (convergent thinking).

APPLIED QUESTIONS

▶ What are the educational implications of the views of intelligence advanced by Das, Sternberg, or Gardner?

▶ Explain why correlation does not prove causation.

- ▸ Debate the merits and the educational implications of the belief that intelligence is modifiable.
- ▸ Using library resources, research the proposition that measured intelligence is related to family size, birth order, and spacing of children.

- ▸ How might lessons be modified to encourage creativity in students?
- ▸ Can you think of classroom examples of divergent and convergent thinking?

STUDY TERMS

componential theory of intelligence **237**
confluence model **254**
content **261**
contextual theory of intelligence **237**
convergent thinking **261**
creativity **255**
crystallized abilities **235**
divergent thinking **261**
flexibility **259**
fluency **259**
fluid abilities **234**

g **235**
group tests **244**
individual tests **244**
intelligence quotient (IQ) **244**
knowledge acquisition components **239**
LAPD **243**
metacomponents **238**
negative correlation **242**
operations **261**
originality **259**
PASS **237**
performance components **239**

planning **236**
positive correlation **242**
PREP program **237**
products **261**
psychometrics **233**
reliability **248**
simultaneous processsing **236**
SOMPA **246**
successive processing **236**
tests of divergent thinking **258**
theory of multiple intelligence **239**
validity **248**
variables **242**

SUGGESTED READINGS

The following two-volume encyclopedia contains more than 250 current articles dealing with all aspects of intelligence and intellectual functioning, including most of the topics covered in this chapter:

STERNBERG, R. J. (ed.) (1994). *Encyclopedia of human intelligence.* New York: Macmillan.

The pros and cons of intelligence testing, and some of the myths surrounding the meaning of IQ, are presented clearly in the following three books:

LUTHER, M., & QUARTER, J. (1988). *The genie in the lamp: Intelligence testing reconsidered.* North York, Ontario: Captus Press.

MENSH, E., & MENSH, H. (1991). *The IQ mythology: Class, race, gender, and inequality.* Carbondale: Southern Illinois University.

SELIGMAN, D. (1992). *A question of intelligence: The IQ debate in America.* New York: Carol Publishing Group.

Current thinking and research in creativity are summarized in:

CROPLEY, A. J. (1992). *More ways than one: Fostering creativity.* Norwood, N.J.: Ablex.

SHAW, M. P., & RUNCO, M. A. (eds.) (1994). *Creativity and affect.* Norwood, N. J.: Ablex.

FINKE, R. A., WARD, T. B., & SMITH, S. M. (1992). *Creative cognition: Theory, research and applications.* Cambridge, Mass.: MIT Press.

A useful overview of intelligence measures, with detailed comparisons and evaluations of the Stanford-Binet and WISC-III, is:

KAMPHAUS, R. W. (1993). *Clinical assessment of children's intelligence.* Boston: Allyn & Bacon.

During hibernation, all the metabolic processes are slowed to an absolute minimum. The animal is exceedingly torpid and approaches death as closely as possible without actually dying. Bears do not truly hibernate, although they do "den-up" during severe weather (Matthews, 1969).

CHAPTER 8

How dull it is to pause, to make an end,
To rust unburnished, not to shine in use!
As tho' to breathe were life.

ALFRED, LORD TENNYSON, *Ulysses*

Ah, yes! I wrote the "Purple Cow"—
I'm sorry, now, I wrote it!
But I can tell you anyhow,
I'll kill you if you quote it!

GELETT BURGESS, *Burgess Nonsense Book,*
  The Purple Cow

Diversity in the Classroom

PREVIEW

Today's school is vastly different from my father's school—or my childhood school. And not just because of the appearance of new-fangled technologies like computers but maybe more because today's average, ordinary classroom typically contains a sometimes bewildering diversity of students. For one thing, North American societies are becoming increasingly multicultural; for another, legislation now mandates that wherever possible, exceptional children be educated in ordinary classrooms with more average students. As a result, the teacher's roles and responsibilities have become increasingly complex, as we see in this chapter.

FOCUS QUESTIONS

▶ How is *giftedness* defined for educational purposes?

▶ What are some techniques for promoting creativity?

▶ How do teacher's attitudes and styles affect creativity?

▶ What are the dimensions of exceptionality?

▶ What are the teacher's responsibilities with respect to intellectual exceptionality?

▶ What is ADHD?

"Suppose," my father said, "suppose you have a wild cow . . . no, make that a demented goose. . . ." Some of us chuckled a bit, squirming ahead in our seats to get closer and not miss anything. My father often began his lessons that way, especially when we were hot and sweaty and unsettled from recess. All he had to say was something like "suppose"—a rich word, pregnant with implications—and we would collectively draw a quick breath and listen for what was to come next. And when, in the same short sentence, he would wave in front of us an image like that of a wild cow or a demented goose, he had us—attention riveted, unwavering.

"A demented, cross-eyed goose," he continued. "A goose with a completely unnatural passion for Ford cars." Barney tittered suddenly, loudly, perhaps knowing or suspecting something about demented geese or unnatural passions of which the rest of us were not yet aware.

"Now suppose this loco goose is flying along at 30 miles an hour and he looks down and sees that he just happens to be over a nice Ford that's going in the same direction, only it's just going 20 miles an hour. Well, the goose is tempted to go right down and get closer to this Ford." Barney tittered once more.

"But," my father continued, "when the goose looks out in the distance with his crossed eyes, he sees another Ford. This other Ford is exactly 120 miles away and it's coming directly toward the first Ford at a steady speed of 40 miles an hour.

"Well, the mad goose can't resist, so it leaves the first Ford and flies straight toward the second one at 30 miles an hour. But when he gets to the second Ford, he remembers the first, changes his mind, and turns right around. Without slowing down a bit, he flies right back to the first Ford. Well, as I told you, this goose is a little strange, so when he gets back to the first Ford, he turns around again and flies right back to the second, always at 30 miles an hour and always without slowing down—back and forth and back and forth, honking madly and looking in both directions at once with his crossed eyes, until finally the two Fords run, kaboom! smack into each other!

"The question is," my dad announced into the expectant silence—and we knew that we had again been seduced into a math problem—"the question is, how far will that goose have flown before the two cars run into each other?"

Stan raised his hand at once. "I know the answer! Can I tell it?"

"Just write it down and hand it to me." We knew that Stan's answer would be correct, although I couldn't for the life of me see how he could have figured it out so fast. Most of the rest of us wrestled with the problem, writing numbers, dividing, multiplying, drawing lines, trying to figure out how many turns the goose would make, how much shorter each one would be. For his part, Barney drew exquisite replicas of two Ford cars, one in each of the bottom corners of a sheet of paper. Then he sketched a clearly delirious cross-eyed goose in one upper corner, drew a line from that corner to the other, curved the line down and back part of the way, curved it back again (but a shorter distance this time), and continued doing this, back and forth, until he had drawn what looked like a continuous series of diminishing esses down to the bottom center of the page. He then measured this line with a ruler and a string and announced, "374 miles—give or take a few." There was something about demented geese that Barney apparently didn't know.

THE TALENTED AND THE GIFTED

"That is an excellent goose!" my dad announced. He seemed truly proud, as if he were somehow responsible for the fact that Barney could draw and paint so well. "May I show it to the others, even if the goose didn't fly quite 374 miles?"* And even Barney was proud. One of my father's greatest gifts as a teacher was that he recognized gifts and talents in others and that he encouraged these attributes and made their owners feel proud.

Education does not always recognize giftedness and talent. One problem is that historically, with some notable exceptions, most school jurisdictions have not offered special programs for gifted children. And those that have were never quite certain about which children to include in these programs. As Adamson (1983) notes, our "fuzzy" concept of giftedness might include superior academic achievement, high measured intelligence, exceptionally rapid learning, evidence of a single extraordinary ability or talent, or combinations of these.

---

*PPC: How far did the goose fly?
AUTHOR: I don't remember. But I could figure it out. Now, to reach the second Ford the first time . . .

GIFTEDNESS DEFINED

Like creativity, *giftedness* is not easy to define. Unfortunately, however, a fuzzy concept of giftedness is of little value to teachers and school administrators who need to identify students for gifted programs.

A distinction is sometimes made between those who are gifted and those who might be termed **prodigies.** Whereas giftedness is usually seen as a relatively generalized characteristic evident in superior performance and ability in a number of areas, a child who is a prodigy is characterized by a more highly focused but typically very outstanding skill or ability (Feldman, 1993). Child prodigies have often been identified as those with extraordinary musical or artistic talent. As another example, Lupkowski-Shoplik and Assouline (1994) present case studies of two boys and two girls marked by extreme mathematical precocity.

Public Law 91-230. The concept of giftedness was clarified somewhat in 1969, following the

---

prodigies A distinct form of giftedness characterized by a highly focused talent or ability, such as in music or art, for example.

passage of U.S. Public Law 91-230. A section of this law (806) relates directly to the gifted and talented and includes the following definition:

Gifted and talented children are those identified by professionally qualified persons who by virtue of outstanding abilities are capable of high performance. These are children who require differentiated educational programs and/or services beyond those normally provided by the regular school programs in order to realize their contribution to self and society.

The law goes on to state that capacity for high performance may be defined in terms of demonstrated achievement and/or potential for achievement in one or more of the following aptitudes and abilities:

▶ General intellectual ability
▶ Specific academic aptitude
▶ Creative or productive thinking
▶ Leadership ability
▶ Visual and performing arts
▶ Psychomotor ability

Interestingly, a modification of this legislation in 1978 deletes the category "psychomotor ability" as a means of identifying gifted children. This was done not because children who are exceptional in this area are not considered gifted but simply because psychomotor giftedness is generally evident in superior athletics, an area that is well funded under other programs (Harrington, Harrington, & Karns, 1991).

Defining giftedness and establishing criteria for admission to this group is particularly important where special programs are available for gifted and talented children. The definition and criteria we use determine which children will be eligible for special programs. By the same token, they determine which children are not eligible—that is, they implicitly label a large group of children "not gifted." There are, as Grossman (1995) notes, important ethical and equity issues here, particularly in light of the serious problems with the procedures used to identify gifted children, as well as those whose exceptionalities are less advantageous. Because of biases in identification procedures, those who are non-European and poor tend to be misrepresented in special education programs. Not only are they overrepresented among programs for those with learning disabilities, emotional disorders, and related disabilities, but they are underrepresented among the talented and the gifted.

IDENTIFYING GIFTED CHILDREN

In practice, those who are gifted are typically identified through their performance on group intelligence tests, through teachers' nominations—usually as a function of superior achievement in schools—and perhaps through an individual intelligence test. But a great deal of ambiguity and confusion surrounds the use of intelligence tests. As we saw in Chapter 7, what these tests measure isn't entirely clear. What we do know is that they tell us very little about some important things such as motivation, persistence, and other personality variables. And whatever they measure, they don't always measure very accurately.

In effect, then, what happens in practice with respect to identifying gifted children often does not reflect official definitions of giftedness. In the majority of cases, general intellectual ability and academic achievement are taken into consideration, but these are only two of the five criteria identified by the U.S. public law that defines giftedness. Although special talents and abilities in the other criteria (creative ability, leadership qualities, and talents in visual and performing arts) may affect teachers' nominations, they are seldom part of formal identification procedures.

Many researchers have attempted to develop assessment procedures and definitions of giftedness that reflect these concerns. Renzulli, Reis, and Smith (1981), for example, define giftedness in terms of a variety of characteristics. They suggest, however, that from the teacher's point of view, giftedness can be recognized in terms of a combination of three things—either demonstrated or potential:

MIRO VINTONIV/STOCK, BOSTON

Among the culturally different, there are some remarkably gifted and talented individuals. Unfortunately, schools often overlook these people when selecting candidates for gifted and talented programs. This is partly because of biases in the selection procedures used, and also because the culturally different are sometimes underachievers.

▶ High ability (might be evident in high achievement and/or high measured intelligence)

▶ High creativity (sometimes evident in production of novel ideas or in problem-solving ability)

▶ High commitment (manifested in a high level of persistence and task completion)

Renzulli's Scale for Rating Behavioral Characteristics of Superior Students gives teachers a preliminary instrument for identifying gifted and talented students (Renzulli, 1986). Such instruments are essential if teachers and administrators are to identify candidates for special programs fairly. It's also very important that teachers and schools employ a variety of measures in their attempts to identify gifted children—and that they not use any single one of these measures as a means for excluding a given child from the program. That is, even if a child functions at an average or below average level with respect to one measure, other measures should also be looked at before making a final decision. Among the measures most often looked at by teachers and administrators are scores on IQ tests, academic achievement, performance in visual or performing arts, self nomination, parent nomination, peer nomination, teacher nomination, and scores on measures of creativity.

Prevalence of Giftedness. Estimates of the number of gifted and talented children vary considerably. Some researchers (Renzulli, 1986, for example) argue that as many as 20 percent or more of all children have the potential to be gifted. However, special programs are available for nowhere near this proportion of students (Harrington, Harrington, & Karns, 1991). Heward and Orlansky (1992) report that gifted programs are provided for 3.6 percent of all students in forty-four American states.

Overlooking Culturally Different Gifted Learners. As we noted, among the gifted who are systematically overlooked are a number of identifiable groups. Perhaps most obvious are the culturally different, for whom the usual measures of achievement and potential are sometimes highly inappropriate. For example, Kitano (1991) notes that minority groups are underrepresented in gifted programs in spite of education's growing concern about meeting the needs of these children. Matthew and associates (1992) report that the use of the SOMPA, a testing procedure deliberately designed to be fairer to ethnic minorities, results in the identification of gifted children who would otherwise be missed by more conventional testing practices (see Chapter 7 for more information on the SOMPA).

Gifted children who are culturally different also are often overlooked because many of them are underachievers (Wilgosh, 1991). Because they don't do as well as majority-group children in ordinary classroom programs, they are hardly likely to be viewed as potentially gifted. Similarly, Urban (1991) reports that gifted youngsters who have behavioral disorders are seldom found in programs for the gifted.

There are four principal reasons why many gifted youngsters are overlooked, reports Shaklee (1992): (1) our definitions are too limiting, (2) there is confusion about identifying gifted learners as well as about the options available for them, (3) we place too much emphasis on biased measures of ability and achievement, and (4) there are insufficient programs for gifted learners.

PROGRAMS FOR THE GIFTED

Following the passage of PL 91-230 in 1969, which, among other things, attempted to define giftedness, a massive survey of programs for the gifted and talented was undertaken in the United States. The survey, which involved thousands of parents and educators, revealed several things. One was that the education of the gifted and talented was typically perceived as a very low-priority issue: Only twenty-one states had any legislation to provide facilities for the gifted, and in most cases this legislation represented intent rather than concrete action. Another revelation was that those programs that did exist typically did not reach the gifted and talented from ethnic and social minorities and that there were some serious problems in identifying the gifted and talented (S. P. Marland, 1972).

A similar survey, conducted some six years after the passage of PL 91-230, found that all but eight states had some type of legislation concerning programs for the gifted and talented. And the National Research Center on the Gifted and Talented has been receiving nearly $10 million per year since 1990 to direct and coordinate research on the gifted and to establish gifted programs (Harrington, Harrington, & Karns, 1991). However, the majority of states (and provinces) still provide services to relatively small numbers of children in this category—a situation that may be attributed to lack of funding, lack of trained personnel, and lack of widely accepted procedures and criteria for identifying the gifted and talented. Sadly, an observation made by Terman (1925) more than six decades ago might still be true today: When comparing potential and achievement, we find that the most "retarded" group in our schools is the highly gifted.

Acceleration Versus Enrichment. There are two broad approaches to educating the gifted: **acceleration** and **enrichment.** The terms are essentially self-explanatory. Programs that accelerate simply move students more rapidly through the conventional curriculum, exposing them to the same material as other students. These programs attempt to compress or compact the regular curriculum into fewer lessons, and are sometimes referred to as compaction programs (Evans & King, 1994a, 1994b). Programs that enrich provide gifted students with additional and different school experiences in an attempt to deepen and broaden their knowledge and capabilities. Both enrich-

---

acceleration An approach in the education of the gifted. Acceleration programs attempt to move students through the conventional curriculum more rapidly than normal.

enrichment An approach in the education of gifted children. Enrichment involves providing students with additional and different school experiences rather than simply moving them more rapidly through the conventional curriculum. Also termed the *revolving door* model.

ment and acceleration can occur in the regular classroom, or both might involve grouping gifted students together, sometimes within the classroom and sometimes in special classes or even special schools.

The enrichment approach is well illustrated by Renzulli's (1977) enrichment model, also called the **revolving door model** (Renzulli, Reis, & Smith, 1981). This model advocates selecting gifted individuals on the basis of three characteristics: high academic ability, high creative potential, and high motivation. No rigorous cutoff scores are used; instead, all students whose achievement or apparent potential places them in the upper 25 percent of students in the school are designated as talented. Any of these students may then enter enrichment programs and drop out of them as they wish (hence, the revolving door). The programs vary according to the expressed interests of the students. When they identify a project and commit themselves to it, they are allowed to enter a resource room and work on the project. Under this model, enrichment programs tend to be schoolwide rather than restricted to specific classes or students (Renzulli & Reis, 1994).

The acceleration approach is perhaps best illustrated by Stanley's (1976) **radical acceleration model,** developed primarily for students gifted in mathematics. It attempts to compress the ordinary curriculum so as to enable gifted individuals to master a course of studies in a fraction of the time ordinarily required. Subsequently, many of these accelerated youngsters are enrolled in university-sponsored courses for additional acceleration.

The relative merits of acceleration and enrichment have long been debated among educators. One of the most common arguments against acceleration is that it might be harmful to move students much beyond their social and psychological levels of development. Educators have been concerned that one effect of accelerating gifted students might be that they would eventually no longer "fit in" socially with their peers—a possibility that might have harmful consequences. Interestingly, the most common argument for enrichment is precisely the argument used against acceleration; that is, educators simply assume that enrichment will not have the same social and psychological implications as acceleration. After all, enrichment does not remove gifted children from their age and grade levels as does acceleration; it simply provides them with an opportunity to deepen and broaden their knowledge at each level.

Research has not yet established that one of these methods is clearly superior to the other. In fact, there is some evidence that the two may not be all that different in practice. Slavin (1993a) suggests that most accelerated programs do not really involve acceleration at all, but are far more likely to be enrichment programs. And relatively recent studies that have looked at the effects of various combinations of enrichment and acceleration typically report that a balance between the two is most effective (for example, Kulik & Kulik, 1992; Keirouz, 1993).

It now seems clear that most acceleration programs do not lead to negative social or emotional consequences (Janos & Robinson, 1985). What may be most important, in the final analysis, is not whether gifted students are in enriched or accelerated programs, but whether they are *grouped* with other students for instruction (Kulik & Kulik, 1992). Grouping, reports Rogers (1993), is clearly effective for gifted and talented students.

Mentoring and Tutoring. An increasing number of programs for the gifted use mentors or tutors (Emerson-Stonnell & Carter, 1994); mentoring

---

revolving door model An enrichment program for gifted children advocated by Renzulli, available to the top 25 percent of students in a program (high ability, high creativity, high motivation) on an optional basis, so that students can opt in and out of the program (hence, the revolving door).

radical acceleration model Stanley's acceleration program for gifted children, designed specifically for very high achievers in mathematics. Also termed a *compression* or *compaction* program, it attempts to compress the mathematics curriculum so that it can be covered in a fraction of the time that would ordinarily be required.

and tutoring are also used for students with learning disabilities (Phillips, Fuchs, & Fuchs, 1994).

A **mentor** is an individual who serves as a sort of intellectual and psychological guide. Mentoring implies a close relationship within which the mentor may be a role model, consultant, advisor, source of wisdom—even a sort of protector. Hence, the term *protégé* to signify the one who is mentored (Jacobi, 1991). A **tutor**, on the other hand, is a teacher rather than a mentor; but unlike the regular classroom teacher, the tutor teaches only one student at a time (Raines, 1994).

Tutoring, says Bloom (1984), is clearly the most effective way to teach. His review of the research suggests that one-on-one tutoring will move the average learner from the middle of the pack (where, by definition, average learners are found) to about the ninety-eighth percentile. In addition, tutoring has beneficial effects on the tutors themselves—they develop more positive attitudes and gain in understanding. And it has beneficial effects on children identified as being at risk of failure (Snow & Swanson, 1992).

Mentoring, which requires a more encompassing relationship between two individuals, has become more common in education in recent years, and is especially useful in career development (Holland, 1994). For example, a large number of school jurisdictions have instituted mentor programs wherein expert teachers are designated as mentors to assist the early development of novice teachers (Bainer & Didham, 1994). Similarly, mentoring programs are used at some universities, at both the graduate, and the undergraduate level.

---

mentor Individual engaged in a one-to-one teaching/learning relationship in which the teacher (mentor) serves as a fundamentally important model with respect to values, beliefs, philosophies, and attitudes, as well as a source of more specific information.

tutor Teacher involved in a one-on-one teaching situation. Tutors are frequently other students, or may be other teachers or experts.

Individualized Educational Plans (IEPs). Another approach to the education of the gifted involves self-directed and independent study, often using learning/thinking strategies of the kind discussed in Chapter 5. Some self-directed study programs also use *individualized educational plans (IEPs)*, individually designed for students according to their special needs and talents. IEPs are widely used for special-needs

---

CASE: YOUR DAD'S NOT THE TEACHER

THE SETTING: Ms. Adèle Bourgeois' grade 3 arithmetic class. The class has been learning odd and even numbers.

MS. BOURGEOIS: So who can tell me, you should all know this by now, which numbers between 1 and 10 can be divided by 2?

THOMAS: All the even ones—2, 4, 6, 8, and 10!

MS. BOURGEOIS: Very good, Thomas. That's exactly right.

CLAIRE: That's not right.

MS. BOURGEOIS (annoyed): What's that, Claire?

CLAIRE: That's not right. I mean, not just the even numbers.

MS. BOURGEOIS (quite angry): You always think you know better than the book, don't you?

CLAIRE (more timidly, but sticking to her guns): But the odd ones too. My dad said . . .

MS. BOURGEOIS: Your dad isn't the teacher, smarty pants. How d'you suppose you'd divide 5 by 2, hunh? Weren't you paying any attention at all when we talked about how all even numbers can be divided by 2?

Claire, red-faced, shrugs and whispers "2½" too softly for Ms. Bourgeois to hear.

children, their use having been mandated in the United States by a 1975 law (PL 94-142). (IEPs are described and illustrated later in this chapter.) Torrance (1986) notes that IEPs are becoming more popular for use with gifted children, for whom the plans usually involve a combination of approaches and materials such as self-directed study, mentoring, enrichment, perhaps acceleration, and programs for development of learning/thinking strategies and motivation.

Special Schools. In addition to these approaches to the education of the gifted, a number of schools cater solely to these children, as do Saturday and summer programs and a variety of community or university enrichment programs. Some of their offerings can sometimes be included in IEPs designed for gifted children.

In spite of these special programs, many gifted and talented children—like many whose gifts and talents are less than average—are in regular classrooms and lack access to any formal "special" education. This does not mean, however, that there is nothing that teachers of regular classes can (or should) do for them. In fact, as we discuss later in this chapter, mainstreaming legislation now makes it mandatory for many children who would otherwise receive special instruction to spend most of their time in regular classrooms. It has therefore become necessary for teachers in regular classrooms to learn about exceptionality and about what they can do for these children. Many suggestions included in this chapter are appropriate for both ordinary students and for those who are more extraordinary.

PROMOTING CREATIVITY AND GIFTEDNESS

"In the final analysis," write Harrington, Harrington, and Karns, "[we] must provide educational challenge for [our] bright people or else tomorrow we will be led by the mediocre, and on the day after, by the incompetent" (1991, p. 41).

Do schools do what they can (or should) for the gifted and creative? Perhaps not, if Ms.

Bourgeois' class is any indication—which Cropley (1992) suggests it might be (see the case "Your Dad's Not the Teacher"). The behaviors and personalities most characteristic of the highly creative, notes Cropley, are not the qualities most preferred by teachers. Podd'iakov (1992) makes the same point, claiming that the normal socialization of children works against their creativity, mainly because it discourages exploration. Schools are geared toward developing students who are obedient, accepting of other people's ideas, popular, punctual, courteous, and respectful. And academic success is fostered by memorization and the ability to recognize and replicate accepted answers and procedures. Note that flexibility, risk taking, originality, inventiveness, and nonconformity are absent in these lists. Claire, like all other students in her class, was expected to learn a simple odd-even rule and to repeat it when asked.

A *good* teacher would not have responded as Ms. Bourgeois did. Not only was she unwilling to consider the possibility that Claire's response might have merit—or at the very least, to have her explain her response—but she resorted to name calling. And even if Claire's response had been totally incorrect and inappropriate, it was nevertheless different, innovative, exploratory. As Matson (1991) notes, there is much to be said for rewarding *failure*—that is, for rewarding the brave and creative attempts of students even when they are incorrect and fail.

As the world's problems multiply, the need for creativity becomes ever more pressing and more apparent—as does the need for teachers to learn how they can contribute to the development of the gifted and creative.

WHAT TEACHERS CAN DO: SOME TECHNIQUES

After you have been teaching for a while, it might be a good idea to pause and ask yourself what it is that you have been teaching. If you are honest (as most teachers are), you will probably find that you have been teaching information relating to one or more conveniently labeled and categorized bodies of knowledge that we call "subjects" and perhaps a number of practical skills having to do with reading, writing, and manipulating numbers. You might also note that some of your students, some of the time, have also begun to learn how to understand and appreciate, how to analyze and synthesize. Some will show signs of being able to compare and summarize, will perhaps even know how to interpret and criticize, find and test assumptions, and observe and classify.

Sadly, however, unless you are one of those rare teachers who have taken pains to work toward these ends, or unless you are part of an experimental project designed to develop learning/thinking strategies (see Chapter 5), most of this learning will have occurred incidentally—almost accidentally.

Although we have long paid lip service to the desirability of developing creative and thinking skills in students, schools have paid little attention to programs deliberately designed to foster these skills. In fact, we have naively assumed that the abilities involved in creating and thinking are largely innate. Worse yet, we have assumed that systematic exposure to increasingly large bodies of information and increasingly difficult problems and concepts would automatically develop the ability to think. With respect to creativity, we have been less certain; we have preferred, instead, to assume that some have it and others don't. At the same time, we have assumed that the worst thing a teacher might do with respect to creativity is to stifle it and that the best thing a teacher might do is not stifle it.

But there are specific things teachers can do to teach students different ways of thinking and perhaps to foster creative thinking. Among them are a number of different problem-solving techniques.

Brainstorming. Brainstorming, for example, is among the most common group approaches for solving problems creatively. It has been used extensively, and successfully, in many school programs designed to foster creativity (for example, Alvino, 1993; Naval-Severino, 1993; Herschel, 1994).

Developed by Alex Osborn (1957), **brainstorming** is a technique for producing a wide variety of solutions while deliberately suspending judgment about the appropriateness of any of them. This, the principle of deferred evaluation, is the most important characteristic of brainstorming—and, in fact, of most approaches to creative thinking. Putting off evaluation is an extremely difficult thing for inexperienced problem solvers to do, but it leads to the production of 23 to 177 percent more good-quality solutions than when simply following instructions to "produce good ideas" (Parnes, 1962). Delaying evaluation allows much greater scope in the responses emitted. Evaluation during production has a dampening effect on both groups and individuals.

In a brainstorming session, several rules are followed closely:

▶ Criticism of a contributed idea is absolutely barred (deferred evaluation).

▶ Modification or combination with other ideas is encouraged.

▶ A large quantity of ideas is sought.

▶ Unusual, remote, or wild ideas are sought.

In industry, a brainstorming session may last for two or more hours and involve five to twelve people from a wide variety of backgrounds. The leader explains the rules, describes the problem to be solved, and the session begins. Ideally, it is a free-wheeling, wide-ranging affair, with ideas coming rapidly from all sources. All forms of evaluation are forbidden. Evaluative comments such as "that sounds good" or "no, that won't work," ridicule, laughter, or nonverbal expressions of either admiration or disgust are stopped immediately. Habitual offenders may even be removed from the group.

---

brainstorming A technique popularized by Osborn and used in the production of creative solutions for problems. A brainstorming session usually involves a small group of people who are encouraged to produce a wide variety of ideas, which are evaluated later.

During a brainstorming session, a number of specific aids to creativity are used. Most common are checklists used to stimulate ideas. For example, Parnes (1967) provides a checklist of nine actions that could be applied to a variety of problems. Each of these nine possibilities is illustrated here with reference to the question, "How many suggestions can you make for different ways to manage a classroom?"

▶ *Other uses.* The class might be used as something other than a learning situation. For example, students might be given the responsibility for entertaining the school at a social evening.

▶ *Adapt.* Adaptation involves using ideas from other sources; perhaps the class could be run like a factory, like a prison, or like a playground.

▶ *Modify.* Modification suggests changing the composition of the class, changing teaching methods, or changing the approach to discipline problems.

▶ *Magnify.* Class size could be increased, as could the number of teachers, number of assignments, or magnitude of punishment or reinforcement.

▶ *"Minify."* Class size could be decreased, as could the number of assignments, number of reprimands, or number of school days.

▶ *Substitute.* A new teacher might be substituted, the entire class might be exchanged, or a few members of the class might be replaced by students from other classes.

▶ *Rearrange.* The physical setup of the room could be changed, or the seating plan could be rearranged to separate troublemakers.

▶ *Reverse.* Perhaps the desks should all face the rear. Or the teacher might face the front as a sort of reversal. Another reversal would be to have the students take turns teaching.

▶ *Combine.* A combination of the previous suggestions might provide a solution. Or the teaching/learning function could be combined with other functions, such as entertainment, problem solving, or discussion of noncurricular topics of interest.

The Gordon Technique. A slight modification of brainstorming, the **Gordon technique,** differs from brainstorming in that it presents participants with an abstraction of a problem rather than with a complete, detailed problem (W. J. J. Gordon, 1961). For example, if the problem is one of parking cars in New York, the leader of a Gordon group might begin by saying, "The problem today is one of storing things. How many ways can you think of for storing things?" Such an approach sometimes leads to ideas that would not otherwise occur (for example, "put them in bags," "pile them up," "hang them," "can them," "put them on conveyer belts," "fold them," "put them in boxes," "cut them up," and so on).

Later in the session, the leader of the group begins to narrow down the problem. The next step might be to say, "The things to be stored are quite large." Later, more restrictions will be specified: "The objects cannot be folded or cut up," and so on.

Morphological Analysis. This procedure, described by Osborn (1957) and Arnold (1962), was originated by Fritz Zwicky of Aero-Jet Corporation. It involves dividing a problem into a number of independent variables, thinking of as many potential solutions as possible for each one, and then combining the results in all possible ways. Arnold illustrates **morphological analysis** using the problem of developing a new type of vehicle. Three different aspects of this problem are (1) the type of vehicle, (2) the type of power, and (3) the medium in which the vehicle will be used. Each of these aspects lends itself to various solutions. For

---

Gordon technique A creativity-enhancing technique very similar to brainstorming except that an abstraction of a problem rather than a specific problem is presented.

morphological analysis A creativity-enhancing technique, advanced by Arnold, involving the analysis of problems into their component parts and subsequent attempts to brainstorm each of these component parts.

example, the type of vehicle might be a cart, a sling, a rocket, a box, and so on. Figure 8.1 presents 180 potential solutions for the problem; there are thousands more. Some of these have already been invented; some are completely impractical; others might be worth pursuing. Imagine, for example, a sling-type vehicle, drawn by horses, going through oil; or imagine an atomic rocket going through a tube.

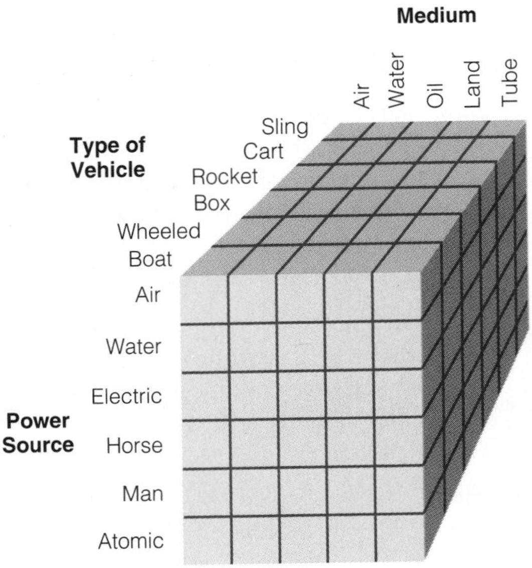

Lateral Thinking. According to de Bono (1970), if you want to dig a hole deeper, it is necessary to dig vertically. But if the object is to have a hole that, so to speak, covers different ground, you have to dig laterally. In the same way, if the object is to discover more about something or to arrive at a conventional, accepted, "convergent" solution to a problem, **vertical thinking** is entirely appropriate; but if the object is to find unusual, divergent, creative solutions for problems, **lateral thinking** would be better. It arrives at solutions by attacking problems sideways—hence laterally.

De Bono argues that lateral thinking is a way of using the mind that leads to creative thinking and to creative solutions but that it is not the same thing as creative thinking. He maintains that although lateral thinking is closely related to insight, creativity, and humor, these last three can only be prayed for, whereas lateral thinking can be developed deliberately. Accordingly, he has devised a program for teaching lateral thinking, as well as one designed to teach vertical thinking (de Bono, 1976). Vertical (or critical, or logical) thinking is necessary for creative problem solving, argues de Bono, but it isn't sufficient. That is because we need the ability not only to critique ideas, but also to create them (Brodinsky, 1985).

FIGURE 8.1 A model of morphological analysis for the problem of developing a new vehicle. One hundred and eighty possible solutions are shown.

Unlike brainstorming and other techniques designed to foster creative behavior, de Bono's program for teaching lateral thinking does not require students to solve specific problems; instead, it encourages them to develop new ways to approach all problems. In de Bono's words, it attempts to teach lateral rather than vertical approaches.

Many exercises in de Bono's program are similar to items used on various tests of creativity. Students might be presented with various geometric designs, for example, and asked to describe them in as many ways as possible. Other activities are designed to encourage students to ask why, to suspend judgment, to identify and challenge assumptions, to brainstorm, to produce analogies, and so on. Throughout, emphasis is on creating new ideas and challenging old ones, but care is taken to assure that the learner does not overemphasize the negation of the old. Negation, de Bono says, is one of the principal techniques in vertical thinking because "logical" thinking is based on negation and selection, with the major role being played

vertical thinking De Bono's term for thought processes that lead to correct, appropriate, and accepted solutions. This term is in contrast to *lateral thinking*, which leads to creative solutions.

lateral thinking De Bono's term for a way of thinking that leads to creative solutions.

by rejection. Hence, the centrality of a word such as *no* in logical (vertical) thinking.

Lateral thinking does not have a central word—that is, it didn't. In addition to offering a large number of exercises, de Bono also presents his students with a new word, **po,** intended to be to lateral thinking what *no* is to vertical thinking. The word *yes* is clearly unsuitable, for it implies uncritical acceptance. But the word *po* is entirely suitable; it means nothing and everything. It is a word that permits us to do or say anything, a word that requires no justification, a word that de Bono terms the "laxative" of language and thinking. Po is neither affirmation nor negation; it is simply an invitation to think laterally. As such, it is an invitation to examine, challenge, modify, combine, brainstorm, or analogize. Po might have some place in your teaching.

Conceptual Models. Education, we argued in Chapter 1, must do far more than simply teach facts and procedures. Students should not only learn; they should also learn how to learn. Although they need to accumulate facts and formulas, they should also grow in their ability and in their willingness to think. One of the grand goals of all education, we insisted, is to empower students; that is, students should be given the skills, the attitudes, and the information that will enable them to deal most effectively with life—that will empower them to solve their problems (as well as yours and mine).

To be truly empowered, students must also be creative. Mayer asks the question, "What can be done to empower students to be creative when they are faced with problems?" (1989, p. 43). One important answer, he claims, can be found in the use of conceptual models as an instructional and learning technique.

---

po A word invented by de Bono, meant to stimulate lateral (creative) thinking. Even as *no* is central to vertical (critical or logical) thinking, *po* is intended to be central to creating. Its meaning is neither to affirm nor to deny but rather to invite creativity, challenge, change, resistance.

1. TRANSMISSION: A pulse travels from an antenna.

2. REFLECTION: The pulse bounces off a remote object.

3. RECEPTION: The pulse returns to the receiver.

4. MEASUREMENT: The difference between the time out and the time back tells the total time traveled.

5. CONVERSION: The time can be converted to a measure of distance because the pulse travels at a constant speed.

seconds =   miles

FIGURE 8.2 A conceptual model of how radar functions. Adapted from R. E. Mayer (1989), "Models for Understanding." *Review of Educational Research, 59,* 1, 43–64. Copyright 1989 by the American Educational Research Association. Reprinted by permission of the publisher.

A **conceptual model** (also termed a *concept map*) is a verbal or graphic presentation designed to assist the learner in developing a clear and useful mental representation of whatever is being studied. Such models, note

---

conceptual model A verbal or graphic representation of concepts and important relationships that exist among them. Designed to assist the learner in developing a clear and useful mental representation. Also termed a *concept map*.

Rafferty and Fleschner (1993), are especially useful in promoting meaningful learning and understanding. They are as Mayer (1989) puts it, a special form of advance organizer of the kind we discussed in connection with Ausubel's theory (see Chapter 6). Conceptual models used as advance organizers are typically developed by teachers. Students might also be encouraged to develop their own conceptual models (concept maps) as a way of organizing information and increasing understanding and retention (Novak & Musonda, 1991).

Figure 8.2 is an example of a conceptual model that includes the most important elements required to understand how radar functions. Students who were allowed to examine this model for 1 minute before a short lecture on radar later recalled 57 percent more of the important concepts than did students who had been given the lecture without the model (Mayer, 1989). Perhaps more important, students who had examined the conceptual model were able to produce solutions that were 83 percent more accurate than the other group's for problems that required transferring what they had learned to new situations. Put another way, these students were able to use creatively what they had learned, in the sense that they could then apply it to new situations.

Mayer (1989) cites a number of other studies that support the argument that conceptual models significantly increase students' creative solutions to problems not presented in the initial lesson. In addition, models of this kind increase recall of important concepts, although they tend to decrease rote, or verbatim, recall. Like Ausubel's advance organizers, conceptual models provide the learner with important concepts that organize previous learning and that provide essential elements of cognitive structure to which new material can be related.

From the teacher's point of view, it is important to know both how to devise models and which models are most likely to be effective. Mayer (1989) describes a number of characteristics of good conceptual models.

First, such a model is *complete* in the sense that it contains all essential aspects of a system,

so that the learner sees and understands how the system works. At the same time, the model needs to be both *concise* (so that it doesn't overwhelm with detail) and *coherent* (so that it makes sense). The model must be *concrete* in that it deals with events and functions that are familiar to the learner, but it also needs to be *conceptual* in that it deals with meaningful ideas. It goes almost without saying that it must also be *correct*. And finally, a good conceptual model must be *considerate* in that it takes into consideration the learner's sophistication and level of understanding.

Clearly, there might have been better terms with which to describe the characteristics of conceptual models most likely to lead to understanding and creativity, but note that in the alliteration there is a useful mnemonic.*

Research with conceptual models suggests that they can be particularly effective in science (Roth & Bowen, 1993). "Better learning," argues Papert, "will not come from finding better ways for the teacher to *instruct*, but from giving the learner better opportunities to *construct*" (1993, p. 3). Computer programming is one way to construct—to make models; making graphic representations with paper and pencil is another; inventing mental models is yet another. This new constructionist emphasis in teaching and learning encourages learners to discover and build their own representations, their own models.

FAMILY CONTEXT, CLASSROOM CLIMATE, AND THE CREATIVE AND GIFTED

Follow-up studies of children in Terman's longitudinal investigation of gifted children indicated that, in the end, many of these children were not outstanding achievers—although, on average, they tended to be better adjusted and more successful than comparable but non-

---

*PPC: I'm not sure all students will understand this. Even those who know what alliteration is may not c the relevance of this sentence. Do you get it?
AUTHOR: [Groan].

280 PART FOUR DIVERSITY AND TEACHING

gifted individuals (see Fetterman, 1994). Some, however, were far more successful than others not only in terms of academic achievement, but also in terms of career and general happiness.

Family Context. In an effort to find out why some were more successful than others, Terman and Oden (1959) compared a group of the 100 most successful with a second group of the 100 least successful participants in this study. Their most important finding: The family backgrounds of the two groups were significantly different. Subjects from the successful group were from highly educated families that encouraged exploration, independence, achievement, and ambition far more than did the families of the less successful participants. It appears that family context is extremely important in determining later achievement. This finding was confirmed again in a later followup of the same two Terman study groups, each consisting of 100 very high and 100 lower achievers (Pyryt, 1993). The Pyryt followup also confirmed the importance of schooling for later achievement.

Psychology has taken too simple and too cognitive a view of giftedness, notes Torrance (1993). As a result, we have been guilty of neglecting important personality, family, and school variables that are closely involved in creative achievement. These factors include such things as love of one's work, a sense of purpose in life, high motivation and persistence, love of challenge, and high energy—all of which may be more important than measured intelligence or creative ability. And these factors are strongly influenced not only by the family, but also by the school.

Classroom Climate. Encouraging exceptionality in students needs to go far beyond occasionally making use of specific techniques developed to encourage creative problem solving or lateral thinking: It is also highly dependent on the climate in the classroom.

Lowe (1983) suggests that creative teaching and learning stem from a belief in the importance of self-initiated learning, from flexible and nonauthoritarian instructional methods, and from approaches that value reasoning,

questioning, and the manipulation of ideas and materials. Creativity and high achievement are fostered by teachers (and parents) who have an attitude that recognizes and encourages individuality and creativity in students (Fahrmeler, 1991) and by a culture that rewards rather than punishes those who are gifted (Scott, 1991). Schools that reflect these values might also do much to foster the development of gifted—talented—creative youngsters.

Haddon and Lytton (1968) contrasted two types of schools, which they labeled "formal" and "informal." The formal schools were characterized by an authoritarian approach to learning and teaching, whereas the informal schools tended to emphasize self-initiated learning and greater student participation. Not surprisingly, students in informal schools consistently did better on measures of creative thinking than did students of comparable intelligence and socioeconomic status who attended the formal schools. Similar results were found in relatively unstructured classrooms (informal classes) where students spent time programming computers using Logo (see Chapter 12). These students typically did better on subsequent measures of creativity (Clements, 1991).

One important aspect of classroom climate is the extent to which students perceive school activities as cooperative or competitive. Adams (1968) reports that students tested under noncompetitive conditions score higher on tests of spontaneous flexibility than do those tested under competitive conditions. Further, if the examiner is warm and receptive, students do even better. These findings have been corroborated in a large number of studies, twenty-eight of which are reviewed and summarized by Slavin (1980). Among other things, the studies indicate that cooperative teaching methods (in which students work in small groups and receive rewards based on group rather than individual performance) lead to "increased student achievement, positive race relations in desegregated schools, mutual concern among students, student self-esteem, and other positive outcomes" (p. 315). (See Chapter 9 for a detailed discussion of cooperative learning.)

Factors Related to Creative Eminence. When Torrance (1993) conducted a thirty-year follow-up investigation of gifted students (now adults), he found that the highest achievers are those who are both highly intelligent and specially gifted. But, as we noted, not all of the highly intelligent and highly creative become high achievers. And among the highest achievers, only a small number become truly, outstandingly eminent. These appear to be individuals with just the right combination of talents and personality characteristics and, perhaps most important, individuals fortunate enough to have been born into the right family context and schooled in classroom climates that encouraged their development.

Albert and Runco (1986) summarize the most important factors that appear to be involved in the development of eminence. If children are to become eminent, they claim, it is best that they:

▶ Be both highly intelligent and highly creative
▶ Develop the values, motivation, and abilities that allow them to undertake important or highly unusual work
▶ Be reared in a family context that encourages the development of these values and drives
▶ Find a "fit" between talents and career demands, such that the demands of the career are sufficiently challenging to lead to eminence
▶ Be provided with the right combination of experiences (that is, musical, athletic, academic, social, political, and so on)
▶ Come from a family whose history includes eminence
▶ Be subjected to family direction consistent with the development of specific talents, but not unrealistic, overly demanding, or uncaring

Notice how prominently the family and other early experiences (academic, for example) figure among these factors. Karges-Bone (1993), too, argues that the most important source of influence in the life of the gifted child is the family. And Christian and Morgan (1993) sug-gest that how parents of gifted children cope with their interests and their energy levels, and with other challenges of raising gifted children, is central in determining their adjustment and achievement. Also central are teachers' attitudes toward creativity.

TEACHERS' ATTITUDES AND CREATIVITY

Some evidence suggests that humanistic approaches to teaching are more likely to lead to creativity among students. Research reviewed in Chapter 9, for example, indicates that open education often leads to higher creativity scores, but it also often leads to lower scores on standardized achievement tests. Similarly, Turner and Denny (1969) found that warm, spontaneous, and caring teachers are more likely to encourage creative behavior in their students than are teachers characterized as highly organized and businesslike.

It should be kept in mind, however, that humanistic concerns and attitudes are not clearly and irrevocably incompatible with businesslike approaches to learning. The important variables are probably not specific teaching methods so much as teachers' attitudes and other personality characteristics.

Torrance (1962) gives a list of suggestions for teacher attitudes and behaviors designed to promote creativity in students. Consider how each might be implemented in the classroom:

▶ Value creative thinking.
▶ Make children more sensitive to environmental stimuli.
▶ Encourage manipulation of objects and ideas.
▶ Teach how to test each idea systematically.
▶ Develop tolerance of new ideas.
▶ Beware of forcing a set pattern.
▶ Develop a creative classroom atmosphere.
▶ Teach children to value their creative thinking.
▶ Teach skills for avoiding peer sanctions.
▶ Give information about the creative process.
▶ Dispel the sense of awe of masterpieces.
▶ Encourage self-initiated learning.

- Create "thorns in the flesh" (that is, awareness of problems).
- Create necessities for creative thinking.
- Provide for active and quiet periods.
- Make available resources for working out ideas.
- Encourage the habit of working out the full implications of ideas.
- Develop constructive criticism—not just criticism.
- Encourage the acquisition of knowledge in a variety of fields.
- Develop adventurous teachers.

In contrast with these behaviors and attitudes that might foster creativity, Hallman (1967) lists some common inhibitors of creativity:

- Pressure to conform
- Authoritarian attitudes and environments
- A teacher with a rigid personality
- Ridicule and sarcasm
- Overemphasis on evaluation
- Excessive quests for certainty
- Hostility toward divergent personalities
- Overemphasis on success
- Intolerance of playful attitudes

It follows that if these behaviors discourage creativity, their opposites might promote it. This list suggests what not to do—as opposed to Torrance's list, which suggests what teachers should do. Both, taken in combination, can serve as useful guides for teacher behavior.

TEACHING STYLES AND CREATIVITY

A **teaching style** is an identifiable and related group of teaching activities and routines. Thus, researchers speak of styles that reflect specific methods of instructing (for example, the lecturing style, the questioning style, the role-playing style). Or they speak of styles that reflect the teacher's predominant relationship with students or the major roles that each assumes (for example, authoritarian versus democratic, teacher centered versus pupil centered, traditional versus progressive). Research has also examined several broad classifications, such as formal–informal styles or direct–indirect styles.

Although teaching style often reflects a teacher's personality, it also reflects many other factors, including personal philosophy, educational goals, the influences of teacher-training programs, maturity, wisdom, and the use of inspiring or less inspiring textbooks. Nor do most teachers invariably display only a single style. For example, most use a variety of instructional procedures and choose different ones depending on the lesson being taught, who the learners are, the amount of preparation time and resources available, and other factors. However, many teachers have a definite tendency to be more formal than informal (or vice versa) or to use more direct rather than less direct approaches to instruction.

From the teacher's point of view, it may be important to know the likely effects of these different styles on students' achievement, on students' motivation, and on the development of the skills and attitudes related to being thoughtful and creative.

Formal–Informal Styles. One of the broadest classifications of teaching styles describes **formal teaching style** and **informal teaching style** (Bennett, 1976). Teachers whose styles are most formal teach each subject separately, emphasize individual rather than group work, assign class

---

teaching style An identifiable way of teaching. Teaching activities and routines marked by common features and often characteristic of specific teachers (formal or informal teaching styles, for example).

formal teaching style An approach to teaching that emphasizes competition, individual work, discipline, order, achievement, and external motivators.

informal teaching style A teaching approach that grants students a relatively high degree of freedom and autonomy and that emphasizes individual growth and fulfillment rather than academic achievement and external rewards.

Some classes, like the one shown on the left, are highly formal: They emphasize order, individual work, discipline, and achievement. Others, like that on the right, are more informal: They grant students a higher level of autonomy and tend to emphasize personal growth rather than achievement and external rewards. To some

seating, restrict students' movement, emphasize assessment and achievement, and make extensive use of external motivators such as grades. Those whose styles are more informal tend to integrate subjects, provide students with considerable freedom in determining their activities, typically allow students to select their seating, do not emphasize tests and academic achievement, and tend to rely on internal sources of motivation like self-satisfaction.

Do these styles significantly affect students' achievement? Research suggests that they do. As we see in Chapter 12, formal styles are associated with higher academic achievement than are informal styles. However, informal styles may be associated with higher levels of creativity.

Direct–Indirect Styles. Flanders (1970) describes two types of teacher–learner verbal interaction that define a **direct teaching style** and an **indirect teaching style.** The direct style is in some ways much like the formal style just described. Teachers whose behavior reflects this style direct classroom activity: They lecture, elaborate their opinions, give directions, and criticize or justify on the basis of their authority and

that of other experts. In contrast, the indirect teaching style involves asking questions rather than providing information and is characterized by an acceptance of the student's feelings and attitudes, by the encouragement of student-initiated behaviors and opinions, and by the solicitation of ideas from students. Flanders' analysis of teacher–student classroom interaction led him to conclude that the direct style predominates in approximately two-thirds of all classrooms.

Research that has evaluated both direct and indirect teaching styles reports mixed results—perhaps, as Silvernail (1979) notes, because using verbal interaction alone to evaluate teaching style oversimplifies a complex situation. In some situations and for some stu-

direct teaching style A relatively authoritarian approach to teaching in which teachers are the primary source of information.

indirect teaching style A relatively humanistic approach to teaching that favors student-initiated activities and that views the teacher's role as questioning and facilitating learning rather than directing it.

extent, these teaching styles reflect the teacher's personality; they also reflect the influences of other factors such as teacher training programs, school goals and philosophy, and the wider influences of culture, politics, and religion. Neither approach is clearly superior for all purposes.

dents, a direct style may be best; in different situations or for different students, indirect styles may be superior.

In spite of these ambiguous conclusions, a number of specific characteristics of teaching styles are clearly related to the outcomes of the educational process. As we have seen elsewhere in this text, such things as praise, feedback, criticism, advance organizers or conceptual models, classroom climate, and cooperative reward structures all relate importantly to student achievement and perhaps to creativity and thoughtfulness as well.

TEACHERS' EXPECTATIONS
AND STUDENTS' PERFORMANCE

There are numerous examples of **self-fulfilling prophecies**—of situations in which what we expect will happen does, perhaps simply because we expect it will. Often we assume that

---

self-fulfilling prophecies Expectations that are realized because they are expected to be. Teachers' expectations for students are sometimes self-fulfilling prophecies.

our expectations somehow affect outcomes. But surely, there are just as many examples of situations in which what we expect does not happen. Do the expectations of teachers have any effect on the behaviors of their students?

The Research. The classic study of teacher expectations is Rosenthal and Jacobson's (1968a, 1968b) "Oak School" experiment. Teachers in this school were told that they were participating in the validation of a new test designed to predict academic "blooming." They were also told that children, especially slow achievers, often show sudden intellectual spurts and that the new test could identify "spurters." But the tests that the Oak School children were given were actually only intelligence tests (the Flanagan Tests of General Ability). These were administered in the spring; the following September, the teachers were given false information about the test results. Specifically, they were casually given the names of students designated as spurters but actually chosen randomly from the student body. This group comprised about 20 percent of the school's population. The only difference, then, between the spurters and other students (control groups) was that the teachers had reason to expect increased performance on the part of the spurters.

Amazingly, report Rosenthal and Jacobson, their expectations were fulfilled. What is more surprising is that not only did academic achievement—which is to some degree under a teacher's control—increase but so did intellectual ability as measured by the Flanagan tests. The most dramatic spurts were for first-grade students, probably those who had the greatest room for improvement. In addition, indications are that intelligence is more malleable at an earlier age (see Chapter 2).

The results of the Rosenthal and Jacobson study have since been questioned by some reviewers who noted that there seemed to have been some misjudging, misrecording, and misrepresentation of the original data (see Rosenthal, 1987; Wineburg, 1987). Furthermore, many attempted replications have failed. But others have not.

Brophy and Good (1974) reviewed sixty attempted replications and concluded that many were confusing and inconclusive and that none provided strong evidence of results as dramatic as those first reported by Rosenthal and Jacobson. But, they hasten to point out, many of these studies reveal quite consistent patterns of expectations among teachers, and these expectations are probably linked in important ways to such crucial things as the student's self-concept and self-esteem, as well as to achievement.

Similarly, Braun (1976) reviewed a wealth of teacher-expectation literature and also found remarkably consistent patterns for teachers' expectations. It seems that teachers often develop more positive expectations (with respect to academic achievement) for children who come from higher socioeconomic backgrounds, who are obedient and compliant, who are attractive, and who sit close to the teacher and speak clearly. And there is evidence, as well, that expectations might be communicated in subtle but measurable ways. For example, Brophy and Good (1974) report that some teachers pay less attention to lower achievers, give them less time to answer questions, and are more likely to criticize their answers than identical answers given by higher achievers.

In summary, although the effects of teacher expectations might not be as dramatic as first reports might have indicated, most researchers now accept that teacher expectations can be an important influence on student achievement (Wang, Haertel, & Walberg, 1993). And investigators continue to try to clarify the conditions under which teachers' expectations develop and the effects they might have on the teaching/learning process. For example, Rolison and Medway (1985) found that both the type of label applied to the student and the information the teacher has about the student's recent performance are important in determining the teacher's expectations. Teachers had higher expectations for students labeled "learning disabled" than for those labeled "mentally retarded"; they also had higher expectations for students whose recent performance showed an ascending rather than a descending pattern. Similarly, Babad (1985) reports a significant bias in the grading of worksheets by teachers relative to whether or not teachers believe the work to have been done by excellent or weak students. And Chandler (1994) found that many elementary teachers have expectations for their students that are clearly affected by gender. For example, many expect female students to do less well in science and mathematics—and perhaps better in art.

Implications of Research on Expectations.
Obviously, the conclusion that teachers' expectations undeniably and consistently affect pupils' behavior is not fully warranted by the evidence. It appears, nevertheless, that teachers do develop expectations and that these may be important (see, for example, Ozar, 1994). In some instances, negative expectations may adversely affect students' behavior or teachers' assessments—just as positive expectations might have more positive effects. As Bardwell (1984) notes, positive expectations might do much to increase students' motivation and, indirectly, students' performance.

Given the apparent relationship between teacher expectations and student performance, a large number of studies have been designed to *change* teacher expectations. Their goals are simply to raise expectations, especially for students for whom teachers might otherwise have unjustly low expectations (Babad, 1993). These studies often provide specific recommendations for equalizing teacher expectations and teaching practices, and for making teachers more aware of their expectations. And although their results have not always been measurably positive, in general, they support the belief that teacher expectations can be made more positive and can result in happier and more successful students. They also indicate that teacher expectations, like most of our beliefs, are not simple, easily changed ideas. As Weinstein, Madison, and Kuklinski (1995) note following a two-year in-school program designed to modify teacher expectations, teacher expectations go well beyond the teacher and the student. Attempts to change them need to take into consideration the context in which these expectations are embedded—for example, the wealth of long-established beliefs about race, sex, and gender that affect what teachers expect of students. As well, researchers need to be aware of beliefs teachers have about the malleability of students, about the importance and meaning of characteristics like intelligence, and about the extent to which they can bring about significant change.

Another Possibility. Clearly, positive expectations don't always have beneficial effects, nor are the effects of negative expectations always negative. Is the opposite possible? That is, might positive expectations lead to negative results, and vice versa?

Goldenberg (1992) describes an investigation in which nine students were studied during their first year of school. Two of these students, Hispanic American girls who shared the same first-grade teacher, had scored poorly on a scale of reading readiness—which would predict that each would do poorly in first-grade reading achievement. Unaware of their nearly identical reading readiness scores, the teacher had high expectations for one girl but low expectations for the other.

But the teacher was wrong. In fact, the girl for whom the teacher had high expectations did poorly; the other did remarkably well. Amazing? No, claims Goldenberg. These apparently contradictory results are easily explained by the fact that the teacher provided more assistance, more personal attention, more support for the girl for whom she had the lowest expectations—having determined that this girl needed the additional help. The most reasonable conclusion, argues Goldenberg, is that what matters most is not what the teacher *expects* but rather what the teacher *does*. Negative expectations might lead one teacher to give up on a student, to pay little attention, to provide no help, perhaps even to stop interacting with that student—and the self-fulfilling effects of the expectation may seem clear. But another teacher might react with additional assistance and attention, as did this teacher; the final results might be in direct opposition to expectations.

OTHER FACES OF EXCEPTIONALITY

Most of the human population is what we consider normal or average—although each of us is different from every other. But there are some who, in one or more ways, are different from the average. These are children who, from an educational, social, and sometimes medical point of view, can be described as having **special needs.**

Among them are those about whom we have been talking: those who are far more intelligent, far more creative. There are others who are endowed with superior motor skills or outstanding physical appearance; others are socially

---

special needs Phrase used to describe individuals whose social, physical, or emotional exceptionalities require special treatment and services if they are to develop their potential.

gifted. These are individuals for whom the label "exceptional" is appropriate.

Unfortunately, there is another dimension of **exceptionality**—one that includes those less intelligent, less creative; those with physical and motor disabilities; those with emotional and adjustment problems. In short, the term *exceptional* applies equally to those to whom nature and nurture have been noticeably generous and to those to whom they have been much less kind.

PUBLIC LAW 94-142

Knowing how to identify exceptional children—and knowing, as well, how to administer the programs and resources available for them—has always been an essential part of the training of **special education teachers.** These are teachers whose express function is to provide educational services for children with disabilities.

In recent years, however, the special needs of exceptional children have also become important to the regular classroom teacher—particularly since the passage of **Public Law 94-142** in 1975. This law was in part an attempt to correct some of the injustices that have sometimes existed in the treatment of exceptional children. The law was amended in 1990 by the **Individuals with Disabilities Education Act (IDEA)** and reauthorized by the U.S. Congress in 1995 (see Fuchs & Fuchs, 1995). Its provi-

sions, and related court interpretations, have been largely instrumental in revolutionizing how schools deal with exceptionality.

Among other things, the law provides four principal guarantees for children with special needs:

► Education in the "least restrictive environment"

► Free and appropriate educational services

► Fair, nondiscriminatory evaluation and due process of law

► An individualized educational plan (IEP)

The clearest practical implication of these four requirements is apparent in what is termed *inclusion* **(inclusive education)** or **mainstreaming.**

Least Restrictive Environment: Mainstreaming. Mainstreaming is a direct result of PL 94-142's requirement that school jurisdictions provide special services for qualified children in the "least restrictive environment" possible. In most instances, this environment has been judged to be the regular classroom; this is why an increasing number of regular classroom teachers (as opposed to special education teachers) are called upon to teach exceptional children in what are termed **inclusive classrooms.**

Mainstreaming resulted not only from the passage of PL 94-142, but was also influenced by at least two other related events in the field of special education. The first involves the recognition—sometimes by courts of law—that many who had been labeled "emotionally disturbed" or "mentally retarded" and who had therefore not been admitted into regular classrooms were indeed capable of learning and functioning effectively when given access to these classrooms. At the same time, a relatively new classifi-

---

exceptionality Term used to describe significant deviation from the average in terms of physical, intellectual, or emotional behaviors, abilities, or skills. A two-dimensional concept in that it can indicate significant superiority or significant handicaps.

special education teachers Teachers whose training and/or functions have to do specifically with the education of exceptional children.

Public Law 94-142 A 1975 U.S. education act that guarantees for special students: a free and appropriate education, nondiscriminatory evaluation, due process, an individualized educational plan (IEP), and education in the least restrictive environment. Amended in 1990 by the Individuals with Disabilities Education Act (IDEA).

mainstreaming The practice of placing students in need of special services in regular classrooms rather than segregating them. Also termed *inclusive education*.

inclusive classrooms Classrooms that contain one or more children with special needs in addition to a number of more average children.

JEAN-CLAUDE LEJEUNE/STOCK, BOSTON

Mainstreaming, or inclusive education, involves educating children with special needs in regular classrooms—as is illustrated here with this blind pupil who is reading a braille book. There is some concern that full inclusion might lead to injustices as serious as those that might result from the routine segregation of all children with special needs.

Contemporary thinking in special education, note Scruggs and Mastropieri (1994), clearly emphasizes the value of inclusion for children with special needs and assumes, as well, that inclusion is also a positive experience for the nondisabled children in inclusive classrooms. But subsequent research has not always confirmed the belief that all children with special needs would do better in regular classrooms. Fuchs and Fuchs (1995), for example, argue that many of the special education techniques that work well with children who have specific needs are seldom found in inclusive classrooms where most of the children are not disabled. Specifically, the techniques that work best with many exceptionalities are highly individual; in contrast, the main instructional methods in today's inclusive classroom is oriented toward the group rather than the individual.

Kauffman, Lloyd, and Riedel (1995) also agree that not all children with special needs should be included in regular classrooms. Such **full inclusion,** they note, denies some students a full and effective education. Students with the more serious emotional and behavioral problems, for example, often do not fare well in regular classrooms where overtaxed and undertrained teachers cannot provide the most optimal services for them.

In spite of the widespread support that the inclusive classroom has recently enjoyed in North American education, some negative reaction has occasionally come from parents of nondisabled students who have feared that the education of their children might suffer—as well as from some parents of disabled students who also fear that their children might not be provided the education that is best for them (Diamond & LeFurgy, 1994). Negative reaction has also come from student teachers—whose attitudes tend to become more positive during teacher training, but more negative again after student teaching (Wilczenski, 1994). Similarly, some practicing teachers react negatively to

cation of learning difficulty was introduced: **learning disability.** This category, described in more detail later in this chapter, generally includes individuals who do not have obvious disabilities (blindness, deafness, or profound mental retardation, for example) and have therefore not been eligible for special classes but have not functioned well in regular classrooms.

Thus, there is, on the one hand, a recognition that some "special" children have been mislabeled and that, even if they have not been mislabeled, they can benefit from regular classroom experiences. On the other hand, educators now recognize that there are a number of children in regular classrooms for whom special attention would be highly desirable.

---

learning disability A depression in the ability to learn specific things (for example, reading or arithmetic), in which the learning difficulties are not related to mental retardation or emotional disturbance.

---

full inclusion The inclusion of all special needs children in regular classrooms regardless of the nature and severity of their handicaps.

mainstreaming, especially if they have not been trained specifically for inclusive education (Volk & Stahlman, 1994). Finally, nondisabled students in inclusive classrooms may also react negatively to the presence of students with severe learning difficulties (Whitaker, 1994).

In spite of these difficulties, much of the recent research on mainstreaming indicates that the needs of special students can be met in regular classrooms (McDonald, 1993). And evidence is mounting that the self-concepts and social adjustment of children who are mainstreamed are more positive than those of segregated children (Macmillan, Keogh, & Jones, 1986). Mainstreaming nevertheless remains highly controversial, and the support for it somewhat qualified (Klassen, 1994). This is at least partly because inclusion of special needs children in regular classrooms is expensive and difficult for school administrators, given legal requirements concerning unbiased and extensive testing and the need to consult parents and obtain their consent. In addition, integration complicates the lives of teachers, not all of whom are well prepared, both in terms of personality characteristics and in terms of training, to deal intelligently and effectively with inclusive classrooms. The inclusive classroom requires changes in teacher education programs, with considerably more emphasis on identifying and providing programs for disabled and gifted children (see the case "Robert Goldberg, Bad Teacher").

It is perhaps not surprising that Chester (1992) found that teachers in inclusive classrooms are relatively likely to rate their learning-disabled students as "underachieving, uninterested, non-studious, not striving for success, ashamed, and lacking in self confidence" (p. 93). Strikingly, non-learning-disabled students in these same classrooms rated the learning-disabled students significantly more positively than did the teachers, giving them negative ratings only with respect to popularity and self-confidence. And, in fact, research indicates that learning-disabled students do have lower self-concepts than average children, whether they are mainstreamed or not (Chapman, 1988).

A Free and Appropriate Education. The controversy over mainstreaming is not really a question of whether classrooms should or should not be inclusive. Rather, it concerns the *extent* to which they should be inclusive. And there now appears to be growing consensus that in the same way as the practice of segregating all special needs children led to serious injustices and poor educational practice, so too might *full* inclusion. As Huefner (1994) notes, what school administrators need to do is avoid either extreme: the full inclusion model or blanket separation of all children with special needs. Decisions about the placement of a child, she argues, should be made individually and should honor the concept of least restrictive environment. For some children, that environment may be a segregated classroom; and for others, it may be an inclusive classroom.

Not only should decisions about services for children with special needs respect the principle of the least restrictive environment, but

CASE: ROBERT GOLDBERG, BAD TEACHER

A RECOLLECTION: By Blooma, a teacher in training

Mr. Goldberg was boring, dressed sloppily, and rarely talked to me. He spent more time with the smarter people and at many times I felt "left out." I recall an instance in the beginning of the school year when I sat in the front of the class with my best friend behind me. By the middle of the year he had moved the "smarter" people to the front and the "dumb" people to the back. You guessed it—I was classified as dumb and was separated from my friend, who was very smart. I was deeply hurt and I have never forgiven Mr. Goldberg.

legislation mandates that these decisions should also conform to the principle that all children are entitled to education that is not only *free* but also *appropriate*. This might mean special materials, special instructional procedures, even a special curriculum. It might also mean only minor adjustments to the offerings of the regular classroom.

Fair Evaluation and Due Process. The decision that a student has special needs is typically based on a variety of evaluation and assessment procedures. Usually parents or teachers are first to notice that there might be a problem and to seek referral for further evaluation. PL 94-142 mandates that an interdisciplinary assessment team be employed to determine whether comprehensive assessment is required. Assessment may involve various diagnostic and achievement tests, the stipulation being that these instruments will be as appropriate and as fair and unbiased as possible. That is, not only must they be given by people trained in their administration and interpretation, but they must be selected so as to provide a complete and accurate assessment of the student's functioning. Thus, where there might be language problems, for example, tests should be given in the child's native language; and if there are physical disabilities, special steps might be taken to enable the child to respond.

If the final decision is that the student requires special services, an IEP is prepared—often by the assessment team in consultation with the teacher and the parents.

Individualized Educational Plans (IEPs). Individualized educational plans (IEPs) (sometimes called individualized program plans or IPPs) are written programs, mandated by law and required for every disabled child. In inclusive classes, IEPs are often prepared by the class-

---

individualized educational plans (IEP) Individualized instructional programs tailored to a child's specific pattern of needs and abilities. IEPs may be used for gifted, learning-disabled, retarded, or average children. Also termed *individualized program plans* or *IPPs*.

room teacher and an education team made up of the principal, other specialists, parents, and sometimes students. As Van Reusen and Bos (1994) note, there can be motivational advantages in actively involving students in IEP conferences. IEPs are almost invariably implemented by the teacher, although sometimes with the assistance of one or more specialists. Hence, it is essential that all teachers know what is required in these plans, how to interpret them, and how to prepare them.

A number of steps typically occur before an IEP is prepared. First, someone—often a teacher, sometimes a parent—becomes aware that a student might require special services. Following this, if parents consent, the student may be referred for assessment, perhaps by school personnel, sometimes by outside agencies.

Public Law 94-142 stipulates that IEPs must contain the following:

- ▶ A description of the student's current performance and achievement
- ▶ A statement of annual goals, as well as of shorter-range objectives
- ▶ A list of services and programs to be provided for the student
- ▶ The expected duration of the program, including specific dates
- ▶ Evaluation procedures that will be used to determine whether the program's goals are being met

An example of an IEP is provided in Figure 8.3.

Even when they are mainstreamed, not all exceptional children have their needs met only by their teachers and entirely in inclusive classrooms. Some may stay in a regular classroom, but the regular teacher may be assisted by an aide, an assistant teacher, or an itinerant specialist; others may be sent to a special resource room for part of each day or week; some may be in special classrooms part of the time and in a regular classroom for the remainder of the time; some may be in a segregated, special class full time. Still others may be in residential schools (some of the deaf or blind, for example) or in hospitals or other institutions.

STRATHCONA COUNTY BOARD OF EDUCATION

INDIVIDUALIZED EDUCATIONAL PLAN

NAME OF STUDENT Thea Murray

GRADE ECS   SCHOOL Wye

TEACHER C. Munoz

IEP TEAM MEMBERS

SIGNATURE	POSITION	SIGNATURE	POSITION
	Teacher		Special Needs Aide
	Assistant Principal		
	Counsellor		
	Speech Clinician		

PROGRAM GOALS (S)	INSTRUCTIONAL OBJECTIVES	STRATEGY/MATERIALS/ RESOURCES	DATE START	DATE END	EVALUATION CRITERIA	PLACEMENT/PERSON RESPONSIBLE
1. develop intelligibility	– to improve intelligibility *NB "r" "b" following has in library*	– through one-to-one assistance, provide Thea with the correct speech model – have Thea repeat the model speech – provide Thea with the opportunity to interact with her peers with appropriate levels of intelligibility	Oct. 3 *check use of "got" at times intended – "forgot" – is "forgot" also syntax*	June 28	– ongoing assessment – notes will be kept on ongoing basis – periodic reassessment by L. Brent	– C. Munoz – E. Takata – H. Murphy – L. Brent * * L. Brent is responsible to train the assigned teacher aide to carry out the appropriate assistance program for goals 1–4.
2. develop correct production of /L/	– to improve production of /L/ *much improved*	– through one-to-one assistance, provide Thea with the correct speech model – have Thea repeat the model speech – encourage Thea to find words with 'L' in her environment – provide Thea with the opportunity to interact with her peers with appropriate /L/ usage	Oct. 3	June 28		

FIGURE 8.3 Sample individualized educational plan (IEP). Reprinted by permission of Strathcona County School.

STRATHCONA COUNTY BOARD OF EDUCATION

INDIVIDUALIZED EDUCATIONAL PLAN

NAME OF STUDENT Thea Murray

GRADE ECS   SCHOOL Wye   TEACHER C. Munoz

PROGRAM GOALS (S)	INSTRUCTIONAL OBJECTIVES	STRATEGY/MATERIALS/ RESOURCES	DATE START	DATE END	EVALUATION CRITERIA	PLACEMENT/PERSON RESPONSIBLE
3. develop receptive and expressive syntax	– to improve receptive and expressive syntax	– through one-to-one assistance, provide Thea with the correct speech model – have Thea repeat the model speech – provide Thea with the opportunity to interact with her peers with appropriate receptive and expressive syntax	Oct. 3	June 28		
4. develop fine motor skills	– to improve fine motor skills	– through one-to-one assistance, Thea will participate in a variety of fine motor skills including pasting, painting, drawing, manipulating, etc.	Oct. 3	June 28	– ongoing assessment – progress relative to expected performance	

Handwritten annotations:

i.e., "I don't got a turn."

Second item of improved - effort improved - now not using very where not intended.

FIGURE 8.3 (continued)

Summary of Major Provisions of PL 94-142. In addition to the provision for education in the least restrictive environment, Public Law 94-142 brought about a number of other significant changes in the schools' treatment of exceptionality by stipulating that

▶ Extensive effort be made to identify disabled children using procedures that are not racially or culturally biased.

▶ Parents have a right to be informed and to grant or withhold consent regarding assessment and educational plans for special needs children.

▶ School jurisdictions are compelled to provide special services for children who need them at no cost to parents or guardians.

▶ A written individualized educational plan (IEP) must be provided for every disabled child.

For obvious reasons, PL 94-142 is often described as the Bill of Rights for the disabled. But, as we saw, even though it has done a tremendous amount to reduce bias and unfair practices in the treatment of exceptional children, it has also presented some real difficulties of interpretation and implementation for educators. IEPs, for example, are difficult and time-consuming to prepare and are therefore extremely costly, and they have not proved popular. Nor is it always easy or even possible to find tests for specific forms of exceptionality or to find tests in the child's native language. In addition, the law's most obvious practical manifestation—the inclusive classroom or mainstreaming—remains controversial. (See Table 8.1 for a summary of PL 94-142.)

DIMENSIONS OF EXCEPTIONALITY

Given the classroom teacher's role in identifying and providing services for children with special needs, it has become increasingly important for all teachers to be familiar with the various manifestations of exceptionality they are most likely to encounter.

Exceptionality, as we saw, has two dimensions: the exceptionally gifted and those who are disabled.* Exceptionalities are found in each of the three main areas of human functioning—the cognitive, the physical, and the social-emotional. In each area, abilities range continuously from some point just noticeably beyond the average to the furthest extreme in either direction. People at the extreme of the negative end include, for example, the severely mentally disabled, those with severe multiple physical disabilities (such as being blind, deaf, and quadriplegic), and those with serious emotional disorders (such as schizophrenia).

PL 94-142 provides an important official definition for the term *handicapped*: "Handicapped children means those evaluated as being mentally retarded, hard-of-hearing, deaf, speech impaired, visually handicapped, seriously emotionally disturbed, orthopedically impaired, other health impaired, deaf-blind, multihandicapped, or as having specific learning disabilities, who because of these impairments need special education and related services" (U.S. Office of Education, 1977, p. 42478).

The sections that follow examine exceptionality in all three areas—physical, cognitive (intellectual), and social (emotional)—with special emphasis on cognitive disabilities, which often are more relevant for the regular classroom teacher (see Figure 8.4). Teachers who major in special education would be expected to know much more than can be included in these few pages.

---

*PPC: I noted the bear is now using *disabled* where he used *handicapped* in an earlier edition. I know that *disabled* is more acceptable, but it too strikes me as more negative than necessary. Many of my special education colleagues now use the word *challenged*. Might that be better?

AUTHOR: In even earlier editions, other terms such as *deficient* were often used. And before the bear, words like *idiot, imbecile,* and *moron* were widely accepted psychological terms. Now these terms are carefully avoided. Terms such as these often have highly negative connotations and are quite uninformative. Maybe, as you suggest, *challenged* would be better. It's certainly more emotionally neutral. But it's also stunningly vague.

TABLE 8.1 MAIN PROVISIONS OF THE INDIVIDUALS WITH DISABILITIES EDUCATION ACT (IDEA OR PL 94-142)

PROVISION	PRACTICAL IMPLICATION
Education in the least restrictive environment	Mainstreaming (or the inclusive classroom) because the "least restrictive environment" is interpreted by the courts to mean the most normal environment that can meet the child's special needs
Free and appropriate educational services	Publicly funded special education programs provided without charge to all children with special needs
Fair, nondiscriminatory evaluation and due process of law	Students must be evaluated by experts using instruments that are free from bias and that take into consideration specific disabilities and problems the child might have (such as a different first language); parents have a right to be informed and to grant or withhold consent regarding assessment and educational plans for their children
Individualized educational plans (IEPs)	An individually designed educational plan for each child with special needs, developed by a team of teachers, administrators, specialists, and parents, and containing statements of goals, instructional programs, and assessment procedures together with specific time lines for each

Physical Exceptionality. At one extreme among the physically exceptional are those who are endowed with superior capabilities that might be manifested in athletic skills and in other activities requiring motor coordination, strength, rhythm, and so on. At the other extreme are those with physical disabilities, sensory deficits, cerebral palsy, or a number of diseases that might or might not lead to problems in school. Among these, blindness and deafness may require special assistance beyond the capabilities and resources of the regular classroom teacher. On occasion, however, corrective devices (glasses and hearing aids) and special learning aids (large-print books, for example) can be used within the regular classroom in compliance with mainstreaming regulations.

Social-Emotional Exceptionality. At the positive end of social-emotional exceptionality are those more socially adept, better adjusted, more immune to the stresses and tensions of life than are ordinary individuals. These exceptional individuals often go unrecognized and unheralded, although they might on occasion be envied.

At the other extreme are those variously described as "behavior-disordered," "emotionally disturbed," or "socially maladjusted." What these labels have in common is that each

describes individuals who are troubled and often unhappy and who are also usually a source of difficulty for teachers, peers, parents, and others. Over 70 percent of students with behavioral disorders are very low achievers (Nelson & Pearson, 1991). Estimates of the prevalence of emotional disorders vary tremendously. Knitzer, Steinberg, and Fleisch (1990) suggest that between 3 and 5 percent of children are seriously emotionally disturbed. Only about 20 percent of these are identified and receive special services (Heward & Orlansky, 1992).

For the most severe manifestations of emotional disturbance (for schizophrenia, for example), institutional care is generally required. In many cases, however, children who might be described as suffering from emotional disorders continue to function in regular classrooms. Of special interest to the teacher is **attention deficit hyperactivity disorder (ADHD),** an emotional disorder commonly called **hyperactivity.** ADHD is considered in more detail in a later section of this chapter.

---

attention deficit hyperactivity disorder (ADHD) A disorder marked by excessive general activity for the child's age, attention problems, high impulsivity, and low frustration tolerance. Also termed *hyperactivity.*

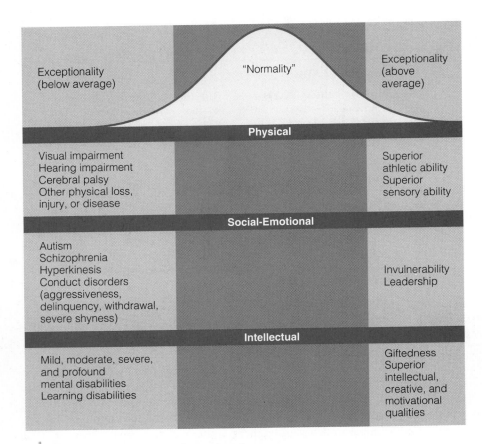

Exceptionality (below average)

"Normality"

Exceptionality (above average)

Physical

Visual impairment
Hearing impairment
Cerebral palsy
Other physical loss, injury, or disease

Superior athletic ability
Superior sensory ability

Social-Emotional

Autism
Schizophrenia
Hyperkinesis
Conduct disorders (aggressiveness, delinquency, withdrawal, severe shyness)

Invulnerability
Leadership

Intellectual

Mild, moderate, severe, and profound mental disabilities
Learning disabilities

Giftedness
Superior intellectual, creative, and motivational qualities

FIGURE 8.4 Dimensions of exceptionality.

INTELLECTUAL EXCEPTIONALITY:

MENTAL RETARDATION

On the one hand are the gifted and creative, about whom we spoke earlier in this chapter; on the other are children who have significant difficulty in learning some, if not all, things learned relatively easily by others. This dimension of exceptionality includes two important categories: the mentally disabled (or retarded) and the learning disabled.

Definition of Mental Retardation. The most obvious feature of **mental retardation** is a depression in the ability to learn; a second important

feature relates to problems in adapting. These features are apparent in the widely accepted definition presented by the American Association on Mental Deficiency (AAMD), which reads as follows (AAMD, 1992, p. 5):

> Mental retardation refers to substantial limitations in present intellectual functioning. It is characterized by significantly subaverage intellectual functioning existing concurrently with related limitations in two or more of the following applicable adaptive skill areas: communication, self-care, home living, social skills, community use, self-direction, health and safety, functional academics, leisure, and work. Mental retardation manifests before age 18.

The meaning of this definition can be clarified by looking at each of its key components.

---

mental retardation A significant general depression in the ability to learn, usually accompanied by deficits in adaptive behavior.

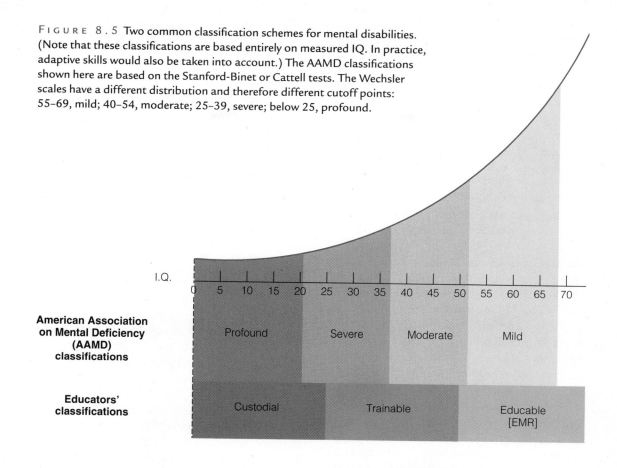

FIGURE 8.5 Two common classification schemes for mental disabilities. (Note that these classifications are based entirely on measured IQ. In practice, adaptive skills would also be taken into account.) The AAMD classifications shown here are based on the Stanford-Binet or Cattell tests. The Wechsler scales have a different distribution and therefore different cutoff points: 55–69, mild; 40–54, moderate; 25–39, severe; below 25, profound.

First "significantly subaverage intellectual functioning" is generally defined in terms of test scores on one or more of the well-known individual intelligence tests such as the Stanford-Binet or the Weschler. An IQ score of 70 is the generally accepted, but highly inexact, cutoff between normality and retardation.

Second, "limitations in . . . adaptive skill areas" are apparent as significant maturational deficits, most evidently in an inability to learn and in failure to reach the levels of independence, social effectiveness, and social responsibility that would normally be expected of others of similar age and experience—such as a 4-year-old not yet knowing how to talk. Various standardized inventories are available for assessing level of adaptive behavior (see Reschly, 1990).

Classifications of Mental Retardation. Figure 8.5 presents some commonly used classification

schemes for mental retardation. Note that the labels are based primarily on performance on standard measures of intelligence, most commonly the Stanford-Binet. In practice, approximately 1 percent of the general population appears to be mentally disabled—when level of adaptive behavior is taken into account (Patton & Polloway, 1990). This is why it is so important to take adaptation into consideration (Reschly, 1992).

Causes of Mental Retardation. While psychcologists and educators tend to classify mental retardation in terms of level of retardation (as is shown in Figure 8.5), geneticists and psychiatric researchers (among others) tend to classify it in terms of causes (Hodapp & Dykens, 1994). However, most of the time we don't actually know the specific cause of the retardation. In fact, the causes are so varied that classification in terms of degree is far more common than classification in terms of cause. Nevertheless, researchers often identify two groups of causes: those that are organic, whether they be pre- or postnatal, and the familial (Zigler & Hodapp, 1991). Organic causes of mental retardation include cerebral injury, chromosomal aberrations and defects such as Down's syndrome, maternal infections at critical periods of fetal development, and so on. Familial causes include inadequate genetic endowment, growing up in unstimulating environments, or a combination of environmental and genetic factors.

Characteristics of the Mentally Retarded. The largest group of retarded children (about 75 percent) is marked by **mild retardation** (Hallahan & Kauffman, 1994). Relatively few of these children are identified as intellectually impaired before they have been in school for a period of time. Many are eventually capable of acceptable academic achievement in elementary school—at perhaps the sixth-grade level, and can adapt quite well socially. The majority are usually mainstreamed, and may be described as **educable mentally retarded (EMR).**

Severe retardation and **profound retardation** are generally associated with highly limited motor learning—virtually no communication skills in the case of profound retardation and only rudimentary skills for the severely retarded—and institutionalization throughout life. In the case of profound retardation, institutional care is often of a custodial nature, involving feeding and clothing.

Moderate retardation is characteristic of about 20 percent of those classified as mentally retarded (Hallahan & Kauffman, 1994). These children learn to talk during the preschool period, and the majority also learn to walk, although their verbal and motor skills are generally noticeably inferior to those of other children. Many are educated in inclusive classrooms where, with the help of special programs and teachers, they may progress through the primary grades, but not usually much further academically. Training in occupational skills is sometimes highly helpful for these children.

INTELLECTUAL EXCEPTIONALITY: LEARNING DISABILITIES

Whereas mental retardation usually affects all areas of cognitive functioning, another type of intellectual impairment manifests itself in only a few areas of functioning—and frequently only in one. That is, there are children who, in the absence of any perceptible physical or emotional disturbance, nevertheless experience significant difficulty in learning specific skills. These children have sometimes been described as suffering from a learning dysfunction, hyperactivity, cerebral dysfunction, minimal brain damage, perceptual disabilities, dyslexia, perceptual disability, or simply as being slow learners. Unfortunately, these terms are nonspecific, often confusing, and sometimes meaningless. Largely for this reason, Samuel Kirk proposed the term *learning disability* in 1963. It does not have the same negative connotations as do expressions like "cerebral dysfunction" or "slow learner," and its meaning can be expressed relatively clearly (Hammill, 1993).

---

mild retardation A classification of mental retardation identified by degree and usually defined in terms of an IQ range between 50 and about 70. Also termed *educable,* children with mild retardation are capable of achievement at about the sixth grade level, and of adequate social adaptation.

severe retardation A level of mental retardation defined in terms of an IQ range between 20 or 25 and 35 or 40. Can learn to communicate and, with systematic training, to take care of simple hygiene.

profound retardation A degree of mental retardation defined in terms of a measured IQ below 20 or 25 and marked by limited motor development and a need for nursing care.

moderate retardation A degree of mental retardation defined in terms of an IQ range between 35 or 40 and 50 or 55. Can achieve at about the second-grade level, and can profit from training in social and occupational skills.

Prevalence. Children with learning disabilities make up the largest group of special needs students in North America. In fact, they comprise almost 5 percent of the entire student body in U.S. public schools (U.S. Department of Education, 1991)—about two-thirds of all children with special needs. This may be because, as Lerner (1995) notes, the term is often applied to any student who is having problems in school and for whom no other label seems entirely appropriate.

Defining Learning Disabilities. The term *learning disability* is now used to describe a variety of conditions. And although Public Law 94-142 includes a definition of learning disabilities that serves as a guideline for the allocation of funds, the definition is open to several interpretations. As a result, many school jurisdictions have established their own criteria for identifying children with learning disabilities. These criteria do not specify exactly what learning disabilities are, but instead describe generally associated symptoms and behaviors (Kavale, Forness, & Lorsbach, 1991). Also, more precise descriptions are often provided for specific learning disabilities (Cole, 1993; Stanovich, 1993).

Most descriptions of learning disabilities emphasize four groups of characteristics:

▶ There is a marked disparity between expected and actual behavior. This disparity is often apparent in general academic achievement that is significantly below what would be predicted on the basis of measured IQ.

▶ The learning-disabled child displays an uneven pattern of academic achievement, doing quite well in some subjects but very poorly in others. Often, such a child is unable to do certain things that other children do very easily.

▶ Learning disabilities are often evident in problems in one of the basic psychological processes involved in language or in arithmetic. Hence, the disorder is apparent in disorders of listening, thinking, talking, reading, writing, spelling, or arithmetic.

▶ Problems associated with learning disabilities are not the result of other problems relating to hearing, vision, or general mental retardation.

The clearest identifying characteristic of learning disabilities, according to government regulations, is a significant discrepancy between IQ and achievement, caused by problems in such basic psychological processes as remembering and perceiving. Children whose ability to learn is generally depressed or who suffer from environmental deprivation, emotional problems, or sensory defects are specifically excluded from the category of the learning disabled. But, as Shepard, Smith, and Vojir (1983) found following a survey of 800 children classified as learning disabled, many supposedly learning-disabled children have characteristics that do not conform to the definitions found in government regulations. In fact, more than half this sample had emotional disorders, mild retardation, or specific language problems; they should not have been classified as learning disabled. Unfortunately, this misclassification may lead to the use of inappropriate treatment strategies with some of these children. It will almost certainly confound the results of research designed to investigate the incidence of learning disabilities and the effectiveness of various treatments.

Symptoms and Identification of Learning Disabilities. For the classroom teacher, first indications of learning disabilities are usually very tentative and uncertain. As we saw, the most obvious characteristic, and the one most likely to be noticed by teachers, is general academic retardation. Academic retardation by itself, however, does not define a learning disability—although it is often a result of the learning-disabled child's problems with reading, writing, and other aspects of the language arts.

A variety of other symptoms may also be associated with learning disabilities. These include inattentiveness, mood shifts, hyperactivity, and impulsiveness (see Table 8.2). In

TABLE 8.2 SOME SYMPTOMS THAT MAY BE ASSOCIATED WITH LEARNING DISABILITIES

Inattentiveness (short attention span)

Impulsiveness

Hyperactivity

Frequent shifts in emotional mood

Impaired visual memory (difficulty in recalling shapes or words)

Motor problems (difficulty in running, hitting a ball, cutting, writing)

Disorders of speech and hearing

Specific academic difficulties (reading, writing, spelling, arithmetic)

Source: Based on Clements (1966).

addition, short-term memory problems are common among those with learning disabilities (Swanson, 1993). Drug use may also be more common among these children, perhaps because of their problems in school and subsequent adjustment problems (Karacostas & Fisher, 1993). For the same reason, adolescents with learning disabilities may be at slightly higher risk of suicide (Huntington & Bender, 1993).

Various tests are available to help identify the learning disabled. These are used to measure general intelligence as well as to examine basic psychological processes involved in learning and remembering. It's important to also look at the possibility that other factors—such as visual problems, hearing deficits, physical or health handicaps, low intelligence, or environmental disadvantages—might be involved. While measuring intelligence and eliminating other defects are relatively straightforward procedures, assessing basic psychological processes presents greater problems, largely because there isn't widespread agreement on what these processes are. Tests such as the Detroit Tests of Learning Aptitude attempt to look at processes involved in activities such as reading and are sometimes useful for identifying specific weaknesses.

Categories of Learning Disabilities. The causes of specific learning disabilities remain largely unknown although brain damage or some other neurological impairment is suspected in many cases (Mercer, 1990). Various diseases and infections, malnutrition, and other environmental or genetic factors might also be involved. However, like mental retardation, learning disabilities are not classified by cause but by symptom. In the case of learning disabilities, they are most often classified according to the specific area in which the disability is most apparent. Thus, they are typically labeled according to whether they involve oral or written speech, comprehension or production of speech, or particular problems in spelling or arithmetic.

By far the most frequently diagnosed learning disabilities are those that have to do with language—especially with reading. Thus, a common learning disability is **developmental reading disorder**—also called *dyslexia,* or *specific reading disability* (Stanovich, 1992). Its main fea-

---

developmental reading disorder A learning disability manifested in reading problems of varying severity—sometimes evident in spelling difficulties. Also termed *dyslexia* or *specific reading disability*.

ture, according to the American Psychiatric Association (1987), is impairment in recognizing words and understanding what is read, in spite of normal or above normal intelligence and absence of problems such as deafness, blindness, or inadequate schooling. Developmental reading disorder is usually first noticed when the child has difficulty learning to read. It may later be evident in spelling difficulties or in a lag of several years in reading skills. Remedial teaching can sometimes be highly effective in overcoming some of the effects of dyslexia.

A second specific learning disability is labeled **developmental arithmetic disorder** (American Psychiatric Association, 1987). Its principal feature is significant difficulty in developing arithmetic skills in the absence of other problems such as mental retardation. Consequently, developmental arithmetic disorder is usually most apparent in computational problems (difficulties in adding, subtracting, multiplying, or dividing) or in problems in processing visual or auditory information. As a result, children with arithmetic disabilities also often have reading problems (Semrud-Clikeman & Hynd, 1992).

In addition to reading and arithmetic disorders, learning disabilities include what are referred to as **process disorders.** These are defined as deficits in a basic psychological process. Thus, there may be deficits having to do with perception (confusion of words that sound or look alike), memory (problems associated with remembering and generalizing what has been learned), and attention (a condition

---

developmental arithmetic disorder A learning disability evident in specific problems in developing arithmetic skills in the absence of other problems such as mental retardation.

process disorders A type of learning disability that involves a deficit in a basic psychological process such as perceiving, remembering, or paying attention. In practice, process disorders are difficult to separate from other specific learning disabilities such as developmental reading or arithmetic disorder.

labeled "attention deficit disorder" associated with restlessness, hyperactivity, low frustration tolerance, and distractibility). In practice, however, it is often difficult to separate a basic process disorder from a disorder that is manifested in a specific subject area.

Treatment. In most instances, learning disabilities are treated in the context of the regular classroom, often with the help and advice of learning disability specialists. These children are not typically different from other children in regular classrooms, other than for the specific learning difficulty they experience. Most of the learning disabled are well adjusted and well liked. When Juvonen and Bear (1992) compared the social adjustment of learning-disabled children with that of non-learning-disabled children, they found no differences between the two in the proportion of each ranked as well liked or as rejected on sociometric scales.

Here, as in other areas of exceptionality, the onus of initial identification rests with the classroom teacher. In fact, the teacher's opinion may be relied on in place of more formal—and more expensive—testing. As Clarizio (1992) reports, the regular classroom teacher's opinion is often the most influential data with respect to determining whether a child is learning disabled. Unfortunately, the results of Clarizio's research indicate that relying solely on teachers' judgments would nearly double the number of students identified as learning disabled, resulting in a huge number of false identifications. Hence, the need for clear definition and strict adherence to accepted criteria when identifying all special needs children.

ATTENTION DEFICIT HYPERACTIVITY DISORDER (ADHD)

Attention deficit hyperactivity disorder (ADHD), or hyperactivity, is a relatively common emotional exceptionality that is closely related to learning disabilities. In fact, many children who suffer from one of these conditions will also manifest symptoms of the other (Korkman & Pesonen, 1994). As a result, some researchers suggest diagnosis might be more accurate if the two categories were combined (Cherkes-Julkowski & Stolzenberg, 1991).

Prevalence. Although as many as 3 percent of current elementary school children may suffer from varying degrees of hyperactivity (American Psychiatric Association, 1987), not all of these will be classified as having attention deficit hyperactivity disorder. Also, attention problems can exist without hyperactivity (termed *attention deficit disorder* or *ADD*).

Estimates of ADHD vary enormously depending on the criteria used, and depending as well on whether diagnosis is based on teacher ratings, parent ratings, or both (Cohen, Riccio, & Gonzalez, 1994). One survey of 14,229 students in a school district identified 136 children with ADHD—slightly less than 1 percent (Reid et al., 1994).

Symptoms and Diagnosis. In general, ADHD is marked by excessive general activity for the child's age (often taking the form of incessant and haphazard climbing, crawling, or running); difficulty in sustaining attention and apparent forgetfulness; and impulsivity (tendency to react quickly, difficulty taking turns, low frustration tolerance). As a result, many ADHD children experience considerable difficulty adjusting to school and home and are considered to be relatively serious problems (Zentall, 1993). The criteria described by the American Psychiatric Association also stipulate that the duration of the child's hyperactivity be at least 6 months.

Diagnosis of ADHD is often made inappropriately by parents and teachers who are confronted by children who are restless and who find it difficult to do the quiet things that adults sometimes demand—and who, consequently, are often discipline problems. But, as Kirby and Kirby (1994) note, the disruptive behavior of the ADHD child is not usually intentional. And if authorities were to rely primarily on the judgments of parents and teach-

ers, far too many children would be classified as ADHD. The diagnostic criteria most often used place too much emphasis on impulsivity, argue Tynan and Nearing (1994). As a result, they are far too inclusive, especially when applied to very young children. In fact, they note, fewer than half of all toddlers diagnosed as impulsive later become ADHD.

Strictly speaking, attention deficit hyperactivity disorder, as defined by the American Psychiatric Association (1994), needs to be apparent before the age of seven to differentiate it from disorders that might arise as reactions to stressful events or illness. In addition, it requires the presence of five criteria presented in Table 8.3.

Not all children with ADHD manifest the same combination and seriousness of symptoms. However, because the condition is defined largely in terms of observable behaviors, it is easy to diagnose and can therefore easily be overdiagnosed. Extreme caution should be exercised before applying the label to any child.

Causes. The causes of ADHD are unclear although the fact that between 80 and 90 percent more males than females are hyperactive suggests that it is at least partly genetic. Evidence also indicates that it results from a dysfunction of the central nervous system (Ward, 1994). As such, it may be partly a maturational problem. Not only is the activity level of hyperactive children often similar to that of children of 4 or 5 years, but many hyperactive children—though not all—seem to outgrow their symptoms after adolescence (Henker & Whalen, 1989).

Other explanations for hyperactivity have sometimes implicated neurological impairment or brain damage and dietary or vitamin-linked causes. However, the evidence for either of these causes is weak (Erickson, 1992). There is some suggestion, too, that between 5 and 10 percent of hyperactive children react badly to certain food dyes and that these children might therefore be helped through dietary means (Ross, 1980).

TABLE 8.3 DSM-IV DIAGNOSTIC CRITERIA FOR ATTENTION-DEFICIT HYPERACTIVITY DISORDER

A. Symptoms from either group 1 or 2 must be present.

   1. Six (or more) of the following symptoms of inattention have persisted for at least six months to a degree that is maladaptive and inconsistent with developmental level:

      a. often fails to give close attention to details or makes careless mistakes in schoolwork, work, or other activities

      b. often has difficulty sustaining attention in tasks or play activities

      c. often does not seem to listen when spoken to directly

      d. often does not follow through on instructions and fails to finish schoolwork, chores, or duties in the workplace (not due to oppositional behavior or failure to understand instructions)

      e. often has difficulty organizing tasks and activities

      f. often avoids, dislikes, or is reluctant to engage in tasks that require sustained mental effort (such as schoolwork or homework)

      g. often loses things necessary for tasks or activities (for example, toys, school assignments, pencils, books, or tools)

      h. is often easily distracted by extraneous stimuli

      i. is often forgetful in daily activities

   2. Six (or more) of the following symptoms of hyperactivity-impulsivity have persisted for at least six months to a degree that is maladaptive and inconsistent with developmental level:

   Hyperactivity

      a. often fidgets with hands or feet or squirms in seat

      b. often leaves seat in classroom or in other situations in which remaining seated is expected

      c. often runs about or climbs excessively in situations in which it is inappropriate (in adolescents or adults, this may be limited to subjective feelings of restlessness)

      d. often has difficulty playing or engaging in leisure activities quietly

      e. is often "on the go" or often acts as if "driven by a motor"

      f. often talks excessively

   Impulsivity

      g. often blurts out answers before questions have been completed

      h. often has difficulty awaiting turn

      i. often interrupts or intrudes on others (for example, butts into conversations or games)

B. Some hyperactive–impulsive or inattentive symptoms that caused impairment were present before age seven years.

C. Some impairment from the symptoms is present in two or more settings (for example, at school [or work] and at home).

D. There must be clear evidence of clinically significant impairment in social, academic, or occupational functioning.

E. The symptoms do not occur exclusively during the course of a pervasive developmental disorder, schizophrenia, or other psychotic disorder and are not better accounted for by another mental disorder (for example, mood disorder, anxiety disorder, dissociative disorder, or a personality disorder).

Source: *Diagnostic and Statistical Manual of Mental Disorders* (4th ed.) DSM-IV (pp. 83–85), 1994. Copyright © 1994 American Psychiatric Association. Reprinted with permission.

Treatment. The most common treatment for a child diagnosed as having an attention deficit disorder with hyperactivity involves the use of stimulant drugs such as dextroamphetamine (Dexadrine) and methylphenidate (Ritalin) (Busch, 1993). This might seem strange because stimulants ordinarily increase activity and the ADHD child already suffers from excessive activity. However, these drugs appear to have what is termed a **paradoxical effect** on children. That is, they appear to sedate rather than stimulate (Swanson et al., 1991). Some evidence suggests that they are about twice as effective as behavior modification (primarily the use of rewards) in controlling problem behavior in many ADHD children, as well as in improving academic achievement (Pelham et al., 1993).

Although the use of stimulants to treat ADHD children is often associated with preventing continued achievement declines in school (Busch, 1993), as well as with increasing the manageability of the children in question, it remains a controversial treatment. These drugs can also have some negative side effects such as weight loss, growth retardation, and mood changes (Henker & Whalen, 1989). However, these negative effects are rare when the child has been properly diagnosed (Guffey, 1991).

Another form of treatment for children with attention deficit disorders involves the use of computer-based instrumentation that monitors the children's brain-wave activity and provides them with information about their brain functioning. Researchers have found that the brain activity of these children is measurably different from that of children without attention deficits (see, for example, Janzen et al., 1995). It appears that the children can be trained to alter their brain-wave activity so that it more closely resembles that of normal children. Training involves providing them with feedback—termed **biofeedback** or **neurofeedback**—about their brain activity while they are engaged in actual tasks. The procedure, which is time-consuming and requires expensive instrumentation, is still experimental but initial results are positive (Lubar et al., 1995).

As we saw, ADHD, or hyperactivity, is a relatively common emotional exceptionality. It does not generally require special services outside the school. ADHD children are characterized by a variety of persistent symptoms, the most common of which are extreme difficulty in sustaining attention, a very high level of physical activity, and high levels of vocalization (Platzman et al., 1992). In school, such children, the majority of whom are boys, are easily distracted, inattentive, fidgety, loud, and restless. Not surprisingly, they are often a problem for teachers.

Attempts to change the behavior of ADHD children through counseling or reinforcement programs have had only limited success (Gordon, et al., 1991). As a result, ADHD is most often treated medically with Ritalin. Because of the behavior problems associated with high activity in schools, some children who do not have ADHD are nevertheless diagnosed as such and prescribed Ritalin. Unfortunately, Ritalin can have some negative effects

---

neurofeedback Refers to information subjects are given about the functioning of their nervous systems. Unlike biofeedback, which refers to feedback relating to all biological systems, neurofeedback relates specifically to information about brain functioning (EEG feedback).

biofeedback Information we obtain about our biological functioning. In a specialized sense, biofeedback refers to information subjects receive about the activity of their nervous system when they are connected to one of various sensors or instruments designed for that purpose.

---

paradoxical effect Literally, a surprising or contradictory effect. Phrase used to describe the apparently sedating effect that some stimulants (such as Ritalin) have on children who suffer from excessive activity (hyperactivity).

(emotional and physical), although, as mentioned above, these are rare when the child has been properly diagnosed (Guffey, 1991).

A variety of other personality and conduct disorders (sometimes manifested in lying, cheating, extreme insolence, and other socially maladaptive behaviors) occasionally present serious management and teaching problems for teachers. In most cases, however, such students remain in regular classrooms, barring major transgression of school regulations or criminal activity that might lead to expulsion from school and/or to detention in an institution for juvenile offenders.

IDENTIFYING EXCEPTIONAL CHILDREN

Mild mental retardation, learning disabilities, and emotional disturbances are seldom identified before the child goes to school. A number of stages appear to be common in the identification of each of these manifestations of exceptionality.

Initially, these children begin school as ordinary students. Some will achieve at a sufficiently deficient level that they may be kept in first grade an extra year, a practice that seems to be more common for the mildly retarded from lower socioeconomic backgrounds (Mercer, 1973).

The next stage described by Mercer begins when the teacher realizes that the child has not progressed sufficiently to be promoted to the next grade. At this point, the decision is made to refer the child for further diagnosis. In some cases, the child may simply be promoted to the next grade—a "social promotion," reflecting the school's reluctance to separate the child from age peers.

Lynch, Simms, von Hippel, and Shuchat (1978) provide a number of suggestions to help teachers in the early stages of tentative diagnosis—when the important decision is whether professional assessment is warranted. First, teachers are urged to learn to observe carefully to identify children who seem difficult, hard to get along with, or slow. Having identified these children, teachers can attempt to determine

what might work with them and can try several different approaches. Frequently, it turns out that there is no problem.

Second, Lynch and colleagues suggest that teachers ask themselves key questions: Does the child learn so slowly, or is the child's adaptive behavior (ability to use language, to play with other children, and to be reasonably independent) so poor that the child cannot participate fully with other children?

Third, and very important, teachers must be careful to distinguish between exceptionality and simple cultural differences. Very intelligent children whose dominant language and values are significantly different from those of the majority can sometimes appear less than normally bright.

Fourth, just as it is important to distinguish between the culturally different and those in need of special education, it is also important to recognize normal individual differences in temperament, motivation, interests, and so on. And teachers must always be aware of the possibility that difficulties between themselves and certain children might have to do with differences in personal style rather than with specific failings in the children.

Once teachers have determined that there is a real possibility of a problem requiring special attention, the next stage is to obtain professional help. Subsequent diagnosis—typically undertaken by professionals—usually involves assessments using prescribed instruments and consultation among members of an interdisciplinary team. Following diagnosis, remedial action will depend on the specific diagnosis, especially for learning disabilities for which remedial prescriptions are based on as detailed a diagnosis as possible. As we saw, most children diagnosed as having mild mental retardation, an emotional disturbance, or a learning disability will continue to attend regular classes, although they may also be segregated for group or individual special services. For each of these children, an IEP will need to be prepared and implemented. (See box "Identifying Exceptionality.")

IDENTIFYING EXCEPTIONALITY

Some extremes of exceptionality are obvious and can easily be detected by parents and others not specifically trained in such things. However, most instances of exceptionality are not extreme, and their diagnosis and assessment are often difficult.

Although the final diagnosis and assessment of an exceptionality that requires special intervention are usually made by a professional team following extensive testing, initial identification of those in need of further evaluation is often made by parents or teachers; hence, it is useful to know what to look for. However, parents and others need to be extremely cautious in their tentative judgments of exceptionality, especially in cases in which children (and sometimes adults) experience mild problems with subjects such as reading or arithmetic. It is extremely easy to misinterpret a common learning problem as evidence of a learning disability or mental retardation.

Some symptoms parents and teachers might notice are listed here. Further assessment and evaluation, or referral, can usually be provided by school psychologists.

Cerebral Palsy
Diagnosis is made by a physician. Symptoms can include

any, none, or most of the following and can range from very mild to very severe:

 uneven gait

 jerky movements

 speech problems

 rigidity

 drooling

 balance problems

 uncontrolled fluttering movements

 involuntary facial gestures

 shaking movements

 possible convulsions

Epilepsy
Diagnosis requires medical assessment. Observable symptoms are seizures. In *petit mal,* seizures are momentary lapses of attention lasting only seconds and may be accompanied by fluttering of the eyelids and suspension of activity. *Grand mal* seizures (also called fits, attacks, or convulsions) may involve sudden stiffening, falling, thrashing around, and moaning. Seizures may last only a few seconds and seldom last more than 5 minutes. Seizures that last longer require urgent medical attention.

Hearing Problems
 frequent earaches

 inattentiveness

 speech problems

high volume on TV or radio

failure to respond

discharge from one or both ears

turns head to listen

speaks in abnormally loud voice

Vision Problems
 rubbing of eyes

 redness of eyes

 headaches

 difficulty seeing chalkboard

 squinting

 high sensitivity to light

 holds material close to see

Schizophrenia
Requires psychiatric diagnosis. May be characterized by one or more of the following:

 aloofness

 refusal to cuddle

 self-injurious behavior (head banging, for example)

 no verbal communication

 repetitive behaviors (twirling, rocking, for example)

 abnormal object attachments

 insensitivity to pain

 poor balance

 withdrawal

 extreme distress when faced with change

---

cerebral palsy Label for a collection of congenital motor problems associated with brain damage and manifested in motor problems of varying severity, and occasionally in other problems such as convulsions or behavior disorders.

epilepsy A seizure disorder, sometimes genetic in origin, varying in severity; it is often treatable or controllable with drugs.

high sensitivity to pain

poor coordination

Attention Deficit Hyperactivity Disorder

Primarily a male disorder. Characterized by at least some of the following characteristics, present for at least 6 months and before the age of 7, and more frequent and severe than in most other children of the same mental age:

- often fidgets
- difficulty remaining seated
- easily distracted
- difficulty awaiting turn
- often blurts out answers
- difficulty following instructions
- difficulty sustaining attention
- shifts often from one activity to another
- difficulty playing quietly
- talks excessively
- often interrupts
- often does not seem to listen
- often loses things
- often takes physical risks

Conduct and Personality Disorders

These disorders require psychological or psychiatric assessment. They span a wide range of behaviors and symptoms,

some of which might include the following (note that only extreme and persistent manifestations of these behaviors would be considered disorders):

- high aggressiveness and hostility
- extreme withdrawal and social isolation
- extreme shyness
- lying
- stealing
- temper tantrums
- highly negative self-concept

Mental Disabilities: Moderate to Severe Retardation

Diagnosis and assessment require administration of individual intelligence tests by a trained psychologist. The most obvious feature is deficient ability to learn, ranging from mild to severe, defined in terms of significantly subaverage performance on intelligence tests (IQ below 70) and deficits in adaptive behavior. Early symptoms of moderate to severe mental retardation include:

- significant developmental lag in learning to crawl, walk, and talk
- failure to learn developmental tasks such as eating, dressing, tying shoes
- poor motor coordination
- markedly inferior verbal skills

Mild Retardation

Ordinarily not detected before school age; once in school, the child may show the following symptoms:

- significant difficulty in learning
- problems with short-term memory
- language deficits
- motor problems
- short attention span

Learning Disabilities

Identification and assessment are difficult even for trained professionals. Learning disabilities may be manifested in:

- uneven pattern of academic achievement
- academic retardation
- learning problems not related to intelligence or environmental disadvantage
- specific learning problems in language-related subjects or arithmetic
- erratic spelling
- frequent failure to recognize simple words
- confusion of letters or numbers
- persistent difficulty with simple arithmetic computations
- inattentiveness, impulsivity, mood shifts
- poor visual memory

schizophrenia A serious mental disorder that may take a variety of forms, sometimes characterized by bizarre behaviors, obsessions, distorted views of reality, and so on. Schizophrenia in infants and children is sometimes confused with autism, although it does not ordinarily begin as early.

LABELS IN SPECIAL EDUCATION

"Learning disabled," "educable mentally retarded," "attention deficit hyperactivity disorder"—these and their highly common letter substitutes, LD, EMR, and ADHD, respectively, are widely used labels in special education. But they are just that: labels. Labels do nothing more than name; they don't explain anything. To say that Eric has difficulty recognizing numbers because he is LD might mislead us into thinking we understand why Eric hesitates and struggles when he picks up the six of spades. But all the label "LD" tells us is that Eric's behavior manifests a combination of symptoms that we have agreed to label "LD." The label can be useful because it permits us to communicate with one another, and it gives us some basis for developing educational programs for children like Eric.

Still, labels do have disadvantages, and many argue against their use. Common arguments insist that labels are often unfair (given the social and cultural biases of intelligence tests), that they lead to lower expectations and thus present an additional disadvantage to those who are labeled, and that there is a remarkable lack of homogeneity among those who are given identical labels. In addition, there is a growing tendency to treat disabled children as quantitatively rather than qualitatively different from normal children. The use of generally pejorative labels is clearly incompatible with this trend.

We have come some distance from labels that were once as widely accepted as those we use today: "idiot," "moron," "imbecile," "cretin" . . .

MAIN POINTS

1. Prodigies are those with a very specific, highly extraordinary talent. Giftedness is a more general characteristic. Talented and gifted children are identified by professionals as being capable of high performance by virtue of outstanding capabilities that might be reflected in general intellectual ability, specific academic aptitude, creative or productive thinking, leadership, or artistic talent. In practice, these children are often nominated by teachers and identified on the basis of ability and achievement measures. The culturally different are often overlooked and are underrepresented among programs for the gifted.

2. Two main approaches to educating the talented and gifted are acceleration (students progress through the conventional curriculum at an accelerated pace—for example, Stanley's radical acceleration) and enrichment (students go beyond the conventional curriculum—that is, Renzulli's revolving door model). Other approaches include mentoring, self-directed and independent study, IEPs, special schools, and out-of-school programs and courses.

3. Brainstorming is a group approach for producing ideas and solving problems, using the principle of deferred evaluation. The Gordon technique modifies brainstorming by beginning with an abstraction of the problem. Morphological analysis divides a problem into its attributes and brainstorms these. De Bono presents suggestions for developing skills involved in lateral (creative) and vertical (logical) thinking. The use of conceptual models can also increase creative thinking and problem solving.

4. Family variables are very important for encouraging the qualities that lead to eminence, as is school climate, with informal schools (as opposed to those that are more formal) and warm, receptive teachers being more likely to encourage creativity. Similarly, formal teaching styles (structured, teacher controlled, achievement

oriented, emphasizing individual work) may lead to higher academic achievement; informal styles (student centered, integrative, intrinsically motivated—characteristic of open classrooms) are sometimes associated with higher creativity and motivation.

5. Disputed evidence shows that teachers' expectations can serve as self-fulfilling prophecies and affect students' performance positively or negatively in accordance with expectations. Expectations are often higher for students from higher socioeconomic levels, for obedient children, for students with the most positive labels (for example, "learning disabled" rather than "mentally retarded"), and for those who sit front and center and speak clearly. There is also the opposite possibility—that low expectations might lead teachers to provide additional help for a student, thus leading to higher achievement.

6. In addition to mandating education in the "least restrictive environment" (mainstreaming or inclusive education), Public Law 94-142 and the Individuals with Disabilities Education Act establish the child's right to due process and nondiscriminatory evaluation, free and appropriate educational services, and an IEP for each child with special needs.

7. Mainstreaming (also called integration or inclusion) attempts to meet the needs of exceptional children in the regular classroom. For some children with special needs, full inclusion may be difficult and not entirely appropriate. IEPs must be prepared for all special needs children, following assessment and parental involvement and consent. These include statements of goals, duration of the program, and evaluation procedures.

8. Exceptionality describes significant deviation from the norm in cognitive, social-emotional, or physical functioning. It can be associated with either superior or deficient functioning.

9. Physical exceptionality may be manifested in exceptional athletic ability or extraordinary grace and elegance; at the other extreme, it may be apparent in sensory or motor impairments, physical disabilities, diseases, and so on.

10. Social-emotional exceptionality includes manifestations of emotional disturbance, behavioral disorders, and attention deficit hyperactivity disorder (ADHD), among others. All but the most severe forms of social-emotional exceptionality are ordinarily dealt with in the regular classroom.

11. Mental retardation is characterized by a marked depression in general ability to learn and limited adaptation, and may vary from mild to profound. The majority of the mentally retarded are mildly retarded and are capable of acceptable achievement in elementary school.

12. Learning disabilities are generally evident in disparity between actual and expected achievement, with an uneven pattern of achievement often marked by one or more specific learning impairments (for example, developmental reading disorder or developmental arithmetic disorder).

13. Attention deficit hyperactivity disorder (ADHD) is a relatively common emotional disorder marked by excessive activity, attention problems, and impulsivity far in excess of what might be considered normal. ADHD is often treated with stimulant drugs (the paradoxical effect) and, more experimentally, with brain activity feedback instrumentation.

14. Initial identification of exceptionality is often made by classroom teachers after the child has begun school. Mild retardation and learning disabilities are seldom diagnosed before this time.

15. Labels are useful in categorizing children and in providing for their special needs. But they simply name rather than explain, and should not be pejorative.

APPLIED QUESTIONS

▶ Explain the most important elements of the legal definition of the talented and gifted.

▶ What are some techniques for promoting creativity?

▶ Write a personality and teaching-style profile of a hypothetical teacher whose approach is most likely to foster creativity.

▶ What are the two dimensions of physical, intellectual, and emotional exceptionality?

▶ Distinguish between mental retardation and learning disabilities.

▶ Describe the most important symptoms of attention deficit hyperactivity disorder.

STUDY TERMS

acceleration **272**
attention deficit hyperactivity disorder (ADHD) **295**
biofeedback **304**
brainstorming **276**
cerebral palsy **306**
conceptual model **279**
developmental arithmetic disorder **301**
developmental reading disorder **300**
direct teaching style **284**
educable mentally retarded (EMR) **300**
enrichment **272**
epilepsy **306**
exceptionality **288**
formal teaching style **283**
full inclusion **289**

Gordon technique **277**
hyperactivity **295**
inclusion (inclusive education) **288**
inclusive classrooms **288**
indirect teaching style **284**
individualized educational plans (IEPs) **291**
individualized program plans (IPPs) **291**
Individuals with Disabilities Education Act (IDEA) **288**
informal teaching style **283**
lateral thinking **278**
learning disability **289**
mainstreaming **288**
mental retardation **296**
mentor **274**
mild retardation **298**

moderate retardation **298**
morphological analysis **277**
neurofeedback **304**
paradoxical effect **304**
po **279**
process disorders **301**
prodigies **269**
profound retardation **298**
Public Law 94-142 **288**
radical acceleration model **273**
revolving door model **273**
schizophrenia **307**
self-fulfilling prophecies **285**
severe retardation **298**
special education teachers **288**
special needs **287**
teaching style **283**
tutor **274**
vertical thinking **278**

SUGGESTED READINGS

The following two references should be of value for teachers concerned with the creative behavior of their students. The first has been translated into many different languages and continues to be popular. The second is a useful analysis of current thinking and research in creativity. The last three chapters deal specifically with approaches that foster creativity in the classroom:

OSBORN, A. (1957). *Applied imagination.* New York: Scribner's.

CROPLEY, A. J. (1992). *More ways than one: Fostering creativity.* Norwood, N.J.: Ablex.

The following is a highly practical guide for teachers of exceptional children in the early childhood classroom. It deals with the characteristics of exceptional younger children as well as their identification, and provides useful ideas for working with them:

SPODEK, B., & SARACHO, O. N. (1994). *Dealing with individual differences in the early childhood classroom.* New York: Longman.

The two following references are practical classroom guides for teachers in inclusive classrooms. The first outlines a large number of specific strategies teachers can use in different situations; the second is a two-part video program produced by Phi Delta Kappa that looks not only at the usefulness of mainstreaming, but also at some of the practical issues involved:

POLLOWAY, E. A., & PATTON, J. R. (1993). *Strategies for teaching learners with special needs* (5th ed.). New York: Macmillan.

Facing inclusion. Two tapes and a guide available for $185 from Phi Delta Kappa, P.O. Box 789, Bloomington, Ind. 47402-0789. (800-766-1156)

A detailed look at diversity in today's schools and at various approaches to diversity is

GROSSMAN, H. (1995). *Special education in a diverse society.* Boston: Allyn & Bacon.

A far more comprehensive introduction to special education than can be provided here is found in this general textbook:

HALLAHAN, D. P., & KAUFFMAN, J. M. (1994). *Exceptional children: Introduction to special education* (6th ed.). Boston: Allyn & Bacon.

In the summer, a bear's heart normally beats approximately forty times per minute. In winter, when the bear is denned up, heart rate may drop as low as ten beats per minute. Amazingly, extreme cold rouses the bear as readily as does warmth. If this were not the case, many bears would freeze to death because it is necessary for the bear to awaken and warm up when the temperature drops too low (Matthews, 1969).

CHAPTER 9

I am going to where life is more like life than it is here.

SEAN O'CASEY, *Cock-a-Doodle Donkey*

There is surely a piece of divinity in us, something that was before the elements, and owes no homage unto the sun.

SIR THOMAS BROWNE, *Religio Medici*

Humanistic Approaches to Teaching

PREVIEW

Humanists object to what they see as the mechanistic, dehumanizing, and inhumane emphases of traditional approaches to psychology and education. They urge the adoption of new attitudes, concepts, and approaches in these fields. This chapter describes the fundamental characteristics of humanistic approaches to understanding people and to teaching. The most important point it makes is that humanism, behaviorism, and cognitivism are not incompatible. You can be and do all the good things that humanism implies and still use the knowledge offered by other approaches.

- How is humanism different from other approaches?

- What are the principles of Carl Rogers' theory?

- What is humanistic education?

- What is an open classroom?

- What are the main strategies of cooperative learning?

When I came home at Christmas that first year of college, I still believed that psychologists had devious and clever ways of peering into our minds and of uncovering all sorts of dark things hidden there. That, after all, was why I had decided to study psychology. And, as a budding psychologist, I brought great armloads of explanations home to my grandmother, like chunks of firewood to stoke her fires and inflame her imagination. Because she wanted to know, I told her with stunning behavioristic clarity why pigs lie in their muddy wallows on hot summer days and why chickens crow in the morning and roost at night. I explained to her why cows always go into the same stall and why horses stand with their backs to a storm.

"Bah!" harrumphed my grandmother, refusing to see the magic in my explanation. "If I were a pig," she said, "I'd lie in the mud. And if I were a chicken I'd crow in the morning and roost at night."

"But . . ."

"And if I were a cow," she continued, keeping me from telling her how my explanations were still bang-on . . . "if I were a cow, I'd be a wild cow. I'd never go into stalls!"

"But the point," I said (brilliantly, I thought), "is that you're not a pig, a chicken, or a cow. You're a people, and there are explanations for that too!" Quickly, I launched into a powerful behavioristic explanation of Frank's fear of cats and Louise's embarrassing attachment to the tattered remains of a dirty-green baby blanket.

"But," countered my grandmother, "what about why Frank isn't scared of dogs, and he was bitten about eight times? And cats hardly ever bit him. And what about how Louise doesn't even like any other blankets or pillows? And why doesn't Lucy like *her* baby blanket?"

A practiced skeptic, my grandmother could always ask questions more rapidly than I could answer them. And although I had enough of the beginnings of some answers to eventually convince her that Skinner, Freud, Piaget, and others each had important and useful things to say about Frank's fear of cats and Louise's love of a dirty rag, there was no way I could ever convince her that they, or I, knew more about Frank or Louise than she did.

As my grandmother so pointedly put it, "I personally know pigs that don't care to wallow in mud, chickens that never roost or crow, cows that park their arses wherever, and horses so contrary they'll face whichever way they bloody please."

My grandmother was a humanist.*

HUMANISTIC PSYCHOLOGY

Humanistic psychology is concerned with the uniqueness, the individuality, the humanity of each individual. It is an orientation that readily admits that some people smile when they wallow in mud, some turn up their noses but endure the embarrassment, and others find such behavior quite unacceptable. In more human terms, it is an orientation based on the fundamental observation that although we might resemble each other in many important ways, each of us is quite different from every other. Our uniqueness is our "self." And self is the most central concept in humanistic psychology.

---

*PPC: Don't you think the language is a little strong, especially for a grandmother? After all, some students reading this have had pretty sheltered lives.

AUTHOR: That's the way she talked. If she felt like it. Sheltered students, please don't take offense. . . . On second thought, if you want to take offense . . .

Science, humanists insist, tends to dehumanize people. It reduces them to averages and generalizations; it looks for what is common and predictable. And it ignores those things that are private and individual and uniquely human. In fact, it simply isn't equipped to deal with these things.

What Humanists Object To. It is largely for these reasons that there has historically been conflict between humanism and behavioristic or cognitive approaches—a conflict based on orientations that are fundamentally different in terms of their most basic beliefs and attitudes toward human beings. In a nutshell, what humanists object to is what they see as the technological orientation of approaches such as behaviorism. In its most extreme form, this technological orientation asserts that certain identifiable teaching processes, when used with such and such a type of student for such and such a kind of content, will predictably result in the attainment of specific, previously identified, and clearly intended objectives.

Humanists object strongly to this process-product orientation. As Shulman (1986) observes, they see it as focusing too strongly on techniques that "should" be practiced by teachers and as placing far too much emphasis on the measurable outcomes of the teaching/learning process, especially in terms of gains on standardized tests. They are alarmed that the conclusions and recommendations of process-product research have often been used by school authorities as a basis for evaluating school systems, teachers, and teaching. Traditional emphases on teaching styles and teaching outcomes, notes Ornstein (1993), ignores the humanistic aspects of teaching.

Humanistic Emphases. The humanistic view emphasizes two things: the uniqueness of the pupil and the teacher's attitudes toward students. Hence, humanistic teachers are especially sensitive to diversity in their classrooms. As Bartolome (1994) notes, humanistic teaching is culturally sensitive. It respects and tries to enhance the history, culture, and different perspectives of individual students. Thus, the preparation of humanistic teachers, as Patterson and Purkey (1993) argue, needs to devote as much attention to teachers' beliefs and attitudes as is now given to subject matter and instructional strategies.

Stretching the Truth. If teaching is both an art and a science—as we claimed in Chapter 1—humanists are on the side of art and behaviorists on the side of science. But before we rush forward to describe what it is the humanists have to say about the art of teaching, it's important to note that our use of terms in this section, and in much of this chapter, is almost shamefully loose and general. Real life is not so simple. Behaviorists are not often as technology oriented as an exaggerated humanistic description of their views might suggest; nor are all process-product researchers behaviorists, or cognitivists. In fact, later in this chapter we look at two important and quite specific instructional methods (one based on learning styles and the other on cooperative learning), each of which reflects much of the humanist's concern with the individual and with emotional growth but each of which is fundamentally concerned with both the processes and the products of instruction. The results of process-product research do not really suggest that teachers should ideally be quasirobotic classroom mechanics who repair cognitive and behavioral deficits and impairments and produce wonderful little academic achievers.

Keep in mind that most educators do not fall neatly into the humanist, the behaviorist, or the cognitive camps. Most are quite eclectic; they borrow from here and there.

So what we do in this chapter is stretch the truth on two counts: We exaggerate the differences between humanism and, especially, behaviorism; and we pretend that all that is not clearly humanistic is, by default, behavioristic.

Exaggeration can be a useful pedagogical device—so long as you are not deceived.*

ROGERIAN PHENOMENOLOGICAL THEORY

As an introduction to humanism, we look first at a summary of those aspects of the writing of Carl Rogers that deal with personality and behavior; then we look at several approaches to education that reflect humanistic orientations. (Rogers is among the most influential theorists in this area; Abraham Maslow, another important humanist, is discussed in Chapter 10.)

Rogers' writings are based not so much on objective data as on his answers for questions about what individuals think of the world. How do they feel? How do they perceive their relationships to others? What are the conditions required for them to change? Thus, Rogers' theory, which contrasts sharply with the more rigorous approaches of other theorists, is especially important in the fields of psychotherapy and counseling, where it has had (and continues to have) an enormous influence (see, for example, Brodley, 1993; Patterson, 1993). And it provides the teacher with a different way of looking at and communicating with students. In the words of his daughter, Natalie, ". . . he verified the notion that a safe, supportive environment allowed each person (including children) to journey down the path of self-discovery, self-esteem and self-directed learning" (Rogers & Freiberg, 1994, p. iii).

---

*PPC: This is an important point. Perhaps you should repeat it.
AUTHOR: Okay: Exaggeration can be a useful pedagogical device—so long as you are not deceived.
PPC: That's not what I meant. Can you make the point in a different way, to make it more memorable?
AUTHOR: Okay. Real life is seldom like the simple black-and-white pictures that we draw to depict our little theories and our precious ideological stances. We are still like children using crude wooden pencils. In our drawings we miss all the color, most of the nuances, and thousands of other poses that we could have drawn. We draw only frozen stick-men and stick-women, and then we pretend we have drawn something with a soul.

IMPORTANT TERMS

Different terms are used to describe the various emphases of Rogerian theory. The first, **client-centered therapy** (also **person-centered therapy**), describes several aspects of the system. It indicates, first, that the theory is a therapeutic one; that is, it is designed to be useful to a counselor who deals with behavioral and emotional problems. Second, the label highlights the major difference between this and other approaches to **counseling**—namely, that the counseling procedures revolve around the person. It proposes client-centered as opposed to **directive therapy.** The counselor's role in client-centered therapy is accordingly deemphasized; instead of giving advice or solving problems for clients, the therapist sets the stage so that clients themselves define their problems, react to them, and take steps toward their solution. (The process is actually much more complex than it may seem from the preceding statements; see Rogers, 1951.)

The second term is **phenomenology,** a term that denotes concern with the world as it is perceived by an individual rather than as it may actually be. Rogerian theory is phenomenological in that it is concerned primarily with the individual's own view of the world—that is,

---

client-centered therapy Type of patient–counselor relationship in which the counselor (therapist or psychiatrist) is not directive in the sense of telling clients how they should behave but rather attempts to allow patients to express themselves and discover within themselves ways of dealing with their own behavior. This therapeutic approach is generally contrasted with directive therapy. Also termed *person-centered therapy.*

counseling The act of giving advice.

directive therapy Type of counselor–client relationship in which the counselor takes the major responsibility for directing the client's behavior.

phenomenology An approach concerned primarily with how individuals view their own world. Its basic assumption is that each individual perceives and reacts to the world in a unique manner and that it is this phenomenological world view that is important in understanding the individual's behavior.

with the world as a person sees it rather than as it appears to others.

The third term is **humanism.** Humanism in literature, philosophy, and psychology has historically been concerned with human worth, with individuality, with humanity, and with the individual's right to determine personal actions. Accordingly, the development of human potential tends to be highly valued while the attainment of material goals is deemphasized. Thus, Rogers describes **self-actualization** as the end toward which all humans strive. In addition, his encouragement of client-centered therapy is compatible with the humanist's emphasis on self-determination. In fact, the question of self-determination versus external control, together with a consideration of the ethical and practical problems of applying a science of behavior, was the subject of a debate by Rogers and Skinner (1956).

THE BEHAVIOR CONTROL DEBATE:
ROGERS VERSUS SKINNER

The central issue in this debate concerns the application of behavior control techniques for personal control in social groups, for educational procedures, and for control by governments. Skinner argues strongly for abandoning techniques of aversive control (see Chapter 4) and for consciously and openly applying techniques of positive control toward the betterment of society. (This topic was the subject of his 1948 novel, *Walden II,* an account of a fictitious society developed through the application of a behavioral technology.)

But, claims Rogers, Skinner underestimates the problem of power by making the false assumption that techniques of social control will be used in the best interests of society. Furthermore, he fails to specify goals for this behavioral technology. Rogers dismisses Skinner's claim that if behavioral scientists experiment with society, "eventually the practices which make for the greatest biological and psychological strength of the group will presumably survive" (Skinner, 1955, p. 549). Rogers argues instead that a society's goals should be concerned primarily with the process of "becoming," with achieving worth and dignity, with being creative—in short, with the process of self-actualization.*

The debate resolves no issues; it simply exposes the fundamental conflict between those who favor human control (for our benefit) through the thoughtful application of a science of behavior and those who believe that science should be used not to change or control us but simply to enhance our capacity for self-control and self-determination.

PRINCIPLES OF ROGERS' THEORY

In the eleventh chapter of *Client-Centered Therapy* (1951), Rogers presents an integrated account of his position in the form of nineteen propositions (see also Rogers, 1992, a reprint of a 1957 article). Most of these ideas continue to this day to underlie Rogerian counseling practices and humanistic applications to education (Kirschenbaum, 1991). The most important of these are summarized here (also see Table 9.1).

---

humanism A philosophical and psychological orientation that is primarily concerned with our humanity—that is, with our worth as individuals and with those processes that are considered to make us more human.

self-actualization The process or act of becoming oneself, of developing one's potentialities, of achieving an awareness of one's identity, of self-fulfillment. The term is central in humanistic psychology.

---

*PPC: Students would probably like to know who, in the opinion of most contemporary researchers and educators, wins the debate. Could the bear provide some enlightenment—without risking his precious political correctness?

AUTHOR: As the next line notes, the debate resolves no issues. Besides, winning a debate does not prove the correctness of the winning side—although it might say something about the strength of its arguments or the persuasiveness of its defenders. And the bear's political correctness is not at issue here. The bear is politically correct not because he lacks the courage of his convictions but simply because . . . well, he doesn't want to offend anybody. Okay?

TABLE 9.1 MAJOR CHARACTERISTICS OF HUMAN PERSONALITY ACCORDING TO ROGERS (1951)

PRINCIPLE	CLARIFICATION
1. *Our worlds are private; reality is phenomenological.*	The significant aspects of reality consist of the world of private experience. Our realities are therefore completely individualistic. They can be *intuited* but not *known* by others.
2. *Our reality is immediate, personal consciousness.*	Our private experience determines our reality. Our phenomenal field makes up our immediate consciousness.
3. *The goal of human existence is self-actualization.*	Each of us has a basic tendency to strive toward becoming a complete, healthy, competent individual through a process characterized by self-government, self-regulation, and autonomy.
4. *Behavior can be understood only from the individual's point of view.*	Because behavior occurs within the context of personal realities, the best way to understand a person's behavior is by attempting to adopt his or her point of view; hence, humanism emphasizes the importance of open communication.
5. *We construct our own selves.*	We discover who we are on the basis of direct experiences and on the basis of beliefs and values that we incorporate in our self-concepts from information provided by people who communicate to us what we are.
6. *Behaviors are consistent with notions of self.*	In general, we select behaviors that do not contradict who and what we think we are.

Understanding these principles is important for understanding the rationale underlying the various approaches to humanistic education described later in this chapter.

Principle 1. One of the most fundamental assertions of the phenomenologist is that every individual is the center of a continually changing world of personal experiences. This recognizes two features of human functioning that are particularly important for the teacher. First, it implies that for any individual, the significant aspects of the environment are private. Second, it suggests not only that the individual's phenomenological world is private but also that it can never be completely known by anyone else. Consider, for example, the simple complaint of a child to his mother after waking up from a nightmare, "Mama, I'm scared." The fear that the child expresses is a real and significant aspect of his world, and his mother may draw on her own stored-up memories of past fears to imagine how her son feels. But she cannot really know his fear. The phenomenological world can never be fully shared.

Principle 2. We react to the world as we experience and perceive it; that is our reality. What we perceive and feel, labeled the **phenomenal field,** makes up our immediate consciousness. And because this field is defined in terms of the individual's private experience, reality is also private. Therefore, what is real for one individual is not necessarily real for another. A student who likes her teacher, no matter how unbearable that teacher appears to other students, has

phenomenal field The feelings, perceptions, and awareness that an individual has at any given moment.

The world is understood only from the individual's point of view.

a likable teacher in her phenomenal field—and her behavior toward that teacher will reflect this reality. This is why it's important for a teacher to understand that students perceive their worlds in different ways. It is no accident that the teacher who seems to understand students best is often described as empathetic (able to intuit how others feel).

Principle 3. The individual has one basic, overriding tendency—to actualize, maintain, and enhance the experiencing individual. It is neither necessary nor useful to list a variety of needs or drives to account for human behavior, claims Rogers; we strive for only one goal—*self-actualization.*

One way of defining self-actualization is to say that it involves becoming whatever one can become through activities determined by oneself (Maslow, 1970). In other words, to actualize oneself is to develop one's potentialities. Rogers attempts to clarify this definition by describing some characteristics of the process of self-actualization.

Self-actualization is a directional process in two senses: First, it tends toward maturation, increasing competence, survival, reproduction, and so on. These important, motivation-related objectives of human functioning are viewed as tendencies that characterize the overriding process of actualizing—of becoming.

Self-actualization is also directional in that it moves toward increasing "self-government, self-regulation, and autonomy." At the same time it moves away from "heteronymous control, or control by external forces" (Rogers, 1951, p. 488). This is one reason for the basic incompatibility between behavior control in a Skinnerian sense and the process of growth in a Rogerian sense.

In summary, Rogers believes that humans have an inner, directing need to develop themselves in the direction of healthy, competent, and creative functioning. This notion is absolutely basic to an understanding of the humanist's view of people as essentially good and forever striving toward a better state.

Principle 4. The individual's reality is private and personal, says Rogers; no one can really know it. But if we are to come close to understanding someone else, we have to try to adopt their point of view—as did Arnold Jackson (see the case "Are You Sure It's His Problem?").

Rogers claims that much of our inability to understand behavior results from our failure to recognize that responses are meaningful only from the individual's own point of view.

Principle 5. As a result of interacting with the environment, and especially with other people, we develop notions of who and what we are. In other words, we begin to construct notions of "self." The self is a consistent pattern of beliefs we have about our "I" or "me." As we receive feedback about ourselves from others, we incorporate this information into our concept of self. Most children receive signs at a very early age from parents and others indicating that they are lovable and good. Consequently, notions of themselves as being good become part of their perceived selves. In the same manner, a child may learn that he is cute from the comments of others; he may also learn that he is anything but cute ("My, my, look at that kid's nose, will you!"). As a result of receiving high grades, a student may develop a concept of self that includes the belief that she is intelligent.

CASE: ARE YOU SURE IT'S HIS PROBLEM?

THE SITUATION: Arnold Jackson, who has now been teaching for thirteen years, reflecting on his first year teaching:

I was only 22 and I had this grade 10 class, and, I'll admit, I was scared. What scared me most was I might have bad discipline, they wouldn't listen to me. So I watched real hard for misbehavior and rebellion because I was determined I'd wipe it out quick.

Well, there was this student, big guy named Randy, a bit older than all the others, and he wasn't doing very well. He'd already failed at least once but I think twice, and he could never answer any questions in class, and I just knew he was going to be trouble.

Which he was. Only maybe the second or third day of English class, and already he was slouched down in his seat, his legs sprawled way out into the aisle. So I straightened him out, just a quick, firm, verbal reprimand—which worked, but I had to do it twice more that class, and again the next day, until, finally, totally exasperated, I just walked down the aisle, put my foot under his outstretched leg, and flung it back under his desk.

At that moment, he looked at me like raw hate, and I knew I'd got me a bad enemy. And from there, it just seemed to get worse, day by day. Every time I looked at him in class, it's like he was doing something else, mostly not paying attention, deliberately not handing in his assignments on time, slouching his feet out in the aisle, and then drawing them back quickly as if he'd just thought of it.

Finally, I talked to Franklin Lohde, the vice principal who was pretty well in charge of discipline in the school. I explained to him how Randy'd been behaving. "He's got a real problem," I concluded. And I'll never forget what Franklin Lohde said:

"Are you sure it's his problem?" he said.

"What?"

"You sure it's his problem—that he's deliberately inattentive and defiant? Or is it maybe your problem?"

That one simple question turned me right around, turned my whole career around for sure. It made me think maybe I should ask, is this really Randy's problem? Is it possible there's a problem only because in my mind I think there is? Is it possible maybe this big kid slouches not because he doesn't have respect but just because he's so big in that desk? The more I thought about it, the more it made sense that maybe Randy didn't deliberately decide not to finish his work, but maybe he just couldn't.

I started to see him, and a lot of my other students, in a completely different way, almost like asking well, what would that feel like or be like if I was them?

One of the most important facts of the human condition, claim the Humanists, is that the individual's world is private. How much can even a very sensitive teacher know of this Mexican-American child's world?

Conversely, she may come to think of herself as being stupid if the information she receives is negative.

Two important sources of information are related to the development of the self. The first is the child's direct experiences—experiences of being loved and wanted and of feeling good as a result, experiences of being hurt and the consequent realization that the self does not like to be hurt, experiences of gratification (for example, eating) together with the realization that gratification is pleasant. These direct experiences lead to the development of an awareness of self. The child also experiences self-related events indirectly, often by being told things ("You're real smart, Guy. Good boy"). These experiences too contribute to the development of self-notions.

Sometimes an individual's direct and indirect experiences are contradictory and lead to conflicting notions of the self. Consider, for example, the student whose indirect experiences have led him to believe that he is academically gifted (that is, his mother has often said to him, "You're academically gifted, son") but whose direct experience is that he constantly fails in school. The resolution of this conflict may take several forms. One, of course, involves accepting the direct evidence and concluding that he is not especially brilliant. An alternative would be for him to accept the indirect value

and distort his perception of direct experience. He might, for example, conclude that he is, indeed, quite brilliant but that his teachers don't like him. Or he might look for additional information to resolve the dilemma. Rogers suggests that the seeds for later maladaptive behavior are often found in the early failure to resolve the conflicting pictures of self that emerge from direct experience and what he terms **introjected values.**

Principle 6. Most of the ways of behaving that are adopted by the individual are those that are consistent with the concept of self. Consider, for example, the man who thinks of himself as a gifted orator and who has been invited to address the local chapter of the Ear Realignment and Onion Society (EROS). This proposition predicts clearly that in line with his image of self, this individual will accept the invitation. By the same token, a man who thinks of himself as inhibited and verbally inept would be likely to turn down such an invitation. In both

---

introjected values Rogers' phrase for values that result not from direct experience but that are, in a sense, borrowed—sometimes from the reactions of others to the individual, sometimes from observations of how others appear to be, sometimes from the individual's unrealistic fantasies about the self.

these cases, and indeed in most instances of human behavior, the activity selected is compatible with the self-image.

Consider what happens, however, when the image of self is somewhat distorted—when, for example, the person who believes himself to be a gifted speaker has derived this notion not from direct experience (that is, applause following past orations) but from the words of his wise and ancient grandmother: "You shpeak zo vell, Ludvig, you mus be a gud spichmakerrr." In line with his self-image, he accepts the invitation; but as the day approaches, he becomes afraid—not consciously but organically. This individual may suddenly find himself physically ill in a literal sense. How can a sick man be expected to address a large audience of ear realigners and onion lovers? And to refuse to do so when ill is quite congruent with this man's image of self-as-great-orator. In Rogers' words, "The behavior which is adopted is such that it satisfies the organic need, but it takes channels which are consistent with the concept of self" (1951, p. 588). This—the individual's attempt to satisfy a "real" need that is not consistent with the image of self—is assumed to be one of the primary sources of neurotic behavior in humans.

EVALUATION OF
ROGERIAN PHENOMENOLOGY

Many important aspects of Rogers' views of behavior seem intuitively correct. It appears obvious that each individual perceives the world in a manner not experienced by anyone else. It also seems obvious that to understand others completely, it may be useful to adopt their points of view. However, some aspects of the propositions are not so obvious. In particular, the meanings of terms such as *self-actualization* are not always clear. Nor are Rogers' conclusions about human behavior necessarily as general as he implies.

Rogers' approach is clearly highly subjective and not very scientific. That is, it is not based on rigorous, replicable research. Never-theless, its merits in the progress of science may be considerable; even very speculative theorizing can sometimes generate fruitful ideas. The theory has had, and continues to have, tremendous impact on counseling and teaching (Ryan, Hawkins, & Russell, 1992).

The important question now should not be whether this is a correct view of humanity but rather whether this is a useful way to look at people. It is.

HUMANISM IN THE CLASSROOM

When Agne, Greenwood, and Miller (1994) looked at differences between teachers who had been selected as Teacher of the Year and in-service teachers, they found that the Teachers of the Year were significantly more humanistic in the way they interacted with their students. So, for those of you who aspire to be Teachers of the Year, being humanistic may be a good thing. The question is, What does it mean to be a humanistic teacher? (See "Behavior Control à la Rogers.")

In line with their basic beliefs, humanists such as Rogers and Maslow (see Ryan, Hawkins, & Russell, 1992) and Combs (1982) present a strong plea for **student-centered teaching.** Student-centered teaching advocates a philosophy of teaching in which students are given a far more important role in curriculum decisions than has traditionally been the case. Such teaching advocates that teachers should be learning facilitators rather than didactic instructors and that to be successful as learning facilitators, they must be trained to be sensitive and caring, genuine and empathetic.

Not surprisingly, humanistic approaches to education emphasize healthy social and per-

---

student-centered teaching Rogers's expression for an approach to teaching based on a philosophy of self-discovered learning. The approach requires that the teacher genuinely care for students as individuals and that students be allowed to determine for themselves what is important in their lives.

BEHAVIOR CONTROL À LA ROGERS

As an alternative to Skinner's behavioral technology, Rogers proposes the following five-point model for the control of human behavior (Rogers & Skinner, 1956, pp. 1063–1064):

1. It is possible for us to choose to value humanity as a self-actualizing process of becoming—and also to value creativity and the processes by which we acquire knowledge.

2. Science can help us discover the conditions that lead to the development of these processes and may provide better ways of achieving these purposes.

3. It is possible for individuals or groups to set the conditions for growth without resorting to a great deal of external control or power. Current knowledge suggests that the only authority necessary is the authority to establish certain qualities of interpersonal relationship.

4. Exposed to these conditions, individuals become more self-responsible, make progress in self-actualization, become more flexible, and become more creatively adaptive.

5. Choosing these humanistic values would lead to the beginnings of a social system in which values, knowledge, adaptive skills, and even the concept of science would be continually changing and growing. The emphasis would be upon the human being as a process of becoming.

---

sonal development and, at the same time, deemphasize rigorous, performance-oriented, test-dominated approaches to subject matter. They strongly advocate providing students with experiences of success rather than failure; their orientation is toward discovery rather than reception learning. The humanistic view of human functioning accepts individuals for what they are, respects their feelings and aspirations, and holds that every person has the right to self-determination. Such a view of the student leads naturally to child-centered schools. And the basic premise in these schools, claim Rogers and Freiberg (1994), "is that if we are genuine, caring, empathic and congruent as teachers, parents, or counselors, we will be fostering the growth and learning capacity of others" (p. iii).

But the child-centered school is not concerned solely with the emotional and personal development of the child—although it sometimes seems that way, partly because its emphasis is on affective growth and partly because this aspect of the humanistic movement has been exaggerated as a reaction against more rigorous approaches. Most humanistic programs, several of which are described next, are responsive to the important requirements of curricula. After all, even the most self-actualized individuals still need to know how to read, write, and name the major capitals of Europe. In fact, becoming self-actualized—that is, becoming all that one can and should be—may well depend on both knowledge of the three Rs and the wealth of cognitive and metacognitive strategies that our new cognitive instructional sciences use to build their programs. Clearly, cognitive concerns can also be part of a thoughtful, humanistic approach to teaching.

HUMANISTIC MOVEMENTS IN EDUCATION

The thinking exemplified in humanistic theory has become part of the so-called **third-force psychology**—the other two forces being behav-

---

third-force psychology A general expression for humanistic approaches to psychology such as those exemplified by the work of Carl Rogers and Abraham Maslow. The first two forces are psychoanalysis and behaviorism (S–R psychology).

ioristic S-R theory and Freudian theory. In education, third-force psychology represents a movement pervaded by (1) a belief in the uniqueness and importance of the human individual and (2) a strong reaction against overly mechanistic and allegedly dehumanizing approaches to understanding humans.

The humanistic movement in education is represented by a variety of alternative approaches to education that go by labels such as "free schools," "open classrooms," "process education," and "community-centered education." The rationale for these methods is based on a genuine concern for the welfare of children —and a firm belief that humanistic approaches are better for that welfare—and the conviction that current methods of schooling leave much to be desired. Thus, in his description of an alternative to traditional schooling, Dennison (1969) speaks of the profound beneficial effects of that alternative on the lives of students. He also criticizes (very politely) the "military discipline, the schedules, the punishments and rewards, the standardization" of more conventional approaches (p. 9). His book, however, like many similar books, is not in itself a criticism of existing educational methods but rather an attempt to describe an approach that might be better. "There is no need to add to the criticism of our public schools," Dennison informs us. "The critique is extensive and can hardly be improved upon" (p. 3).

PRINCIPLES OF HUMANISTIC EDUCATION

The concerns and goals of humanistic education and those of more traditional schools are basically compatible. All schools are concerned with the current and future welfare of students; all recognize the worth and the rights of the individual; all pay lip service to such human and humane values as openness, honesty, selflessness, and altruism. But, as we see shortly, the emphases of humanistic approaches are incompatible with the pressures of overcrowded classrooms, the regimentation and anonymity of bureaucratic educational systems, the fierce competition for academic success. Rather, these approaches strive for meaningful communication, for the exploration of values, and for the development of affect and of self. The challenge for the humanistic teacher is to remain true to these ideals in the context of a traditional classroom situation.

Common Emphases. Humanistic approaches to education are highly varied, but share a number of common emphases. Chief among them is a greater attention to thinking and feeling than to the acquisition of knowledge. In this respect they are sometimes quite different from more traditional approaches.

A second common emphasis of humanistic approaches is on development of notions of self and individual identity. For example, Borton (1970) presents a highly humanistic, three-phase teaching model designed to identify students' concerns so that students might be *reached* as individuals, *touched* or motivated as human beings, and still *taught* in a systematic fashion compatible with traditional schools. (Labels for these three phases form the title of Borton's book: *Reach, Touch, and Teach*). Similarly, Purkey (1984), also concerned with the developing self-concepts of students, draws a useful distinction between teacher behaviors that are "inviting" and those that are "disinviting." One of his major premises is that there are more students who are disinvited than disadvantaged. Disinvitation is often communicated to the child through a teacher's apparent indifference and through failure to respond to students as people. A teacher invites students by communicating to them (in any of numerous different ways) that they are valuable, able, and self-directed, and by expecting behaviors and achievements that are compatible with their worth and their self-directedness—in short, by having and communicating highly positive feelings about students. Examples of disinvitations are listed in the box entitled "Disinvited Students."

A third major emphasis is on communication. As an example, T. Gordon's (1974)

DISINVITED STUDENTS

Purkey (1984) presents a strong argument for the encouragement of teacher behaviors that *invite* students to see themselves as valuable, responsible, worthwhile, and important people. It would be naive to assume that all teachers have attitudes toward students that lend themselves to inviting behaviors. Listed here is a sample of experiences that are clearly *disinviting* in that they label students as irresponsible, incapable, or worthless—and sometimes all three (from Purkey, 1984).

The teacher said I didn't want to learn, that I just wanted to cause trouble.

She told the class we were discipline problems and were not to be trusted.

The teacher put me out in the hall for everyone to laugh at.

They put me in the dummy class, and it had SPECIAL EDUCATION painted right on the door.

The teacher said to me in front of the whole class: "I really don't think you're that stupid!"

When the principal hit me he said it was the only language I understood.

She said I was worse than my brother, and I don't even have a brother.

My name is Bill Dill, but the teacher always called me "Dill Pickle" and laughed.

I transferred to a new school after it had started. When I appeared at the teacher's doorway, she said, "Oh, no, not another one!"

Teacher Effectiveness Training (TET) program illustrates this emphasis. It presents teachers with specific advice on methods of bringing about good teacher–learner relationships, and it is based on the notion that teachers should be taught the principles and skills of "effective human relations, honest interpersonal communication, [and] constructive conflict resolution" (1974, p. ix).

A final emphasis shared by most humanistic approaches is the recognition and development of personal values. Students are encouraged to know themselves and express themselves, to strive toward feelings of self-identity, to actualize themselves (see Table 9.2).

Common Instructional Methods. These four common emphases—affect, self-development, communication, and values—lend themselves to a number of instructional methods more readily than do the more traditional emphases on mastery of academic content, good citizenship, and sportsmanship. Thus, group process approaches, rooted in the **sensitivity group** and **encounter group** movements (sometimes referred to collectively as **growth groups**), are common instructional approaches in humanistic education. In groups, students can be encouraged to express their feelings more openly, to discover and clarify these feelings, to explore interpersonal relationships, and to articulate their personal value systems. Various communication games can enhance the genuineness and openness of interpersonal relationships. Role-playing games also offer a way to explore emotions and human relationships.

Teacher Effectiveness Training (TET) Gordon's humanistic training program for teachers. It emphasizes good teacher–learner relationships, honest interpersonal communication, and conflict resolution.

growth groups A general label for group process approaches to therapy and sometimes to instruction. These typically involve the use of techniques designed to foster communication, openness, self-discovery, sharing, conflict resolution, and so on, usually in small-group settings. Also termed *sensitivity groups* or *encounter groups*.

TABLE 9.2 COMMON EMPHASES OF HUMANISTIC APPROACHES TO EDUCATION

EMPHASIS	PRACTICAL IMPLICATION
1. *Affect*	School places much greater emphasis on feeling and thinking and less on the acquisition of information
2. *Self-Concept*	One of the most important educational goals is the development of positive self-concepts in children
3. *Communication*	Teachers pay particular attention to the development of human relationships and honest interpersonal communication
4. *Personal Values*	Schools recognize the importance of personal values and try to facilitate the development of positive values

Perhaps the most important contribution humanistic concerns can make to teachers' preparation is in the realm of attitudes rather than methods. The humanistic educator strives toward a real caring for people, toward open and effective communication, and toward genuineness, empathy, and warmth.

But these are vague terms, and vagueness is not what we need; we need examples and methods. Because no matter how appealing and convincing arguments for humanizing the teaching/learning process are, if they leave us short of methods and strategies, we may pay no attention to them.

In the final sections of this chapter, we look at three alternatives to traditional education. The first—open education—is most concerned with the affective (emotional) development of students and, by that token, is most clearly humanistic. The other two alternatives—learning styles approaches and cooperative learning—although also driven by some of humanism's concerns for the individual, retain more emphasis on academic and cognitive growth.

THREE HUMANISTIC CLASSROOM APPROACHES

Schools and children don't always fit very well. As a result, the experience of going to school is not a happy and effective one for all children. As Hess and Azuma (1991) note:

Although learning is a natural process schools are not naturally conducive to learning. Children are compelled to attend; they have little choice in the content of a curriculum whose value may not be apparent; they must share the teacher's time and other resources with peers; classmates differ from one another in ability and experience, requiring many of them to deal with an instructional tempo not suited to their interest or preparation; and they are governed by a set of rules about personal acts such as talking, moving around, and attending to physical needs. In short, schools are not user-friendly (p. 2).

Different cultures react differently to the sometimes poor fit between students and schools. The Japanese culture, claim Hess and Azuma (1991), is most likely to require that students change to conform to the demands of the system. In contrast, North American cultures are more likely to try to make changes in the system to conform to the needs and wishes of students.

In spite of this, most classrooms in North America are what we might term *traditional*—that is, they are very much like the not very "user-friendly" school described by Hess and Azuma. We know what these classrooms are like; most of us have been through them. And most of us, given that we are here in this rarefied academic atmosphere—you there and me here—have not been treated too badly by this thing called traditional education.

But that alternatives exist is what this chapter is all about. In the sections that follow we look at three of them.

THE OPEN CLASSROOM

Several decades ago, a phenomenon called **open education,** or the *open classroom,* became something of a North American fad. The open classroom differs from the traditional classroom in a number of important ways. First, the principal goals of open education—specifically, individual growth, critical thinking, self-reliance, cooperation, and a commitment to lifelong learning—are not the kinds of goals that are ordinarily sought in traditional classrooms (Walberg, 1986). Second, in open education, the most important person is the student, not the teacher. And third, the open classroom typically does not adhere to the same curriculum-bound, age-locked, grade-locked system that typifies the traditional school but is instead far less formal.

The flavor of open education is perhaps best conveyed by Dennison's (1969) description of an open classroom. He describes an approach that emphasizes student-centered and intensive but relaxed teacher–pupil contact (made possible in his example by the extremely low teacher–pupil ratio). It is an approach that deemphasizes schedules—following Rousseau's notion that time is not meant to be saved but to be lost (Dennison, 1969, p. 13). The philosophy of open education, as expressed by Dennison, is that a school should be concerned with the lives of its children rather than with education in a narrow sense, that abolishing conventional classroom routines can lead to important

insights about the roles of emotions and other features of the human condition, and that running an elementary school can be a very simple thing once it is removed from "the unworkable centralization and the lust for control that permeates every bureaucratic institution" (p. 9).

It is impossible, in this short section, to fully convey the atmosphere that permeates the type of school of which Dennison speaks. Indeed, it seems futile and perhaps misleading to describe such a school as one that has no administrators, no report cards, no competitive examinations, and extremely modest facilities; where every child is treated with "consideration and justice"; where the unfolding lives of the children are the primary concern. Whereas this is an accurate description of the school, it is only a partial description. As Kohl (1969, p. 15) points out, it is difficult to say exactly what an open classroom is. Similarly, it is difficult to say what freedom is or to draw the line between chaos and student-determined order, between rebelliousness and the legitimate expression of individual rights, between wasting time and the productive use of time for activities outside the curriculum.

Open education is now rare in North America, although elements of it are found in some forms of **distance education,** where student interests are influential in determining course content, delivery, evaluation, and pacing (Norris & Pyke, 1992; Guri-Rozenblit, 1993). Interestingly, however, most of the many studies that evaluated open education and compared it with more traditional approaches found that open education was usually effective in reaching its most important goals; that is, students exposed to open classrooms typically had better self-concepts and were more creative

---

open education A student-centered alternative to traditional education that emphasizes personal growth, independence, and cooperation, and that is not committed to the curriculum-bound, pass–fail, age-locked, grade-locked system of the traditional school. Also termed *open classroom.*

distance education An educational delivery system that involves little or no face-to-face contact, but where instructional material is presented at a distance, often using one or more of a combination of computers, electronic networking facilities, telephone conferencing, facsimile transmitters, radio, television, film, videocassette recordings, or other communication media.

and cooperative (see, for example, Horwitz, 1979). However, these gains were usually at the expense of academic achievement as defined by more traditional measures. And, given a zeitgeist* that appears to emphasize academic achievement, open learning systems are not highly popular at present.

THE LEARNING STYLES APPROACH

In discussing traditional education, Dunn and Griggs claim: "The system works well for some, but not for others" (1988, p. 1). Why?

Different Styles. Because, Dunn and Griggs explain, some students do not learn at all well in the morning but perform very well in the afternoon. Some work well in bright, noisy environments; others do their best work in quiet places with subdued lighting. Some excel with highly structured, teacher-directed instructional methods; others do far better in informal, unstructured environments. Some students need and want to be told what to do and when and how to do it; others perform best when working on their own initiative. In short, each student has a personal and unique **learning style.** Some of these are evident in clearly different preferences with respect to variables like time of day, method of presentation, the physical and the sociological learning environment (for example, individual versus group instruction) (Klavas, 1994).

---

*PPC: Is the bear German? Why does he use such a big word? Maybe he should explain it.

AUTHOR: Okay. *Zeitgeist* means something like spirit of the times. As for the bear's ancestry—well, the less said the better.

---

learning style A unique and important learner variable manifested in differences in biological rhythms (morning versus evening people), perceptual strengths (visual versus auditory learners), sociological preference (whole-group versus small-group instruction), attention span (long or short), and a wealth of personality variables (dependence or independence, for example).

Unfortunately, traditional schools do not often take individual learning styles into account. As a result, they reward students whose personal styles happen to match that for which the traditional school was designed—and, by the same token, they unwittingly punish those whose rhythms are sounded on a different drum. Students whose biological rhythms make it difficult to concentrate in the morning must nevertheless come to school and sit through the same offerings as everyone else. Those who respond best to visual stimuli—or to tactile stimulation—are forced to listen as much as those who are more responsive to auditory stimuli. Children with shorter attention spans are compelled to sit as long as those who are not so easily distracted.

This situation is not fair, argue Dunn, Dunn, and Perrin (1994); it is not an optimal learning situation. Schools, they insist, must take into account these fundamentally important differences in learning styles. But how?

Adapting Schools to Styles. First, schools need to develop a profile of each student's learning styles. A number of instruments are available for this purpose, including Gregorc's (1982) Style Delineator and Renzulli and Smith's (1978) Learning Styles Inventory. The Gregorc instrument provides a measure of perceptual strengths (how people obtain information, including a concrete/abstract dimension) and differentiates among learners on the basis of their predispositions toward reason, emotion, and intuition. It also looks at the individual's preferred ways of dealing with and ordering information.

The Renzulli and Smith inventory is designed to help teachers customize their instructional procedures to match individual learners' attitudes toward such common instructional procedures as lectures, simulations, discussions, projects, games, drills, recitations, peer teaching, independent study, and programmed instruction.

Another approach, described by Reay (1994), classifies learners in terms of whether they are *activists, reflectors, theorists,* or *pragmatists.*

TABLE 9.3 ONE CLASSIFICATION OF LEARNERS AND POSSIBLE INSTRUCTIONAL STRATEGIES

TYPE OF LEARNER	CHARACTERISTICS	PREFERENCES	INSTRUCTIONAL APPROACHES
Activists	Impetuous; impulsive; open-minded; flexible	Variety; excitement; involvement; activity	Group processes; activity-based learning
Reflectors	Cautious; careful; deliberate; judicious	Evidence; time to think and reflect; opportunity to deliberate	Private study; reading assignments; self-paced learning
Theorists	Logical and rational; disciplined; inquisitive; objective	Rationality; coherence; careful explanation; models and theories	Computer-based instruction; conceptual models; scientific approaches
Pragmatists	Practical and down to earth; applied	Eager to try things out; new ideas and methods; practical solutions and applications	Supervised experience; hands-on experience; personal coaching

Source: Based on Reay (1994).

Characteristics associated with each of these types of learners, and the best instructional approaches for each, are described in Table 9.3.

Identifying individual learning styles is only the beginning; dramatic changes are required in schools and in teachers' behavior if schools are to be truly responsive to students' individual differences. Dunn and Griggs (1988) visited ten schools at which attention to learning styles had become the determining factor in educational offerings. Although there were many differences among these schools, they had a number of things in common. A description of these is, in a sense, an idealized description of a humanistic school.

The Learning Styles-Driven School. This idealized school gives learners an almost staggering assortment of options. It allows children to work alone on soft carpets or to work in groups at conference tables. It provides highly structured teacher-presented lessons, peer teaching, programmed instruction, computer-assisted instruction, and self-learning. It rotates presentation of core subjects so that they are offered at all times of the day, including early in the morning and later in the afternoon. It allows students to take examinations and do projects at times that are compatible with their biological rhythms.

The idealized humanistic, learning style–driven school is identifiable not only by its attention to differences among individual learners but also by its values and objectives. Far more than the traditional school, it stresses students' involvement at all stages of learning, and it emphasizes problem solving and creativity.

Finally, this idealized school's most common instructional technique, especially for presenting new material, is a highly participatory, cooperative, small-group approach that is sometimes called **circles of knowledge.** This approach is described in the next section, which discusses cooperative learning.

This brief description of the translation of learning styles information into classroom practice cannot do justice to the complexity of the topic. There is no single, best program that

---

circles of knowledge A generic term sometimes used to describe a variety of small-group learning approaches. These approaches stress face-to-face interaction, peer help, and rewards for cooperative, group activities rather than for individual activity. Such approaches are highly cooperative rather than competitive or individualistic.

we can describe simply and accurately; programs continue to change and develop. As we noted, most require profound changes in schools and in teachers, and the changes required must be continual. They involve experimentation in and modification and clarification of programs, as well as refocusing of objectives and of efforts, and on and on.

Evaluation of Learning Styles Approaches. We cannot begin to evaluate the effectiveness of this approach, other than very tentatively. Dunn and Griggs (1988) report that in the ten learning styles-driven schools they visited, learners performed exceptionally well on a variety of measures of academic performance. Some had won national awards, and many had succeeded in passing subjects they had previously failed. And most said they liked—no, loved—school.

In general, notes Guild (1994), the research indicates that students of all learning styles can succeed academically. But it also indicates that students tend to do better when the instructional approaches to which they are exposed allow them to use the strengths of their personal learning styles. Not surprisingly, then, good teaching requires far more than a single instructional approach.

Unfortunately, as Snow and Swanson (1992) note, the current lists of learning styles, and the instruments used to measure them, are unorganized, lengthy, and include a large range of habits, personality characteristics, and abilities. For example, in a short booklet, Reiff (1992) describes several dozen different learning styles that have been identified in the literature. And research has not yet established whether any of them are useful. Nor has it shown clearly which specific instructional approaches are best with which styles and under what circumstances this might be so. Learning styles, argue Thompson and Crutchlow (1993) are an important factor for teachers to consider; but they are only one factor, and their impact may well be overrated in the enthusiasm that often accompanies educational movements.

Perhaps when the bear is a very, very old bear, history will look back and say, "Hey, that learning styles stuff just before the turn of the millennium was another one of those educational fads, like open schools and teaching machines." Or maybe, just maybe, history's judgment will be "Hey, just before the millennium—that's when it all started."

COOPERATIVE LEARNING

According to Johnson and Johnson (1994), teachers have three basic choices: "In every classroom, no matter what the subject area," they write, "teachers may structure lessons so that students:

1. engage in a win–lose struggle to see who is best (competitive)

2. work independently on their own learning goals at their own pace and in their own space to achieve a preset criterion of excellence (individualistic)

3. work cooperatively in small groups, ensuring that all members master the assigned material (cooperative)" (1994, p. 3).

Unfortunately, these authors claim, most students see schools as competitive because that is how grades are typically assigned. Not everyone can do well; in order to achieve at the highest level, students must compete with, and outachieve, the others. And when schools are not competitive, they are most often individualistic; that is, students are urged to work toward the attainment of their own individual goals—without help, proudly and independently! Only rarely are school experiences truly cooperative, where, as Cohen (1994) puts it, students work "together in a group small enough that everyone can participate on a collective task that has been clearly assigned . . . [and where] students are expected to carry out their task without direct and immediate supervision of the teacher" (p. 3).

Another way of distinguishing among these three alternatives is in terms of rewards

Humanistic classrooms are a highly student-centered alternative to more formal traditional approaches. They are often marked by low pupil-teacher ratios, a cooperative rather than a competitive orientation, and a more relaxed atmosphere.

(Bossert, 1988). In a **cooperative learning** situation (also termed **collaborative learning**), the individual is rewarded in proportion to others in the group; in a **competitive learning** situation, individual rewards are inversely related to those others receive; and in an **individualistic learning** situation, there is no relationship among individual rewards.

---

cooperative learning An instructional method in which students work together in small groups so that each member of the group can participate in a clearly assigned, collective task. Also termed *collaborative learning*. (See also *competitive learning*, *individualistic learning*.)

competitive learning One of the most common instructional approaches in North America. Involves students working against each other to see who is best. In competitive learning, student rewards are inversely related to the performance of others.

individualistic learning A common instructional approach in which students work independently and at their own pace, and in which student rewards are independent of the performance of other students.

Occasionally, some schools present a few activities that are cooperative. Only rarely do schools and teachers make cooperative learning a fundamental part of their instruction. Schools that do, claim Schniedewind and Davidson (1988), are humanistic schools because cooperative learning is essentially a humanistic approach to education. It combines the cognitive and affective aspects of learning, and it emphasizes participation and active engagement, both of which are humanistic concerns. But perhaps more than other explicitly humanistic approaches, cooperative learning also stresses academic achievement and clearly defined curricular goals. In most schools that use cooperative learning methods, students do not have the unstructured freedom that they might be given in an open classroom, nor does the system cater to their personal strengths and preferences as it might in a school organized to respond to individual learning styles.

The Rationale for Cooperative Learning. Why is it important to learn to cooperate? Advocates of this approach present a variety of reasons. Among the most compelling is the nagging suspicion that it is our only hope for salvation—that if we do not learn to cooperate, we and our planet are doomed.

There are other reasons why we must learn to cooperate—if survival does not seem sufficiently important, or if our doom seems too distant, or if we simply prefer not to think about it. Cooperation, Bossert (1988) tells us, is the cornerstone of modern democracy. Nations cannot be governed without cooperation among leaders; cooperation is essential for political and economic survival.

At a more immediate level, teaching cooperation in the schools might do much to reduce students' dependence on teachers and to decrease divisiveness and prejudice among students. Cooperative learning, Johnson and Johnson (1994) claim, may resolve two important crises: declining academic performance and pervasive feelings of alienation, isolation, purposelessness, and social unease among students.

Another reason for using cooperative learning is that it works. In Snow and Swanson's words, "The evidence clearly shows its effectiveness in achieving cognitive goals, but the methods also promote more positive attitudes toward school, improved student self-esteem, and improved relations among different types of students" (1992, p. 612).

Finally, students prefer cooperative approaches. When researchers asked students from three different cultures (Germany, Canada, and Iran) which approach to learning they most preferred, they chose cooperative learning (Huber et al., 1992).

Features of Cooperative Learning. Cooperative learning occurs when students work together to achieve a common goal. Unlike competitive learning, rewards depend not on doing better than someone else but on doing well *with* someone else.

Although there are a variety of approaches to cooperative learning in the classroom, most have a number of features in common (Johnson & Johnson, 1994; Slavin, 1995):

▶ Cooperative learning requires face-to-face interaction among group members—usually four to six students.

▶ The relationship among group members can be described as one of positive interdependence; that is, members must cooperate in allocating resources, assigning roles, and dividing labor if they are to achieve their goals.

▶ Cooperative learning usually assigns some degree of individual responsibility for sharing, cooperating, and learning. Accordingly, various techniques are used to ensure that goals and rewards are contingent on the performance and contribution of all group members.

▶ Cooperative learning involves the use of interpersonal and small group skills, such as those involved in taking turns, facilitating, collaborating, and so on.

A large number of cooperative group activities have been developed and used in schools. They have a variety of names but are sometimes included under the generic labels "circles of knowledge" or "circles of learning." Although each activity is distinct from the others, all share the common features described earlier, the most important of which is the interdependence of group members.

Learning Together. One of the most widely used cooperative instructional techniques is **learning together,** developed by Johnson and Johnson (see Johnson et al., 1984). In learning together, groups of four to six students are given a lesson or worksheet that they must learn or complete together. Members must help each other to ensure that everyone learns the lesson or completes the assignment. Members of each group are also encouraged to help other groups once they have completed the assignment. Praise is given for cooperating and finishing the assignment. In this approach, there is no competition among groups. Learning together emphasizes four things: (1) face-to-face interaction (students are in groups of four to six); (2) postitive interdependence (students work together to achieve a common goal); (3) individual accountability (all students must later demonstrate that each has mastered and understands the material); and (4) interpersonal and small-group skills (students are taught how to work together and how to evaluate the functioning of their groups).

Student Teams–Achievement Divisions (STAD). **Student teams–achievement divisions (STAD)** is one of several forms of student "team learning," in which individual groups are teams that

---

learning together A cooperative instructional technique in which groups of four to six students work together on a jointly assigned task using small-group interaction skills, and in which each member of the group is individually responsible for mastering the material.

compete against one another (Slavin, 1995). In STAD, students are divided into heterogeneous teams of four to six students. Ideally, each team includes high- and low-ability children, children of different ethnic backgrounds, and children of both sexes. The instructional technique typically involves five steps:

1. *Presentation*. New material is typically presented to the class using conventional approaches like lectures, discussions, and videos.

2. *Teamwork*. Groups are given material to study and worksheets to complete. They can work on these individually, in pairs, or in larger groups. They are encouraged to help each other and to make sure that everybody understands and knows the material, the emphasis being on the performance of the team.

3. *Quizzes*. At the end of the study period, which typically lasts a week, students write quizzes based on that week's material—individually, and without helping each other.

4. *Individual improvement scores*. Team scores are then calculated. And although recognition is given to teams that obtain the highest total scores, winning teams are those whose individuals improved the most. In that way, lower-achieving students can contribute as much to the team's total score as more able students (sometimes even more).

5. *Team recognition*. Teams are then rewarded, perhaps with certificates, tokens, prizes, and praise. Team scores may also be used as a factor in determining individual grades.

STAD produces dramatic changes in the classroom, claims Slavin (1995). "[Students] begin to see learning activities as social instead of isolated, fun instead of boring, under their own control instead of the teacher's" (1983, p. 7). Also, he claims, they now help each other learn instead of resenting those who learn more easily or making fun of those who learn with more difficulty.

Teams–Games–Tournaments (TGT). **Teams–games–tournaments (TGT)** begin in exactly the same way as STAD, with the same teams, instructional sessions, and cooperative learning sequence. The difference is that at the end, students engage in tournaments rather than in quizzes. In these tournaments, team members are assigned not as a group, but as individuals, to a table. Each table consists of three competitors of approximately equal ability (as selected by instructors). Games occur at all tables simultaneously and involve drawing numbered cards, trying to answer questions corresponding to the numbers on the cards, and challenging incorrect answers. Players retain cards when they answer (or challenge) correctly and lose them for incorrect challenges. At the end of the game (or period), points are assigned according to the number of cards in each player's possession, and total tournament points are computed for each team.

More complete rules for TGT can be found in Slavin (1995). Materials for STAD and TGT are available for a wide range of subjects in elementary and secondary schools from The Johns Hopkins Team Learning Project, Center for Social Organization School, Johns Hopkins University, 3505 North Charles St., Baltimore, Md. 21218 (410-338-8249).

---

student teams–achievement divisions (STAD) A cooperative instructional technique in which students are assigned to heterogeneous groups of four to six (including high- and low-ability students and different ethnic groups) to work on certain tasks, after which they are given quizzes (to be answered individually, without cooperation) and rewarded *by team* on the basis of the group's performance on the quizzes.

teams–games–tournaments (TGT) A cooperative instructional technique identical to student teams–achievement divisions (STAD) except that instead of being given quizzes at the end, students play tournaments of competitive games that center around content-relevant questions.

Jigsaw. In **jigsaw,** developed by Aronson and colleagues (1978), the material to be learned is divided into separate units. Individual members of the group are then given separate, *different,* parts of the whole to learn, and they must teach what they have learned to other members of the group. No one member is given sufficient information to solve the problem at hand or complete the assignment in question, but when all the information is put together—Voilà!* The jigsaw is complete.

In a modification of the original jigsaw, labeled "jigsaw II," students are given the *same* narrative material to read rather than different parts of the whole, a procedure that eliminates the need to prepare a lot of different material. Individual students are then assigned the responsibility for mastering different topics. They are encouraged to discuss these with members of other teams who have been assigned the same topics, and then return to their own teams to teach their teammates what they have learned. Hence the central feature of jigsaw is the interdependence of team members; performing well depends on how well individual members learn and teach their topics. As in STAD, teams are given quizzes and rewarded on the basis of team performance, taking into account individual improvement scores.

Group Investigation. Group investigation, described by Sharan and Sharan (1992), is a cooperative technique that combines academic scholarship and inquiry with the principles of cooperation. Using this approach, students in a class select an area for study, typically some problem that lends itself to investigation. The area is then divided into subtopics, and the class divides itself into small groups of investigators on the basis of shared interest in a topic. Each group then formulates a plan by which to investigate and assigns responsibilities. Members can now work individually, in pairs, or as larger groups. Having completed their inquiry—perhaps over a period of some weeks—group members meet and share the fruits of their investigations. They decide, as well, how to present their integrated information to other members of the class. Finally, all groups meet for the final sharing of information. Throughout the process, teachers are involved in guiding students, helping them with both the academic skills required for successful inquiry and the social skills involved in group processes.

Implementation of Cooperative Learning Techniques. The techniques just described are only a few of the many that have been developed and evaluated. For those interested in still more approaches, the Suggested Readings section at the end of this chapter lists important sources of information.

Unlike the learning styles approach, cooperative learning does not require a major restructuring of the school day or a reordering of curriculum offerings. Whereas the learning styles approach attempts to cater to individual differences in learning styles and learning preferences, cooperative group methods typically include all students simultaneously. In fact, one advantage of cooperative approaches is that they foster cooperation among students with different strengths and weaknesses and perhaps those of different ethnic backgrounds, ages, and sexes.

Cooperative learning techniques are most often introduced as an adjunct to regular class-

---

*PPC: Ha ha! A bilingual bear!
THE BEAR: But of course!

---

jigsaw A cooperative instructional technique in which individual members of groups are given the responsibility for mastering different aspects of specific tasks and teaching them to other members of their group. The key feature of jigsaw is that successful performance depends on the different contributions of each member.

group investigation A collaborative instructional technique in which students identify topics and related sources of information, form themselves into groups on the basis of shared interests, assign responsibility for collecting material, gather and study relevant material alone and in groups, prepare group reports, and present these to the class.

room offerings. In a typical situation, they might be used for 60 or 90 minutes a day. However, the most vocal advocates of this approach recommend that as much as 70 percent of class time involve cooperative activities, with 20 percent devoted to individualistic approaches and only 10 percent to competitive activities (Johnson & Johnson, 1975).

Although cooperative approaches normally make up only a small part of the total curriculum, their implementation usually requires careful materials preparation. Depending on the specific approach used, the teacher will need to prepare worksheets, questions, resource materials, and so on, all carefully structured to foster cooperation while promoting learning.

Evaluation of Cooperative Learning. How well do these cooperative techniques work? Johnson and colleagues (1981) analyzed 122 studies that had examined cooperative learning. Most of these studies contain direct comparisons between specific cooperative approaches and traditional classroom instruction. Johnson and associates conclude that cooperative learning leads to better achievement at virtually all grade and age levels studied and for all subjects. They suggest that increases in achievement occur because group discussion and cooperation promote discovery, lead to the development of higher-quality cognitive strategies, increase motivation to learn, increase comprehension by requiring students to teach each other, enrich the learning experience by blending students of a variety of ability levels and experiences, and promote highly positive relationships among group members. This last statement is also supported by results of a study involving a school with a mixture of Israeli and Arab students in which students exposed to a cooperative approach not only performed better academically than those exposed only to a traditional approach but also displayed far fewer signs of ethnic tension in their language (Sharan & Shachar, 1988).

A direct comparison of competitive and cooperative instructional approaches is provided by a meta-analysis of forty-six different studies (Qin, Johnson, & Johnson, 1995). Taken together, these studies indicate that members of cooperative teams typically outperform those in more competitive situations, regardless of whether achievement is measured in terms of verbal or nonverbal performance and whether the problems used to assess achievement are highly structured and clear or more poorly defined.

A more recent study corroborates many of these positive findings (Stevens & Slavin, 1995). In this study, which spanned a two-year period, an entire elementary school switched to a cooperative instructional philosophy; this study is in marked contrast to the majority of studies that have typically been short term and have involved only one or two teachers. In this school, cooperative learning approaches were used extensively in all academic subjects. In addition, disabled students were mainstreamed throughout the school and were also closely involved in cooperative learning. As well, teachers were encouraged to use collaborative approaches in their instructional planning—for example, peer coaching, as well as direct collaboration with parents and the principal. The results? After the second year of this program, both the academically handicapped and the nonhandicapped students achieved at significantly higher levels in reading vocabulary, reading comprehension, language expression, math computation, and math application. Furthermore, the gifted students also seemed to benefit significantly, outperforming their peers in noncooperative programs.

In general, much of the research supports this positive evaluation. Cooperative learning approaches most often result in measurably superior academic performance (Patrick, 1994), higher motivation (Nichols & Miller, 1994), greater interest in school (Elmore & Zenus, 1994), and better relations among students (Patterson, 1994). However, Bossert (1988) suggests that some of the positive academic effects of cooperative learning may owe more to the fact that lessons typically are more highly structured and more systematic than simply to peer interaction.

Why Cooperation Works. Dividing classes into groups may not always be the most effective way to teach. In fact, on occasion, and for some students, it does not work. Nor is it appropriate for all subjects and all lessons, note Roy and Hoch (1994). In addition, it's possible for students to work *in* groups but not *as* groups. Students working in groups but not as groups can easily waste time talking about irrelevant matters or develop procedures wherein some group members dominate and others are ignored.

Research and theory clearly emphasize that two things are essential if cooperative learning is to work (for example, Slavin, 1995; Stevens & Slavin, 1995): (1) incentive to cooperate and (2) individual accountability. In most applications of cooperative learning—such as STAD or TGT, for example—group recognition and/or interteam competition provide the incentive. And there is individual accountability to the extent that group or team performance depends on the performance of each individual in the group.

Vygotsky's (1978) theory suggests yet another reason why cooperative learning might work. Learning, he claims, is highly dependent on social interaction. To a large extent, it depends on interactions with others who are better informed, and the results of learning are manifested in social interaction as well. Furthermore, learning—and all higher mental processes—depend on language. One of the great contributions of cooperative group learning is that it fosters the development and exercise of language skills.

To Cooperate or Not? Cooperative learning, it seems, can be highly effective in imparting academic content and strategies and also seems to have beneficial effects on the social development and interpersonal relationships of students. S. L. Mueller (1992) reports that it also enhances self-esteem and the learner's sense of purpose and autonomy. Does this mean that all teachers and schools should now become cooperative—that is, entirely cooperative? (See "How Should I Teach?")

Bossert (1988) advises caution. Even though it seems clear that cooperative approaches have substantial academic and social benefits, they also have some disadvantages. For example, low-achieving students are sometimes embarrassed by their performances and ashamed of the fact that they lower the group's score. As a result, they may become progressively more reluctant to participate in cooperative activities as their motivation and self-concepts deteriorate. The long-term effects of this situation might be lower achievement for these students—and perhaps lower achievement for their groups as well. However, the use of performance improvement as the basis for scores, as is done in STAD and TGT, may do much to invalidate this caution.

Bossert also cautions that those who advocate that cooperative techniques should be the dominant feature of classroom activity may be overlooking the possibility that one reason cooperative learning is effective is precisely because it presents a clear contrast to conventional classroom procedures. The shifts in attention and in procedures required of students serve to increase concentration, to motivate, and ultimately to enhance performance. But if all or most classroom activity were cooperative, these shifts might not occur, and performance might not improve so dramatically—if at all.

Finally, Bossert (1988) argues that even though it is important for children to learn to cooperate with one another, it is also important to learn competitive and individualistic skills.

It is worth noting, as well, that there are certain situations and subjects that don't lend themselves particularly well to cooperative, group approaches. For example, expert contributions (sometimes in the form of guest speakers) may be far more efficient and effective as didactic presentations. In addition, some students' individual preferences—in other words, their learning styles—favor individual or competitive rather than cooperative approaches.

HOW SHOULD I TEACH?

The school system that hires you (and that also can fire you) will almost certainly operate within a relatively well-defined set of regulations governing the conduct of teachers in classrooms, prescribed curricula, reporting and testing procedures, disciplinary actions, and so on. Yet, in the final analysis, you will determine your own approach to teaching; you will develop your own personal style of interacting with students. No one is likely to force you to violate personal conviction. And if you firmly believe in the importance of the right of all children in your care to be treated as human beings and to be allowed to develop in such a way as to enhance their human qualities, it might happen that you will be frustrated by the system (or by your interpretation of that system).

Many humanistic alternatives work within even the most traditional school contexts. If you want to know more about them, you would be well advised to read some of the references annotated at the end of this chapter.

SOME REACTIONS TO HUMANISTIC EDUCATION

To the extent that humanistic education represents concern for the individual lives and self-concepts of students and concern for the healthiest and happiest development of human potential, it is beyond reproach. All teachers must be humanistic.

However, humanistic education too often appears to deal with vague qualities and speculative conclusions. Terms such as *authentic, open, real, genuine, fully functioning,* and *meaningful* are often meaningless. How do you distinguish between an authentic experience and one that is not authentic? between a genuine teacher and an impostor? between a fully functioning student and one who is only three-quarters functioning? Unfortunately, although these terms are vague, they seem to represent good things and are therefore highly appealing. Equally unfortunate, the things they represent cannot be easily defined or measured, and as a consequence the evidence upon which advocates of humanistic reforms base their arguments is not always convincing.

Perhaps the most telling criticism of general humanistic approaches to teaching is that most are highly dependent upon the personal qualities and skills of individual teachers. More conventional approaches to classroom practice are, in this respect, much more "teacher proof."

These criticisms are not entirely fair, however. They apply primarily to global approaches to humanistic education, such as those represented by "open" (or what have sometimes been called "free") schools. As we saw earlier, evidence from research suggests that although students who emerge from these schools appear to be more creative and more cooperative and have better self-concepts, these gains typically come at the expense of academic achievement. A large-scale evaluation in the United States found that these students performed more poorly than comparison groups on almost all achievement measures (Kennedy, 1978) (although few of these measures tap creative-thinking skills, the ability to reason logically, or other important personality characteristics). Perhaps it is not surprising that most of these schools have now closed. We should note, however, that various forms of nongraded schools (no age or grade placement and no graded report cards) can have positive effects on student achievement (Gutiérrez & Slavin, 1992). But these schools are somewhat different from open schools in that they typically present a structured curriculum but in an ungraded, no-fail environment.

These criticisms of humanistic education—of vagueness, overattention to affective growth, and disregard of both standard curricula and cognitive development—are not relevant with respect to two expressions of humanistic concerns detailed in this chapter: learning styles-oriented schools and cooperative learning. As we saw, both approaches can lead to superior academic achievement. Interestingly, among the important techniques of learning styles schools are the group methods that define cooperative learning.

One of the reasons why various humanistic, student-centered approaches to instruction have been criticized, notes Waterhouse (1991), is that instructors have often been guilty of what he terms "technical mistakes" and mistaken assumptions about humanistic education. Chief among these are:

▶ The belief that students should immediately be granted complete autonomy

▶ The belief that the best instructional plans are always tailored for specific individuals (rather than for entire classes)

▶ The belief that student-centered instruction requires special material

▶ The belief that humanistic education should be highly permissive

▶ The belief that traditional instruction must be abandoned to make way for humanistic approaches

It is extremely important to bear in mind that humanism is not a specific educational technique, although it manifests itself most clearly in specific techniques. In effect, humanism is an educational philosophy characterized by the sorts of admirable attitudes toward students and toward educational goals that should be characteristic of all teachers. These attitudes, as mentioned earlier, are not subject to the same criticisms that have been applied so generously to specific humanistic approaches to education. In the end, it may not be important to copy the models or take the advice presented by the more visible of humanistic educators.

What is important is that you genuinely care about students as people.

THE LAST WORD—FROM WATSON!

It may seem strange to conclude a discussion of humanism by referring to the recognized initiator and principal spokesman for the position usually considered most directly opposed to humanism. Interestingly, however, some of the writings of John B. Watson describe a highly humanistic society. More than six decades ago, Watson concluded a book with a section entitled "Behaviorism as a Guide for All Future Experimental Ethics" (1930, pp. 303–304):

> Behaviorism ought to be a science that prepares men and women for understanding the principles of their own behavior. It ought to make men and women eager to rearrange their own lives, and especially eager to prepare themselves to bring up their own children in a healthy way. I wish I could picture for you what a rich and wonderful individual we could make of every healthy child if only we could let it shape itself properly and then provide for it a universe in which it could exercise that organization—a universe unshackled by legendary folklore of happenings thousands of years ago; unhampered by disgraceful political history; free of foolish

customs and conventions which have no significance in themselves, yet which hem the individual in like taut steel bands. I am not asking here for revolution; I am not asking people to go out to some God-forsaken place, form a colony, go naked and live a communal life, nor am I asking for a change to a diet of roots and herbs. I am not asking for "free love." I am trying to dangle a stimulus in front of you, a verbal stimulus which, if acted upon, will gradually change this universe. For the universe will change if you bring up your children, not in the freedom of the libertine, but in behavioristic freedom—a freedom which we cannot even picture in words, so little do we know of it. Will not these children in turn, with their better ways of living and thinking, replace us as society and in turn bring up their children in a still more scientific way, until the world finally becomes a place fit for human habitation?

MAIN POINTS

1. Humanistic psychology is concerned with the uniqueness, the worth, and the dignity of the self. It presents an ideological conflict with the more mechanistic orientation of other approaches. It also objects to the school's emphasis on academic achievement and its neglect of affective growth.

2. Carl Rogers' theory is phenomenological (the phenomenal world is the environment as it is perceived by one individual), humanistic (concerned with the individual, with self-actualization), and student centered. His position is opposed to Skinner's expressed concern with control through the application of the principles of operant learning.

3. Rogers believes that an individual's real world is private (phenomenological), the purpose of behavior is to achieve self-actualization (development of maximum potential), self-actualization is related to healthy and creative functioning, and the development of the "self" results from interactions with the world (direct experience) and from values about the "me" that are borrowed from the actions of other people (indirect experience).

4. Rogerian theory suggests that in order to promote full, healthy functioning, schools should be student centered. The instructional procedures that Rogers sees as best for these schools are discovery oriented.

5. The major emphases of humanistic approaches are greater attention to thinking and feeling than to the acquisition of knowledge, the development of self, communication, the clarification of values, openness, honesty, and self-determination. Group process and cooperative approaches to education are most compatible with these emphases.

6. Open education is most concerned with the affective growth of students—with critical thinking, self-reliance, and commitment to learning. It is student rather than teacher centered, typically ungraded, and emphasizes personal growth rather than measurable academic achievement. Research suggests that graduates of open schools may be more creative, more cooperative, and have better self-concepts—but they usually score lower by traditional academic measures.

7. Learning styles are individual preferences and strengths as they relate to the best conditions for learning (for example, morning versus evening; visual, auditory, or kinesthetic; individual versus group; structured versus unstructured; and so on).

8. Learning styles-driven schools develop profiles for individual students and attempt to match instructional methods, curriculum offerings, scheduling, and other aspects of instruction to each

learner's personal style. Students in learning styles schools appear to do very well on standard academic measures.

9. Cooperative learning involves small-group techniques structured so that learners are rewarded for the group's results but are nevertheless individually responsible for learning and for helping other members of the group to learn. It is characterized by face-to-face interaction, positive interdependence, individual responsibility, and the use of interpersonal and small-group skills.

10. Some techniques for cooperative learning include learning together (pure cooperation, common goal, no intergroup competition), student teams–achievement divisions (STAD) (groups are teams that compete against each other on the basis of performance improvement), teams–games–tournaments (TGT) (STADlike procedure but with three-member head-to-head competitions following learning), jigsaw (each group member given only part of the information; interaction with whole required to solve a problem or learn a lesson), and group investigation (whole class investigates single inquiry-type problem by dividing in groups for investigation and coming together to integrate and share).

11. Evidence suggests that cooperative learning techniques lead to superior academic achievement, high motivation, and the enhancement of social skills. These positive effects may be due partly to the greater curriculum structure required for cooperative learning and to the contrast these approaches present to the traditional classroom. They may also be due to the language and social skills they foster. They are most effective when two conditions are met: Students are given incentive to cooperate, and learners are individually accountable for their learning outcomes.

12. General humanistic approaches to education are often highly dependent upon individual teachers' qualities and sometimes use vague and speculative terms. Humanism in education is less vulnerable to criticism as an attitude or philosophy than as a technique—and as an attitude it is perhaps more valuable to teachers. In this sense, all teachers should be humanistic.

APPLIED QUESTIONS

▶ Compare and contrast the educational implications of humanism and behaviorism.

▶ Can you describe the principal beliefs and attitudes of a prototypical humanistic educator?

▶ List some of the characteristics that might differentiate an open classroom from a more conventional classroom.

▶ What is your preferred learning style? How would you outline the educational approach(es) most compatible with it?

▶ Prepare a lesson that incorporates one or more specific cooperative learning techniques.

STUDY TERMS

Suggested Readings

The following revision of Carl Rogers' classic book not only describes his theory but also describes classrooms that put his ideas into practice. It includes many vignettes and interviews with teachers, and many useful suggestions for teaching and for developing discipline:

ROGERS, C. R., & FREIBERG, H. J. (1994). *Freedom to learn* (4th ed.). New York: Merrill.

The learning styles approach to education is well described in the following two books. The first is a detailed and highly practical description of the learning styles approach; the second is a brief booklet explaining a large variety of approaches for identifying student learning styles and suggesting ways teachers can accommodate them:

DUNN, R., DUNN, K., & PERRIN, J. (1994). *Teaching young children through their individual learning styles: Practical approaches for grades K–2.* Boston: Allyn & Bacon.

REIFF, J. C. (1992). *Learning styles.* Washington, D.C.: National Education Association.

The book by Johnson and Johnson is an excellent description of cooperative learning and of a number of different schools that use this approach. Slavin's book describes specific approaches to cooperative learning, including sample exercises and classroom examples. The collection edited by Sharan contains many articles written by people who have developed and applied cooperative instructional approaches:

JOHNSON, D. W., & JOHNSON, R. T. (1994). *Learning together and alone: Cooperative, competitive, and individualistic learning* (4th ed.). Boston: Allyn & Bacon.

SLAVIN, R. E. (1995). *Cooperative learning: Theory, research, and practice* (2nd ed.). Boston: Allyn & Bacon.

SHARAN, S. (ed.). (1994). *Handbook of cooperative learning methods.* Westport, Conn.: Greenwood Press.

The Laplanders venerated the bear and called it the Dog of God. The Norwegians called it "the old man with the fur cloak" (Engel, 1976).

PART FIVE

I have measured out my life with coffee spoons.

T. S. ELIOT, *Love Song of J. Alfred Prufrock*

More Effective Instruction

WE DON'T OFTEN USE *coffee spoons to measure out our students. We use other measures: tests, scales, checklists, questionnaires, anecdotes, portfolios, observations . . . and on and on. Teaching is not a simple business. There are hundreds of choices to be made. And the nitty-gritty of classroom practice requires much more than what we have gleaned from educational psychology and reported in the preceding chapters. Among other things, it demands of the teacher interpersonal and management skills of the highest order; it requires patience and imagination, a measure of genius and a touch of humility, enthusiasm and warmth, and other good things often more characteristic of angels than of teachers. The four chapters in the last part discuss these and related topics.*

CHAPTER 10

Motivation and Teaching

Boredom is a sign of satisfied ignorance, blunted apprehension, crass sympathies, dull understanding, feeble powers of attention and irreclaimable weakness of character.

JAMES BRIDIE, *Mr. Bolfry*

Persons attempting to find a motive in this narrative will be prosecuted; persons attempting to find a moral in it will be banished; persons attempting to find a plot in it will be shot.

MARK TWAIN, *Huckleberry Finn,*
INTRODUCTION

PREVIEW

My grandmother, an astute observer of human affairs, spent much of her knitting and quilting time in quiet contemplation of human motives. "Why do geese go south and ravens stay?" she would mutter as her needles clicked. "Why did Réné go out in the storm?" "Why does Frank study so hard and Lucille won't do zip?" "Why doesn't Robert want to go to school anymore?" This chapter might have been of some value to her, although the questions it examines are surely no more important than the questions she asked. But it does provide some answers for why we do or don't do things and some suggestions for teachers, whose role in motivating students can hardly be overstated.

FOCUS QUESTIONS

▶ How valid and useful are instinct-based and hedonistic explanations of human behavior?

▶ What is arousal theory? What are its educational implications?

▶ How are extrinsic and intrinsic motivation related?

▶ What is Maslow's humanistic theory of motivation?

▶ What is self-efficacy? attribution theory?

Most of the time, I was about as average a student as there was in that high school—although I spent a lot of time looking through the windows, hoping to see a bear. The nun who taught us, Sister Ste. Mélanie, didn't much care about that as long as people did their work and paid enough attention to answer the odd question.

I spent a lot of time looking at girls, too. Always had, I think, starting back with Gloria in third grade. But that had never alarmed any of the grownups, who recognized and dismissed it as chronic puppy love. But about halfway through that first year of high school, I discovered the incomparable Clarisse. When the good sisters first noticed me turning my mongrel eyes on Clarisse, they apparently decided it was no longer a canine thing, and they were cautious and watchful rather than amused. I later discovered that Sister Ste. Mélanie even spoke of it with my grandmother, with whom I was then living.

By then I was absolutely smitten with a doglike (though not puppylike) devotion to this wonderful creature. I followed her around the schoolyard constantly, at what I thought was a discreet distance. I stared at her while she ate her lunch, trying to be inconspicuous, sometimes imagining myself to be a cucumber sandwich or a pickle. And I gazed longingly at her back when she stood at the chalkboard declining copulative verbs. That's when I first noticed that she had trouble with her verbs. Me, I knew copulative verbs inside out.*

"I'll help you with your grammar," I finally blurted the line I had been rehearsing all morning. "At my grandma's after school."

"'Kay," she nodded, making me so happy I almost died.

At lunchtime, between spoonfuls of pea soup, I casually outlined my plan for my grandmother, informing her how some girl who was having trouble with her verbs would be coming over and we'd go to my room where I'd teach her, which would be excellent practice, wouldn't it, for when I was a teacher, and at the same time it would help her, which is surely a fine and noble thing to do and . . .

"No!" my grandmother announced very firmly. "No, that wouldn't be right. Right here in the kitchen would be fine."

"All I want is a quiet place with no distractions so that I can teach her some verbs," I insisted.

"I won't distract you at all," my grandmother said. "And it's not that I don't trust you. It's just not right. People would wonder about your motives."

"My motives are just to help . . ."

"Your motives, like everybody else's," my grandmother interrupted, "are selfish. Everybody's motives are selfish. All of what I call our creature motives, like for food and drink and you-know-what, they're selfish. I'm not saying, mind you, that you-know-what is your motive for helping Clarisse."

"It isn't for you-know-what. She needs help. That's all."

But my grandmother disagreed at length, citing many convincing instances of behaviors whose motives might seem obvious and scrupulously moral, but where careful examination revealed baser and far more selfish motives.

"But there are, of course, exceptions," she concluded generously.

---

*PPC: Are you sure it was "copulative" verbs, not transitive or intransitive or something? I mean, is this just for effect? And is it maybe going too far?

AUTHOR: I've checked my notes. It was definitely copulative verbs.

"I'm one!" I insisted.

"I don't think so," she said. "I think you have an ulterior motive."

MOTIVES: EXPLANATIONS FOR BEHAVIOR

Ulterior motives—a strange and wicked disorder from which I think I still suffer. You see, **ulterior motives** are, by definition, hidden and unknown; they do not show themselves. More than once I have wished that my true motives had been more obvious—had been more apparent to others.

In this chapter we look not at **motives** that are ulterior but at those that are more obvious. Motives are what move us; they are the **causes** of what we do—causes being agents or forces that produce an effect or an action. As Dweck (1986) notes, motives are the causes of all our goal-directed activity.

But motives are more than causes; they are also **reasons** for behavior, in the sense that reasons are explanations. Thus, motives explain the *why* of our behavior, whereas learning theories are more concerned with the *how* and the *what*.

From the teacher's point of view, the most important motives are those that have to do with learning and achievement. The teacher needs to be especially concerned with why some students expend a great deal of effort in achievement situations and others do not.

Teachers need to understand why some students spend a great deal of effort in achievement situations and why others don't—and why some activities are more likely than others to capture and maintain student interest.

Keith and Cool (1992) tried to determine some of the factors that most contributed to the achievement scores of more than 25,000 students. Not surprisingly, the strongest direct effect they found was for ability. Two factors had strong indirect effects: motivation and quality of instruction. "It appears," conclude Keith and Cool, "that students enrolled in a high-quality school and curriculum are more highly motivated by that curriculum. . . . Students with high academic motivation take more academic course work . . . and do more homework . . . and as a result, achieve at a higher level" (1992, p. 215).

The importance to the teacher of understanding motivation and the factors that affect it can hardly be overemphasized. Uguroglu and Walberg (1979) estimate that motivation accounts for a proportion of student achievement sufficient to be the difference between success and failure. Unfortunately, research reviewed by Anderman and Maehr (1994)

---

ulterior motives Hidden motives. Reasons for behavior that are not what they seem. Ulterior motives often involve an element of deception.

motive The causes of behavior. Our motives are the reasons why we engage in some behaviors and not in others. They are what initiate behavior and what direct it.

causes Agents or forces that produce an effect or a result. Causes are one aspect of motivation.

reasons Explanations for or defenses of an action. In psychology, reasons are often treated as motives.

indicates that there is often a significant decline in motivation during the middle grades of school. This decline is evident in negative attitudes as well as in behaviors not especially conducive to high achievement. To the extent that this is true, it becomes even more urgent that teachers understand student motivation and take steps to maintain it at a high level.

Recent research makes it clear that a wide variety of classroom variables have a direct effect on students' motivation—variables such as "classroom organizational, instructional and climatic variables, including task structure, task complexity, grouping practices, evaluation techniques, locus of responsibility for learning, and quality of teacher-student and student-student relationships" (Matthews, 1991).

This chapter explores various explanations for human behavior, with special emphasis on how each factor listed by Matthews can affect students' motivation. Initially, it touches briefly on some historical approaches to motivation, then it moves to a series of more detailed discussions of contemporary views of motivation, organized according to the major models discussed in earlier chapters: behaviorism, humanism, and cognitivism. Keep in mind that these divisions continue to be artificial and therefore somewhat misleading. As we study them, we sometimes feel compelled to judge them and choose only one among them. But different theories are simply reflections of different world views and different underlying emphases and metaphors. One is not correct and the others incorrect; rather, something of each may be useful for our different purposes.

HISTORICAL VIEWS OF HUMAN MOTIVATION

History, as is often its custom, can teach us about an assortment of past beliefs, not all of which are relevant to our current views. Nevertheless, there is often something in these historical views that may be useful to our understanding of human behavior in general and of children in particular.

INSTINCTS

In the case of one of the first views of human motivation—that concerning **instincts**—what history can tell us may be more relevant to our understanding of animals than of people.

When Zoe, our dog, gave birth to her first litter, 4-year-old Laurier watched bug-eyed as the bitch eased each little pup in turn from its sac, nipped its umbilical cord close to its belly, ate the afterbirth, and nudged it toward her nipples. "Where'd she learn to do that?" he asked. But she hadn't really learned; somehow, she already knew. How to birth pups was one of the instincts with which she was born.

A Definition. Instincts are innate, complex, species-specific, relatively unmodifiable behavior patterns. What do these terms mean?

> *Innate*: Instinctual behaviors are not learned but are genetically determined. That is, they are present at birth or develop naturally later as a result of appropriate experiences.
>
> *Complex*: Behaviors such as blinking in response to air blown in the eye, sucking behavior, and other simple behaviors of which we are capable at birth are not instincts; they are *reflexes*. Instincts are more complex groupings of behaviors such as those involved in courting or nesting among some birds.
>
> *Species specific*: Instincts are general within species. Thus, *all* wild ducks are characterized by a migratory instinct, and *all* bears (except for polar bears) by the urge to den up in winter.
>
> *Relatively unmodifiable*: Because instincts are largely innate, they are not much affected by the environment—although, in the absence of some environmental experi-

---

instinct A complex, species-specific, relatively unmodifiable pattern of behaviors such as migration or nesting in some birds and animals. Less complex inherited behaviors are usually referred to as *reflexes*.

ences, instinctual behaviors can be changed somewhat. For example, female rats reared in deprived environments do not exhibit the maternal and nesting instincts characteristic of female rats reared normally.

Human Instincts. There are many examples of instinctual behavior patterns among animals, most having to do with nesting, migration, and mating—all behaviors related to survival. The question is whether people engage in behavior that can be similarly explained in terms of instincts.

Some early theorists thought so. For example, L. L. Bernard (1924) listed some six thousand human instincts, ranging from the common ones (sexual, maternal) to remote inclinations, such as the tendency "to avoid eating apples that grow in one's own garden" (p. 212).

But these are not instincts at all. As we saw, instincts are more complex than this; they are general to all members of the species (which is not the case for the tendency to avoid eating apples from one's garden); and they are relatively unmodifiable (again, not the case for eating apples). But even if these were instincts, they would not be particularly valuable because naming an instinct neither explains a behavior nor predicts it. At best, the reasoning process is entirely circular. If we make love, it's obvious that we have an instinct for doing so. Why, then, do we make love? Well, because we have this instinct, you see. How do we know that this instinct exists? Well, because people make love. And so on, *ad infinitum*.

Currently, the notion of instinct is applied more to animal than to human behavior, although a related phenomenon, **imprinting,** is sometimes linked to some features of infant development. Imprinting is the appearance of complex behaviors, apparently as a result of exposure to an appropriate object or event (releaser) at a **critical period** in the animal's life. For example, newly hatched ducklings will follow the first moving object they encounter and become attached to it. Fortunately, this object is usually the mother duck. However, Lorenz (1952) reports the case of a greylag goose that imprinted on him and followed him around like a dog. Much to his embarrassment, when it matured it insisted on foisting its affections on him during mating season.*

Although there do not appear to be critical periods in the infant's life during which it must be exposed to appropriate experiences in order to have some behavior imprinted, researchers such as Bowlby (1982) suggest that the first six months might be a **sensitive period** during which a parent or other caregiver must be present for the infant to develop strong attachment bonds.

PSYCHOLOGICAL HEDONISM

A second historical explanation of human motivation is **psychological hedonism,** the belief that we act so as to avoid pain and obtain pleasure. Unfortunately, psychological hedonism does little to explain behavior because it does

---

*PPC: Among other demonstrations of undying love, Lorenz's birds persisted in depositing beakfuls of minced worms in his ears. Lorenz did not reciprocate.
AUTHOR: Yecch!

---

imprinting Unlearned, instinctlike behaviors that are not present at birth but that become part of an animal's repertoire after exposure to a suitable stimulus during a critical period. The "following" behavior of young ducks, geese, and chickens is an example.

critical period A period in development during which exposure to appropriate experiences or stimuli will bring about specific learning much more easily than is the case at other times.

sensitive period A period during which specific experiences have their most pronounced effects—for example, the first six months of life during which the infant forms strong attachment bonds to the mother or caregiver.

psychological hedonism The belief that humans act primarily to avoid pain and to obtain pleasure.

"Mother" Lorenz.

NINA LEEN/LIFE MAGAZINE, © TIME MAGAZINE INC.

not specify those conditions that are pleasurable or painful. Even if it is true that the pain/pleasure principle governs our activities, we can predict and control these activities only if we know what gives pleasure and what gives pain.

NEED–DRIVE THEORIES

Need–drive theories offer one way to define pain and pleasure. **Needs** are states of deficiency or lack within an organism. **Drives** are the energies or the tendencies to react that are aroused by needs. For example, we have a need for food; this need gives rise to a hunger drive.

---

need–drive theory A motivation theory that attempts to explain human behavior on the basis of the motivating properties of needs. Such theories typically assume that humans have certain learned and unlearned needs, which give rise to drives, which in turn are responsible for the occurrence of behavior.

needs Ordinarily refers to a lack or deficit in the human organism. Needs may be either unlearned (for example, the need for food or water) or learned (the need for money).

drive The tendency to behave that is brought about by an unsatisfied need—for example, the hunger drive is related to the need for food.

If we assume that satisfying needs is pleasant and that a state of need is unpleasant, the relationship between need theory and psychological hedonism is obvious: Identifying and describing needs makes clear the nature of pain and pleasure. A list of needs is a list of conditions that when satisfied are pleasant and when unsatisfied are unpleasant.

Needs can be divided into two broad categories: psychological and physiological. **Physiological needs** include the need for food, water, sleep and rest, activity, and sex. They are manifested in actual tissue changes. **Psychological needs** include the need for affection, belonging, achievement, independence, social recognition, and self-esteem. They are more closely related to mental functioning. One important

---

physiological needs Basic biological needs, such as the need for food and water.

psychological needs Human needs other than those dealing with basic physical requirements such as food, sex, water, and temperature regulation (physiological needs). Psychological needs described by Maslow include the need to belong, to feel safe, to love and be loved, to maintain a high opinion of oneself, and to self-actualize.

difference between the two categories is that psychological needs are never completely satisfied, whereas physiological needs can be. In addition, psychological needs are probably more often learned than are physiological needs.

SUMMARY AND IMPLICATIONS
OF HISTORICAL APPROACHES TO MOTIVATION

From the teacher's point of view, the most useful explanations of motivation are those that provide us with the greatest insight about the circumstances under which students will be most interested in doing certain things—and least interested as well.

Explanations such as those based on instincts may be valuable explanations for a bear's habit of denning up in the winter, but they tell us little about why Frank will study all night before his science exam or why Sam will watch television instead and will then have to explain how he forgot all about the exam.

Nor does psychological hedonism tell us much about Sam or Frank. True, the belief that we do things that we expect will lead to pleasant outcomes—and that we avoid behaviors that lead elsewhere—does little violence to our naive convictions about human behavior. But, as we saw, the belief by itself explains little; we need to know what is pleasant and unpleasant.

Theories about needs and drives begin to spell out some of the conditions and outcomes we find pleasant or unpleasant. We know that people who are hungry and thirsty will go to extraordinary lengths to obtain food and drink. People who are lonely may also go to staggering lengths to ease their solitude.

Teachers need to be aware of needs in their students. It is clear, for example, that certain basic biological needs must be satisfied if the teaching/learning process is to be effective. A hungry or thirsty student is almost certain to find concentration difficult. By the same token, a hungry teacher is a sad sight as well and is probably seldom as effective as a well-fed one. Other basic needs, such as the need for sex, are not likely to present a serious problem for younger students; the same cannot be said about adolescents or about teachers—young or old.*

Because most children's basic needs are adequately taken care of in our society, teachers aren't often called upon to walk around with a bag of cookies and a jug of milk. Psychological needs are quite another matter. Recall that these include the need for affection, for belonging, for achievement, for social recognition, and for self-esteem. A useful exercise for a prospective teacher might be to consider what a "bag" filled with the wherewithal to satisfy these needs would look like. Teachers who through their actions can give each student a sense of accomplishment and belonging are probably carrying such a bag.

AROUSAL THEORY:
MAGNITUDE OF MOTIVATION

How much effort a student is willing to make (in other words, how motivated the student is) is a function of three things, claim Brehm and Self (1989): internal states such as needs or desires, potential outcomes, and the person's estimate of the likelihood that a specific behavior will lead to a given outcome. In this view, motivation is both physiological and psychological. And because it is physiological, they claim, it can be measured. That is, the physiological changes that accompany increasing motivation are changes in the **sympathetic nervous system,** the part of the nervous system responsible for changes that accompany

---

*PPC: And old bears? What can be said of their sexual needs?
AUTHOR: Actually, quite a lot, much of which has been said by Marian Engel in the novel *Bear* (Toronto: McClelland and Stewart). But little of that is directly relevant in this serious textbook.

---

sympathetic nervous system Part of the nervous system that instigates the physiological responses associated with emotion.

emotion. These changes are evident in increasing **arousal.**

WHAT IS AROUSAL?

Arousal is both a psychological and a physiological concept. Psychologically, it refers to alertness or attentiveness. It is, in a sense, the individual's degree of wakefulness. At the lowest levels of arousal, the individual is asleep (or in a coma) and is totally inattentive; at higher levels of arousal, the individual is intensely aware and alert; at still higher levels of arousal, the individual might be in a state of panic or shock.

Accompanying these psychological states—ranging from sleep to panic—are underlying physiological changes evident in the functioning of the sympathetic nervous system. At the lowest levels of arousal, respiration and heart rate, brain-wave activity, conductivity of the skin to electricity, and so on, are all at low levels. But with increasing arousal, respiration and heart rate may increase, the skin's electrical conductivity increases as a function of perspiration, and brain-wave activity changes predictably.

SOURCES OF AROUSAL

The main sources of arousal are the **distance receptors**—hearing and vision—but arousal may be affected by all other sources of stimulation, including activity of the brain. Some properties of stimuli—meaningfulness, intensity, surprisingness, novelty, and complexity (Berlyne, 1960)—make them more arousing than others.

---

arousal As a physiological concept, arousal refers to changes in functions such as heart rate, respiration rate, electrical activity in the cortex, and electrical conductivity of the skin. As a psychological concept, arousal refers to degree of alertness, awareness, vigilance, or wakefulness. Arousal varies from very low (coma or sleep) to very high (panic or high anxiety).

distance receptors The senses that receive stimulation from a distance (for example, hearing and vision).

Therefore, amount of stimulation is probably less critical in determining level of activation than the nature of stimulation.

AROUSAL AND MOTIVATION:
THE YERKES-DODSON LAW

Increasing arousal, claim Brehm and Self (1989), is more or less equivalent to increasing motivation—more or less because the relationship is not completely linear. That is, at very low levels of arousal, motivation tends to be low and behavior ineffective. In fact, at the lowest level of arousal—sleep—there is little or no response to external stimulation. Try asking a sleeping person where Moose Jaw is. *Nada.* Ask her again just as she is waking up. "What the #$@#%##?" says she. But as she becomes more fully awake, she may respond correctly (if she knows the answer). However, if in your zeal for observing the relationship between arousal and behavior you go ahead and set your subject's house on fire, awaken her with a bucket of cold water, inform her that her house is on fire, and then ask her where Moose Jaw is, you will probably observe the ineffectiveness of behavior that accompanies excessive arousal.*

This inverted U-shaped relationship between arousal and behavior is referred to as the **Yerkes-Dodson law** (see Figure 10.1). What

---

*PPC: By the way, just exactly where is Moose Jaw? It always frustrates me when an author asks a question but doesn't answer it. Besides, this might be important to somebody.
AUTHOR: Moose Jaw is in southern Saskatchewan—which is important to the people who live there. Apparently, it was once important to Al Capone, as well. He is rumored to have used it as a base for running whiskey across the U.S.–Canada border. In fact, one of the cellars he reportedly used as a whiskey storeroom is located under present-day Charlotte's, a restaurant on Main Street.

Yerkes-Dodson law Law that states that the effectiveness of performance is an inverted U-shaped function of arousal, such that very low and very high levels of arousal are associated with least effective behavior.

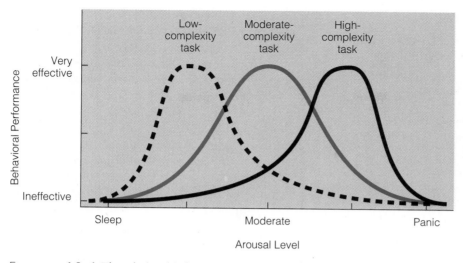

FIGURE 10.1 The relationship between behavioral performance and arousal level. The level of arousal that is optimal for effective behavior varies with the complexity of the task.

this law says, in effect, is that motivation (and the effectiveness of behavior) increases with increasing arousal until an optimal level is reached; following this, further increases in arousal will result in decreasing motivation and decreasing effectiveness of behavior.

The relationship between arousal and motivation can be summarized by two assumptions:

Assumption 1. For any given activity, for an individual there is a level of arousal at which performance will be optimal. Certain activities can best be performed under conditions of relatively high arousal, whereas others are best performed under conditions of lower arousal. Activities involving routine, habitual responses such as counting one's fingers or driving a car, do not ordinarily require a high level of arousal. On the other hand, intense, concentrated activities such as taking examinations require higher levels of arousal.

As we saw, people under great stress often engage in inappropriate behavior. There are the tragic examples of panic-stricken people in crowds trampling one another to death in their haste to escape danger (Schultz, 1964). There are the studies of Marshall (cited by Bruner,

1957b), who found that fewer than one-quarter of the infantrymen in combat during World War II actually fired their rifles when under heavy fire. Fortunately, the enemy probably did no better.

Assumption 2. An individual behaves in such a way as to maintain the level of arousal that is most nearly optimal for ongoing behavior. In other words, if arousal level is too low, the individual will try to increase it; if it's too high, steps will be taken to lower it. For example, when people experience great fear, their first reaction may be to flee the object of their fear. The effect is to reduce arousal level. When people are bored, their level of arousal is probably too low. They may then engage in more stimulating activity: reading, sports (participating or observing), or, if they are students, daydreaming. The effect should be an increase in arousal level. In this connection it is worth noting that Mac Iver, Reuman, and Main (1995) report evidence that the level of student boredom in schools is closely related to instructional procedures. Specifically, schools that emphasize memorization, drill, and repeated practice are more likely to have students who are highly bored.

AROUSAL AND LEARNING

And highly bored students are less likely to be effective learners. In fact, like effective behavior, maximally effective learning takes place under conditions of optimal arousal. Low levels of arousal are characterized by low attentiveness—and less effective learning. As a teacher, you can illustrate this point. Prepare a good lesson full of content, write it out, and read it to your class very slowly in a soothing monotone. Then deliver the same lesson to another, comparable class in your usual, "today" kind of style. Test the relative retention of your two classes. It is little wonder that common synonyms for the term *motivating* are expressions such as "interesting," "captivating," "arousing," "moving," "useful," "involving," "stimulating," "compelling," "attention getting," "challenging," and "curiosity whetting."

WHEN AROUSAL IS TOO HIGH:

ANXIETY AND LEARNING

One manifestation of increasing arousal is **anxiety**—a feeling characterized by varying degrees of fear and worry. Research on anxiety and its relationship to learning (and more specifically to performance on tests) dates back more than four decades but has been quite sporadic and unsystematic. However, recent years have seen a marked upsurge in research on the nature of anxiety, its relationship to performance, and techniques that can be used to reduce it. Much of this research is of a psychiatric nature, because anxiety is implicated in many mental disorders (American Psychiatric Association, 1987). Research that deals more specifically with anxiety and education is reviewed briefly here.

Text Anxiety. Sarason (1959, 1961, 1972, 1980) was among the first to show that anxiety related to test-taking decreases test performance. This important finding has been well documented by subsequent research. Hembree (1988) summarized 562 separate studies that have investigated **test anxiety.** The conclusion is clear, claims Hembree: Test anxiety causes poor test performance. In addition, it is related to lower self-esteem. Females tend to be somewhat more test anxious than males, although their greater anxiety does not manifest itself in lower performance. Research also indicates that in addition to performing less well on tests, highly anxious students do not profit as much from instruction. Some of these highly anxious students, explain Birenbaum and Nasser (1994), simply have poorer study skills; others lack test-taking skills. As a result, anxiety appears to have a detrimental effect not only on test-taking but on learning as well. This observation is apparently true for a wide variety of instructional methods. However, highly anxious students tend to learn better with more structured instructional approaches, such as programmed learning, computer-assisted instruction, and teacher-directed lessons in which student interaction is not expected or required. Thus, high anxiety does not always mean poorer test performance—although it often does (see J. H. Mueller, 1992a, 1992b).

Reducing Test Anxiety. Following an extensive review, G. S. Tryon (1980) concludes that many different anxiety-reducing techniques can work. Most of these techniques are aimed at changing students' attitudes about their personal competence and at focusing attention on the tasks at hand rather than on feelings of worry. Accordingly, they often take the form of attempting to develop learning/thinking strategies.

Other possibilities for reducing anxiety, suggested by Hill and Wigfield (1984), include a variety of changes in instructional and evaluation procedures. For example, teachers can reduce time pressure on students by providing

---

anxiety A feeling of apprehension, worry, tension, or nervousness.

test anxiety A characteristic evident in a fear of taking tests and an expectation of poor performance. Evidence suggests that test anxiety can impair performance on tests.

more time for assignments and tests and by teaching students simple time management strategies. They can also try to prevent failure by changing the difficulty level of assignments and tests, thereby matching them more carefully to students' skill levels.

Hembree's review of 562 studies indicates that many of these approaches are effective in reducing test anxiety and that improved performance typically follows anxiety reduction. In light of these findings, he argues that tests such as intelligence or standardized achievement measures—and even teacher-made examinations—consistently underestimate the abilities of test-anxious students—at least after fifth grade. Before this time, test anxiety is not ordinarily a significant factor in test performance.

The implications of these findings are twofold: First, steps should be taken to reduce test anxiety for highly anxious students, both through treatment programs and through changes in test-taking directions. And second, research is needed to discover ways to prevent test anxiety from developing in the first place.

Biofeedback, a procedure whereby participants are given direct information about the functioning of their sympathetic nervous systems (for example, their brain-wave activity, their heart rate, or the conductivity of their skins to electricity), is another procedure that may be effective in reducing anxiety. But it is not a procedure ordinarily available to classroom teachers. (See the box "Biofeedback.")

AROUSAL: IMPLICATIONS FOR THE TEACHER

The relevance of arousal theory for education depends on the teacher's control over variables that affect arousal. Ideally, all students in a given class should be working at a moderate level of arousal. Students who are asleep, nearing sleep, or just waking up are at too low a level of arousal for most classroom activities; those who show signs of panic and impending flight are at too high a level. The really central question for teachers is how arousal level can be controlled.

We saw that the primary sources of arousal are the distance receptors, vision and hearing, but that all other sources of stimulation also have some effect. Furthermore, it is less the amount than the intensity, meaningfulness, novelty, and complexity of stimulation that affect arousal. There are other factors as well. Degree of risk or personal involvement is directly related to arousal level, as is illustrated by the arousing effects of risk-taking behavior.

Teachers control a significant part of the stimulation to which students are exposed. The intensity, meaningfulness, and complexity of what teachers say, of what they do, of how they look, and of what they write all directly affect the attention (arousal) of their students. Thus teachers can keep students at an uncomfortably high level of arousal by overemphasizing testing, making tasks unrealistically difficult, using threats, or presenting material that is too complex—and students may reduce that arousal by withdrawing attention and effort. Teachers can also keep students at too low a level of arousal by boring them—and again students may cease to pay attention.

The important thing for a teacher to remember is that arousal increases in proportion to the intensity, meaningfulness, novelty, and complexity of stimulation. Presenting Napoleon Bonaparte in the classroom is clearly novel, meaningful, and highly motivating (see the case "The Emperor Comes to Class"). Similarly, all changes in teachers' behavior that intensify the meaningfulness and novelty of stimuli may also increase attention. One key feature of highly arousing (motivating) approaches to classroom teaching is clearly *variety.*

A BEHAVIORISTIC VIEW OF MOTIVATION

Motivational theories can be categorized in much the same way as approaches to learning: behavioristic, humanistic, and cognitive. Recall that behaviorism is concerned with how the consequences of behavior regulate and control

Biofeedback

If we care to, we can determine the texture of objects by touching them, their colors by looking, their sounds by listening, their smells, their tastes. . . . Our senses permit us to detect external feedback—information that comes back to us from "out there." But under normal circumstances, we know little of the internal functioning of our nervous systems; we have little biological feedback. However, psychology has invented ways of giving us biofeedback and has conducted experiments to determine whether subjects can learn to control their own arousal.

In one kind of experiment, subjects are connected to an **electroencephalograph** (EEG) recorder, also called a polygraph or alpha recorder (or sometimes a lie detector). Simple alpha recorders differentiate between **alpha waves** (normal, resting arousal level) and **beta waves** (more vigilant, excited) brain waves. The object of the experiment is to have the subject control brain functioning and increase the proportion of alpha waves.

It has repeatedly been demonstrated that this is quite possible without any direct instruction, using the principles of operant conditioning. Whenever subjects emit a sufficient proportion of alpha waves, a tone sounds. Because they have been told that the object is to keep the tone going as long as they can, the sound serves as reinforcement. Eventually, most subjects find that they can reach the alpha state much more easily than they could originally. Interestingly, practitioners of Zen, yoga, and transcendental meditation can, through the practice of their respective meditative techniques, arrive at similar states of low arousal—a condition that is believed to be highly conducive to physical and mental health.

Biofeedback instruments and techniques are being used to bring about relaxation, to treat migraine headaches, to deal with mental and emotional problems involving tension and anxiety, and in the treatment and prevention of cardiovascular problems such as hypertension (Parloff, London, & Wolfe, 1986). And, as we saw in Chapter 8, they are also being used in attempts to train children with attention deficit hyperactivity disorder (ADHD) to develop control over aspects of their brain functioning (Lubar, 1991; Janzen et al., 1995; Lubar et al., 1995).

---

actions; that humanism is concerned with the autonomy, the dignity, and the worth of the self; and that cognitivism deals with how we know, think, and remember. Accordingly, behavioristic approaches emphasize **extrinsic motives** (external motives) such as those having to do with praise and reward; humanistic approaches emphasize the importance of **intrinsic motives** (internal motives) such as those related to the need to be autonomous, to develop competence, to actualize potential; and cognitive approaches emphasize the individual's need to know and understand.

---

electroencephalograph (EEG) A graphlike representation of changes in electrical potential that occur in the brain.

alpha waves Relatively high amplitude but low frequency brain waves associated with a relaxed but wakeful state.

beta waves High frequency, low amplitude brain waves associated with alertness and higher arousal.

---

extrinsic motives Motives associated with external sources of reinforcement—like food, money, sex.

intrinsic motives Motives associated with internal sources of reinforcement—like satisfaction.

Psychological hedonism—the **pain/pleasure principle**—is a simple summary of the most basic behavioristic motivational principle: We behave to obtain pleasure and avoid pain. However, as we saw earlier, pain and pleasure are subjective emotional evaluations that violate the behaviorist's determination to be objective. Instead, the behaviorist attempts to identify situations (stimuli) that have the effect of increasing the probability of a behavior. These are termed *reinforcers*. Reinforcers can then be used in various ways to bring about desirable behaviors and sometimes to eliminate those that are less desirable.

Recall from Chapter 4 that reinforcement can be positive or negative. Positive reinforcement increases the probability of a behavior when it follows as a consequence of the behavior (a food reward given for an action, for example). Negative reinforcement also increases the probabilty of a response, but does so as a function of being *removed* as a consequence of behavior (for example, detention terminates following an apology).

Positive and negative reinforcement (and sometimes punishment as well) is used in virtually all classrooms, even by the most humanistic or cognitively oriented of teachers. Teachers praise and admonish students, they give high and low grades, they smile and frown. These and a thousand other indicators of approval or disapproval are examples of reinforcement. When used judiciously and systematically, reinforcement can have profound effects on behavior (for example, Vaughn, 1993). (See Chapter 11 for a detailed discussion of the systematic use of reinforcement in the classroom.)

But we are not simply hungry rats in some experiment, Weiner (1984) informs us. If we look into the classroom, we will see that behavior is not driven simply by external rewards like candy bars or gold stars or high marks. Rather, behavior is *informed*. That is, it is driven by cognitions and by emotions.

It should come as no surprise that current applications of reinforcement theory in the classroom take the student's thinking into account. As Stipek (1988) notes, the most powerful reinforcers for students are stimuli such as **praise,** the effectiveness of which clearly depend on the student's interpretations of the teacher's behavior.

Praise. Praise is not like food in an empty belly, warm and pleasurable even in the absence of learning. Rather, it is a complex event that says

---

pain/pleasure principle A common expression for psychological hedonism—the belief that we are motivated to seek pleasure and avoid pain.

---

praise Positive verbal comments or other signs of approval. For example, most of what my grandmother said to or about me (heh! heh!).

CASE: THE EMPEROR COMES TO CLASS

THE SITUATION: Boris Randolph, a good teacher, as recollected by Elizabeth, teacher in training

He had a wealth of knowledge of history, and he would allow 10 minutes at the beginning of each class for questions on any topic relating to history, not just the specific time frame we were dealing with in class. After an extensive unit on Napoleon, he presented to us a man who was dressed as the Emperor Napoleon. We were given the entire class period to question "Napoleon" about his life, his career, and the state of France and Europe during his reign. The gentleman who disguised himself as Napoleon was a history professor at the local university so he was able to correctly answer our questions. This man also came to us as Adolph Hitler, Joseph Stalin, and Otto von Bismarck.

not only "you have done well" but also "you have behaved in a socially approved manner." Praise—and its absence, too—give us fundamentally important information with which to build notions of self. It says things about how worthwhile and competent we are. And, as is made clear shortly, these are fundamentally important concepts in human motivation.

But teachers do not always use praise well. Brophy (1981) notes that much teacher praise is determined not so much by the student's actual behavior as by the teacher's perception of what the student needs. As a result, praise is often used too infrequently to be effective, or it is used so often as to be almost meaningless. Praise used in these ways is not clearly contingent (dependent) upon a specific desired behavior, as a good reinforcer is, nor is it sufficiently credible to be very rewarding.

Praise alone, note Hitz and Driscoll (1994), is not always highly effective. But it can become very effective when it is designed to increase the student's self-esteem. For example, if praise is accompanied by constructive encouragement, it has longer-term and more powerful effects than might a simple "Good work!" Furthermore, note Hitz and Driscoll, encouragement should be specific rather than vague and general. It should also focus on the student's efforts rather than simply on the outcomes of that effort. And it goes without saying that praise should be sincere. Hitz and Driscoll caution, as well, that teachers should avoid labeling students or making comparisons among them.

Brophy (1981) makes many of the same points. If praise is to be effective, he argues, then it should not be too frequent. Furthermore, it should be contingent upon some specific behavior, it should be credible, and it should be informative. In addition, it should focus on the student's efforts. It should not be random and unsystematic, nor should it reward mere participation rather than quality of performance. (See Table 10.1 for a summary of Brophy's suggestions.)

Although reinforcement (in the form of praise and otherwise) is used extensively by virtually all teachers, some object to its systematic and deliberate use because they sense that there might be something mechanistic and dehumanizing about the systematic application of rewards and punishments (of extrinsic reinforcement, in other words) to shape behavior. Others object because they fear that if students are trained to respond too readily to extrinsic reinforcers, they might become too dependent on them. And some humanists fear that such students will never learn to listen to their own motives—to their intrinsic and fundamentally human urge to excel, to become something worthwhile and actualized.

A HUMANISTIC VIEW OF MOTIVATION

But praise is quite different from extrinsic rewards like tiny gold stars and high grades. At its simplest level, praise is a verbal affirmation that the student has done well; at a more complex level, praise is a highly informative event that has much to say not only about the outcome of the student's efforts, but also about the value and uniqueness of the student. Thus, praise might do much to increase the student's reliance on intrinsic (or internal) motivation (Fair & Silvestri, 1992). In this sense, praise is more humanistic than are gold stars.

Humanistic psychology's concern with intrinsic motives is most clearly apparent in Maslow's (1970) theory of human needs and especially in his conception of self-actualization.

BASIC NEEDS AND METANEEDS

Maslow proposes two general need systems: **basic needs** and **metaneeds.**

Basic Needs. The basic needs include

> *physiological needs*: the basic biological needs—for example, the need for food, water, and temperature regulation

---

basic needs Maslow's term for lower-level needs, such as the physiological needs as well as the need to belong, to love, and to have high self-esteem. Also termed *deficiency needs.*

TABLE 10.1 GUIDELINES FOR EFFECTIVE PRAISE

EFFECTIVE PRAISE	INEFFECTIVE PRAISE
1. Is delivered contingently	1. Is delivered randomly or unsystematically
2. Specifies the particulars of the accomplishment	2. Is restricted to global positive reactions
3. Shows spontaneity, variety, and other signs of credibility; suggests clear attention to the student's accomplishment	3. Shows a bland uniformity that suggests a conditioned response made with minimal attention
4. Rewards attainment of specified performance criteria (which can include effort criteria, however)	4. Rewards mere participation without consideration of performance processes or outcomes
5. Provides information to students about their competence or the value of their accomplishments	5. Provides no information at all or gives students information about their status
6. Orients students toward better appreciation of their own task-related behavior and thinking about problem solving	6. Orients students toward comparing themselves with others and thinking about competing
7. Uses students' own prior accomplishments as the context for describing current accomplishments	7. Uses the accomplishments of peers as the context for describing students' current accomplishments
8. Is given in recognition of noteworthy effort or success at difficult (for this student) tasks	8. Is given without regard to the effort expended or the meaning of the accomplishment (for this student)
9. Attributes success to effort and ability, implying that similar successes can be expected in the future	9. Attributes success to ability alone or to external factors such as luck or ease of task
10. Fosters endogenous attributions (students believe that they expend effort on the task because they enjoy the task and/or want to develop task relevant skills)	10. Fosters exogenous attributions (students believe that they expend effort on the task for external reasons—to please the teacher, win a competition or reward, and so on)
11. Focuses students' attention on their own task-relevant behavior	11. Focuses students' attention on the teacher as an external authority figure who is manipulating them
12. Fosters appreciation of and desirable attributions about task-relevant behavior after the process is completed	12. Intrudes into the ongoing process, distracting attention from task-relevant behavior

Source: From J. Brophy, "Teacher Praise: A Functional Analysis," *Review of Educational Research, 51,* No. 1, 5–32 (p. 26). Copyright 1981 by the American Educational Research Association. Reprinted by permission of the publisher.

safety needs: needs that are manifested in people's efforts to maintain sociable, predictable, orderly, and therefore nonthreatening environments

metaneeds Maslow's term for higher needs. Concerned with psychological, self-related, functions rather than with biology. Include the need to know truth, beauty, justice, and to self-actualize. Also termed *growth needs.*

love and belongingness needs: the need to develop relationships involving reciprocal affection; the need to be a member of a group

self-esteem needs: the need for cultivating and maintaining a high opinion of oneself; the need to have others hold one in high esteem

These needs are hierarchical in the sense that higher-level needs will be attended to only

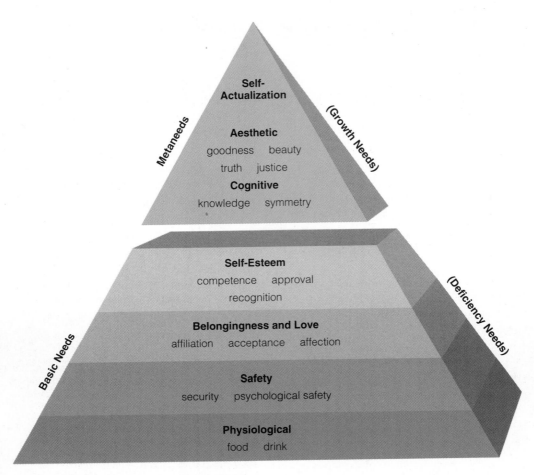

FIGURE 10.2 Maslow's hierarchy of needs.

after lower-level needs are satisfied (see Figure 10.2). When people need food, they are not likely to be concerned with love or with self-esteem. History provides striking examples of the potency of lower-level needs. In the 1933 famine in eastern (Soviet) Ukraine, for example, in which at least 4.5 million people died, more than half the victims were infants. In the words of one of the survivors ("Ukrainian Famine Survivors," 1983):

> All you think about is food. It's your one, your only, your all-consuming thought. You have no sympathy for anyone else. A sister feels nothing for her brother; a brother feels nothing for his sister; parents don't feel anything for their children. You

become like a hungry animal. You will throw yourself on food like a hungry animal. That's what you're like when you're hungry. All human behavior, all moral behavior collapses.

Metaneeds. Maslow's basic needs are also termed **deficiency needs** because they motivate (lead to behavior) when the organism has a defi-

---

deficiency needs Maslow's expression for basic needs, so called because they motivate the person to act when a related deficiency is sensed—for example, a deficiency of food leads to eating, a deficiency of self-esteem leads to behaviors intended to increase esteem.

"How about that? I rescently became my own person, too."
Drawing by Lorenz; © 1984 The New Yorker Magazine, Inc.

ciency with respect to a need (for example, lacks food or water). The metaneeds are termed **growth needs** because they motivate behaviors that result not from deficiencies but from a natural human tendency toward growth. The growth will be attended to only after the basic needs are reasonably satisfied.

The metaneeds include aesthetic and cognitive urges associated with such virtues as truth and goodness, the acquisition of knowledge, and the appreciation of beauty, order, and symmetry. The highest need in Maslow's system is our tendency toward *self-actualization*—the unfolding and fulfillment of self.

Recall from Chapter 9 that self-actualization is a process rather than a state. It is a process of growth—of becoming—a process that, interestingly, is in many ways highly similar to the ideals of Chinese Taoism and Zen

Buddhism (Chang & Page, 1991). Most humanistic psychologists consider self-actualization absolutely central to the healthy experience of being human. But, laments Maslow (1991) in one of several of his recently published papers* there are relatively few truly self-actualizing people. Why? One of the reasons is that growth requires will and effort and perhaps a great deal of sacrifice. And many of us, notes Maslow, suffer from the **Jonah complex.** Like that biblical character, we deliberately avoid the commitment and the effort required for our personal growth and development. We choose, instead, to struggle along eating and drinking and satisfying our other needs. And in the end, we are somehow less human than we might have been. And perhaps less happy as well, notes Umoren (1992), who argues that our well-being is closely tied to how well we satisfy higher-level needs.

Although abstractions such as beauty, goodness, truth, and self-actualization are difficult to describe and even more difficult to examine scientifically, they do represent motivating concerns and processes for a great many individuals.

COMPETENCE MOTIVATION

R. W. White (1959) argues that one of our most important intrinsic needs is the need to feel competent. **Competence motivation** is manifested in the child's struggle to perform competently and in the feelings of confidence and worth that accompany successful performance.

---

*A series of Maslow's previously unpublished papers, most of them written in the 1960s, have now been published in the *Journal of Humanistic Education and Development* (vol. 29, no. 3, 1991).

---

growth needs Another expression for Maslow's metaneeds. So called because they motivate behaviors not as a result of deficiencies but because of an intrinsic need to grow, to become, to actualize. Include cognitive, aesthetic, and self-actualization needs.

Jonah complex A phrase used by Abraham Maslow to describe those who avoid and deny their personal capacity for growth and self-actualization.

competence motivation R. W. White's phrase for our innate need to achieve competence and to feel competent. According to White, competence motivation has especially important adaptive value in a species that is born with little innate competence.

MICHAEL DWYER/STOCK, BOSTON

We have an innate need, says White, to be and to feel competent. This drive for competence goes a long way toward explaining why some students strive to learn a second language, why some students spend hours practicing shooting baskets—and why others become so good at drawing on sidewalks.

In the sense that it involves efforts directed toward the growth and development of potential, competence motivation can be seen as one aspect of self-actualization.

R. W. White believes that competence motivation is an especially important concept for understanding species such as ours in which individuals are born with so few innate competencies. Unlike the young of many nonhuman species, our infants cannot run or hide, they cannot feed themselves; they have little recognition of enemies or of danger. Perhaps even more important, they know few of the signals, gestures, and sounds they need to master to understand the world and to communicate competently. To be human is to learn a thousand competencies.

Competence motivation, suggests White, explains a tremendous range of behaviors engaged in by children. It is the drive for competence—for mastery—that explains curiosity and information-seeking behavior. Competence motivation is evident in the repetitive, circular reactions of Piaget's infant (see Chapter 3); it also explains why schoolchildren practice skills over and over again until they achieve competence.

R. W. White explains the child's struggles for competence in terms of the feelings of pride and efficacy (personal effectiveness) that result from mastering a skill or understanding a concept. Albert Bandura (1986) expands this concept of self-efficacy in a theory that is as much cognitive as humanistic (it's often labeled a "social cognitive theory"). We look at self-efficacy later in this chapter.

EDUCATIONAL IMPLICATIONS
OF HUMANISTIC ORIENTATIONS

Humanistic approaches to motivation emphasize internal or intrinsic factors that affect behavior. As we saw in Chapter 9, humanistic schools are child rather than teacher or subject centered. Their emphasis is on affective growth and on the development of self-concept. Note, however, that humanistic concerns need not be incompatible with more traditional values that emphasize curriculum content and the development of basic skills.

As we saw, three educational alternatives that illustrate humanistic concerns are open education, learning styles schools, and cooperative learning. These alternatives translate into practice some of the educational implications of humanistic approaches to motivation (see Chapter 9 for a discussion of their strengths and weaknesses).

The greatest contribution of humanistic approaches to instructional practice is embodied perhaps less in specific recommendations for the nitty-gritty of classroom practice than in teachers' attitudes toward students. The humanistic educator is a concerned individual who places great value on the personal development of students. Accordingly, self-actualization is one of the important goals of humanistic instruction—as is the concomitant development of positive feelings about the self and about personal effectiveness and competence (self-efficacy). As a case in point, consider the case "A Leaf Has a Soul."

COGNITIVE VIEWS OF MOTIVATION

Once again, it's important to realize that our categories in psychology are seldom as neat as we would like; the real world is not as simple as the models we invent to represent it. For example, aspects of R. W. White's competence motivation theory are every bit as cognitive as they are humanistic, and in some ways they are behavioristic as well. And some of the theories we consider in this section have behavioristic and humanistic overtones.

The earliest accounts of motivation viewed the human organism as a passive being, unmoved and unmoving in the absence of external or internal conditions that define needs, drives, and arousal levels, that trigger instinctual or primitive learned behavior, or that are clearly associated with pain or pleasure. In other words, early psychology has, inadvertently or otherwise, described an organism that is highly reactive but considerably less active. Hence, the contention that older theories have painted an overly passive and mechanistic picture of human beings.

Newer approaches are clearly more cognitive and social. We are seen not as victims of internal or external prods moving us willy-nilly through our daily activities but as organisms whose ongoing activity is mediated largely by conscious evaluation, anticipation, and emotion. Bolles (1974), agreeing with one of Freud's basic beliefs, makes the point that there are no unmotivated behaviors. Thus, motivation is not some special force that should be isolated and classified like needs are isolated and listed. It is simply a characteristic of ongoing behavior. And perhaps the single most important feature of human motivation is our ability to delay gratification. So much of our behavior is motivated by our anticipations of distant outcomes that the analysis of human behavior in terms of conditions that seem relevant to the behavior of very young children is often fruitless for older children and adults. For example, a promise of twenty dollars tomorrow—all you have to do is wait—is unlikely to satisfy the 3-year-old who wants a dollar so that he can buy ice cream now. We, on the other hand, would be more than happy to forgo one dollar

CASE: A LEAF HAS A SOUL

THE SITUATION: Miss Cook, eighth-grade English; a good teacher, as recollected by Eleanor, teacher in training

Miss Cook sensed I was shy and never called upon me to answer any questions in class. We had been told to write an assignment on personification. My topic had been a leaf that had a soul and how it was tossed by the wind. After returning our papers, Miss Cook asked if I would kindly share my writing with the class. She asked with such quiet respect, and with such gentleness, I could not refuse. I read the paper in a shaky voice, and she thanked me. As I was walking out of the class, she suggested I keep a diary and think about a career in writing. I did both and find on thinking back that the experience of being in Miss Cook's English class affected a large portion of my life.

today in exchange for twenty tomorrow. We have learned to delay gratification by virtue of some uniquely human abilities involved in thinking, imagining, and verbalizing. It is through a study of these ongoing cognitive processes that social cognitive theorists such as Bandura search for understanding and for explanations of human behavior.

The clear emphasis of theories such as Bandura's is on our cognitive and information processing capacities and how these affect our behavior (Grusec, 1992). Among other things, Bandura looks at what is termed *self-referent thought*—thought that has to do with our selves and with our own mental processes. Metacognition, as we saw in Chapter 5, is one aspect of self-referent thought. Another, which has important implications for motivation, relates to our personal estimates of our effectiveness and competency, or to what is termed **self-efficacy.**

SELF-EFFICACY

Self-efficacy, Bandura (1986, 1991) informs us, has to do with our estimates of our personal effectiveness. The most efficacious people are those who can most effectively deal with situations—in other words, those who are most competent. Accordingly, self-efficacy has two related components: The first has to do with the skills—the actual competencies—that are required for successful performance; the second has to do with the individual's personal estimates of competence.

Personal estimates of competence are extremely important in education. As Zimmerman, Bandura, and Martinez-Pons put it, "Numerous studies have shown that students with a high sense of academic efficacy display greater persistence, effort, and intrinsic interest in their academic learning and performance" (1992, p. 664). Accordingly, it is important for teachers to understand the origins of judgments of self-efficacy. Much of what teachers do—and can do—has an effect on self-efficacy.

Influences on Self-Efficacy Judgments. Bandura (1986) identifies four important influences on a person's judgments of self-efficacy (or personal competence). He terms these *enactive, vicarious, persuasory,* and *emotive* influences.

Enactive influences are evident in the results of the individual's own actions. Whether a person is habitually successful in a given task clearly influences personal judgments of competence. Those who are never successful are less likely to have highly positive evaluations of self-efficacy than are those who most often succeed. It does not follow, however, that success is invariably attributed to personal competence and inevitably results in high self-efficacy judgments. As we see later, some individuals habitually attribute their successes to good fortune or to other factors over which they have no control, rather than to their own competence and effort. By the same token, these individuals take little personal blame for their failures, attributing them instead to bad luck (see the later section on attribution theories for more information).

A second influence on self-efficacy judgments is *vicarious* (secondhand); it has to do with observing the performance of others. Clearly, if we see that others around us always produce nicer paintings than we do, we are not likely to develop high evaluations of our artistic competence. Similarly, children who always receive the poorest grades—or the highest—are being provided with comparative information that might be highly instrumental in determining their judgments of personal worth.

Bandura (1981) suggests that the most important comparisons for making judgments of personal competence are those the child makes with peers. It is not particularly helpful for my self-concept to beat the trousers off a 12-year-old at racquetball. It would be considerably more informative (and unlikely) to decimate the local champion.

---

self-efficacy A term that refers to judgments we make about how efficacious (effective) we are in given situations. Judgments of self-efficacy are important in determining our choices of activities and in influencing the amount of interest and effort we expend.

TABLE 10.2 MAIN SOURCES OF INFORMATION AFFECTING JUDGMENTS OF SELF-EFFICACY

	EXAMPLES OF INFORMATION THAT MIGHT LEAD JILL TO POSITIVE ESTIMATES OF HER PERSONAL EFFICACY
ENACTIVE	She wins a scholarship to attend agricultural college.
VICARIOUS	She learns that Ronald worked harder than she did but wasn't given a scholarship.
PERSUASORY	Her teacher tells her she should enroll in the advanced program for gifted farmers.
EMOTIVE	She was tense before her pest control exam, but felt exhilarated afterward.

Vicarious sources of influence on self-judgments are most important in competitive school situations—which means, of course, that they are important in most school situations because, as we saw earlier, most are competitive. In more cooperative settings, however, comparisons with peers are not nearly so important.

Persuasion can also sometimes be an important source of information about competence. Those who lack confidence—and whose self-efficacy judgments are therefore presumably low—can sometimes be persuaded to do things they would otherwise be reluctant to do. Implicit in the persuasion ("Come on, Emily, play your bandura* for us") is a positive judgment ("You play your bandura so well, Emily").

The fourth source of influence on judgments of self-efficacy is termed *emotive* and has to do with arousal. As we saw in an earlier section of this chapter, arousal refers to alertness or vigilance and ranges from sleep or comatose states to states of high, intense alertness or even panic.

High arousal, Bandura (1986) suggests, can affect self-judgments in different ways. For example, great fear might lead to judgments of low personal competence. A mountain climber overcome by fear might decide he is incapable of continuing—as might a person about to

speak in public. In contrast, great fear might lead a hiker to judge that she is capable of outrunning a bear.

In summary, our feelings of competence are a combined function of the results of our behavior (enactive influence: our successes and failures tell us much about how competent we are), our comparisons with others (vicarious influence: our performance is as good as, better than, or poorer than that of others), the persuasions of others (persuasory influence: when others persuade us, their behavior tells us positive things about our competence), and the intensity of arousal (emotive influence: judgments of competence can be raised or lowered by the intensity of an immediate emotional reaction). (See Table 10.2 for a summary of influences on self-efficacy.)

Implications of Self-Efficacy. Our personal judgments of our own effectiveness—our notions of self-efficacy—are extremely important determiners of what we do and don't do. Hence they are extremely important in understanding human motivation. In fact, says Bandura (1993), measures of self-efficacy are sometimes a better predictor of behavior than are relevant skills. That's because under most circumstances, children—and adults—don't attempt to do things that they expect to do badly. "Efficacy beliefs," Bandura explains, "influence how people feel, think, motivate themselves, and behave" (1993, p. 118).

Judgments of self-efficacy affect not only what we choose to do, and sometimes where we

---

*PPC: I don't get this. Are you trying to make fun of Albert Bandura?

AUTHOR: Not really. A bandura is an ancient, many-stringed Ukrainian musical instrument. It looks a little like what we might imagine an angel's harp looks like.

choose to do it, but also the amount of effort we are willing to expend when faced with difficulties. The stronger an individual's perceptions of efficacy, the more likely the individual is to persist and the greater the effort expended will be. But if notions of self-efficacy are not highly favorable, difficult activities may be abandoned after very little effort and time—or might not be undertaken at all.*

Self-efficacy judgments have also been shown to be related to goals. Zimmerman, Bandura, and Martinez-Pons (1992) show that students set their academic goals in relation to notions of their self-efficacy for academic achievement. Children who do not see themselves as being effective learners set lower goals for themselves than do those who have higher estimates of self-efficacy. Goals are especially important, says Bandura (1986), because they set the criteria for personal failure or success. Reaching them, or failing to, is therefore accompanied by strong emotional reaction. Hence, the goals learners set for themselves are powerful sources of motivation.

Judgments of efficacy also motivate our behavior by influencing our thoughts and our emotions. Those whose judgments of personal competence are low are far more likely to evaluate themselves negatively and to suffer from poorer self-esteem. Significantly, Coopersmith's (1967) research with adolescent boys indicates that positive self-concepts are closely related to success both in school and in interpersonal affairs.

The importance of positive self-evaluations for achievement—that is, of expectations of high achievement—is highlighted in a study that looked at the math and verbal achievement of nearly seven hundred sixth- and ninth-grade Norwegian students (Skaalvik & Rankin, 1995). For this study, the investigators developed scales that looked specifically at how students perceived their ability in mathematics and in verbal arts. Not surprisingly, they found a high positive relationship between high expectations of success and actual achievement. And, as they note, high expectations of success are one manifestation of high self-efficacy.

In conclusion, highly favorable judgments of personal competence (high self-efficacy), together with accompanying positive evaluations of the self (positive self-esteem), can be extremely important positive influences on a child's achievement in school—and on the child's happiness as well. By the same token, low self-efficacy judgments may have highly negative effects.

ATTRIBUTION THEORIES

Success and failure clearly affect our judgments of personal competence—of self-efficacy. But we are not simple, highly predictable creatures, you and I; we don't necessarily react to our failures or successes in exactly the same way. **Attribution theory** recognizes that we attribute the outcomes of our behavior to different causes. Some believe that they do well because they are intelligent; others are convinced that they are simply lucky. Our attributions, notes Weiner (1994), depend very much on our personalities—specifically, on one aspect of our personalities: our **locus of control**. Locus (place) of control refers to the causes to which we attribute our behaviors. Some of us are internally ori-

---

*PPC: Can the bear illustrate this?

AUTHOR: Yes. For example, if a bear (or a student) did not consider himself a very good diver—that is, if he had a low estimate of self-efficacy with respect to this skill—he might, on a kick-in-the-rump sort of hot day, choose to dive into the pond where no one could see him. Similarly, students who have highly positive self-efficacy judgments with respect to their reading skills might enthusiastically volunteer to read out loud. Those with less positive judgments might prefer to read privately.

attribution theory A cognitive motivational theory concerned with predictable consistencies in what people interpret as the causes of the outcomes of behavior.

locus of control An aspect of personality evident in the individual's consistent tendency to attribute behavioral outcomes to a specific class of causes—causes over which the individual does, or does not, have control.

ented; others are externally oriented. Furthermore, claims Weiner (1992), there are those who accept responsibility for the outcomes of their behaviors and others who don't. And some attribute the causes of behavior to highly stable factors—that is, to factors that don't change much like how difficult a task is. Others are more likely to attribute the causes of behavior to highly unstable factors—that is, to factors that are subject to change, like the amount of effort the individual expends on a task.

These three factors, *locus of control, personal responsibility,* and *stability,* are the cornerstones of Weiner's theory of motivation. They are extremely important in cognitive motivational theory's attempt to understand the achievement-oriented behavior of students (or their lack of achievement effort).

Locus of Control. If I have an **internal orientation,** I might attribute my successes and failures to my ability, to my effort, or to some combination of the two. Note that these are factors *within* the individual. But if I have an **external orientation,** I am more likely to attribute my performance to factors that are *outside,* like luck or task difficulty.

Personal Responsibility. Behaviors can also be attributed to causes over which I have no control and for which I therefore have no responsibility. External causes like luck, for example, are uncontrollable and are therefore associated with highly limited personal responsibility. In contrast, if I attribute the outcome of my behavior to an external cause like the interference of my friends, this may well be a cause over which I have some degree of control. That is, I can do things like avoid my friends, pay no attention to them, make them into enemies,

Causal Attributions

	Internal	External
Unstable	Effort (controllable)	Luck (uncontrollable)
Stable	Ability (uncontrollable)	Difficulty (controllable)

FIGURE 10.3 Four important possible attributions for success and failure. Our explanations of why we succeed or fail may be internal or external; in addition, they may involve causes that are either stable or unstable, and that are controllable or uncontrollable.

make new friends, or all of the foregoing. Because I accept that I have some control over this cause, I also accept personal responsibility for the outcomes of my actions.

Stability and Instability of Causes. The causes to which people attribute the outcomes of their behaviors can be highly stable and unchanging. The difficulty of a subject is one such possible attribution. If I attribute my failing an educational psychology course to a stable cause like the tremendous complexity of the subject, I will not expect to do any better in the future than I have in the past. But if, on the other hand, I attribute my failure to an unstable cause like the difficulty of the exam, I can at least hope that the instructor will devise a less difficult examination next time.

The three dimensions of possible causes to which our successes and our failures can be attributed give rise to eight different possibilities. These are illustrated in Table 10.3. Figure 10.3 summarizes the characteristics of four of the most important possible attributions that students can make when analyzing the outcomes of their efforts in school. That is, they can decide that they have done well or less well because of effort, ability, luck, or the difficulty of the task (or the lack of each of these).

---

internal orientation A tendency to attribute the outcomes of behavior to factors within the individual (such as effort or ability).

external orientation A tendency to attribute the outcomes of behavior to factors outside the individual (such as luck or the difficulty of a task).

TABLE 10.3 THE EIGHT CLASSES OF CAUSAL ATTRIBUTIONS IN WEINER'S MOTIVATIONAL THEORY

CHARACTERISTICS OF CAUSAL ATTRIBUTIONS	ILLUSTRATION (RICK'S EXPLANATION OF WHY HE FAILED HIS EDUCATIONAL PSYCHOLOGY TEST)
Internal-unstable-controllable (high responsibility)	He spent the previous night at his girlfriend's house instead of studying.
Internal-unstable-uncontrollable (low responsibility)	He had sprained his wrist and couldn't write rapidly enough to complete the test.
Internal-stable-controllable (high responsibility)	He refuses, as a matter of principle, to study for any education subject.
Internal-stable-uncontrollable (low responsibility)	He has a learning disability that makes it almost impossible for him to do well on multiple choice tests.
External-unstable-controllable (high responsibility)	There didn't happen to be enough questions on all the stuff he knew so well.
External-unstable-uncontrollable (low responsibility)	The course outline assigned the wrong chapters to study.
External-stable-controllable (high responsibility)	Left-handed, red-headed males never do well at this university.
External-stable-uncontrollable (low responsibility)	Educational psychology is bleeping tough.

Source: Based on Weiner, 1992.

Clearly, there are other causes to which performance can be attributed (mood, illness, or fatigue, for example), but these are more personal, more variable, and not easily amenable to scientific investigation.

Development of Attribution Tendencies. The tendency to attribute success and failure to either internal or external causes seems to be a relatively predictable and stable personality characteristic. However, it is less apparent in children younger than 9, who have not yet differentiated between such factors as ability and effort. Nicholls (1978) reports that these children equate effort with intelligence; they believe that smart people are those who work hard (and consequently succeed). At about 9 or 10, the child begins to consider ability as a separate factor that contributes to success. But even at this age, smartness is still equated with hard work. By age 11, however, the child typically shares our intuitive notions about the distinctions among ability, luck, effort, and task difficulty.

Performance Versus Mastery Goals. Children, Dweck (1986) informs us, seem to behave as though they subscribed intuitively to one of two views of intelligence: the **entity theory** or the **incremental theory.** If they subscribe to the entity theory, they behave as though they believe that intelligence is fixed and unchanging. Accordingly, their achievement goals are **performance goals;** that is, they will be moved

---

entity theory Dweck's label for the belief that ability is a fixed, unchanging entity. Associated with performance goals—that is, with doing well so as to be judged positively by others.

incremental theory Dweck's label for the belief that ability is malleable through work and effort. Associated with mastery goals—that is, with increasing personal competence.

performance goals Goals directed toward performing well rather than toward mastering a subject and increasing one's competence.

TABLE 10.4 ACHIEVEMENT GOALS AND ACHIEVEMENT BEHAVIOR

THEORY OF INTELLIGENCE	GOAL ORIENTATION	CONFIDENCE IN PRESENT ABILITY	BEHAVIOR PATTERN
Entity theory (Intelligence is fixed.)	*Performance goal* (Goal is to gain positive judgments/ avoid negative judgments of competence.)	*If high*	*Mastery oriented* (Seeks challenge; high persistence)
		If low	*Helpless* (Avoids challenge; low persistence)
Incremental theory (Intelligence is malleable.)	*Learning goal* (Goal is to increase competence.)	*If high or low*	*Mastery oriented* (Seeks challenge that fosters learning; high persistence)

Source: Adapted from Dweck (1986).

to obtain favorable judgments about their competence (about their ability) and to avoid unfavorable judgments. On the other hand, if they subscribe to the incremental theory, they behave as though they believe that intelligence is malleable. Accordingly, the goals of their achievement-oriented behavior will be **mastery goals** (also termed *learning goals*) rather than performance goals; that is, they will focus on effort and will attempt to increase their competence.

Dweck's analysis of attribution research strongly suggests that students whose basic orientation is toward performance goals (view intelligence as being fixed) need to have extremely high confidence in their ability if they are willing to accept challenges. Students whose confidence is lower are more likely to be characterized by what Dweck describes as "helplessness," primarily because they see failure as a direct reflection of their ability. In contrast, students who are oriented toward mastery (those who view intelligence as malleable) are far more likely to seek challenges and to be persistent. That is, when students view ability as being a function of effort, they are more likely to strive toward high achievement because for them the

cost of failure is not as high as it is for those who see ability as fixed and unchangeable (Dweck & Leggett, 1988; Erdley & Dweck, 1993). (See Table 10.4.)

Attribution and Achievement Motivation. The implications of attribution theory for understanding students' behavior become clearer when considered in relation to what is termed **achievement motivation.** Some individuals behave as though they have a high need to achieve, to be successful, to reach some standard of excellence; others behave as though they are more afraid of failing than desirous of success (McClelland et al., 1953). Research indicates that individuals who score high on measures of achievement motivation also tend to be the high achievers in school (Atkinson & Raynor, 1978).

Other relevant findings are that high-need achievers are typically moderate risk takers. They attempt tasks that are moderately difficult, thus providing themselves with a challenge while keeping their probability of success

---

mastery goals Goals directed toward increasing one's personal competence.

achievement motivation A need that, if high, is evident in a strong desire to achieve, to excel, to reach a high level of excellence. Achievement motivation can also be low.

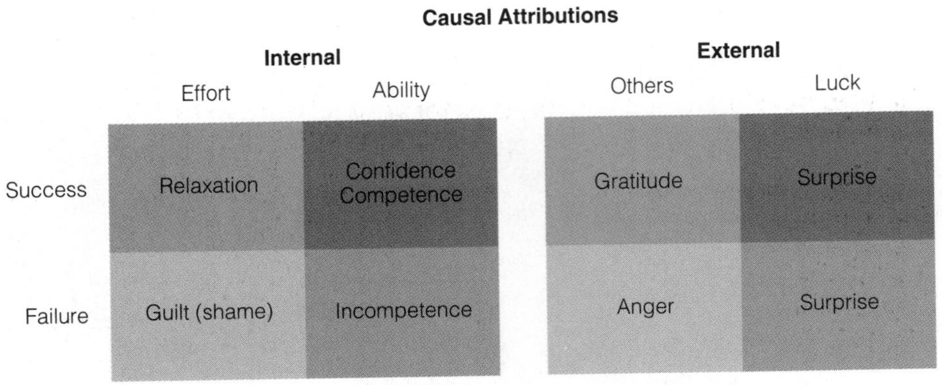

Causal Attributions

	Internal		**External**	
	Effort	Ability	Others	Luck
Success	Relaxation	Confidence Competence	Gratitude	Surprise
Failure	Guilt (shame)	Incompetence	Anger	Surprise

FIGURE 10.4 Relations between causal attributions and feelings associated with success and failure.

Locus of Control

	Internal	External
Success	Pride Confidence Competence	Grateful Thankful
Failure	Guilt	Anger Surprise

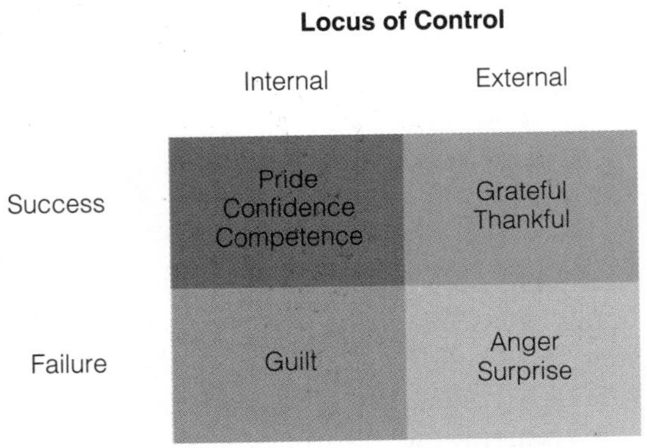

FIGURE 10.5 Relations between locus of control and feelings associated with success and failure.

fairly high (McClelland, 1958; Thomas, 1980). In contrast, low-need achievers typically attempt tasks that are quite difficult or quite easy. Why?

The answer may lie in attribution theory. If I attempt a very difficult task and fail, I will probably attribute my failure to task difficulty, a factor over which I have no control; hence, I will assume no personal responsibility and therefore experience no negative affect (emotion). If I am successful, there is again little positive affect because my success is not due to factors over which I have any control but to external factors. Moderate risk takers, on the other hand, can attribute success to skill or effort; similarly, they can attribute failure to

personal factors. In either case, there is considerably more emotional involvement in the outcomes of their performances (see Figures 10.4 and 10.5).

It appears reasonable to suppose, then, that high-need achievers will tend to be internally oriented, whereas low-need achievers will more likely attribute their performance to external factors. This supposition is, in fact, borne out by research (Greene, 1985; Wittrock, 1986).

CLASSROOM APPLICATIONS OF COGNITIVE VIEWS

Cognitive approaches to understanding motivation have a wealth of educational implications. This is not surprising because many of these approaches have been developed specifically in order to understand achievement in the classroom.

CHANGING ATTRIBUTIONS AND ACHIEVEMENT MOTIVATION

We know that attributions are related to motivation and performance and that internally oriented individuals typically manifest higher achievement motivation and set more realistic goals. There are indications, as well, that students with high achievement motivation are more satisfied with school and that they are less bored (Duda & Nicholls, 1992). An important question for educators is, Can externally oriented individuals be made more internally oriented?

A number of attribution-changing programs have been developed and investigated. As Weiner (1994) notes, the major objective of most of these programs is to move students in the direction of effort attributions; that is, the programs attempt to lead students to the understanding that their successes and failures ought to be attributed to their personal efforts. For example, a program developed by de Charms (1972) attempts to teach students to shift their locus of control from an external orientation—in which they see themselves as helpless "pawns" who have no responsibility for their own learning and achievement—to an internal orientation, in which they perceive themselves as "origins" and assume greater responsibility for the outcomes of their behavior. Similarly, a program developed by McCombs (1982) attempts to develop motivation not only by changing the student's attributions to internal causes but also by teaching cognitive strategies and metacognitive skills. It follows that as students become more adept at the management of these skills and strategies (as they learn more about learning) they will also begin to realize that they can exercise a great deal of control over learning and achievement—that it isn't all just a matter of luck and faith.

In most school-related tasks, luck should have little bearing on performance, although there are those students who will invoke that lady repeatedly in any case. They blame her when they have studied the wrong sections, inadvertently misaligned their answer sheets, or had the misfortune of being presented with inferior teachers. Teachers can exercise some control over the other three major categories to which performance outcomes can be attributed (effort, ability, and task difficulty), but luck can only be left to chance.

It should come as no great surprise that repeated failures are likely to have a negative effect on self-concept and on feelings of competence and that individuals who have failed more than they have succeeded will be reluctant to attribute their failures to lack of ability. Indeed, it appears reasonable to predict that repeated failures will contribute to external attribution and corresponding feelings of powerlessness. By the same token, repeated successes in tasks of moderate or high difficulty (rather than tasks too absurdly simple) are most likely to lead to positive self-concepts, feelings of competence, acceptance of personal responsibility for performance, and high achievement drives.

The key phrase undoubtedly is "personal responsibility." To the extent that students accept personal responsibility for their performance they will be emotionally involved, success will enhance their self-concepts, motivational forces will be largely intrinsic rather than extrinsic, and the problems of classroom management (discussed in the next chapter) will become interesting pedagogical problems rather than discipline problems.

CHANGING ACHIEVEMENT GOALS

Goal theory, another emphasis in cognitive explanations of motivation, looks at how the individual's goals affect behavior. An achievement goal, says Ames (1992), is a pattern of beliefs and attributions that produces an intention to do or accomplish something. Goal theory is based on two important observations, which have been mentioned earlier in this chapter:

1. Students who believe that the outcomes of their behaviors result from personal effort tend to develop mastery goals—goals that focus on the intrinsic value of the learning. (Recall that Dweck also labeled these "learning goals.") Such students focus on developing skills, understanding their work, becoming more competent—in short, mastering what they study. Mastery goals are associated with high need for achievement, with risk taking, and with positive attitudes toward learning (see Ames, 1992).

TABLE 10.5 INSTRUCTIONAL STRATEGIES DESIGNED TO PROMOTE A MASTERY ORIENTATION

▶ Present students with a variety of tasks with short-term goals that can be accomplished with reasonable effort.

▶ Assign work that is personally involving—hence less likely to lead to comparisons with other students.

▶ Emphasize competence and mastery in your evaluation procedures.

▶ Avoid comparative evaluations.

▶ Focus on the processes of learning and on comprehension.

▶ Avoid the social comparisons implicit in singling out students for public praise.

▶ Give students meaningful choices regarding important issues like curriculum, methods and pace of studying, and evaluation.

▶ Encourage students to set meaningful, competence-oriented goals.

▶ Reward students for effort and improvements rather than for performance and product.

▶ Emphasize individual progress in evaluations.

2. Students who believe that behavioral outcomes are a function of ability rather than effort develop performance goals. Their focus is on doing better than others, on achieving public recognition, on succeeding according to external norms. Learning and understanding are secondary for these students; doing well (performing) is all-important. Performance goals are associated with the avoidance of challenging tasks, use of short-term learning strategies, and negative affect following failure.

These two goal orientations are strongly influenced by whether students perceive classrooms as being oriented toward mastery. And that perception, says Ames (1992), is affected by at least three aspects of the classroom experience: tasks, evaluation, and authority. In an analysis of these three factors are numerous suggestions for teacher behaviors that might enhance student motivation. (Some of these are summarized in Table 10.5.)

1. *Tasks.* "Embedded in tasks," says Ames, "is information that students use to make judgments about their ability, their willingness to apply effortful strategies, and their feelings of satisfaction" (1992, p. 263). There are at least three important motivational

dimensions of tasks: variety, challenge, and meaningfulness.

Variety, notes Blumenfeld (1992), is associated with sustained motivation. And when tasks are defined in terms of specific, short-term goals, students are more likely to decide they can accomplish them with reasonable effort (to see themselves as efficacious). Similarly, tasks that are personally involving are less likely to lead students to compare their performance with that of others—and less likely to lead to performance goals.

2. *Evaluation.* One of the surest ways to develop a performance orientation is to use evaluation procedures that emphasize ability and that underline comparisons among students. When the focus in classrooms is on students' products and on correctness and memorization, rather than on the processes of learning and on comprehension, students soon become performance oriented. Unfortunately, as Mac Iver, Reuman, and Main (1995) point out, our traditional evaluation practices are, in fact, based largely on comparing the performance of a given student to that of other students.

Social comparisons are among the most obvious of performance-oriented evaluation

Drawing by Benard Schoenbaum; © 1989
The New Yorker Magazine. Inc.

procedures. They are evident, says Ames (1992), in the practice of making public the highest and lowest scores, of singling out students' papers and performances, of displaying students' achievements. The effect on those who do not compare favorably can be devastating.

There are evaluation practices such as criterion-referenced assessment or portfolios, described in Chapter 13, that avoid the most direct forms of social comparison, and that might contribute significantly to the development of more intrinsically motivated, mastery goals.

3. *Authority*. The extent to which teachers give students meaningful choices is directly related to students' mastery orientation. Research reviewed by Ames (1992) suggests that teachers who provide students with meaningful opportunities for autonomy are more likely to foster mastery orientations. Teachers who are highly controlling and who make all important decisions encourage performance goals. Ames notes that in most contemporary classrooms, students have little opportunity to make meaningful decisions regarding curriculum, methods and pace of studying, or assessment.

A REVIEW OF THE COGNITIVE VIEW

Why do some learners set challenging but attainable goals and others not? Why do some persist in the face of difficulty while others don't? How can teachers keep students interested?

Big questions, these, with no short or simple answers. But we have too little space here to be long-winded and no wish to be complex. So what follows is only a little bit of an answer squeezed from the contemporary cognitive view we have just reviewed.

A Cognitive View of the Learner. The learner, this view insists, is first of all a reflective, thinking being (that is, a cognitive being). In this view, motivation boils down to the individual learner's decisions about goals, how these decisions result from and interact with some of the learner's beliefs, and how the learner's behavior is guided by both beliefs and goals. In a sense, it is as though the learner evaluates the self in terms of wishes, inclinations, and abilities and evaluates goals in terms of likely rewards. And, as we have seen, for some learners, intrinsic rewards (often associated with mastery or learning) are more important than external rewards (often associated with performance or product).

The Importance of Self-Evaluation. We asked what is important. The cognitive view suggests that the student's self-evaluation is one thing that is important. Believing that we are bright and capable—and loved because we are lovable—is fundamentally important to each of us. Most of our lives, Kegan (1982) says, we struggle to be meaningful—to mean something to others. If we mean nothing, that is the measure of our personal worth.

The Role of the Teacher. Do teachers affect students' self-evaluations? Clearly, yes. Much of what teachers do—and can do—directly and indirectly influences students' perceptions of their competence and their meaningfulness. But the classroom factors that contribute to these evaluations do not mold them in simple ways. As Marshall and Weinstein (1984) put it, influences are complex and interactive. Often students' self-evaluations are based at least in part on comparisons with other students. But many factors (in complex interaction) are involved in the final evaluation. For example, in most competitive situations, success increases self-evaluations of ability; failure has the opposite effect. But if children are each given different tasks, the opportunity for comparison is much less than if all work on identical tasks. In much the same way, whole-class instructional procedures often provide more opportunity for direct comparisons than do small group approaches such as those used in cooperative learning.

In addition, students' self-evaluations clearly depend on the outcomes of their behaviors and on the responses of teachers and others. Other things being equal, success leads to positive self-evaluations more often than does failure. And teachers' responses to students are typically loaded with information. Gestures, attention, facial expressions, grades, and verbal comments are just a few sources of information that tell the student, "Gee, you're pretty dumb, kid" (or worse), or that say, "Hey, way to go!"

The Importance of Outcomes. Unfortunately, not everyone can do very well. In fact, not everyone is equally competent. But, as Marshall and Weinstein (1984) put it, the outcome of social comparisons need not always be negative for low achievers. If teachers and students alike see competence and intelligence as a matter of

Social comparisons, such as are implicit in the act of singling out the class valedictorian (who also happens to be class president) are a clear form of performance-oriented evaluation. Some argue that social comparisons of this nature can be quite devastating for other close competitors who are not so honored.

accumulating skills and knowledge through effort (Dweck's incremental theory), rather than as a fixed, unchangeable quality (entity theory), those who achieve less well need not suffer from unfavorable comparisons. Teachers who hold these views, claim Marshall and Weinstein, will favor noncompetitive learning, flexible grouping, mastery-oriented learning, and comparisons of a student's current performance with previous performance instead of with the performance of others.

Main Points

1. Theories of motivation attempt to answer questions about the causes of and reasons for behavior. Among historical explanations are instinct theory (complex, unlearned patterns of behavior common to an entire species account for behavior), psychological hedonism (people behave to obtain pleasure and avoid pain), and need theories (the urge to satisfy physical and psychological needs drives behavior).

2. Increasing arousal is defined by physiological changes (for example, in respiration and heart rate) accompanied by increasing alertness or wakefulness. Amount, intensity, meaningfulness, surprisingness, and complexity of stimulation are directly

related to the level of arousal. There is an optimal level of arousal for maximally effective behavior, and the individual will behave in such a way as to maintain arousal level at or near the optimal.

3. One responsibility of teachers is to maintain moderate levels of arousal in students. Overly high arousal, sometimes manifested in anxiety, often has a detrimental effect on students' learning and performance. In particular, test anxiety has repeatedly been shown to decrease grades. Highly anxious students do better when exposed to instructional methods that are more structured, less demanding of public interaction, and consequently less anxiety arousing.

4. Behavioristic approaches to motivation stress the importance of positive and negative extrinsic reinforcers. One very important reinforcer is praise; the effectiveness of the praise depends largely on the student's interpretation of the situation (hence praise has important cognitive connotations). It should be used systematically, deliberately, and intelligently.

5. Humanistic approaches emphasize intrinsic (internal) motives such as those relating to autonomy, competence, and self-actualization. The humanistic educator is especially concerned with both the personal development of students and the enhancement of positive self-concepts. Maslow's humanistic theory presents a hierarchical arrangement of need systems, with physiological needs at the lowest level (basic needs) and the need for self-actualization at the highest (metaneeds). R. W. White believes that an intrinsic need to develop competence motivation is an important human motive.

6. Cognitive theories describe humans as active, exploring, evaluating organisms capable of delaying gratification and of explaining the outcomes of their own behaviors (contrasted with traditional theories' more passive view).

7. Bandura suggests that ideas of self-efficacy (of personal effectiveness) are important in determining which behaviors will be undertaken (children are least likely to attempt activities in which they expect failure) and the amount of effort that will be expended (greater if success is anticipated). Judgments of self-efficacy are affected by enactive influences (successful outcomes increase positive judgments), vicarious influences (comparisons with others), persuasory influences (persuasion by others), and emotive influences (high arousal can increase or decrease judgments of self-efficacy).

8. Weiner's attribution theory says that individuals tend to attribute their successes or failures to internal (ability and effort) or external (difficulty or luck) causes. Some of these imply a high level of responsibility; others don't. Similarly, some causes imply a high degree of personal control; others don't.

9. Mastery-oriented learners try to increase their competence; performance-oriented learners focus on achievement. Dweck suggests that children who subscribe to the entity theory (intelligence is fixed) tend to be oriented toward performance goals. Children who subscribe to the incremental theory (intelligence increases with effort) are more likely to be oriented toward mastery (learning) goals.

10. Students whose need for achievement is high are typically more internally oriented (have an internal locus of control) and consequently are more likely to accept personal responsibility for the outcomes of their efforts. Achievement orientation can be modified by specific training programs that invite children to take risks, make predictions, modify predictions, establish realistic goals, and assume personal responsibility for the results of their behaviors.

11. Attribution-changing programs attempt to move students in the direction of making more effort attributions—that is, attributing successes and failures to the results of effort rather than to causes over which the individual has no personal control.

12. Most cognitively oriented, motivation-driven classroom interventions attempt to foster the development of mastery rather than performance goals by manipulating factors such as tasks (variety, personal meaningfulness and surmountable challenges foster commitment and persistence), evaluation (social comparisons encourage performance orientations), and authority (opportunities for meaningful autonomy enhance commitment and mastery goals).

APPLIED QUESTIONS

▶ Using library resources, describe some historical approaches to explaining human behavior.

▶ Outline a lesson in which the teacher makes deliberate use of the educational implications of arousal theory.

▶ Do you think that excessive use of external rewards might reduce intrinsic motivation? Why or why not?

▶ Illustrate how human needs are hierarchical. What educational implications can you draw from this observation?

▶ List a number of teacher attitudes and behaviors that are likely to contribute to the development of positive judgments of self-efficacy in students.

STUDY TERMS

achievement motivation **369**
alpha waves **356**
arousal **352**
attribution theory **366**
basic needs **358**
beta waves **356**
biofeedback **356**
causes **347**
competence motivation **361**
critical period **349**
deficiency needs **360**
distance receptors **352**
drives **350**
electroencephalograph (EEG) **356**
entity theory **368**

external orientation **367**
extrinsic motives **356**
growth needs **361**
imprinting **349**
incremental theory **368**
instincts **348**
internal orientation **367**
intrinsic motives **356**
Jonah complex **361**
locus of control **366**
mastery goals **369**
metaneeds **358**
motives **347**
need-drive theories **350**
needs **350**
pain/pleasure principle **357**

performance goals **368**
physiological needs **350**
praise **357**
psychological hedonism **349**
psychological needs **350**
reasons **347**
reflexes **348**
reinforcers **357**
self-actualization **361**
self-efficacy **364**
self-referent thought **364**
sensitive period **349**
sympathetic nervous system **351**
test anxiety **354**
ulterior motives **347**
Yerkes-Dodson law **352**

Suggested Readings

A practical guide to motivating students in school, with particular attention to the development of achievement motivation, is the following:

STIPEK, D. J. (1988). *Motivation to learn: From theory to practice*. Englewood Cliffs, N.J.: Prentice-Hall.

For a fascinating account of the effect of high arousal on human behavior, see:

SCHULTZ, D. P. (1964). *Panic behavior*. New York: Random House.

Cognitive theories of motivation are presented clearly at a sophisticated level in the following book:

WEINER, B. (1992). *Human motivation: Metaphors, theories and research*. Newbury Park, Calif.: Sage.

The Hamilton and Ghatala book presents practical educational applications of many of the theories discussed in this chapter. Especially relevant here is the ninth chapter, which looks at the practical implications of various motivational theories. Bandura's book is an excellent overview of current cognitive approaches to motivation; the Ames and Ames' collection of articles, and especially the more recent Ames article, look specifically at the application of cognitive motivational concepts to the classroom:

HAMILTON, R., & GHATALA, E. (1994). *Learning and instruction*. New York: McGraw-Hill.

BANDURA, A. (1991). Social cognitive theory of self-regulation. *Organizational Behavior and Human Performance, 50,* 248–287.

AMES, R., & AMES, C. (eds.). (1984). *Research on motivation in education (Vol. I): Student motivation*. New York: Academic Press.

AMES, C. (1992). Classrooms: Goals, structures, and student motivation. *Journal of Educational Psychology, 84,* 261–271.

The brown bear (*Ursus arctos*) is still found in small numbers in very limited mountainous areas of western Europe, in Russia, Asia, India, and northern China, as well as in North America. It is extinct in the British Isles (Southern, 1964).

CHAPTER II

Most people sell their souls and live with a good conscience on the proceeds.

LOGAN PEARSALL SMITH, *Afterthoughts*

Few men have virtues to withstand the highest bidder.

GEORGE WASHINGTON, *Moral Maxims*

Oh wad some power the giftie gie us
To see oursels as others see us!
It wad frae monie a blunder free us
An' foolish notion.

ROBERT BURNS, *To a Louse*

Classroom Management

PREVIEW

It may not come as a surprise to you that one of the principal reasons for teachers' unhappiness and premature retirement is discipline problems. This chapter, one of the more practical chapters in this text, outlines a number of strategies and principles that might be effective in preventing and/or correcting disruptive behavior. It looks too at the application of behavior modification in the classroom. The single most important point it makes is that here, as in medicine, prevention is far more valuable than correction.

Focus Questions

▶ Why is good classroom management essential for effective teaching?

▶ What are the principal characteristics of each of the following management models:

Roger's humanistic model
Kounin's teacher with-it-ness
Webster's democratic procedures
Dreikurs' logical consequences
Skinner's behavior modification
Canter's assertive discipline
Meichenbaum's cognitive behavior modification

▶ What are some strategies for preventive classroom management?

It was the day after Mouche, Marc Voisin's dirty-yellow dog, died. I hadn't ever actually seen anything die before, other than flies and gophers, and it had shaken me up some. Even though Mouche and I had not been that close, I felt like I'd lost a friend. Also, to tell the truth, I was a little afraid I might die too. One minute Mouche had been running, full of life, through the raspberry patch; the next, the bear he had stumbled across had clouted him up the side of the head and he was lying there dead. Deep down, I was afraid that could happen to me too. And not just in a dream.

I had a bit of trouble concentrating in school that day, and, as a distraction, I sharpened my pencil as pointed as it would get without breaking the lead, and then I used it to try to make a hole in my rubber eraser, pounding it against the eraser with my ruler. The teacher, my dad, didn't appreciate the distraction and told me to stop—which I did for a while, but then I forgot. Maybe his day wasn't much better than mine because it seems like there weren't all that many warnings before he called me to the front of the class, pulled out the strap from the top right-hand drawer, and whacked me once on each hand.

That straightened me right out for most of the year—especially after Horseface and his

brother, Paul, got into a fight during afternoon recess and my dad stood them in front of the whole school, bloody noses and all, each of them already crying. Then he strapped them one after the other, and after that we corrected our spelling test from the morning period.

That double strapping actually straightened everybody out for a long time. But there was once, later that year, when my dad kept me in after school and ordered me to scrub the inside walls of the outhouse. It seems that someone had chosen to be offended by a tiny bit of graffiti penciled above the small hole (there was a larger one). For a long time, I was convinced that God does watch all transgressors and reports directly to their teachers, but later I remembered that the spelling test we had been given that afternoon had contained most of the words found in the graffiti. In those days, I spelled turkey "t-e-r-k-e-e."*

That was my last major punishment that year other than the time I had to write "I will not squirt ink on Louise" 150 times. It was about then that they first started to talk about sending me to a private boarding school—a place for bright kids, I was told, although I did hear one of my cousins remark unkindly, "They're afraid he's turning into a discipline problem."

Classroom Management and Discipline

Teachers have always been highly concerned with **discipline** and **classroom management**—although the methods they have used to maintain classroom order have varied considerably.

---

*PPC: As a matter of academic interest, what was the graffiti?
Author: Luc Doré is a bird
And he is a terkee
I don't know if you herd
He is full of peapea.
(Hey, I was only in second grade.)

---

discipline The control aspects of teaching.

Strapping and even lashing were once a normal part of most teachers' teaching strategies, a fact to which I can testify. At other times, authorities have advocated highly permissive, nonpunitive techniques. What has remained constant, however, is the importance of classroom management in determining teaching success. As Wang, Haertel, and Walberg (1993) put it, "Effective classroom management has been shown to increase student engagement, decrease disruptive behaviors, and enhance use of instructional time, all of which results in improved student achievement" (p. 262).

SOME DEFINITIONS

Some of the various meanings of the term *discipline* are evident in these common statements:

> One of the reasons she's a good teacher is that she maintains such good discipline.

> They had to be disciplined again after they released the pigeons in the classroom.

> Now, Jack, for example, is a well-disciplined young man.

> What sort of discipline do you use in your classroom?

Although the term *discipline* is used frequently by teachers, administrators, and students, it is not always the correct word. Often, *classroom management* would be better.

In Kounin's words, discipline is simply "how a teacher handles misbehavior" (1970, p. v). As such, discipline includes a wide range of options such as punishments of various kinds, behavior modification programs, and various kinds of classroom management practices. *Classroom management* is a more inclusive term than *discipline*. It refers to the arrangement of classroom activities to facilitate teaching and learning.

---

classroom management A comprehensive term for the variety of teacher actions designed to facilitate teaching and learning in the classroom. Classroom management includes disciplinary actions, as well as daily routines, seating arrangements, and scheduling of lessons.

Hence, classroom management may include procedures designed to prevent misbehavior or to deal with it—in other words, classroom management includes discipline. In addition, it includes a wealth of procedures, routines, and practices that have much less to do with discipline than with teaching and learning.

Clearly, management and disciplinary acts may occur simultaneously or in close sequence, depending on the requirements of the immediate situation. Accordingly, this chapter discusses classroom management and discipline together. The emphasis throughout is on the practical and ethical aspects of disciplinary and management processes, rather than on the distinctions between the two.

IMPORTANCE IN TEACHING

As Doyle notes, some educators view management and discipline as a prerequisite to instruction—something to "get out of the way so that teaching can occur" (1986, p. 394). Not so. Neither classroom management nor classroom discipline can be taken care of and then put aside so that instruction and learning can take place. Rather, both are centrally involved in the ongoing process of teaching.

Discipline problems are one of the principal reasons for teachers' failure and stress (Blase & Pajak, 1985). Not surprisingly, when Merrett and Wheldall (1993) interviewed 176 secondary school teachers, they found that the topic of classroom management was one of the primary preoccupations. Unfortunately, however, classroom management techniques are often not included as a compulsory component of many teacher education programs, report Tonnsen and Patterson (1992). And where classroom management is included, the emphasis is too often on authority and control—that is, on the disciplinary aspects of classroom management—rather than on managing classrooms to optimize learning. That is, teachers are given lists of classroom management techniques designed to develop obedience and compliance in their students—rather than techniques designed to develop creative problem solvers, self-regulated risk takers, and independent thinkers who respond to their own intrinsic rewards rather than to pressure to achieve high grades.

This chapter deals with both aspects of classroom management: first, the facilitation of learning; and second, the prevention and correction of misbehaviors.

SOME CHARACTERISTICS OF CLASSROOMS

To put the subjects of this chapter into perspective, it's important to consider the environment (the context) in which teaching and learning occur—and the teacher manages.

Variety in the Classroom. In the same way that the "average student" is an abstraction that does not exist in the real world, there is no "average class." Every class is unique. Each has its special blend of personalities that interact with one another, and with the personality and style of the teacher, to create its own dynamic ecology—that is, its own ever-changing environment. Some classrooms are filled with obedient and compliant children; others are riddled with violence. Each day, note McCaslin and Good (1992), some 135,000 children in the United States bring guns to school! Thousands of others have been suspended or are on detention; thousands more are in institutions for juvenile offenders.

Some classes are a complex mix of different ethnic groups, different abilities, different language skills, different interests; others are a homogeneous collection of majority-group children. Some include only children of highly similar abilities and interests; others are inclusive classes, characterized by an unpredictable mix of special needs.

Some Common Characteristics. Yet, says Doyle (1979), certain characteristics are descriptive of most classes and need to be taken into account in the business of teaching students and managing classes. Specifically, claims Doyle, the events that occur in classes are:

multidimensional: They can include a variety of individuals participating in many different activities and working toward a number of goals.

simultaneous: Seldom is only one thing happening at a time. Even when they are engaged in direct, whole-class instruction, teachers may recognize different degrees of attentiveness among individual students and different behaviors (or misbehaviors) that may require them to interrupt the instructional process. As they phrase questions, they must also make decisions about who will answer, assess the pace of the lesson relative to time constraints, and constantly monitor individual students for signs of inattention or for potentially disruptive behaviors.

immediate: Many of the events that occur simultaneously in the classroom require a teacher's immediate response. Decisions must be made and implemented rapidly if the flow of classroom activity is to remain smooth and purposeful.

unpredictable: Given the immediacy, the multidimensionality, and the simultaneity of classroom events, their course at any given moment is highly unpredictable.

What Is Required of Teachers? To manage such an environment—one that demands a continuous, rapid sequence of immediate decisions and is as complex and unpredictable as a classroom—requires a special set of managerial skills. Unfortunately, these managerial skills are not like simple recipes that can be memorized and applied as needed. Rather, they are a complex set of skills whose effective use depends to a great extent on the personal philosophies and teaching styles of teachers, on their knowledge and understanding of pedagogical principles, and on the composition of their classes. It is not a simple task.

But it is not a completely overwhelming task either—although it might seem that way to the beginning teacher. Expert teachers do not need to consciously analyze all the elements simultaneously present in the classroom; they don't need to deliberately and sequentially monitor and appraise the immediate activities of each student, responding when necessary and all the while maintaining a wonderful pedagogical flow, never failing to recognize and capitalize on those brief, unpredictable opportunities that recent jargon labels "teachable moments." The expert teacher, Kagan (1988) tells us, does all these things, many of them unconsciously. Such teachers develop sequences of routines and strategies that become almost automatic.

Can the skills and the strategies used by expert teachers be learned?

In a word, yes. Some skills and strategies have been identified, and simply being aware of them might prove helpful to beginning teachers. For example, certain important pedagogical (instructional or teaching) skills concern sequencing, structuring, and managing the content of instruction. Many of these skills can be gleaned from what psychology knows about learning and development, and many are described in the chapters of this text.

But teaching is more than organizing content. Teaching also requires important classroom management skills having to do with paying attention to students and being aware of ongoing classroom events. As we see later in this chapter, some teachers are more "with it" than others; they are more aware of what is going on in their classrooms and are better able to direct the flow of activities to keep students on-task (involved) and interested. Some teachers are more gifted in the art, although not necessarily the science, of teaching. Such teachers can more skillfully build the classroom environments— the contexts—that are most conducive to learning and to happiness and least conducive to management and discipline problems.

In addition to the artistic, pedagogical, and with-it-ness skills that teachers require are a wealth of specific strategies and potential responses to classroom events that can be learned and applied in the discipline and management of classes. These strategies and responses are the subject of this chapter.

CONTROL VERSUS PERMISSIVENESS

At certain times in the history of educational practice, the notion that teachers are responsible for controlling activity in their classrooms— that is, for controlling the behavior of their students—has been highly unpopular. Some of this unpopularity can be traced to educational and philosophical writings that have stressed the importance of freedom, self-determination, self-worth, individuality, and other humanistic concerns. These writings have often been associated with liberal and permissive childrearing and educational methods. And, to a large extent, the same concerns define much of the spirit of our times. Most parents and teachers like to think of themselves as liberal and permissive rather than conservative and restrictive. Most would choose to be democratic rather than autocratic.

The Need for Control. Is control therefore necessary? Is it ethical? Does it violate our commitment to value the autonomy, the self-direction, of the child?

There are no simple answers. If there were, there would be little controversy, and behaviorists and humanists would have much less about which to disagree.

Consider, first, that control of student behavior may be absolutely necessary in some situations—as, for example, when Johnny insists on repeatedly setting fire to the library.* Teachers, by virtue of their position and by virtue of their duties, have a responsibility to exercise control over student behavior. Indeed, it is not at all unreasonable to insist that the exercise of control is one of the teacher's most important duties because, as Evertson and Harris (1992) point out, without classroom

---

*PPC: It might be worth noting that Johnny is not the only one who feels compelled to burn books. Here, for example, a group of parents recently decided that a whole raft of books used in high school English courses should be banned. And they actually had a bonfire in front of the school board offices.

AUTHOR: Fear of fire is not why this bear is so insistently politically correct.

control, instruction may be totally ineffective. Note, however, that we are not speaking here of a fear-enforced control that might have been characteristic of some of yesterday's schools. Control can be achieved, or at least facilitated, in a variety of gentle ways, some of which can be learned.

Parents too control their children (or at least try), often by setting limits for their behavior. Part of the successful socialization process requires that children be prevented from engaging in behaviors that might be injurious to themselves or to others. Thus, parents do not permit their children to play with dinner as it is cooking on the stove, to insert knives in electrical outlets, to jump off ladders, or to discharge firearms in the garage. Less extreme instances of control involve the teaching of socially appropriate behavior, of values and morals—of "shoulds" and "should nots." It is less by accident than by virtue of parental control that children learn not to deface walls, steal other people's property, or kill the neighbor's dog. In short, certain standards of behavior are learned at least partly as a function of parental control. Whether such control involves reinforcement, punishment, models, reasoning, or a combination of these and other strategies cannot hide the fact that control is being exercised.

Control in the Classroom. The classroom situation is not really very different. Teachers have often been described as acting *in loco parentis*— in the place of parents. They are urged to act in all ways as might a wise, judicious, and loving parent. And there is, in fact, no great incompatibility between values held in highest esteem by those who describe themselves as humanists and the techniques of behavior control that have been described by science. Love, empathy, warmth, genuineness, and honesty can go a long way toward ensuring a classroom climate conducive to learning and development. In spite of these highly desirable qualities, however, discipline problems are not uncommon in classrooms. That teachers should judiciously administer rewards and punishment in an effort to maintain an effective educational environment does not mean that they care less for their students; indeed, it might well indicate that they care more.

SOME SPECIFIC CLASSROOM MANAGEMENT MODELS

In the classroom, as in medicine, prevention should be valued more highly than correction, argues Black (1994b). And it is reassuring that research is paying increasing attention to **preventive strategies**—the methods by which teachers might prevent the occurrence of discipline problems. Perhaps the most important (though not entirely surprising) finding of this research is that the degree of order in a classroom depends far less on the frequency and insistence with which the teacher acts to maintain or restore order than on the nature of ongoing classroom activity. As Black points out, teachers who are most effective at managing classrooms are those who design engaging and motivating lessons, who communicate goals and expectations clearly to students, and who use unobtrusive and subtle techniques for maintaining students' attention and on-task behavior. These teachers, claims Black, can "throw away the hickory stick."

The second most important finding of this research concerns the timing of a teacher's interventions. The most successful classroom managers are those teachers who seem to antic-

---

in loco parentis A Latin expression meaning, literally, in the place of parents. Teachers are said to have rights and responsibilities *in loco parentis* to the extent that society charges them with the care and education of children.

---

preventive strategies Instructional strategies designed to prevent the occurrence of discipline problems. Preventive strategies are an intrinsic part of good classroom management.

Models of classroom management range from highly permissive, where the teacher tries to intervene as little as possible, to highly directive, where the teacher assumes primary responsibility for establishing and enforcing rules of conduct. But even where there are clear rules, as in this classroom, classroom management might still be highly democratic and humanistic.

ipate most accurately when misbehaviors are likely to occur and intervene early to prevent them. In addition, the most effective interventions are subtle, brief, and often almost private, and as a result they do not interfere with ongoing classroom activities.

Preventive strategies are part of effective classroom management. That is, they depend on the arrangement of classroom activities to facilitate teaching and learning. There is a great deal of advice about the best ways of doing this, much of it based on the collective experience of successful teachers and on the systematic observation of teachers in their classrooms. For what it might be worth to you, this chapter presents a distillation of such advice. Bear in mind, however, that your personality is one of the most important factors in the classroom situation. Students find reasons to like or to dislike teachers in the combination of elusive and abstract qualities that define personality. Unfortunately, however, desirable personality characteristics cannot easily be acquired if you don't already have them—nor can those less desired simply be thrown away like a worn-out pair of jeans. Not everybody should be a

teacher. For example, if you don't really care for children, and if they don't like you very much either, please . . .*

MODELS OF CLASSROOM MANAGEMENT

The advice that the various experts give teachers about how to manage their classrooms and discipline their students varies enormously—which is not always a very reassuring thing, especially for beginning teachers. Much of the variation stems from fundamentally different philosophical orientations. That is, these experts often have very different notions about what the causes of misbehavior are, as well as very different notions about what sort of intervention is most effective and most appropriate.

At one extreme are management models that recommend the least amount of intervention possible: for example, open schools and

---

*PPC: Perhaps the author should finish the sentence. Those who should take it to heart the most probably won't bother finishing it.

AUTHOR: Those of you who didn't bother finishing this sentence, well . . .

TABLE 11.1 MODELS OF CLASSROOM DISCIPLINE

	THEORETICAL UNDERPINNING	BELIEFS ABOUT CAUSES OF MISBEHAVIOR	PRINCIPAL RECOMMENDATIONS	ADVOCATES
MOST PERMISSIVE– LEAST DIRECTIVE	Humanistic	Poor self-concept	Minimal intervention; teacher should provide supportive environment, encourage self-development	Carl Rogers Michael Marland
	Democratic	Inappropriate goals; faulty understanding of consequences; illogical assumptions and conclusions	Teacher should be democratic rather than autocratic; set reasonable limits; use techniques of reasoning and logic to identify goals; point out logical consequences of behaviors; use class meetings for rule setting and discussion	Jacob Kounin Rudolf Dreikurs Staten Webster
LEAST PERMISSIVE– MOST DIRECTIVE	Behavioristic	Misbehaviors are learned; failure to learn appropriate alternative behaviors	Behavior modification techniques such as reinforcement, modeling, punishment	Burrhus F. Skinner Lee Canter

humanistic approaches like that of Carl Rogers. At the other extreme are the more restrictive behavior modification models that make extensive use of systematic rewards and punishments. And in between are various models that try to balance permissiveness with restrictiveness, and that offer a variety of suggestions about how this might be accomplished.

The remainder of this chapter describes several of the most representative classroom management and discipline models, loosely classified in terms of their principal orientation and in terms of the degree of permissiveness and restrictiveness they advocate. Table 11.1 summarizes them, as it also previews much of what follows.

FREEDOM TO LEARN: CARL ROGERS

The clear goal of the humanistic teacher, claims Carl Rogers (Rogers & Freiberg, 1994), is to develop self-discipline in students. Broadly defined, self-discipline is "knowledge about one-self and the actions needed to grow and develop as a person" (p. 221). That, says Rogers, is the goal of most teachers, but not all take the right path.

And what is the right path? Simply put, it is among the most nondirective of classroom management models. Rogers, like Maslow, believed that all students have a basic desire to grow, to develop, to *become*. Ideally, the role of parents and teachers is to provide the sort of supportive environment that facilitates and fosters growth. Because of the importance of the child's self-concept for growth and happiness, Rogers argues that children should be loved—no, more than simply loved, children should be loved unconditionally. Hence, the sort of environment that teachers are encouraged to provide for children is one that accepts them unconditionally, that values them for what they are, and that fosters their growth. In this model, the teacher is a facilitator rather than a director, and students are active and fundamentally important participants in the teaching/

learning process. To illustrate what he means, Rogers describes a number of model classrooms in which children develop self-discipline and, at the same time, also develop a strong sense of personal responsibility. A scenario from one of these classrooms is summarized in the case "So Where's the Teacher?"

Unfortunately, Rogers does not provide a list of specific classroom management techniques that teachers should learn and apply to their classrooms. Doing so would, in a sense, violate his belief in the autonomy of the student. This does not mean that he advocates the total permissiveness that sometimes characterized the open classrooms that were briefly popular in the early 1970s (see Chapter 9). As we saw, he argues that students should be helped to become self-disciplined. And what is most important for helping students grow and become self-disciplined is the atmosphere of trust, of warmth, and of acceptance that the teacher fosters.

Student-Centered Schools. As we saw in Chapter 9, humanistic education is student rather than teacher centered. The role of the teacher in a student-centered school is nondirective

or, to use Rogers' term, *facilitative*. In such schools, students are self-motivated and self-directed and require a minimum of direction. Common instructional techniques include inquiry approaches, group projects, and self-assessment. At the other extreme, that of teacher-centered schools, teachers are highly directive, and students are controlled through external rewards and punishments. Common instructional techniques in teacher-centered schools include lecturing, questioning, drill and repetition, and teacher demonstrations.

Between these two extremes, according to Rogers and Freiberg (1994), are schools where the teacher's role is somewhere between being facilitative and directive. Common instructional techniques in such schools include cooperative learning approaches and guided discovery. Figure 11.1 summarizes these distinctions.

General Guidelines for Nondirective Classroom Management. Although Rogers is not highly prescriptive with respect to the specifics of what teachers should and should not do to manage their classrooms, a number of instructional recommendations are implicit in his general description of the techniques and the language

CASE: So Where's the Teacher?

THE SITUATION: A day in Ms. Wilcox's classroom
Early one morning, Ms. Wilcox, history teacher, phones in to say she's sick and won't be able to come to school. The principal's wife answers the phone, but forgets to pass on the message.

In her class, Ms. Wilcox has set up a program entitled Consistency Management. This program gives students responsibility for the conditions *they* have decided are necessary for the classroom to work for them. These conditions are expressed in a series of jobs for which different students volunteer. When necessary, students have been helped by Ms. Wilcox to learn these jobs, which rotate to different students every three weeks.

Now that Ms. Wilcox is sick, different students in each class simply go ahead and assume their normal responsibilities. Some serve as student facilitators, essentially teaching lessons, presenting projects, leading discussion groups, sending in attendance slips, and doing other routine and not-so-routine things.

During the final period of the day, someone in the office needs to have Ms. Wilcox sign a form. But they can't find her anywhere. So self-disciplined are her students that her absence has gone absolutely unnoticed all day.

Source: Based on Rogers & Freiberg (1994).

TEACHER CENTERED	
TEACHER'S ROLE	**INSTRUCTIONAL TECHNIQUES**

TEACHER'S ROLE	INSTRUCTIONAL TECHNIQUES
Highly directive Teacher directs student behavior and controls through external rewards and punishments **Semidirective/semifacilitative** Teacher and students cooperate in designing the classroom and in establishing its important activities **Nondirective/facilitative** Teacher encourages student autonomy and self-discipline	lecturing questioning drill and practice demonstration discussion cooperative groups guided discovery contracts role playing projects inquiry self-assessment

STUDENT CENTERED

FIGURE 11.1 Teacher-centered versus student-centered discipline and learning.

Source: Based on C. R. Rogers and H. J. Freidberg, *Freedom to Learn* (4th ed.), 1994. New York: Merrill. Reprinted by permission of Prentice-Hall.

of facilitative, nondirective teaching. Specifically, nondirective teachers

> *are reflective.* They reflect important aspects of the learner's behavior and conversation to get them to think about their own thoughts. (For example, the teacher says, "What I sense you're saying is . . .")
>
> *provide support for learners.* Communicate unconditional regard and support.
>
> *encourage self-assessment.* For example, "How do you feel about your acting?"
>
> *develop responsibility in students.* "What do *you* think you should do?"
>
> *foster self-actualization.* Provide opportunities for learning and growth. Encourage the development of special talents.

Strengths and Weaknesses. The major strength, and the major appeal, of Carl Rogers' model is its attention to the uniqueness and the worth of the individual. Its emphasis on the development of personal responsibility, the importance of the teacher's attitudes toward children, and a

climate of trust and love in the classroom are also among its strengths.

Its principal weakness from the beginning teacher's point of view is that it presents few specific recommendations for teacher behaviors that might prevent or correct discipline problems.

CARING FOR CHILDREN: MICHAEL MARLAND

Michael Marland (1975) also describes a number of classroom management strategies and recommendations that are clearly humanistic; however, they are more specific than those suggested by Rogers.

Caring for Children. It's important, says Marland, not only to care for children but to let them know they are cared for. In this connection, one obvious but highly useful classroom strategy is to memorize pupils' names as soon as possible. More important, perhaps, is to learn as much as you can about each student. Relevant information can be obtained from conversations with other teachers (but beware of their prejudices and the consequent expectations that you might develop), from records, from involvement in extracurricular activities, and from parents and others. The children you teach should be more than just names and faces. The extent to which you care about them is reflected in the knowledge and understanding that you have of each. And the depth of your caring also affects how much they care about you, about each other, and about their own selves.

Setting Rules. Classroom management and discipline would be much simpler if we could just give teachers a clear and simple list of rules and regulations that should govern all students in classrooms—complete with prescribed punishments for violation of these rules.

It's not quite so simple. Rules for student conduct are not and should not be fixed and absolute, says Marland. Instead, they must be relative to teachers, to situations, and to students. Because of their different temperaments and styles, not all teachers expect or approve of similar student behaviors. Nor should teachers expect conformity to the same rules among students of widely differing ages and experience. And the rules of conduct imposed in a physical education class are quite different from those imposed during a recitation or a final examination.

Despite the relativity of rules, research suggests a number of generally valid observations. Probably the most important is that effective classroom management depends to a large extent on the successful establishment of rules and procedures early in the school year (Doyle, 1986). However, because rules are highly relative to situations, they are not usually established formally; that is, teachers seldom tell students that this is a rule and that is a rule and that is another rule and so on. Instead, students tend to learn most rules indirectly, often when infractions of those rules occur. Many rules are never made explicit but are simply implied by the teacher's interventions.

In contrast, many routines are taught explicitly and directly. Particularly in the elementary grades, such routines are indispensable to the smooth operation of the class and govern the activities of teachers and students. They specify where books and supplies are to be kept, how questions are to be asked and answered, how games are to be played, where reading circles are to be placed, and dozens of other details of classroom activity. The establishment of such routines is an important aspect of classroom management that provides a context within which learning can be greatly facilitated.

Routines need to be established early in the school year. As Doyle (1986) observes, the most successful classroom managers are those who, in a sense, hover over activities at the beginning of the year, guiding and directing students until procedures have become routine and the routines have been learned and accepted by all students. Although rules and routines need to be predictable and consistent, this does not mean that they must always be enforced inflexibly. Even in the highly controlled, isolated one-room school that I attended, the "no talking" and "no leaving your desk without permission" rules occasionally could be bent and sometimes broken.

I remember this happening one day when a bear ambled across the schoolyard and the teacher (my father) allowed the entire class to crowd up against the windows and watch. Later that day, he delivered a marvelous lesson on how bears socialize in the woods beyond the river, how they den up in the winter to dream of wild blueberries, and what their cubs look like when they are first born.

For days after that, I kept looking out the window, hoping to see a bear. Even now, years later, when I'm bored and tired I sometimes catch myself looking for a bear through my window. . . .

But there are few places for bears here.

Giving Legitimate Praise. Praise, claims M. Marland (1975), is one of the most powerful of the teacher's tools. Hence teachers need to arrange situations so that they can make frequent but legitimate use of praise. However, they need to be careful to observe two simple guidelines concerning the use of praise and criticism:

1. Praise, given its effect on self-esteem and self-concept, should be public. On occasion, it should be communicated to parents and other interested adults as well.

2. Criticism, in contrast, also because of its effects on self-esteem and self-concept, should be given privately.

In addition, both praise and criticism should be specific rather than general. As we saw in Chapter 10, research clearly demonstrates that praise and punishment that are not contingent on behavior or that are not clearly related to a specific behavior are much less likely to be effective. Thus, Marland suggests that a student should not be admonished in general terms such as "Behave yourself" or "Be good." Instead, students should be directed to engage in a specific behavior and given a reason for that behavior. For example, the teacher might say, "Please put down your water pistol and your hunting knife because you are disturbing the class." Presumably, the rule relating to the inadvisability of disturbing the class will already have been explained and justified and the penalties for repeated infraction of that rule will have been made explicit.

Using Humor. The effectiveness of humor is often overlooked by teachers who do not consider themselves spontaneously humorous. And teacher training facilities have not gone out of their way to encourage prospective teachers to learn either how to make others laugh or, perhaps most important, how to laugh at themselves. Potentially explosive confrontations can often be avoided by turning aside an implied student challenge with a skillful and humorous parry.

Consider, for example, Ms. Howard, who, because of her reputation for maintaining order in the classroom, has been assigned a ninth-grade class that might generously be described as predelinquent. (Less generous descriptions are entirely inappropriate in a polite textbook.) On the first day of class, she is challenged. One Rodney Phillips, closely modeled after a popular television personality who is himself modeled after a stereotype of the 1950s, finds an excusable error in Ms. Howard's arithmetic computations on the chalkboard. "She can't even add proper and they call her a teacher," he says for the benefit of his classmates. Whereupon Ms. Howard immediately falls to her knees and, in an amateurish imitation of the television hero, prays loudly to some undisclosed source to "Make me perfect again like I used to be!" Laughter that might otherwise have been directed at her is now with her. Ms. Howard simply has the knack of not taking herself too seriously.

Shaping the Learning Environment. Everything involved in teacher–learner interactions and in the teaching/learning environment can facilitate or impede classroom discipline. M. Marland (1975) suggests various ways to personalize the learning environment. For instance, there is something impersonal and cold about the traditional, dominating position of the teacher's desk at the front-center of the class. Similarly, students' desks traditionally are aligned in straight, even-length rows with uniform spaces front, back, and sides. Eyes front! Of course, certain definite advantages are inherent in this traditional placement, not the least of which are that there must be some focal point for students' attention and that it is considerably easier for students to look to the front to see their teacher than it is to look to the rear. My eleventh-grade teacher moved her desk to the back of the room—not because she was experimenting with ways to personalize the classroom environment but because she could more easily watch those among us who had already dedicated their lives to mischief. We suspected as well that she had tired of being bombarded with our crude, elastic-propelled spitballs.

Marland's advice that the learning environment be personalized goes beyond a search for a more personal arrangement of desks. It includes those small decorative touches that are often more visible in the early rather than the later grades. Posters, charts, wall hangings, and other instructional and/or decorative objects need not be provided solely by the school and by teachers but might also be provided by students.

Classroom climate is more than the physical environment. As was shown in Chapter 8, for example, creativity appears to be fostered in certain climates (warm, friendly, and so on) and to be impeded in others (cold, authoritarian). So, too, certain classroom climates are more conducive to preventive discipline than others. Glasser (1969), for example, says that discipline problems will be minimized in warm, personal environments in which all students are accepted as capable.

The case "A City-Class" is one example of a personally meaningful classroom environment, which also involves the use of some reinforcement principles for classroom management and learning.

Strengths and Weaknesses. The major strengths of Marland's recommendations have to do with their attention to the dignity and worth of individual students, as well as with their relatively specific nature. Particularly useful are the suggestions for setting rules and using praise and humor, as well as the suggestions for establishing a classroom climate conducive to learning.

Like most models of classroom management, however, Marland's suggestions cannot cover all possible situations. As a result, they are far more appropriate in some circumstances than others—for example, in lower rather than higher grades. In addition, they provide few suggestions for correcting discipline problems but are more useful for preventing them.

TEACHER WITH-IT-NESS AND DESISTS: JACOB KOUNIN

Kounin (1970) argues that what successful teachers do to prevent misbehavior is probably more important than whatever they might do to handle misbehavior once it has occurred. Following detailed analysis of teachers' behavior in actual classrooms, he describes a handful of specific behaviors that appear to be closely related to successful classroom management, and he identifies a number of teacher behaviors more likely to lead to student misbehaviors.

With-It-Ness. The most successful teachers, says Kounin, seem to be more aware than less successful teachers of what is going on in their classrooms, of who is responsible for infractions of rules, and of when intervention is

CASE: A CITY-CLASS

THE SITUATION: Mrs. Fitzsimmons, a good teacher, as recollected by George, teacher in training

In third grade, Mrs. Fitzsimmons designed a "city" in which my fellow students and I could actively take part. Every two weeks we elected a mayor, who was given privileges such as opening the "city gate" so the students could come into the classroom. Along the outside edges of the classroom we set up stores, restaurants, offices, and a zoo with large cardboard boxes, assigning students to each vocation. The currency in "our city" was silver-painted bottle caps with numbers; merchandise in the store was brought from home. If we behaved well all day and lessons were completed, we were given time to transact in "our city," which was a learning experience in itself. By rewarding good behavior there was peer pressure to pay attention. As we got older, extra-credit assignments were given to those who had completed their work and could be a distraction in the classroom.

necessary. These teachers are more *with it*. **With-it-ness** is important for maintaining order in the classroom. A teacher who is with it knows what is going on and is more likely to be respected by students.

Precisely what with-it-ness is and how it can be developed are important matters for the teacher. Unfortunately, we know little about its development, although we may know more about its nature. Kounin (1970) arrived at teacher with-it-ness scores by looking at how often a teacher successfully directed a student to **desist**—that is, to stop engaging in some off-task behavior. Teachers with the highest scores were those whose "desists" were on target and on time (neither too early nor too late). Teachers who were less with it tended to instruct the wrong students to desist, or they tended to deliver their desist requests either after an off-task behavior had been going on for some time or too far ahead of its occurrence.

In an attempt to define with-it-ness in concrete terms, Kounin describes several components of with-it "teacher desist behaviors." According to Kounin, the most with-it teachers use desists that

▶ Are clear in the sense that they provide enough information for the student to understand specifically what is required. (For example, the desist, "Quit that!" is not nearly as clear as "Edward, stop writing on the window.")

▶ Suggest some alternative, on-task behavior rather than simply requesting cessation of the off-task behavior. (For example, the teacher continues "Please return to your seat, Edward.")

---

with-it-ness Kounin's expression for a quality of teacher behavior manifested in the teacher's awareness of all the important things happening in a classroom. Teachers who are high in with-it-ness make more effective use of desists.

desist To stop, to refrain from. In education, desists are teacher behaviors intended to make a student stop (desist from) some ongoing or impending misbehavior. Desists may take the form of threats, simple requests, orders, pleas, and so on.

▶ Praise on-task behavior while ignoring concurrent off-task activities. (For example, again directed at Edward, "Edward, could you write those words in your notebook as neatly as you did yesterday? You have such a nice notebook.")

▶ Provide descriptions of desirable behaviors or of relevant classroom rules. ("Hey, Edward, the caretaker gets very upset when someone writes on the window because he has to clean them.")

▶ Provide timely desists (they occur before the misbehavior spreads and/or intensifies).

▶ Provide desists that are on target (they are directed toward the principal wrongdoer).

Also, highly effective teachers seemed more aware of what Kounin calls the **ripple effect.** The ripple effect is simply the tendency of the effects of a teacher's behavior to spread to other students to whom they were not directed. For example, a teacher's desists directed toward me ("Stop eating your pencil, Guy, or I'll just have to strap you. Again.") always seemed to ripple over and work for Luc Doré, who would immediately stop doing whatever he had been doing. He feared the strap even more than I did.

Kounin's (1970) research on teacher with-it-ness led to the conclusion that timely and on-target desists are associated with less deviant behavior in the classroom and more involvement in classroom activities. This conclusion was later corroborated in a study by Brophy and Evertson (1976) and again in research conducted by Copeland (1987). In Copeland's study, teachers interacted with a computer simulation of a classroom situation. The simulation allowed the investigator to assess teachers' multiple-attention and vigilance skills—described in much the same terms as Kounin's with-it-ness. Teachers were then observed in their classrooms, and measures were obtained of the extent to which their students remained

---

ripple effect Kounin's term for the tendency of the effects of teacher desists to spread to students other than those to whom they were directed.

on-task or were disruptive. Copeland reports that the highest on-task scores were associated with high teacher vigilance and attentiveness.

Overlapping. Classrooms, as we noted earlier, are characterized by multiple sequences of events occurring simultaneously.

Successful teachers, says Kounin, are able to deal with several matters occurring at one time—a situation termed **overlapping.** Overlapping occurs in two different kinds of situations: when a desist is required in the course of a lesson or when something intrudes on the flow of the lesson. Both situations are illustrated in the case "In the Counting House." The bathroom request is a mild intrusion but one that would have been disruptive had Kightly interrupted himself to say, "Yes, okay, you can go to the bathroom, Sam." And the intercep-

tion of the Evelyn West note is a nondisruptive desist—again, a situation that would have been clearly disruptive had Kightly stopped in mid-sentence (as Ms. Regina Donnelly typically does in her class) and said, "Evelyn West! Would you like to read that note out loud to the class?"

The guiding principle in dealing with overlapping, notes Kounin, is that the ongoing flow of classroom activities be interrupted as little as possible.

Smoothness and Momentum. Successful teachers keep the pace of classroom activity flowing smoothly. This means not only that the teacher must be able to deal with overlapping but also that transitions between classroom activities occur smoothly. Kounin reports that a normal school day contains an average of more than thirty-three major changes in learning activities (not including nonacademic transitions such as going to recess or lunch). These include transitions from one subject to another, as well as transitions from one major activity to another within lessons (say, from listening to reading, from reading to writing, from individual work to group activity).

---

overlapping Kounin's term for the simultaneous occurrence of two or more events in the classroom, each requiring the teacher's attention. Good class managers can handle overlapping events without disrupting the flow of classroom activities.

CASE: IN THE COUNTING HOUSE

THE PLACE: Walnut Creek Elementary
THE SETTING: Dennis Kightly's sixth-grade class
THE SITUATION: Mr. Kightly is reading a passage from Charles Dickens' *A Christmas Carol*

". . . At length the hour of shutting up the counting-house arrived. With an ill-will Scrooge dismounted from his stool, and tacitly admitted the fact to the expectant clerk in the Tank, who instantly snuffed his candle out, and put on his hat.

" 'You'll want all day to-morrow, I suppose?' said Scrooge. . . ."

While reading, the very with-it Mr. Kightly notices that Sam Taylor, who today has a touch of the galloping something, has raised his hand tentatively in the beginning of the signal that

means, "Sorry but I gotta go quick." At the same time, he sees that Evelyn West has just completed a note and is reaching to pass it to her cousin, Mary West.

" 'If quite convenient, sir . . .' "

Mr. Kightly continues, at the same time nodding almost imperceptibly to Sam, who immediately lurches, bent over, from his desk.

" 'It's not convenient,' said Scrooge, 'and it's not fair. If I was to stop half-a-crown . . .' "

By now Mr. Kightly has reached Evelyn's desk. He intercepts the message in mid-air, returns to his desk, and drops it in the wastebasket without missing a beat.

" '. . . for it, you'd think yourself ill-used . . .' "

Reading from Dickens, 1843/1986, p. 23.

Good teachers, says Kounin, have smooth transitions that maintain the momentum of classroom activities. In fact, reports Kounin, **jerky transitions** and lesson interruptions are among the principal causes of students' inattentiveness, restlessness, and misbehavior. He describes several major causes of lesson slowdown or interruption, or of jerky transitions:

"Stimulus-boundedness"—the teacher's attention is interrupted by some extraneous stimulus. For example, if Mr. Kightly had interrupted his reading when he saw Evelyn West writing her note, and said, "That reminds me. I want each of you to write a note to your parents about getting permission to get back late from the field trip on Friday. So remind me after I finish this story."

"Thrusts"—the teacher interrupts students' activities without prior signal and without consideration for their readiness.

"Dangles"—the teacher interrupts an ongoing activity and then returns to it again.

"Truncations"—the teacher does not return to the original activity after being interrupted.

"Flip-flops"—the teacher makes a transition from one activity to a second and then flip-flops back to the first activity, as though he has changed his mind.

"Overdwelling"—the teacher spends far more time than necessary on some aspect of a lesson or perhaps with some aspect of a student's behavior (or, more often, misbehavior); this is a type of lesson slowdown.

"Fragmentation"—the teacher breaks down an activity (or a group of students) in such a way that individuals are required to wait unnecessarily, resulting in a lesson slowdown; for example, a teacher has students come to the chalkboard, one at a time, to complete a simple arithmetic problem—

"Now it's your turn, Bobby"—while the others wait their turns. But if there is nothing to be learned from watching Bobby, all students might come up at once, greatly reducing waiting time and improving the momentum of the lesson.

Maintaining Focus. The most important factor in determining classroom order is not the frequency or strength of teachers' interventions so much as the nature of ongoing classroom activity.

There are a large number of different classroom activities. These include seat work, student presentations, small group activities, discussions, recitations, demonstrations, lectures, giving instructions, tutoring, and so on. In the elementary school, an activity typically lasts somewhere between 10 and 20 minutes; in the higher grades, activities often last somewhat longer. Between activities are transitions, also sometimes considered a type of activity.

In an extensive study of student involvement and classroom activity, Gump (1969) found that small group activities led by the teacher brought about the greatest involvement. In contrast, student presentations elicited the least student involvement—at least on the part of nonpresenters. Subsequently, a number of researchers have reported that involvement is lowest when students are doing seat work and highest when teachers are actively leading the class (see, for example, Burns, 1984; Ross, 1984). Accordingly, disruptions and misbehaviors are most likely to occur during seat work, during student presentations, and during transitions.

Kounin (1970) describes three different ways by which successful teachers attempt to maintain students' focus on ongoing activities:

▶ They develop ways of making each student accountable—usually by having each individual in the class demonstrate some product or some competence or understanding. Other ways of making students accountable is to require that they answer questions in unison, and to ask that they engage in some

---

jerky transitions Kounin's expression for disruptive and abrupt changes in learning activities in the classroom.

meaningful activity (like taking notes or making specific observations) while another student is making a presentation.

▶ They use *group-alerting cues,* which are signals designed to maintain attention or alertness. Asking questions at random and keeping children in suspense about who will be called on next are common group-alerting cues. Interspersing questions that require a single individual to answer with questions that require a group answer is another.

▶ They alter the format of classroom activities to maintain focus and prevent boredom. Lesson formats that require only one student to perform at a time (as in reading, for example) often lead to inattentiveness on the part of other students. One lesson format to counteract this requires other students to do something else while one student is reading (for example, answer a question, think of a question, listen for an answer).

Strengths and Weaknesses. The major strength of Kounin's system is its emphasis on *preventing* discipline problems. And it provides teachers with highly specific and sometimes very useful recommendations for doing so. "A management system based on Kounin's principles," write McCaslin and Good, "provides expectations and understandings around which there is generally shared meaning between teachers and students, although teacher behaviors will be interpreted variously by individual students. The system allows the class to function in a relatively smooth and predictable way" (1992, p. 13).

But classes—and teachers—are quite different one from another. And students change with age, so that management principles that work well with very young children don't work at all well with older children. As McCaslin and Good (1992) point out, teachers' rules, behaviors, and expectations need to be flexible and sometimes need to change dramatically. Certainly, if one of the important objectives of education is to develop independent thinkers, the continued application of teacher-determined rules and procedures may be quite inappropriate.

The major weaknesses of this system are that its use is limited largely to teacher-directed classroom activities and that it offers few suggestions for solving discipline problems. And, unlike Carl Rogers' model, it is not intended to develop personal responsibility in students.

DEMOCRATIC PROCEDURES: STATEN WEBSTER

Staten Webster (1968) describes a number of principles to guide teachers in their efforts to maintain a nonautocratic form of classroom order—that is, to maintain a democratic order. Like the more humanistic approaches, one of the primary goals of these principles is to promote the development of self-discipline in students.

The principles are based on what Webster describes as the three Rs of good discipline: reason, respect, and relevance. Thus, discipline should be reasonable and interpreted as such by students; it should reflect one of the most important of society's values—respect for individuals; and it should be relevant to the behaviors giving rise to disciplinary action. Several of the principles listed by Webster are shown in Table 11.2.

Strengths and Weaknesses. Even though there is little that is surprising, obscure, or difficult about Webster's advice, it is nevertheless valuable. It is all too easy to act instinctively when faced with a discipline problem. And although the teacher's instincts might often be entirely appropriate, there might be occasions when other behaviors would have been considerably more appropriate. Perhaps knowledge of these principles can increase instances of appropriate action.

LOGICAL CONSEQUENCES: RUDOLF DREIKURS

Rudolf Dreikurs describes a well-known, though sometimes complex, democratic model of classroom management. It is a model based closely on the work of Adler, a personality theorist.

TABLE 11.2 WEBSTER'S PRINCIPLES OF NONAUTOCRATIC ORDER

1. Teachers must make sure that all students understand rules and standards and the reasons for their existence.

2. The first violation of a rule should lead to a warning, a discussion of alternative ways of behaving, and clarification of the consequences of repeated infractions.

3. Teachers should endeavor to discover the causes underlying misbehavior.

4. Whenever possible, teachers should address students in private regarding their misbehavior.

5. Sarcasm, ridicule, and other forms of discipline that lead to public humiliation should be avoided.

6. When teachers make mistakes (if they ever do), they should apologize.

7. The punishment should fit the crime. Minor infractions should not bring about harsh punishment.

8. Extra class work and assignments, academic tests, and other school-related activities should never be used as a form of punishment.

Source: Webster (1968), p. 50.

Goals: Adler's Theory. Among other things, Adler believed that all human behavior is clearly motivated by the individual's desire to reach certain goals. Hence, to understand the behavior of students, it's important to know what these goals are, as well as how the child is likely to interpret them, and what behaviors are most likely to lead to them.

Adler identifies four principal classes of goals that drive a child's behavior. These are manifested in the child's need for gaining attention, exercising power, obtaining revenge, and appearing inadequate.

These goals, explains Adler, are hierarchical. That is, children (or students) first do things designed to gain attention. If that fails, they may try to obtain power, perhaps asserting themselves and becoming rebellious and defiant. If this goal, too, is not reached, the child may then strongly desire and try to obtain revenge. Finally, if all else fails, the child may try to appear helpless and inadequate.

Mistaken Assumptions. What is important for the teacher to know, explains Dreikurs, is that children often make mistakes in their assumptions about what sorts of behaviors are most likely to lead to the goals they seek. In fact, the cornerstone of Dreikurs' model of classroom management is the belief that all student misbehaviors result from these mistaken assumptions.

As an illustration, the most important of the child's goals revolve around finding a place, gaining status—in other words, obtaining attention. Among the many acceptable ways of getting attention are to achieve at a high level or to display socially adaptive behaviors. Unfortunately, many children assume that the way to gain the attention they want is to misbehave, to be disruptive and lazy, to ask for favors, to throw things, to cry, to yell and fight, and on and on.

Similarly, when children don't get all the attention they want, they may then enter into a power struggle with authorities. If they fail to establish their will—that is, to obtain power—they may be frustrated and respond with even more inappropriate behavior. Such children may become stubborn, argumentative, and rebellious.

When the frustrated child realizes that power is unlikely, revenge becomes the next goal, says Adler. In an effort to exact revenge for perceived injustices of a system that denies both attention and power, the child may become vicious and sullen, and may take steps to hurt others, or perhaps to hurt animals.

Finally, in line with the fourth of Adler's hierarchical goals, the thoroughly frustrated child may begin to feel hopeless and may give up. One manifestation of this, notes Adler, is the appearance of behaviors designed to make the child seem helpless and inadequate. Thus children may engage in patently stupid behaviors, and may show signs of a deep-seated inferiority complex.

Suggested Teacher Responses. How should teachers respond to misbehaviors of this nature? Dinkmeyer and Dinkmeyer (1976) suggest a number of steps that clarify Dreikurs' model—a number of sequential actions that teachers might take:

▶ Attempt to determine the student's motives and help the student understand them.

▶ Help students change their mistaken goals and assumptions for some that are more useful.

▶ Teach children to apply logical consequences, perhaps using group discussions to develop class rules and analyze problems.

Determining student motives is accomplished by direct and relatively aggressive questioning. For example, if the student is showing off and being unruly, and the teacher suspects that the motivating goal relates to obtaining attention, the teacher might ask: "Do you want me to pay more attention to you?" "Do you want me to do something for you?" For a child who has become vicious and defiant and when the teacher suspects a revenge-related motive, the teacher might ask: "Is it possible that you want to hurt your dog? And your fellow students?"

Dreikurs provides relatively specific suggestions with respect to how teachers should go about helping students understand their mistaken assumptions and exchange them for some that are more acceptable. The most important of these, regarding the four major goals that Dreikurs assumes motivate children's behavior, are summarized in the following sections.

Responding to Attention-Seeking Behavior. The most important rule here, says Dreikurs, is ignore the child's attention-seeking misbehav-ior (Cassel & Dreikurs, 1972). Teachers who become visibly annoyed and impatient, or who react in any other way to the child's bid for attention, are simply reinforcing that behavior. Hence, do not punish, nag, do things for, advise, or admonish the attention seeker. But, says Dreikurs, the teacher should make a point of paying special attention at other times when the child is not misbehaving. It's especially important that the teacher be aware of when students are working well, or paying close attention to the teacher, so that the teacher can reward them with attention for desirable behaviors.

Responding to Power-Seeking Behavior. When the child becomes stubborn and argumentative and shows other signs of wanting to dominate, and when the teacher has determined that power is the underlying goal, the most important rule, says Dreikurs, is neither fight nor give in. This contradicts the common belief that teachers should be firm in the face of student challenges, that they should meet an attempted show of strength with an even greater show of strength. Not so, claims Dreikurs. Struggling for power with students simply leads to greater feelings of hostility. Instead, the teacher should

▶ Recognize that the child does have legitimate power

▶ Grant the child power where appropriate

▶ Avoid a power struggle

▶ Ask for the student's help when possible

▶ Respect the child

▶ Reach an agreement, perhaps using logical consequences (discussed shortly)

Responding to Revenge-Seeking Behavior. The desire for revenge, according to Dreikurs, rises primarily from a frustrated struggle for power. The most important rule for teacher responses to revenge seeking is simple: Never show that you have been hurt. Because the objective of revenge is to hurt someone, admitting or showing hurt is an effective way of reinforcing revenge-seeking behavior. Among specific responses that Dreikurs recommends is that of doing the unexpected. The vengeful and rebellious student always knows how to respond to an expected teacher reaction, explains Dreikurs. But an unexpected reaction can sometimes defuse the situation before a serious problem results. Another possibility is that of enlisting the help of one or more members of the class in an effort to befriend the vengeful student. The objective is to persuade the student that others like him or her.

Responding to Displays of Inadequacy. Among children's actions that attempt to project inferiority and inadequacy are unexpectedly stupid actions, failure to accept challenges, giving up easily, asking to be left alone, and refusing to participate. Students who manifest inadequacy are often overly ambitious, notes Dreikurs, and find it difficult to succeed at the level they desire. Others are simply overly competitive and don't respond well to not being first. Others, too, are simply overly sensitive to pressure and give up rather than responding to it.

The most important rule for responding to displays of inadequacy, says Dreikurs, is to encourage the child's efforts even when they result in mistakes. The objective is to make children feel worthwhile, to lead them to realize that no one has given up on them. It's especially important, argues Dreikurs, that the teacher remain highly supportive and constructive. And it's often useful to enlist the help and cooperation of other students.

Teaching Children to Apply Logical Consequences. A student's misbehaviors can have two sorts of consequences, explains Dreikurs: **Natural consequences** are simply the natural, uncontrived outcomes of behavior. For example, a natural consequence of not getting up with the morning alarm is to miss school. Similarly, a natural consequence of not studying for an examination is to do less well than would otherwise have been the case, and perhaps to fail.

In contrast to natural consequences, **logical consequences** are contrived consequences (Dreikurs & Grey, 1968). That is, they are consequences of behaviors, or more often, of misbehaviors, that have been arranged by teachers and by students as well. Unlike natural consequences, these are outcomes that would not normally follow the behavior, although they are intended to seem natural and logical. Nor are logical consequences like punishment. Punishment, notes Dreikurs, is an expression of authority that often involves moral judgments and sometimes anger as well. Furthermore, punishment is rarely related directly to a specific misbehavior but tends to be general. The parent who spanks Albert for frying up the goldfish would also be likely to spank Albert were he to make holes in the kitchen window.

Punishment, claims Dreikurs, might have been acceptable some decades ago. But now it's outdated and ineffective. Far more effective is the practice of setting up logical consequences with students—consequences that have been explained, understood, and agreed upon by students. The main objective of these consequences is to bring about good behavior, not to punish. Thus, Albert and his father might agree that a logical consequence of his frying of the goldfish would be that Albert walk to the market and buy replacement goldfish; or that he buy a nice fillet of trout and fry that up. Similarly, a logical consequence of his making holes in the window would be that he arrange to have them repaired, perhaps paying the cost.

Table 11.3 presents several examples of possible logical consequences for specific misbehaviors, some of which are based on work by

---

natural consequences Dreikurs' phrase for the ordinary consequences of behavior—or, more specifically, of misbehavior. Natural consequences are the effects and outcomes of behavior that are not arranged or contrived.

logical consequences Dreikurs' phrase for a disciplinary tactic that involves contriving or inventing consequences for children's misbehavior in an attempt to modify that behavior. Unlike natural consequences, which follow naturally from a misbehavior, logical consequences are arranged, explained, discussed, and agreed upon by teachers and students.

TABLE 11.3 EXAMPLES OF LOGICAL CONSEQUENCES

MISBEHAVIOR	LOGICAL CONSEQUENCE
Sandy writes her name on her desk.	She may either clean the desk or pay the caretaker to do so.
William scribbles his assignment in nearly illegible pencil on a wrinkled and torn scrap of paper.	The teacher will not read or grade the assignment until it has been rewritten.
Jane gets into a hair-pulling fight with Melissa after school.	Jane and Melissa are required to work out a schedule that prevents them from leaving school simultaneously until they have developed a written plan detailing why they fought and how they will avoid doing so in the future.
Susan disrupts the class by repeatedly speaking to Sarah out loud.	Susan and Sarah are invited to communicate only at recess or out of school, or to work out a seating arrangement that will prevent them from disrupting the class.

Dreikurs, Grunwald, and Pepper (1982). Note that the logical consequences described in that table do not involve punishment in the normal sense of the word. Rather, these consequences are logical outcomes of the misbehaviors that are agreed upon and understood by the students.

Strengths and Weaknesses. The main strength of Dreikurs logical consequences has to do with the role it gives students in establishing the consequences of their misbehaviors. As a result, it tends to promote a high degree of autonomy and responsibility. And, as Edwards (1993) notes, it also promotes respect between teachers and students.

Unfortunately, however, it can be very difficult for teachers to establish the motives that underly children's misbehaviors. Furthermore, it may be overly simplistic to try to ascribe all misbehaviors to one of four classes of goals and mistaken assumptions. And, perhaps most serious, it simply isn't always possible to arrive at clear, well-understood, and acceptable logical consequences for all misbehaviors and for all students. Unfortunately, the theory says little about what the teacher should do if Melissa simply refuses to stop fighting with Jane, blast the consequences, be they natural or logical.

And it has little concrete advice for Albert's father if Albert agrees to replace the goldfish, but then fries them up again the next day.*

BEHAVIOR MODIFICATION: BURRHUS F. SKINNER

What Albert's father may require, in the end, is a different model, a more corrective one. The main emphasis of the classroom management models considered so far has been preventive. In contrast, the principal emphasis of those aspects of behavior modification, considered in this section, is *corrective*.

The immediate objective of corrective discipline is to change or eliminate a particular behavior. Reinforcement and punishment are among the most common elements of corrective discipline. Not surprisingly, then, the strategies of corrective discipline often use principles of conditioning theory (described in Chapter 4). Collectively, these strategies define behavior

---

*PPC: Frying of goldfish is perhaps too far-fetched an illustration to be very meaningful.

Author: The truth is that the illustration was not fetched from very far at all. And Albert, one of my second cousins, swears to this day that fried goldfish is as tasty as any wild trout.

modification—sometimes also referred to as behavior management or behavioral intervention.

Behavior modification refers specifically to strategies based on behaviorist learning theory. These strategies include the use of reinforcement, models, extinction, and punishment. In addition, some applications of behavior modification use principles of cognitive theory; these are labeled "cognitive behavior modification." Examples of each of these strategies is discussed here with specific reference to discipline problems.

Presland (1989) describes the most common sequence for a behavioral intervention program for an individual student:

1. *Defining the problem.* Often a written list is developed of behaviors that are too frequent (speaking out in class) or too infrequent (volunteering answers for questions). The student might be involved in this step.

2. *Measuring the problem.* The teacher attempts to determine how serious (frequent or infrequent) the behavior actually is, perhaps by counting occurrences.

3. *Determining antecedents and consequences.* What conditions precede the behavior? What are its apparent consequences? In other words, how is it triggered and what reinforces it?

4. *Deciding whether and how to change antecedents and consequences.* Are there existing consequences that serve to reinforce a too-frequent behavior? Are there new consequences that might reinforce an infrequent behavior? For example, one of the consequences of undesirable behavior might be increased teacher attention. This might serve to maintain the behavior. If so, teacher inattention might have the opposite effect. Similarly, increased teacher attention for less frequent but more desirable behaviors might increase their frequency.

5. *Planning and implementing the intervention.* Having determined behaviors in need of change and having identified certain antecedents (stimuli) and consequences (poten-

tial reinforcers) associated with them, it's now possible to devise a program designed to modify the behavior in question. The program should specify, often in contract with the student, how antecedents and consequences will be used and how the student will be involved.

6. *Following up.* Following the program's implementation, the teacher (and student) evaluate its effectiveness and determine whether additional or different intervention is desirable.

Systematic Reinforcement Programs. Applying positive reinforcement as a corrective strategy often involves rewarding behaviors that run counter to those that are a problem. Instead of focusing on eliminating undesired responses, the teacher focuses on reinforcing the opposite behavior. For example, if a teacher's attention reinforces Sally's disruptive behavior, one reinforcement strategy that might be effective is to pay attention when she is not being disruptive and to ignore her when she is.

Teachers have at their disposal a wide variety of potent reinforcers, not the least important of which are praise, smiles, grades, and attention. When these social reinforcers prove ineffective, more elaborate reinforcement systems can be established. The best known are **token systems** whereby students earn points or tokens for good behavior and sometimes lose them for less desirable behavior. The tokens can later be exchanged for tangible rewards.

An Example of a Token System. Psychology journals offer numerous examples of the use of positive reinforcement in the classroom. For example, Ross and Braden (1991) used a reinforcement system where students with learning disabilities could earn tokens for the develop-

---

token system A behavior modification system in which tokens are given as rewards for desirable behaviors. These can be accumulated and later exchanged for other rewards.

ment of math skills during a four-week period. Tokens could then be exchanged for other reinforcers. The result was significant gains in achievement following the study.

Although the effectiveness of reinforcement in establishing and maintaining acceptable behaviors can hardly be disputed, there are a number of problems involved in the systematic use of token systems. The establishment of such a system requires a great deal of time and care and presents some real problems in selecting reinforcers for which tokens can be exchanged. In addition, tokens are ineffective for some students and distracting for others (Kazdin & Bootzin, 1972). Some students spend so much time counting and sorting their tokens that they experience considerable difficulty attending to the tasks desired of them.

A Red Light–Green Light System. An interesting classroom behavior management system is the **red light–green light system** (see, for example, Nay et al., 1976; Barbetta, 1990). In a typical application of this system, tape or chalk is used to demarcate an area around each student's desk—their personal spaces, to be named and decorated by them and to be occupied by them alone. Clear, unambiguous signals, such as red or green lights, are then used to indicate when certain behaviors are permissible, and when not—behaviors like leaving one's personal space, for example, or speaking out loud. The assumption is that being allowed to remain in one's territory is reinforcing, particularly if infractions of rules result in one's removal from that territory. Desks may also be set aside in a "no man's land," and children guilty of leaving their seats or of talking when these activities are prohibited are sent to no man's land for periods of exile of varying lengths depending on the seriousness of the infraction.

---

red light–green light system A behavior management system that make use of clear, unambiguous signals, such as green or red lights, to indicate to students whether or not specific behaviors are permissible.

Extrinsic Reinforcement. As we saw in Chapter 4, **extrinsic reinforcement** includes all sources of reinforcement that come from outside rather than from within the individual. Among the extrinsic reinforcers most commonly used in the classroom are attention, praise, tokens, stars, grades, and promotion. Another important and apparently quite effective source of reinforcement is defined by the **Premack principle** (Premack, 1965), which states that behavior that ordinarily occurs frequently can be used to reinforce less frequent behavior. Parents and teachers use this principle constantly: A child is allowed to play outside after eating supper; a student is permitted to read a library book after completing an assignment.

Bijou and Sturges (1959) identify five distinct categories of extrinsic reinforcers:

consumables—like food and drink

manipulatables—meaning things that can be manipulated like toys

visual and auditory stimuli—like green lights and gold stars and one-armed bandit buzzers that mean, "Well done! You win!"

social stimuli—like smiles and hugs and pats on the head

tokens—like plastic disks that can be used to buy other rewards

It is interesting, and potentially valuable, to consider how each of these might be used in the classroom. Consumables are relatively inconvenient. A teacher walking around a classroom with a bag of cookies, dispensing them as she observes desirable student behavior, might occasion some concern among parents.

---

extrinsic reinforcement Reinforcement that comes from outside rather than from within—for example, high grades, praise, or money.

Premack principle The recognition that behaviors that are chosen frequently by an individual (and that are therefore favored) may be used to reinforce other, less frequently chosen behaviors. (For example: "You can watch television when you have finished your homework.")

Manipulatables, objects such as toys or trinkets, can be used successfully, particularly with young children. Reinforcing auditory and visual stimuli are less likely to be readily available to a teacher. Such reinforcers are signals that have been given reinforcing properties. For example, if a teacher told students that he would ring a bell every time he was happy with them, the bell would be an auditory reinforcer. This is not to be confused with social reinforcers, which take the form of praise, approval, or simply attention, and which are by far the most prevalent and powerful reinforcers available to a teacher. In this connection, it should also be kept in mind that peer approval is often as powerful or more powerful a reinforcer than teacher approval. Tokens are sometimes used as direct extrinsic reinforcement for desirable behavior. In a token system, tokens can commonly be exchanged for other reinforcers: consumables, manipulatables, or perhaps time for some pleasant activity.

Intrinsic Reinforcement. Unlike extrinsic reinforcement, **intrinsic reinforcement** is not under a teacher's direct control. Recall that intrinsic reinforcement includes all sources of reinforcement that come from within rather than from outside—things like satisfaction and a sense of accomplishment. The teacher can nevertheless structure learning situations in ways that are more likely to lead to intrinsic satisfaction. Presenting students with tasks that are too difficult is not likely to lead to satisfaction with learning. Likewise, excessively simple tasks are not self-reinforcing. As we saw in Chapter 10, teachers can foster an intrinsic (mastery) orientation by manipulating tasks (personal involvement in challenging but achievable tasks), type of evaluation (social comparisons foster a performance orientation and a reliance on extrinsic sources of reinforcement like grades), and use of authority (providing students with opportunities for meaningful autonomy—say in determining questions worth investigating—fosters an intrinsic orientation).

Effects of Extrinsic Rewards on Intrinsic Motivation. The teacher's use of external rewards, especially in the early grades, is another potential source of influence on intrinsic motivation. If rewards are initially administered for behaviors related to learning, it follows that the process of learning may acquire the characteristics of a generalized reinforcer. In fact, it is customary in structured teaching programs based on reinforcement principles to use external rewards only in the initial stages of the program (see, for example, Hewitt, 1992). It is assumed that intrinsic reinforcement will eventually suffice to maintain the behavior.

There is some possibility, however, that the excessive use of reinforcement can have harmful effects on subsequent motivation (Lepper, 1981). In one representative experiment, Lepper and Greene (1975) asked two groups of children to solve a number of geometric puzzles. One group was told that they would be allowed to play with some attractive toys as a reward; the other was also allowed to play with the puzzles but was not led beforehand to expect a reward. Later, children were observed unobtrusively to see whether any of them spontaneously played with the puzzles, which were freely available in the classroom. As is shown in Figure 11.2, significantly more of those who had not expected a reward continued to be motivated to play with the puzzles.

Why? Lepper and Greene suggest that the most reasonable explanation is a cognitive one. It is important for us to try to make sense of our behaviors—to understand why we do things. Typically, we resort to two classes of explanations for our behaviors: extrinsic or intrinsic causes; that is, we generally recognize that we do things for certain external rewards (money, prestige, being allowed to play with toys), for internal rewards (satisfaction, sense of accomplishment, personal interest), or sometimes for both internal and external rewards. When external rewards are large and obvious,

---

intrinsic reinforcement Reinforcement that comes from within the individual rather than from outside (satisfaction, for example). Also termed *internal reinforcement.*

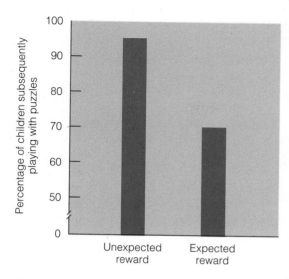

FIGURE 11.2 Significantly more of the children who had not expected a reward showed intrinsic interest by subsequently playing with the geometric puzzles. Based on data from M. R. Lepper and D. Greene (1975), "Turning Play into Work: Effects of Adult Surveillance and Extrinsic Rewards on Children's Intrinsic Motivation," *Journal of Personality and Social Psychology, 31,* 479–486.

our motivation becomes largely extrinsic, but when we expect no great extrinsic rewards, we must look to intrinsic causes. Thus, children who expect reinforcement can understand and justify their behavior in terms of extrinsic factors; those who do not expect external rewards must justify their behavior in terms of such things as the pleasure and enjoyment associated with it. Children who do not expect rewards are subsequently more highly motivated (intrinsically motivated) to continue the activity. To the extent that this observation is true, there may clearly be some danger associated with the indiscriminate and excessive use of external rewards. However, these findings have not always been replicated, and a meta-analysis of ninety-six studies that looked specifically at the extent to which extrinsic rewards might reduce intrinsic motivation concludes that, in general, "reinforcement does not harm an individual's intrinsic motivation" (Cameron & Pierce, 1994, p. 363).

Clearly, extrinsic reinforcers can be extremely useful for teachers. But care should be taken to ensure that they are not used excessively, and attention needs to be paid to the development of intrinsic motivation. As we saw in Chapter 10, children who are intrinsically motivated tend to be mastery oriented. Not only do these children achieve at a higher level but their emphasis is on learning and understanding, rather than on simply performing and competing—hence, the advisability of encouraging intrinsic motivation.

Home-Based Reinforcement Programs. Teachers are not the only ones who have control over reinforcers that are important to the lives and learning of their students; parents, too, control some extremely powerful reinforcers—and punishments, too. For this reason, it has sometimes proven helpful to involve parents in systematic reinforcement programs.

Barth (1979) reviews several dozen studies in which investigators deliberately and systematically enlisted the help of parents in providing reinforcement for school-related activities. These studies involved students in group homes, in special classes, and in ordinary classes. Reinforcers varied from tokens and social praise to consumables and special privileges and were administered for an extremely wide range of behaviors. In many cases, money was also used as a reinforcer. For example, students would earn varying amounts of money for different school grades—and sometimes would lose money for failing to complete assignments or for getting low grades.

Taken as a whole, the studies reviewed by Barth indicate that home-based reinforcement can be extremely influential in bringing about measurable and significant positive changes, both in behavior and in academic achievement, for many students in a wide range of subjects and situations.

Seven Principles for Using Reinforcement. Michael (1967) describes seven principles that should be kept in mind when attempting to control behavior through its consequences.

TABLE 11.4 A REINFORCEMENT MENU*

REWARD	COST
1. One free period in the library	10
2. One free period in class	10
3. One day off from clean-up duty	5
4. Lunch with Ms. Clements (the teacher)	15
5. Lunch prepared by Ms. Clements	25
6. Extra help with one subject	2
7. Get to choose the game for gym	10
8. Get to sit anywhere in class for one day	3

*Members of a fifth-grade class could purchase activities from this menu, using points earned in school-related activities.

Some of these have been discussed earlier, but all are important enough to bear repeating.

First, the consequences of behavior, whether rewarding or punishing, are defined only in terms of their effect on the learner. Teachers should not always assume that a stimulus they consider pleasant for a student will strengthen behavior. Peer attention, for example, is generally strongly reinforcing; for a very inhibited student, however, peer attention may be quite punishing. Nor can a teacher simply ask students what is reinforcing for them, because this might well render some reinforcers almost meaningless. If, for example, students were to indicate that praise was reinforcing, subsequent praise might be interpreted as less genuine and hence would be less reinforcing.

A useful concept in relation to this first principle (that reinforcement is highly individualistic) is that of the **reinforcement menu,** introduced by Addison and Homme (1966). Based largely on the Premack principle, a reinforcement menu is a list of potentially reinforcing activities from which the student is allowed to select following some behavior that merits reinforcement. Table 11.4 presents one example

of a reinforcement menu. Interestingly, however, research with very young children (between 2 and 6 years) indicates that rewards selected by experimenters are sometimes more effective than rewards children are allowed to select for themselves (Baer et al., 1992).

The second principle states that the effects of reinforcement are automatic; that is, the teacher need not explain to students that if they learn well, they will receive some specific reinforcement that will then lead them to study even harder. The point is that if students do learn and consequently are reinforced, they will probably study even harder without ever having discussed this marvelous phenomenon with their teacher. However, as Kalish (1981) points out, praise (or punishment) by itself, especially for young children, is not as effective as praise accompanied by a description of what was done to deserve praise or by an explanation of why it is deserved.

The third principle stresses that reinforcement or punishment should be closely related to the desirable (or undesirable) behavior. As Pica and Margolis (1993) point out, teachers must have some short-range goals clearly in mind so that they can reinforce behavior that matches those goals.

Fourth, reinforcement should be consistent. This does not mean that reinforcement must occur for every correct response. It does

---

reinforcement menu A list of activities, objects, or other consequences from which students can select reinforcers.

mean, however, that a specific behavior should not be reinforced one time and punished the next.

Fifth, consequences should follow behavior closely. Delayed reward or punishment is much less effective than immediate consequences. Adherence to this principle is clearly one of the major strengths of programmed instruction in which learners receive knowledge of results immediately (discussed in Chapter 12). Another implication of this principle is that the period of time between giving a quiz and returning the results should be kept as short as possible.

The sixth of Michael's principles is that the amount and potency of reinforcement necessary for behavioral change is usually underestimated. This is particularly true for the early stages of learning.

The seventh principle relates to the structuring of a learning situation. It maintains that the student's work should be set up as a series of clear steps, each of which can be reinforced. Programmed instruction (see Chapter 12) can meet this requirement much more easily than can a classroom teacher who is responsible for a relatively large number of students.

Modeling. Another behavior modification technique, that of *modeling*, is often used unconsciously by teachers who inadvertently serve as models for students. In much the same way, students also serve as models for each other. The deliberate and systematic use of models is perhaps rarer, but it can be highly effective.

Recall from Chapter 4 that one effect of models is the suppression or reappearance of previously suppressed deviant behavior. This effect, the *inhibitory-disinhibitory effect*, apparently occurs as a result of seeing a model being punished or rewarded for deviant behavior.

The inhibitory effect is common in schools. It is, in fact, what Kounin calls the ripple effect. When a teacher selects for punishment one offender from among a group of offenders, the hope is that the effects of the punishment will spread to the remainder of the group. This is why leaders are often punished for the transgressions of their followers.

Extinction. Animal studies indicate that responses maintained by reinforcement can usually be eliminated through the complete withdrawal of reinforcement—usually but not always. For example, a pigeon that has been taught to peck at a disk for its food will usually cease to peck when food is no longer provided as a consequence of disk pecking. But some pigeons will continue to peck at the disk indefinitely, even when the pecking no longer leads to reinforcement. A humanist might simply insist that to be a pigeon is to peck and that a fully actualized pigeon gets high by pecking disks and remains unmoved by the crass material rewards that might move other pigeons. Others might argue that pigeons have a biological predisposition for pecking. Whatever the reason might be, it remains true that not all behaviors can be extinguished through the removal of reinforcement. Furthermore, many disruptive behaviors in the classroom are reinforced by peers rather than by teachers. To the extent that teachers are not in control of relevant reinforcers, there is little that they can do to remove them.

More optimistically, some disruptive behaviors appear to be maintained by teacher attention, in which case it might be a relatively simple matter to cease paying attention. However, the matter might not be quite so simple if the behavior in question is highly disruptive of class activities. But there are other alternatives, the most common of which is punishment.

Punishment. *Punishment* can take a variety of forms. Recall from Chapter 4 that there are, in principle, two distinct types of punishment: The first involves the presentation of a noxious (unpleasant) stimulus; the second involves the removal of a pleasant stimulus.

Specific punishments used on a schoolwide basis, notes Bacon (1990), include expulsion, suspension, and physical punishment. Classroom teachers are more likely to use facial gestures of disapproval, reprimands, detention, unpleasant activities, time-outs, and, occasionally, physical punishment (see the case "The Old Bag's Chair Trick").

There are many passionate objectors to the use of punishment and a number of practical objections as well. At the same time, there is a need to reexamine the effectiveness of various forms of punishment.

Corporal Punishment. **Corporal punishment,** also termed *physical punishment,* is the use of physical force to bring about pain. Often, it is also associated with fear and humiliation.

Although physical punishment is no longer nearly as common as it was some decades ago, McFadden, Marsh, Price, and Hwang (1992) report that it is still used in a large number of schools. In fact, it has been used consistently in North American schools throughout history (Ryan, 1994). And, in spite of many objections to its use, in some school systems the majority of students approve of its use (see, for example, Anderson & Payne, 1994).

Interestingly, courts as high as the U.S. Supreme Court have affirmed the rights of schools to use corporal punishment, providing it is not grossly excessive. In contrast, some apparently milder forms of punishment such as suspension and expulsion present schools with much clearer legal liabilities because a number of courts have ruled that to suspend students is to deprive them of their right to an education.

McFadden and associates (1992) looked at 4,391 discipline files from 9 Florida schools.

---

corporal punishment Punishment that uses physical force to inflict pain.

These schools had clear written rules concerning violations and disciplinary options. For example, they identified twenty-five different classes of infractions ranging from serious (assault, possession of weapons), which were quite rare, to mild (bothering others). They found that seven categories of violations accounted for more than 80 percent of all misbehaviors. And the most common punishment for misbehaviors requiring counselor or principal intervention was in-school suspension; second most common, strikingly, was corporal punishment; third, suspension from school.

McFadden and associates (1992) also report marked race and gender bias in the application of corporal punishment. Not only did males account for more offenses than females but physical punishment was administered for a higher proportion of these offenses. Similarly, some 45 percent of all African-American students referred were punished physically but only 22 percent of the white students and 23 percent of the Hispanics.

It's interesting to note that the probability of a teacher using corporal punishment is closely related to the sorts of experiences the teacher had as a child. Kaplan (1992) found that teachers' own disciplinary experiences were good predictors of what they would do in situations requiring disciplinary intervention. Teachers who had themselves experienced corporal punishment were more likely to use it with their own students.

CASE: THE OLD BAG'S CHAIR TRICK

THE SITUATION: Mrs. Neigel, a bad teacher, as recollected by Rhonda, teacher in training

In fourth grade, I left my chair (we sat at tables) to retrieve my eraser from another student. When I returned to my chair, the teacher was standing behind my chair and proceeded to shout at me to sit down. As I sat down, she pulled my chair away from me and, you guessed it, I landed on the floor. She did this twice. The third time I managed to sit on the chair but before she returned to the blackboard, she smacked me across the face. Being a fourth grader, I was very frightened and extremely humiliated. The class was shocked. At the time, I thought she was an old bag, and I wished I wasn't in her class.

The Case Against Punishment. That it does not often work is one of the important objections to the use of punishment. In the McFadden and associates (1992) study just described, for example, punishment seemed to have little effect on recidivism (repetition of offenses). The large majority of the students referred for punishment in these schools were repeat offenders. As McFadden and colleagues put it, "punishments may actually serve to increase the frequencies of the very behaviors they are intended to eliminate" (1992, p. 145).

In addition, there are some obvious ethical and humanitarian objections to corporal punishment, and a number of more practical ones. Among these is the observation that punishment by itself draws attention to socially undesirable behavior but fails to illustrate suitable alternatives. (Note that punishment used in conjunction with reasoning and other corrective measures need not be subject to the same objection.)

Additional evidence suggests that punishment sometimes has effects opposite of those intended. This is particularly obvious when parents or teachers attempt to eliminate aggressive or violent behavior through physical punishment, as we saw in the McFadden and associates study (1992). In effect, those who punish violence with violence provide a model of aggression for the child—a model that might be interpreted to mean that aggressiveness is permissible under certain circumstances.

Other objections to the use of punishment are summarized by Clarizio and Yelon (1974, p. 50) as follows:

▶ Punishment does not eliminate an undesirable response, although it might result in its suppression or in a reduction in its frequency.

▶ Punishment may have unpleasant emotional side effects that are themselves maladaptive (for example, fear, anxiety, and tension).

▶ Punishment is a source of frustration and may therefore lead to other undesirable or maladaptive behaviors.

The Case for Punishment. Most of the objections just cited apply only to one type of punishment: the presentation of unpleasant stimuli. Furthermore, these objections are most applicable to corporal punishment and much less applicable to verbal punishment. The forms of punishment that involve the removal of pleasant stimuli (for example, loss of privileges) are not subject to the same practical and philosophical objections and should be considered legitimate methods by which teachers can maintain the degree of control essential for humane and personal teaching.

The case to be made for punishment can be based on a number of studies demonstrating that punitive methods can be effective in suppressing disruptive and sometimes dangerous behaviors (Parke, 1974). Some situations demand immediate and decisive intervention and do not lend themselves to the more gentle strategies of reinforcement, modeling, and reasoning. A child caught lighting matches and touching them to the draperies may be reasoned with and physically removed, but if he persists in burning the curtains at every opportunity, punishment may well be in order.

Although reinforcement, modeling, and reasoning have proved highly effective for promoting desirable behaviors, it is extremely difficult for a child to learn to recognize unacceptable behaviors simply by generalizing in reverse from situations that have been reinforced (Ausubel, 1958). In many cases, then, punishment of specific behaviors can be highly informative. And even though considerable evidence shows that punishment administered by an otherwise warm and loving parent is more effective than punishment administered by a habitually cold and distant parent (Aronfreed, 1968), no evidence shows that punishment administered by a loving parent disrupts emotional bonds between parent and child (Walters & Grusec, 1977).

One theoretical objection to the use of punishment is that it does not work—that although it might serve to suppress behavior or reduce its frequency, it does not lead to the elimination (extinction) of a response. Consider, however, that a punisher's intent clearly is to *suppress* a behavior; complete elimination is, in fact, absolutely irrelevant. If Timmy has been punished for burning curtains, we should not dare hope that he will, as a result, have forgotten how to burn curtains. But we are justified in hoping that he will refrain from doing so in the future.

Interestingly, most of the data that we have regarding punishment are derived from animal studies. For obvious reasons, it's easier to do research with animals than with children (although even the lowly rat is now treated with considerably more respect than was once the case). It's possible to administer electric shocks to animals; there are no directly comparable stimuli that can be used with children. Hence, controlled research of the effects of punishment on children typically use "annoyers" such as loud buzzers. Evidence from a number of studies suggests that these annoyers can be effective in suppressing unwanted behavior. (In many of these experiments, children are asked not to play with a toy; the buzzer sounds if they do.)

This section is not meant to minimize the dangers of punishment. Several important points need to be made. The most important is that the majority of researchers and theorists remain virtually unanimous in their rejection of physical punishment. Not only is physical punishment a humiliating violation of the person but it presents a highly undesirable model. If your task were to teach children that the best way to obtain what they want is by force, excessive use of physical punishment might well be your best teaching method.

If we do reject physical punishment (in practice, the rejection is far from complete), a number of alternatives remain. The least objectionable are those involving the withdrawal of reinforcement.

If you are like most teachers, you are apt to make use of both major types of punishment in your classroom: withdrawal of pleasant consequences and the administration of unpleasant consequences. A careful review of the punishment literature and of humanistic counterarguments reveals that three effective forms of punishment that do not have the disadvantages usually associated with punishment are reprimands, time-outs, and response cost.

Reprimands. **Reprimands** can be mild or harsh, they can be verbal or nonverbal, and they can be administered by teachers, parents, or peers. A simple "No" is a verbal reprimand; a negative head shake is a nonverbal reprimand.

Reprimands are the most common form of punishment, both in the home and in school. This is not particularly surprising given that reprimands are simply expressions of disapproval. As such, they are available to anyone in power, and they are extremely easy to administer. Furthermore, given our social natures, reprimands can influence us in a way that they cannot influence most animals.

Researchers have compared the frequency of praise and of reprimands by teachers. In a large-scale survey, M. A. White (1975) found that the proportion of praise and reprimands changes markedly through school. Praise is more frequent than reprimands during first and second grade; in subsequent grades, reprimands are more common. The actual rate of reprimands through the remaining elementary and junior high school grades was approximately one every 2 minutes but dropped to about half that rate in high school. In college, it drops even more drastically. M. A. White also found that reprimands are somewhat more common with respect to students of lower ability. Merrett and Wheldall (1992) found that boys tended to be reprimanded more often than girls in secondary school, although not in primary school.

Research suggests that the effectiveness of reprimands depends on some of their characteristics. In general, effective reprimands

---

reprimand A common form of mild punishment that takes the form of an expression of disapproval. Reprimands are often verbal ("You shouldn't do that") but can also be nonverbal (a head shake).

identify the undesirable behavior and provide specific rationales for doing (or not doing) something. These are more effective than reprimands that simply express disapproval. For example, it is more effective to say, "Robert, please do not stick out your tongue because you distract the other children and you confuse me when I'm trying to explain something" than to say, "Don't do that, Robert!"

are given at a close distance. In a study conducted by Van Houten and colleagues (1982), students were reprimanded from a distance of 1 meter or 7 meters (approximately 3¼ feet or 23 feet). Tone and intensity of reprimand were kept constant. Reprimands from a distance of 1 meter were most effective.

are given softly. (O'Leary & Becker, 1968; O'Leary et al., 1974). However, as Van Houten and Doleys (1983) note, this might be because soft reprimands are generally given in closer proximity to the student. There is also the possibility that, at close proximity, the teacher will reinforce the reprimand by means of eye contact and other nonverbal gestures that have been found to increase the effectiveness of reprimands.

consist of simple, unobtrusive squelches such as "shh," "wait," "no," or simply a look or a gesture. Reprimands such as these have the advantage of minimizing class disruption.

Reprimands of the type discussed in this section are clearly not always appropriate or effective for the most severe instances of disruptive behavior. Those who engage in crimes such as physical violence, robbery, drug use and sale, rape, and vandalism in schools are likely to sneer at gentle reprimands. For these behaviors, more drastic measures are clearly warranted and, often, schoolwide security systems need to be put in place (Myles & Simpson, 1994). In most cases, these misbehaviors occur in corridors, lunchrooms, washrooms, and playgrounds rather than in the classroom, and they are sufficiently rare in most schools that when they occur, they are usually dealt with by school administrators—although there are now chilling indicators that school violence may be rising dramatically (see, for example, Bachus, 1994; Natale, 1994). Still, the most common misbehaviors the classroom teacher must deal with on a daily basis are truancy, tardiness, inattentiveness, talking, and forgetting books and assignments. For these misbehaviors, a simple reprimand might suffice—or perhaps a time-out or response-cost procedure might work.

Time-Outs. In a **time-out** procedure, students are removed from a situation in which they would ordinarily expect reinforcement and are placed in a situation in which they cannot be reinforced. For example, if classroom activities are such that the students like to be in class, being removed from the classroom for a time-out is a form of punishment.

Brantner and Doherty (1983) distinguish among three different time-out procedures that the classroom teacher might use. The first involves **isolation.** This is clearly illustrated when a child is physically removed from the area of reinforcement (typically, the classroom; perhaps also the playground, the lunchroom, or the library) and isolated in a different place. Although isolation is not entirely uncommon in schools, it is somewhat controversial because it violates our more humanistic values. It reminds us of the types of seclusion that have sometimes been used with criminals.

A second time-out procedure does not isolate misbehaving children but simply excludes them from ongoing activities. A common

---

time-out A procedure in which students are removed from situations in which they might ordinarily be rewarded. Time-out procedures are widely used in classroom management.

isolation A time-out procedure in which a child is removed from an area of reinforcement (typically the classroom, although sometimes the playground or other areas) and isolated in a different place.

exclusion time-out procedure in a school might require a child to sit at the back of the room, facing in the opposite direction or perhaps sitting behind a screen.

The third time-out procedure is labeled **nonexclusion.** In this, the mildest of the three, the child is removed from the ongoing activity (removed from the immediate source of reinforcement) and is required to observe others engaging in the activity. The child might, for example, be asked to stand apart from a game (or at the side of the class) and simply watch.

Following a thorough review of the time-out literature, Brantner and Doherty (1983) conclude that this is an extremely common classroom management practice but that research results are too few and too inconsistent to identify the characteristics of effective time-out procedures. In addition, although time-out procedures are usually effective, they do not always work.

Response Cost When students have been given tangible reinforcers for good behavior but stand to lose some of these reinforcers for disruptive behaviors, the loss is referred to as **response cost.** It too constitutes a mild form of punishment—similar to preventing a child who has misbehaved from watching television. Response-cost systems are frequently used in token reinforcement programs. An experiment reported by Kaufman and O'Leary (1972) clearly illustrates the difference between a response-cost method and a reinforcement sys-

tem. The experiment was conducted in two classes in a children's unit of a psychiatric hospital. In one class, students earned points for good behavior (token reinforcement); in a second class, children were awarded all their points at the beginning of a class period and had points subtracted from their total for specific misbehaviors. Although both methods were highly effective in reducing disruptive behavior, neither was more effective than the other.

Pazulinec, Meyerrose, and Sajwaj (1983) report that the majority of studies of the effectiveness of response-cost procedures have found positive results. Such procedures successfully reduce disruptive classroom behavior and bring about significant increases in class achievement and in performance on standardized tests. Among the relative advantages of response-cost procedures for classroom management is that they do not remove the child from the learning situation (as time-out procedures typically do). In addition, they are usually combined with a reinforcement procedure (use of tokens, for example) and can therefore benefit from the many advantages of reinforcement.

Strengths and Weaknesses. One of the principal strengths of behavior modification is that it provides very specific recommendations for managing classrooms. Although all teachers make use of reinforcers and reprimands almost intuitively, there are few teachers who cannot benefit from a clearer understanding of the types of available reinforcers, of how reinforcement can be applied in the classroom, and of when and how negative consequences such as reprimands are most effective. Behavior modification offers the well-informed teacher a wide array of detailed programs and concrete recommendations involving the systematic use of extrinsic and intrinsic reinforcers, as well as the use of models, token reinforcement systems, and even punishment in its various forms.

But, argue the more liberal and more humanistic educators, behavior modification smacks too much of behavior control. It pays too little attention to the dignity and worth of the student. More than this, it fails to recognize

---

exclusion A time-out punishment procedure whereby a child is not removed from the situation but is excluded from ongoing activities, often by being made to sit behind a screen, in a corner, or facing away from the class.

nonexclusion The mildest form of time-out procedure; the child is not allowed to participate in ongoing activity but is required to observe.

response cost A mild form of punishment whereby tangible reinforcers that have been given for good behavior are taken away for misbehaviors. Response-cost systems are often used in systematic behavior management programs.

the value of autonomy and self-direction—opting, instead, for externally imposed control and direction. In addition, some of its more aversive methods of control—those involving the use of punishment and negative reinforcement—can not only be highly ineffective but can also have negative consequences, evident in undesirable behaviors and personality characteristics.

ASSERTIVE DISCIPLINE: LEE CANTER

Another highly behavioristic management program is the well-known **assertive discipline** model advocated by Lee Canter (Canter & Canter, 1992). The model is based on the premise that teachers (and school systems) have become too permissive, too lenient. They have paid too little attention to the rights and responsibilities of teachers. Teachers possess three important classes of these rights and responsibilities.

▶ To establish rules and directions that clearly define the limits of acceptable and unacceptable student behavior

▶ To teach students to follow these rules and directions consistently throughout the school day and school year

▶ To ask for assistance from parents and administrators when support is needed in handling the behavior of students (Canter & Canter, 1992, p. 5)

These are extremely important rights and responsibilities, argues Canter, because they provide a blueprint for the kind of classroom environment the teacher will establish. And they dovetail, as well, with the rights of students—specifically, the right to

▶ A teacher who will set firm and consistent limits

---

assertive discipline The take-charge, aggressive, classroom management model advocated by Canter, based squarely on the notion that not only should teachers reinforce desirable behaviors, but that they should punish those that are undesirable.

▶ A teacher who will provide consistent positive encouragement to motivate them to behave

▶ Know what behaviors they need to engage in that will enable them to succeed in the classroom

▶ A teacher who will take the time to teach them how to manage their own behavior (Canter & Canter, 1992, p. 13)

The responsibility for putting these rights and responsibilities into effect is clearly the teacher's, says Canter. Hence the need to be assertive.

A Classroom Discipline Plan. The assertive teacher bears not only the right but the responsibility to provide students with the best learning environment possible. Doing that, Canter insists, requires a classroom discipline plan, the purpose of which is not only to make the management of students easier, but also to protect their rights. In addition, such a plan increases the likelihood of parental and administrative support.

A classroom discipline plan specifies three things: (1) the rules that students must follow, (2) the positive recognition they will receive for following the rules, and (3) the consequences of not following the rules.

Rules need to be clear and observable, rather than vague. For example, "Don't push or pull other students when you're in line" is a clear, simple rule. In contrast, "Don't fool around," is vague, difficult to interpret, and difficult to enforce. Important and general rules include admonitions such as "Follow the teacher's directions," "No profanity," "No teasing or bullying," "No eating during class," "Walk, don't run, in the classroom."

Clearly, rules, and the consequences for following or not following them, need to be different for different grade levels. Also, students should be involved in the formulation of rules, and, of course, need to be fully aware of the consequences for rule infractions. Important positive consequences described by Canter include praise, notes sent home and phone calls, special privileges, awards, classwide recognition, and other tangible rewards.

Consequences for Misbehaving. The consequences for misbehaving in my father's school were clear. First would be a warning. Second might be another warning often accompanied by a verbal reprimand, the strength of which depended on the severity of the transgression and the age of the transgressor. And third would be what we thought of as a real consequence: sometimes an unpleasant task like cleaning one of the little houses out in the yard; more often, a strapping. Parents supported this classroom management model wholeheartedly. And they didn't even know it was a form of assertive discipline.

The consequences of which the Canter model speaks are somewhat more gentle than those in vogue in the isolated community in which I was schooled. But they are, nevertheless, clearly a form of punishment. Teachers should follow three guidelines in setting up consequences, advises Canter:

1. Consequences should be something students do not like, but they should not be physically or psychologically harmful.*

2. Consequences should be a choice.

3. Consequences do not have to be very severe to be effective.

Among the consequences that Canter advocates are most of those we have discussed in connection with the use of punishment in behavior modification programs: time-outs, response cost, detention, and being sent to the principal's office. The model of assertive disci-

---

*PPC: It might be worth pointing out that whether a specific form of punishment is psychologically harmful may depend more on the context in which it is given than on the specific nature of the punishment. A "strapping" in the author's school was apparently a socially accepted—even *expected*—form of punishment, and is far less likely to have been psychologically harmful than it might now be in a relatively punishment-free contemporary school. AUTHOR: Yes.

pline also recommends that parents be called upon to help in disciplining their children. Teachers are advised to occasionally make tape recordings of the misbehaviors of children so that these can later be played for administrators and parents who might be slightly skeptical when faced with the possibility that Angela, such a model little girl, would actually use profanity in public.

In summary, Canter describes four steps in establishing and implementing a program of assertive discipline in school: (1) establish rules and expectations, (2) identify misbehavior, (3) use punishment to enforce rules and expectations, and (4) implement a system of positive consequences for desired behaviors.

This program also provides a large number of highly specific teacher suggestions concerning how to respond in different situations, how to implement consequences, how to deal with student anger, and how to handle the 5 to 10 percent of students who are truly difficult.

Strengths and Weaknesses. One of the principal strengths and appeals of Canter's assertive discipline is its insistence on the rights and responsibilities of teachers and of students. It provides teachers with a clear and workable set of procedures for establishing and maintaining classroom order, and, to a large extent, it legitimizes the use of punishments that might be shunned by more humanistic models. In addition, the model is clear and simple, and has the advantage of involving both parents and administrators in the management of students.

But assertive discipline does not lack critics, many of whom object to its use of punishment. Clearly, all of the common objections to the use of punishment also apply to assertive discipline: It often does not work; it can have undesirable side effects; it teaches children that violence and aggressiveness are permissible under certain circumstances. Others object on the grounds that assertive discipline can belittle and humiliate students, that it may lead to even greater defiance and rebelliousness, and that it does not address the basic causes of misbehavior.

COGNITIVE BEHAVIOR
MODIFICATION: DONALD MEICHENBAUM

Behavior modification, as we saw, focuses not on what the student has or is but on what the student does. This is true of management techniques based on the principles of behavioristic conditioning theories. It is also true of an approach that merges cognitive with behavioristic principles: cognitive behavior modification.

Changing Cognitions. Cognitive behavior modification is based on the recognition that what we *think* is fundamentally important to what we do. As Meichenbaum (1977) notes, the effects of the consequences of our behavior may have more to do with our ability to imagine and to anticipate these consequences than with the consequences themselves. I know clearly that I am hurrying as I write these words this evening because I have not yet eaten, and I can predict and anticipate that when I am done, I will be able to go to where I can eat. I don't hurry like some mindless rat simply because I have been conditioned to expect food at the end of my labors; I hurry because I see lasagna on the table of my reason.

Accordingly, the cognitive behavior therapist looks not just at visible manifestations of behavior and at the consequences that influence them, but also at cognitions (thoughts). The causes of behavior, says Hughes (1988), are "cognitive mediating processes." And our cognitions, our thoughts, are subject to change in the same way as are our behaviors.

In essence, cognitive behavior modification uses the principles of behavior modification and incorporates cognitive activities (thinking processes) in an effort to bring about change (Hughes, 1988).

---

cognitive behavior modification An approach that combines the behavioristic principles of operant conditioning (mainly principles of reinforcement) with the power of reasoning and with the human ability to imagine the consequences of behavior in an effort to bring about behavior change.

An Illustration of Cognitive Behavior Modification. Cognitive behavior modification is well illustrated in Meichenbaum and Goodman's (1971) attempt to reduce the impulsivity of overly active children. They devised a five-step cognitive behavior modification training procedure using a simple line-drawing task:

1. The experimenter performed the task, serving as a model, and speaking out loud throughout the performance. The verbalization focused on the problem, responses to the problem, and monitoring of ongoing activity (the "cognitive modeling" phase):

   Okay, what is it I have to do? You want me to copy the picture with the different lines. I have to go slow and be careful. Okay, draw the line down, down, good; then to the right, that's it; now down some more and to the left. Good, I'm doing fine so far. Remember go slow. Now back up again. No, I was supposed to go down. That's okay. Just erase the line carefully . . . Good. Even if I make an error I can go on slowly and carefully. Okay, I have to go down now. Finished. I did it. (p. 117)

2. The child is asked to perform the same task but is guided by the experimenter while doing so.

3. The child performs the task while speaking "self-instructions" out loud.

4. The child performs the task but only whispers the directions.

5. The child performs the task, guided only by silent "inner speech."

These five steps were used with progressively more difficult tasks during four different sessions. Subsequently, impulsive children appeared to have become more reflective. They took more time to complete tasks and committed significantly fewer errors while doing so.

Cognitive behavior modification programs have been successfully used for a variety of behavior as well as learning problems (for example, Kamann & Wong, 1993; Loera &

Meichenbaum, 1993). Self-instructions or self-talk are an important component of most of these programs (Meichenbaum, 1993). A second important characteristic is an emphasis on our ability to think—to *reason*. In fact, reasoning, although often used less systematically than might be appropriate for a cognitive behavior modification program, is one of the most effective—and most common—classroom management strategies.

Strengths and Weaknesses. Among the main strengths and appeals of cognitive behavior modification is its recognition of the role that thinking plays in our behavior. We are not, note the cognitive psychologists, just some mindless rats or pigeons scurrying about in ways that have previously been rewarded—or rushing desperately to avoid sources of previous punishment. Rather, we are thinking creatures who understand much about the relationship between our behaviors and their outcomes, and who have a unique ability to imagine and anticipate rewards that may still be a long time in coming. This view does far less violence to our humanistic notions of what it is to be human than does a more behavioristic view. At the same time, however, cognitive behavior modification techniques tend to be complex, require considerable preparation and expertise on the part of the teacher, and may not be suitable for a wide variety of immediate classroom problems—problems for which some of the more direct, if less humanistic, methods of behaviorism may seem more effective and appropriate.

MORE GENERAL CLASSROOM MANAGEMENT STRATEGIES

Preceding sections have dealt with a number of specific models of classroom management and discipline. First were the highly humanistic, student-centered approaches of Rogers and Marland. These were followed by a series of models described as democratic (those of Kounin, Webster, and Dreikurs). Finally, we looked at the more authoritarian and assertive models of Skinner, Canter, and Meichenbaum. In the remaining sections, we deal with a handful of more general approaches and strategies for maintaining classroom order and solving discipline problems. Most of these approaches share elements of one or more of the models already considered.

REASONING

Reasoning, for example, which is one of the most important alternatives to the more direct forms of corrective intervention, is a fundamental component of humanistic and democratic approaches to classroom management. And, because of its appeal to the intellect, it is also closely related to cognitive behavior modification.

Essentially, to reason is to provide rational explanations; hence, reasoning as a corrective strategy involves presenting children with reasons for not engaging in deviant behavior and/or reasons for engaging in some alternative behavior. There is a fundamental difference between saying to a student, "Don't snap your fingers because you are distracting the others and making it difficult for them to study," and saying, "Don't snap your fingers or you will have to stay after school." The first uses reasoning; the second involves a threat of punishment. Note, however, that the first statement, while appealing to reason, might also be interpreted as implying a threat, depending on the child's prior experience with the person attempting the correction. If children have learned through experience that the likely consequences of not acceding to authority's wishes, no matter how reasonably those wishes might be phrased, is some form of punishment, the effectiveness of reason might well be due to the implied threat.

---

reasoning As a disciplinary strategy, the process of providing a rationale for doing or not doing certain things. May be used as both a corrective and a preventive classroom management tactic. Forms an important part of humanistic and democratic approaches to classroom management.

Reasoning is considerably more appealing to parents and teachers than are most other disciplinary alternatives. It seems somehow more humane to deal with children on an intellectual level than to deal with them from our positions of power as dispensers of rewards and punishments. And, happily, research and good sense both confirm our suspicions that reasoning can be an effective means of controlling or correcting student behavior (Vasquez-Levy, 1993).

Effectiveness of Different Reasons. A number of researchers have investigated the comparative effectiveness of various kinds of reasons that might be given children to prevent them from engaging in some behavior. In a typical experimental situation, children are asked not to play with a toy and are then left alone with that toy; they have no reason to believe that they will be admonished if they do play with the toy. Investigators give the children specific reasons for not playing with the toy.

Parke (1974) reports that rationales that stress the object ("The toy might break") are more effective for younger children than are more abstract rationales relating to rights of possession ("You should not play with toys that belong to others"). However, Hoffman (1970) found that for older children rationales that emphasize the consequences of their behavior for other people ("other-oriented induction") are more persuasive than rationales that emphasize the consequences to the child. In other words, if the experimenter says, "Do not play with that toy because you will make the child it belongs to unhappy," subjects are more likely not to play with the toy than if the experimenter says, "Do not play with that toy because it might break and that would make you unhappy."

Walters and Grusec (1977) also argue that reasoning that arouses empathy for others is usually more effective than reasoning that focuses on personal consequences, particularly after the age of 6. Thus, with advancing intellectual and moral development, children are more likely to respond to rationales relating to abstractions and ideals and to become less con-cerned with immediate objective consequences. This observation is further corroborated by what is known about the sequence of moral development in children (see Chapter 2). The implications of the foregoing observations are obvious: It is wise to provide younger children with specific, concrete reasons for requests that are made of them. After children have reached school age, however, more abstract rationales are preferable. Perhaps most important, rationales that are other directed and that consequently arouse empathy for others appear to be most effective.

Why Reason? In addition to humanitarian and ethical considerations that clearly favor reasoning over punishing, reasoning is preferable to punishment for several practical reasons. First, a punishing agent provides a model of aggressiveness for the learner. In effect, the punisher's activities signify that one acceptable method of dealing with difficult situations is through the assertion of punitive power. Reasoning provides a rather different model. To reason with a child—to provide a rationale for required behavior—is to say, in effect, that one way to cope with difficulty is the deliberate application of thought.

A second advantage of a reasoning strategy is that such an approach lends itself naturally to the description of alternative acceptable behaviors. In other words, reasoning need not be restricted to providing rationales for why a behavior should not be engaged in but can also be directed toward explaining why certain behaviors should be undertaken. Various forms of altruistic and prosocial behavior (cooperation, sharing, helping) cannot easily be taught by punitive means but instead lend themselves more readily to the use of models, reasoning, reinforcement, or a combination of these.

TEN PROCEDURES FOR PREVENTIVE CLASSROOM MANAGEMENT

Grossnickle and Sesko (1990) provide a list of ten procedures they consider an important basis for classroom management. Many of these have been mentioned earlier in this chapter but are worth repeating in this simple, organized form:

1. *Establish clear behavior guidelines.* Expectations, standards, and rules should be clear to teachers, students, and parents. Preferably, they should be written and distributed to all concerned.

2. *Adopt a teamwork approach.* Teachers, administrators, and parents are a team and should all work together to support, follow, and enforce agreed-upon management procedures.

3. *Design a complete discipline ladder.* This is a clear description of available corrective disciplinary measures and the order in which they are to be invoked (for example, first an in-class warning, followed, in order and if necessary, by an after-class conference, a phone call to parents, referral to the principal, help from counselors . . .).

4. *Teach self-management and self-discipline.* This is a gradual process but an essential function of schools.

5. *Invite good discipline.*

6. *Focus on students' success and self-esteem.*

7. *Implement firm, fair, and calm enforcement.*

8. *Plan lessons thoroughly.*

9. *Continually monitor the classroom environment.*

10. *Minimize problems early.*

CREATING A CLASSROOM CONTEXT FOR PREVENTIVE CLASSROOM MANAGEMENT

The preceding sections might seem a little like a catalogue from which a clever teacher might select an assortment of tricks and tactics for managing classrooms, all the while keeping students happily on-task. But good teaching is not so simple; in teaching, there are no recipes that, when followed one-two-three, always lead where they are intended.

Good teaching—which implies effective classroom management—requires far more than the deliberate and judicious application of principles and tactics in specific classroom situations. As we saw at the beginning of this chapter, classes are characterized by a multiplicity of often unpredictable events occurring simultaneously; they demand of the teacher an exceptional level of attention and vigilance (with-it-ness). And they require as well an ongoing series of instantaneous decisions and their immediate implementation.

In addition to the ongoing decision making and problem solving that good teaching requires, it involves a large number of decisions that are made in advance. These might be in response to specific, immediate questions, such as "What do I teach next?" "What assignments are appropriate for this unit?" "How should I arrange the seats in my classroom?" Or they might be in response to more global questions, such as "Should I incorporate cooperative learning activities in my classroom?" "Should I involve students in decisions about rules?" "Should I include programs designed to increase prosocial behavior?" "Should I emphasize a whole-class, teacher-directed teaching style?" "Should I implement more small-group learning activities?" And so on.

The important point is that learning and classroom management occur in a classroom context that is determined by at least four influences: the blend of students that compose the class, your beliefs and personality, your application of the science that texts such as this provide, and a measure of art.

You may have some control over the third and fourth of these influences but not over the first two. You cannot easily change your beliefs and personality, and you are not likely to be allowed to select students for your classes. Still, enough is under your control to make worthwhile the struggle to become the best teacher you can. All that relates to good and effective teaching also relates to maintaining classroom order.

But even enormously effective teachers are sometimes called on to deal with disturbances and disruptions in the classroom. That this should be the case does not necessarily mean that you are a failure, that the system is at fault, or that teacher-training institutions have been remiss. Although each of these might be wholly or partly responsible, the point is not to lay the blame but to deal with the situation.

In dealing with any disciplinary problem, two concerns are of paramount importance. The first is that the individual not be harmed— that whatever the teacher does is done in the best interests of the student, with full consideration of that person's self-esteem and humanity. The second is that the disciplinary measures invoked should be applied in the interests of the entire group. In short, the teacher as a humanitarian practitioner of skills (with a little art, to be sure) must strike a delicate balance between the well-being of the group and that of the individual. The resolution is not always simple.

DEVELOPING MORALITY IN STUDENTS

The most effective and comprehensive management systems for classrooms, argue Smith and Misra (1992), are those that concentrate on reaching the academic and social goals that schools have for children. In other words, they are systems where the emphasis is on antecedent conditions that are designed to prevent or minimize disruptions, and on consequences that reinforce appropriate behavior rather than punishing that which is less appropriate.

This philosophy is reflected in the first part of this chapter, which has intentionally emphasized preventive and management strategies, rather than **corrective strategies,** in the hope that with proper attention to the aspects of teacher–learner interaction that are conducive to enthusiasm, warmth, and caring, seriously disruptive behavior will be infrequent and the need for corrective action rare. As a result, the teacher may have more time and energy to address the larger but sometimes less visible problems of social adjustment, self-discipline, and the development of *morality*.

Rules and regulations in a classroom exist primarily to ensure the order necessary for teaching and learning, but they have other effects as well. School is more than preparation for later life; it is a fundamental part of the child's immediate life. And it is perhaps fortunate that, in many respects, schools mirror the larger society. The penalties for infraction of school rules might not be as harsh as those that apply to the infraction of society's laws, but the rewards for compliance are no less. And although we might strenuously object that schools should not teach compliance, we must nevertheless admit that society would be incredibly more chaotic than it sometimes appears to be were it not that most of us have learned to live within social, legal, and moral prescriptions, that we have learned how to resolve a majority of our conflicts without resorting to knives, guns, and fists, and that we behave in morally acceptable ways most of the time.

It is probably somewhat presumptuous of schools to assume that the development of high moral standards, the internalization of values, and the development of principles and ideals will result incidentally from the experiences that life provides for children—that nothing can, or should, be done deliberately to foster their development. In fact, it is likely that much is accomplished incidentally by wise and sensitive teachers who might accomplish much more were they to address themselves deliberately to the development of **character.** A grab-bag

---

corrective strategies Strategies designed to correct discipline problems. Often involve the systematic use of rewards and punishments.

character An inclusive and ill-defined term signifying those aspects of human personality that include the individual's values, moral strength, principles, virtues, and vices. Relates to what we think of as the goodness or moral strength of the individual.

expression for values, moral strength, principles, and virtues, *character* is an ill-defined and rare term in today's social sciences. Otherwise, these sciences might have more advice to offer the teacher who is concerned with issues other than classroom management and the curriculum-bound teaching/learning process.

PROSOCIAL PROGRAMS

Humanistic approaches to education represent an attempt to cater directly to children's social and emotional needs and to help them develop the social skills that are useful and necessary for effective interaction with others. The humanistic emphasis on affective education points clearly in this direction, as do the various group-process approaches that have become popular in humanistic schools, as well as a handful of values clarification and conflict management programs developed for use in schools.

Conflict Management. Palmares and Logan (1975) have developed an extensive **conflict management** curriculum, both audiovisual and textual, intended to teach children a variety of methods they can use to resolve conflicts. Many of these methods are used spontaneously by children and are learned incidentally as a function of the give-and-take of social interaction. However, some children experience more difficulty than others in acquiring these social skills. For these children, the program should prove particularly effective.

Among the conflict resolution skills taught by the program are negotiating, compromising, taking turns, explaining, listening, apologizing, soliciting intervention, using humor, and invoking chance (for example, flipping a coin). Seven-

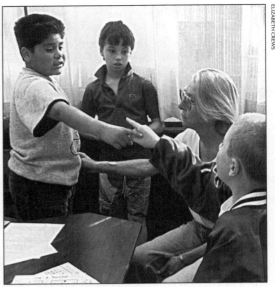

ELIZABETH CREWS

Helping children learn the many ways of resolving conflicts is one of the teacher's important reponsibilities. Among conflict resolution skills that can be taught and learned are negotiating, compromising, taking turns, listening, explaining, apologizing, using humor—perhaps even pointing fingers on occasion.

teen specific strategies are developed, fourteen of which are primarily positive and clearly useful in adult interaction as well. Three are more negative (violence, flight, and tattling), although they too might occasionally be resorted to.

This program, and variations of it, have been used extensively in several situations. For example, Beekman and Holmes (1994) developed a program that teaches parents five approaches that can work in resolving parent–child conflict: collaborating, compromising, accommodating, avoiding, and directing. Similarly, Black (1994a) describes how students who are confident, caring, and intelligent, and who are trained, can serve as **mediators** to intervene

---

conflict management Label given to a program designed to teach individuals acceptable ways of resolving conflicts. Common conflict management techniques include negotiating, compromising, taking turns, explaining, listening, apologizing, mediation, using humor, and invoking chance.

mediator Students who are specially trained to intervene between two or more other students who are in conflict.

between two or more other students who are in conflict. And Rubin (1994) also describes how negotiators (or mediators) can help resolve conflicts.

An Experimental Prosocial Program. A general approach to developing prosocial behavior is illustrated by an experimental program implemented and evaluated during a five-year period in three elementary schools (Solomon et al., 1988). The program emphasizes commitment to accepted and shared values, a sense of community, and the development of concern and care. It includes five separate kinds of activities for students. Among the most important of these are small group cooperative activities of the kind described by Johnson, Johnson, Holubec, and Roy (1984) and intended primarily to develop values associated with fairness, respect, responsibility, and helping one another.

The second aspect of the program, developmental discipline, is a student-centered approach to classroom management and discipline wherein students are given an opportunity to participate in formulating and enforcing rules. The emphasis is on understanding the principles that underlie rules, and the goal is to foster student development toward autonomy.

A third component of the Solomon and associates (1988) program involves activities promoting social understanding and is exemplified in instances in which the teacher uses classroom situations to discuss and reinforce prosocial values. In addition, role-playing games, formal discussions, books, films, and other activities are used to increase children's sensitivity to one another and to promote tolerance of differences.

Fourth, the program encourages activities that involve highlighting prosocial values. For example, teachers are instructed to draw attention to instances of prosocial behavior in the classroom, such as sharing and comforting.

Films, books, and other models of prosocial behavior are also used.

The fifth component of this program stresses helping activities. It consists of encouraging children to engage directly in prosocial behaviors by helping one another and their community. To this end, "buddy" systems and tutoring programs are set up, and various school and community improvement activities are organized.

This program was evaluated by comparing students in three experimental schools with comparable students in three other schools. The results? In the authors' words, "[The program] had substantial positive effects on children's interpersonal behavior in the classroom (without impeding their achievement)" (Solomon et al., 1988, p. 545). Children in these programs were found to be more supportive, more cooperative, friendlier, and more helpful toward one another than comparable children not in the program.

Although implementing this program required that teachers undertake week-long training sessions, attend weekly and monthly meetings, and be provided with considerable supportive material, elements of the program can profitably be incorporated in any classroom. As Solomon and associates (1988) note, two general aspects of life in the classroom seem clearly related to the development of prosocial values and behaviors: One is the establishment of a warm teacher–student relationship; the other is the provision of opportunities for cooperation and collaboration among students.

Intentionally or otherwise, schools do much to teach children how to get along with one another. Unfortunately, students sometimes learn *not* to get along instead. Perhaps if teachers attend to these two things—the teacher–student relationship and interstudent cooperation—schools will intentionally do much more that is positive.

MAIN POINTS

1. The expression "classroom management" refers to the arrangement of classroom activities to facilitate teaching and learning; "discipline" relates to the interventions made necessary by student behaviors that disrupt (or threaten to disrupt) classroom activities.

2. Classrooms are characterized by tremendous student and teacher diversity but share some common features: multidimensionality of classroom events (many individuals, many activities, many goals), simultaneity (many events occurring at any one time), immediacy (many events requiring instant teacher decision and action), and unpredictability (the course of classroom events cannot easily be predicted). Hence, managing classes requires special pedagogical and information processing skills (vigilance and with-it-ness), which may eventually become unconscious and automatic.

3. Despite some valid ethical and humanitarian objections to control, to the extent that teachers act *in loco parentis* and care for their students, discipline may be necessary. Preventive strategies are essential to effective classroom management.

4. Humanistic models of discipline (Rogers) recommend minimal teacher intervention and advocate highly supportive, student-centered schools. The humanistic teacher aims to develop self-discipline in students.

5. Marland's model provides more specific humanistic strategies for classroom management. He advises that teachers should set reasonable limits and rules, give legitimate praise, use humor, and establish a supportive classroom environment.

6. Kounin describes these important characteristics of successful classroom management: with-it-ness (timely, noninterruptive, on-target desists); overlapping (responding effectively to potential classroom disruptions without interrupting ongoing activity); smoothness and momentum (as opposed to jerky transitions, lesson slowdowns, and interruptions caused by stimulus-boundedness, thrusts, dangles, truncations, flip-flops, overdwelling, or fragmentation); maintaining focus (making students accountable, using group-alerting cues, and using lesson formats that involve all students).

7. Webster's democratic principles are based on reason, respect, and relevance. They emphasize clear, well-understood, and well-accepted rules and appropriate punishments for infractions.

8. Dreikurs' logical consequences model interprets child misbehavior in terms of their need for attention, for power, for revenge, or perhaps for appearing inadequate. It provides procedures for determining student motives and suggests specific teacher responses for behaviors related to each motive. It also advises setting up logical consequences as outcomes of misbehaviors—outcomes accepted as just by students and intended to encourage good behavior rather than to punish misbehavior.

9. Behavior modification applies behavioristic principles in order to change behavior and typically involves specific steps: define the problem, measure it, determine response antecedents and consequences, decide how these can be changed, plan and implement intervention, and follow up (evaluate and terminate or perhaps modify the program).

10. Systematic reinforcement programs in schools typically use positive reinforcement, sometimes in the form of tokens or a combination of teacher praise and other tangible rewards (such as the Premack principle that calls for a desirable activity to be used as a reinforcer). Some disputed evidence suggests that excessive reliance on external rewards may have a dampening effect on intrinsic motivation.

11. Extrinsic reinforcers include consumables, manipulatables, visual and auditory stimuli, social stimuli, tokens, and items on reinforcement menus (lists of rewards from which students select). The teacher's attention is extremely important. Important principles governing the use of reinforcement in the classroom include these: Reinforcement is individualistic (defined only in terms of its effects on the individual); its effects are automatic; reinforcement and punishment should be consistent, should be related closely to the relevant behavior, and should occur as soon as possible; the amount of reinforcement required should not be underestimated; and students' work should be organized in such a way that it is possible to reinforce small steps frequently.

12. Models provide children with standards of appropriate behavior. On occasion, punished models may serve to inhibit deviant behaviors as well. Perhaps the most important classroom model is the teacher.

13. Extinction involves an attempt to eliminate undesirable behavior through the withdrawal of reinforcement. Punishment involves the presentation of an unpleasant stimulus or the removal of a pleasant stimulus as a consequence of behavior. Among objections to the use of punishment are claims that it does not always work, that it presents an undesirable model of violence, that it might have undesirable emotional side effects, and that it might lead to maladaptive behaviors through the introduction of frustration. Research indicates that punishment may suppress undesirable behaviors and that it may be particularly appropriate in cases in which it is necessary for a child to learn about behaviors that are not permitted.

14. Common punishments include reprimands (expressions of disapproval, generally verbal but sometimes nonverbal), time-outs (the removal of a student from a reinforcing situation—includes isolation [physical removal], exclusion [removal of the child from ongoing activities but not from the classroom], or nonexclusion [removal of the child from the ongoing activity to a place where the child continues to observe the activity], and response cost (loss of previously earned reinforcers).

15. Canter's assertive discipline argues against teacher permissiveness and advocates that teachers establish classroom discipline plans that include clear rules, ways of teaching students to follow those rules, and provisions for involving parents in disciplining children.

16. Cognitive behavior modification (Meichenbaum) uses the principles of behavioral intervention and the person's thoughts (cognitions) to change behavior. Typically, it attempts to make people aware of their thought processes and of the reasons for their behaviors.

17. Reasoning, often in combination with other disciplinary measures, appears to be a highly effective and humane way of handling classroom problems. Concrete reasons appear to be more effective with younger children; abstract reasons work better with older children. In addition, reasons that appeal to the effect of behavior on others are particularly successful and may be important in developing higher levels of moral orientation.

18. In addition to maintaining classroom order, teachers should also attend to the development of social and affective skills in children. Humanistic educators suggest that teachers should pay attention to students' emotional and moral development, perhaps by using specific prosocial programs and techniques (such as those that deal with conflict management).

APPLIED QUESTIONS

▶ Why is good classroom management so important? Write an essay outlining your answer.

▶ List specific instructional strategies relating to each of the following management models:

Rogers' humanistic model

Marland's caring for children model

Kounin's teacher with-it-ness

Webster's democratic procedures

Dreikurs' logical consequences

Skinner's behavior modification

Canter's assertive discipline

Meichenbaum's cognitive behavior modification

▶ If you were to develop a series of lessons that incorporate strategies for preventive classroom management, what would you come up with?

STUDY TERMS

SUGGESTED READINGS

There are a large number of books that present recipes and strategies relating to classroom management and discipline. The first two of the following seven books are highly practical, general guides to different models of classroom management; the second three books present humanistically oriented approaches to management; and the final two describe approaches that are clearly more restrictive and assertive:

HEWITT, J. D. (1992). *Playing fair: A guide to the management of student conduct*. Vancouver, B.C.: EduServ.

EDWARDS, C. H. (1993). *Classroom discipline and management*. New York: Macmillan.

NELSEN, J. (1987). *Positive discipline: A warm, practical, step-by-step sourcebook for parents and teachers*. New York: Ballantine.

KAMEENUI, E. J., & DARCH, C. B. (1995). *Instructional classroom management: A proactive approach to behavior management*. White Plains, N.Y.: Longman.

FROYEN, L. A. (1993). *Classroom management: The reflective teacher-leader* (2nd ed.). New York: Macmillan.

CANTER, L., & CANTER, M. (1992). *Lee Canter's assertive discipline: Positive management for today's classroom*. Santa Monica, Calif.: Lee Canter & Associates.

DOBSON, J. (1992). *The new dare to discipline*. Wheaton, Ill.: Tyndale.

Bears are extremely confident and capable climbers, particularly when young. With increasing weight, however, they trust only the stoutest of branches, although a fall is not likely to prove disastrous. Polar bears, for example, can climb an almost sheer ice wall and will then routinely jump down from heights of fifteen to twenty feet. And this in spite of their ponderous weights. One bear reportedly dived more than fifty feet into the water to escape hunting dogs and then set off in the direction of the closest land mass— an impressive twenty-two miles away (Perry, 1966; Matthews, 1969).

CHAPTER 12

I am a Bear of Very Little Brain, and long
words Bother me.

A. A. MILNE, *Winnie-the-Pooh*

Madam, I have been looking for a person
who disliked gravy all my life; let us swear
eternal friendship.

SYDNEY SMITH, *Memoirs*

Computer Technology and Other Approaches to Individualizing Instruction

PREVIEW

My Funk and Wagnall's tells me that technology is the application of science and of technical advances in industry, the arts, and other fields. Education is presumably among these other fields, and this, the twelfth chapter, is this textbook's technology chapter. It details the application of science (to the extent that psychology is a science) and of technical advances in the business of educating. Accordingly, this chapter describes programmed instruction, the use of computers in education, and a number of specific teaching techniques founded on distinct theoretical principles.

Focus Questions

▶ What is tracking?

▶ What are the characteristics of branching and linear programs?

▶ How might computers be used in education?

▶ What is mastery learning? PSI? IPI? IGE?

▶ Which instructional strategies are best for which kinds of learners?

In our school in Pascal, there were usually about forty students scattered through eight grades, and then maybe one or two students working their way through ninth or tenth grade, following what were called correspondence courses—a sort of mail-order course for students in isolated areas. Those who took correspondence courses were expected to work almost entirely on their own. After all, the teacher had eight other grades to look after.

The year I reached eighth grade, there were two students who signed up for ninth-grade correspondence courses: Jimmy Giggs, whom we called Jigs although he couldn't dance a step; and Rejean Lajeunesse, whose name, following a stunningly successful attempt at growing facial hair to ward off winter's cold, we changed to Barbu (and later on to Whiskers when we had all learned enough English).

Jigs was not an especially gifted student, although he could kick a soccer ball a mile and shoot a puck through fenceboard. He had struggled through most of elementary school and might never have passed out of it had it not been that my father, the teacher, had a policy of not failing anybody in eighth grade.

"Shoot, if I passed him that far," my dad explained, "why would I fail him now and he couldn't get a good job, eh?"

"Yeah," Walter Charpentier, the storekeeper, agreed. "Besides, he always has lots of chores to do at home, and it wouldn't be fair."

Whiskers, on the other hand, had breezed through elementary school, gold stars on all his report cards.

"He'll do good, that Rejean, in the correspondence courses," my dad wisely predicted. As for Jigs, all he would say was, "Well, it's better than hanging around the pool room."

Which, as it turned out, it was. It seems that Jigs got a charge out of studying lessons one at a time, all carefully laid out one after the other, each with a clear assignment that some nameless person in the government somewhere dutifully corrected and sent back by mail every second week. In the end, he not only passed his ninth-grade correspondence courses but enthusiastically registered for tenth grade the next year and eventually went on to finish high school and complete a welding course.

Sadly, Whiskers didn't fare so well. He had little motivation to study his lessons, and often couldn't find quite enough time to finish his assignments and send them in. Maybe this was partly because that was the year that he discovered Saturday night dances and other diversions, along with growing whiskers and learning to speak in a man's voice. His final correspondence course evaluation simply said "incomplete."

Making the Lesson Fit the Student

Most of us believed that Jigs was not very bright and that he would have to struggle hard for whatever he achieved. We were equally certain that Whiskers would breeze through school. And, all things being equal, perhaps we were more right than wrong. But things are not always equal. Some students are bright, alert, inquisitive, and interested; others are less capable or less interested—or both. A lesson, or a course, does not necessarily fit all students equally well. Much of mass education is, well, for the masses; often, lessons are designed for all and sundry with little attention to individual differences. A fundamentally important question is what can an ordinary classroom teacher do to individualize instruction?

One solution is for the teacher to spend time with each student individually, respond-

ELIZABETH CREWS

Although there often isn't enough time, money, or energy to implement completely individualized programs for all students, individualization on a more limited scale is possible in every classroom. Individualization of instruction does not mean that all students work individually at all times throughout the school day. But it does mean that whenever possible the teacher takes into consideration the needs, strengths, weaknesses, and wishes of individual students.

ing to the student's immediate needs and interests, explaining, probing, imparting strategies, and doing other things good teachers do. Unfortunately, teacher–pupil ratios, the time available, and the demands of the curriculum make this a difficult and often impractical solution. As a result, teachers often resort to one or more educational strategies that take into consideration individual differences among learners. These strategies include ability grouping (or tracking), the learning styles approach discussed in Chapter 9, programmed instruction, computer-based or computer-assisted programs, and a number of specific individualized instructional programs such as Bloom's mastery learning and Keller's PSI. The details and merits of these strategies are the subject of this chapter.

TRACKING

Tracking involves grouping students for instructional purposes. Oakes and Guiton (1995) point out that tracking is generally based on one of three sets of criteria: Students are separated into groups on the basis of cultural factors like race, social class, and apparent intelligence—with low-income and minority students being significantly overrepresented among the lower-ability groups.

Tracking may also reflect job prospects and aspirations. This type of tracking is evident, for example, in the distinction between vocational

tracking An instructional procedure that involves dividing the members of a class into groups according to their ability.

(or technical) high schools and those that are more academic.

Finally, tracking decisions may reflect personal choice factors such as individual interests or parental pressure. Thus, parents may select certain programs for their children largely because of the aspirations and hopes they have for them. Or, in some cases, they may select schools on the basis of their reputations (or for social, cultural, or religious reasons).

SOME ARGUMENTS FOR TRACKING

Tracking students into high- and low-ability classes was once a relatively common way of attempting to match school offerings more closely to students' differences. When ability was used as the basis for tracking, the expectation was that the needs of lower-ability students could be met more effectively if they received instruction in groups composed of individuals of similar ability. By the same token, educators argued that higher-ability students would do better in an instructional environment designed specifically to cater to their needs and abilities. Gallagher (1993), for example, argues that ability grouping is especially useful for brighter children—although not necessarily for those of lower ability.

SOME ARGUMENTS AGAINST TRACKING

In fact, the research is remarkably consistent in its negative evaluation of tracking. As Braddock and Slavin (1993) argue, at best, tracking is totally ineffective; at worse, it is harmful.

What are some of the problems associated with tracking? George (1993) lists the following:

▸ Many student placements are unfair and inaccurate.

▸ Ability grouping tends to lock in students for extended periods of time regardless of their subsequent performance.

▸ Tracking stresses ability but minimizes the value of effort.

▸ Racial, ethnic, and income differences among groups tend to be highlighted.

▸ Students assigned to lower-ability groups often suffer serious loss of self-esteem.

▸ The curriculum used in lower-ability groups is not always sufficiently challenging.

Black (1993) also points out that tracking often violates rights of equal protection guaranteed by statute, and may, therefore, be illegal. And Burks (1994) cites evidence that ability grouping may, in fact, have effects opposite to those intended, especially for lower-ability students. That is, ability grouping tends to be justified at least partly in terms of expected increments in the performance of lower-ability students following instruction ostensibly tailored more closely to their needs. But, says Burks, tracking often results in a magnification of initial differences between lower- and higher-ability groups.

For these reasons, argues Slavin (1993b), between-class ability grouping must go. But there are many alternatives. One is ability grouping *within* classes, in which groups of students are separated for specific learning experiences more closely suited to their needs, but they remain an integral part of the regular classroom. Others include cooperative learning, mastery learning, peer tutoring, and computer-aided instruction.

Detracking. Although being placed in a high track may have a positive effect on some students, Slavin (1993b) reviewed twenty-seven studies of tracking effects and concludes that tracking has essentially no effect, either positive or negative, on the performance of high, middle, or low "tracks." And the bulk of the research indicates that being assigned to a low track often has negative effects on the achievement, self-esteem, and motivation of students (for example, see Snow & Swanson, 1992). Yet, note Wells and associates (1995), "tracking is an entrenched practice in most American schools" (p. 18). And getting rid of the practice, or reducing its use, is a major educational reform that will require far-reaching social and political changes.

THE LEARNING STYLES APPROACH

Another way of individualizing instruction, perhaps the one that goes furthest toward making the lesson fit the student, is the **learning styles approach** discussed in Chapter 9 (see Dunn & Griggs, 1988; Dunn, Dunn, & Perrin, 1994). The learning styles philosophy recognizes that students learn in different ways—that each has a unique learning style. Some students learn well in the morning; others awaken reluctantly and don't function well until later in the day.* Some excel with highly structured, teacher-directed, whole-class approaches; others perform much better with less-structured, self-initiated, individual approaches; still others achieve better in small group, cooperative settings. Some students prefer to work in bright, well-lit surroundings with loud music; others require quiet, more subdued environments. Some learners have a marked preference for the visual or the auditory mode, some respond better than others to praise or criticism, some have longer attention spans than others . . . and on and on.

To truly individualize instruction, advocates of learning styles approaches argue, it is necessary to develop a profile of each learner. This profile provides a detailed description of strengths and weaknesses, as well as of preferences and dislikes. Schools and classes can then be tailored to cater to each individual's style. As we saw in Chapter 9, in practice this approach requires a tremendous assortment of alternatives. Core school subjects must be presented at different times of the day; classes must be organized so that individuals can select among small group, individual, or whole-class approaches; rewards must be restructured so that classes include individual, cooperative, and competitive situations; and instructional materials must be developed to appeal to visual, auditory, and kinesthetic sensory modes.

LEARNING STYLES IN
THE REGULAR CLASSROOM

For many practical reasons, truly individualizing instruction as completely as is suggested by a learning styles approach is often difficult or even impossible. Even if everyone concerned were convinced that this is the best of all possible instructional alternatives, in most instances there simply isn't enough time, money, or energy to implement all aspects of the program. But individualization on a more limited scale is possible in virtually every classroom. In fact, not only is it possible but it is essential, especially in the now common *inclusive classroom* that may include any number of children with unique special needs. But even in a relatively homogeneous classroom, argues Bacdayan (1994), if instruction is not individualized to some extent, the result will be an inefficient and ineffective use of educational resources. The poorer students will struggle needlessly and perhaps unsuccessfully; and the better students will waste much of their time in a boring and unchallenging environment.

Keep in mind that individualization of instruction does not mean that all students work individually at all times throughout the school day. What individualization means is that instructional methods, class organization, evaluation procedures, and other components of the teaching/learning process are selected and modified in response to learners' characteristics, course and lesson goals, and practical constraints. In practice, this usually means that some students are exposed to different experiences at least some of the time; some of these experiences might well be individual, but many will occur in small groups. And even in classes in which the teacher individualizes instruction, much can take place in whole-class situations (see the case "Digging Up the Truth").

---

*PPC: We'd have a lazy bunch of students if we let them sleep all morning just because that's their learning style.
AUTHOR: The bear is not lazy, but he sleeps all winter. That's his *life*style.

---

learning styles approach An individualized instructional system that is designed specifically to cater to the learning style of each student.

Among the instructional methods available to teachers are lecturing, discussing, reciting, questioning, facilitating guided discovery, using small or large group strategies, tutoring, peer teaching, and so on. Each has advantages for different purposes, but even the methods that research has identified as potentially "best" (for example, one-to-one tutoring; Bloom, 1984) cannot, for practical reasons, be used exclusively. Even the methods represented by such global terms as *lecturing, discussing,* and so on are virtually never used to the exclusion of all other methods by any teacher worth even slightly more than his or her salt. Thus, teachers do not typically lecture or discuss; they present lessons, an activity that involves talking, listening, questioning, demonstrating, using instructional materials, and sometimes standing on one's ear or nose. These activities might be directed toward an entire class of students (large or small), a single student, or a handful of students, or they might alternate among the various possibilities. And they might occur in connection with any of a number of specific techniques that have been developed to individualize, to systematize, to computerize, and/or to personalize instruction.

Several of these techniques, some derived directly from psychological theory and experimentation, are described in the remainder of this chapter: programmed instruction, computer-assisted instruction (CAI), mastery learning, Keller's personalized system of instruction (PSI), individually guided education (IGE), and individually prescribed instruction (IPI). Aspects of the methods and principles of each of these approaches might be profitably incorporated in the increasingly sophisticated arsenal of every contemporary teacher.

PROGRAMMED INSTRUCTION

The term **programmed instruction** can be used in a general sense to describe any organized **autoinstructional device**—that is, any device that presents information in such a way that the learner can acquire it without the help of a teacher. In this sense, textbooks are a kind of programmed material, as are computers. A more specific definition of programmed instruction, however, limits it to material that is specifically designed to be autoinstructional and is arranged according to one of two patterns, linear or branching, or a combination of the two.

---

programmed instruction An instructional procedure that makes use of the systematic presentation of information in small steps (frames), in the form of a workbook or some other device. Programs typically require learners to make responses and provide immediate knowledge of results.

autoinstructional device Any instructional device that is effective in the absence of a teacher. Common examples are workbooks and computers.

CASE: DIGGING UP THE TRUTH

THE SITUATION: Edward Stewin, a good teacher, as recollected by Serge, teacher in training

Mr. Stewin, my grade 3 and 4 teacher, always made sure he knew what each student was most interested in and he found ways of letting us work on these interesting subjects, sometimes alone and sometimes in groups. For example, some of us were quite interested in native people, so he had us research a particular tribe and then build articles that they would have used. We then buried them in the schoolyard, and another team of students had to dig them up and assess their lifestyle. Then we got together and more or less taught the rest of the class about this tribe.

Skinner (1954) is usually associated with the **linear program,** whereas Crowder (1961, 1963) introduced the **branching program.**

LINEAR PROGRAMS

The Skinnerian, or linear, program is one in which all learners move through the same material in exactly the same sequence. Linear programs individualize instruction by permitting students to progress at their own rate.

Linear programs are based directly on an operant conditioning model. They present material that leads the student to emit a correct response and that provides reinforcement for that response. In effect, the students' responses are operants, and the knowledge that they have responded correctly is a reinforcer. Accordingly, linear programs have the following characteristics that ensure that a student will almost always answer correctly:

- ▶ The material is broken down into small steps, referred to as **frames,** which are presented in logical sequence. Each frame consists of a minimal amount of information so that a student can remember this information from frame to frame.

- ▶ Students are required to make frequent responses—usually one in every frame and often as many as four or five in each frame.

---

linear program The presentation of programmed material in such a manner that all learners progress through the same material in the same order. Linear programs typically make no provision for individual differences in learning; the material, however, is broken up into very small steps (frames).

branching program Programmed material that, in contrast to a linear program, presents a variety of alternative routes through the material. Such programs typically make use of larger frames than do linear programs, and they frequently use multiple choices. Also termed *Crowder programs.*

frames Units of information presented in programmed instruction. A frame not only presents information but also usually requires the student to make a response.

They are given **prompts** to ensure that they answer correctly.

- ▶ Linear programs provide immediate **knowledge of results.** Students know at once that they have answered correctly (or not). This knowledge is assumed to act as reinforcement. Because linear programs attempt, through the use of prompts and small frames, to ensure that the student makes few errors, most of the feedback is positive—it having been established that positive feedback is more effective than negative feedback (knowledge that one is wrong).

To try your hand at a linear program, see the box entitled "Piagetian Jargon: A Linear Program," and follow the directions.

BRANCHING PROGRAMS

Crowder, or branching, programs present learners with much longer frames than linear programs (sometimes an entire page at a time). And, unlike linear programs, they require learners to select from among several alternative answers rather than making up their own. But the most striking difference between the two is that in branching programs, not all students go through the program in exactly the same way. Students who give all responses correctly go through in the shortest way possible. Students who make errors receive remedial instruction and further clarification. Typically, learners who answer incorrectly are sent to a **remedial frame**

---

prompts Devices used in programmed instruction to ensure that the student will probably answer correctly. They may take a variety of forms.

knowledge of results Knowledge about the correctness or incorrectness of a response. Knowledge of results is usually immediate in programmed instruction.

remedial frame A frame in a branching program to which students are referred when they make an incorrect response. The purpose of the remedial frame is to provide information required for a subsequent correct response.

PIAGETIAN JARGON: A LINEAR PROGRAM

Directions: Fold a sheet of paper or use a strip of cardboard to cover the answers, which are given in the right-hand margin. With the answers covered, read frame 1 and write your answer in the blank provided. Move the paper or cardboard down to check your answer before proceeding to frame 2.

1. Jean Piaget has developed a theory that deals with human adaptation. It is a developmental theory of human _____.

   adaptation

2. As children learn to cope with their environment and to deal effectively with it, they can be said to be _____ to it.

   adapting

3. Adaptation therefore involves interacting with the environment. The process of adaptation is one of organism–environment _____.

   interaction

4. One of the central features of Piaget's developmental theory is that it attempts to explain _____ through interaction.

   adaptation

5. Interaction takes place through the interplay of two complementary processes: One involves reacting to the environment in terms of a previously learned response. This process is called assimilation. Assimilation involves a _____ learned response.

   previously

6. Whenever children use an object for some activity they have already learned, they are said to be assimilating that object to their previous learning. For example, when Jennifer sucks a pacifier, she is _____ the pacifier to the activity of sucking.

   assimilating

7. Sam is given a paper doll. He looks at it curiously and then puts it in his mouth and eats it. He has _____ the doll to the activity of eating.

   assimilated

8. Assimilation is one of the two processes involved in interacting with the environment. It is part of the process of _____.

   adapting or adaptation

9. Adaptation involves two processes. The first is assimilation. The second is called accommodation. It occurs whenever a change in behavior results from interacting with the environment. Accommodation involves a _____ in behavior.

   change or modification

10. When children cannot assimilate a new object to activities that are already part of their repertoire, they must _____ to them.

    accommodate

11. Johnny West was presented with a very long pacifier on the occasion of his first birthday. Before that time he had been sucking a short "bulb" pacifier. The long pacifier matched his nose. He had to elongate his mouth considerably more than usual in order to suck this new pacifier. Johnny West had to _____ to the new pacifier.

    accommodate

12. If Johnny West had been given his old, short pacifier, he could more easily have _____ it to the activity of sucking.

    assimilated

13. . . .

or sequence of frames and eventually return to the main branch. They then proceed from there (see Figure 12.1). An example of a branching program is presented in the box entitled "Bear Tracking: A Branching Program."*

*PPC: Does this program have anything to do with the subtitle of this book? Some of my students wondered, last year.

AUTHOR: It's always a good sign when students wonder. Especially if they do so out loud and ask intelligent questions.

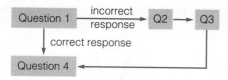

FIGURE 12.1 A branching program.

USEFULNESS OF PROGRAMMED INSTRUCTION

Programmed instruction, as originally conceived and developed, is largely of historical interest. Searches of common educational and psychology databases indicate that very little research has been conducted on programmed instruction since its heyday as an educational fad in the early 1960s—although there is still a scattering of studies that continues to attest to its relative effectiveness (for example, Fernald & Jordan, 1991; Strawitz, 1993). In the end, the legacy of this fad may be in the learning principles it revealed. Markle and Tiemann (1974; Markle, 1978) point out that these principles constitute the rudiments of an instructional theory that can be applied to simple tasks of motor learning or to highly complex cognitive learning tasks. The three fundamental concepts of this programmed instruction theory are active responding, errorless learning, and immediate feedback.

Applying these principles to classroom practice involves presenting small units of information so as to maximize immediate comprehension and minimize the number of errors students make while learning, providing for continual student involvement through active responding, and providing students with immediate confirmation of correct responses. And although it is very time-consuming to structure lessons as logically as the programs require, such a sequence is conducive to learning.

THE COMPUTER AND INSTRUCTION

Some principles of programmed instruction are also evident in another development that can contribute dramatically to individualizing instruction—the use of computers in schools. In fact, many computerized instructional programs are highly similar in format to the programmed texts that were briefly popular a handful of decades ago. And some researchers note that there has been a natural transition from traditional programmed instruction to computer-assisted instruction (Jonassen, 1993). The computer is an especially powerful interactive tool for presenting systematic instructional sequences like those that define programmed instruction.

THE COMPUTER REVOLUTION

"The computer revolution is upon us!" we are told almost daily—and have been told for some time now. A big word, *revolution*. Small wonder that so many of us should ask what this computer revolution is, whether it actually is upon us, and whether it is good or bad.

The Third Wave. Yes, the computer revolution is upon us, according to Alvin Toffler (1980), who earlier (1970) warned us that the coming of this revolution might send many of us into a state of shock. Toffler sees the computer revolution as the **third wave** in a series of monumental changes that have swept over humanity. The first wave, which occurred more than ten thousand years ago, was the agricultural revolution—a revolution that transformed our hunting and foraging ancestors into domesticators of animals and growers of food, changing the very meaning of what it was to be human in those times. The second wave, far more recent in our history, was the industrial revolution, the ultimate effects of which were to transform our workplaces, our homes, and our lives. Only history can ultimately tell us how profound will be the effect of the third wave—the computer revolution that is sweeping over us now.

---

third wave Toffler's expression for the computer revolution (the first two waves of monumental change being the agricultural and the industrial revolutions).

BEAR TRACKING: A BRANCHING PROGRAM

Objectives: After you have read this program, you should be able to:

1. recognize a forest
2. recognize a bear's tracks
3. recognize a bear
4. run very rapidly in all directions

Note: Because only part of the program is presented here, only the first two objectives can be attained.

Directions: Read each frame very carefully; reread it if it appears confusing. Then select what you think best completes the statement presented, and follow the directions that correspond to that answer.

1. A forest is a collection of trees. It is a large collection of trees, just as a city is a large collection of people. A wood is a small collection of trees, just as a town is a small collection of people. A bush is a collection of small trees. What is a collection of small people? Never mind. Bears are often found in large collections of trees.

   If you were looking for a bear, you would go to:

   (a) a large collection of people.

   (b) a forest.

   (c) an ocean.

   If you answered (a), go to frame 10.
   If you answered (b), go to frame 3.
   If you answered (c), go to frame 7.

2. Correct. Good. Now that you have found a forest, you must find some tracks. Remember, a bear's tracks look like this:

   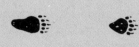
   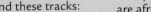

   After you have found the tracks, follow them. Somewhere, a bear is standing in them. If you find these tracks:

   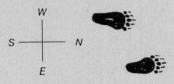

   you should go

   (a) N.

   (b) S.

   (c) E or W.

   If you said (a), go to frame 8.
   If you said (b), go to frame 12.
   If you said (c), go to frame 4.

3. You are correct. Bears are often found in forests. Occasionally, however, bears are also found elsewhere. You should keep this in mind. The best way to find a bear is to do two things: First, look for a forest: second, look for a bear's tracks. They look something like this:

   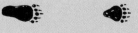

The best way of finding a bear is to:

(a) look for an ocean.

(b) look for its tracks.

(c) look for a forest.

If you answered (a), go to frame 7.

If you answered (b), go to frame 9.

If you answered (c), go to frame 2.

4. Your answer is incorrect, but it may not be unwise. If you are afraid of bears, you might even consider going south. Go to frame 12 to see what would happen if you went south.

5. It is obvious that you are afraid of bears. Your instructions are to go directly to your local university library (do not pass Go, do not collect $200, heh, heh). You are asked to read about counterconditioning, paying special attention to systematic desensitization. If you can afford to, you might consider hiring this textbook's author as a therapist. If you can't afford me, hire someone else.

6. Good! Good! You should do something else. But first you must return to the large collection of people. Having done that . . .

   (Now go to frame 13.)

7. You are not paying attention. Go back to frame 1 and start again.

8. Good. You noticed the arrow. You may eventually see a bear. It is interesting, don't you think, that a bear always stands facing toward the front of its tracks, *sniffing around*? This makes it a lot easier to locate. After you have found the bear, you will have to make a decision:

   Will you:

   (a) stop and pray?

   (b) run home?

   (c) do something else?

   If you said (a), go to frame 11.

   If you said (b), go to frame 5.

   If you said (c), go to frame 6.

9. That is not correct. If you begin to look for a bear's tracks before finding a forest, you may never find either track or bear. Go back to frame 3.

10. That is not correct. A large collection of people is a city. Bears are not usually found in cities, but they are often found in large collections of trees (forests). You might waste a lot of time looking for bears in cities. Now go back and read frame 1 again.

11. Piety is an admirable quality in a student, but it is not the desired response here. You might seriously consider, at this point, whether you really want to track bears. If you are sure that you do, you are instructed to begin with frame 1.

12. Stop! You are going in the wrong direction. A bear faces toward the front of its tracks. This is an important point. Now you may go back to frame 2, or you might want to rest for a minute before continuing. You may do so, but you should probably begin at frame 1 when you are well again.

13. The beginning of this program is included here simply as an illustration of a branching program. Frustrated would-be bear trackers are invited to consult their local library—or they can hire me as a guide (high-quality service at reasonable rates).

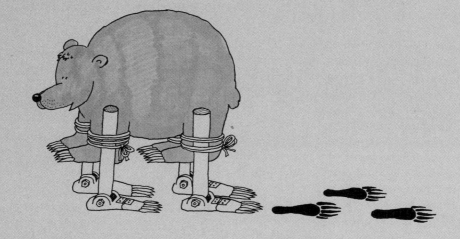

Resistance to the Revolution. "Tomorrow," writes Wilson (1988), "we're going to need to do something entirely different. And that's frightening because people have to let go of who they think they are. A good caterpillar only wants to know how to be a better caterpillar. 'A butterfly?' she says. 'No way you're going to get me up in one of those things'" (p. 14).

Some teachers, and some students, simply want to be good caterpillars. They are uneasy about the computer, afraid of the changes the revolution might require. But there are signs of change. Kristiansen (1992) studied teachers' attitudes toward computers in education over a twenty-year period (1970 to 1990) and found marked increases in acceptance of, even enthusiasm for, computers in school—and a dramatic decline in fear. Yet even today, many college students suffer from varying degrees of "technophobia"—they are apprehensive of the new computer technologies—and more of these are females than males (Bernhard, 1992).

All this may well change, however, as today's generation of children grows. When Todman and Lawrenson (1992) compared 9-year-olds with first-year psychology students, they not only found that the children were less anxious about computers than the college students but also that they had significantly more experience with them. For them, the new technologies will not seem anything like a revolution.

Evidence of the Revolution. Evidence of the computer revolution is all around us. Some twenty-five years ago, I wrote the first edition of this book using a 25-cent ballpoint pen and two dozen pads of yellow paper. Now I write to you on a computer linked to a laser printer—and linked as well to a university computing system, a network of library systems, an assortment of databases, a CD-ROM, and uncountable individuals throughout the world via *their* personal computers. Not that there were no computers in 1972. Quite the contrary, there were many of them, and, surprising as it might seem, in many important ways they were not very different from today's computers in terms of their

Computers are rapidly becoming almost indispensable tools in the teaching/learning process. But not all estimates of their impact are entirely positive.

capabilities. But some important differences between first-generation computers and today's computers account for the revolution. Chief among those differences are the reduced size and price of today's desktop, or personal, computers, made possible by the microchip, a fingernail-size wafer that contains all of the computer's processing units. In addition, new computer technologies have succeeded in linking the world by means of a vast electronic web known as the **Internet.** And these same technologies now make it possible to use computers to immerse people in simulated environments

Internet Label for a worldwide, amorphous, changing web of computer linkages, mainly via telephone lines and satellites. The Internet uses the computing resources of many universities and industries and can be accessed by virtually anyone with a computer and a telephone link (modem). The Internet makes inexpensive electronic communication possible worldwide.

that seem so real they are labeled "virtual reality" (Dykman, 1994).

Now people (and schools) can own personal computers as easily as they can own television sets. In addition, today's personal computer is far easier to operate than its grandparents. It is, in the jargon of the trade, far more user friendly. Small wonder that personal computers proliferate on the market. But what will their effect be on education?

THE POTENTIAL EFFECTS
OF COMPUTERS IN EDUCATION

Computer enthusiasts and other optimists predict sweeping, somewhat radical, and highly beneficial effects of the widespread introduction of computer technologies into schools.

Positive Effects. Among other things, they see schools becoming a part of large information exchange-and-retrieval systems in which individual students will have virtually instant access to an almost unlimited quantity of high-quality information. For example, Alberta Education (1987) summarizes research that indicates that the application of technology in education will

make education more productive

make education more immediate and relevant

make education more powerful

give instruction a more scientific base

make education more individual

make education more accessible

make education more responsive to special and individual needs

make education more cost effective and efficient (p. 5)

There are others who also predict that smaller, friendlier, more personal schools will again proliferate once the resource disadvantages that sometimes characterize smaller schools disappear with the coming of the computer. Some of these enthusiasts insist that problems with reading, writing, and arithmetic

will end as people master the new computer skills. Indeed, some go so far as to suggest that many of the ill effects of television will be replaced by the creative activities encouraged by computers and that family ties will be strengthened as more and more of the third-wave generation are able to work from their homes, linked to their offices (if there still are such things) and to the world via spun-glass fibers, gold filaments, infrared rays, satellite systems, or more mundane telephone lines.

Less Positive Possibilities. There is, of course, a less optimistic view of the likely impact of computers. This view suggests that our basic computational skills may decline dramatically as computers take care of our computational needs, that reading skills are likely to suffer as children spend more time being amused by computers and their fantasy games and less time reading, and that violence may increase as a function of computer video games. Others believe that computers are not likely to make knowledge and power more accessible to the masses but rather to have the opposite effect.

Parsons (1983), for example, argues that according to our best historical evidence, computers are more likely to increase than to decrease the gap between the haves and the have-nots. Schools, notes Muffoletto (1994) have to be especially careful to apply democratic principles of social justice in their introduction of computers in schools. It seems clear that at least in the first decades of the computer in the school, poor and ethnic-minority students (and females) have had less access to computers than wealthier, ethnic-majority students (and males) (Sutton, 1991; Martinez, 1994).

Also, says Parsons, computer enthusiasts are sometimes guilty of exaggerating and misrepresenting the benefits of computers in education. For example, he points out that these enthusiasts use the term *interaction* widely and inaccurately. Parsons sees interaction as a "meeting of minds," a sort of sharing of meaning (exemplified in conversation or in reading a book). Typically, however, interaction with a computer is quite different: It primarily involves the giving of information. Furthermore, although computers often are described as expert systems of one kind or another, they do not resemble human experts in most fields (doctors, lawyers, professors, psychiatrists); computers are generally ill-equipped to provide us with advice—information, yes, but advice only occasionally.

In the final analysis, these opposing optimistic and pessimistic views of how computers are likely to affect our lives are no more than speculation based perhaps on reason and probability, but certainly based also on hope and fear. What will come to pass in the end may not be affected a great deal by our often premature speculations. From the teacher's point of view, given the invasion of the computer in our lives and our schools, what is most important is to understand the uses of the computer that will provide the greatest benefits to students.

USES OF COMPUTERS IN EDUCATION

With their peculiar tendency toward jargon and acronyms, educators have given us a whole series of computer-related expressions: CAI (computer-assisted instruction), CML (computer-managed learning), CBE (computer-based education), CAT (computer-assisted training), CBT (computer-based testing), CBT again (computer-based training), CMI (computer-managed instruction), CMT (computer-managed training), ITS (intelligent tutoring system), ICAI (intelligent computer-assisted instruction), and CAL (computer-assisted learning). Of these, **CAI** is perhaps the most general term.

Basically, there are three related things students can do with computers; they can learn *about* them, they can learn *with* them, and they can use them simply as tools.

Computer Literacy. Learning about computers is what computer literacy is all about. In the same way as learning something about cars is essential for most of us whose daily activities require that we drive, learning something about computers may well be essential for today's children who will in all likelihood be required to do far more with computers than we are. If the effects of the computer revolution are anywhere near the magnitude of the agricultural and industrial revolutions, those who remain computer illiterates may be swept under and drowned by the third wave.

Or will tomorrow's computers, like today's computerized banking machines, be so simplistic that even the nearly illiterate will be able to operate them? Will they be dumbed down like fast-food cash registers with pictures of tiny hamburgers on their keys?*

Computers as Tools. Computers can be useful tools in the management of schools. They simplify routine clerical tasks such as registering students, storing data, solving scheduling problems, issuing report cards, and so on. And they are also tremendously useful computing and writing instruments for school administrators, staff, and teachers.

Computers can also be word processing and computing tools for students, as well as extremely important sources of information. New compact disk technology has not only increased the amount of information a **stand-alone computer** can store for the learner, but has made its retrieval almost instantaneous. In this sense, the computer can be very much like an encyclopedia. But information in the

---

*PPC: Or like highway signs that hardly ever have numbers or words on them anymore, just symbols and pictures.
AUTHOR: Ironically, for those of us who are literate, words might be far more precise than symbols and pictures.

CAI One of many acronyms related to the application of computer technology in education. Specifically, CAI refers to computer-assisted instruction, the use of computers for instructional rather than administrative purposes.

---

stand-alone computer A computer system that is complete by itself in that it includes a processing unit, a monitor, and an input device (keyboard)—in contrast with computer terminals linked to a central computing system.

printed encyclopedia can only be accessed sequentially—or specific related topics can be searched for separately and found in their scattered locations. In contrast, information on a computer's compact disk can be accessed almost instantly—and all related information can be displayed (or printed).

Computers as sources of information are not dependent solely on their own stored information, but can easily be connected to any of a variety of **databases.** A database is a source of information typically organized in terms of one or more subject areas. While doing research for this revision, for example, I repeatedly accessed databases such as PSYCHINFO, ERIC, and MEDLINE. Doing so allowed me to quickly scan (and print out if necessary) summaries of a large number of articles on related topics.

Computers can also be used as a source of advice on career decisions. Their great advantage in career guidance is that they can store a tremendous wealth of information concerning career opportunities and requirements that relate to a rapidly changing job market. They handle routine career-related questions quickly and efficiently, and they can be programmed to find relationships among a student's achievement, aptitudes, and interests and the likelihood of success in various careers. Many career advice computer programs are now available and widely used in schools. Some of these provide information on thousands of careers, and most are designed to be used with the personal computers found most commonly in homes and schools.

Although these are extremely valuable functions, they are more remotely associated with the actual business of instruction than some of the computer's other uses.

Computers for Drill and Practice. Computers can be used as a sort of teaching machine—as an ultrasophisticated piece of audiovisual equipment designed to present programs or lessons, with or without the assistance of teachers. For example, the first uses of the computer in education were often to present Skinnerian or branching programs. The computer is particularly suitable for presenting programs individually, as well as for repetitive, drill-type exercises (in mathematics or language learning, for example, or in learning things like keyboarding skills). Used for these purposes, computers can do a great deal to free the classroom teacher for other activities.

Research indicates that these relatively unimaginative uses of computers are expensive and work better for lower- than higher-ability students but that they are effective for many students, that they can result in time savings, and that students' attitudes toward computers are generally positive (Scott, Cole, & Engel, 1992).

Simulations. Happily, the computer's uses are not limited to drill and practice exercises but include **computer simulations** as well. Computer simulations mimic certain actions or phenomena. For example, programs are available that mimic the circulatory system, a chemical laboratory, or the in-flight responses of a Boeing 737. Simulations allow the learner to discover the results of specific responses without the risk and expense of actually performing them. Thus, in using a computer-controlled simulator, a pilot can learn that a particularly unlucky combination of aileron and rudder movements can cause a crash—without actually destroying either a multimillion-dollar aircraft or human lives.

At a less dramatic level, a clever simulation of a chemical laboratory might allow students

---

databases Sources of information accessible by computers. Common databases include library cataloguing systems or abstracts of current journal articles. Databases are often organized by topics. For example, PSYCHINFO is a vast database that contains summaries of an enormous number of articles published in journals relevant to psychology.

---

computer simulations Mimicking or modeling certain actions, procedures, or phenomena using computers. For example, computers might be used to simulate (copy the actions of) weather patterns or chemical reactions.

to discover the potentially disastrous effects of combining, chilling, heating, pressurizing, or eating different chemicals, without losing a school building or a human body in the process.

Computer simulation can also be used for teaching perceptual and cognitive skills involved in sports, report Starkes and Lindley (1994), who developed a video and slide simulation of basketball. It can also be used for teaching problem-solving skills, report Woodward, Carnine, and Gersten (1988), whose health and lifestyles program (called *Health Ways*) is designed to lead students to determine combinations of factors that are related to longevity.

Virtual Reality Simulations. Imagine you are a student studying ancient Mayan civilizations. Today, you have chosen to explore a Mayan ruin. You climb the precipitous slope of the main pyramid's north face, skipping along the lower steps, then clawing your way up to where the ancient stones have crumbled. Finally, you stand on top. Deliberately, you look in each of the four directions. Now you take out your compass, turn it so that it points to 280 degrees, and search the jungle for signs of the opening into the sacrificial *cenote*. Finding it, you switch to "museum mode" and explore a database, complete with photographs, filled with information on Mayan sacrifices and related topics.

Possible? Almost, with interactive videodisk environments used to produce computer simulations labeled **virtual reality (VR).** Such simulations typically involve one or more of the sensory systems to heighten the sense of realism (Franchi, 1994). As a result, virtual reality describes a particular kind of computer–learner relationship (interface, in computer jargon) wherein the learner experiences aspects of an environment and makes choices or moves

within that environment in such a way that the experience seems virtually real. In a virtual reality system described by Ferrington and Loge (1992), individuals wear the computer's display systems on their heads using something that looks like a helmet and goggles. This system presents the individual with three-dimensional visual and corresponding auditory displays and includes sensors that respond to the user's movements. If users look up, they might see the sky; to the left, another landscape; to the right, yet another. Furthermore, users make choices suggested by the visual display by manipulating an icon (termed a "puppet") that appears on the visual display. The puppet is controlled by a "dataglove" that is so engineered that finger and hand movements are translated directly into corresponding movements of the puppet. Thus, the user can open doors, grasp and move objects, and point in any direction to "move" in that direction.

Although virtual reality systems are still largely experimental, various interactive instructional/entertainment programs are available—including the Mayan program, called *Palenque,* just described (Wilson & Talley, 1990). Although it doesn't use headset receivers or datagloves, it presents learners with individual point-of-view camera angles and permits a variety of places to explore physically, or of other modes such as "museum," which then permit still further choices such as different "rooms" within the museum (Kozma, 1991).

The simulations that VR systems might make possible are staggering to contemplate. They include flight simulators with changing kinesthetic and visual feedback made possible by manipulating the "pilot's" seat and controlling visual images as well as auditory stimulation, highly realistic game simulations, military training simulations, and other educational and entertainment possibilities (Auld & Pantelidis, 1994; Lewis, 1994).

Integrated Learning Systems. Computer-based courses are widely available for a tremendous variety of topics and ages. Delivery systems might include a computing center and a num-

---

virtual reality (VR) A computer simulation that is so realistic it appears almost real. Virtual reality simulations typically involve more than one of the senses and are often designed so that the participant's movements are reflected in realistic changes in visual, auditory, or kinesthetic stimulation.

ber of student terminals or might consist of one or more stand-alone units, each with its own computer and terminal. Typically, the learner interacts with the computer program by means of a monitor and a keyboard or some other control device such as a mouse or a joystick. This physical paraphernalia is collectively labeled **hardware;** the programs, which are really the brains of the computer—its information, instructions, and capabilities—are termed **software,** or sometimes *courseware.*

The phrase **integrated learning system (ILS)** is used to refer to any of a variety of computer-based learning systems typically developed for mass marketing. The systems usually include hardware and software and may also involve links with external databases (Hativa & Becker, 1994). For example, McCullough (1992) describes an integrated learning system at Graham Elementary School in Shelby, N.C., that was created by Computer Systems Research, Inc. (a division of CTB-Macmillan-McGraw Hill). This courseware provides various programs and activities in the three basic areas: reading, writing, and arithmetic. The ILS allows for different levels of objectives and activities and permits ongoing evaluation of students' performance. As a result, it also provides for diagnosis and automatically prescribes a series of courses for each student.

Research indicates that ILS systems can be highly effective in meeting measurable curriculum objectives (West & Marcotte, 1993–94). However, their use can be expensive, and not all teachers are prepared to implement such systems in the classroom (Cook, 1994).

---

hardware The physical components of a computer, including monitors, controllers, keyboards, chips, cards, circuits, drives, printers, and so on.

software Computer instructions; programs. Also termed *courseware.*

integrated learning system (ILS) A computer-based learning/instructional system that includes both hardware and software, often with links to external databases, and that is designed to guide students through part or all of a curriculum.

Most ILS programs emphasize course content rather than the student's cognitive processes. Few approach the current ideal in the field of computer applications to education: intelligent systems.

Intelligent Tutor Systems (ITS). An **intelligent tutor system (ITS)** is a program that takes into account the learner's strengths and weakness and modifies its offerings accordingly—very much as a good teacher does. Intelligent tutor systems try to determine what a student knows (or needs to know) on the basis of the student's interactions with the system—that is, typically on the basis of the student's answers. The system then draws from its databases experiences and instructions that will be most effective given this student and the goals programmed into the system (Mills, 1994).

Intelligent tutor systems are best described in terms of five separate aspects or "modules" (Farnham-Diggory, 1992; Scott, Cole, & Engel, 1992). The "expert module" is the source of knowledge—in computer jargon, a database. Like a good teacher, the ITS's database allows it to select from its expert knowledge information and activities that are appropriate for specific learners. Hence, it is a far more complex database than would be found in most integrated learning systems.

The "student module" is the computer's representation of what the student is like. This representation is built from the student's responses but must necessarily be based on certain preconceptions about learners that are built into the system. The system also has to be designed so that it can obtain information it needs about the learner. That is, just as a good human tutor asks the learner to explain an answer, so too might an ITS—and it would then use this information to make qualitative judgments about the learner.

---

intelligent tutor system (ITS) A computer-based learning system that takes into account the individual learner's strengths and weaknesses, and that modifies its presentations accordingly.

The "instructional module" consists of pedagogical, or teaching, rules built into the system. The rules might take forms such as, "If a student qualified as X gives response (explanation) A, then . . ."

The communication component consists of the interface, or link, between student and machine. It includes the ways in which the learner can interact with the system (a keyboard, a mouse, a joystick, a finger) and the ways in which the system can interact with the learner (visual display, auditory signals).

ITS systems are still largely experimental. One of the major problems, notes Farnham-Diggory (1992), is that computers do not process human language as we do; they cannot easily, in their own words so to speak, explain the meaning of a prose passage—or comment sincerely on the learner's new shoes.

Logo. Another fundamentally important use of the computer is evident in the learning of programming skills. As Papert (1987, 1993) has shown, these skills can be learned by very young children—children who program computers rather than being programmed by them.

"If you've ever watched youngsters use Nintendo and other computer games," Soloman tells us, "you know there are powerful forces at work—concentration, commitment, and control. Schools need to harness that power . . ." (1992, p. 10). Teaching children to program computers seems to be one way to harness that power.

In order to teach young children how to program computers, Papert and his associates have developed a simple computer language, **Logo,** which is powerful enough to let children explore the world of differential equations or move to an understanding of HyperCard, a Macintosh courseware package (Yoder, 1992), but simple enough to enable children with no mathematical sophistication whatsoever to explore the world of plane geometry. For this purpose, Logo (which runs on most personal computers) introduces the turtle—a triangular little creature on the computer monitor that can be moved by means of ordinary words rather than the more abstract and complex terminology of most computer languages. For example, the child simply types FORWARD 50 to make the turtle move straight ahead fifty little turtle-steps, dragging a "pen" behind it so that you can see its path; FORWARD 50 RIGHT 90 FORWARD 50 makes it go ahead fifty steps, turn to the right, and go forward another fifty steps at right angles to the first path. It is only a short child-step from here to the design of a complete square and but one small additional step to learn that all the instructions required for making this square can be shortened because they involve repetition (REPEAT 4 FORWARD 50 RIGHT 90) and can be given a name—such as SQUARE. Subsequently, when the child types SQUARE, the turtle draws a square. The child has easily and painlessly created a simple program.

As the child learns new instructions and continues to "play turtle," the programs can become more complex and the designs of plane geometry more intricate. Playing turtle simply involves imagining how the turtle will respond to all the possible combinations of instructions. Thus can a child learn to program the computer to draw a cartoon figure, a house, a tree, an anything. Thus, too, can the child learn geometry, mathematics, the systematic and clear thinking required to write programs, and other aspects of what has come to be called **computer literacy.** For example, in one study involving the use of Logo, fourth graders designed and developed

---

Logo Seymour Papert's computer language, designed for young children to allow them to learn programming skills easily and painlessly as they might learn an exciting new game. The program uses a "turtle"—a small creature that can be instructed (that is, programmed) to move in different ways, tracing various geometric designs as it moves.

computer literacy The minimal skills required for interaction with computers. Does not require knowing how a computer functions internally or how to program it.

software to teach other schoolchildren about fractions (Harel & Papert, 1990).

COMPUTER APPLICATIONS EVALUATED

Among the advantages of computers are their impressive memory capacities, the rapidity and accuracy with which they can deliver information, their problem-solving and computation capabilities, and the versatility of their presentation modes. Computers also present a number of advantages not directly related to their role in assisting instruction—advantages that have relatively little to do with how they are used to help in the ordinary business of teaching (and learning) the conventional curriculum. These advantages have to do with the computer's unique qualities and with the cognitive processes it can foster. As Papert (1993) notes, computers are intellectual tools that require a degree of explicitness and precision in the use of language—and, therefore, in thinking—that is not found in ordinary conversation. Computers do not understand ambiguous statements; they are not programmed to guess or to read between the lines. Instead, they respond logically and rationally. As a result, to be intelligent in the computer society—to be truly computer literate—requires learning how to be completely explicit, context free, repeatable, logical, and rational (Calfee, 1985). This type of communication is quite different from our natural, spoken language, which tends to be highly implicit, specific to context, idiosyncratic, and intuitive.

Better or Not? Because of the important differences between computers and other instructional media such as teachers, texts, and television, Salomon and Gardner (1986) caution against attempting to evaluate computer-related instruction by asking such naive and largely uninformative questions as "Does it teach better than . . . ?" The important point in evaluations is the recognition that computers both do things that are different from other instructional methods and do them differently as well. For example, computers allow us to teach programming and perhaps to foster the types of cognitive processes involved in programming. The function of programming courses, notes Papert (1987) is to teach problem solving as well as programming. That is, when children learn Logo, they also learn something about learning. And subsequent assessments reveal that children who become skilled in Logo not only increase their mastery of metacognitive skills but improve in measured creativity as well (Salomon & Gardner, 1986).

A comprehensive review of evaluations of computer-assisted instruction (CAI) at the college level looked at fifty-nine separate studies (Kulik, Kulik, & Cohen, 1980). This review provides additional evidence that CAI in general produces significant positive changes in both achievement and attitude among college students. Perhaps equally important, it substantially reduces instruction time.

Schofield, Eurich-Fulcer, and Britt (1994) looked at eight classrooms in which intelligent tutoring systems were being used. They found not only that students preferred the tutoring system to conventional instruction by a teacher, but also that they learned more when using such systems. But perhaps this study's most positive finding was that the use of tutoring systems freed teachers' time, enabling them to give students far more individualized help. Furthermore, students tended to have more control over the kind of help they received from teachers, because they were more aware of where they needed help. Tutoring systems don't replace teachers at all, note Schofield, Eurich-Fulcer, and Britt; rather, they provide an additional resource.

Revolution or Not? But are we in the midst of a computer revolution in education and in society at large? *Revolution* implies sudden, dynamic, sweeping changes that ultimately transform significant aspects of our lives. Looking back through the ages, social historians have no difficulty identifying and naming revolutions: the agricultural, the industrial, the French. We recognize these revolutions clearly; sometimes we even think we understand them.

But recognizing current social change—or predicting future change—is more difficult. We are too much a part of our cultures to easily sense change in them. Perhaps we are too much a part of the change itself.

Computers, Papert (1993) tells us, are a fundamental part of our culture. They are more than simply tools that we can use for various purposes; they change our very way of thinking and acting. We are part of the computer revolution, and as a result, perhaps we do not see it very clearly.

But if a computer revolution is actually happening in education, it certainly doesn't seem sudden. Laurillard (1988) notes that computers should provide an excellent learning environment for our students, given their amazing powers for storing, retrieving, and processing information and in light of their interactive capabilities. However, in her words, "computer assisted learning has never become a principal teaching method at any level of education" (p. 215).

We have now had a full two decades to examine the use of computers in schools and to incorporate them in our programs, says Laurillard. Yet those who advocate their use must continue to rely on their promise rather than on evidence of what they have done. As Bracey (1994) points out, the enthusiasm with which many school jurisdictions embraced the computer a decade or so ago has resulted in a large number of schools that now have badly outdated computer equipment. As a consequence, and because many children have not had access to computers at home, measures of computer literacy are often disappointingly low. Nor have computers and their instructional potential been well integrated into the curriculum of most schools. Too many schools, notes Papert (1993), keep computers in back rooms and teach computer literacy as a separate subject, not well integrated into the day-to-day activities of the classroom. In addition, computers are too often used simply as a new technology for teaching the same old unimaginative curriculum.

In fact, however, students have not had wide access to computers until recently, so we have not really had two decades to develop their educational uses or to assess their impact. It is only during the last few years that computers have become sufficiently compact and affordable to be widely available—in some schools and homes, although by no means all.

Change in education is seldom rapid—especially from the perspective of those who are part of it. In the end, history might look back and judge that, yes, this was a sudden and most dramatic revolution that produced a truly marvelous outcome. The ultimate contributions of computer-based instructional systems may be even greater than we can yet imagine. All the caterpillars might yet decide they really do want to go up in that thing called a butterfly.

It is also possible that historians will look back and say, "There was no revolution of any kind back there near the end of the twentieth century. There was only the rather slow proliferation of that primitive tool they called the computer. Of course, now it's obsolete."

OTHER INDIVIDUALIZED INSTRUCTIONAL PROGRAMS

Programmed instruction—in all its variations, with or without computers—is but one of the instructional modes that clearly reflect the influence of psychological theory on education. There are more. Among them, perhaps no others have received greater attention than Bloom's suggestions for mastery learning and Keller's outline for a personalized system of instruction (PSI), sometimes called the Keller plan. Also well known are individually prescribed instruction (IPI) and individually guided instruction (IGE).

BASIC ASSUMPTIONS

These approaches have much in common. Most important, each is based on a single fundamental assumption: There are faster learners and slower learners (Bloom, 1976). Accordingly, aptitude is primarily a function of the speed with which a student acquires information, concepts, or skills. As long as all students receive identical instruction, the correlation between aptitude and achievement will be high. In other words, with identical instruction, faster students will achieve better, and slower students will achieve at a lower level. However, if each student is presented with optimal learning conditions, the relationship between aptitude and achievement will be very slight, and most learners will reach the same level. In Bloom's terminology, all learners, provided they are given optimal instruction, will achieve *mastery* of important objectives.

A second important assumption of most individualized instructional systems is that learning requires constant evaluation—not for grading the learner but for guiding the learning/instruction process. This type of evaluation, termed **formative evaluation,** is not to be confused with more formal evaluation provided at the end of a unit or course, termed **summative evaluation.** Whereas summative evaluation is intended primarily to provide a grade, formative evaluation is an essential diagnostic tool in the teaching process. In both Bloom's and Keller's systems, for example, the attainment of a specific grade is not the most important criterion; mastery of course objectives is.

MASTERY LEARNING

AND OUTCOME-BASED EDUCATION

Bloom's **mastery learning model** is based largely on John B. Carroll's (1963) model of

---

formative evaluation Evaluation undertaken before and during instruction, designed primarily to assist the learner in identifying strengths and weaknesses. Formative evaluation is a fundamental part of the process of instruction.

summative evaluation The type of evaluation that occurs at the end of an instructional sequence and that is designed primarily to provide a grade.

mastery learning model An instructional approach described by Bloom in which a learning sequence is analyzed into specific objectives, and progress requires that each learner master sequential objectives.

school learning. Simply stated, this model specifies that degree of learning is primarily a function of the time spent learning relative to the amount of time required to learn. Amount of time required is, in turn, a function of both aptitude and quality of instruction received.

Carroll's emphasis is on providing all learners with both high-quality instruction and the time required to learn. His objective is "equality of opportunity," which contrasts with Bloom's objective of "equality of attainment" (Carroll, 1989, p. 30).

Bloom's basic notion is that it is possible to analyze any learning sequence in order to specify a number of specific objectives and to teach in such a way that most, if not all, students attain these objectives. Although the teaching methods suggested by Bloom are not fundamentally different from those ordinarily used by teachers, they differ in two important respects: First, they are directed specifically toward the mastery of previously identified objectives; and second, they make extensive use of formative evaluation to diagnose learners' difficulties, to suggest modifications in instructional strategies, and to identify subject areas in which more time needs to be spent. A third important characteristic of Bloom's mastery learning is that it requires the use of a great variety of systematic and deliberate corrective procedures in conjunction with formative evaluation (Bloom, 1987). Among these corrective procedures are study sessions, individualized tutoring, reteaching, students helping each other in small, cooperative groups, and a selection of alternative instructional materials in a variety of forms, such as programs, films, audiotapes, and so on. (See Table 12.1.)

One final characteristic of Bloom's mastery learning is the provision that classes typically progress from one unit to another as a group. This is accomplished by providing enrichment for students who master course objectives first. Thus, the pace of progress through the curriculum is determined largely by those who require the longest time to reach mastery. Ultimately, all students who have mastered course objectives are given "A's"; those who have not

TABLE 12.1 BASIC ELEMENTS OF BLOOM'S MASTERY LEARNING

UNDERLYING ASSUMPTIONS	1. There are *faster* learners and *slower* learners (not better learners and poorer learners).
	2. Learning requires constant *formative* evaluation, designed specifically to guide the teaching/learning process.
BROAD CHARACTERISTICS OF TEACHING METHODS	1. Instruction is directed toward the attainment of specific, explicit, and previously identified objectives.
	2. Instruction is guided by the results of formative evaluation.
	3. Numerous corrective instructional procedures in the form of study sessions, cooperative student groups, individualized tutoring, reteaching, and alternative instructional materials are provided.

succeeded are given "I's" (for incomplete, but meaning "mastery in the making"). No students fail in this system.

Closely related to Bloom's mastery learning is an individualized instructional approach that is generally termed **outcome-based education (OBE)** (Evans & King, 1994b). Like mastery learning, outcome-based education is directed toward the mastery of important learning objectives. The basic difference between the two approaches is that mastery learning derives its objectives from the material to be learned; in contrast, OBE determines the skills and knowledge that students will need after graduation and is directed toward bringing about these outcomes in learners (O'Neil, 1993; Brandt, 1994).

KELLER'S PERSONALIZED
SYSTEM OF INSTRUCTION (PSI)

The Keller **personalized system of instruction (PSI)** plan is an elaboration of Bloom's mastery learning (Keller, 1968). Originally developed for teaching introductory psychology at the college level, PSI (also called the Keller plan) has since

been used in a variety of college courses. And although its applicability at the elementary or secondary school level has not been extensively demonstrated, the principles upon which it is based and the methods it suggests might prove useful there as well.

Essentially, a PSI approach requires that the course be broken down into small units, that appropriate instructional materials be developed for each of these units, and that students be allowed to take as much time as necessary to learn each unit. Whenever students feel they are ready, they are given a short unit quiz, the quiz is marked immediately, and they are told whether they need to spend more time studying the same unit or whether they can proceed to the next unit. At the end of the course, an examination covering all material is given (see Table 12. 2).

Unlike mastery learning, the Keller plan does not advocate the use of traditional instructional methods, nor does it rely as heavily on corrective procedures, although alternative learning materials are available. Instead, the onus for mastering a unit rests largely on

---

outcome-based education (OBE) An outgrowth of mastery learning. An individualized instructional program designed to bring about important learning outcomes defined in terms of the skills and knowledge the learner will need upon completion of a course of studies.

personalized system of instruction (PSI) An instructional approach developed by Keller, based in part on Bloom's mastery learning, in which course material is broken down into small units, study is largely individual, a variety of study material is available, and progress depends on performance on unit tests. Sometimes termed *the Keller plan.*

Table 12.2 Main Elements of Keller's Personalized System of Instruction (PSI)

- ▶ Directed toward mastery
- ▶ Objectives to be mastered clearly specified
- ▶ Self-paced instructional system
- ▶ Material is carefully sequenced and in small steps
- ▶ Repeated testing is employed
- ▶ Learner is given immediate feedback following testing
- ▶ Emphasis is on credit for success, not penalty for errors
- ▶ Lectures are used for motivation, as a reward

the student. In many cases, the unit in question corresponds to a chapter in a textbook and/or to a programmed version of the same material. Tutoring often occurs after a student proctor marks the unit quiz, but it is not an essential part of the course. Nor, indeed, is the traditional lecture. In fact, students attend lectures only after they have successfully completed specified units. Lectures are intended to serve as reinforcement for success rather than as a basis for it (Sherman, 1992).

Keller's PSI, like Bloom's mastery learning, is designed to provide experiences of success for all learners. And although both approaches recognize important individual differences among learners, they contradict the ancient belief that there are good and bad learners. Learners are faster or slower, perhaps, but not better or poorer. Accordingly, each approach attempts to provide learning experiences that will optimize the attainment of specific objectives for each learner. Those objectives might be behavioral or performance objectives or a specified score on a quiz.

The advantages claimed for approaches such as these center on the attention that each pays to individual differences in rate of learning. Whereas traditional approaches to instruction and evaluation make it almost inevitable that some of those who learn more slowly than their age/grade peers will fail, these highly individualized approaches ensure that almost all students will eventually succeed.

Another advantage of mastery approaches may be increased student motivation. As Stallings and Stipek (1986) note, repeated exposure to a mastery approach should lead students to the expectation that they will succeed if they work hard enough. It follows that students who are externally oriented may, as a result, eventually become more internally oriented and consequently more willing to accept challenges (see Chapter 10).

INDIVIDUALLY PRESCRIBED INSTRUCTION (IPI)

To individualize teaching is to make it more responsive to the needs and the characteristics of the individual learner. This does not mean that instruction must occur only in a private, individual setting and in a self-paced situation (Anderson & Block, 1977). The essential requirement is simply that some of the characteristics of instruction (such as level of material presented, mode of presentation, and instructional goals) take into account at least some of the student's characteristics (such as aptitude, interest, and previous achievement). **Individually prescribed instruction (IPI),** for example, is a complex system based on the reorganization of the entire curriculum for each subject into a large number of sequential units, each with its own objectives and tests. Students work individually on a unit, making extensive use of written materials. Once they have completed a unit, they take the accompanying test; if their performance is satisfactory, they proceed to the next unit. Units are essentially ungraded so that a learner can progress as rapidly or as slowly as ability and inclination allow. Thus at any one time, students in what would otherwise be a single grade might be working at levels that elsewhere would fall within a wide spread of

individually prescribed instruction (IPI) A complex instructional system that involves reorganizing the entire curriculum for each subject (and over a wide range of grades) into a series of sequential units with clearly defined objectives and tests for each unit. Students progress at their own rate as they master each unit.

grades (Scanlon, Weinberger, & Weiler, 1970). In fact, IPI's advocates claim that this is one of the chief advantages of the system.

INDIVIDUALLY GUIDED EDUCATION (IGE)

Individually guided education (IGE) originated at the University of Wisconsin in the early 1970s. Like IPI, it requires a reorganization of school systems, for it too is based on the principle of ungraded schools. In addition, IGE makes use of teams of teachers, extensive workshops to coordinate the objectives and activities of teachers, a systematic program of home and school cooperation, individual programming for students, and ongoing research to develop and improve IGE materials (Haney & Sorenson, 1977; Klausmeier, Rossmiller, & Saily, 1977). Both IGE and IPI use their own curriculum materials or extensively modify existing materials. Partly for this reason, both can involve considerable expense, particularly in their early stages.

EVALUATION

OF INDIVIDUALIZED INSTRUCTION

Do individualized approaches to instruction work? In a word, yes. But to say that they work better than more conventional approaches all (or even most) of the time would require more convincing evidence than we now have. Approaches such as IGE and IPI, which require extensive reorganization of schools and school systems, cannot easily be compared to more traditional instructional methods.

Investigations of Keller's PSI at the college level and of Bloom's mastery learning primarily in elementary schools have found these ap-

proaches to be quite effective, both in terms of reaching course goals and in terms of general attitude toward course work. In a review of studies that have investigated the effectiveness of mastery approaches, Slavin (1987) found a number of studies with positive results—and several showed no advantage for mastery learning. Bloom (1987) suggests that results are usually positive when students make full use of the "corrective feedback" process that is part of formative evaluation.

Kulik, Kulik, and Bangert-Drowns (1990) subsequently analyzed 108 investigations of mastery learning. Their conclusion: In general, mastery learning increases achievement, most notably for weaker students. In fact, average increases for all groups were from approximately the fiftieth to the seventieth percentile. In addition, mastery learning has positive effects on students' attitudes toward school. On the other hand, self-paced mastery programs are associated with lower completion rates in college courses.

Kulik, Kulik, and Cohen also analyzed seventy-five studies that compared Keller's PSI with conventional approaches (see Figure 12.2 for one comparison). Their conclusion: "The analysis establishes that PSI generally produces superior student achievement, less variation in achievement, and higher student ratings in college courses, but does not affect course withdrawal or student study time in these courses" (1979, p. 307).

Lest we madly run off selling another educational panacea, it should be noted that PSI and mastery learning have their faults and weaknesses as well and that not all evaluations are as positive and as optimistic as that of Kulik and associates. For example, a number of researchers have noted that student attrition is often higher with these methods than with more conventional approaches (Robin, 1976). And other critics have observed that an emphasis on the mastery of objectives that all (or most) learners can achieve might, in fact, penalize the fast learner (M. Arlin, 1984). At best, such a system does not maximize the faster learner's achievement; at worst, it leads to bore-

---

individually guided education (IGE) An individual approach to instruction based on the principle of ungraded schools. It makes use of teams of teachers, extensive inservice teacher training, individual programming for each student, home involvement, and the continual development of new curriculum material. Like IPI, it is also based on mastery learning.

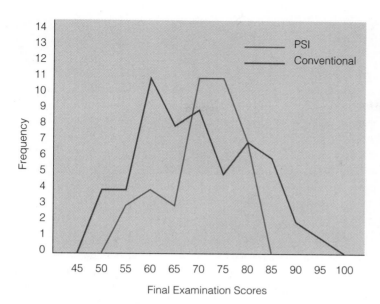

FIGURE 12.2 Distribution of final examination averages for forty-eight PSI and forty-eight conventional classes (PSI = personalized system of instruction). From J. A. Kulik, C. C. Kulik, and P. A. Cohen, "A Meta-Analysis of Outcome Studies of Keller's Personalized System of Instruction," *American Psychologist, 34,* 307–318. Copyright 1979 by the American Psychological Association. Reprinted with permission of the authors.

dom, destroys motivation, and renders meaningless the assignment of grades because all who work long enough obtain "A's." Furthermore, we cannot completely discount the possibility that undue emphasis on specifiable objectives might restrict the teaching/learning process and prevent the occurrence of important incidental learning—and that it might, in fact, lead to an extrinsically motivated, performance-based orientation rather than a mastery orientation.

In summary, individualized instruction is at least as effective as more conventional approaches in secondary schools and often is significantly more effective at the college level. In general, the approaches require considerable effort on the part of schools and teachers with respect to systematizing and simplifying instruction. And they demand that schools and teachers make a conscious effort to specify their immediate goals and sometimes also their long-range goals. Among their virtues, these approaches provide important experiences of success for learners who might otherwise lack them by making it possible for learners of all aptitudes to master units and courses. In addition to these and other positive features of systematic individualized instruction, the greatest

contribution of this approach may turn out to lie in the impetus it provides for research on attribute–treatment interaction (ATI). Such research is designed to uncover the relationships among specific instructional modes, identifiable learner characteristics, and the attainment of instructional goals.

ATTRIBUTE–TREATMENT INTERACTION

Approaches such as Keller's PSI and Bloom's mastery learning are based on the assumption that all learners can achieve the same instructional goals—that each is capable of mastery. However, they also recognize that some people learn faster than others and that some need more assistance. Even approaches that try to minimize the importance of differences in learners' characteristics must, in the end, recognize that these differences are sometimes quite important.

Other programs, such as learning styles approaches, are based directly on a recognition of differences among learners. Such programs require information about the relationship between learners' characteristics and specific instructional methods—or what is termed

attribute–treatment interaction (Cronbach & Snow, 1977).

The basic premise of attribute–treatment research is simple: Specific instructional methods are better for students with a particular characteristic, whereas different instructional methods might be better for students with other characteristics. Put another way, an attribute–treatment interaction exists whenever the effectiveness of instruction (the treatment) is shown to depend, at least in part, on the learner's characteristics. The ultimate goal of attribute–treatment research is to identify the best combinations of attributes and treatments.

FINDINGS AND CONCLUSIONS

Researchers have looked at numerous student characteristics (including anxiety, dependence, conformity, various dimensions of intellectual abilities, and many others) and have attempted to relate these to various instructional methods (such as lecturing, small group interaction, programs, computers, demonstrations) and to various characteristics of each of these—including, for example, whether the approach is structured or unstructured (Ross, Rakow, & Bush, 1980; Whitener, 1989).

Although findings from ATI studies are by no means clear and simple, researchers advance several tentative conclusions. One of the most replicated findings is the interaction between anxiety and the degree to which an instructional method is structured or requires active learner participation. Specifically, highly anxious students do better with instructional approaches that do not require a high degree of student interaction but instead are more "teacher centered" (see, for example, Snow &

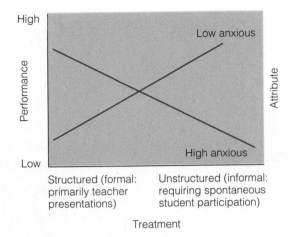

FIGURE 12.3 A schematic representation of an attribute–treatment interaction—specifically, an interaction between anxiety and degree of structure in teaching method. Note that highly anxious students tend to perform better with more structured approaches, but that the opposite is true of students who are less anxious.

Swanson, 1992; see Figure 12.3). Similarly, there appears to be an interaction between general ability and structure, such that students of lower ability do relatively better with highly structured approaches (such as programmed instruction) that use small steps together with frequent responding and reinforcement (Swing & Peterson, 1982). This interaction may result in part from the fact that highly structured approaches reduce information processing requirements—that is, they demand fewer cognitive strategies of the learner (Resnick, 1981). Recall that Kulik, Kulik, and Bangert-Drowns (1990) also found that mastery learning tended to be more effective with lower-ability students.

Whitener (1989) also reports an interaction between prior achievement (as opposed to aptitude) and lesson structure. Highly structured lessons increase the difference between high and low achievers; in contrast, self-paced, relatively unstructured lessons tend to decrease that difference. In effect, what this means is that higher achievers benefit more than lower achievers from an increase in instructional structure.

---

attribute–treatment interaction The relationship of students' characteristics (attributes), teaching methods (treatments), and outcomes. These relationships are sometimes quite complex. Thus, a given treatment (instructional method, for example) may be more effective for students with certain attributes than it is for others with different attributes.

In conclusion, then, at least three separate interactions between lesson structure and student attributes have been uncovered by research:

▶ Highly structured approaches benefit students of lower ability.

▶ Highly structured approaches are better for more anxious students.

▶ Highly structured approaches help students whose prior achievement is higher.

Some Cautions. Several important cautions are in order. First, these conclusions are extremely tentative at best. Furthermore, simple summaries of complex studies tend to make the results seem far clearer and more definite than they actually are. In fact, the results of research on attribute-treatment interaction are highly inconsistent and often contradictory. As a case in point, consider that two of our three conclusions are almost contradictory: Students of lower ability do better with highly structured approaches, but higher-achieving students also improve more with increasing structure than do students who have previously achieved at a lower level.

Interestingly, when students' preferences are taken into account in an attempt to discover the best combinations of attributes and teaching approaches, the picture becomes blurrier rather than clearer. For example, research tells us (tentatively to be sure) that students of lower ability tend to perform better in more highly structured classroom environments, but that the opposite is true of higher-ability students (Snow & Lohman, 1984). However, R. E. Clark (1982) found that lower-ability students prefer unstructured and highly permissive classrooms—perhaps because their lack of achievement is more likely to go unnoticed in this environment. In contrast, better students express a strong preference for highly structured approaches—approaches that make it unnecessary for them to plan and think and that they suspect will make it easier for them to direct their efforts and achieve well. Thus, students' preferences directly contradict what research suggests is best for them.

Ability and Achievement. If this sounds impossibly complex to you, do not despair. Its complexity and lack of clarity mean that no very valuable suggestions can yet be derived and applied directly to classroom practice. Besides, as Gagné and Dick (1983) observe, measures of relationships uncovered thus far have been extremely modest. In the end, the most powerful variables related to school achievement continue to be intellectual ability and previous school achievement. Consequently, the most fruitful approach to matching instruction to students' characteristics is probably one that takes these two variables into account. And that is what happens, at least to a small degree, when students are sorted into groups on the basis of achievement and sometimes of ability. We should not be misled into thinking, however, that these two variables—achievement and ability—account for most of the variation in observed student achievement. In fact, they account for only about 25 percent of the variation; some of the remaining 75 percent is linked to other factors such as home background, type and quality of instruction, and personality characteristics, particularly as they are reflected in motivation and attitudes (Bloom, 1976).

MAIN POINTS

1. Tracking (ability grouping) is now uncommon; detracking is an important part of school reform in many jurisdictions—largely because tracking may have negative effects on members of lower groups and sometimes zero effects on other groups.

2. Learning styles approaches attempt to tailor a variety of instructional features—instructional method, teaching mode, curriculum, evaluation, and rewards—to individual students' strengths and weaknesses.

3. A program is a sequential arrangement of information in small steps (frames), each of which requires the learner to make a response that is then reinforced through immediate feedback (knowledge of results). A linear program (Skinner) requires all learners to progress through the same material in exactly the same sequence and to construct their own responses; a branching program (Crowder) requires learners to select an answer and then directs them to the next frame on the basis of that answer. Those who make errors are provided with further help.

4. The optimistic view of the computer revolution suggests that computers will provide students with immediate access to high-quality information; may lead to smaller, friendlier, and more personal schools; can reduce problems with basic reading, writing, and mathematical skills; and might do a great deal to counter the negative effects of television. A more pessimistic view suggests that computers may lead to a decline in computational and reading skills; might encourage violence; might help widen the gap between the haves and the have-nots; might lead us to rely on expert computer systems, the expertise of which rests on information rather than on wisdom; and might depersonalize schools. Some resist the apparent revolution.

5. Computers are used in schools to teach computer literacy; as tools to manage instructional programs (data storage and analysis, for example), obtain information (databases), provide career information, and for word processing and computation; for drill and practice instructional exercises; for simulations, including possibilities opened up by virtual reality; for computational purposes; as sophisticated teaching machines or audiovisual aids to present programs, sometimes in integrated learning systems; and as intelligent tutoring systems (ITS) in which the computer modifies its interactions on the basis of its analysis of the student. Students can also

be taught to program computers, with resulting cognitive benefits.

6. Bloom's mastery learning is based on the assumption that most learners are capable of mastering important school objectives, but that some people require more time and more nearly optimal instruction than others. This "no-fail" program breaks the curriculum into small units that must be mastered before the student proceeds.

7. Keller's personalized system of instruction (PSI), closely related to Bloom's mastery learning, is designed for teaching at the college level. It places the onus for attainment of unit and course objectives primarily on the student. Students are allowed to repeat unit quizzes until they reach a specified performance criterion and then progress to the next unit.

8. Individually guided education (IGE) and individually prescribed instruction (IPI) require the reorganization of entire school systems because both are nongraded approaches. In IPI, the entire school curriculum is divided into small units, each with related tests. In IGE, students also work individually on specially prepared and sequenced material developed by teams of teachers and also involving the home.

9. Evaluations of these approaches to individualizing instruction indicate that they typically have positive effects on achievement and attitudes. They are sometimes associated with higher student attrition, however.

10. Attribute–treatment interactions exist when there is a consistent relationship between the effectiveness of an instructional approach and some identifiable characteristic (or grouping of characteristics) of the learners. The clearest example of an attribute–treatment interaction involves anxiety and instructional structure (highly anxious students often do better with structured approaches like programmed instruction).

11. A bear always faces the front of its tracks.

APPLIED QUESTIONS

▶ What are some arguments for and against tracking?

▶ Can you give brief examples of branching and linear frames in one of your areas of expertise?

▶ Describe how you think computers might be used most effectively in the classroom.

▶ How can some of the principles of mastery learning be used in a traditional classroom?

▶ List some of the implications of the most important findings related to attribute–treatment interaction.

STUDY TERMS

SUGGESTED READINGS

Papert's two books present an important vision of the potential of computers in the cognitive development of children. The book by Merrill and associates is a clear and comprehensive survey of the various uses to which computers can be put in education. And the Geisert and Futrell book is a very clear and practical introduction to the use of computers in schools:

PAPERT, S. (1980). *Mindstorms: Children, computers, and powerful ideas.* New York: Basic Books.

PAPERT, S. (1993). *The children's machine: Rethinking school in the age of the computer.* New York: Basic Books.

MERRILL, P. F., HAMMONS, K., TOLMAN, M. N., CHRISTENSEN, L., VINCENT, B. R., & REYNOLDS, P. L. (1992). *Computers in education* (2nd ed.). Boston: Allyn & Bacon.

GEISERT, P. G., & FUTRELL, M. K. (1995). *Teachers, computers, and curriculum: Microcomputers in the classroom* (2nd ed.). Boston: Allyn & Bacon.

Classic references for PSI and Bloom's mastery learning include:

BLOOM, B. S. (1976). *Human characteristics and school learning.* New York: McGraw-Hill.

KELLER, F. S. (1968). Good-bye, teacher.... *Journal of Applied Behavior Analysis, 1,* 79–89.

Seals are the staple food of the polar bear. Infant seals are particularly easy to capture when they are still in the aglos (calving dens). The aglo is a small ice cave hollowed out by a mother seal and accessible only from the water. It is covered with a 3- to 5-foot layer of snow and a thick cover of ice. The polar bear can scent aglos from a remarkable distance. Having found one, the bear rapidly excavates the overburden of snow with quick blows of paws and then attempts to break through the ice by rearing up and smashing downward with both front paws. If the ice is too thick, the bear may move back a short distance, run toward the aglo, leap high in the air, and come thundering down with all four paws, crashing noisily through the ice. It is then a simple matter to reach inside and pull out the squirming infant (Perry, 1966).

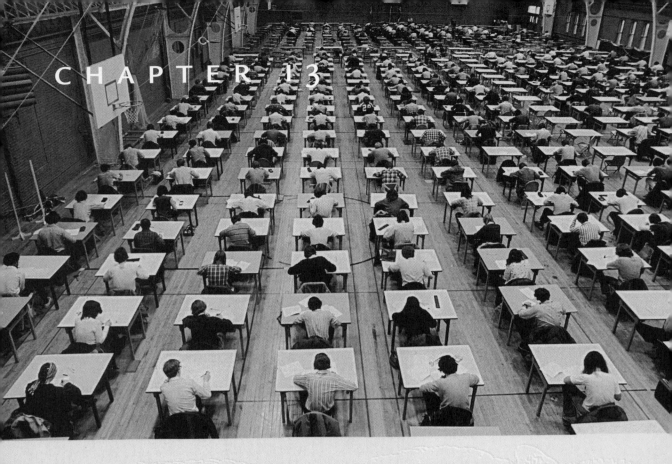

CHAPTER 13

All animals are equal, but some animals are more equal than others.

GEORGE ORWELL, *Animal Farm*

The low man goes on adding one to one
His hundred's soon hit:
This high man, aiming at a million
Misses a unit.

ROBERT BROWNING, *A Grammarian's Funeral*

Instructional Objectives and School Assessments

PREVIEW

In spite of the intuitive appeal of "schools without failures," "schools without tests," and other hypothetical situations in which everyone is highly motivated, absolutely dedicated, and deliriously happy, the nitty-gritty of classroom practice sometimes (perhaps frequently) requires assessment. This chapter describes the various methods by which students' and teachers' performances can be measured and evaluated, why assessment is important, some of the abuses and misuses of assessment procedures, and some trends toward new assessment procedures.

FOCUS QUESTIONS

▶ What is the difference between measurement and evaluation?

▶ What are the most useful kinds of instructional objectives?

▶ What are the characteristics of good measuring instruments?

▶ What are standardized tests, and what are their uses?

▶ How are criterion-referenced and norm-referenced evaluation different?

▶ What are performance-based assessments?

When I reached twelfth grade, they sent me to Collège Notre Dame—not the Notre Dame of academic, football, or hockey fame, but just a small, all-boys residential French-Catholic high school up in Prince Albert. The school, which was staffed and run by the Brothers of the Sacred Heart, had been established for bright French-Catholic students who had no easy access to a local high school. Eventually, it became home to an assortment of problem students sent to the Collège to be straightened out. Also, the school included a relatively large number of lads who were destined for the priesthood. I qualified on almost all counts.

The year I attended Notre Dame, there were about eighty of us in the school in grades 8 to 12. Rules and routines governed all aspects of our existence. On a typical day we would get up at 6, be in the chapel at 6:30, have breakfast at 7:15, and begin classes at 8. School days (which included Saturdays), classes lasted until 4, with short breaks in the morning and afternoon and a brief lunch break. We had 30 minutes of free time before dinner followed by 90 minutes of organized sports, the nature of which depended on the season. Following this, there would then be an hour of study time before bed. By 9, the lights went out.

In most of our classes at Notre Dame, there were no more than five or six students. As a result, much of the instruction took the form of one-on-one tutoring. Quizzes and tests were not a normal part of our classroom fare; we had tests only at Christmas and at the end of the year. But at least once a week, one of the Brothers would call each of us in for a discussion of our goals and our progress.

"You need to do better, Guy," was how most of the Brothers opened their discussions with me. This could have meant that with my startling intelligence and astonishing command of languages, the Brothers expected an uncommon display of genius from me.

"When the tests come," I promised, "I'll do awful good." And, in the meantime, I continued to dream of other things.

But when the tests came, they asked unexpected questions. Brother Alphonse called me into his office.

"Guy," said he, "You didn't do awful good. You got just a 61, here, on your Latin."

MEASUREMENT AND EVALUATION IN SCHOOLS

A statement such as, "You need to do better, Guy," implies **evaluation.** To evaluate is to judge certain qualities—to place a value on them. A statement such as "You got just a 61, here," illustrates **measurement.*** Measurement involves

---

*PPC: Not to be too personal, but how did you get to where you are with grades like that?

AUTHOR: That was just one test, one grade, following a long term filled with difficult adjustments and much homesickness. On the next test, I scored 63. Besides, hardly anybody speaks Latin anymore.

---

evaluation In contrast to measurement, involves making a value judgment—deciding on the goodness or badness of performance. Also denotes the highest-level intellectual skill in Bloom's taxonomy of educational objectives, in which it is defined as the ability to render judgments about the value of methods or materials for specific purposes, making use of external or internal criteria.

measurement The application of an instrument to gauge the quantity of something, as opposed to its quality. Assessing quality involves evaluation, not measurement.

Calvin and Hobbes

by Bill Watterson

Calvin and Hobbes © Watterson. Dist. by Universal Press Syndicate. Reprinted with permission. All rights reserved.

the use of an instrument (for example, a ruler, a tape measure, or a test) to assess a specific quantity. In general, measuring is a more precise and more objective procedure; evaluating is less precise and more subjective. The term **assessment** is often used as a general term for the process of appraising student performance, and may include elements of both measurement and evaluation.

Both measurement and evaluation are important parts of the instructional process. As we saw in Chapter 1, instruction can be described as a sequence of procedures conducted before teaching, during teaching, and after teaching (see Figure 13.1). In the before-teaching phase, assessment may be involved in placing students, in selecting instructional procedures, and in determining students' readiness. Plans for final assessment should also be made at this stage. During the teaching phase, assessment might be used to determine whether goals are being met, as a basis for modifying instructional procedures, or as a learning event. And in the after-teaching phase, assessment is used not only to determine the extent to which

instructional goals have been met but also to gauge the effectiveness of instructional strategies and to reevaluate students' placement and readiness. Measurement is being used when actual tests are used; it is essentially a *quantitative* process. Evaluation is being used when teachers make decisions concerning the adequacy of instructional procedures, the readiness of students, and the extent to which curriculum goals are being met; it is a more *qualitative* process.

Evaluation need not be based on measurement. Indeed, much teacher assessment of students' behavior is not based on measurement. The countless value judgments made by teachers about the abilities of students, their motivation, their persistence, their pleasantness, and so on are often examples of evaluation without measurement. In addition, a number of important assessment procedures such as **portfolios** frequently do not involve tests. In fact, there are those who argue that one of the educational reforms most in need of implementation would involve replacing multiple-choice tests with forms of assessment that look at the student's performance in more realistic, real-life situations (see, for example, Brown, 1993). This type

---

assessment A judgmental process intimately involved in the teaching/learning process. A general term for the process of appraising student performance. May include elements of both measurement and evaluation.

---

portfolio In educational assessment, a collection of actual samples of students' performances and achievements.

of assessment is often referred to as **performance assessment** or **authentic assessment.** These topics are covered later in this chapter.

In this chapter, as in most other educational writing, the terms *assessment* and *evaluation* are used interchangeably to include one or more of the following: subjective valuations, measurement with tests, or appraisal by some other means.

THE IMPORTANCE
OF EDUCATIONAL ASSESSMENT

Because evaluation is a central component of each stage of the teaching model presented in Figure 13.1, it might be expected that teacher education programs would devote a considerable amount of time and effort to this topic. Sadly, however, this does not always seem to be the case. As a case in point, a survey of 397 teachers revealed that almost half of them felt that their training in assessment was inadequate, and that they had been forced to learn through trial and error (Wise, Lukin, & Roos, 1991). Interestingly, however, even those who had learned through trial and error thought they actually knew quite a lot.*

Given the importance of assessment at all stages of the instructional process, it might also

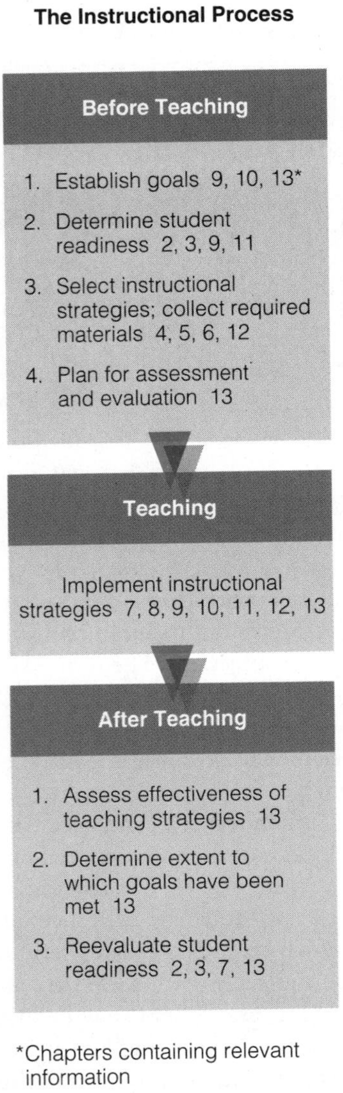

---

*PPC: The bear should perhaps point out that this is most often a form of self-delusion, and that teachers not well trained in assessment will never know important concepts and procedures.

AUTHOR: That is correct. It's a common and easy deception, well expressed in my grandmother's admonition that "you never know what you don't know." It follows that poorly trained teachers might well remain unaware of deficiencies in their knowledge.

---

performance assessment Assessment that looks at the actual performance of students in situations as close to real life as possible.

authentic assessment Refers to assessment procedures designed to allow students to demonstrate their ability to apply learning in real-life situations. Often contrasted to assessment based solely on objective tests, especially of the multiple-choice variety. Also termed *performance assessment*.

The Instructional Process

Before Teaching

1. Establish goals 9, 10, 13*
2. Determine student readiness 2, 3, 9, 11
3. Select instructional strategies; collect required materials 4, 5, 6, 12
4. Plan for assessment and evaluation 13

Teaching

Implement instructional strategies 7, 8, 9, 10, 11, 12, 13

After Teaching

1. Assess effectiveness of teaching strategies 13
2. Determine extent to which goals have been met 13
3. Reevaluate student readiness 2, 3, 7, 13

*Chapters containing relevant information

FIGURE 13.1 **A three-stage model of the teaching process.**

be expected that assessment procedures would occupy a significant portion of classroom time.

Prevalence. This is in fact the case. Gullickson (1985) reports that an average of 5 to 15 percent of class time is actually spent on tests. (In lower elementary grades, the percentage is closer to 5; in high school, it is closer to 15.)

In addition to time spent actually writing, correcting, and going over tests, a tremendous range of other evaluative activities fills school days: asking students questions, commenting on students' responses and presentations, evaluating nontest performances in such subject areas as art, drama, music, and writing, informal observations of ongoing student work, correcting and grading homework assignments, evaluating written work, informal assessments of attitudes and efforts, and many more. In fact, the bulk of the teacher's evaluations, especially in lower elementary grades, is based on informal observation and on grading of assignments and performance rather than on test results.

Measurement-Driven Instruction. How do these evaluative procedures affect students? Profoundly. In fact, it is difficult to overestimate the influence of evaluation on students' behavior. Ramsden (1988a) argues that students' beliefs about assessment are among the most important influences on learning. He explains that the types of assessments used determine what students study and how they learn. This is the reasoning that, in the early 1980s, was partly responsible for the development of a broad instructional approach sometimes labeled **measurement-driven instruction.** Measurement-driven instruction is instruction geared specifically toward increasing student performance on specific achievement measures.

One of the clear effects of measurement-driven instruction is an increase in student grades. Unfortunately, however, it also has some negative effects, among which Cizek (1993b) includes a "dumbing down" and a "narrowing" of the curriculum. In addition, our most common approaches to evaluation encourage a passive form of learning in which rote memorization of facts and formulas is heavily rewarded. Put another way, there are two broad approaches to learning: a surface approach that emphasizes memorization of unrelated facts, and a deep approach that involves a deliberate and active search for underlying principles and concepts and that attempts to discover relationships (Crooks, 1988). Because our tests emphasize the simple, surface components of curriculum content and largely ignore the more complex, deeper aspects of knowledge, the surface components are what students learn. And teachers whose instructional methods are most clearly measurement driven may well be most responsible for developing surface learners.

How do we change surface approaches to deep ones? How do we get learners to pay attention to relationships and principles, and how do we get them to achieve understanding instead of memorization?

This text provides several possible answers. For example, there are programs with the express goals of teaching thinking, developing cognitive strategies, imparting learning/thinking skills, or developing metacognitive awareness. And there are cognitive learning theories, such as those described by Bruner and by Ausubel, that emphasize meaningfulness and comprehension while deemphasizing "meaningless rote learning." These theories provide a number of recommendations for helping students attend to the underlying structures of knowledge, to relationships, and to meaningfulness.

But perhaps, in Elton and Laurillard's words, "the quickest way to change student learning is to change the assessment system" (1979, p. 100) because in the final analysis students try to learn what teachers test, not what teachers suggest is important. It is not sufficient to pay lip service to the importance of complex cognitive processes such as synthesizing or evaluating, or what Bruner calls "going beyond the information given." If teacher-made tests and final examinations ask students only to repeat what they have read in textbooks or heard in class, that is what students will learn to learn.

The point is clear: Teachers must evaluate students on the right things; that is, they must evaluate students on those things they consider most important—the things they want students to learn.

---

measurement-driven instruction A general approach to instruction wherein the overriding objective is to increase student performance on specific achievement measures.

A second point should also be clear: Evaluation needs to be fair, consistent, and reliable. Whenever possible, it should be based on the best measurements available, although often it will also result from informal observation.

EDUCATIONAL GOALS AND ASSESSMENT

The relationship between assessment in schools and **educational goals** is simple: Goals are what tell the teacher not only what to teach but also which behaviors need to be evaluated. We cannot assess the effectiveness of our instructional procedures unless we know what they are intended to accomplish, and we cannot determine what they have accomplished without some form of assessment.

A comprehensive theory of instruction, argue Glaser and Bassok (1989), must pay attention to at least three important aspects of the teaching/learning process:

1. Describing the desired outcomes of the learning process—the knowledge and skills that learners are to acquire

2. Analyzing the pre-instruction state of the learner's knowledge and skills

3. Suggesting the means by which the learner can be guided to make the transition from the pre-instruction state to the desired outcomes of instruction

As we saw in Chapter 1, the desired outcomes or objectives of education can be expressed in broad terms such as "The goal of education is to develop decent, worthwhile citizens" or "The goal of education is to empower students." Among broad educational goals advanced by a former president of the United States is the following statement:

By the year 2000, American students will leave grades four, eight, and twelve having demonstrated competency in challenging subject matter including English, mathematics, science, history, and geography; and every school in America will ensure that all students learn to use their minds well, so that they may be prepared for responsible citizenship, further learning, and productive employment in our modern economy. (George Bush, cited in R. Walker, 1990, p. 16)

Although general statements of objectives such as these are useful in guiding the development of curriculum and in influencing the behavior of administrators and students, they are not nearly as useful in the day-to-day business of teaching as are more specific instructional objectives.

INSTRUCTIONAL OBJECTIVES

Instructional objectives are statements about the type of performance that can be expected of students once they have completed a lesson, a unit, or a course. Note that objectives do not describe the course itself but instead describe the intended performance of students. Because performance implies behavior, the phrase "behavioral objectives" is sometimes used interchangeably with "instructional objectives."

TEACHERS' ACCOUNTABILITY AND INSTRUCTIONAL OBJECTIVES

In recent years a renewed emphasis on the use of instructional objectives in schools has become apparent. This emphasis stems not only from the recognition of their importance in teaching but also from a growing concern with what is called "teacher accountability" (Mac Iver,

---

educational goals The intended or desired outcomes of the educational process. Often expressed in terms of instructional *objectives* that can range from highly general to very specific.

instructional objectives The goal or intended result of instruction. Objectives may be short-range or long-range. Also termed *behavioral objectives*.

I'VE FINISHED SIR— —AND YOU SCORED 75 PERCENT FOR TEST CONSTRUCTION!

Reuman, & Main, 1995). The phrase implies that teachers should in some way be held accountable for their performance in the classroom—accountable perhaps to students, perhaps to parents, but most certainly to the administrative authorities who hire and fire them.

Evaluating Teachers' Competence. Implicit in the notion that teachers should somehow be held accountable for the results of their teaching is the assumption that if they are rewarded for effective teaching, they will work harder and become more effective. The practical implication of these beliefs is that many school jurisdictions have looked for ways to evaluate **teacher competence**—as well as ways to reward teachers (perhaps with **merit pay** or with other incentives, such as more rapid advancement up

---

teacher competence Phrase used to describe the measurable performance of teachers—often assessed through the achievement of students.

merit pay Monetary incentive used to reward teacher competence.

the career ladder or recognition through involvement in teacher mentor programs, inservice workshops, and so on.)

Unfortunately (or perhaps fortunately), there is no easy way to assess teachers' performance. But there have been many attempts to assess teachers' basic competence (see Millman & Darling-Hammond, 1990). For example, in 1986 some 210,000 teachers in Texas were administered a specially developed test of basic communication skills (Texas Examination of Current Administrators and Teachers, or TECAT). The test was designed to identify teachers whose basic literacy was so poor that they could not justifiably be classed as anything but incompetent. Shepard and Kreitzer (1987) report that following a massive preparatory program involving workshops, review courses, and study books, almost 97 percent of the teachers passed the test on the first administration and 99 percent had passed after a second examination. But 1,950 educators who were unable to pass the test lost their jobs. Although this might seem like a very high number, it represents fewer than 1 percent of all teachers who took the test. (Interestingly, some 8,000 teachers and administrators did not take the test but still retained their positions.) Of the 1,950 individuals who failed the test, 887 had held academic positions (principals, superintendents, and teachers of academic subjects) and 1,063 had held nonacademic positions (including teachers of physical education, industrial arts, music, art, English as a second language, and health, as well as school counselors).

Shepard and Kreitzer (1987) estimate the total cost of test development, teachers' preparation, and test administration and scoring at more than $35 million. Among the unexpected outcomes of this testing program was significant demoralization of teachers, many of whom objected to the implicit questioning of their competence and to the largely negative portrayal of teachers' competence widely disseminated by the media. Furthermore, the questionable validity of the test and the fact that considerable effort and expense were devoted to remediation before teachers took the test detracted considerably from its usefulness. It is perhaps revealing that such massive screenings of teachers' competence are extremely rare. Part of the problem, notes Reynolds (1992) is that we don't know very clearly what competent teaching is or what the differences are between highly competent and less competent teachers.

Although it is easy to understand the administration's and the public's wish to monitor teachers' behavior and its effects more closely, it is also easy to understand why a large number of teachers are reluctant to conform to increasing demands for manifested competence. Some subjects are more difficult than others to teach and to learn; some students learn more slowly or more rapidly; some teachers are better than other teachers at their profession.

One way to increase (and monitor) teachers' responsiveness to parental and administrative expectations is through the widespread requirement that teachers specify instructional objectives for their courses. But this is not the most important reason for using instructional objectives; their contribution to good teaching and learning is even more important.

MAGER'S INSTRUCTIONAL OBJECTIVES

To be useful, says Mager (1962), instructional objectives must specify clearly what the learner must be able to do following instruction. A useful instructional objective is a statement of the instructor's goals *in behavioral terms*—that is, worded in terms of the actual, observable performance of the student. This type of **behavioral objective** serves as a description of course goals and as a guide for instructional strategy. And, equally important, because it describes specific, observable behaviors as goals of the instructional process, it serves as a guide for assessing students' and teachers' performance.

Characteristics of Good Behavioral Objectives. Consider the following statements of instructional objectives:

1. The student should understand evolutionary theory.
2. The student should be able to state the two Darwinian laws of evolution and give examples of each.

Mager argues that the second objective is more useful than the first for several reasons. The second objective specifies exactly what students must do to demonstrate that they have reached the course goal, it provides the teacher with specific guidelines for determining whether course goals have been reached, and it suggests what must be taught if course goals are to be reached.

In contrast, the first statement, because of its use of the ambiguous term *understand* and the global phrase "evolutionary theory," does none of these things. It is clearly open to misinterpretation. Similarly, terms such as *know, appreciate,* and *master* are rarely found in the kind of objectives Mager recommends—unless, of course, the nature of knowing, appreciating,

---

behavioral objective Phrase used to describe an instructional objective that can be expressed in terms of specific, observable, measurable behaviors. Mager's instructional objectives are behavioral objectives.

or mastering is also clearly spelled out. For example, President Bush's phrase "use the mind well" needs to be made more specific if it is to be useful. We need to know what is involved in using the mind well.

A second quality of meaningful instructional objectives is that they often establish specific criteria of acceptable performance. Consider the following statements:

1. The learner will be able to translate a simple passage from French to English.

2. The learner will be able to translate a simple passage from French to English without use of a dictionary. The passage will be taken from the prescribed text, and the translation will be considered correct if there are no more than 5 errors for each 100 words of text and acceptable if the translation is completed in no more than 20 minutes for each 100 words.

The second statement is more precise than the first, and again it is more useful for both the instructor and the learner. It specifies the nature of the expected behavior and the constraints under which it is to be performed to be considered acceptable.

Writing good instructional objectives is a time-consuming task. However, carefully prepared objectives can be of tremendous assistance to teachers in planning instructional strategies and in evaluating both their own performance and that of their students. In addition, if statements of behavioral objectives are given to each student at the beginning of courses, units, or lessons, they can be of tremendous value to the learner. In Mager's words, "If you give each learner a copy of your objectives, you may not have to do much else" (1962, p. 53).

EISNER'S EXPRESSIVE OBJECTIVES

Not all educators agree that Mager's approach to instructional objectives is the best. Recent decades have seen a marked shift away from a behavioral orientation in psychology and educa-

tion—an orientation that emphasized measurable outcomes that could be expressed in Mager-type behavioral objectives. The behavioral orientation, notes Winn (1990), has gradually been replaced by a more cognitive orientation—an orientation that emphasizes understanding and other less easily measured outcomes, and that is reflected in a movement from the more objective multiple-choice assessment to performance and portfolio assessment (discussed later).

The use of behavioral objectives presents several definite disadvantages, claims Eisner (1967). Strict adherence to behavioral objectives restricts the development of curriculum, discourages other important learning outcomes, and fails to recognize that attitudes are among the most important outcomes of instruction.

Accordingly, he argues that a teacher's instructional objectives should include not only performance objectives of the kind described by Mager but also **expressive objectives.** Expressive objectives involve a conscious recognition by the teacher that the visible and measurable outcomes of a learning experience are not the only outcomes of that experience (and, in many cases, not always the most important). For example, a reading teacher should not only intend to teach reading (an outcome that can easily be expressed in terms of Mager's instructional objectives), but should also try to instill positive attitudes toward reading (an outcome less easily expressed in Mager's terms).

GRONLUND'S GENERAL AND SPECIFIC OBJECTIVES

Gronlund (1972, 1975) agrees with both Mager and Eisner. Emphasis on precise, performance-oriented objectives is both appropriate and effective for simple skills and for content areas that can be described in terms of specific items of information, he claims. But such emphasis is

---

expressive objectives Instructional objectives that are concerned with the affective (emotional) components of learning rather than simply with content or performance.

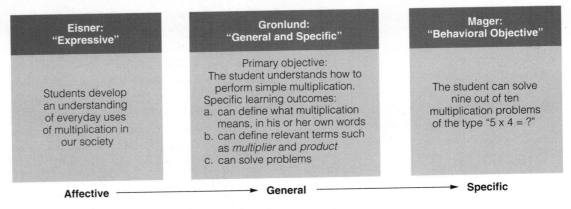

Eisner: "Expressive"	Gronlund: "General and Specific"	Mager: "Behavioral Objective"
Students develop an understanding of everyday uses of multiplication in our society	Primary objective: The student understands how to perform simple multiplication. Specific learning outcomes: a. can define what multiplication means, in his or her own words b. can define relevant terms such as *multiplier* and *product* c. can solve problems	The student can solve nine out of ten multiplication problems of the type "5 x 4 = ?"

Affective ———————————→ General ———————————→ Specific

FIGURE 13.2 Different types of instructional objectives.

considerably less appropriate for more complex subjects and more advanced cognitive behaviors. And, as Nahl-Jakobovits and Jakobovits (1993) point out, it does not recognize the importance of affective outcomes. The most effective teachers, they argue, are those who integrate all the great variety of objectives they have for their students.

In line with this, Gronlund (1972) suggests that teachers express main objectives in general rather than specific terms. Each main objective should then be elaborated in terms of more specific learning outcomes or, in many cases, in terms of actual examples of behaviors that would reflect the primary objective. These examples can then be used as a basis for what is termed *performance* or *authentic assessment*.

The former president's admonition that schools should "ensure that all students learn to use their minds" is a highly general objective. However, the extent to which it has been accomplished (or is being accomplished) can be ascertained far more easily if we can describe specific examples of performances or products that illustrate "using the mind." There is an important difference between these examples of behaviors and Mager's instructional objectives. Mager's objectives specify actual behaviors that constitute instructional objectives in and of themselves. What Gronlund recommends, however, are not objectives per se but are instead

examples of the type of evidence that a teacher can look for to determine whether the primary objective has been attained. This approach, as is shown in the examples that follow, may be used to describe expressive objectives as well. For instance, the primary objective might be the development of a certain attitude; specific behaviors would serve as evidence of attainment of that attitude. (Figure 13.2 summarizes the differences among these three viewpoints.)

Examples of Different Types of Objectives. To illustrate and clarify the preceding passage, consider the following objectives for a poetry unit. Objectives based on Mager's approach might include such statements as

1. The student should be able to name the titles and authors of five poems in the unit.

2. The student should be able to recite, with no more than three errors, ten consecutive lines from a single poem in the unit.

Eisner's expressive objectives might center on the desirability of having a student develop positive feelings for poetry and/or for specific poems and poets:

1. The student should develop an appreciation for the Romantic poets.

Finally, Gronlund's objectives might begin with an expressive objective such as the preceding one and then elaborate further with specific behavioral examples:

1. The student should develop knowledge and appreciation of, and liking for, the Romantic poets.

2. The student chooses to read (or write) poetry during a free reading period.

3. The student attempts to evaluate poetry as being good or bad (or to compare different poems).

In summary, each of these three approaches to the formulation of instructional objectives has its advantages and disadvantages. Mager's approach emphasizes specificity and objective behaviors and is particularly useful for simple skills and factual content areas. Eisner's approach recognizes the importance of affective outcomes of instructional procedures. Gronlund's suggestions are useful for more complex subject areas and for higher-level intellectual processes and can also be used to formulate expressive objectives. There is clearly room for each in the conscientious teacher's repertoire.

BLOOM'S TAXONOMY
OF EDUCATIONAL OBJECTIVES

Objectives are desired outcomes. School-related objectives include both the specific instructional objectives of teachers and the wider objectives of curricula, programs, principals, and communities—things like "using the mind" and "being responsible citizens." Questions relating to the wider objectives of education have traditionally been in the domains of philosophy, politics, and economics rather than psychology, and such objectives are seldom evaluated directly in schools—although perhaps they should be. Most classroom evaluation has to do with a teacher's more specific objectives.

As an aid to teachers trying to sort out the most useful and appropriate objectives for their instructional efforts, Bloom, Engelhart, Furst, Hill, and Krathwohl (1956) and Krathwohl, Bloom, and Masia (1964) have provided exhaustive lists of cognitive and affective educational objectives (referred to as a **taxonomy of educational objectives).** The usefulness of lists such as these is that they can serve as guides in determining the goals for a lesson or course. In addition, notes Ross (1993), they can be used as a model in designing educational computer-based programs such as those that use **hypertext,** an organizational method that allows the user to move freely among related topics. The taxonomy of objectives for the **cognitive domain,** for example, describes a class of objectives, a list of educational objectives that correspond to this class, and test questions that illustrate it (see Table 13.1). The six hierarchical classes of objectives in that domain are, from the lowest to the highest level; knowledge (factual information), **comprehension** (obtaining meaningfulness), **application** (using information; applying it in practical situations), **analysis** (breaking down into components to arrive

---

taxonomy of educational objectives An exhaustive list of possible educational outcomes that can serve as a guide in compiling instructional objectives. The best-known taxonomy of educational objectives is Bloom's, which provides objectives in both the cognitive and the affective domain.

hypertext A basic organizational mode for computer-based information that allows the user to jump from topic to topic and back again.

cognitive domain Bloom's expression for the area of educational activity and educational objectives relating to acquiring information, understanding, analyzing, synthesizing, and so on.

comprehension The lowest level of understanding in Bloom's hierarchy of educational objectives; defined as the ability to apprehend the meaning of communication without necessarily being able to apply, analyze, or evaluate it.

application An educational objective described by Bloom. Consists primarily of the ability to use abstractions in concrete situations.

analysis The process of breaking down into component parts. As an intellectual activity, it consists primarily of examining relationships among ideas in an attempt to understand them better. It is a relatively high-level intellectual skill in Bloom's taxonomy of educational objectives.

Table 13.1 Bloom's Cognitive Domain, Defined and Illustrated

CLASS OF OBJECTIVES	EXAMPLE
1. Knowledge (items of factual information)	Who wrote *A Midsummer Night's Dream*?
2. Comprehension (understanding; obtaining meaning from communication)	What was the author trying to say?
3. Application (using information, principles, and so on to solve problems)	Given what you know about the authenticity of the first quarto and about weather conditions in England in the summer of 1594, when do you think the play was written?
4. Analysis (arriving at an understanding by looking at individual parts)	Find the most basic metaphors in Act I and explain their meaning.
5. Synthesis (arriving at an understanding by looking at the larger structure or by combining individual elements)	Identify the four themes in *A Midsummer Night's Dream* and discuss how they contribute to the central action.
6. Evaluation (arriving at value judgments)	Do you agree with the statement that *A Midsummer Night's Dream* is Shakespeare's first undisputed masterpiece? Explain your answer.

at comprehension), **synthesis** (understanding by looking at larger organization), and **evaluation** (arriving at value judgment; weighing value).

Bloom and associates also list objectives in the **affective domain.** These deal with the learner's emotional reactions—that is, with motivational aspects of behavior including such things as interest, involvement, commit-

---

knowledge A generic term for the information, the ways of dealing with information, the ways of acquiring information, and so on that an individual possesses; also the lowest level objective in Bloom's taxonomy of educational objectives.

synthesis Putting together of parts in order to form a whole; complementary to analysis; a high-level intellectual ability in Bloom's taxonomy of educational objectives.

evaluation In contrast to measurement, involves making a value judgment—deciding on the goodness or badness of performance. Also denotes the highest-level intellectual skill in Bloom's taxonomy of educational objectives, in which it is defined as the ability to render judgments about the value of methods or materials for specific purposes, making use of external or internal criteria.

ment, and positive or negative evaluation. See Bloom's handbook of objectives (Bloom et al., 1956) for a more detailed consideration of Bloom's taxonomy of educational objectives.

GAGNÉ'S LEARNING OUTCOMES

Closely related to Bloom's taxonomy of educational objectives are Gagné's learning outcomes, which we described in Chapter 6 (Gagné, Briggs, & Wager, 1992). Recall that there are five classes of these: intellectual skills, cognitive strategies, verbal information, attitudes, and motor skills.

Like Bloom's taxonomy of educational objectives, Gagné's learning outcomes can serve as a guide for formulating instructional objectives—as is illustrated in Table 13.2.

In an earlier section we noted the importance of what teachers test—how what they test determines what and how students learn. We noted also that schools tend to evaluate stu-

---

affective domain Bloom's expression for the grouping of educational goals that relate to affect (emotion), and that are evident in behaviors relating to motivation, interest, and values.

TABLE 13.2 GAGNÉ'S LEARNING OUTCOMES AND INSTRUCTIONAL OBJECTIVES

LEARNING OUTCOMES	EXAMPLES OF RELATED INSTRUCTIONAL OBJECTIVES
1. Intellectual Skills	
Higher-order rules	Learner figures out how to calculate the volume of a cone.
Rules	Learner discovers relationship between air pressure and boiling point of water.
Concepts	Learner learns the defining characteristics of birds.
Discriminations	Learner learns to distinguish between p and b.
Simple types of learning (signal; stimulus–response; chaining)	Learner is conditioned to respond positively to mathematics.
2. Verbal Information	Learner can list the major classes of objectives in Bloom's cognitive domain.
3. Cognitive Strategies	Learner uses a mnemonic device to remember the distinction between expressive and behavioral objectives.
4. Attitudes	Learner chooses to do homework rather than play.
5. Motor Skills	Learner plays a passage on the piano.

dents on the basis of how many textbook- and teacher-presented facts they remember rather than on the basis of how much they understand, how cleverly they generalize and extrapolate, or how elegantly they formulate hypotheses and generate new concepts. Research on Bloom's taxonomy corroborates this unhappy finding. Fleming and Chambers (1983) analyzed more than 8,800 questions used primarily in high school tests. Nearly 80 percent dealt only with knowledge of facts and specifics—the lowest level in Bloom's taxonomy (see the box entitled "Remembering and Thinking").

BLUEPRINTS FOR TEACHER-MADE TESTS

We should emphasize at the outset that a test—whether it is a **teacher-made test** or a **standardized test**—is not like other common measuring instruments, such as rulers, scales, and thermometers. Rulers measure whatever they measure directly; our psychological and educational instruments measure indirectly.

In effect, a student's test performance consists of a sample of behaviors (selected from a large number of potential behaviors) that (we assume) represents some knowledge, ability, or attitude. We then use this sample of behaviors as a basis for making inferences. The inferences we make about knowledge, ability, or other student characteristics are never based on direct measurement; they are simply inferences—educated bits of speculation based on nothing more than a sample of behavior. Hence, the question of precisely which behaviors to sample is important.

As you probably know, the business of preparing tests, exams, and quizzes is frequently a pretty haphazard process. Teachers,

---

teacher-made test Any of the wide variety of tests written, developed, or organized by teachers, usually for the purpose of evaluating students or assessing the effectiveness of instruction.

standardized test A professionally developed—rather than teacher-made—test that provides the user with norms (standards) and that typically indicates the average or expected performance of groups of subjects of certain grades and/or ages.

who have a general idea of the sorts of things they want their students to learn, sit down near the end of the unit or term and fashion a compilation of questions that they hope will measure reasonably accurately some of the things they intended to teach. Some teachers are better than others at putting together appropriate questions. Many, however, might be helped considerably by learning more clearly the characteristics of good and bad test items (discussed later in this chapter) and by systematically attempting to blueprint their tests even before they begin to teach the relevant series of lessons.

A **test blueprint** is, in effect, a table of specifications for a test. It details the topics to be tested, the nature of the questions to be used, how many questions will relate to each topic, and the sorts of cognitive processes to be

sampled. Test blueprints need not be developed only by the teacher; they can also involve the collaboration of students. Constructing the blueprint can do a great deal to clarify instructional goals, both for the teacher and for students. It can also contribute in important ways to the teacher's selection of instructional strategies and to the students' monitoring of their own learning processes.

Detailed test blueprints that take into consideration differences among possible learning outcomes can be based on systems such as Bloom's taxonomy or Gagné's learning outcomes. A typical test blueprint based on portions of Bloom's taxonomy, for example, takes the form of a table that lists all relevant topics as well as all classes of objectives, and that specifies the number of items for each topic relating to each class of objectives (see Table 13.3). One alternative to this, as Popham (1981) suggests, is to use simpler classifications that teachers and students might find easier and more useful. For example, items might be divided simply in terms of whether they involve recall or go beyond recall.

---

test blueprint A table of specifications for a teacher-made test. A good test blueprint provides information about the topics to be tested, the nature of the questions to be used, and the objectives (outcomes) to be assessed.

NUMBER OF ITEMS BY CLASS OF OBJECTIVES

CHAPTER 6 TOPICS	KNOWLEDGE	COMPREHENSION	APPLICATION	ANALYSIS	SYNTHESIS	EVALUATION
Gagné's theory	4	3	3	2	3	1
Bruner's theory	3	4	3	2	2	1
Ausubel's theory	3	3	2	2	2	1
Other models	4	3	3	2	2	3
Totals	14	13	11	8	9	6

There are a number of other ways to devise test blueprints, some of which are easier and more useful in certain subjects. In physical education classes, for example, for which Bloom's taxonomy and other similar classifications are not highly relevant, teachers might simply make a list of the skills that students are expected to acquire. This list of skills, together with an indication of the criteria that will be used as evidence of skill mastery, serves as a test blueprint. Unfortunately, this kind of test blueprint in physical education classes is rare. Most often, teachers rely on informal, intuitive evaluation. And although there is clearly a need for such evaluation, it is seldom as impartial as more formal evaluation. Nor does it serve nearly as well as a guide to instruction.

CHARACTERISTICS OF A GOOD MEASURING INSTRUMENT

Probably the most important characteristic of a good test from the students' point of view is that it be fair. Essentially, this means that the test should reflect instructional objectives as they are understood by students—that is, it should reflect what was to be learned (and, presumably, taught).

From a measurement point of view, good measuring instruments have two important qualities: validity and reliability.

VALIDITY

A test is valid if it measures what it is intended to measure; many tests don't, or they measure many other things as well and are consequently not very dependable. *Validity* is the most important characteristic of a measuring instrument. If a test does not measure what it purports to, the scores derived from it are of no value whatsoever.

Face Validity. There are several different ways to measure or estimate validity—several indexes of validity (see Figure 13.3). The first, **face validity,** is the extent to which the test appears to measure what it is supposed to measure. This is probably the easiest type of validity to determine; if a test *looks* valid, it at least has face validity. Face validity is especially important for teacher-made tests. Students should know just by looking at a test that they are being tested on the appropriate things. A mathematics test that

face validity The extent to which a test appears to be measuring what it is intended to measure.

REMEMBERING AND THINKING

The six classes of objectives described by Bloom and associates (1956) fall into two broad classes: those that involve remembering and those that require thinking. Only the knowledge objectives fall into the first category (knowledge of specifics, knowledge of ways and means of dealing with specifics, and knowledge of the universals and abstractions in a field). All these objectives emphasize remembering.

Most teachers want to teach for understanding (comprehension, application, and so on) as well as for recall. Yet few know clearly the precise skills involved in intellectual activities such as comprehension, application, synthesis, analysis, or evaluation. The two most frequently confused skills are comprehension and application.

Comprehension is the lowest level of understanding, implying no more than the ability to apprehend the substance of what is being communicated without necessarily relating it to other material. It can be tested through items that require the students to translate (change from one form of communication to another, express in their own words), interpret (explain or summarize), or extrapolate (predict consequences or arrive at conclusions).

Application, on the other hand, requires that learners be able to use what they comprehend—that they abstract from one situation to another. Application cannot be tested simply by asking that students interpret or translate; they must also be required to abstract the material to see its implications.

Two final points should be made. The first is a simple appeal: Familiarize yourself with this taxonomy because of its implications both for teaching and for testing. The second is a reiteration of an obvious point: Your instructional objectives (what you want of your students) are communicated directly and effectively to your students through your measurement devices. Even if you emphasize repeatedly that you want to teach for comprehension and other high-level skills, you will probably not be successful unless you construct achievement tests that reflect these objectives. In the final analysis, your students will study what you test.

---

has face validity will consist of items that look like mathematics items.

In some circumstances, however, test makers carefully avoid any semblance of face validity. Tests designed to measure personality characteristics such as honesty or openness, for example, are likely to be highly invalid if they appear to measure what they are actually intended to measure. Because we know that dishonest people might well lie to us, we are not likely to obtain an accurate measure of their honesty if we let them know that that is what we are interested in. Better to deceive them, lie to them, to determine what liars and scoundrels they really are.

Content Validity. A second important index of the extent to which a test measures what it purports to measure, **content validity,** is assessed by analyzing the content of test items in relation to the objectives of the course, unit, or lesson. Content validity is perhaps the most crucial kind of validity for measurements of school achievement. A test with high content validity includes items that sample all important course objectives (both content [product] and process objectives) in proportion to their importance. Thus, if some of the objectives of an instructional sequence are the development of cognitive processes, a relevant test will have content validity to the extent that it samples these processes. And if 40 percent of the course content (and, consequently, of the course objectives) deals with knowledge (rather than with

---

content validity Test validity determined by a careful analysis of the content of test items and a comparison of this content with course objectives.

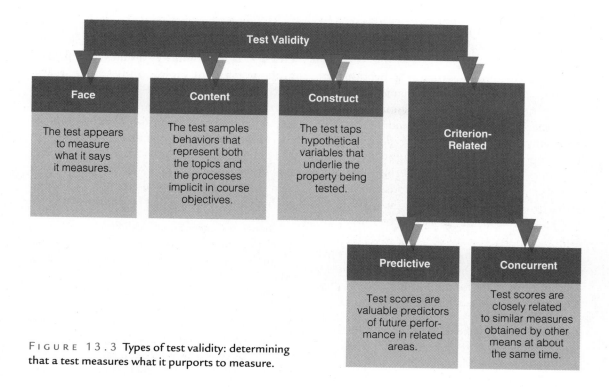

FIGURE 13.3 **Types of test validity: determining that a test measures what it purports to measure.**

comprehension, analysis, and so on), 40 percent of the test items should assess knowledge.

Determining the content validity of a test is largely a matter of careful, logical analysis. As Oosterhof (1994) notes, one of the main advantages of preparing a test blueprint (table of specifications) of the kind described earlier is that it ensures content validity (providing, of course, that the test maker follows the blueprint).

Note that tests and test items do not possess validity as a sort of intrinsic quality; that is, a test is not generally valid or generally invalid. Rather, it is valid for certain purposes and with certain individuals and invalid for others. For example, if the following item is intended to measure comprehension, it does not have content validity:

How many different kinds of validity are discussed in this chapter?

a. 1 b. 2 c. 3 d. 5 e. 10

If, on the other hand, the item were intended to measure knowledge of specifics, it would have content validity. And an item such as the fol-

lowing might have content validity with respect to measuring comprehension:

Explain why face validity is important for teacher-constructed tests.

Note, however, that this last item measures comprehension only if students have not been explicitly taught an appropriate answer. That is, it is possible to teach principles, applications, analyses, and so on as *specifics,* so that questions of this sort require no more than recall of knowledge. What an item measures is not inherent in the item itself so much as in the relationship between the material as it has been taught to the student and what the item requires.

Construct Validity. A third type of validity, **construct validity,** is conceptually more difficult than either face or content validity. It is somewhat less relevant for teacher-constructed tests

construct validity An estimate of test validity based on the extent to which test results agree with and reflect the theories that underlie the test.

but highly relevant for many other psychological measures (personality and intelligence tests, for example).

In essence, a construct is a hypothetical variable—an unobservable characteristic or quality, often inferred from theory. For example, a theory might specify that individuals who are highly intelligent should be reflective rather than impulsive—reflectivity being evident in the care and caution with which the individual solves problems or makes decisions, and impulsivity being apparent in the individual's haste and failure to consider all aspects of a situation. One way to determine the construct validity of a test designed to measure intelligence would then be to look at how well it correlates with measures of reflection and impulsivity. (See Chapter 7 for a discussion of correlation.)

Criterion-Related Validity. A primary use of tests is to predict future performance. Thus, we assume that all students who do well on year-end fifth-grade achievement tests will do reasonably well in sixth grade. We also predict that those who perform poorly on these tests will not do well in sixth grade, and we might use this prediction as justification for having them fail fifth grade. The extent to which our predictions are accurate reflects **criterion-related validity.** One component of this form of validity, just described, is labeled **predictive validity** and is easily measured by looking at the relationship between performance on a test and subsequent performance. Thus, a college entrance examination designed to identify students whose chances of college success are high has predictive validity to the extent that its predictions are borne out.

Concurrent validity, a second aspect of criterion-related validity, is the relationship between a test and other measures of the same behaviors. For example, the most accurate way to measure intelligence is to administer a time-consuming and expensive individual test; a second way is to administer a quick, inexpensive group test; a third, far less consistent approach, is to have teachers informally assess intelligence on the basis of what they know of their students' achievement and effort. Teachers' assessments are said to have concurrent validity to the extent that they correlate with the more formal measures. In the same way, the group test is said to have concurrent validity if it agrees well with measures obtained in other ways.

A Changing Conception of Validity. Tests have a profound influence not only on those who take them but on the entire educational system. Maguire (1992) shows how departmental exams that are common to an entire school system influence how teachers teach. And Wolf, Bixby, Glenn, and Gardner make the point that current testing practices in schools are "exercises in detection and selection rather than generation" (1991, p. 32). As such, they foster a narrow, predictable, memory-based approach to teaching and learning. These authors argue that teachers need new forms of assessment that "permit the assessment of thinking rather than simply the possession of information" (p. 33).

Recognition of the influence of assessment on learning and teaching suggests a new way of looking at validity, says Moss (1992). This view of the validity of assessment takes into consideration the effects of tests on learning. For example, if one of the purposes of testing is to foster thinking, we have to look at the extent to which our tests succeed in promoting thinking in order to determine their validity.

The development of approaches to assessment that emphasize students' performance (portfolios, for example) is one manifestation of this new view of validity. Portfolio assessments, argue Porter and Cleland (1995), are, in effect, an instructional strategy. (Performance assessments are described later in this chapter.)

RELIABILITY

A good measuring instrument must not only be valid; it must also be *reliable*. This means that

---

criterion-related validity A measure of the extent to which predictions based on test results are accurate (predictive validity) and the extent to which the test agrees with other related measures (concurrent validity). Also termed *predictive validity*.

the test should measure whatever it measures consistently. An intelligence test that yields a score of 170 for a student one week and a score of 80 the next week is probably somewhat unreliable (unless something has happened to the student during the week).

Types of Reliability. An instrument that is highly unreliable cannot be valid. Put another way, if a test measures what it purports to, and if what it measures does not fluctuate unpredictably, the test will yield similar scores on different occasions. Hence, one way to assess *reliability* is to correlate results obtained by giving the test twice or by giving two different forms of the same test. These are called **repeated-measures** and **parallel-forms reliability.**

Another way to determine reliability, called **split-half reliability,** is to divide the test into halves and correlate the scores obtained on each half. If all items are intended to measure the same things, the scores on the halves should be similar.

Factors that Affect Reliability. One factor that contributes to the reliability of a test is the stability of what is being measured. Clearly, if a characteristic fluctuates dramatically over time, measurements of the characteristic will also fluctuate. However, most of what we measure in psychology and education is not expected to fluctuate unpredictably; that is, although we

expect change in many characteristics, we can often predict the nature of the change. Students are expected to read better, understand more clearly, solve more problems, and generally improve cognitively throughout the course of their schooling. Tests that are valid and reliable should reflect these changes.

A second important factor, particularly with respect to teacher-constructed, multiple-choice, or true–false tests, is chance. As an example, consider a test consisting of twenty true–false items. The chance of getting any single item correct, if the student knows next to absolutely nothing, is one out of two. Hence, unless Lady Luck is looking pointedly in the other direction, the average score of a large class of hypothetical know-nothings should be about 50 percent. And some of the luckier individuals in this class may have astoundingly high scores. But a subsequent administration of this or of a parallel examination might lead to startlingly different results.

One way to increase test reliability is obvious: Make tests longer. Of course, this does not mean that all short objective tests must be avoided. In the long run, the effects of chance tend to even out; 100 short tests, taken all together, make up one long, sometimes highly reliable test. The most important admonition is simply that the teacher should not place undue confidence in the results of only a handful of short tests in which the effects of chance cannot easily be controlled.

Another way of increasing the reliability of multiple-choice tests is to use a preponderance of items of moderate difficulty, rather than throwing in a number of very difficult or very easy items (Feldt, 1993). Other things being equal, very easy and very difficult items tend to result in less consistent patterns of responding.

Although a test cannot be valid without also being reliable, it can be highly reliable without being valid. Consider the box, Lefrançois' Dumb Scale of Intelligence. This intelligence test has been demonstrated to be extremely reliable (as well as extremely democratic). In other words, it is extremely consistent: Testees obtain the same scores repeatedly.

---

repeated-measures reliability An estimate of the consistency (reliability) of a test based on the degree of agreement among scores obtained from different presentations of the same test.

parallel-forms reliability A measure of test consistency (reliability) obtained by looking at the correlation between scores obtained by the same individual on two different but equivalent (parallel) forms of one test.

split-half reliability An index of test reliability (consistency) derived by arbitrarily dividing a test into parallel halves (odd- and even-numbered items, for example) and looking at the agreement between scores obtained by each individual on the two halves.

LEFRANÇOIS' DUMB SCALE OF INTELLIGENCE

Instructions
Join the dot to the square with four separate, parallel, but orthogonal lines.*

Scoring
Minimum score: 100

Add 50 for half a correct answer (i.e., two lines) _____

Add 25 for another half

_____

Total (maximum 175) _____

Interpretation
If you scored:
100—you are very bright
150—you are a genius
175—you are God

_____

*PPC: I don't think that's possible.
AUTHOR: You score 100. Bravo!

Bright people usually score 100; geniuses, 150; and God, 175. Unfortunately, however, it is desperately invalid.

STANDARDIZED TESTS

A test is a collection of tasks (items or questions) assumed to be a representative sample of the behaviors that the tester wishes to assess. Given that human beings vary in countless ways, there are countless types of tests and countless examples of each type. A few examples of some psychological tests (creativity and intelligence) were given in Chapter 7. These tests are referred to as *standardized tests*. They are so called because they provide standards (also called "norms") by which to judge the performance of individual students. Thus, intelligence tests are typically standardized in such a way that average performance is reflected in a score close to 100. In addition, the norms for intelligence tests tell us what distribution of scores we might expect for a large group.

A large collection of tests that are particularly important for classroom teachers is **standardized achievement tests.** These professionally developed tests are available for virtually every school subject and are designed to provide teachers, school administrators, and parents with information about the relative performance of individual students, classes, or schools. The indication of relative performance typically is derived by comparing the students' test results to the norms provided with the test. Hence, almost all standardized tests include the testing material itself and a manual that specifies the objectives of the test (what it is designed to measure), the age and grade levels for which it is appropriate, the samples on which it was standardized, and tables for converting the students' raw scores to scores that can be compared directly with the test norms.

Many school jurisdictions make routine use of achievement tests. One study reports that students between first and fifth grades can expect to take an average of one and one-half standardized achievement tests a year (Levin, 1983). Unfortunately, teachers don't often use the results of these tests to modify their instructional procedures, although they might use them to make decisions about students' placement.

---

standardized achievement tests Professionally developed and normed tests that are designed to measure achievement and provide some basis for judging the relative quality of that achievement given the student's age and grade placement.

USES OF STANDARDIZED TESTS

There are at least five distinct and important uses for standardized tests in schools (R. L. Linn, 1986). The first is for placement in special education programs. As we saw in Chapter 7, intelligence tests are widely used for this purpose. However, legal challenges of their fairness have often been successful, especially when it could be shown that a test was biased toward a certain group. These legal challenges have resulted in the modification of some tests to reduce their biases, the translation of tests into different languages, and the use of a variety of assessment procedures in addition to intelligence tests. Recall that Public Law 94-142 mandates each of these changes.

The second use of standardized tests is to certify students' achievement. Minimum competency tests are a clear example of this use, as are the variety of standardized entrance examinations used to decide whether to accept an applicant for a course of studies, as well as standardized final examinations used to determine success or failure after a course of studies.

In addition to these two principal uses, standardized tests are being used in some jurisdictions to determine the competency of teachers, to evaluate schools (through the performance of students), and for instructional diagnosis.

USING STANDARDIZED TEST NORMS

To use and interpret standardized tests, it's necessary to know about the types of scores and norms that are used with them.

Grade-Equivalent Norms. Grade-equivalent scores are the most common among the various norms that are typically provided with standardized tests. These norms allow teachers to convert a **raw score** on a test to a grade equivalent (raw score means the actual, untransformed score on the test). Thus, students who take a standardized reading test will typically have their scores converted to a grade-equivalent score, meaning, essentially, that this student is reading at a grade level of 3, or 3.5, or 5, or whatever.

Several cautions are in order when interpreting grade-equivalent scores. First—and this applies to all standardized tests—it is extremely important to make sure that the test is suitable for the children being tested, and that the norms are appropriate. In the same way that intelligence tests are often biased against groups for whom they were not normed, so too achievement tests are often biased against students whose school curriculum is different from that of the norming population or whose social, language, and ethnic backgrounds are different.

Once you have determined that an achievement test is suitable and that grade-equivalent scores are therefore meaningful, it is important to know precisely what their meaning is. A grade-equivalent reading score of 5 obtained by a fourth-grade student does not mean that the student should be in fifth grade. In fact, the raw score that corresponds to this grade-equivalent score is simply the average score of a large number of fifth-grade students. A few fifth-grade students will have scored much higher or much lower. Similarly, many fourth-grade students in the norming group will have raw scores as high as some of the fifth-grade pupils. Hence, an achievement test does not separate cleanly among different grade levels—it does not give us an absolutely accurate index of what grade level a student should be. Furthermore, achievement tests given at different times of the year can produce markedly different results. For example, scores obtained immediately after summer vacation are often much lower than scores obtained just before the previous term ended.

---

grade-equivalent scores Standardized test norms that allow users to convert raw scores to grade equivalents—that is, that allow the user to conclude that the testee has performed at a level comparable to that of average children at a specified grade level.

raw score The actual numerical score a testee obtains on a test. The testee's score before it is converted to a grade- or age-equivalent score, an IQ, or some other norm.

Age-Equivalent Norms. Although most achievement tests designed for use in schools provide grade-equivalent scores, many also provide one or more of a variety of other types of norms, including age equivalents (and others, such as Z-scores, T-scores, percentiles, and stanines, explained in the box entitled "Norms and the Normal Distribution"). **Age-equivalent scores,** as the label implies, are norms expressed in terms of ages rather than grades. Such norms make provisions for converting raw scores to age equivalents that can be interpreted as meaning that a student is functioning at a level comparable to the average for a specific age group. Age-equivalent scores are more common for intelligence tests and other measures of ability or aptitude than they are for achievement tests. This is largely because it is more meaningful to say that a person is intellectually at the level of a 4-year-old or a 9-year-old than to say that someone reads at a 4-year-old or a 9-year-old level. When interpreting age-equivalent scores, observe the same cautions as when interpreting grade-equivalent scores. The most important caution is that these scores represent averages; hence, there is a wide range of scores within most groups. In addition, because standardized tests are far from completely valid or completely reliable, we should be careful not to rely on them too heavily.

SOME PROS AND CONS
OF STANDARDIZED TESTS

There is an ongoing controversy concerning the use of standardized tests in schools. On the one hand, many educators feel that the tests are unfair, biased, unreliable, and often invalid—that they are excellent examples of "science and technology run amok" (Wigdor & Garner, 1982). On the other hand, many argue that in spite of their weaknesses, standardized tests are more likely to be valid, reliable, objective, and fair than are other forms of evidence upon which teachers and educators base their judgments.

During the middle decades of this century, it seemed that the antitesting movement might become dominant. Increasing numbers of school jurisdictions began to abandon the use of standardized tests; their use seemed incompatible with the cry for equity (R. L. Linn, 1986). But the pendulum now seems to have swung in the opposite direction once more. One important reason for this most recent swing was the publication of the report *A Nation at Risk* (National Commission on Excellence in Education, 1983). Among other things, the report put forth a cry for excellence rather than simply for equity and raised the frightening possibility that American schoolchildren might be seriously deficient in basic reading, writing, and arithmetic skills. The report lent support to the concept of **minimum competency testing,** a general term for batteries of tests, often administered statewide, to determine whether students have achieved some minimum standard of competency.

Minimum competency tests have been legally challenged on the grounds that they are unfair and discriminatory (Madaus, 1994). However, challenges have typically been unsuccessful (Perkins, 1982).

Some object to the wide-scale use of standardized tests for other reasons. First, as Haladyna, Nolen, and Haas (1991) point out, raising educational achievement is equated too often with raising test scores. M. L. Smith's interviews of teachers indicate that when the results of standardized tests are made public, teachers often experience "feelings of shame, embarrass-

---

age-equivalent scores Standardized test norms that allow users to convert raw scores to age equivalents. Such norms allow test users to interpret the subject's performance in terms of the average performance of a comparable group of children of a specified age.

minimum competency testing A global term for the administration of batteries of tests designed to determine whether students, or teachers, have reached some minimum level of competency in basic areas such as language and mathematics.

ment, guilt, and anger" (1991, p. 9). As a result, it is not uncommon for teachers to prepare their students specifically to write a given test—a practice that can seriously change the validity of the test. Furthermore, note Nolen, Haladyna, and Haas (1992), while teaching to a test might improve students' marks, it does not actually raise achievement. In fact, it typically encourages memorization of specifics rather than the growth of understanding and thinking. Additionally, some research suggests that minimum competency testing does not increase measured achievement in many students (Winfield, 1990).

Sternberg (1992) suggests that standardized tests have changed little since their appearance early in this century—except that they are a little easier to administer, a little more reliable, perhaps more attractively packaged. But they still measure pretty much the same things they've always measured: basic memory and some analytical abilities. We need alternatives, he claims, that also measure the more creative and pragmatic facets of intelligence and that begin to tap how people think and learn. As Black (1994c) notes, in the main, standardized tests measure only language and mathematical skills: They omit the other five of Gardner's seven intelligences (discussed in Chapter 7).

One other objection to standardized competency testing, claim Paris, Lawton, Turner, and Roth (1991), is that it may have a progressively more negative effect on students. In their surveys of large numbers of students, they found that many of them, especially the lower achievers, became increasingly more anxious about tests. As a result, some cheated, and some simply stopped trying.

TEACHER-MADE TESTS

Standardized tests are widely used in most school systems, more than 80 percent of them being standardized achievement tests (García & Pearson, 1994). But a majority of the tests used in the classroom are made by classroom teachers. Some of these tests are highly representa-

tive of course objectives, are at an appropriate level of difficulty, and are used reasonably and wisely. Other tests are less well made.

Teacher-made tests can be used for a variety of purposes, only one of which is the assigning of grades. Other than this, a test can be used to determine whether students are ready to begin a unit of instruction, to indicate to the teacher how effective instructional procedures are, to identify learning difficulties, to determine what students know and what they don't know, to predict their probability of success on future learning tasks, to motivate students to learn, and as a learning experience.

Teacher-made tests are usually of the paper-and-pencil variety, although sometimes a sample of nonverbal behavior might be used for assessment. For example, in physical education, in art, in drama, and in some workshop courses, students are sometimes asked either to produce something or to perform. Increasingly, performance-based assessment may also be required in other subjects such as mathematics, where teachers are interested in examining the processes by which students arrive at answers rather than simply the products (more about this approach later in this chapter).

At present, the dominant form of classroom assessment continues to be teacher-made, written tests that are typically **objective tests** or **essay tests.** An essay test requires a written response of some length for each question. Objective tests, however, normally require little writing, and the scoring procedure is highly uniform (hence, objective).

The four major types of objective test items are completion, matching, true–false, and multiple choice. Examples of each are given in Figure 13.4.

---

objective tests Label used for tests in which the scoring procedure is simple, clear, and objective. Includes multiple-choice, completion, matching, and true-false formats.

essay tests Tests that require testees to construct responses of varying length in sentence, paragraph, or essay form.

NORMS AND THE NORMAL DISTRIBUTION

If you were to throw 100 coins onto a table 1,000 times and record the number of heads and tails that came up each of the 1,000 times, a figure representing your tallies would probably look very much like the one in this box (in which the "0" represents 50 heads and 50 tails and the scale on either side represents an increasing proportion of heads or tails).

The figure shows a **normal curve**—a mathematical abstraction to which the majority of the observations that concern us in the social sciences and in education conform. When we know that a set of observations, such as test scores, is distributed normally, we also know what a graphic representation of these scores would look like if we had enough of them. We know that most of the scores would cluster around the **mean** (arithmetic average) and that there would be fewer and fewer scores as we got farther and farther away from the mean.

Thus, if we knew the average, we might have some idea of what a score meant. But we would have an even better idea of its meaning if we also knew the **standard deviation**—an index of how scores are distributed around the mean. Knowing the standard deviation allows us to determine how unusual a score is, because we know that approximately 66 percent of all observations will fall within 1 standard deviation of the mean, and approximately 95 percent will fall within 2 standard deviations of the mean. Hence, those who score more than 2 standard deviations above a mean will be in the top 2.5 percent of the population.

It follows, then, that to interpret a test score (providing we can assume that a large collection of such scores would be normally distributed), we especially need to know the mean and the standard deviation. This is, in fact, what most manuals accompanying standardized tests tell us when they describe test norms.

Test norms can take a variety of forms, including age and grade equivalents or simply means and standard deviations. They can also be expressed as **percentiles, Z-scores, T-scores,** or **stanines.**

Percentiles indicate the percentage of scores that falls below a given point. Thus, the seventy-fifth percentile is the point at or below which 75 percent of all observations fall. If a student scores at the fiftieth percentile on a standardized test, that student's score is

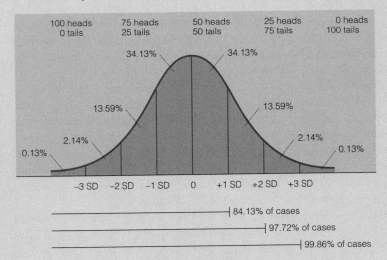

| 100 heads
0 tails | 75 heads
25 tails | 50 heads
50 tails | 25 heads
75 tails | 0 heads
100 tails |

84.13% of cases
97.72% of cases
99.86% of cases

---

normal curve A mathematical function that can be represented in the form of a bell-shaped curve. A large number of naturally occurring events are normally distributed (the vast majority of the events, or scores, cluster around the middle of the distribution, around the mean or median, with progressively fewer scores being farther and farther away from the average).

mean The arithmetic average of a set of scores. In distributions that are skewed (top- and bottom-heavy), the mean is not the best index of central tendency; that is, it is not necessarily at the middle of the distribution.

standard deviation A mathematical measure of the distribution of scores around their mean. In a normal distribution, approximately two-thirds of all scores fall within 1 standard deviation of the mean, and almost 95 percent fall within 2 standard deviations of the mean.

exactly in the middle. Note that a score corresponding to the fortieth or the thirty-fifth percentile is not a failing score; it is simply the score at or below which 40 or 35 percent of the observations fall.

Z-scores, T-scores, and stanines are all standard scores with a predetermined mean and standard deviation. They are used to simplify interpretation of test results. Because raw scores on different tests vary a great deal, as do means and standard deviations, simply knowing that a person has a score of 112 or 23 or 1,115 is meaningless unless we know what the mean and standard deviation are for a comparable group on that test. But if these raw scores are transformed into one of the standard scores, they become highly meaningful.

Z-scores are standard scores with a mean of 0 and a standard deviation of 1; T-scores have a mean of 50 and a standard deviation of 10; and a stanine score uses a mean of 5 and a standard deviation of 2. The meaning of these standard scores, relative to each other, is depicted in the figure here. As you can see, a T-score of 80 would be an extremely high score (3 standard deviations above the mean is above the ninety-ninth percentile); the equivalent Z-score would be 3. There is no exactly equivalent stanine score because the highest score possible on this 9-point scale is 9, which is 2 standard deviations above the mean.

Converting raw test scores to one of these standard-score scales is usually extremely simple because virtually all tests that use them provide transformation tables. These tables typically allow you to read the standard-score equivalent directly once you know the student's raw score and age or grade. And if you can remember what the mean and standard deviation are for these standard scores, they will be meaningful. Otherwise, they are just numbers.

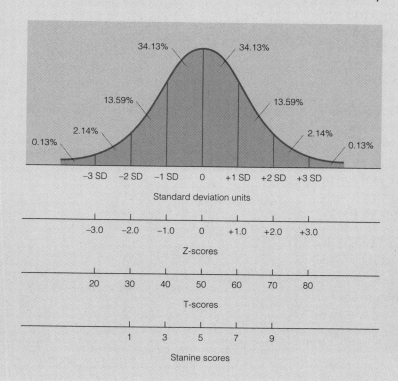

percentile The point at or below which a specified percentage of scores fall. For example, the fiftieth percentile is the point at or below which 50 percent of all scores fall. A score of 50 percent is not necessarily at the fiftieth percentile.

Z-score A standardized score with a mean of 0 and a standard deviation of 1. Hence, a Z-score of +3 is very high; a score of –3 is very low.

T-score A standardized score with a preset mean of 50 and a standard deviation of 10. A T-score of 70 is therefore quite high because 70 is 2 standard deviations above the mean and only approximately 2.5 percent of all scores ordinarily fall beyond that point.

stanines Standard scores that make use of a 9-point scale with a mean of 5 and a standard deviation of 2.

ESSAY VERSUS OBJECTIVE TESTS

Objective tests of the kind just described and the more subjective essay tests can be used to measure almost any significant aspect of students' behavior. However, some course objectives are more easily assessed with one type of test than with the other. Several of the major differences between essay and objective tests are given here. These differences can serve as a guide in deciding which to use in a given situation. Often, a mixture of both can be used to advantage (see the box entitled "To Be Objective or Subjective?"):

1. It is easier to tap higher-level processes (analysis, synthesis, and evaluation) with an essay examination. That is, essay examinations can more easily be constructed to allow students to organize knowledge, to make inferences from it, to illustrate it, to apply it, and to extrapolate from it. However, good multiple-choice items can measure much the same things as free-response items (Thissen, Wainer, & Wang, 1994).

2. The content of essay examinations is often more limited than the content of the more objective tests. Because essay exams usually consist of fewer items, the range of abilities or of information sampled may be reduced. The objective question format, in contrast, permits coverage of more content per unit of testing time.

3. Essay examinations allow for more divergence. Students who do not like to be restricted in their answers often prefer essays over more objective tests.

4. Constructing an essay test is considerably easier and less time-consuming than making up an objective examination. In fact, an entire test with an essay format can often be written in the same time it would take to write no more than two or three good multiple-choice items.

5. Scoring essay examinations usually requires much more time than scoring objective tests. This is especially true when tests can be scored electronically (as objective tests

1. *Completion*
   Test blueprints are often based on _____ taxonomy. Predictive and concurrent validity are two types of _____ validity.

2. *Matching*

_____	Z-scores	1.	mean = 50; standard deviation = 10
_____	T-scores	2.	mean = 0; standard deviation = 1
_____	stanine	3.	mean = 5; standard deviation = 2

3. *True-False*
   a. A good achievement test should result in a grade-equivalent score of between 4 and 5 for an average fourth-grade class.
   b. Content validity can be determined by making a careful, logical analysis of the relationship of test items to course objectives.

4. *Multiple choice*
   The extent to which a test appears to measure what it is intended to measure defines:
   a. content validity
   b. face validity
   c. construct validity
   d. test reliability
   e. criterion-related validity

FIGURE 13.4 **The four major types of objective test items.**

are in most universities and in an increasing number of schools). The total time involved in making and scoring a test is less for essay examinations than for objective tests if classes are small (twenty students or fewer, perhaps) but is considerably less for objective tests than for essay tests as the number of students increases (see Figure 13.5).

6. The reliability of essay examinations is much lower than that of objective tests, primarily because of the subjectivity involved in their scoring. In one study, 300

The question is purely rhetorical. Not only does it have no answer, but it deserves none. Very few teachers will ever find themselves in situations in which they must always use either one form of test or the other. Some class situations, particularly those in which size is a factor, may lend themselves more readily to objective test formats; in other situations, essay formats may be better; sometimes a combination of both may be desirable. The important point is that each has advantages and disadvantages. A good teacher should endeavor to develop the skills necessary for constructing the best items possible in a variety of formats without becoming a passionate advocate of one over the other.

The good teacher also needs to keep in mind that there are alternatives to assessment other than the usual objective or essay tests, or standardized tests. Many of these are assessments of students' performances rather than simply products. They might involve keeping portfolios of students' work, writing anecdotal records, or looking for other evidence of the quality of students' learning and thinking. The assessment procedure chosen, cautions Boodoo (1993), should be determined by the purposes of the assessment.

essays were rated by 53 judges on a 9-point scale (Educational Testing Service, 1961). Slightly more than one-third of the papers received all grades possible; that is, each of these papers received the highest possible grade from at least one judge, the lowest possible grade from at least one other, and every other possible grade from at least one judge. Another 37 percent of the papers each received eight of the nine different grades; 23 percent received seven of the nine.

Other studies have found that a relatively poor paper that is read after an even poorer one will tend to be given a higher grade than if it is read after a good paper, that some graders consistently give moderate marks whereas others give extremely high and low marks, although the average grades given by each might be similar; that knowledge of who wrote the paper tends to affect scores, sometimes beneficially and sometimes to the student's detriment; and that if the first few answers on an essay examination are particularly good, overall marks tend to be higher than if the first answers are poor.

There are a number of methods for increasing the scorer's reliability for essay examinations, not the least of which is simply being aware of possible sources of unreliability. Some of the suggestions given in the box entitled "Norms and the Normal Distribution" may be of value in this regard.

Suggestions for Constructing Tests. The advantages of a particular type of test can often be increased if its items are constructed carefully. By the same token, the disadvantages can also be made more severe through faulty item construction. Essay examinations, for example, are said to be better for measuring "higher" mental processes. Consider the following item:

List the kinds of validity discussed in this chapter.

If the tester's intention is to sample analysis, synthesis, or evaluation, this item has no advantage over many objective items. However, an item such as the following might have an advantage:

Discuss similarities and differences among three of the different types of validity discussed in this chapter.

Several specific suggestions follow for the construction of essay tests and of multiple-choice tests, the most preferred among objective-item forms.

Essay Tests. The following suggestions are based in part on Gronlund (1968):

1. Essay questions should be geared toward sampling processes not easily assessed by objective items (for example, analysis, synthesis, or evaluation).

2. As for all tests, essay questions should relate directly to the desired outcomes of the learning procedure. This should be clearly understood by the students as well.

3. Questions should be specific if they are to be scored easily. If the intention is to give marks for illustrations, the item should specify that an illustration is required.

4. A judicious sampling of desired behavior should make up the substance of the items.

5. If the examiner's intention is to sample high-level processes, sufficient time should be allowed for students to complete the questions.

6. The weighting of various questions, as well as the time that should be allotted to each, should be specified for the student.

7. The questions should be worded so that the teacher's expectations are clear to both the student and the teacher.

There are ways to make the scoring more objective as well. One is to outline model answers before scoring the test (that is, write out an answer that would receive full points). Another is to score all answers for one item before going on to the next; this should increase uniformity of scoring. A third suggestion is simply that the scorer be objective. For example, if poor grammar in a language arts test results in the loss of five points on one paper, grammar that is half as bad on another paper should result in the loss of two and a half points.

Multiple-Choice Items. A multiple-choice item consists of a statement or series of statements (called the *stem*) and three to five alternatives, only one of which is the correct or best solu-

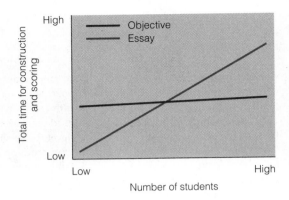

FIGURE 13.5 The relationship between class size and total time required for test construction and scoring for two types of test.

tion. The other alternatives are referred to as *distractors*. Each of the distractors is a response that should appear plausible if students do not know the answer. If students do know the correct answer, distractors should, of course, appear less plausible. Listed here are a number of suggestions for writing multiple-choice items. Most are common sense (which makes them no less valid):

1. Both stems and alternatives should be clearly worded, unambiguous, grammatically correct, specific, and at the appropriate level of difficulty. In addition, stems should be clearly meaningful by themselves (Hoepfl, 1994).

2. Don't use no double negatives. They are highly confusing and should be avoided. Are single negatives highly recommended? Not—especially, says Tamir (1993), for items requiring a high degree of cognitive reasoning.

3. Test items should sample a representative portion of subject content, but they should not be taken verbatim from the textbook. This is defensible only when the intention clearly is to test memorization.

4. All distractors should be equally plausible so that answering correctly is not simply a matter of eliminating highly implausible

distractors. Consider the following example of a poor item:

10 + 12 + 18 =
a. 2,146   b. 7,568,482   c. 40   d. 1

5. Unintentional cues should be avoided. For example, ending the stem with *a* or *an* often provides a cue.

6. Qualifying words such as *never, always, none, impossible,* and *absolutely* should be avoided in distractors (though not necessarily in stems). They are almost always associated with incorrect alternatives. Words such as *sometimes, frequently,* and *usually* are most often associated with correct alternatives. In stems, both kinds of qualifiers tend to be ambiguous.

7. Provide students with feedback following testing. Going over and explaining test items leads to more learning, Snowman (1993) reports, than simply giving students more time to study.

REPORTING TEST RESULTS

Having constructed, administered, and scored a test, the teacher is faced with the responsibility for making the wisest possible use of the information derived from it. Obviously, some uses are separate from the actual reporting of test results to students or parents. The teacher is concerned instead with instructional decisions: Are the students ready to go to the next unit? Should they be allowed to study in the library again? Should educational television be used? Should a review be undertaken? Should the teacher look for another job?

Even if the test is primarily intended to answer questions such as these, results should also be reported to students. The feedback that students receive about their learning can be of tremendous value in guiding future efforts. It can also be highly reinforcing in this achievement-oriented society.

Making Scores Meaningful. Although raw scores can be reported directly to the student, they

might not be very meaningful. A score of 40 on a test with a maximum possible score of 40 is different from a score of 40 on a test in which the ceiling is 80.

The traditional way to give meaning to test scores is to convert them either to a percentage or to a letter grade that has clearly defined (though arbitrary) significance. And if students are also told what the *mean* (arithmetic average) and the range of scores (low and high scores) are, they become even more meaningful.

The mean is called a measure of **central tendency** because it indicates approximately where the center of a distribution of scores is. Two other common measures of central tendency are the **median** and the **mode.** The median is the exact midpoint of a distribution. It is the fiftieth percentile—the point above and below which 50 percent of all scores lie. The mode is simply the most frequently occurring score; as such, it is not particularly valuable for educational and psychological testing. It is of considerable interest to shoe and clothing manufacturers, however, because they are not interested in manufacturing average or median sizes but those that occur most often.

A measure of central tendency is not nearly as valuable by itself as it is when combined with a measure of variability (see box entitled "Norms and the Normal Distribution"). And the most useful measure of variability for normally distributed observations is the standard deviation. If students are sufficiently sophisticated, the standard deviation might be reported as an important dimension of test scores. A formula for computing the standard deviation is presented in Table 13.4.

---

central tendency The tendency for the majority of scores in a normal distribution to cluster around the center of the distribution. Measures of central tendency include the mean, the mode, and the median.

median The midpoint or fiftieth percentile of a distribution; the point at or below which 50 percent of all scores fall.

mode The most frequently occurring score(s) in a distribution.

TABLE 13.4 FORMULAS FOR SUMMARIZING TEST SCORES

	INDIVIDUAL	TEST SCORE	$\bar{X}$	$(X - \bar{X})$	$(X - \bar{X})^2$
SCORES ON TEST	Bill	37	33	4	16
	Joan	36	33	3	9
	Evelyn	35	33	2	4
	Renée	35	33	2	4
	Otis	33	33	0	0
	Sam	33	33	0	0
	Jose	33	33	0	0
	Rita	32	33	–1	1
	Odetta	30	33	–3	9
	Guy	26	33	–7	49
	Sums (Σ)	330	330	0	92
	N = 10				

FORMULAS

$$\text{Mean } (\bar{X}) = \frac{\Sigma \text{ (sum) } X}{N \text{ (number of scores)}} = \frac{330}{10} = 33$$

$$\text{Mode} = 33 \text{ (most frequently occurring score)}$$

$$\text{Median} = 33 \text{ (fiftieth percentile)}$$

$$SD \begin{vmatrix} standard \\ deviation \end{vmatrix} = \sqrt{\frac{\Sigma(X - \bar{X})^2}{N}} = \sqrt{\frac{92}{10}} = \sqrt{9.2} = 3.03$$

CRITERION-REFERENCED TESTING

There is a small kingdom hidden in a steamy jungle somewhere. One of its borders is a great river, which describes a serpentine half-circle around most of its perimeter; the other border consists of an impenetrable row of mountains. So the inhabitants of this kingdom are trapped by the river on one side (they're afraid to try to cross it) and by the mountains on the other (although they can climb the mountains to their very tops, the other side is an unbroken row of sheer cliffs with a vertical drop of no less than 8,000 feet at any point). In this kingdom are many extremely ferocious, people-eating beasts. Fortunately, all are nocturnal. I say "fortunately" because, although the human inhabitants of the kingdom live on the mountainsides well beyond where the predators can climb, every day they must descend the mountain to find food.

TESTING IN THE JUNGLE

In this kingdom a test is given to all able-bodied men, women, and children each day of their lives. It is a simple test. Before nightfall, each must succeed in climbing the mountain to a point beyond the reach of their predators. Failure to do so is obvious to all because the individual who fails simply does not answer roll call that evening. Success is equally obvious.*

---

*PPC: Where is this place? I want to send some of my students there.
AUTHOR: Why?

This jungle test is quite different from the ordinary testing practices of most schools. Passing the test does not require that individuals be the first to reach safety; it doesn't even require that they be among the first 90 percent to do so. Nor do they need to climb higher than everyone else. In fact, they will have been just as successful if they are among the very last to reach the fire. They will be just as alive as the first (and maybe less hungry).

TESTING IN TODAY'S SCHOOLS

Consider the situation in most of our schools. Assume that all students are expected to attain a certain level of performance in a variety of subjects, a level of performance that we will denote by the symbol X. Reaching X is analogous to climbing the cliff before the snarling beasts grab you.

Now, in the course of the school year, teachers prepare a number of tests that allow them to determine, probably relatively accurately, that certain individuals usually do better than others. These students are, in effect, comparable to the people in the aforementioned kingdom who typically reach safety first, or who climb higher than the others. They are the students that the teacher can rightly assume have reached (or even gone beyond) X.

But in assessing students' performance and reporting grades, teachers don't often ask themselves which students have reached X and which haven't. Instead, they compare each child to the average performance of all children and on that basis make judgments about the relative performance of students. Thus, in a very advanced class, students who have in fact reached X but who fall well below average performance may be assigned mediocre marks. In a less advanced class, these same students might be assigned much higher grades. This illustrates what is labeled **norm-referenced testing.** Norm-referenced tests are therefore tests in which the student's performance is judged and reported in terms of some standard or norm that is derived from typical student performance on the test. In other words, the results of such a test are based on comparisons among students. Such testing is highly compatible with competitive approaches to teaching but lends itself poorly to more cooperative approaches.

In a second alternative, students are not compared one to the other; instead, performance is judged only in relation to a criterion— hence, **criterion-referenced testing.** In the jungle example, the criterion is simply the ability to climb beyond the reach of predators; success is survival, and failure is death.

Criterion-referenced testing can also be used in schools and is in fact used extensively in mastery learning, PSI, and other forms of individualized instruction. If teachers are able to specify what is involved in achieving X, they can judge whether a student has reached the criterion without having to compare the student to any other. Obviously, it is sometimes difficult and certainly very time-consuming to define X in such a way that its attainment can be assessed. On the other hand, it may be possible to define aspects of X in measurable terms, in which case criterion-referenced tests can be used. A teacher can decide, for example, that all fifth-grade students should be able to read a selected passage within 5 minutes and subsequently answer three questions about the content of the passage. This amounts quite simply to establishing a criterion. Students can then be tested to determine whether they have reached the criterion.

norm-referenced testing A test in which the student is competing against the performance of other students rather than in relation to some preestablished criterion of acceptable performance.

criterion-referenced testing Test in which the student is judged relative to a criterion rather than relative to the performance of other students. The teacher decides beforehand the specific performance expected and tests to see whether the student has reached this criterion.

Which Approach? The principal difference between criterion-referenced tests and norm-referenced tests lies not in the nature of the tests themselves but in the use that the teacher makes of them. In criterion-referenced testing, the student's performance is compared to a criterion; in norm-referenced testing, an individual's performance is compared to that of other students. Individual differences are far less important in criterion-referenced testing. Indeed, the objective is to have all students succeed (Ornstein, 1993b).

Literature on educational testing has sometimes been preoccupied with a minor controversy surrounding the relative merits of these two approaches to testing. Advocates of criterion-referenced testing point to the inherent justice of their approach. No student need consistently fail for performing less well than others after a predetermined period of time. When students reach the criterion, they will have succeeded. Indeed, at that point they will be as successful on that particular task as all other students. And students who have more to learn at the onset of instruction will not fail simply because they start at a different place and consequently lag behind others in the beginning. If they reach the mountain heights before the beasts, they will survive just as surely as will those who climbed first, fastest, and highest. Criterion-referenced testing argues strongly for the individualization of instruction and of evaluation; it fosters cooperation rather than competition, it encourages students to work toward the goals of the system rather than against other students, and it forces teachers to make those goals explicit.

But criterion-referenced testing has certain limitations, as critics have been quick to point out. Although it is relatively simple to specify that after taking typing lessons for six weeks a student should be able to type thirty words per minute with no more than two errors, it is considerably more difficult to determine precisely what a student should know or understand after sitting in a social studies class for six weeks. A criterion-referenced test is clearly appropriate in the first instance but is more difficult to apply in the second. Among other things, it requires that teachers specify their standards and criteria with a clarity that is not always easily obtained (Cizek, 1993a).

A second limitation is that some students are able to go beyond the criterion, given sufficient motivation to do so. Some educators fear that exclusive reliance on criterion-referenced testing may thwart students' initiative and stifle their motivation.

An advantage of norm-referenced testing is that it provides both students and those who would counsel them with valuable information concerning their likelihood of success in academic situations in which they will, in fact, be required to compete with others.

What should you do while the controversy rages around you? Simply use both types of test. There are situations in which norm-referenced tests are not only unavoidable but also useful. There are also many situations in which students will respond favorably to the establishment of definite criteria for success and in which both their learning and your teaching will benefit as a result. This, as is so often the case, is no either-or matter; your decisions should be based on the purposes of your instructional procedures in specific situations.

CURRENT TRENDS: PERFORMANCE-BASED ASSESSMENTS

Recent literature on educational assessment contains ever-increasing references to what are often termed *new approaches* to assessment. And although many of these approaches have been around for a long time, their popularity has increased dramatically in recent years (Swanson, Norman, & Linn, 1995). Collectively, these approaches to assessment are termed *performance-based assessment* (or simply *performance* *assessment.*) Alternately, they are sometimes referred to as *authentic assessment.**

Essentially, performance-based assessment attempts to determine students' competence by looking at examples of what they do—real-life performances. As R. L. Linn (1994) puts it, performance assessment requires that actual levels or standards of performance be expressed in terms of concrete examples and explicit definitions. The assumption is that performance assessment requires a level of understanding and an ability to apply learning that is not always necessary in more conventional forms of assessment. Farr and Tone (1994) point out that a conventional, multiple-choice test might well determine that carpentry students know the difference between a ballpeen, a sledge, or a claw hammer; but it would not demonstrate that the students actually know how to build a house. In their words, "There's a big difference between naming hammers and pounding nails in a wall" (p. viii).

The increasing popularity of performance-based assessment, notes Messick (1994), is based largely on its promise that it can provide more authentic, direct appraisals of student competence, and that it will therefore have clearly positive consequences for learning and teaching. In fact, educational literature repeatedly claims that one of the principal components of current educational reform is increasing use of performance-based assessment.

CHANGING ASSUMPTIONS

In addition to teaching reading, writing, arithmetic, and other related things, one of the purposes of your instructional procedures may be, in the president's words, to teach students to use their minds well. If that is really what you want to do, then, as we have argued a number of times in these pages, you have to change your assessment procedures so that what is being assessed is not limited to items of information well remembered—or forgotten—but includes actual evidence of minds working well. Put another way, if cognitive strategies training programs (see Chapter 5) and new theories of motivation (Chapter 10) deliver their promise of empowering students to become autonomous, reflective, thinking learners, we absolutely need assessment procedures based on new assumptions and new models.

Current testing practices, says G. Grant (1991), deal with behaviors that are easy to measure rather than with those that are more abstract. And they encourage individual accomplishment and competitiveness rather than group accomplishment and cooperation. These practices are evident in the predominant role that ranking plays in reporting assessments, in the widespread use of one-correct-answer-only objective tests, in assessment procedures that look only at individual learning rather than group performance, and in the view of tests as quasiscientific measuring instruments like thermometers or altimeters (Wolf et al., 1991).

But there is clearly a shift in the assumptions that underlie current testing practices. As Ewell (1991) notes, we are moving from a "production process" view of education to a view that recognizes more explicitly the range of differences that exist among students, that admits more readily that there are different ways to think, learn, and express oneself. There is little room for multiple and divergent responses, for assessing specific thought processes, for evaluating social skills—in short, for looking at how well a mind works—in a conventional objective achievement test.

Are there alternatives? Yes. As we saw, performance-based assessment allows teachers to measure student competence by observing their actual performance in real-life or simulated situations (Bergen, 1993–94). It includes a variety of procedures and approaches, the most important of which are described here.

---

*PPC: I've never liked the expression "authentic assessment" because it implies that every other type of assessment must, by definition, be unreal or not authentic. It's an emotionally loaded label that, basically, is meaningless.

AUTHOR: The bear, being politically correct, would not have put it quite so strongly.

Developmental Assessments. **Developmental assessments** are a form of performance-based assessment that attempt to document evidence of progressive accomplishments. They look at real, actual accomplishments rather than at relative accomplishments. That is, they look at characteristics of the student's actual behavior rather than at accomplishments relative to other, comparable students.

Developmental assessments typically use detailed, performance-based lists of expected or desired behaviors as a guide for interpreting the student's progress. The most common approach to developmental assessments takes the form of checklists that present detailed, sequential lists of accomplishments or capabilities in any of a variety of areas (see Figures 13.6 and 13.7). In some school systems, checklists have completely replaced more traditional, grade-oriented assessments.

Less rigorous approaches to developmental assessment have long been common in elementary schools where, as McClean (1992) notes, tests are not nearly as common as they later become. Instead, teachers rely more on observation and relatively informal evaluation. That is, they make informal judgments about the competency of their students based on their observations of students' actual performance.

Sampling Thinking Performances. **Sampling thinking performances** is a form of performance-based assessment that requires that students answer questions, solve problems, write, or do other things in real rather than contrived circumstances. The objective is to sample performances that provide evidence of competency in the skills involved in cognition. Sampling performances is what happens when a novice driver takes a road test or a singer auditions. In these cases, the objective is to demonstrate the ability to perform the activity being assessed by actually performing it. In much the same way, argue Wolf and associates (1991), if we want to assess a student's ability to think, we must sample actual performances of thought.

An example of a thinking-performance assessment is found in an experimental program involving ten separate Alberta school systems. Collectively termed the *Educational Quality Indicators Initiative,* this project focused on a different goal in each system (see McEwen, 1992). For example, teams in one district attempted to identify the blend of academic, social, and other activities most closely related to quality education; one concentrated on developing criteria suitable for assessing portfolios, and one dealt with a thinking-performance approach to assessing problem solving in mathematics (Sereda, 1992). This approach asks students to write or speak their thought processes while solving problems. Assessment is based on evidence of specific cognitive strategies rather than simply on the production of a correct response. Teachers identify the presence or absence of these strategies on the basis of sequentially ordered criteria. Thus, the child's verbal explanation for the solution or attempted solution of a problem in mathematics might be "preliminary" (does not reflect the problem), "partial," "complete," or "elegant." For each of these categories, additional highly specific descriptors are supplied. For example, a partial response might include any or all of the following characteristics:

> *Begins the problem in a manner that could lead to a solution but fails to complete it:*
> *—omits a significant part of the problem*
> *—makes a major computational error*
> *—uses an inappropriate strategy for solving the problem*
> *Provides a solution, but explanation unclear:*
> *—argument or explanation incomplete*

---

developmental assessments A performance-based assessment that looks at the student's performance in relation to developmental or course-based expectations rather than in relation to the performance of other students. Often uses checklists of expected (desired) behaviors.

sampling thinking performances An approach to performance-based assessment in which students are given an opportunity to perform real-life activities that require and illustrate the use of specific cognitive processes.

—*diagram is inappropriate or unclear*
(A correct answer with no evidence to support the solution must be further supported by an interview or else there is no basis on which to judge the process [Sereda, 1992, p. 84].)

Assessment procedures include not only criteria for assessing samples of thinking, but checklists for describing "mathematical dispositions"—for example, motivation, creativity, confidence, and strategic processes and approaches. Again, specific behavioral criteria are supplied for each category. As a result, assessors can develop a **profile** of each student—that is, a description of the individual's strengths, weaknesses, and other characteristics.

Exhibitions. Exhibitions are public displays of performance. They differ from other performance-assessment procedures in that they underline the social nature of thinking and learning. Common examples of exhibitions include oral examinations by expert or peer committees, musical recitations, and science fairs. This form of assessment requires students to synthesize their knowledge, to extrapolate it, and to explain and demonstrate it in social situations.

Portfolios. Portfolios are ongoing records of achievement or performance. They are collections of actual samples of the student's work, often gathered by students themselves. In the primary grades, for example, portfolios might consist of drawings—preferably with the student's story/explanation written on the back, often by the teacher; of samples of the student's writing; of records of simple computations; perhaps of tests and quizzes that tap meaningful

processes. In later grades, portfolios include not only samples of early and later work but also a more systematic and structured range of work representing different subjects and different cognitive processes. McClean (1992) suggests that a useful approach to portfolios is to have students collect ongoing working portfolios. This active portfolio contains works in progress as well as earlier work. From this working portfolio, teachers and students select samples to be placed in a more permanent cumulative portfolio.

Portfolios can also be used in higher education. For example, as part of a teacher assessment project, teacher candidates were asked to develop portfolios (Haertel, 1991). Among other things, the portfolios included overviews of instructional units, samples of several lessons, lists of instructional references and resources, copies of handouts for students; samples of students' work, photos or written records of blackboards and bulletin boards, videotapes of different aspects of instruction, evaluator/observer notes and assessments. These portfolios were later scored using a detailed system of specific criteria for each category of entry.

Portfolios such as these provide teachers and students with a continuous body of physical evidence about important changes. Thus, they are useful not so much for assessing current attainment as for identifying acquisitions, detecting interests and special skills, and perhaps pointing out weaknesses. A well-organized portfolio is, in a sense, a biography of the learner's mind, a history of change and progress.

Portfolios provide teachers with a basis for assessment of changes in performance and are a means by which students develop increasing awareness and understanding of their own changing thought processes. Thus, the purpose of using portfolios is not simply to assess performance but, perhaps even more important, to provide ongoing occasions for learning (Porter & Cleland, 1995). In this connection, portfolios have been found to be especially valuable for gifted children, for whom they can

---

profile A description of individual patterns of strengths, weaknesses, or abilities.

exhibitions A performance-based assessment procedure that requires the public display of competence. Exhibitions are most common in the visual or performing arts, as well as in oral examinations for graduate degrees. They underline the social nature of thinking.

INDIVIDUAL STUDENT PROGRESS REPORT
FULTONVALE ELEMENTARY SCHOOL

Name: *Magee, Wayne*
Grade: *02* **Homeroom:** *55*
Teacher: *Ms. A. Sanders*

Term: _____
Program Type: Regular _____
Modified _____

The checks (✓) in the columns show your child's development at this time. **Any items not checked do not apply.** The skills and behaviors observed are:

Not yet apparent...
  Is developing...
    Developed as expected...

	Not yet apparent	Is developing	Developed as expected
PERSONAL & SOCIAL DEVELOPMENT			
Reflects positive attitudes about self			✓
Works independently			✓
Concentrates on tasks			✓
Organizes materials and space			✓
Makes effective use of time			✓
Works and plays cooperatively			✓
Respects the rights and properties of self and others			✓
Follows class/school rules and routines			✓
ATTITUDES TOWARD LEARNING			
Demonstrates initiative			✓
Accepts new challenges			✓
Demonstrates commitment to completing tasks			✓
THINKING SKILLS AND LEARNING STRATEGIES			
Demonstrates critical thinking skills (organizes, reasons logically, plans, asks questions, evaluates...)			✓
Demonstrates creative thinking skills (generates varied ideas, elaborates, shows originality...)			✓
Demonstrates decision making and problem solving strategies			✓
LANGUAGE LEARNING			
Language is developed and used in all subjects. It is an essential component of all learning.			✓
Applies reading skills		✓	
Applies writing skills		✓	
Applies listening skills			✓
Applies talking skills			✓
MATHEMATICS			
Participates in mathematical activities			✓
Understands the concepts			✓
Applies problem-solving strategies			✓
Computes accurately			✓
SOCIAL STUDIES			
Participates in class activities and discussions			✓
Understands the concepts			✓
Applies skills and strategies related to responsible citizenship			✓
SCIENCE			
Participates in class activities and discussions			✓
Understands the concepts			✓
Applies scientific process skills and strategies			✓
HEALTH			
Participates in class activities and discussions			✓
Understands the concepts			✓
Applies skills and strategies related to personal well-being			✓
PHYSICAL EDUCATION			
Participates in physical education activities			✓
Demonstrates personal competency in motor skills and physical activities			✓
Cooperates in group/team activities			✓
ART			
Participates in art activities			✓
Applies skills and concepts			✓
MUSIC			
Participates in musical activities			✓
Demonstrates an understanding of musical skills and concepts			✓

COMMENTS:

Wayne continues to demonstrate a positive attitude and is eager to learn. He works diligently and his homework is usually completed in the allotted time. He takes pride in his work and enjoys sharing ideas that might enrich and/or extend the activities. He is enthusiastic and shows initiative and originality when encountering new activities. At times these ideas are counter-productive as the method he chooses is labor intense, but he perseveres and adapts.

Wayne continues to demonstrate an increased fluency and an increased sight-word vocabulary base. However, Wayne is not an independent reader. His daily reading fluency is inconsistent. He has a good knowledge of the many word-recognition skills but the transfer and application of these skills is not consistent. Wayne's oral/verbal story fluency far exceeds his written ability. His spelling skills greatly inhibit his writing. Often, Wayne can't reread his written stories with his inconsistent spelling patterns. His stories are very creative, imaginative, and interesting. It is frustrating to him when he cannot make the written words flow like his thoughts.

Wayne has a good understanding of the math concepts studied this term. He can apply these concepts in problem-solving situations. Wayne computes accurately, but he relies on manipulation rather than memory with his addition and subtraction facts to 18.

Wayne continues to demonstrate personal competency and good sportsmanship. He cooperated in the team activities involved in our Floor Hockey unit and is enjoying the individualistic focus in our Gymnastics unit.

A special thank you to Mrs. Magee for her help Mondays in the computer room. Thanks AS

Parent/Guardian Signature: _____

FIGURE 13.6 A sample checklist report card. Used by permission of Strathcona County Schools.

Friendly
Sharing
Exciting
School

Fort Saskatchewan Elementary School
9802 – 101 Street
Fort Saskatchewan, Alberta
T8L 1V4
Office: (403) 998-7771
Child Safe: (403) 998-0484

INTERIM REPORT CARD

Date:

Dear Parents:
This interim report card is designed to give you a general indication of
your child's progress in school. If you have any questions, please call.
PLEASE RETURN TO YOUR CHILD'S HOME ROOM TEACHER by Wed., Oct. 21

STUDENT'S NAME: **GRADE:**

	Satisfactory Development	Requires Further Development
Showing a positive attitude toward school		
Developing good work habits		
Language learning		
Math		

TEACHER COMMENTS:

Teacher's Signature:

PARENT COMMENTS:

Parent/Guardian's Signature:

FIGURE 13.7 A sample checklist interim report card. Used by permission of Strathcona County Schools.

have important motivational consequences (Hadaway & Marek-Schroer, 1994). In addition, the use of portfolio assessment, and the making up of portfolios, can result in significant changes in teaching styles (Valencia & Place, 1994).

Portfolios kept by teachers of their own performance can also be useful in improving teaching. Athanases (1994) reports a case in which a teacher kept a portfolio of her instruction over a one-year period. The portfolio included samples of lessons as well as reflections on their effectiveness, thoughts about how they might be changed, and so on. (See the case "What I Want to Be When I Grow Up.")

AN ASSESSMENT
OF PERFORMANCE ASSESSMENT

"Expanding interest in performance assessment," writes Moss, "reflects the growing consensus among educators about the impact of evaluation on what students learn and what teachers teach, about the role that multiple-choice assessments have played in narrowing the curriculum to reflect the form and content of these tests, and about the potential power of carefully designed performance assessments to document and encourage critical, creative, and self-reflective thought" (1992, pp. 229–230).

Still, it isn't entirely clear that performance assessment is delivering all that has been promised (Guskey, 1994). In addition, there are a number of serious problems with the wholesale implementation of performance-based assessment, not the least of which are questions concerning how to determine standards by which student performances are to be judged (Baker, 1994).

Arguments for Performance-Based Assessment. There is little doubt that emphases on learning how to learn and on autonomous, reflective, independent, creative thinking are in many ways incompatible with current testing practices. To the extent that our assessments demand the sort of linear thinking that is evident in acceptance and reproduction of single correct answers, they foster a type of teaching and of learning that results not in minds that work well but in minds that reproduce well.

Performance-based assessment appears to have a number of distinct advantages:

> It is better attuned to our changing educational emphases.
>
> It may be more equitable than more traditional approaches.
>
> It provides more ways of viewing competence and even excellence.
>
> It might expose social and intellectual skills that more traditional measures would overlook.
>
> It bases assessment on a wider range of evidence than has been customary.
>
> To the extent that it is more authentic, it might be more relevant to competency in the real world.

Arguments Against Performance-Based Assessment. But these new forms of assessment are clearly more cumbersome, more time-consuming, and in most cases less exact. That is, they require more time, more effort, more knowledge—in short, more resources—on the part of teachers (Guskey, 1994). In addition, they are not as easily quantifiable and are therefore not as useful for educational decisions that require comparison. That is, they provide a less certain basis for answering such questions as "Which 120 of these 500 college applicants should be admitted?" or "Which 1 of these 120 should be given the Earnest Q. Honest Memorable Scholarship?"

From a measurement point of view, performance-based assessment suffers from relatively lower standards of reliability and validity than more conventional assessment procedures (Bateson, 1994). This is partly because performance measures often cannot be quantified. It is also because results on performance-based tasks usually need to be interpreted by teachers who, notes Marzano (1994), are prone to being influenced by the student's overall performance in other areas.

In addition, notes Ewell (1991), these approaches to assessment generate a tremendous volume of material and information but no simple way to interpret or summarize it. There is perhaps little hope for them unless we can develop clear and effective procedures for collecting and displaying samples of performances and clear criteria for understanding their meaning.

ASSESSMENT IN TODAY'S SCHOOLS

Assessment is a fundamental part of the teaching/learning process with important potential benefits to both teacher and learner. Deale (1975) suggests that teachers need to assess students for the following reasons: to determine whether what has been taught has also been learned, how well it has been learned, and by how many; to monitor the progress of individual students as well as of groups; to evaluate instructional materials and procedures; to amass and retain accurate records of students' attainment; and to aid learning.

THE ETHICS OF ASSESSMENT

For each of these purposes, teachers can use their own teacher-made tests or standardized tests complete with administration, scoring, and norming procedures. But tests are not always appropriate for all purposes, nor are they always used or interpreted fairly. With the increasing use of tests, particularly of the standardized variety, and with increasing concern for privacy, individual rights, and equality, some ethical issues implicit in the administration and use of tests have become matters of political and social concern. Tests are frequently seen as a threat, as a violation of privacy, and as unjust. Unfortunately, these concerns are not entirely unfounded. For example, personality tests can invade privacy when they probe into matters that would not ordinarily be publicly revealed; tests can be threatening when school placement, job opportunities—indeed, success and failure—depend upon their results; and they can be patently unjust when used for purposes for which they were not intended or with groups for whom they were not designed. And, as McGill-Franzen and Allington (1993) point out, when the results of standardized tests are made public or are used as a basis for rewarding teachers or funding school programs, they can easily lead to a variety of unethical practices, including narrowing the curriculum so that teachers teach more directly to the tests and flunking or reclassifying students who don't do well on these tests in order to improve reported results.

None of these observations is intended as justification for abandoning the use of teacher-made and standardized tests in the schools; rather, they are intended as an argument for the sane and restrained use of both tests and the results obtained therefrom.

CASE: WHAT I WANT TO BE WHEN I GROW UP

THE SITUATION: Carolyn White, a good teacher, as recollected by Lillian, teacher in training

My eighth-grade language arts teacher, Mrs. White, was able to make writing weekly essays the highlight of the week. Each week we would write an essay on something about us. For example, we wrote on topics such as: "What I want to be when I grow up," "A hard decision I had to make," "My best friend," and so on. Then, after she had corrected each essay, we wrote a final copy and put it into our "dossier," which was a book-style collection of all our writing. This idea made writing fun as well as enabling us to learn a lot about ourselves. Also, Mrs. White would go through the dossier when she made up our report cards and base her evaluation and her comments on the dossier. Then, at the end of the year, she gave us our dossiers back to keep. Mine is among my prized possessions now.

It is reassuring to note that in the United States increasing concern with the ethics of testing and records is now reflected in a public law affecting all schools funded by the U.S. Office of Education. Among other things, this law (Public Law 93-380) grants parents of children younger than 18 the right of access to education records kept by schools and relating to their own children, the right to challenge the accuracy and appropriateness of these records, the right to limit public access to these records and to receive a list of individuals and/or agencies that have been given access to them, and the right to be notified if and when the records are turned over to courts of law. All these parental rights become the student's rights after the age of 18 or after the student enters a postsecondary educational institution.

SOME CONCLUDING THOUGHTS

In most schools, far more emphasis is placed on the use of assessment for grading (summative evaluation) than on its instructional roles in identifying strengths and weaknesses, in suggesting remediation, and so on (formative evaluation). This situation, suggests Crooks (1988), needs to be rectified. Evaluation needs to be used more often to provide students with feedback about their performance. This feedback should emphasize progress toward important educational goals and should occur in the course of learning rather than only at the end of a unit.

Our evaluation procedures are often weak not only in terms of how test results are used but, perhaps far more important, in terms of what we choose to evaluate. Crooks (1988) notes that although class evaluation has a profound effect on what students learn, many teachers spend little time and effort in developing good assessment procedures or attempting to ensure that what they test is really what they want students to learn. As we saw, one result is that a great deal of class evaluation emphasizes the lowest-level cognitive objectives—specifically, knowledge of specifics. Accordingly, schools teach students to remember isolated facts rather

than to understand, to look for relationships, and to go beyond the information given.

The solution? At least in part, the solution lies in changing evaluation procedures. If we want to teach students to think, to evaluate, to be critical, and to solve problems, we need to stop loading our tests with items that ask for a simple regurgitation of text- and teacher-sanctified facts. We can tell our students what our grand goals are, but unless our tests reflect what we say, our students will not believe us.

We have to change our attitudes toward measurement, insist Wolf and associates (1992). First, instead of ranking students, we have to develop sequential criteria of accomplishments—in other words, we have to move to criterion- rather than norm-referenced assessment. Second, we have to change our notion that high reliability is an essential aspect of educational assessment. Portfolio-based assessments, for example, might vary considerably from one assessor to another. And third, we have to stop insisting that we need a single summary number to describe—and compare—students.

OLD WINE . . .

Are these new approaches to assessment really new? After all, observation of students' performance, anecdotal records, cumulative files, including samples of student work, exhibitions such as science fairs, evaluation in social situations such as in oral examinations, and various other performance-based approaches to assessment have been around for a long time.

Is this old wine in new bottles, new labels and all?

Is it just our assumptions, our emphases, and our goals that are changing? Or are these too old wines now being rebottled? It's interesting to read what William James wrote in his *Talks to Teachers* almost a century ago:

No elementary measurement, capable of being performed in a laboratory, can throw light on the actual efficiency of the subject; for the vital thing about him, his emotional and moral energy and doggedness, can be measured by no single experiment, and becomes known only by the total results in the long run . . . Be patient, then, and sympathetic with the type of mind that cuts a poor figure in examination. It may, in the long examination which life sets us, come out in the end in better shape than the glib and ready reproducer, its passions being deeper, its purposes more worthy, its combining power less commonplace, and its total mental output consequently more important. (James, 1915, pp. 135–143; quoted in Wolf et al., 1991, p. 51)

Old wine is often better than new wine.

MAIN POINTS

1. Measurement is the use of an instrument (a ruler, a thermometer, a test) to gauge the quantity of a property or behavior. Evaluation is making a decision about quality, goodness, or appropriateness. Assessment includes aspects of both. What teachers assess is important in determining what students learn. If schools emphasize learning unrelated facts (surface learning) rather than understanding relationships (deep learning), that is what students learn.

2. Statements of instructional objectives should specify both what the learner must do and the criteria of acceptable performance. They may be highly performance oriented and specific (Mager), more expressive (affective, Eisner), or both general and specific (Gronlund).

3. Bloom's taxonomy can be valuable in setting up educational objectives and in designing tests to determine the extent to which these goals have been obtained. Bloom's taxonomy of cognitive educational objectives includes six classes of goals: knowledge (facts, specifics), comprehension (obtaining meaning from communication), application (using principles to solve problems), analysis (understanding by looking at parts), synthesis (understanding by combining individual parts), and evaluation (judging value). Gagné's learning outcomes can also be used as a guide for setting up instructional objectives.

4. A test blueprint is a table of specifications for a test. It should specify topics or behaviors to be sampled as well as the number or proportion of items that will relate to each.

5. Good measuring instruments need to be valid (measure what they purport to measure) and reliable (measure consistently). A test cannot be valid without also being reliable; however, it can be reliable without being valid. Aspects of validity include face validity (the test appears to measure what it says it measures), content validity (judged by analyzing test items to determine whether they sample appropriate content), construct validity (how well the test reflects underlying hypothetical variables), and criterion-related validity (the measure agrees with other current measures [concurrent validity] or predicts future performance [predictive validity]).

6. Reliability can be measured by looking at correlations between repeated presentations of the same test (repeated-measures reliability), between different forms of the same test (parallel-forms reliability), or between halves of a single test (split-half reliability).

7. Standardized tests are professionally developed instruments—usually measures of intelligence, personality, or achievement—that provide norms or standards by which to judge individual performance. Common uses of standardized tests are for special education placement, to certify students' achievement, to judge the competency of teachers, to evaluate schools, and for instructional diagnosis.

8. Standardized achievement tests typically provide one or more of the following norms: age-equivalent scores (provide a comparison to average like-aged

performance), grade-equivalent scores (provide comparison to expected performance for different grades), or percentiles (indicate percentage scoring below given point). Scores may be transformed to standard scores such as Z-scores (mean = 0, standard deviation = 1), T-scores (mean = 50, standard deviation = 10), or stanines (mean = 5, standard deviation = 2).

9. Teacher-made paper-and-pencil tests are either objective (true-false, completion, matching, or multiple choice) or essay type. Essay tests are better for tapping higher mental processes, allow for more divergence, and are less time-consuming to prepare; they are more limited in content, less reliable, and more time-consuming to score.

10. Good essay examinations should sample processes not easily measured with objective tests. Questions should be specific and clearly worded, sufficient time should be allowed for answering, and relative weightings of different questions should be clear. Good multiple-choice items have clear, meaningful stems, distractors of approximately equal plausibility, and no double negatives, absolute qualifiers (*always, never*), or other unintentional cues (*a, an,* singulars, plurals).

11. One way to give raw scores on achievement tests meaning is to convert them to percentage scores or letter grades. The average score, the range of scores, the class distribution, and the standard deviation are also useful. Measures of central tendency include the mean (arithmetic average),

the mode (most frequently occurring score), and the median (fiftieth percentile; midpoint).

12. Schools have traditionally used norm-referenced tests (performance is judged in relation to the performance of other students). Criterion-referenced tests compare performance to a preestablished criterion rather than to the performance of other students.

13. Current testing practices emphasize ranking, are geared toward providing numerical summaries of students, and encourage a reproductive rather than productive approach to teaching and learning. An alternative is performance-based assessment, which might include developmental assessment (for example, progressive, criterion-specific checklists), sampling thinking performances (assessment of the actual performance of a thoughtful activity such as solving a math problem), evaluating exhibitions (public displays of samples of meaningful achievements and processes), or evaluating portfolios (actual collection representing ongoing records of samples of performance).

14. New assessment approaches are more compatible with current emphases on developing autonomous, reflective thinkers, may be more equitable, and are geared toward learning (formative evaluation) rather than simply assessing achievements (summative evaluation). But they are time-consuming, difficult, and inexact.

APPLIED QUESTIONS

▶ How would you illustrate how measurement and evaluation might be involved in the assessment of student performance in the classroom?

▶ Write instructional objectives that illustrate the approaches of Mager, Eisner, and Gronlund.

▶ Define *reliability* and each of the following kinds of validity: face, content, construct, and criterion-related (predictive and concurrent).

▶ If you were to debate the systemwide use of standardized achievement tests, what would be your pros and cons?

▶ Evaluate the relative merits of criterion-referenced and norm-referenced evaluation.

▶ What are portfolios and why might they be used to evaluate student performance?

STUDY TERMS

SUGGESTED READINGS

Harris and Bell's book is a useful and practical discussion of assessment. It reflects education's increasing concern with teaching students to learn rather than simply teaching them facts, and it discusses approaches compatible with goals that are cooperative and individual rather than competitive. The Oosterhof book is a clear and simple introduction to educational measurement:

HARRIS, D., & BELL, C. (1994). *Evaluating and assessing for learning.* New York: Nichols (London: Kogan Page).

OOSTERHOF, A. (1994). *Classroom applications of educational measurement.* New York: Maxwell Macmillan.

The following three books are useful sources for information about performance-based approaches to assessment—especially the use of portfolios:

FARR, R., & TONE, B. (1994). *Portfolio and performance assessment: Helping students evaluate their progress as readers and writers.* Fort Worth: Harcourt Brace.

PORTER, C., & CLELAND, J. (1995). *The portfolio as a learning strategy.* Portsmouth, N.H.: Boynton/Cook.

MARZANO, R. J., PICKERING, D., & MCTIGHE, J. (1993). *Assessing student outcomes: Performance assessment using the Dimensions of Learning model.* Alexandria, Va.: Association for Supervision and Curriculum Development.

Purring among suckling young has been reported in the black bear. Growling among adult bears has also been reported (Ewer, 1973).

EPILOGUE

What we call the beginning is often
the end
And to make an end is to make
a beginning
The end is where we start from.

We shall not cease from exploration
And the end of all our exploring
Will be to arrive where we started
And know the place for the first time.
T. S. ELIOT, *Little Gidding*

Epilogue and a Growing Footnote

We have now come full circle. And, in the manner of that wonderful design, we are ready to go back to the beginning, again. . . .

Or at least we can go somewhere very near the beginning. There you were given a word of caution, which is just as fitting here at the end as it was at the beginning: A science of humanity tends to dehumanize, we warned. It transforms living, breathing beings into "organisms"; it reduces our enormously complex behavior to stimuli and responses and the activity of our minds to inventions, to hypothetical structures. At the beginning, we said that students are more than all this. At the end, we say again that they are much more. Psychology has only begun to understand; the last word has not been said or written. . . .

Yet something has been said in the pages of this text. On thirteen occasions, that something was reduced to a set of statements that were called "Main Points." Here, in this epilogue, all those main points are reduced to a single, final, all-embracing Main Point. This, reader, is what this text has been all about:

*A bear always faces the front.**

The relevance of this statement to teaching cannot easily be explained in anything shorter than a full-length book. Because this book is now concluding, suffice it to say that a teacher should try to behave as sensibly as a bear, who persistently faces the front of its footprints. Teaching has been described as an art and a science. The comment was made in Chapter 1 that where science fails, art should be used. The point being made here is that both the art and the science share common sense.

---

*When I wrote the first edition of this book in 1972, I had no doubt that this statement was absolutely true, but by 1975 I realized that it is only a very stupid bear who does not occasionally look backward. Accordingly, the second edition loudly proclaimed, "A bear ~~always~~ *usually* faces the front." Truth is a precarious luxury. By 1979 the bear had been approached from the rear much more often, had become far wiser, and consequently spent a great deal of time facing backward. Accordingly, the title of the third edition announced with considerable assurance: "A bear ~~always usually~~ *sometimes* faces the front." How fickle truth. Perhaps more pertinent, how fickle bears. In 1982, with inflation rampant and the world situation tensing, we knew that the sagest of bears only very *rarely* faced the front. And a mere three years later, by 1985, it had finally happened. Confused by the awesome uncertainties of those years, though still moved by poetic visions of a peaceful and happy world, the bear looked boldly in all directions except, as the title page so unabashedly proclaimed, the front: "A bear ~~always usually sometimes rarely~~ *never* faces the front." But by 1988 things had again changed. In a cunning about-face, the bear began once more to face the front, only occasionally casting a furtive, sidelong glance in other directions. Until 1991. By then the bear had begun to sniff some new winds of change, winds that carried the stench of methane gases. After all these years, he thought he had begun to recognize the enemy: Wild cows. He saw evidence of their passage in the dried-up stream beds and in the taste of dead clover. He followed their spoor along the Saskatchewan River Valley and into the decimated boreal forests of the North. He watched them playing cards, drinking whiskey, and smoking cigars. He heard them sing their country songs. He was not impressed, and he was very uneasy. Accordingly, in 1991, the bear absolutely *would not commit himself.* No way. But by 1994, the bear had had enough of sitting on his duff, looking here and there. Driven by a burning resolve to teach wild cows better values, he hurled himself headlong into the environmental crusades. Now, as the title insisted ("A bear ~~always usually sometimes rarely never always faces the front will not commit himself just now~~ faces the future"), he began to look to the future.

Who said an old bear cannot learn new tricks? It's 1997, for crying out loud! A today kind of bear can no longer afford old prejudices and attitudes and deep-seated, ethnically based convictions of rightness and goodness. Today's bear is tolerant and multicultural and multilingual and outstandingly cool, and, above all else, *politically correct.* Absolutely!

BIBLIOGRAPHY

AAMD Ad Hoc Committee on Terminology and Classification. (1992). *Mental retardation: Definition, classification, and systems of support* (9th ed.). Washington, D.C.: American Association on Mental Retardation.

Adams, J. C., Jr. (1968). The relative effects of various testing atmospheres on spontaneous flexibility, a factor of divergent thinking. *Journal of Creative Behavior, 2,* 187–194.

Adamson, G. (1983, January). The coin with more than two sides. *ATA Magazine,* 28–30.

Addison, R. M., & Homme, L. E. (1966). The reinforcing event (RE) menu. *Journal of the National Society for Programmed Instruction,* 8–9.

Agne, K., Greenwood, G. E., & Miller, L. D. (1994). Relationships between teacher belief systems and teacher effectiveness. *Journal of Research and Development in Education, 27,* 141–152.

Ahsen, A. (1977a). *Psych eye: Self-analytic consciousness.* New York: Brandon House.

——. (1977b). Eidetics: An overview. *Journal of Mental Imagery, 1,* 5–38.

Albert, R. S., & Runco, M. A. (1986). The achievement of eminence: A model based on a longitudinal study of exceptionally gifted boys and their families. In R. J. Sternberg & J. E. Davidson (eds.), *Conceptions of giftedness.* New York: Cambridge University Press.

Alberta Education. (1987). *Visions 2000: A vision of educational technology in Alberta by the year 2000.* Edmonton: Department of Education.

Alexander, P. A., & Judy, J. E. (1988). The interaction of domain-specific and strategic knowledge in academic performance. *Review of Educational Research, 58,* 375–404.

Alvino, J. (1993). Teaching our children to solve "fuzzy" problems. *PTA Today, 18,* 13–14.

Ambert, A. N. (1991). *Bilingual education and English as a second language: A research handbook, 1988–1990.* New York: Garland.

American Psychiatric Association. (1994). *Diagnostic and statistical manual of mental disorders* (4th ed.). Washington, D.C.: American Psychiatric Association.

Ames, C. (1992). Classrooms: Goals, structures, and student motivation. *Journal of Educational Psychology, 84,* 261–271.

Amir, R., & Tamir, P. (1994). In-depth analysis of misconceptions as a basis for developing research-based remedial instruction: The case of photosynthesis. *American Biology Teacher, 56,* 94–100.

Amsel, A. (1989). *Behaviorism, neobehaviorism, and cognitivism in learning theory: Historical and contemporary perspectives.* Hillsdale, N.J.: Erlbaum.

Anderman, E. M., & Maehr, M. L. (1994). Motivation and schooling in the middle grades. *Review of Educational Research, 64*, 287–309.

Anderson, C. W., & Smith, E. L. (1984). Children's preconceptions and content-area textbooks. In G. G. Duffy, L. R. Roehler, & J. Mason (eds.), *Comprehension instruction: Perspectives and suggestions.* New York: Longman.

Anderson, J. R. (1983). *The architecture of cognition.* Cambridge, Mass.: Harvard University Press.

Anderson, L. W., & Block, J. H. (1977). Mastery learning. In D. J. Treffinger, J. K. Davis, & R. E. Ripple (eds.), *Handbook on teaching educational psychology.* New York: Academic.

Anderson, S., & Payne, M. A. (1994). Corporal punishment in elementary education: Views of Barbadian school children. *Child Abuse and Neglect: The International Journal, 18*, 377–386.

Arlin, M. (1984). Time, equality, and mastery learning. *Review of Educational Research, 54*, 65–86.

Arnold, J. E. (1962). Useful creative techniques. In S. J. Parnes & H. F. Harding (eds.), *A sourcebook for creative thinking.* New York: Scribner's.

Aron, R. H. (1994). Atmospheric misconceptions. *Science Teacher, 61*, 30–33.

Aronfreed, J. (1968). Aversive control of socialization. In D. Levine (ed.), *Nebraska Symposium on Motivation.* Lincoln: University of Nebraska Press.

Aronson, E., Blaney, N., Stephan, C., Sikes, J., & Snapp, M. (1978). *The jigsaw classroom.* Beverly Hills: Sage.

Ashman, A. F., Wright, S. K., & Conway, R. N. F. (1994). Developing the metacognitive skills of academically gifted students in mainstream classrooms. *Roeper Review, 16*, 198–204.

Athanases, S. Z. (1994). Teachers' reports of the effects of preparing portfolios of literacy instruction. *Elementary School Journal, 94*, 421–439.

Atkinson, J. W., & Raynor, J. O. (1978). *Personality, motivation, and achievement.* New York: Wiley.

Atkinson, R. C., & Shiffrin, R. M. (1968). Human memory: A proposed system and its control processes. In K. W. Spence & J. T. Spence (eds.), *The psychology of learning and motivation* (Vol. 2). New York: Academic.

Aubrey, C. (1993). An investigation of the mathematical knowledge and competencies which young children bring into school. *British Educational Research Journal, 19*, 27–41.

Auld, L. W. S., & Pantelidis, V. S. (1994). Exploring virtual reality for classroom use: The virtual reality and education lab at East Carolina University. *Techtrends, 39*, 29–31.

Ausubel, D. P. (1958). *Theory and problems of child development.* New York: Grune & Stratton.

——. (1963). *The psychology of meaningful verbal learning.* New York: Grune & Stratton.

——. (1977). The facilitation of meaningful verbal learning in the classroom. *Educational Psychologist, 12*, 162–178.

Ausubel, D. P., & Robinson, F. G. (1969). *School learning: An introduction to educational psychology.* New York: Holt, Rinehart & Winston.

Babad, E. (1993). Pygmalion—25 years after: Interpersonal expectancies in the classroom. In P. D. Blanck (ed.), *Interpersonal expectations: Theory, research, and application.* Cambridge: Cambridge University Press.

Babad, E. Y. (1985). Some correlates of teachers' expectancy bias. *American Educational Research Journal, 22*, 175–183.

Bacdayan, A. W. (1994). Time-denominated achievement cost curves, learning differences and individualized instruction. *Economics of Education Review, 13*, 43–53.

Bachus, G. (1994). Violence is no stranger to rural schools. *School Administrator, 51*, 18–22.

Bacon, E. H. (1990). Using negative consequences effectively. *Academic Therapy, 25*, 599–611.

Baer, J. (1993–94). Why you shouldn't trust creativity tests. *Educational Leadership, 51*, 80–83.

Baer, R. A., Tishelman, A. C., Degler, J. D., Osnes, P. G., & Stokes, T. F. (1992). Effects of self- vs. experimenter-selection of rewards on classroom behavior in young children. *Education and Treatment of Children, 15*, 1–14.

Bainer, D. L., & Didham, C. (1994). Mentoring and other support behaviors in elementary schools. *Journal of Educational Research, 87*, 240–247.

Baker, E. L. (1994). Making performance assessment work: The road ahead. *Educational Leadership, 51*, 58–62.

Baker, L., & Brown, A. L. (1984). Metacognitive skills and reading. In P. D. Pearson (ed.), *Handbook of reading research.* New York: Longman.

Baltes, M. M., & Silverberg, S. B. (1994). The dynamics between dependency and autonomy: Illustrations across the lifespan. In D. L. Featherman,

R. M. Lerner, & M. Perlmutter (eds.), *Life-span development and behavior* (Vol. 12). Hillsdale, N.J.: Erlbaum.

Banaji, M. R., & Crowder, R. G. (1989). The bankruptcy of everyday memory. *American Psychologist, 44,* 1185–1193.

Bandura, A. (1962). Social learning through imitation. In N. R. Jones (ed.), *Nebraska Symposium on Motivation.* Lincoln: University of Nebraska Press.

——. (1969). *Principles of behavior modification.* New York: Holt, Rinehart & Winston.

——. (1977). *Social learning theory.* Morristown, N.J.: General Learning Press.

——. (1981). Self-referent thought: A developmental analysis of self-efficacy. In J. H. Flavell & L. Ross (eds.), *Social cognitive development: Frontiers and possible futures.* Cambridge: Cambridge University Press.

——. (1986). *Social foundations of thought and action: A social cognitive theory.* Englewood Cliffs, N.J.: Prentice-Hall.

——. (1991). Social cognitive theory of self-regulation. *Organizational Behavior and Human Performance, 50,* 248–287.

——. (1993). Perceived self-efficacy in cognitive development and functioning. *Educational Psychologist, 28,* 117–148.

Bandura, A., Ross, D., & Ross, S. (1963). Imitation of film mediated aggressive models. *Journal of Abnormal and Social Psychology, 66,* 3–11.

Bandura, A., & Walters, R. (1963). *Social learning and personality development.* New York: Holt, Rinehart & Winston.

Banks, J. A. (1993a). Multicultural education: Historical development, dimensions, and practice. *Review of Research in Education, 19,* 3–49.

——. (1993b). The canon debate, knowledge construction, and multicultural education. *Educational Researcher, 22,* 5–14.

Bar, V., Zinn, B., Goldmuntz, R., & Sneider, C. (1994). Children's concepts about weight and free fall. *Science Education, 78,* 149–169.

Barbetta, P. M. (1990). Red light-green light: A classwide management system for students with behavior disorders in primary grades. *Preventing School Failure, 34,* 14–19.

Bardwell, R. (1984). The development and motivational function of expectations. *American Educational Research Journal, 21,* 461–472.

Barnett, W. S. (1993). Benefit-cost analysis of preschool education: Findings from a 25-year follow-up. *American Journal of Orthopsychiatry, 63,* 500–508.

Barrett, G. V., & Depinet, R. L. (1991). A reconsideration of testing for competence rather than for intelligence. *American Psychologist, 46,* 1012–1024.

Barth, R. (1979). Home-based reinforcement of school behavior: A review and analysis. *Review of Educational Research, 49,* 436–458.

Bartolome, L. I. (1994). Beyond the methods fetish: Toward a humanizing pedagogy. *Harvard Educational Review, 64,* 173–194.

Basseches, M. (1984). *Dialectical thinking and adult development.* Norwood, N.J.: Ablex.

Bateson, D. (1994). Psychometric and philosophic problems in "authentic" assessment: Performance tasks and portfolios. *Alberta Journal of Educational Research, 40,* 233–245.

Beekman, S., & Holmes, J. (1994). Resolving conflict with kids: Five approaches that can work for you. *PTA Today, 19,* 11–13.

Belmont, J. M. (1989). Cognitive strategies and strategic learning: The socio-instructional approach. *American Psychologist, 44,* 142–148.

Bennett, N. (1976). Teaching styles and pupil progress. Cambridge, Mass.: Harvard University Press.

Bergen, D. (1993–94). Authentic performance assessments. *Childhood Education, 70,* 99–102.

Berlyne, D. E. (1960). *Conflict, arousal and curiosity.* New York: McGraw-Hill.

Bernard, L. L. (1924). *Instinct: A study in social psychology.* New York: Holt, Rinehart & Winston.

Bernhard, J. K. (1992). Gender-related attitudes and the development of computer skills: A preschool intervention. *Alberta Journal of Educational Research, 38,* 177–188.

Bijou, S. W., & Sturges, P. S. (1959). Positive reinforcers for experimental studies with children—Consumables and manipulatables. *Child Development, 30,* 151–170.

Birenbaum, M., & Nasser, F. (1994). On the relationship between test anxiety and test performance. *Measurement and Evaluation in Counseling and Development, 27,* 293–301.

Black, S. (1993). Derailing tracking. *Executive Educator, 15,* 27–30.

———. (1994a). Handling anger. *Executive Educator, 16,* 27–30.

———. (1994b). Throw away the hickory stick. *Executive Educator, 16,* 44–47.

———. (1994c). Different kinds of smart. *Executive Educator, 16,* 24–27.

Blase, J. J., & Pajak, E. F. (1985). How discipline creates stress for teachers. *Canadian School Executive, 4,* 8–11.

Bloom, B. S. (1964). *Stability and change in human characteristics.* New York: Wiley.

———. (1976). *Human characteristics and school learning.* New York: McGraw-Hill.

———. (1984). The 2 sigma problem: The search for methods of group instruction as effective as one-to-one tutoring. *Educational Researcher, 13,* 4–15.

———. (1987). A response to Slavin's mastery learning reconsidered. *Review of Educational Research, 57,* 507–508.

Bloom, B. S., Engelhart, M. B., Furst, E. J., Hill, W. H., & Krathwohl, D. R. (1956). *Taxonomy of educational objectives: Handbook I: Cognitive domain.* New York: Longman, Green.

Blumenfeld, P. C. (1992). Classroom learning and motivation: Clarifying and expanding goal theory. *Journal of Educational Psychology, 84,* 272–281.

Bolles, R. C. (1974). Cognition and motivation: Some historical trends. In B. Weiner (ed.), *Cognitive views of human motivation.* New York: Academic.

Boodoo, G. M. (1993). Performance assessments or multiple choice? *Educational Horizons, 72,* 50–56.

Boring, E. G. (1923). Intelligence as the tests test it. *New Republic, 35,* 35–37.

Borkowski, J. G., Milstead, M., & Hale, C. (1988). Components of children's metamemory: Implications for strategy generalization. In F. E. Weinert & M. Perlmutter (eds.), *Memory development: Universal changes and individual differences.* Hillsdale, N.J.: Erlbaum.

Borton, T. (1970). *Reach, touch, and teach: Student concerns and process education.* New York: McGraw-Hill.

Bossert, S. T. (1988). Cooperative activities in the classroom. In E. Z. Rothkopf (ed.), *Review of research in education* (Vol. 15). Washington, D.C.: American Educational Research Association.

Bowden, C. L. (1994). Bipolar disorder and creativity. In M. P. Shaw & M. A. Runco (eds.), *Creativity and affect.* Norwood, N.J.: Ablex.

Bower, T. G. R. (1989). *The rational infant: Learning in infancy.* New York: Freeman.

Bowlby, J. (1982). *Attachment and loss (Vol. 1): Attachment* (2nd ed.). London: Hogarth.

Bracey, G. W. (1994). Slouching along the information footpath. *Technos, 3,* 8–11.

Braddock, J. H. II, & Slavin, R. E. (1993). Why ability grouping must end: Achieving excellence and equity in American education. *Journal of Intergroup Relations, 20,* 51–64.

Bradshaw, G. L., & Anderson, J. R. (1982). Elaborative encoding as an explanation of levels of processing. *Journal of Verbal Learning and Verbal Behavior, 21,* 165–174.

Bradshaw, J. L. (1989). *Hemispheric specialization and psychological function.* New York: Wiley.

Brandon, P. R., Newton, B. J., & Hammond, O. W. (1987). Children's mathematics achievement in Hawaii: Sex differences favoring girls. *American Educational Research Journal, 24,* 437–461.

Brandt, R. (1994). On creating an environment where all students learn: A conversation with Al Mamary. *Educational Leadership, 51,* 24–28.

Bransford, J. D., & Johnson, M. K. (1973). Consideration of some problems in comprehension. In W. G. Chase (ed.), *Visual information processing* (pp. 383–438). New York: Academic.

Brantner, J. P., & Doherty, M. A. (1983). A review of timeout: A conceptual and methodological analysis. In S. Axelrod & J. Apsche (eds.), *The effects of punishment on human behavior.* New York: Academic.

Braun, C. (1976). Teacher expectations: Sociopsychological dynamics. *Review of Educational Research, 46,* 185–213.

Brehm, J. W., & Self, E. A. (1989). The intensity of motivation. *Annual Review of Psychology, 40,* 109–131.

Brisk, M. E. (1991). Toward multilingual and multicultural mainstream education. *Journal of Education, 173,* 114–129.

Brodinsky, B. (1985). Tackling problems through lateral thinking. An interview with Edward de Bono. *School Administrator, 42,* 10–13.

Brodley, B. T. (1993). Response to Patterson's "Winds of change for client-centered counseling." *Journal of Humanistic Education and Development, 31,* 139–143.

Bronfenbrenner, U. (1977). Is early intervention effective? In S. Cohen & T. J. Comiskey (eds.), *Child development: Contemporary perspectives.* Itasca, Ill.: Peacock.

———. (1989). Ecological systems theory. In R. Vasta (ed.), *Annals of child development* (Vol. 6). Greenwich, Conn.: JAI Press.

Brophy, J. E. (1981). Teacher praise: A functional analysis. *Review of Educational Research, 51*(1), 5–32.

———. (1983). If only it were true: A response to Greer. *Educational Researcher, 12,* 10–12.

Brophy, J. E., & Evertson, C. M. (1974). *Process-product correlations in the Texas teacher effectiveness study: Final report.* Research Report No. 74–4. Austin: Research and Development Center for Teacher Education, University of Texas.

———. (1976). *Learning from teaching: A developmental perspective.* Boston: Allyn & Bacon.

Brophy, J. E., & Good, T. L. (1974). *Teacher–student relationships: Causes and consequences.* New York: Holt, Rinehart & Winston.

Brown, H. D., & Kosslyn, S. M. (1993). Cerebral lateralization. *Current Opinion in Neurobiology, 3,* 183–186.

Brown, J. S., Collins, A., & Duguid, P. (1989). Situated cognition and the culture of learning. *Educational Researcher, 18,* 32–42.

Bruer, J. T. (1993). The mind's journey from novice to expert: If we know the route, we can help students negotiate their way. *American Education, 17,* 6–15, 38–46.

Bruner, J. (1992). Foreword to the second edition. In S. Farnham-Diggory, *Cognitive processes in education* (2nd ed.). New York: HarperCollins.

Bruner, J. S. (1957a). On going beyond the information given. In *Contemporary approaches to cognition.* Cambridge, Mass.: Harvard University Press.

———. (1957b). On perceptual readiness. *Psychological Review, 64,* 123–152.

———. (1961a). The act of discovery. *Harvard Educational Review, 31,* 21–32.

———. (1961b). *The process of education.* Cambridge, Mass.: Harvard University Press.

———. (1966). *Toward a theory of instruction.* Cambridge, Mass.: Harvard University Press.

———. (1973). Organization of early skilled action. *Child Development, 44,* 1–11.

———. (1983). *Child's talk.* New York: Norton.

———. (1985). Models of the learner. *Educational Researcher, 14,* 5–8.

———. (1986). *Actual minds, possible worlds.* Cambridge, Mass.: Harvard University Press.

———. (1990a). *Acts of meaning.* Cambridge, Mass.: Harvard University Press.

———. (1990b). Metaphors of consciousness and cognition in the history of psychology. In D. E. Leary (ed.), *Metaphors in the history of psychology.* New York: Cambridge University Press.

Bruner, J. S., Goodnow, J. J., & Austin, G. A. (1956). *A study of thinking.* New York: Wiley.

Burks, L. C. (1994). Ability group level and achievement. *School Community Journal, 4,* 11–24.

Burns, R. B. (1984). How time is used in elementary schools: The activity structure of classrooms. In L. W. Anderson (ed.), *Time and school learning: Theory, research and practice.* London: Croom Helm.

Busch, B. (1993). Attention deficits: Current concepts, controversies, management, and approaches to classroom instruction. *Annals of Dyslexia, 43,* 5–25.

Bussey, K., & Bandura, A. (1992). Self-regulatory mechanisms governing gender development. *Child Development, 63,* 1236–1250.

Butcher, J. (1993). The content, structure and meaning of teachers' management schemata: Ordered trees of novice and expert teachers. Special Issue: International conference on teacher thinking: I. *Journal of Structural Learning, 11,* 299–318.

Calderhead, J. (1989). Reflective teaching and teacher education. *Teaching & Teacher Education, 5,* 43–51.

Calfee, R. (1981). Cognitive psychology and educational practice. In D. C. Berliner (ed.), *Review of research in education* (Vol. 9). Washington, D.C.: American Educational Research Association.

———. (1985). Computer literacy and book literacy: Parallels and contrasts. *Educational Researcher, 14,* 8–13.

Cameron, A. W. (1956). *A guide to eastern Canadian mammals.* Ottawa: Department of Northern Affairs and National Resources.

Cameron, J., & Pierce, W. D. (1994). Reinforcement, reward, and intrinsic motivation: A meta-analysis. *Review of Educational Research, 64,* 363–423.

Campbell, F. A., & Ramey, C. T. (1990). The relationship between Piagetian cognitive development, mental test performance, and academic achievement in high-risk students with and without early educational intervention. *Intelligence, 14,* 293–308.

Campbell, R. L. (1993). Epistemological problems for neo-Piagetians. *Monographs of the Society for Research in Child Development, 58,* 168–191.

Canter, L., & Canter, M. (1992). *Lee Canter's assertive discipline: Positive management for today's classroom.* Santa Monica, Calif.: Lee Canter & Associates.

Carey, S. T. (1987). Reading comprehension in first and second languages of immersion and Francophone students. *Canadian Journal for Exceptional Children, 3,* 103–108.

Carpentieri, S. C., & Morgan, S. B. (1994). A comparison of patterns of cognitive functioning of autistic and nonautistic retarded children on the Stanford-Binet—fourth edition. *Journal of Autism and Developmental Disorders, 24,* 215–223.

Carroll, J. B. (1963). A model of school learning. *Teachers College Record, 64,* 723–733.

———. (1989). The Carroll model: A 25-year retrospective and prospective view. *Educational Researcher, 18*(1), 26–31.

Case, R. (1975). Gearing the demands of instruction to the developmental capacities of the learner. *Review of Educational Research, 45,* 59–87.

———. (1991). Stages in the development of the young child's first sense of self. *Developmental Review, 11,* 210–230.

Cassel, P., & Dreikurs, R. (1972). *Discipline without tears.* Toronto: Alfred Adler Institute of Ontario.

Castle, E. M. (1993). Minority student attrition research: Higher education's challenge for human resource development. *Educational Researcher, 22,* 24–30.

Cattell, R. B. (1971). *Abilities: Their structure, growth and action.* Boston: Houghton Mifflin.

Cermak, L. S., & Craik, F. I. (eds.). (1979). *Levels of processing in human memory.* Hillsdale, N.J.: Erlbaum.

Chandler, P. S. (1994). The gender equity quiz. *Learning, 22,* 57.

Chang, R., & Page, R. C. (1991). Characteristics of the self-actualized person: Visions from the east and west. *Counseling and Values, 36,* 2–10.

Chapman, J. W. (1988). Learning disabled children's self-concepts. *Review of Educational Research, 58,* 347–371.

Cheng, Pui-wan. (1993). Metacognition and giftedness. *Gifted Child Quarterly, 37,* 105–112.

Cherkes-Julkowski, M., & Stolzenberg, J. (1991). The learning disability of attention deficit disorder. *Learning Disabilities: A Multidisciplinary Journal, 2,* 8–15.

Cherry, E. C. (1953). Some experiments on the recognition of speech with one and two ears. *Journal of the Acoustical Society of America, 25,* 975–979.

Chester, R. D. (1992). Views from the mainstream: Learning disabled students as perceived by regular education classroom teachers and by non-learning disabled secondary students. *Canadian Journal of School Psychology, 8,* 93–102.

Chi, M., Glaser, R., & Farr, M. (eds.) (1988). *The nature of expertise.* Hillsdale, N.J.: Erlbaum.

Chi, M. T. H., & Glaser, R. (1980). The measurement of expertise: Analysis of the development of knowledge and skill as a basis for assessing achievement. In E. L. Baker & E. S. Quellmalz (eds.), *Educational testing and evaluation: Design, analysis and policy.* Beverly Hills: Sage.

Christian, L., & Morgan, G. (1993). Roses are red, violets are blue, my child is gifted and my family's a zoo. *Gifted Child Today, 16,* 14–17.

Cizek, G. J. (1993a). Reconsidering standards and criteria. *Journal of Educational Measurement, 30,* 93–106.

———. (1993b). Rethinking psychometricians' beliefs about learning. *Educational Researcher, 22,* 4–9.

Clarizio, H. F. (1992). Teachers as detectors of learning disability. *Psychology in the Schools, 29,* 28–34.

Clarizio, H. F., & Yelon, S. L. (1974). Learning theory approaches to classroom management: Rationale and intervention techniques. In A. R. Brown & C. Avery (eds.), *Modifying children's behavior: A book of readings.* Springfield, Ill.: Thomas.

Clark, R. E. (1982). Antagonism between achievement and enjoyment in ATI studies. *Educational Psychology, 13,* 92–101.

Clawson, E. U., & Barnes, B. R. (1973). The effects of organizers on the learning of structured anthropology materials in the elementary grades. *Journal of Experimental Education, 42,* 11–15.

Clements, D. H. (1991). Enhancement of creativity in computer environments. *American Educational Research Journal, 28,* 173–187.

Clements, S. D. (1966). *Minimal brain dysfunction in children: Terminology and identification* (NINDB Monograph No. 3). Washington, D.C.: U.S. Department of Health and Human Service.

Cohen, D. K. (1972). Does IQ matter? *Current, 141,* 19–30.

Cohen, E. G. (1994). Restructuring the classroom: Conditions for productive small groups. *Review of Educational Research, 64,* 1–35.

Cohen, M. J., Riccio, C. A., & Gonzalez, J. J. (1994). Methodological differences in the diagnosis of attention-deficit hyperactivity disorder: Impact on prevalence. *Journal of Emotional and Behavioral Disorders, 2,* 31–38.

Cohn, M. M., & Kottkamp, R. B. (1993). *Teachers: The missing voice in education.* New York: State University of New York.

Colby, A., & Kohlberg, L. (1984). Invariant sequence and internal consistency in moral judgment stages. In W. M. Kurtines & J. L. Gewirtz (eds.), *Morality, moral behavior, and moral development* (pp. 41–51). New York: Wiley.

Cole, P. G. (1993). A critical analysis of Siegel's case for revision of the learning disability construct. Special issue, Festchrift for Professor John McLeod. *International Journal of Disability, Development, & Education, 40,* 5–21.

Collett, J., & Serrano, B. (1992). Stirring it up: The inclusive classroom. *New Directions for Teaching and Learning, 49,* 35–48.

Collins, A., Brown, J. S., & Newman, S. E. (1989). Cognitive apprenticeship: Teaching the craft of reading, writing, and mathematics. In L. B. Resnick (ed.), *Knowing, learning, and instruction: Essays in honor of Robert Glaser.* Hillsdale, N.J.: Erlbaum.

Combs, A. W. (1982). *A personal approach to teaching: Beliefs that make a difference.* Boston: Allyn & Bacon.

Cook, C. (1994). Factors affecting ILS implementation. *Media and Methods—Exploration in Education, 30,* 66–67.

Coon, C. L. (1915). *North Carolina schools and academies.* Raleigh: Edwards and Broughton.

Coopersmith, S. (1967). *The antecedents of self-esteem.* San Francisco: Freeman.

Copeland, W. D. (1987). Classroom management and student teachers' cognitive abilities: A relationship. *American Educational Research Journal, 24,* 219–236.

Corno, L., & Snow, R. E. (1986). Adapting teaching to individual differences among learners. In M. C. Wittrock (ed.), *Handbook of research on teaching* (3rd ed.) (pp. 605–629). New York: Macmillan.

Cowed by cows. *Edmonton Journal,* June 11, 1992, p. B2.

Craik, F. M., & Lockhart, R. S. (1972). Levels of processing: A framework for memory research. *Journal of Verbal Learning and Verbal Behavior, 11,* 671–684.

Crawford, M. A., Doyle, W., Leaf, A., Leighfield, M., Ghebremeskel, K., & Phylactos, A. (1993). Nutrition and neurodevelopmental disorders. *Nutrition and Health, 9,* 81–97.

Crockett, L. J., & Petersen, A. C. (1987). Findings from the Early Adolescence Study. In R. M. Lerner & T. T. Foch (eds.), *Biological-psychosocial interactions in early adolescence: A life-span perspective.* Hillsdale, N.J.: Erlbaum.

Cronbach, L. J., & Snow, R. E. (1977). *Aptitudes and instructional methods.* New York: Irvington.

Crooks, T. J. (1988). The impact of classroom evaluation practices on students. *Review of Educational Research, 58,* 438–481.

Cropley, A. J. (1992). *More ways than one: Fostering creativity.* Norwood, N.J.: Ablex.

Cross, T. L., Coleman, L. J., & Terhaar-Yonkers, M. (1991). The social cognition of gifted adolescents in schools: Managing the stigma of giftedness. *Journal for the Education of the Gifted, 15,* 44–55.

Crowder, N. A. (1961). Characteristics of branching programs. In D. P. Scannell (ed.), *Conference on programmed learning.* Lawrence: University of Kansas, Studies in Education.

——. (1963). On the differences between linear and intrinsic programming. *Phi Delta Kappan, 44,* 250–254.

Csikszentmihalyi, M. (1994). Creativity. In R. J. Sternberg (ed.), *Encyclopedia of human intelligence* (Vol. 1). New York: Macmillan.

Cummins, J. (1986). Empowering minority students: A framework for intervention. *Harvard Educational Review, 56,* 18–36.

Cziko, G. A. (1992). The evaluation of bilingual education. *Educational Researcher, 21,* 10–15.

Daily Report Card, August 14, 1995. Education Commission of the States and the National Education Goals Panel. Washington, D.C.

Damon, W., & Colby, A. (1987). Social influence and moral change. In W. M. Kurtines & J. L. Gewirtz (eds.), *Moral development through social interaction.* New York: Wiley.

Dansereau, D. F. (1985). Learning strategy research. In J. W. Segal, S. F. Chipman, & R. Glaser (eds.), *Thinking and learning skills* (pp. 1, 209–240). Hillsdale, N.J.: Erlbaum.

Darley, J. M., & Shultz, T. R. (1990). Moral rules: Their content and acquisition. *Annual Review of Psychology, 41,* 525–556.

Das, J. P. (1992). Beyond a unidimensional scale of merit. *Intelligence, 16,* 137–149.

Das, J. P., Mishra, R. K., & Pool, J. E. (1995). An experiment on cognitive remediation of word-reading difficulty. *Journal of Learning Disabilities, 28,* 66–79.

Das, J. P., Naglieri, J. A., & Kirby, J. R. (1994). *Assessment of cognitive processes.* Boston: Allyn & Bacon.

Davydov, V. V. (1995). The influence of L. S. Vygotsky on education theory, research, and practice. *Educational Researcher, 24,* 12–21.

Deale, R. N. (1975). *Examinations bulletin 32: Assessment and testing in the secondary school.* London: Evans/Methuen.

Deaux, K. (1985). Sex and gender. *Annual Review of Psychology, 36,* 49–81.

de Bono, E. (1970). *Lateral thinking: A textbook of creativity.* London: Ward Lock Educational.

——. (1976). *Teaching thinking.* London: Temple Smith.

De Bruijn, H. F. M. (1993). Computer-aided learning for adults: A new approach. *International Journal of Lifelong Education, 12,* 303–312.

de Charms, R. (1972). Personal causation training in the schools. *Journal of Applied Psychology, 2,* 95–113.

DeFries, J. C., Plomin, R., & Fulker, D. W. (1994). *Nature–nurture during middle childhood.* Cambridge, Mass.: Blackwell.

Delgado-Hachey, M., & Miller, S. A. (1993). Mothers' accuracy in predicting their children's IQs: Its relationship to antecedent variables, mothers' academic achievement demands, and children's achievement. *Journal of Experimental Education, 62,* 43–59.

DeLong, G. R. (1993). Effects of nutrition on brain development in humans. *American Journal of Clinical Nutrition, 57,* 286s–290s.

Dennison, G. (1969). *The lives of children: The story of the First Street School.* New York: Random House (Vintage Books).

Derry, S. J., & Murphy, D. A. (1986). Designing systems that train learning ability: From theory to practice. *Review of Educational Research, 56,* 1–39.

Deutsch, W. (1992). Teaching machines, programming, computers, and instructional technology: The roots of performance technology. *Performance and Instruction, 31,* 14–20.

Diamond, K. E., & LeFurgy, W. G. (1994). Attitudes of parents of preschool children toward integration. *Early Education and Development, 5,* 69–77.

Diaz, R. M. (1983). Thought and two languages: The impact of bilingualism on cognitive development. In E. W. Gordon (ed.), *Review of research in education* (Vol. 10). Washington, D.C.: American Educational Research Association.

Dickens, C. (1843/1986). *A Christmas carol.* London: Octopus Books.

Dinkmeyer, D., & Dinkmeyer, D., Jr. (1976). Logical consequences: A key to the reduction of disciplinary problems. *Phi Delta Kappan, 57,* 664–666.

Downes, T. (1991). The changing nature of teaching: The increasing complexity of tasks and tools. *Education and Computing, 7,* 239–244.

Doyle, W. (1979). Making managerial decisions in classrooms. In D. Duke (ed.), *78th yearbook of the National Society for the Study of Education: Part 2. Classroom management.* Chicago: University of Chicago Press.

——. (1986). Classroom organization and management. In M. C. Wittrock (ed.), *Handbook of research on teaching* (3rd ed.) (pp. 392–431). New York: Macmillan.

Dreikurs, R., & Grey, L. (1968). *Logical consequences: A new approach to discipline.* New York: Hawthorne.

Dreikurs, R., Grunwald, B. B., & Pepper, F. C. (1982). *Maintaining sanity in the classroom: Classroom management techniques* (2nd ed.). New York: Harper & Row.

Duda, J. L., & Nicholls, J. G. (1992). Dimensions of achievement motivation in schoolwork and sport. *Journal of Educational psychology, 84,* 290–299.

Dunn, R., Dunn, K., & Perrin, J. (1994). *Teaching young children through their individual learning styles: Practical approaches for grades K–2.* Boston: Allyn & Bacon.

Dunn, R., & Griggs, S. A. (1988). *Learning styles: Quiet revolution in American secondary schools.* Reston, Va.: National Association of Secondary School Principals.

Dweck, C. S. (1986). Motivational processes affecting learning. *American Psychologist, 41,* 1040–1048.

Dweck, C. S., & Leggett, E. L. (1988). A social-cognitive approach to motivation and personality. *Psychological Review, 95,* 256–273.

Dykman, A. (1994). Ready for the techno world? *Vocational Education Journal, 69,* 28–32.

Educational Testing Service. (1961). Judges disagree on qualities that characterize good writing. *ETS Development, 9,* 2.

Edwards, C. H. (1993). *Classroom discipline and management.* New York: Macmillan.

Edwards, V., & Redfern, A. (1992). *The world in a classroom: Language in education in Britain and Canada.* Clevedon, England: Multilingual Matters.

Eilers, R. E., & Oller, D. K. (1988). Precursors to speech. In R. Vasta (ed.), *Annals of child development* (Vol. 5). Greenwich, Conn.: JAI Press.

Eisenberg, N., Miller, P. A., Shell, R., McNalley, S., & Shea, C. (1991). Prosocial development in adolescence: A longitudinal study. *Developmental Psychology, 27,* 849–857.

Eisner, E. W. (1982). An artistic approach to supervision. In T. J. Sergiovanni (ed.), *Supervision of teaching* (ASCD 1982 Yearbook). Alexandria, Va.: Association for Supervision and Curriculum Development.

——. (1967). Educational objectives: Help or hindrance? *School Review, 75,* 250–260.

Ellzey, J., & Karnes, F. A. (1993). Comparison of scores on the WISC-R and the Stanford-Binet, fourth edition, for rural gifted students. *Rural Special Education Quarterly, 12,* 10–13.

Elmore, R. F., & Zenus, V. (1994). Enhancing social-emotional development of middle school gifted students. *Roeper Review, 16,* 182–185.

Elton, L. R. B., & Laurillard, D. M. (1979). Trends in research on student learning. *Studies in Higher Education, 4,* 87–102.

Emerson-Stonnell, S., & Carter, C. (1994). Math mentor programs. *Gifted Child Today, 17,* 26–34.

Engel, M. (1976). *Bear.* Toronto: McClelland and Stewart.

Ennis, R. H. (1976). An alternative to Piaget's conceptualization of logical competence. *Child Development, 47,* 903–919.

——. (1978). Conceptualization of children's logical competence: Piaget's propositional logic and an alternative proposal. In L. S. Siegel & C. J. Brainerd (eds.), *Alternatives to Piaget: Critical essays on the theory.* New York: Academic.

Erdley, C. A., & Dweck, C. S. (1993). Children's implicit personality theories as predictors of their social judgments. *Child Development, 64,* 863–878.

Erickson, M. T. (1992). *Behavior disorders of children and adolescents* (2nd ed.). Englewood Cliffs, N.J.: Prentice-Hall.

Erikson, E. H. (1959). *Identity and the life cycle: Selected papers.* Psychological Issue Monograph Series, I (No. 1). New York: International Universities Press.

Erlenmeyer-Kimling, L., & Jarvik, L. F. (1963). Genetics and intelligence: A review. *Science, 142,* 1477–1478.

Evans, K. M., & King, J. A. (1994a). Outcome-based and gifted education: Can we assume continued support? *Roeper Review, 16,* 260–264.

——. (1994b). Research on OBE: What we know and don't know. *Educational leadership, 51,* 12–17.

Evans, R. I. (1989). *Albert Bandura: The man and his ideas—a dialogue.* New York: Praeger.

Evertson, C. M., Anderson, L. M., & Brophy, J. E. (1978). *Texas junior high school study: Final report of process-outcome relationships.* Research Report No. 4061 (Vol. 1). Austin: Research and Development Center for Teacher Education, University of Texas.

Evertson, C. M., & Harris, A. H. (1992). What we know about managing classrooms. *Educational Leadership, 49,* 74–78.

Evra, J. V. (1990). *Television and child development.* Hillsdale, N.J.: Erlbaum.

Ewell, P. T. (1991). To capture the ineffable: New forms of assessment in higher education. In G. Grant (ed.), *Review of research in education* (Vol. 17). Washington, D.C.: American Educational Research Association.

Ewer, R. F. (1973). *The carnivores.* Ithaca, N.Y.: Cornell University Press.

Fabricius, W. V., & Wellman, H. M. (1993). Two roads diverged: Young children's ability to judge distance. *Child Development, 64,* 399–419.

Fahrmeler, L. C. (1991). The child within: Enhancing our creativity. *The Creative Child and Adult Quarterly, 16,* 30–37.

Fair, E. M. III, & Silvestri, L. (1992). Effects of rewards, competition and outcome on intrinsic motivation. *Journal of Instructional Psychology, 19,* 3–8.

Farnham-Diggory, S. (1992). *Cognitive processes in education* (2nd ed.). New York: HarperCollins.

Farr, R., & Tone, B. (1994). *Portfolio and performance assessment: Helping students evaluate their progress as readers and writers.* Fort Worth, Texas: Harcourt Brace.

Feingold, A. (1992). Sex differences in variability in intellectual abilities: A new look at an old controversy. *Review of Educational Research, 62,* 61–84.

———. (1993). Cognitive gender differences: A developmental perspective. *Sex Roles: A Journal of Research, 29,* 91–112.

Feldman, D. H. (1993). Child prodigies: A distinctive form of giftedness. *Gifted Child Quarterly, 37,* 188–193.

Feldt, L. S. (1993). The relationship between the distribution of item difficulties and test reliability. *Applied Measurement in Education, 6,* 37–48.

Fenstermacher, G. D., & Soltis, J. F. (1992). *Approaches to teaching.* New York: Teachers College Press.

Fernald, P. S., & Jordan, E. A. (1991). Programmed instruction versus standard text in introductory psychology. *Teaching of Psychology, 18,* 205–211.

Ferrington, G., & Loge, K. (1992). Virtual reality: A new learning environment. *The Computing Teacher, 20,* 16–19.

Fetterman, D. M. (1994). Terman's giftedness study. In R. J. Sternberg (ed.), *Encyclopedia of human intelligence* (Vol. 2). New York: Macmillan.

Feuerstein, R. (1979). *The dynamic assessment of retarded performers.* Baltimore: University Park Press.

———. (1980). *Instrumental enrichment: An intervention program for cognitive modifiability.* Baltimore: University Park Press.

———. (1994). Learning potential assessment device. In R. J. Sternberg (ed.), *Encyclopedia of human intelligence* (Vol. 2). New York: Macmillan.

Fishkin, J., Keniston, K., & MacKinnon, C. (1973). Moral reasoning and political ideology. *Journal of Personality and Social Psychology, 27,* 109–119.

Flanders, N. A. (1970). *Analyzing teacher behavior.* Reading, Mass.: Addison-Wesley.

Flavell, J. H. (1985). *Cognitive development* (2nd ed.). Englewood Cliffs, N.J.: Prentice-Hall.

Fleming, M., & Chambers, B. (1983). Teacher-made tests: Windows on the classroom. In W. E. Hathaway (ed.), *New directions for testing and measurement: Vol. 19, Testing in the schools.* San Francisco: Jossey-Bass.

Fletcher, J. M. (1992). The validity of distinguishing children with language and learning disabilities according to discrepancies with IQ: Introduction to the special series. *Journal of Learning Disabilities, 25,* 546–548.

Follman, J. (1991). Teachers' estimates of pupils' IQs and pupils' tested IQs. *Psychological Reports, 69,* 350.

Franchi, J. (1994). Virtual reality: An overview. *Techtrends, 39,* 23–26.

Freiberg, H. J., & Driscoll, A. (1992). *Universal Teaching Strategies.* Boston: Allyn & Bacon.

Frisch, R. E., & Revelle, R. (1970). Height and weight at menarche and a hypothesis of critical body weights and adolescent events. *Science, 169,* 397–398.

Fuchs, D., & Fuchs, L. S. (1995). What's "special" about special education? *Phi Delta Kappan, 76,* 542–546.

Fuchs-Beauchamp, K. D., Karnes, M. B., & Johnson, L. J. (1993). Creativity and intelligence in preschoolers. *Gifted Child Quarterly, 37,* 113–117.

Fuller, B., & Heyneman, S. P. (1989). Third world school quality: Current collapse, future potential. *Educational Researcher, 18,* 12–19.

Gabel, D. L., Kogan, M. H., & Sherwood, R. D. (1980). A summary of research in science education—1978. *Science Education, 64,* 429–568.

Gage, N. L. (1964). Theories of teaching. In E. R. Hilgard (ed.), *Theories of learning and instruction: The sixty-third yearbook of the National Society for the Study of Education.* Chicago: University of Chicago Press.

Gagné, E. D. (1985). *The cognitive psychology of school learning.* Boston: Little, Brown.

Gagné, E. D., Yekovich, C. W., & Yekovich, F. R. (1993). *The cognitive psychology of school learning* (2nd ed.). New York: HarperCollins.

Gagné, R. M. (1965). *The conditions of learning.* New York: Holt, Rinehart & Winston.

——. (1974). *Essentials of learning for instruction.* Hinsdale, Ill.: Dryden Press.

——. (1977a). *The conditions of learning* (3rd ed.). New York: Holt, Rinehart & Winston.

——. (1977b). Instructional programs. In M. H. Marx & M. E. Bunch (eds.), *Fundamentals and applications of learning.* New York: Macmillan.

——. (1985). *The conditions of learning* (4th ed.). New York: Holt, Rinehart & Winston.

Gagné, R. M., & Briggs, L. J. (1983). *Principles of instructional design* (3rd ed.). New York: Holt, Rinehart & Winston.

Gagné, R. M., Briggs, L. J., & Wager, W. W. (1992). *Principles of instructional design* (4th ed.). Fort Worth: Harcourt Brace Jovanovich.

Gagné, R. M., & Dick, W. (1983). Instructional psychology. *Annual Review of Psychology, 34,* 261–295.

Gagné, R. M., & Driscoll, M. P. (1988). *Essentials of learning for instruction* (2nd ed.). Englewood Cliffs, N.J.: Prentice-Hall.

Gallagher, J. J. (1960). *Analysis of research on the education of gifted children.* State of Illinois: Office of the Superintendent of Public Instruction.

——. (1993). Ability grouping: A tool for educational excellence. *College Board Review, 168,* 21–27.

——. (1994). Teaching and learning: New models. *Annual Review of Psychology, 45,* 171–195.

Galton, F. (1869). *Hereditary genius: An inquiry into its laws and consequences.* London: Macmillan.

Garcia, E. E. (1993). Language, culture, and education. In L. Darling-Hammond (ed.), *Review of research in education* (Vol. 19). Washington, D.C.: American Educational Research Association.

García, G. E., & Pearson, P. D. (1994). Assessment and diversity. In L. Darling-Hammond (ed.), *Review of research in education* (Vol. 20). Washington, D.C.: American Educational Research Association.

Gardner, H. (1983). *Frames of mind: The theory of multiple intelligences.* New York: Basic Books.

——. (1993). Educating for understanding. *American School Board Journal, 180,* 20–24.

Gardner, H., & Hatch, T. (1989). Multiple intelligences go to school: Educational implications of the theory of multiple intelligences. *Educational Researcher, 18,* 4–10.

Garner, R. (1992). Self-regulated learning, strategy shifts, and shared expertise: Reactions to Palincsar and Klenk. *Journal of Learning Disabilities, 25,* 226–229.

Gaynor, J. L. R., & Runco, M. A. (1992). Family size, birth-order, age-interval, and the creativity of children. *Journal of Creative Behavior, 26,* 108–118.

Gelman, R. (1982). Basic numerical abilities. In R. J. Sternberg (ed.), *Advances in the psychology of human intelligence* (Vol. 1). Hillsdale, N.J.: Erlbaum.

Gelman, R., Meck, E., & Merkin, S. (1986). Young children's numerical competence. *Cognitive Development, 1,* 1–29.

Genesee, F. (1985). Second language learning through immersion: A review of U.S. programs. *Review of Educational Research, 55,* 541–561.

George, P. S. (1993). Tracking and ability grouping in the middle school: Tentative truths. *Middle School Journal, 24,* 17–24.

Getzels, J. W., & Jackson, P. W. (1962). *Creativity and intelligence.* New York: Wiley.

Gilligan, C. (1982). *In a different voice: Psychological theory and women's development.* Cambridge, Mass.: Harvard University Press.

Giroux, A. (1992). Teaching moral thinking: A reconceptualization. *Journal of Educational Thought, 26,* 114–120.

Glaser, R., & Bassok, M. (1989). Learning theory and the study of instruction. In M. R. Rosenzweig & L. W. Porter (eds.), *Annual review of psychology, 40,* 631–666.

Glass, A. L., Holyoak, K. J., & Santa, J. L. (1979). *Cognition.* Reading, Mass.: Addison-Wesley.

Glasser, W. (1969). *Schools without failure.* New York: Harper & Row.

Goldenberg, C. (1992). The limits of expectations: A case for case knowledge about teacher expectancy effects. *American Educational Research Journal, 29,* 517–544.

Goldschmid, M. L., & Bentler, P. M. (1968). *Conservation concept diagnostic kit: Manual and keys.* San Diego: Educational and Industrial Testing Service.

Goodenough, F. (1926). *Measurement of intelligence by drawings.* New York: Harcourt, Brace & World.

Gordon, M., Thomason, D., Cooper, S., & Ivers, C. L. (1991). Nonmedical treatment of ADHD/Hyperactivity: The attention training system. *Journal of School Psychology, 29,* 151–159.

Gordon, T. (1974). *T.E.T.: Teacher effectiveness training.* New York: Peter H. Wyden.

Gordon, W. J. J. (1961). *Synectics: The development of creative capacity.* New York: Harper & Row.

Gould, S. J. (1981). *The mismeasure of man.* New York: Norton.

Grant, G. (1991). Introduction. In G. Grant (ed.), *Review of research in education* (Vol. 17). Washington, D.C.: American Educational Research Association.

Grant, J. P. (1993). *The state of the world's children:1993.* New York: Oxford University Press.

Greene, J. C. (1985). Relationships among learning and attribution theory motivational variables. *American Educational Research Journal, 22,* 65–78.

Greer, R. D. (1983). Contingencies of the science and technology of teaching and prebehavioristic research practices in education. *Educational Researcher, 12,* 3–9.

Gregorc, A. F. (1982). *Gregorc style delineator: Development, technical and administrative manual.* Maynard, Mass.: Gabriel Systems.

Grimmett, P. P., & Mackinnon, A. M. (1992). Craft knowledge and the education of teachers. In G. Grant (ed.), *Review of research in education* (Vol. 18). Washington, D.C.: American Educational Research Association.

Grippin, P. C., & Peters, S. C. (1984). Learning theories and learning outcomes: The connection. Lanham, Md.: University Press of America.

Gronlund, N. E. (1968). *Constructing achievement tests.* Englewood Cliffs, N.J.: Prentice-Hall.

——. (1972). *Stating behavioral objectives for classroom instruction.* New York: Macmillan.

——. (1975). *Determining accountability for classroom instruction.* Itasca, Ill.: F. E. Peacock.

Grossman, H. (1995). *Special education in a diverse society.* Boston: Allyn & Bacon.

Grossnickle, D. R., & Sesko, F. P. (1990). *Preventive discipline for effective teaching and learning.* Reston, Va.: National Association of Secondary School Principals.

Grotevant, H. D., Scarr, S., & Weinberg, R. A. (1977). Intellectual development in family constellations with adopted and natural children: A test of the Zajonc and Markus model. *Child Development, 48,* 1699–1703.

Grusec, J. E. (1992). Social learning theory and developmental psychology: The legacies of Robert Sears and Albert Bandura. *Developmental Psychology, 28,* 776–786.

Guffey, D. G. (1991). Ritalin: What educators and parents should know. *Journal of Instructional Psychology, 19,* 167–169.

Guild, P. (1994). Making sense of learning styles. *School Administrator, 51,* 8–13.

Guilford, J. P. (1950). Creativity. *American Psychologist, 5,* 444–454.

——. (1959). Three faces of intellect. *American Psychologist, 14,* 469–479.

——. (1962). Factors that aid and hinder creativity. *Teachers College Record, 63,* 380–392.

——. (1967). *The nature of human intelligence.* New York: McGraw-Hill.

Gullickson, A. R. (1985). Student evaluation techniques and their relationship to grade and curriculum. *Journal of Educational Research, 79,* 96–100.

Gump, P. V. (1969). Intra-setting analysis: The third grade classroom as a special but instructive case. In E. Williams & H. Rausch (eds.), *Naturalistic viewpoints in psychological research.* New York: Holt, Rinehart & Winston.

Guri-Rozenblit, S. (1993). Differentiating between distance/open education systems: Parameters for comparison. *International Review of Education, 39,* 287–306.

Guskey, T. R. (1994). What you assess may not be what you get. *Educational Leadership, 51,* 51–54.

Gustafsson, J. E., & Undheim, J. O. (1992). Stability and change in broad and narrow factors of intelligence from ages 12 to 15. *Journal of Educational Psychology, 84,* 141–149.

Guthrie, E. R. (1935). *The psychology of learning*. New York: Harper & Brothers.

Gutiérrez, R., & Slavin, R. E. (1992). Achievement effects of the nongraded elementary school: A best evidence synthesis. *Review of Educational Research, 62,* 333–376.

Hadaway, N. L., & Marek-Schroer, M. (1994). Student portfolios: Toward equitable assessments for gifted students. *Equity and Excellence in Education, 27,* 70–74.

Haddon, F. A., & Lytton, H. (1968). Teaching approach and the development of divergent thinking abilities in primary schools. *British Journal of Educational Psychology, 38,* 171–180.

Haertel, E. H. (1991). New forms of teacher assessment. In G. Grant (ed.), *Review of research in education* (Vol. 17). Washington, D.C.: American Educational Research Association.

Haladyna, T. M., Nolen, S. B., & Haas, N. S. (1991). Raising standardized achievement test scores and the origins of test score pollution. *Educational Researcher, 20,* 2–7.

Hall, F. R., & Kelson, K. R. (1959). *The mammals of North America* (Vol. 2). New York: Ronald Press.

Hallahan, D. P., & Kauffman, J. M. (1994). *Exceptional children: Introduction to special education* (6th ed.). Boston: Allyn & Bacon.

Hallman, R. J. (1967). Techniques of creative teaching. *Journal of Creative Behavior, 1,* 325–330.

Halpern, D. F., & Coren, S. (1990). Laterality and longevity: Is left-handedness associated with younger age at death? In S. Coren (ed.), *Left-handedness: Behavioral implications and anomalies.* Amsterdam: Elsevier.

Hammill, D. D. (1993). A brief look at the learning disabilities movement in the United States. *Journal of Learning Disabilities, 26,* 295–310.

Haney, R. E., & Sorenson, J. S. (1977). *Individually guided science.* Reading, Mass.: Addison-Wesley.

Harel, I., & Papert, S. (1990). Software design as a learning environment. *Interactive Learning Environments, 1,* 1–32.

Harrington, J., Harrington, C., & Karns, E. (1991). The Marland report: Twenty years later. *Journal for the Education of the Gifted, 15,* 31–43.

Harris, B. D. (1963). *Children's drawings as measures of intellectual maturity.* New York: Harcourt, Brace & World.

Haskins, R. (1989). Beyond metaphor: The efficacy of early childhood education. *American Psychologist, 44,* 274–282.

Hativa, N., & Becker, H. J. (eds.). (1994). Computer-based integrated learning systems: Research and theory. *International Journal of Educational Research, 21,* 1–119.

Hauser, R. M., & Sewell, W. H. (1985). Birth order and educational attainment in full sibships. *American Educational Research Journal, 22,* 1–23.

Hay, D. F., Stimson, C. A., & Castle, J. (1991). A meeting of minds in infancy: Imitation and desire. In D. Frye & C. Moore (eds.), *Children's theories of mind: Mental states and social understanding.* Hillsdale, N.J.: Erlbaum.

Haywood, H. C., & Switzky, H. N. (1986). The malleability of intelligence: Cognitive processes as a function of polygenic-experiential interaction. *School Psychology Review, 15,* 245–255.

Hebb, D. O. (1966). *A textbook of psychology* (2nd ed.). Philadelphia: Saunders.

Hedges, L., & Friedman, L. (1993). Gender differences in variability in intellectual abilities: A reanalysis of Feingold's results. *Review of Educational Research, 63,* 94–105.

Heinzen, T. E. (1991). A paradigm for research in creativity. *The Creative Child and Adult Quarterly, 16,* 164–174.

Hellige, J. B. (1990). Hemispheric assymmetry. *Annual Review of Psychology, 41,* 55–80.

Hembree, R. (1988). Correlates, causes, effects and treatment of test anxiety. *Review of Educational Research, 58,* 47–77.

Henker, B., & Whalen, C. K. (1989). Hyperactivity and attention deficits. *American Psychologist, 44,* 216–223.

Henshaw, A., Kelly, J., & Gratton, C. (1992). Skipping's for girls: Children's perceptions of gender roles and gender preferences. *Educational Research, 34,* 229–235.

Herschel, R. T. (1994). The impact of varying gender composition on group brainstorming performance in a GSS environment. *Computers in Human Behavior, 10,* 209–222.

Hess, R. D., & Azuma, H. (1991). Cultural support for schooling: Contrasts between Japan and the United States. *Educational Researcher, 20,* 2–8.

Heward, W. L., & Orlansky, M. D. (1992). *Exceptional children: An introductory survey of special education* (4th ed.). New York: Merrill.

Hewitt, J. D. (1992). *Playing fair: A guide to the management of student conduct.* Vancouver, B.C.: EduServ.

Heyns, O. S. (1967, Feb. 4). Treatment of the unborn. *Woman's Own,* p. 18.

Higbee, K. L. (1977). *Your memory: How it works and how to improve it.* Englewood Cliffs, N.J.: Prentice-Hall.

Hill, K. T., & Wigfield, A. (1984). Test anxiety: A major educational problem and what can be done about it. *Elementary School Journal, 85,* 105–126.

Hines, T. (1991). The myth of right hemisphere creativity. *Journal of Creative Behavior, 25,* 223–37.

Hintzman, D. L., & Ludham, G. (1980). Differential forgetting of prototypes and old instances: Simulation by an exemplar-based classification model. *Memory and Cognition, 8,* 378–382.

Hitz, R., & Driscoll, A. (1994). Give encouragement, not praise. *Texas Child Care, 17,* 2–11.

Hodapp, R. M., & Dykens, E. M. (1994). Mental retardation's two cultures of behavioral research. *American Journal of Mental Retardation, 98,* 675–687.

Hoepfl, M. C. (1994). Developing and evaluating multiple choice tests. *Technology Teacher, 53,* 25–26.

Hoffman, M. L. (1970). Conscience, personality, and socialization techniques. *Human Development, 13,* 90–126.

Hoge, R. D. (1988). Issues in the definition and measurement of the giftedness construct. *Educational Researcher, 17,* 12–66.

Holland, J. L., Magoon, T. M., & Spokane, A. R. (1981). Counseling psychology: Career interventions, research, and theory. In M. R. Rosenzweig & L. W. Porter (eds.), *Annual review of psychology* (Vol. 32). Palo Alto, Calif.: Annual Reviews.

Holland, R. W. (1994). Mentoring as a career development tool. *CUPA Journal, 45,* 41–44.

Holstein, C. B. (1976). Irreversible, stepwise sequence in the development of moral judgment: A longitudinal study of males and females. *Child Development, 47,* 51–61.

Horn, J. L. (1976). Human abilities: A review of research and theory in the early 1970s. In M. R. Rosenzweig & L. W. Porter (eds.), *Annual review of psychology* (Vol. 27). Palo Alto, Calif.: Annual Reviews.

Horn, J. L., & Donaldson, G. (1980). Cognitive development in adulthood. In O. G. Brim, Jr., & J. Kagan (eds.), *Constancy and change in human development.* Cambridge, Mass.: Harvard University Press.

Horn, J. M. (1983). The Texas adoption project. *Child Development, 54,* 268–275.

Horowitz, F. D., & O'Brien, M. (1986). Gifted and talented children: State of knowledge and directions for research. *American Psychologist, 41,* 1147–1152.

Horwitz, R. A. (1979). Psychological effects of the open classroom. *Review of Educational Research, 49,* 71–86.

Huber, G. L., Sorrentino, R. M., Davidson, M. A., Epplier, R., & Roth, J. W. H. (1992). Uncertainty orientation and cooperative learning: Individual differences within and across cultures. *Learning and Individual Differences, 4,* 1–24.

Huefner, D. S. (1994). The mainstreaming cases: Tensions and trends for school administrators. *Educational Administration Quarterly, 30,* 27–55.

Hughes, J. N. (1988). *Cognitive behavior therapy with children in schools.* New York: Pergamon.

Humphreys, L. G. (1985). A conceptualization of intellectual giftedness. In F. D. Horowitz & M. O'Brien (eds.), *The gifted and talented: Developmental perspectives* (pp. 331–360). Washington, D.C.: American Psychological Association.

Hunt, E. (1989). Cognitive science: Definition, status, and questions. *Annual Review of Psychology, 40,* 603–629.

Huntington, D. D., & Bender, W. N. (1993). Adolescents with learning disabilities at risk? Emotional well-being, depression, suicide. *Journal of Learning Disabilities, 26,* 159–166.

Husén, T., & Tuijnman, A. (1991). The contribution of formal schooling to the increase in intellectual capital. *Educational Researcher, 20,* 17–25.

Intons-Peterson, M. J. (1988). *Gender concepts of Swedish and American youth.* Hillsdale, N.J.: Erlbaum.

Jacklin, C. N. (1989). Female and male: Issues of gender. *American Psychologist, 44,* 127–133.

Jacobi, M. (1991). Mentoring and undergraduate academic success: A literature review. *Review of Educational Research, 61,* 505–532.

James, W. (1890). *The principles of psychology.* New York: Holt, Rinehart & Winston.

Janos, P. M., & Robinson, N. M. (1985). Psychosocial development in intellectually gifted children. In F. D. Horowitz & M. O'Brien (eds.), *The gifted and talented: Developmental perspectives* (pp. 149–195). Washington, D.C.: American Psychological Association.

Janzen, T., Graap, K., Stephanson, S., Amarshall, W., & Fitzsimmons, G. (1995). Differences in baseline EEG measures for ADD and normally achieving preadolescent males. *Biofeedback and Self Regulation, 20,* 65–82.

Jensen, A. (1980). *Bias in mental testing.* London: Methuen.

Jimenez, M. (1992, Oct. 30). Surviving high school in the '90s. *Edmonton Journal,* pp. A1, A4.

Jiménez, R. T., García, G. E., & Pearson, P. D. (1995). Three children, two languages, and strategic reading: Case studies in bilingual/monolingual education. *American Educational Research Journal, 32,* 67–97.

Johnson, D., & Johnson, R. (1975). *Learning together and alone.* Englewood Cliffs, N.J.: Prentice-Hall.

Johnson, D. W., & Johnson, R. T. (1994). *Learning together and alone: Cooperative, competitive, and individualistic learning* (4th ed.). Boston: Allyn & Bacon.

Johnson, D. W., Johnson, R. T., Holubec, E. J., & Roy, P. (1984). *Circles of learning: Cooperation in the classroom.* Alexandria, Va.: Association for Supervision and Curriculum Development.

Johnson, D. W., Maruyama, G., Johnson, R., Nelson, D., & Skon, L. (1981). Effects of cooperative, competitive and individualistic goal structures on achievement: A meta-analysis. *Psychological Bulletin, 89,* 47–62.

Jonassen, D. H. (1993). Conceptual frontiers in hypermedia environments for learning. *Journal of Educational Multimedia and Hypermedia, 2,* 331–335.

Jones, E. H., & Montenegro, X. P. (1988). *Women and minorities in school administration: Facts and figures, 1987–1988.* Arlington, Va.: American Association of School Administrators.

Justice, E. (1985). Categorization as a preferred memory strategy: Developmental changes during elementary school. *Developmental Psychology, 21,* 1105–1110.

Juvonen, J., & Bear, G. (1992). Social adjustment of children with and without learning disabilities in integrated classrooms. *Journal of Educational Psychology, 84,* 322–330.

Kagan, D. M. (1988). Teaching as clinical problem solving: A critical examination of the analogy and its implications. *Review of Educational Research, 58,* 482–505.

Kaiser-Messmer, G. (1993). Results of an empirical study into gender differences in attitudes towards mathematics. *Educational Studies in Mathematics, 25,* 209–233.

Kalish, H. I. (1981). *From behavioral science to behavior modification.* New York: McGraw-Hill.

Kamann, M. P., & Wong, B. Y. L. (1993). Inducing adaptive coping self-statements in children with learning disabilities through self-instruction training. *Journal of Learning Disabilities, 26,* 630–638.

Kanchier, C. (1988). Maximizing potential of gifted and talented students through career education. *Agate, 2,* 6–13.

Kantor, H., & Lowe, R. (1995). Class, race, and the emergence of federal education policy: From the New Deal to the Great Society. *Educational Researcher, 24,* 4–11, 21.

Kaplan, C. (1992). Teachers' punishment histories and their selection of disciplinary strategies. *Contemporary Educational Psychology, 17,* 258–265.

Karacostas, D. D., & Fisher, G. L. (1993). Chemical dependency in students with and without learning disabilities. *Journal of Learning Disabilities, 26,* 491–495.

Karges-Bone, L. (1993). Parenting the gifted young scientist: Mrs. Wizard at home. *Gifted Child Today, 16,* 55–59.

Kauffman, J. M., Lloyd, J. W., & Riedel, T. M. (1995). Inclusion of all students with emotional or behavioral disorders? Let's think again. *Phi Delta Kappan, 76,* 522–530.

Kaufman, K. F., & O'Leary, K. D. (1972). Reward, cost, and self-evaluation procedures with schizophrenic children. Unpublished manuscript, State University of New York. Cited in K. D. O'Leary & S. G. O'Leary, *Classroom management: The successful use of behavior modification.* New York: Pergamon.

Kavale, K. A., Forness, S. R., & Lorsbach, T. C. (1991). Definition for definitions of learning disabilities. *Learning Disability Quarterly, 14,* 257–266.

Kazdin, A. E., & Bootzin, R. R. (1972). The token economy: An evaluative review. *Journal of Applied Behavior Analysis, 5,* 343–372.

Kegan, R. (1982). *The evolving self: Problem and process in human development.* Cambridge, Mass.: Harvard University Press.

Keirouz, K. S. (1993). Gifted curriculum: The state of the art. *Gifted Child Today, 16,* 36–39.

Keith, T. Z., & Cool, V. A. (1992). Testing models of school learning: Effects of quality of instruction, motivation, academic coursework, and homework on academic achievement. *School Psychology Quarterly, 7,* 207–226.

Keller, F. S. (1968). Good-bye teacher. . . . *Journal of Applied Behavior Analysis, 1,* 79–89.

Kennedy, M. M. (1978). Findings from the follow-through planned variation study. *Educational Researcher, 7,* 3–11.

Kieran, E., & Gardner, H. (1992). An exchange: The unschooled mind: How children think and how schools should teach. *Teachers College Record, 94,* 397–407.

Kirby, E. A., & Kirby, S. H. (1994). Classroom discipline with attention deficit hyperactivity disorder in children. *Contemporary Education, 65,* 142–144.

Kirby, P. C., & Paradise, L. (1992). Reflective practice and effectiveness of teachers. *Psychological Reports, 70* (special issue), 1057–1058.

Kirschenbaum, H. (1991). Denigrating Carl Rogers: William Coulson's last crusade. *Journal of Counseling and Development, 69,* 411–413.

Kitano, M. K. (1991). A multicultural educational perspective on serving the culturally diverse student. *Journal for the Education of the Gifted, 15,* 4–19.

Klassen, R. (1994). Research: What does it say about mainstreaming? *Education Canada, 34,* 27–35.

Klausmeier, H. J., Rossmiller, R. A., & Saily, M. (1977). *Individually guided elementary education: Concepts and practices.* New York: Academic.

Klavas, A. (1994). In Greensboro, North Carolina: Learning style program boosts achievement and test scores. *Clearing House, 67,* 149–151.

Klein, S. S., & Ortman, P. E. (1994). Continuing the journey toward gender equity. *Educational Researcher, 23,* 13–21.

Knitzer, J., Steinberg, Z., & Fleisch, B. (1990). *At the school house door: An examination of programs and policies for children with behavioral and emotional problems.* New York: Bank Street College of Education.

Kohl, H. R. (1969). *The open classroom: A practical guide to a new way of teaching.* New York: Random House (Vintage Books).

Kohlberg, L. (1964). Development of moral character and moral ideology. In M. L. Hoffman & L. W. Hoffman (eds.), *Review of child development research* (Vol. 1). New York: Russell Sage Foundation.

——. (1971). Stages of moral development as a basis for moral education. In C. Beck, E. V. Sullivan, & B. Crittendon (eds.), *Moral education: Interdisciplinary approaches.* Toronto: University of Toronto Press.

Kohlberg, L., & Candee, D. (1984). The relationship of moral judgment to moral action. In W. M. Kurtines & J. L. Gewirtz (eds.), *Morality, moral behavior, and moral development* (pp. 52–73). New York: Wiley.

Kohlberg, L. A. (1980). *The meaning and measurement of moral development.* Worcester, Mass.: Clark University Press.

Kohn, A. (1993). Choices for children: Why and how to let students decide. *Phi Delta Kappan, 75,* 8–16, 18–21.

Korkman, M., & Pesonen, A. E. (1994). A comparison of neuropsychological test profiles of children with attention deficit-hyperactivity disorder and/or learning disorder. *Journal of Learning Disabilities, 27,* 383–392.

Korthagen, F. A. (1993). Two modes of reflection. *Teaching & Teacher Education, 9,* 317–326.

Kothkamp, R. B., Provenzo, E. F., Jr., & Cohn, M. M. (1986). Stability and change in a profession: Two decades of teacher attitudes, 1964–1984. *Phi Delta Kappan, 67,* 559–567.

Kounin, J. S. (1970). Discipline and classroom management. New York: Holt, Rinehart & Winston.

Kozma, R. B. (1991). Learning with media. *Review of Educational Research, 61, 2,* 179–211.

Krathwohl, D. R., Bloom, B. S., & Masia, B. B. (1964). *Taxonomy of educational objectives, the classification of educational goals. Handbook II: Affective domain.* New York: McKay.

Kristiansen, R. (1992). Evolution or revolution? Changes in teacher attitudes toward computers in education, 1970–1990. *Education and Computing, 8,* 71–78.

Kuhn, D. (1984). Cognitive development. In M. H. Bornstein & M. E. Lamb (eds.), *Developmental psychology: An advanced textbook* (pp. 133–180). Hillsdale, N.J.: Erlbaum.

Kulik, C. C., Kulik, J. A., & Bangert-Drowns, R. L. (1990). Effectiveness of mastery learning programs: A meta-analysis. *Review of Educational Research, 60,* 265–299.

Kulik, J. A., & Kulik, C. L. (1992). Meta-analytic findings on grouping programs. *Gifted Child Quarterly, 36,* 73–77.

Kulik, J. A., Kulik, C. C., & Cohen, P. A. (1979). A meta-analysis of outcome studies of Keller's Personalized System of Instruction. *American Psychologist, 34,* 307–318.

——. (1980). Effectiveness of computer-based college teaching: A meta-analysis of findings. *Review of Educational Research, 50,* 525–544.

Labouvie-Vief, G. (1980). Beyond formal operations: Uses and limits of pure logic in life-span development. *Human Development, 23,* 141–161.

——. (1986). Modes of knowledge and the organization of development. In M. L. Commons, L. Kohlberg, F. A. Richards, & J. Sinnott (eds.), *Beyond formal operations. 3: Models and methods in the study of adult and adolescent thought.* New York: Praeger.

Lam, T. C. L. (1992). Review of practices and problems in the evaluation of bilingual education. *Review of Educational Research, 62,* 181–203.

Lambert, W. E. (1975). Culture and language as factors in learning and education. In A. Wolfgang (ed.), *Education of immigrant students.* Toronto: Ontario Institute for Studies in Education.

Landry, R. (1987). Additive bilingualism, schooling, and special education: A minority group perspective. *Canadian Journal for Exceptional Children, 3,* 109–114.

Lapsley, D. K. (1990). Continuity and discontinuity in adolescent social cognitive development. In R. Montemayor, G. R. Adams, & T. P. Gullotta, (eds.), *From childhood to adolescence: A transitional period?* (Advances in Adolescent Development, Vol. 2). Newbury Park, Calif.: Sage.

Laurillard, D. (1988). Computers and the emancipation of students: Giving control to the learner. In P. Ramsden (ed.), *Improving learning: New perspectives.* London: Kogan Page.

Lawson, A. E. (1993). At what levels of education is the teaching of thinking effective? *Theory into Practice, 32,* 170–178.

Lee, E. S. (1951). Negro intelligence and selective migration: A Philadelphia test of the Klineberg hypothesis. *American Sociological Review, 16,* 227–233.

LeGrand-Brandt, B., Framer, J. K., & Buckmaster, A. (1993). Cognitive apprenticeship approach to helping adults learn. *New Directions for Adult and Continuing Education, 59,* 69–78.

Leinhardt, G. (1990). Capturing craft knowledge in teaching. *Educational Researcher, 19,* 18–25.

Lepper, M. R. (1981). Intrinsic and extrinsic motivation in children: Detrimental effects of superfluous social controls. In W. A. Collins (ed.), *Aspects of the development of competence: The Minnesota Symposium on Child Psychology* (Vol. 14). Hillsdale, N.J.: Erlbaum.

Lepper, M. R., & Greene, D. (1975). Turning play into work: Effects of adult surveillance and extrinsic rewards on children's intrinsic motivation. *Journal of Personality and Social Psychology, 31,* 479–486.

Lerner, J. W. (1995). *Attention deficit disorders: Assessment and teaching.* Pacific Grove, Calif.: Brooks/Cole.

Leutner, D. (1993). Guided discovery learning with computer–based simulation games: Effects of adaptive and non-adaptive instructional support. *Learning and Instruction, 3,* 113–132.

Levin, B. (1983, March). Teachers and standardized achievement tests. *Canadian School Executive,* p. 11.

Levy, G. D. (1993). Introduction: An integrated collection on early gender-role development. *Developmental Review, 13,* 123–125.

Lewis, J. E. (1994). Virtual reality: Ready or not! *Technos, 3,* 12–17.

Lindholm, K. J., & Aclan, Z. (1991). Bilingual proficiency as a bridge to academic achievement: Results from bilingual/immersion programs. *Journal of Education, 173,* 99–113.

Linn, R. L. (1986). Educational testing and assessment: Research needs and policy issues. *American Psychologist, 41,* 1153–1160.

——. (1994). Performance assessment: Policy promises and technical measurement standards. *Educational Researcher, 23,* 4–13.

Lockhead, J. (1985). New horizons in educational development. In E. W. Gordon (ed.), *Review of research in education* (Vol. 12). Washington, D.C.: American Educational Research Association.

Loera, P. A., & Meichenbaum, D. (1993). The "potential" contributions of cognitive behavior modification to literacy training for deaf students. *American Annals of the Deaf, 138,* 87–95.

Loftus, E. F. (1979). *Eyewitness testimony.* Cambridge, Mass.: Harvard University Press.

Lohman, D. F. (1993). Teaching and testing to develop fluid abilities. *Educational Researcher, 22,* 12–23.

Lorenz, K. (1952). *King Solomon's ring.* London: Methuen.

Lowe, L. L. (1983, January). Creative learning through fine arts. *ATA Magazine, 63,* 20–23.

Lubar, J. F. (1991). Discourse on the development of EEG diagnostics and biofeedback for attention-deficit/hyperactivity disorders. *Biofeedback and Self-Regulation, 16,* 201–225.

Lubar, J. F., Swartwood, M. O., Swartwood, J. N., & O'Donnell, P. H. (1995). Evaluation of the effectiveness of EEG neurofeedback training for ADHD in a clinical setting as measured by changes in T.O.V.A. scores, behavioral ratings, and WISC-R performance. *Biofeedback and Self-Regulation, 20,* 83–99.

Lund, D. E. (1994). Conceptions of intelligence in an academic community. *Journal of Educational Thought, 28,* 59–87.

Lupkowski-Shoplik, A. E., & Assouline, S. G. (1994). Evidence of extreme mathematical precocity: Case studies of talented youth. *Roeper Review, 16,* 144–151.

Luria, A. R. (1968). *The mind of a mnemonist: A little book about a vast memory.* New York: Avon Books.

Lynch, E. W., Simms, B. H., von Hippel, C. S., & Shuchat, J. (1978). *Mainstreaming preschoolers: Children with mental retardation.* Washington, D.C.: Head Start Bureau; U.S. Government Printing Office.

Mac Iver, D. J., Reuman, D. A., & Main, S. R. (1995). Social structuring of the school: Studying what is, illuminating what could be. *Annual Review of Psychology, 46,* 375–400.

Maccoby, E. E., & Jacklin, C. N. (1974). *The psychology of sex differences.* Palo Alto, Calif.: Stanford University Press.

——. (1980). Sex differences in agression: A rejoinder and reprise. *Child Development, 51,* 964–980.

MacKay, A. (1982). *Project Quest: Teaching strategies and pupil achievement.* Occasional Paper Series, Centre for Research in Teaching, Faculty of Education, University of Alberta, Edmonton, Alberta, Canada.

Macmillan, D. L., Keogh, B. K., & Jones, R. L. (1986). Special educational research on mildly handicapped learners. In M. C. Wittrock (ed.), *Handbook of research on teaching* (3rd ed.) (pp. 686–724). New York: Macmillan.

Madaus, G. F. (1994). A technological and historical consideration of equity issues associated with proposals to change the nation's testing policy. *Harvard Educational Review, 64,* 76–95.

Mager, R. F. (1962). *Preparing instructional objectives.* Palo Alto, Calif.: Fearon.

Maguire, T. O. (1992). Grounded authentic assessment and teacher evaluation. In D. J. Bateson (ed.), *Classroom testing in Canada: Proceedings of the Second Canadian Conference on Classroom Testing, June 1 and 2, 1990.* Vancouver: The University of British Columbia, the Centre for Applied Studies in Evaluation.

Maker, C. J. (1993). Creativity, intelligence, and problem solving: A definition and design for cross-cultural research and measurement related to giftedness. *Gifted Education International, 9,* 68–77.

Mann, C. (1994). New technologies and gifted education. *Roeper Review, 16,* 172–176.

Marfo, K., Mulcahy, R. F., Peat, D., Andrews, J., & Cho, S. (1991). Teaching cognitive strategies in the classroom: A content-based instructional model. In R. M. Mulcahy, R. H. Short, & J. Andrews (eds.), *Enhancing learning and thinking.* New York: Praeger.

Markle, S. M. (1978). *Designs for instructional designers.* Champaign, Ill.: Stipes.

Markle, S. M., & Tiemann, P. W. (1974). Some principles of instructional design at higher cognitive levels. In R. Ulrich, T. Stachnik, & T. Mabry (eds.), *Control of human behavior.* Glenview, Ill.: Scott, Foresman.

Marland, M. (1975). *The craft of the classroom: A survival guide to classroom management at the secondary school.* London: Heinemann Educational Books.

Marland, S. P. (1972). *Education of the gifted and talented.* Washington, D.C.: U.S. Government Printing Office.

Marquis, D. P. (1941). Learning in the neonate: The modification of behavior under three feeding schedules. *Journal of Experimental Psychology, 29,* 263–282.

Marsh, H. W. (1989). Sex differences in the development of verbal and mathematics constructs: The high school and beyond study. *American Educational Research Journal, 26,* 191–225.

Marshall, H., & Weinstein, R. (1984). Classroom factors affecting students' self-evaluations: An interactional model. *Review of Educational Research, 54,* 301–325.

Martinez, M. E. (1994). Access to information technologies among school-age children: Implications for a democratic society. *Journal of the American Society for Information Science, 45,* 395–400.

Marton, F., & Saljo, R. (1984). Approaches to learning. In F. Marton (and others) (eds.), *The experience of learning.* Edinburgh: Scottish Academic Press.

Marzano, R. J. (1993). How classroom teachers approach the teaching of thinking. *Theory into Practice, 32,* 154–160.

——. (1994). Lessons from the field about outcome-based performance assessments. *Educational Leadership, 51,* 44–50.

Maslow, A. H. (1970). *Motivation and personality* (2nd ed.). New York: Harper & Row.

——. (1991). How we diminish ourselves. *Journal of Humanistic Education and Development, 29,* 117–120.

Massaro, D. W., & Cowan, N. (1993). Information processing models: Microscopes of the mind. *Annual Review of Psychology, 44,* 383–425.

Masur, E. F. (1993). Transitions in representational ability: Infants' verbal, vocal, and action imitation during the second year. *Merrill-Palmer Quarterly, 39,* 437–455.

Matson, J. V. (1991). Failure 101: Regarding failure in the classroom to stimulate creative behavior. *Journal of Creative Behavior, 25,* 82–85.

Matthew, J. L., Golin, A. K., Moore, M. W., & Baker, C. (1992). Use of the SOMPA in identification of gifted African-American children. *Journal for the Education of the Gifted, 15,* 344–356.

Matthews, D. B. (1991). The effects of school environment on intrinsic motivation of middle-school children. *Journal of Humanistic Education and Development, 30,* 30–36.

Matthews, L. H. (1969). *The life of mammals* (Vol. 1). New York: Universe Books.

Mayer, R. E. (1979). Can advance organizers influence meaningful learning? *Review of Educational Research, 49,* 371–383.

——. (1989). Models for understanding. *Review of Educational Research, 59,* 43–64.

Mayo, K. E. (1993). Learning strategy instruction: Exploring the potential of metacognition. *Reading Improvement, 30,* 130–133.

McCaslin, M., & Good, T. L. (1992). Compliant cognition: The misalliance of management and instructional goals in current school reform. *Educational Researcher, 21,* 4–17.

McClean, L. (1992). Student evaluation in the ungraded primary school: The SCRP principle. In D. J. Bateson (ed.), *Classroom testing in Canada: Proceedings of the Second Canadian Conference on Classroom Testing, June 1 and 2, 1990.* Vancouver: The University of British Columbia, the Centre for Applied Studies in Evaluation.

McClelland, D. C. (1958). Risk taking in children with high and low need for achievement. In J. W. Atkinson (ed.), *Motives in fantasy, action, and society.* Princeton, N.J.: Van Nostrand.

——. (1973). Testing for competence rather than for "intelligence." *American Psychologist, 28,* 1–14.

McClelland, D. C., Atkinson, J. W., Clark, R. A., & Lowell, E. L. (1953). *The achievement motive.* New York: Appleton-Century-Crofts.

McCombs, B. L. (1982). Transitioning learning strategies research into practice: Focus on the student in technical training. *Journal of Instructional Development, 5,* 10–17.

McCullough, N. T. (1992). Teaching and learning with computers: A school-wide approach. *Computing Teacher, 20,* 8–9.

McDonald, L. (1993). *Task force on integration: Draft discussion paper.* Unpublished paper, Edmonton: University of Alberta.

McEwen, N. (Chair). (1992). *The Educational Quality Indicators Initiative: A success story.* Symposium at the annual meeting of the Canadian Educational Researchers' Association and the Canadian Association for the Study of Educational Administration, Charlottetown, Prince Edward Island, June 6. Edmonton: Alberta Education.

McFadden, A. C., Marsh, G. E., II, Price, B. J., & Hwang, Y. (1992). A study of race and gender bias in the punishment of school children. *Education and Treatment of Children, 15,* 140–146.

McGill-Franzen, A., & Allington, R. L. (1993). Flunk'em or get them classified: The contamination of primary grade accountability data. *Educational Researcher, 22,* 19–22.

McGroarty, M. (1992). The societal context of bilingual education. *Educational Researcher, 21,* 7–9, 24.

McMann, N., & Oliver, R. (1988). Problems in families with gifted children: Implications for counselors. *Journal of Counseling and Development, 66,* 275–278.

Mednick, S. A. (1962). The associative basis of the creative process. *Psychological Review, 69,* 220–232.

Meichenbaum, D. (1977). *Cognitive-behavior modification: An integrative approach.* New York: Plenum.

——. (1993). Changing conceptions of cognitive behavior modification: Retrospect and prospect. *Journal of Consulting and Clinical Psychology, 61,* 202–204.

Meichenbaum, D. H., & Goodman, J. (1971). Training impulsive children to talk to themselves: A means of developing self-control. *Journal of Abnormal Psychology, 77,* 115–126.

Mensh, E., & Mensh, H. (1991). *The IQ mythology: Class, race, gender, and inequality.* Carbondale: Southern Illinois University Press.

Mercer, C. D. (1990). Learning disability. In N. G. Haring & L. McCormick (eds.), *Exceptional children and youth* (5th ed.). Columbus, Ohio: Merrill.

Mercer, J. R. (1973). *Labeling the mentally retarded.* Berkeley: University of California Press.

——. (1979). *System of Multicultural Pluralistic Assessment technical manual.* New York: Psychological Corporation.

Mercer, J. R., & Lewis, J. F. (1978). *System of Multicultural Pluralistic Assessment.* New York: Psychological Corporation.

——. (1979). *System of Multicultural Pluralistic Assessment student assessment manual.* New York: Psychological Corporation.

Merrett, F., & Wheldall, K. (1992). Teachers' use of praise and reprimands to boys and girls. *Educational Review, 44,* 73–79.

——. (1993). How do teachers learn to manage classroom behaviour? A study of teachers' opinions about their initial management. *Educational Studies, 19,* 91–106.

Messick, S. (1994). The interplay of evidence and consequences in the validation of performance assessments. *Educational Researcher, 23,* 13–23.

Meyer, M. M., & Fienberg, S. E. (eds.). (1992). *The case of bilingual education strategies.* Washington, D.C.: National Academy Press.

Michael, J. (1967). *Management of behavioral consequences in education.* Inglewood, Calif.: Southwest Regional Laboratory for Educational Research and Development.

Milgram, S. (1963). Behavioral study of obedience. *Journal of Abnormal and Social Psychology, 67,* 371–378.

Miller, G. A. (1956). The magical number seven, plus or minus two: Some limits on our capacity for processing information. *Psychological Review, 63,* 81–97.

Miller, R. (1990). Beyond reductionism: The emerging holistic paradigm in education. *Humanistic Psychologist, 18,* 314–323.

Millman, J., & Darling-Hammond, L. (eds.). (1990). *The new handbook of teacher evaluation: Assessing elementary and secondary school teachers.* Newbury Park, Calif.: Sage.

Mills, S. C. (1994). Integrated learning systems: New technology for classrooms of the future. *Techtrends, 39,* 27–28, 31.

Moore, K. D., & Hanley, P. E. (1982). An identification of elementary teacher needs. *American Educational Research Journal, 19,* 137–144.

Moss, P. A. (1992). Shifting conceptions of validity in educational measurement: Implications for performance assessment. *Review of Educational Research, 62,* 229–258.

Moynahan, E. O. (1973). The development of knowledge concerning the effects of categorization upon free recall. *Child Development, 44,* 238–245.

Mueller, J. H. (1992a). Anxiety and performance. In A. P. Smith & D. M. Jones (eds.), *Handbook of human performance* (Vol. 3). London: Academic.

——. (1992b). *Test anxiety, study behaviors, and achievement.* Paper presented at the annual meeting of the Western Psychological Association, Portland, Oregon, April 30.

Mueller, S. L. (1992). The effect of a cooperative education work experience on autonomy, sense of purpose, and mature interpersonal relationships. *Journal of Cooperative Education, 27,* 27–35.

Muffoletto, R. (1994). Schools and technology in a democratic society: Equity and social justice. *Educational Technology, 34,* 52–54.

Mulcahy, R. F. (1991). Developing autonomous learners. *Alberta Journal of Educational Research, 37,* 385–397.

Mulcahy, R., Marfo, K., Peat, D., Andrews, J., & Clifford, L. (1986). Applying cognitive psychology in the classroom: A learning/thinking strategies instructional program. *Alberta Psychology, 15,* 9–12.

Mulcahy, R. F., Peat, D., Andrews, J., Darko-Yeboah, J., & Marfo, K. (1990). Cognitive-based strategy instruction. In J. Biggs (ed.), *Learning processes and teaching contexts.* Melbourne: Australian Council for Educational Research.

Murnane, R. J., Singer, J. D., & Willett, J. B. (1988). The career paths of teachers: Implications for teacher supply and methodological lessons for research. *Educational Researcher, 17,* 22–30.

Myles, B. S., & Simpson, R. L. (1994). Understanding and preventing acts of aggression and violence in school-age children and youth. *Preventing School Failure, 38,* 40–46.

Nagle, R. J., & Bell, N. L. (1993). Validation of Stanford-Binet intelligence scale: Fourth edition abbreviated batteries with college students. *Psychology in the Schools, 30,* 227–231.

Naglieri, J. A. (1988). *DAP; draw a person: A quantitative scoring system.* New York: Harcourt Brace Jovanovich.

Nagy, P., & Griffiths, A. K. (1982). Limitations of recent research relating Piaget's theory to adolescent thought. *Review of Educational Research, 52,* 513–556.

Nahl-Jakobovits, D., & Jakobovits, L. A. (1993). Bibliographic instructional design for information literacy: Integrating affective and cognitive objectives. *Research Strategies, 11,* 73–88.

Natale, J. A. (1994). Your life is on the line. *Executive Educator, 16,* 22–26.

National Center for Education Statistics. (1989). *Digest of education statistics. 1989* (25th ed.). Washington, D.C.: U.S. Department of Education.

National Commission on Excellence in Education. (1983). *A nation at risk: The imperative for educational reform.* Washington, D.C.: U.S. Government Printing Office.

Naval-Severino, T. (1993). Developing creative thinking among intellectually able Filipino children from disadvantaged urban communities. *Gifted Education International, 9,* 119–123.

Nay, W. R., Schulman, J. A., Bailey, K. G., & Huntsinger, G. M. (1976). Territory and classroom management: An exploratory case study. *Behavior Therapy, 7,* 240–246.

Neisser, U. (1976). *Cognition and reality.* San Francisco: Freeman.

Nelson, C., & Pearson, C. (1991). *Integrating services for children and youth with emotional and behavior disorders.* Reston, Va.: Council of Exceptional Children.

Nicholls, J. G. (1978). The development of the concepts of effort and ability, perception of academic attainment, and the understanding that difficult tasks require more ability. *Developmental Psychology, 49,* 800–814.

Nichols, J. D., & Miller, R. B. (1994). Cooperative learning and student motivation. *Contemporary Educational Psychology, 19,* 167–178.

Nickerson, R. S. (1986). Why teach thinking? In J. B. Baron & R. J. Sternberg (eds.), *Teaching thinking skills: Theory and practice.* New York: Freeman.

——. (1988). On improving thinking through instruction. In E. Z. Rothkopf (ed.), *Review of research in education* (Vol. 15). Washington, D.C.: American Educational Research Association.

Nicolopoulou, A. (1993). Play, cognitive development, and the social world: Piaget, Vygotsky, and beyond. *Human Development, 36,* 1–23.

Nolen, S. B., Haladyna, T. M., & Haas, N. S. (1992). Uses and abuses of achievement test scores. *Educational Measurement: Issues and Practices, 11,* 9–15.

Norris, D., & Pyke, L. H. (1992). Entrepreneurship in open education. *Australian Journal of Adult and Community Education, 32,* 168–176.

Novak, J. D., & Musonda, D. (1991). A twelve-year longitudinal study of science concept learning. *American Educational Research Journal, 28,* 117–153.

Nunes, T., Carraher, D. W., & Schliemann, A. D. (1993). *Street mathematics and school mathematics.* New York: Cambridge University Press.

Nussbaum, J. (1979). Children's conception of the earth as a cosmic body: A cross age study. *Science Education, 63,* 83–93.

O'Banion, D. R., & Whaley, D. L. (1981). *Behavior contracting: Arranging contingencies of reinforcement.* New York: Springer.

O'Leary, K. D., & Becker, W. C. (1968). The effects of a teacher's reprimands on children's behavior. *Journal of School Psychology, 7,* 8–11.

O'Leary, K. D., Kaufman, K. F., Kass, R. E., & Drabman, R. S. (1974). The effects of loud and soft reprimands on the behavior of disruptive students. In A. R. Brown & C. Avery (eds.), *Modifying children's behavior: A book of readings.* Springfield, Ill.: Thomas.

O'Neil, J. (1993). Making sense of outcome-based education. *Instructor, 102,* 46–47.

Oakes, J., & Guiton, G. (1995). Matchmaking: The dynamics of high school tracking decisions. *American Educational Research Journal, 32,* 3–33.

Ogbu, J. U. (1994). Understanding cultural diversity and learning. *Journal for the Education of the Gifted, 17,* 354–383.

Oosterhof, A. (1994). *Classroom applications of educational measurement.* New York: Maxwell Macmillan.

Ornstein, A. C. (1993a). How to recognize good teaching. *American School Board Journal, 180,* 24–27.

——. (1993b). Norm-referenced and criterion-referenced tests: An overview. *NASSP Bulletin, 77,* 28–39.

Osborn, A. (1957). *Applied imagination.* New York: Scribner's.

Osborne, J. K., & Byrnes, D. A. (1990). Identifying gifted and talented students in an alternative learning center. *Gifted Child Quarterly, 34,* 143–146.

Ozar, L. A. (1994). Diverse assessment—key to richer learning. *Momentum, 25,* 53–56.

Padilla, A. M. (1991). English only vs. bilingual education: Ensuring a language-competent society. *Journal of Education, 173,* 38–51.

Page, E. B., & Grandon, G. M. (1979). Family configuration and mental ability: Two theories contrasted with U.S. data. *American Educational Research Journal, 16,* 257–272.

Pajares, M. F. (1992). Teachers' beliefs and educational research: Cleaning up a messy construct. *Review of Educational Research, 62,* 307–332.

Palardy, J. M. (1991). Behavior modification: It does work, but . . . *Journal of Instructional Psychology, 19,* 127–131.

Palincsar, M. S., & Brown, A. L. (1984). Reciprocal teaching of comprehension—fostering and monitoring activities. *Cognitive Instruction, 1,* 117–175.

Pallas, A. M. (1993). Schooling in the course of human lives: The social context of education and the transition to adulthood in industrial society. *Review of Educational Research, 63,* 408–477.

Pallas, A. M., Natriello, G., & McDill, E. L. (1989). The changing nature of the disadvantaged population: Current dimensions and future trends. *Educational Researcher, 18,* 16–22.

Palmares, U., & Logan, B. (1975). *A curriculum on conflict management.* Palo Alto, Calif.: Human Development Training Institute.

Papalia, D. F. (1972). The status of several conservative abilities across the life-span. *Human Development, 15,* 229–243.

Papert, S. (1987). Computer criticism vs. technocentric thinking. *Educational Researcher, 16* (1), 22–30.

——. (1993). *The children's machine: Rethinking school in the age of the computer.* New York: Basic Books.

Paris, S. G., Lawton, T. A., Turner, J. C., & Roth, J. L. (1991). A developmental perspective on standardized achievement testing. *Educational Researcher, 20,* 12–20.

Parke, R. D. (1974). Rules, roles, and resistance to deviation: Recent advances in punishment, discipline, and self-control. In A. Pick (ed.), *Minnesota Symposia on Child Psychology* (Vol. 8). Minneapolis: University of Minnesota Press.

Parloff, M. B., London, P., & Wolfe, B. (1986). Individual psychotherapy and behavior change. *Annual Review of Psychology, 37,* 321–349.

Parnes, S. J. (1962). Do you really understand brainstorming? In S. J. Parnes & H. F. Harding (eds.), *A sourcebook for creative thinking.* New York: Scribner's.

———. (1967). *Creative behavior workbook.* New York: Scribner's.

Parnes, S. J., & Harding, H. F. (eds.). (1962). *A sourcebook for creative thinking.* New York: Scribner's.

Parsons, J. B. (1983). The seductive computer: Can it be resisted? *ATA Magazine, 63,* 12–14.

Patrick, J. (1994). Direct teaching of collaborative skills in a cooperative learning environment. *Teaching and Change, 1,* 170–181.

Patterson, C. H. (1993). Winds of change for client-centered counseling. *Journal of Humanistic Education and Development, 31,* 130–133.

Patterson, C. H., & Purkey, W. W. (1993). The preparation of humanistic teachers for schools of the next century. *Journal of Humanistic Education and Development, 31,* 147–155.

Patterson, V. E. (1994). Introducing cooperative learning at Princess Elizabeth Elementary School. *Education Canada, 34,* 36–41.

Patton, J. R., & Polloway, E. A. (1990). Mild mental retardation. In N. G. Haring & L. McCormick (eds.), *Exceptional children and youth* (5th ed.). Columbus, Ohio: Merrill.

Pazulinec, R., Meyerrose, M., & Sajwaj, T. (1983). Punishment via response cost. In S. Axelrod & J. Apsche (eds.), *The effects of punishment on human behavior.* New York: Academic.

Pease-Alvarez, L., & Hakuta, K. (1992). Enriching our views of bilingualism and bilingual education. *Educational Researcher, 2,* 4–6.

Peat, D., Mulcahy, R. F., & Darko-Yeboah, J. (1989). SPELT (Strategies Program for Effective Learning/Thinking): A description and analysis of instructional procedures. *Instructional Science, 18,* 95–118.

Pelham, W. E., Jr., Carlson, C., Sams, S. E., Vallano, G., Dixon, M. J., & Hoza, B. (1993). Separate and combined effects of methylphenidate and behavior modification on boys with attention deficit-hyperactivity disorder in the classroom. *Journal of Consulting & Clinical Psychology, 61,* 506–515.

Pérez, B., & Torres-Guzmán, M. E. (1992). *Learning in two worlds: An integrated Spanish/English biliteracy approach.* New York: Longman.

Perez, S. A. (1994). Responding differently to diversity. *Childhood Education, 70,* 151–153.

Perkins, M. R. (1982). Minimum competency testing: What? Why? Why not? *Educational Measurement Issues and Practice, 1,* 5–9.

Perry, P., Pasnak, R., & Holt, R. W. (1992). Instruction on concrete operations for children who are mildly mentally retarded. *Education and Training in Mental Retardation, 27,* 273–281.

Perry, R. (1966). *The world of the polar bear.* Seattle: University of Washington Press.

Petersen, A. C. (1988). Adolescent development. *Annual Review of Psychology, 39,* 583–607.

Phillips, N. B., Fuchs, L. S., & Fuchs, D. (1994). Effects of classwide curriculum-based measurement and peer tutoring: A collaborative researcher-practitioner interview study. *Journal of Learning Disabilities, 27,* 420–434.

Piaget, J. (1932). *The moral judgment of the child.* London: Kegan Paul.

———. (1954). *The construction of reality in the child.* New York: Basic Books.

———. (1961). The genetic approach to the psychology of thought. *Journal of Educational Psychology, 52,* 275–281.

———. (1972). Intellectual development from adolescence to adulthood. *Human Development, 15,* 1–12.

Pica, L., Jr., & Margolis, H. (1993). What to do when behavior modification is not working. *Preventing School Failure, 37,* 29–33.

Pinard, A., & Laurendeau, M. (1964). A scale of mental development based on the theory of Piaget: Description of a project (A. B. Givens, Trans.). *Journal of Research and Science Teaching, 2,* 253–260.

Platzman, K. A., Stoy, M. R., Brown, R. T., Coles, C. D., Smith, I. E., & Falek, A. (1992). Review of observational methods in attention deficit hyperactivity disorder (ADHD): Implications for diagnosis. *School Psychology Quarterly, 7,* 155–177.

Podd'iakov, N. N. (1992). A new approach to the development of creativity in preschoolers. *Russian Education in Society, 34,* 82–89.

Popham, W. J. (1981). *Modern educational measurement.* Englewood Cliffs, N.J.: Prentice-Hall.

Porter, C., & Cleland, J. (1995). *The portfolio as a learning strategy.* Portsmouth, N.H.: Boynton/Cook.

Prawat, R. S. (1991). The value of ideas: The immersion approach to the development of thinking. *Educational Researcher, 20,* 3–10.

Premack, D. (1965). Reinforcement theory. In D. Levine (ed.), *Nebraska Symposium on Motivation.* Lincoln: University of Nebraska Press.

Presland, J. (1989). Behavioural approaches. In T. Charlton & K. David (eds.), *Managing misbehaviour: Strategies for effective management of behaviour in schools.* London: Macmillan Education.

Purkey, W. W. (1984). *Inviting school success: A self-concept approach to teaching and learning* (2nd ed.). Belmont, Calif.: Wadsworth.

Pyryt, M. C. (1993). The fulfillment of promise revisited: A discriminant analysis of factors predicting success in the Terman study. *Roeper Review, 15,* 178–179.

Qin, Z., Johnson, D. W., & Johnson, R. T. (1995). Cooperative versus competitive efforts and problem solving. *Review of Educational Research, 65,* 129–143.

Rafferty, C. D., & Fleschner, L. K. (1993). Concept mapping: A viable alternative to objective and essay exams. *Reading Research and Instruction, 32,* 25–34.

Raines, H. H. (1994). Tutoring and teaching: Continuum, dichotomy, or dialectic. *Writing Center Journal, 14,* 150–162.

Ramsden, P. (1988a). Studying learning: Improving teaching. In P. Ramsden (ed.), *Improving learning: New perspectives.* London: Kogan Page.

——. (ed.). (1988b). *Improving learning: New perspectives.* London: Kogan Page.

Ranzijn, F. J. A. (1991–92). The sequence of conceptual information in instruction and its effect on retention. *Instructional Science, 20,* 405–418.

Raphael, B. (1976). *The thinking computer: Mind inside matter.* San Francisco: Freeman.

Reay, D. A. (1994). *Understanding how people learn.* East Brunswick, N.J.: Nichols.

Reese, H. W., & Overton, W. F. (1970). Models and theories of development. In L. R. Goulet & P. B. Baltes (eds.), *Lifespan developmental psychology: Research and theory.* New York: Academic.

Reid, R. M., John, W., Vasa, S. F., & Wright, G. (1994). Who are the children with attention deficit-hyperactivity disorder? A school-based survey. *Journal of Special Education, 28,* 117–137.

Reiff, J. C. (1992). *Learning styles.* Washington, D.C.: National Education Association.

Renzulli, J. S. (1977). *The enrichment triad model: A guide for developing defensible programs for the gifted and talented.* Mansfield Center, Conn.: Creative Learning Press.

——. (1986). The three-ring conception of giftedness: A developmental model for creative productivity. In R. J. Sternberg & J. E. Davidson (eds.), *Conceptions of giftedness.* Cambridge: Cambridge University Press.

Renzulli, J. S., & Reis, S. M. (1994). Research related to the Schoolwide Enrichment Triad Model. *Gifted Child Quarterly, 38,* 7–20.

Renzulli, J. S., Reis, S. M., & Smith, L. H. (1981). *The revolving door identification model.* Mansfield Center, Conn.: Creative Learning Press.

Renzulli, J. S., & Smith, L. H. (1978). *The learning styles inventory: A measure of student preference for instructional techniques.* Mansfield Center, Conn.: Creative Learning Press.

Reschly, D. J. (1990). Adaptive behavior. In A. Thomas & J. Grimes (eds.), *Best practices in school psychology* (2nd ed.). Washington, D.C.: National Association of School Psychologists.

——. (1992). Mental retardation: Conceptual foundations, definitional criteria, and diagnostic operations. In S. R. Hooper, G. W. Hynd, & R. E. Mattison (eds.), *Developmental disorders: Diagnostic criteria and clinical assessment.* Hillsdale, N.J.: Erlbaum.

Resnick, L. B. (1981). Instructional psychology. *Annual Review of Psychology, 32,* 659–704.

Reynolds, A. (1992). What is competent beginning teaching? A review of the literature. *Review of Educational Research, 62,* 1–35.

Rich, Y. (1993). Stability and change in teacher expertise. *Teaching and Teacher Education, 9,* 137–146.

Richards, R. (1994). Creativity and bipolar mood swings: Why the association? In M. P. Shaw & M. A. Runco (eds.), *Creativity and affect*. Norwood, N.J.: Ablex.

Robin, A. L. (1976). Behavioral instruction in the college classroom. *Review of Educational Research, 46,* 313–354.

Rogers, C. R. (1951). *Client-centered therapy: Its current practice, implications and theory*. Boston: Houghton Mifflin.

——. (1992). The necessary and sufficient conditions of therapeutic personality change. *Journal of Consulting and Clinical Psychology, 60,* 827–832.

Rogers, C. R., & Freiberg, H. J. (1994). *Freedom to learn* (4th ed.). New York: Merrill.

Rogers, C. R., & Skinner, B. F. (1956). Some issues concerning the control of human behavior: A symposium. *Science, 124,* 1057–1066.

Rogers, K. B. (1993). Grouping the gifted and talented: Questions and answers. *Roeper Review, 16,* 8–12.

Rojewski, J. W., & Schell, J. W. (1994). Cognitive apprenticeship for learners with special needs: An alternate framework for teaching and learning. *Remedial and Special Education, 15,* 234–243.

Rolison, M. A., & Medway, F. J. (1985). Teachers' expectations and attributions for student achievement: Effects of label, performance pattern, and special education intervention. *American Educational Research Journal, 22,* 561–573.

Rose, R. J. (1995). Genes and human behavior. *Annual Review of Psychology, 46,* 625–654.

Rosenkoetter, L. I., Huston, A. C., & Wright, J. C. (1990). Television and the moral judgment of the young child. *Journal of Applied Developmental Psychology, 11,* 123–137.

Rosenshine, B., & Meister, C. (1994). Reciprocal teaching: A review of the research. *Review of Educational Research, 64,* 479–530.

Rosenshine, B., & Stevens, R. (1986). Teaching functions. In M. C. Wittrock (ed.), *Handbook of research on teaching* (3rd ed.). New York: Macmillan.

Rosenthal, R. (1987). Pygmalion effects: Existence, magnitude, and social importance. A reply to Wineburg. *Educational Researcher, 16,* 37–41.

Rosenthal, R., & Jacobson, L. (1968a). *Pygmalion in the classroom: Teacher expectations and pupils' intellectual development*. New York: Holt, Rinehart & Winston.

——. (1968b, April). Teacher expectations for the disadvantaged. *Scientific American, 218,* 19–23.

Ross, A. O. (1980). *Psychological disorders of children: A behavioral approach to theory, research, and therapy* (2nd ed.). New York: McGraw-Hill.

Ross, P. A., & Braden, J. P. (1991). The effects of token reinforcement versus cognitive behavior modification on learning-disabled students' math skills. *Psychology in the Schools, 28,* 247–256.

Ross, R. P. (1984). Classroom segments: The structuring of school time. In L. W. Anderson (ed.), *Time and school learning: Theory, research and practice*. London: Croom Helm.

Ross, S. M., Rakow, E. A., & Bush, A. J. (1980). Instructional adaptation for self-managed learning systems. *Journal of Educational Psychology, 72,* 312–320.

Ross, T. W. (1993, Fall–Winter). Bloom and hypertext: Parallel taxonomies? *Ed-Tech Review,* pp. 11–16.

Roth, W. M. (1993). Metaphors and conversational analysis as tools in reflection on teaching practice: Two perspectives on teacher–student interactions in open-inquiry science. *Science Education, 77,* 351–373.

Roth, W. M., & Bowen, M. (1993). Maps for more meaningful learning. *Science Scope, 16,* 24–25.

Roy, P., & Hoch, J. (1994). Cooperative learning: A principal's perspective. *Principal, 73,* 27–29.

Rubin, J. Z. (1994). Models of conflict management. *Journal of Social Issues, 50,* 33–45.

Rubin, K. H., Attewell, P. W., Tierney, M. C., & Tumolo, P. (1973). Development of spatial egocentrism and conservation across the life-span. *Developmental Psychology, 9,* 432–437.

Rushton, J. (1988). Race differences in behaviour: A review and evolutionary analysis. *Journal of Personality and Individual Differences, 9,* 1009–1024.

Rust, F. O. (1994). The first year of teaching: It's not what they expected. *Teaching and Teacher Education, 10,* 205–217.

Ryan, E. R., Hawkins, M. J., & Russell, R. (1992). Education: An exchange of ideas among three humanistic psychologists. *Journal of Humanistic Education and Development, 30,* 178–191.

Ryan, F. J. (1994). From rod to reason: Historical perspectives on corporal punishment in the public school, 1642–1994. *Educational Horizons, 72,* 70–77.

Sadker, M., & Sadker, D. (1986). Sexism in the classroom: From grade school to graduate school. *Phi Delta Kappan, 68,* 512.

Sadker, M., Sadker, D., & Klein, S. (1991). In G. Grant (ed.), *Review of research in education* (Vol. 17). Washington, D.C.: American Educational Research Association.

Salomon, G., & Gardner, H. (1986). The computer as educator: Lessons from television research. *Educational Researcher, 15,* 13–19.

Salomon, G., Perkins, D. N., & Globerson, T. (1991). Partners in cognition: Extending human intelligence with intelligent technologies. *Educational Researcher, 20,* 2–9.

Sarason, I. G. (1959). Intellectual and personality correlates of test anxiety. *Journal of Abnormal and Social Psychology, 59,* 272–275.

———. (1961). Test anxiety and intellectual performance. *Journal of Educational Psychology, 52,* 201–206.

———. (1972). Experimental approaches to test anxiety: Attention and the uses of information. In C. D. Spielberger (ed.), *Anxiety: Current trends in theory and research* (Vol. 2). New York: Academic.

———. (1980). Introduction to the study of test anxiety. In I. G. Sarason (ed.), *Test anxiety: Theory, research, and applications.* Hillsdale, N.J.: Erlbaum.

Sattler, J. M. (1982). *Assessment of children's intelligence and special abilities* (2nd ed.). Boston: Allyn & Bacon.

Savell, J. M., Twohig, P. T., & Rachford, D. L. (1986). Empirical status of Feuerstein's "Instrumental Enrichment" (FIE) technique as a method of teaching thinking skills. *Review of Educational Research, 56,* 381–409.

Scanlon, R., Weinberger, J. A., & Weiler, J. (1970). IPI as a functioning model for the individualization of instruction. In C. M. Lindvall & R. C. Cox (eds.), *Evaluation as a tool in curriculum development: The IPI evaluation program.* AERA Monograph Series No. 5. Chicago: Rand McNally.

Schank, R. C., & Abelson, R. P. (1977). *Scripts, plans, goals and understanding.* Hillsdale, N.J.: Erlbaum.

Schniedewind, N., & Davidson, E. (1988). *Cooperative learning, cooperative lives: A sourcebook of learning activities for building a peaceful world.* Dubuque, Iowa: Wm. C. Brown.

Schofield, J. W., Eurich-Fulcer, R., & Britt, C. L. (1994). Teachers, computer tutors, and teaching: The artificially intelligent tutor as an agent for classroom change. *American Educational Research Journal, 31,* 579–607.

Schultz, D. P. (1964). *Panic behavior.* New York: Random House.

Scott, M. E. (1991). Parental encouragement of gifted–talented–creative (GTC) development in young children by providing freedom to become independent. *The Creative Child and Adult Quarterly, 16,* 26–29.

Scott, T., Cole, M., & Engel, M. (1992). Computers and education: A cultural constructivist perspective. In G. Grant (ed.), *Review of research in education* (Vol. 18). Washington, D.C.: American Educational Research Association.

Scruggs, T. E., & Mastropieri, M. A. (1994). Successful mainstreaming in elementary science classes: A qualitative study of three reputational cases. *American Educational Research Journal, 31,* 785–811.

Sears, R. R., Maccoby, E. P., & Lewin, H. (1957). *Patterns of child rearing.* Evanston, Ill.: Row, Peterson.

Seligman, D. (1992). *A question of intelligence: The IQ debate in America.* New York: Carol Publishing Group.

Semb, G. B., & Ellis, J. A. (1994). Knowledge taught in school: What is remembered? *Review of Educational Research, 64,* 253–286.

Semrud-Clikeman, M., & Hynd, G. W. (1992). Developmental arithmetic disorder. In S. R. Hooper, G. W. Hynd, & R. E. Mattison (eds.), *Developmental disorders: Diagnostic criteria and clinical assessment.* Hillsdale, N.J.: Erlbaum.

Serbin, L. A., Powlishta, K. K., & Gulko, J. (1993). The development of sex typing in middle childhood. *Monographs of the Society for Research in Child Development, 58,* no. 2.

Sereda, J. (1992). Educational quality indicators in art and mathematics. In N. McEwan (chair), *The Educational Quality Indicators Initiative: A success story* (pp. 61–66), symposium at the annual meeting of the Canadian Educational Researchers' Association and the Canadian Association for the Study of Educational Administration, Charlottetown, Prince Edward Island, June 6. Edmonton: Alberta Education.

Shaklee, B. D. (1992). Identification of young gifted students. *Journal for the Education of the Gifted, 15,* 134–144.

Shannon, T. A. (1994). Salmon's laws. *Executive Educator, 16,* 52–54.

Sharan, S., & Shachar, H. (1988). *Language and learning in the cooperative classroom.* New York: Springer-Verlag.

Sharan, Y., & Sharan, S. (1992). *Expanding cooperative learning through group investigation.* New York: Columbia University, Teachers College Press.

Shepard, L. A., & Kreitzer, A. E. (1987). The Texas teacher test. *Educational Researcher, 16,* 22–31.

Shepard, L. A., Smith, M. L., & Vojir, C. P. (1983). Characteristics of pupils identified as learning disabled. *American Educational Research Journal, 20,* 309–331.

Sherman, J. G. (1992). Reflections on PSI: Good news and bad. *Journal of Applied Behavior Analysis, 25,* 59–64.

Shuell, T. J. (1986). Cognitive conceptions of learning. *Review of Educational Research, 56,* 411–436.

Shulman, L. S. (1986). Paradigms and research programs in the study of teaching. In M. C. Wittrock (ed.), *Handbook of research on teaching* (3rd ed.). New York: Macmillan.

Siegler, R. S. (1989). Mechanisms of cognitive development. *Annual Review of Psychology, 40,* 353–379.

Silvernail, D. L. (1979). *Teaching styles as related to student achievement.* Washington, D.C.: National Education Association.

Skaalvik, E. M., & Rankin, R. J. (1995). A test of the internal/external frame of reference model at different levels of math and verbal self-perception. *American Educational Research Journal, 32,* 161–184.

Skinner, B. F. (1948). *Walden II.* New York: Macmillan.

——. (1953). *Science and human behavior.* New York: Macmillan.

——. (1954). The science of learning and the art of teaching. *Harvard Educational Review, 24,* 86–97.

——. (1955). *Transcripts of New York Academy of Science, 17,* 546–587.

——. (1961). *Cumulative record* (rev. ed.). New York: Appleton-Century-Crofts.

——. (1965, October 16). Why teachers fail. *Saturday Review,* pp. 80–81, 98–102.

——. (1968). *The technology of teaching.* New York: Appleton-Century-Crofts.

——. (1971). *Beyond freedom and dignity.* New York: Knopf.

Slavin, R. E. (1980). Cooperative learning. *Review of Educational Research, 50,* 315–342.

——. (1983). *Student team learning: An overview and practical guide.* Washington, D.C.: National Education Association.

——. (1987). Mastery learning reconsidered. *Review of Educational Research, 57,* 175–213.

——. (1993a). Ability grouping in the middle grades: Achievement effects and alternatives. *Elementary School Journal, 93,* 535–552.

——. (1993b). Untracking: The 97 percent solution. A response to James J. Gallagher. *College Board Review, 168,* 27, 35.

——. (1995). *Cooperative learning: Theory, research, and practice* (2nd ed.). Boston: Allyn & Bacon.

Smith, L. (1993). *Necessary knowledge: Piagetian perspectives on constructivism.* Hillsdale, N.J.: Erlbaum.

Smith, M. A., & Misra, A. (1992). A comprehensive management system for students in regular classrooms. *Elementary School Journal, 92,* 353–372.

Smith, M. L. (1991). Put to the test: The effects of external testing on teachers. *Educational Researcher, 20,* 8–11.

Snow, R. E., & Lohman, D. F. (1984). Toward a theory of cognitive aptitude for learning from instruction. *Journal of Educational Psychology, 76,* 347–376.

Snow, R. E., & Swanson, J. (1992). Instructional psychology: Aptitude, adaptation, and assessment. *Annual Review of Psychology, 43,* 583–626.

Snowman, J. (1993). Research alive: How accurate is the conventional wisdom about classroom testing practices? *Midwestern Educational Researcher, 6,* 19–20.

Soloman, G. (1992). Technology and the balance of power. *The Computing Teacher, 19,* 10–11.

Soloman, J. (1993). Four frames for a field. In P. J. Black & A. M. Lucas (eds.), *Children's informal ideas in science.* New York: Routledge.

Solomon, D., Watson, M. S., Delucchi, K. L., Schaps, E., & Battistich, V. (1988). Enhancing children's prosocial behavior in the classroom. *American Educational Research Journal, 25,* 527–544.

Sonnier, I. L. (ed.). (1985). *Methods and techniques of holistic education.* Springfield, Ill.: Thomas.

——. (1991). Hemisphericity: A key to understanding the individual differences among teachers and learners. *Journal of Instructional Psychology, 18,* 17–22.

Sonnier, I. L., & Sonnier, C. B. (1992). The Sonnier model of educational management: Implementing holistic education. *Journal of Instructional Psychology, 19,* 135–140.

Soper, J. D. (1964). *The mammals of Alberta.* Edmonton, Alberta: Hamly Press.

Southern, H. N. (1964). *The handbook of British mammals.* Oxford: Blackwell Scientific Publications.

Sparzo, F. J. (1992). B. F. Skinner's contributions to education: A retrospective appreciation. *Contemporary Education, 63,* 225–233.

Spearman, C. E. (1927). *The abilities of man.* New York: Macmillan.

Springer, S. P., & Deutsch, G. (1989). *Left brain right brain* (3rd ed.). New York: Freeman.

Squire, L. R., Knowlton, B., & Musen, G. (1993). The structure and organization of memory. *Annual Review of Psychology, 44,* 453–495.

Stallings, J. A., & Stipek, D. (1986). Research on early childhood and elementary school teaching programs. In M. C. Wittrock (ed.), *Handbook of research on teaching* (3rd ed.) (pp. 727–753). New York: Macmillan.

Stander, V., & Jensen, L. (1993). The relationship of value orientation to moral cognition: Gender and cultural differences in the United States and China explored. *Journal of Cross-Cultural Psychology, 24,* 42–52.

Stanley, J. C. (1976). The case for extreme educational acceleration of intellectually brilliant youths. *Gifted Child Quarterly, 20,* 66–75.

Stanovich, K. E. (1992). Developmental reading disorder. In S. R. Hooper, G. W. Hynd, & R. E. Mattison (eds.), *Developmental disorders: Diagnostic criteria and clinical assessment.* Hillsdale, N.J.: Erlbaum.

———. (1993). Dysrationalia: A new specific learning disability. *Journal of Learning Disabilities, 26,* 501–515.

Starkes, J. L., & Lindley, S. (1994). Can we hasten expertise by video simulations? *Quest, 46,* 211–222.

Statistics Canada. (1992). *Earnings of men and women: 1990.* Ottawa: Minister of Industry, Science and Technology.

Sternberg, R. J. (1984a). A contextualist view of the nature of intelligence. *International Journal of Psychology, 19,* 307–334.

———. (1984b). Mechanisms of cognitive development: A componential approach. In R. J. Sternberg (ed.), *Mechanisms of cognitive development.* San Francisco: Freeman.

———. (1984c). What should intelligence tests test? Implications of a triarchic theory of intelligence for intelligence testing. *Educational Researcher, 13,* 5–15.

———. (1986). *Intelligence applied: Understanding and increasing your intellectual skills.* New York: Harcourt Brace Jovanovich.

———. (1992). Ability tests, measurements, and markets. *Journal of Educational Psychology, 84,* 134–140.

———. (1993). Would you rather take orders from Kirk or Spock? The relation between rational thinking and intelligence. *Journal of Learning Disabilities, 26,* 516–519.

Sternberg, R. J., & Horvath, J. A. (1995). A prototype view of expert teaching. *Educational Researcher, 24,* 9–17.

Sternberg, R. J., & Lubart, L. I. (1993). Creative giftedness: A multivariate investment approach. *Gifted Child Quarterly, 37,* 7–15.

Stevens, R. J., & Slavin, R. E. (1995). The cooperative elementary school: Effects on students' achievement, attitudes, and social relations. *American Educational Research Journal, 32,* 321–351.

Stewart, D. W. (1993). *Immigration and education: The crisis and the opportunities.* New York: Lexington.

Stipek, D. J. (1988). *Motivation to learn: From theory to practice.* Englewood Cliffs, N.J.: Prentice-Hall.

Stofflett, R. T., & Stoddart, T. (1994). The ability to understand and use conceptual change pedagogy as a function of prior content learning experience. *Journal of Research in Science Education, 31,* 31–51.

Stoll, S. K., & Beller, J. M. (1993). *The effect of a longitudinal teaching methodology and classroom environment on both cognitive and behavioral moral development.* Paper presented at the Annual Meeting of the American Alliance for Health, Physical Education, Recreation and Dance, Washington, D.C., March 24–28.

Strawitz, B. M. (1993). The effects of review on science process skill acquisition. *Journal of Science Teacher Education, 4,* 54–57.

Sutton, R. E. (1991). Equity and computers in the schools: A decade of research. *Review of Educational Research, 61,* 474–503.

Swanson, D. B., Norman, G. R., & Linn, R. L. (1995). Performance-based assessment: Lessons from the health professions. *Educational Researcher, 24,* 5–11, 35.

Swanson, H. L. (1992). The relationship between metacognition and problem solving in gifted children. *Roeper Review, 15,* 43–48.

——. (1993). An information processing analysis of learning disabled children's problem solving. *American Educational Research Journal, 30,* 861–893.

Swanson, H. L., O'Connor, J. E., & Cooney, J. B. (1990). An information processing analysis of expert and novice teachers' problem solving. *American Educational Research Journal, 27,* 533–556.

Swanson, J. M., Cantwell, D., Lerner, M., McBurnett, K., & Hanna, G. (1991). Effects of stimulant medication on learning in children with ADHD. *Journal of Learning Disabilities, 24,* 219–230.

Swing, S. R., & Peterson, P. L. (1982). The relationship of student ability and small-group interaction to student achievement. *American Educational Research Journal, 19,* 259–274.

Sykes, G., & Bird, T. (1992). Teacher education and the case idea. In G. Grant (ed.), *Review of research in education* (Vol. 18). Washington, D.C.: American Educational Research Association.

Tamir, P. (1993). Positive and negative multiple choice items: How different are they? *Studies in Educational Evaluation, 19,* 311–325.

Tavris, C., & Baumgartner, A. I. (1983, February). How would your life be different if you'd been born a boy? *Redbook,* p. 99.

Terman, L. M. (1925). *Genetic studies of genius. The mental and physical traits of a thousand gifted children* (Vol. 1). Stanford, Calif.: Stanford University Press.

Terman, L. M., & Oden, M. (1959). *Genetic studies of genius: Vol. 5: The gifted group at mid-life.* Stanford, Calif.: Stanford University Press.

Thissen, D., Wainer, H., & Wang, Xiang-Bo. (1994). Are tests comprising both multiple-choice and free-response items necessarily less unidimensional than multiple-choice tests? An analysis of two tests. *Journal of Educational Measurement, 31,* 113–123.

Thomas, H., & Lohaus, A. (1993). Modeling growth and individual differences in spatial tasks. *Monographs of the Society for Research in Child Development,* serial 237, vol. 58, whole no. 9.

Thomas, J. W. (1980). Agency and achievement: Self-management and self-regard. *Review of Educational Research, 50,* 213–240.

Thomas, R. M. (1992). *Comparing theories of child development* (3rd ed.). Belmont, Calif.: Wadsworth.

Thompson, C., & Crutchlow, E. (1993). Learning style research: A critical review of the literature and implications for nursing education. *Journal of Professional Nursing, 9,* 34–40.

Thorndike, E. L. (1898). Animal intelligence: An experimental study of the associative processes in animals. *Psychological Review Monograph Supplement, 2,* (8).

——. (1913a). *Educational psychology* (Vol. 1). *The psychology of learning.* New York: Teacher's College Press.

——. (1913b). *Educational psychology* (Vol. 2). *The original nature of man.* New York: Teachers College Press.

——. (1931). *Human learning.* New York: Appleton-Century-Crofts.

——. (1932). Reward and punishment in animal learning. *Comparative Psychology Monographs, 8* (39).

——. (1935). *The psychology of wants, interests, and attitudes.* New York: Appleton-Century-Crofts.

Thorndike, R. L., & Hagen, E. (1977). *Measurement and evaluation in psychology and education* (4th ed.). New York: Wiley.

Thorndike, R. L., Hagen, E., & Sattler, J. M. (1985). *Revised Stanford-Binet intelligence scale* (4th ed.). Boston: Houghton Mifflin.

Thurstone, L. L. (1938). *Primary mental abilities. Psychometric Monographs.* Chicago: University of Chicago Press (No. 1).

Tisak, M. S. (1993). Preschool children's judgments of moral and personal events involving physical harm and property damage. *Merrill-Palmer Quarterly, 39,* 375–390.

Tobin, J. J., Wu, D. Y. H., & Davidson, D. H. (1989). *Preschool in three cultures: Japan, China, and the United States*. New Haven, Conn.: Yale University Press.

Tochon, F. V. (1993). From teachers' thinking to macrosemantics: Catching instructional organizers and connectors in language arts. Special Issue: International conference on teacher thinking: II. *Journal of Structural Learning, 12,* 1–22.

Todman, J., & Lawrenson, H. (1992). Computer anxiety in primary schoolchildren and university students. *British Educational Research Journal, 18,* 63–72.

Toffler, A. (1970). *Future shock*. New York: Random House.

——. (1980). *The third wave*. New York: Morrow.

Tonnsen, S., & Patterson, S. (1992). Fighting first-year jitters. *Executive Educator, 14,* 29–30.

Torrance, E. P. (1962). *Guiding creative talent*. Englewood Cliffs, N.J.: Prentice-Hall.

——. (1966). *Torrance tests of creative thinking (Norms technical manual)*. Princeton, N.J.: Personnel Press.

——. (1974). *Torrance tests of creative thinking*. Lexington, Mass.: Ginn.

——. (1986). Teaching creative and gifted learners. In M. C. Wittrock (ed.), *Handbook of research on teaching* (3rd ed.) (pp. 630–647). New York: Macmillan.

——. (1993). The beyonders in a thirty year longitudinal study of creative achievement. *Roeper Review, 15,* 131–135.

Tryon, G. S. (1980). The measurement and treatment of text anxiety. *Review of Educational Research, 50,* 343–372.

Tryon, R. C. (1940). Genetic differences in maze learning in rats. *Yearbook of the National Society for Studies in Education, 39,* 111–119.

Tsang, M. C. (1988). Cost analysis for educational policymaking: A review of cost studies in education in developing countries. *Review of Educational Research, 58,* 181–230.

Tulving, E. (1989). Remembering and knowing the past. *American Scientist, 77,* 361–367.

——. (1991). Concepts in human memory. In L. R. Squire, N. M. Weinberger, G. Lynch, & J. L. McGaugh (eds.), *Memory: Organization and locus of change*. New York: Oxford University Press.

Turner, N. D. (1993). Learning styles and metacognition. *Reading Improvement, 30,* 82–85.

Turner, R. L., & Denny, D. A. (1969, February). Teacher characteristics, teacher behavior, and changes in pupil creativity. *Elementary School Journal,* pp. 265–270.

Tyler-Wood, T., & Carri, L. (1991). Identification of gifted children: The effectiveness of various measures of cognitive ability. *Roeper Review, 14,* 63–64.

Tynan, W. D., & Nearing, J. (1994). The diagnosis of attention deficit hyperactivity disorder in young children. *Infants and Young Children, 6,* 13–20.

U.S. Bureau of the Census. (1992). *Statistical abstracts of the United States, 1991* (112th ed.). Washington, D.C.: U.S. Government Printing Office.

——. (1994). *Statistical abstracts of the United States, 1994* (114th ed.). Washington, D.C.: U.S. Government Printing Office.

U.S. Department of Education. (1991). *Twelfth annual report to Congress on the implementation of PL 94-142: The education for all handicapped children act*. Washington, D.C.: U.S. Government Printing Office.

U.S. Office of Education. (1977, August 23). Implementation of part B of the Education of the Handicapped Act. *Federal Register, 42,* 42474–42518.

Uguroglu, M. E., & Walberg, H. J. (1979). Motivation and achievement: A quantitative synthesis. *American Educational Research Journal, 6,* 191–206.

Ukrainian famine survivors recall season in hell. (1983, October 20). *Edmonton Journal,* p. A1.

Ulrich, R. E., & Azrin, N. H. (1962). Reflexive fighting in response to aversive stimulation. *Journal of Experimental Analysis of Behavior, 5,* 511–521.

Umoren, J. A. (1992). Maslow hierarchy of needs and OBRA 1987: Toward need satisfaction by nursing home residents. *Educational Gerontology, 18,* 657–670.

Urban, K. K. (1991). Giftedness and behavioural disorders. *International Journal of Special Education, 6,* 12–27.

Urban, K. K., & Jellen, H. (1986). Assessing creative potential via drawing production: The Test for Creative Thinking-Drawing Production (TCT-DP). In A. J. Cropley, K. K. Urban, H. Wagner, & W. H. Wieczerkowski (eds.), *Giftedness: A continuing worldwide challenge*. New York: Trillium.

Uzgiris, I. C., & Hunt, J. (1975). *Assessment in infancy: Ordinal scales of psychological development.* Urbana: University of Illinois Press.

Valencia, S. W., & Place, N. (1994). Portfolios: A process for enhancing teaching and learning. *Reading Teacher, 47,* 666–669.

Valli, L. (1992). Beginning teacher problems: Areas for teacher education improvement. *Action in Teacher Education, 14,* 18–25.

Valsiner, J. (1987). *Culture and the development of children's action: A cultural-historical theory of developmental psychology.* New York: Wiley.

Van Houten, R., & Doleys, D. M. (1983). Are social reprimands effective? In S. Axelrod & J. Apsche (eds.), *The effects of punishment on human behavior.* New York: Academic.

Van Houten, R., Nau, P. A., MacKenzie-Keating, S., Sameoto, D., & Colavecchia, B. (1982). An analysis of some variables influencing the effectiveness of reprimands. *Journal of Applied Behavior Analysis, 15,* 65–83.

Van Reusen, A. K., & Bos, C. S. (1994). Facilitating student participation in individualized education programs through motivation strategy instruction. *Exceptional Children, 60,* 466–475.

Vasquez-Levy, D. (1993). The use of practical arguments in clarifying and changing practical reasoning and classroom practices: Two cases. *Journal of Curriculum Studies, 25,* 125–143.

Vaughn, T. (1993). Rachel and her mother needed positive reinforcement: A seasoned classroom teacher helps mother and daughter. *Gifted Child Today, 16,* 36–37, 42.

Vernon, P. E. (1969). *Intelligence and cultural environment.* London: Methuen.

Volk, D., & Stahlman, J. I. (1994). "I think everybody is afraid of the unknown": Early childhood teachers prepare for mainstreaming. *Day Care and Early Education, 21,* 13–17.

Vosniadou, S., & Brewer, W. F. (1992). Mental models of the earth: A study of conceptual change in childhood. *Cognitive Psychologist, 24,* 535–585.

Vosniadou, S., & Saljo, R. (eds.). (1994). Conceptual change in the physical sciences. *Learning and Instruction, 4,* 1–121 (whole issue).

Voss, J. F., Wiley, J., & Carretero, M. (1995). Acquiring intellectual skills. *Annual Review of Psychology, 46,* 155–181.

Vygotsky, L. S. (1962). *Thought and language* (E. Hamsman & G. Vankan, eds. and trans.). Cambridge, Mass.: MIT Press.

——. (1978). *Mind in society.* Cambridge, Mass.: Harvard University Press.

——. (1986). *Thought and language* (A. Kozulin, ed. and trans.). Cambridge, Mass.: MIT Press.

——. (1991). *Pedagogicheskaia psikhologiia* [Pedagogical psychology, 2nd ed.]. Moscow: Pedagogika. (Original work published in 1926).

——. (1992). *Educational psychology* (M. O'Connor & R. Silverman, eds.). Winter Park, Fla.: PMD Publications.

——. (1993). *The collected works of L. S. Vygotsky. Vol. 2: Fundamentals of defectology (abnormal psychology & learning disability).* New York: Plenum.

Vygotsky, L. S., & Luria, A. R. (1993). *Studies on the history of behavior: Ape, primitive man, & child* (V. I. Golod & J. E. Knox, eds.). Hillsdale, N.J.: Erlbaum.

Wade, R. C. (1994). Conceptual change in elementary social studies: A case study of fourth graders' understanding of human rights. *Theory and Research in Social Education, 22,* 74–95.

Waggoner, D. (1991). *Undereducation in America: The demography of high school dropouts.* New York: Auburn.

Wagner, M. E., Schubert, H. J. P., & Schubert, D. S. P. (1985). Effects of sibling spacing on intelligence, interfamiliar relations, psychosocial characteristics, and mental and physical health. *Advances in Child Development and Behavior, 19,* 196–198.

Wagner, P. A. (1994). Adaptations for administering the Peabody Picture Vocabulary Test-Revised to individuals with severe communication and motor dysfunctions. *Mental Retardation, 32,* 107–112.

Wagner, R. K., & Sternberg, R. J. (1984). Alternative conceptions of intelligence and their implications for education. *Review of Educational Research, 54,* 179–223.

Walberg, H. J. (1986). Syntheses of research on teaching. In M. C. Wittrock (ed.), *Handbook of research on teaching* (3rd ed.). New York: Macmillan.

Walker, H. (1979). *The acting-out child: Coping with classroom disruption.* Boston: Allyn & Bacon.

Walker, R. (1990, February 28). Governors set to adopt national education goals. *Education Week,* p. 16.

Wallach, M. A. (1985). Creativity testing and giftedness. In F. D. Horowitz & M. O'Brien (eds.), *The gifted and talented: Developmental perspectives* (pp. 99–123). Washington, D.C.: American Psychological Association.

Wallach, M. A., & Kogan, N. (1965). *Modes of thinking in young children: A study of the creativity-intelligence distinction.* New York: Holt, Rinehart & Winston.

Walters, G. C., & Grusec, J. E. (1977). *Punishment.* San Francisco: Freeman.

Walters, R. H., & Llewellyn, T. E. (1963). Enhancement of punitiveness by visual and audiovisual displays. *Canadian Journal of Psychology, 17,* 244–255.

Walters, R. H., Llewellyn, T. E., & Acker, W. (1962). Enhancement of punitive behavior by audiovisual displays. *Science, 136,* 872–873.

Wang, M. C., Haertel, G. D., & Walberg, H. J. (1993). Toward a knowledge base for school learning. *Review of Educational Research, 63,* 249–294.

Ward, M. F. (1994). Attention deficit hyperactivity disorder. In R. J. Sternberg (ed.), *Encyclopedia of human intelligence* (Vol. 1). New York: Macmillan.

Waterhouse, P. (1991). *Tutoring.* Stafford, England: Network Educational Press.

Watson, B. (1994). Switch off kids' science misconceptions. *Learning, 22,* 74–76.

Watson, J. B. (1913). Psychology as the behaviorist views it. *Psychological Review, 20,* 157–158.

——. (1916). The place of a conditioned reflex in psychology. *Psychological Review, 23,* 89–116.

——. (1930). *Behaviorism* (2nd ed.). Chicago: University of Chicago Press.

Webster, S. W. (1968). *Discipline in the classroom: Basic principles and problems.* New York: Chandler.

Wechsler, D. (1958). *The measurement and appraisal of adult intelligence* (4th ed.). Baltimore: Williams & Wilkins.

Weinberg, R. (1989). Intelligence and IQ. *American Psychologist, 44,* 98–104.

Weiner, B. (1984). Principles for a theory of student motivation and their application within an attributional framework. In R. Ames & C. Ames (eds.), *Research on motivation in education (Vol. 1): Student motivation.* New York: Academic.

——. (1992). *Human motivation: Metaphors, theories and research.* Newbury Park, Calif.: Sage.

——. (1994). Integrating social and personal theories of achievement striving. *Review of Educational Research, 64,* 557–573.

Weinstein, C. F., & Mayer, R. F. (1986). The teaching of learning strategies. In M. C. Wittrock (ed.), *Handbook of research on teaching* (3rd ed.) (pp. 315–327). New York: Macmillan.

Weinstein, R. S., Madison, S. M., & Kuklinski, M. R. (1995). Raising expectations in schooling: Obstacles and opportunities for change. *American Educational Research Journal, 32,* 121–159.

Wellman, H. M. (1990). *The child's theory of mind.* Cambridge, Mass.: MIT Press.

Wellman, H. M., & Gelman, S. A. (1992). Cognitive development: Foundational theories of core domains. *Annual Review of Psychology, 43,* 337–375.

Wells, A. S., Hirshberg, D., Lipton, M., & Oakes, J. (1995). Bounding the case within its context: A constructivist approach to studying detracking reform. *Educational Researcher, 24,* 18–24.

West, L. (1988). Implications of recent research for improving secondary school science learning. In P. Ramsden (ed.), *Improving learning: New perspectives.* London: Kogan Page.

West, L. W., & MacArthur, R. S. (1964). An evaluation of selected intelligence tests for two samples of Metis and Indian children. *Alberta Journal of Educational Research, 10,* 17–27.

West, R. C., & Marcotte, D. R. (1993–94). The effects of an integrated learning system (ILS) using incremental time allotments on ninth grade algebra achievement. *Journal of Educational Technology Systems, 22,* 283–294.

Whitaker, P. (1994). Mainstream students talk about integration. *British Journal of Special Education, 17,* 13–16.

White, M. A. (1975). Natural rates of teacher approval and disapproval in the classroom. *Journal of Applied Behavior Analysis, 8,* 367–372.

White, R. T., & Tisher, R. P. (1986). Research on natural sciences. In M. C. Wittrock (ed.), *Handbook of research on teaching* (3rd ed.). New York: Macmillan.

White, R. W. (1959). Motivation reconsidered: The concept of competence. *Psychological Review, 66,* 297–333.

Whitener, E. M. (1989). A meta-analytic review of the effect on learning of the interaction between prior achievement and instructional support. *Review of Educational Research, 59,* 65–86.

Wigdor, A. K., & Garner, W. R. (eds.). (1982). *Ability testing: Uses, consequences, and controversies, Part 1: Report of the Committee.* Washington, D.C.: National Academy Press.

Wilczenski, F. L. (1994). Changes in attitudes toward mainstreaming among undergraduate education students. *Educational Research Quarterly, 17,* 5–17.

Wilgosh, L. (1991). Underachievement and related issues for culturally different gifted children. *International Journal of Special Education, 6,* 82–93.

Wilson, K., & Tally, W. (1990). The "Palenque" project: Formative evaluation in the design and development of an optical disc prototype. In B. Flagg (ed.), *Formative evaluation for educational technologies.* Hillsdale, N.J.: Erlbaum.

Wilson, L. (1988). Phase change: Larry Wilson on selling in a brave new world. *Training, 11,* 14.

Wineburg, S. S. (1987). The self-fulfillment of the self-fulfilling prophecy: A critical appraisal. *Educational Researcher, 16,* 28–37.

Winfield, L. F. (1990). School competency testing reforms and student achievement: Exploring a national perspective. *Educational Evaluation and Policy Analysis, 12,* 157–173.

Winick, M. (1976). *Malnutrition and brain development.* New York: Oxford University Press.

Winn, W. (1990). Some implications of cognitive theory for instructional design. *Instructional Science, 19,* 53–69.

Winsten, S. (1949). *Days with Bernard Shaw.* New York: Vanguard Press.

Wise, S. L., Lukin, L. E., & Roos, L. L. (1991). Teacher beliefs about training in testing and measurement. *Journal of Teacher Education, 42,* 37–42.

Wiske, M. S. (1994). How teaching for understanding changes the rules in the classroom. *Educational Leadership, 51,* 19–21.

Wittrock, M. C. (1986). Students' thought processes. In M. C. Wittrock (ed.), *Handbook of research on teaching* (3rd ed.) (pp. 297–314). New York: Macmillan.

———. (1992). An empowering conception of educational psychology. *Educational Psychologist, 27,* 129–141.

Wolf, D., Bixby, J., Glenn, J., & Gardner, H. (1991). To use their minds well: Investigating new forms of student assessment. In G. Grant (ed.), *Review of research in education* (Vol. 17). Washington, D.C.: American Educational Research Association.

Wood, B. S. (1981). *Children and communication: Verbal and nonverbal language development* (2nd ed.). Englewood Cliffs, N.J.: Prentice-Hall.

Wood, D., Bruner, J. S., & Ross, G. (1976). The role of tutoring in problem solving. *Journal of Child Psychology and Psychiatry, 17,* 89–100.

Woodward, J., Carnine, D., & Gersten, R. (1988). Teaching problem solving through computer simulations. *American Educational Research Journal, 25,* 72–86.

Yoder, S. (1992). The turtle and the mouse . . . A tale. *The Computing Teacher, 20,* 41–43.

Zajonc, R. B. (1975, January). Birth order and intelligence: Dumber by the dozen. *Psychology Today,* pp. 37–43.

———. (1976). Family configuration and intelligence. *Science, 192,* 227–236.

———. (1986). The decline and rise of scholastic aptitude scores: A prediction derived from the confluence model. *American Psychologist, 41,* 862–867.

Zajonc, R., & Markus, G. B. (1975). Birth order and intellectual development. *Psychological Review, 82,* 74–88.

Zentall, S. S. (1993). Research on the educational implications of attention deficit hyperactivity disorder. *Exceptional Children, 60,* 143–153.

Zigler, E., & Hodapp, R. M. (1991). Behavioral functioning in individuals with mental retardation. *Annual Review of Psychology, 42,* 29–50.

Zimmerman, B. J., Bandura, A., & Martinez-Pons, M. (1992). Self-motivation for academic attainment: The role of self-efficacy beliefs and personal goal setting. *American Educational Research Journal, 29,* 663–676.

GLOSSARY

This glossary defines the most important terms used (and **boldfaced**) in this book. In each case, the meaning given corresponds to the term's use in the text. For more complete definitions, consult a psychological dictionary, which can be found in most libraries.

acceleration An approach in the education of the gifted. Acceleration programs attempt to move students through the conventional curriculum more rapidly than normal. See also *enrichment*.

accommodation Modification of an activity or ability in the face of environmental demands. In Piaget's description of development, assimilation and accommodation are the means by which individuals interact with and adapt to their world. See also *adaptation, assimilation*.

achievement motivation A need that, if high, is evident in a strong desire to achieve, to excel, to reach a high level of excellence. Achievement motivation can also be low.

adaptation Changes in an organism in response to the environment. Such changes are assumed to facilitate interaction with that environment. Adaptation plays a central role in Piaget's theory. See also *accommodation, assimilation*.

additive bilingualism Phrase used to describe situations in which learning a second language has a positive effect on the first, as well as on general psychological functioning. See *subtractive bilingualism*.

advance organizers Introductory information that is given to learners to help them understand, learn, and remember new material.

affective domain Bloom's expression for the grouping of educational goals that relate to affect (emotion), and that are evident in behaviors relating to motivation, interest, and values. See also *cognitive domain*.

affective learning Changes in attitudes or emotions (affect) as a function of experience.

age-equivalent scores Standardized test norms that allow users to convert raw scores to age equivalents. Such norms allow test users to interpret the subject's performance in terms of the average performance of a comparable group of children of a specified age. See also *grade-equivalent scores, standardized test*.

aggression In human beings, a much-studied characteristic that is generally defined as the conscious and willful inflicting of pain on others.

alpha waves Relatively high-amplitude but low-frequency brain waves associated with a relaxed but wakeful state. See also *beta waves*.

analysis The process of breaking down into component parts. As an intellectual activity, it consists primarily of examining relationships among ideas in an attempt to understand them better. It is a relatively high-level intellectual skill in Bloom's taxonomy of educational objectives.

anxiety A feeling of apprehension, worry, tension, or nervousness.

application An educational objective described by Bloom. Consists primarily of the ability to use abstractions in concrete situations.

arousal As a physiological concept, arousal refers to changes in functions such as heart rate, respiration rate, electrical activity in the cortex, and electrical conductivity of the skin. As a psychological concept, arousal refers to degree of alertness, awareness, vigilance, or wakefulness. Arousal varies from very low (coma or sleep) to very high (panic or high anxiety).

articulation A cognitive apprenticeship technique in which learners are encouraged to put their conclusions, descriptions, and principles into words.

artificial intelligence (AI) Describes models, procedures, devices, or mechanisms intended to simulate or duplicate some of the intelligent functions of human mental activity.

assertive discipline The take-charge, aggressive, classroom management model advocated by Canter, based squarely on the notion that not only should teachers reinforce desirable behaviors, but they should punish those that are undesirable.

assessment A judgmental process intimately involved in the teaching/learning process. A general term for the process of appraising student performance. May include elements of both measurement and evaluation. See also *evaluation, measurement.*

assimilation The act of incorporating objects or aspects of objects into previously learned activities. To assimilate is, in a sense, to ingest or to use something that was learned previously. See also *accommodation, adaptation.*

associationistic Theories that are associationistic are concerned with behavior and the connections or associations that are formed among stimuli and responses.

attention deficit hyperactivity disorder (ADHD) A disorder marked by excessive general activity for the child's age, attention problems, high impulsivity, and low frustration tolerance. Also termed *hyperactivity.*

attitude A prevailing and consistent tendency to react in a certain way. Attitudes can be positive or negative and are important motivational forces.

attribute–treatment interaction The relationship of students' characteristics (attributes), teaching methods (treatments), and outcomes. These relationships are sometimes quite complex. Thus, a given treatment (instructional method, for example) may be more effective for students with certain attributes than it is for others with different attributes.

attribution theory A cognitive motivational theory concerned with predictable consistencies in what people interpret as the causes of the outcomes of behavior. See also *external orientation, internal orientation, locus of control.*

authentic assessment Refers to assessment procedures designed to allow students to demonstrate their ability to apply learning in real-life situations. Often contrasted to assessment based solely on objective tests, especially of the multiple-choice variety. Also termed *performance assessment.* See also *performance assessment.*

autoinstructional device Any instructional device that is effective in the absence of a teacher. Common examples are workbooks and computers.

autonomy Piaget's label for the second stage of moral development, characterized by a reliance on internal standards of right and wrong as guides for action and for judging the morality of an action. See also *heteronomy.*

aversive control The control of human behavior, usually through the presentation of noxious (unpleasant) stimuli. This is in contrast to techniques of positive control, which generally use positive reinforcement.

avoidance learning A conditioning phenomenon usually involving aversive (unpleasant) stimulation, wherein the organism learns to avoid situations associated with specific unpleasant circumstances. See also *escape learning.*

basic needs Maslow's term for lower level needs, such as the physiological needs as well as the need to belong, to love, and to have high self-esteem. Also termed *deficiency needs.* See also *deficiency needs, growth needs, metaneeds.*

bear (a literal bear) A bob-tailed, omnivorous, quadrupedal mammal that walks on the soles of its feet inventing poetic images and humming wonderful love songs. See also *bear (the metaphoric politically correct bear)*.

bear (the metaphoric politically correct bear) A today kind of bear. A bear who has abandoned old prejudices and attitudes and deep-seated, ethnically based convictions of rightness and goodness. A tolerant and multicultural and multilingual and outstandingly cool bear. A good and wise bear, albeit a bear perched somewhat uncomfortably on a pointed fence, overwhelmed by the potential political consequences of commiting himself to one side or the other. See also *bear (a literal bear), wild cow*.

behavior The activity of an organism. Behavior may be overt (visible) or covert (invisible or internal).

behavior management See *behavior modification*.

behavior modification Changes in the behavior of an individual; also refers to psychological theory and research concerned with the application of psychological principles in attempts to change behavior.

behavioral objective Phrase used to describe an instructional objective that can be expressed in terms of specific, observable, measurable behaviors. Mager's instructional objectives are behavioral objectives. See also *expressive objectives*.

behaviorism A general term for theories of learning concerned primarily with the observable components of behavior (stimuli and responses).

behavioristic theories See *stimulus–response (S–R) theories*.

belief The acceptance of an idea as being accurate or truthful. Beliefs are often highly personal and resistant to change. See also *law, model, principle, theory*.

beta waves High frequency, low amplitude brain waves associated with alertness and higher arousal. See also *alpha waves*.

biofeedback Information we obtain about our biological functioning. In a specialized sense, biofeedback refers to information subjects receive about the activity of their nervous system when they are connected to one of various sensors or instruments designed for that purpose. See also *neurofeedback*.

brainstorming A technique popularized by Osborn and used in the production of creative solutions for problems. A brainstorming session usually involves a small group of people who are encouraged to produce a wide variety of ideas, which are evaluated later. See also *Gordon technique*.

branching program Programmed material that, in contrast to a linear program, presents a variety of alternative routes through the material. Such programs typically make use of larger frames than do linear programs, and they frequently use multiple choices. Also termed *Crowder programs*. See also *frames*.

CAI One of many acronyms related to the application of computer technology in education. Specifically, CAI refers to computer-assisted instruction, the use of computers for instructional rather than administrative purposes.

capability A capacity to do something. To be capable is to have the necessary knowledge and skills.

category A term used by Bruner to describe a grouping of related objects or events. In this sense, a category is both a concept and a percept. Bruner also defines it as a rule for classifying things as equal. See also *coding system*.

causes Agents or forces that produce an effect or a result. Causes are one aspect of motivation. See also *reasons*.

central tendency The tendency for the majority of scores in a normal distribution to cluster around the center of the distribution. Measures of central tendency include the mean, the mode, and the median. See also *mean, median, mode*.

cerebral palsy Label for a collection of congenital problems associated with brain damage and manifested in motor problems of varying severity, and occasionally in other problems such as convulsions or behavior disorders.

chains A term used by Robert Gagné to signify the learning of related sequences of responses. A chain is a series of stimulus–response bonds in that each response in the sequence serves as a stimulus for the next response. Motor chains are involved in my keyboarding of this material. In a sense, it's as though when I type Y-O-U, the stimulus Y leads to the response of depressing the "Y" key, which is now a signal (stimulus) that leads to the next response (pressing "O"), and so on.

character An inclusive and ill-defined term signifying those aspects of human personality that include the individual's values, moral strength, principles, virtues, and vices. Relates to what we think of as the goodness or moral strength of the individual.

chunking A memory process whereby related items are grouped together into more easily remembered chunks (for example, a prefix and four digits for a phone number rather than seven unrelated numbers).

circles of knowledge A generic term sometimes used to describe a variety of small-group learning approaches. These approaches stress face-to-face interaction, peer help, and rewards for cooperative, group activities rather than for individual activity. Such approaches are highly cooperative rather than competitive or individualistic.

classical conditioning Also called "learning-through-stimulus substitution" because it involves the repeated pairing of two stimuli so that eventually a previously neutral (conditioned) stimulus comes to elicit the same response (conditioned response) that was previously elicited by the first stimulus (unconditioned stimulus). This was the type of conditioning first described by Pavlov. See also *conditioning, operant conditioning*.

classification The act of grouping in terms of common properties. Classification involves abstracting the properties of objects or events and making judgments concerning how they are similar to or different from other objects or events.

classroom management A comprehensive term for the variety of teacher actions designed to facilitate teaching and learning in the classroom. Classroom management includes disciplinary actions, as well as daily routines, seating arrangements, and scheduling of lessons.

client-centered therapy Type of patient–counselor relationship in which the counselor (therapist or psychiatrist) is not directive in the sense of telling clients how they should behave but rather attempts to allow patients to express themselves and discover within themselves ways of dealing with their own behavior. This therapeutic approach is generally contrasted with directive therapy. Also termed *person-centered therapy*. See also *counseling, directive therapy*.

coaching A technique sometimes used in cognitive apprenticeship approaches to instruction, in which the learner's cognitive behavior is guided by an expert.

cocktail party phenomenon An expression to describe sensory memory. The fleeting and unconscious availability for processing of stimuli to which the individual is not paying attention.

coding system A Brunerian concept; refers to a hierarchical arrangement of related categories. See also *category, hierarchy of classes*.

cognition To cognize is to know. Hence, cognition deals with knowing, understanding, problem solving, and related intellectual processes.

cognitive apprenticeship An instructional model wherein parents, siblings, other adults, and especially teachers serve as a combination of model, guide, tutor, mentor, and coach to foster intellectual growth among learners.

cognitive behavior modification An approach that combines the behavioristic principles of operant conditioning (mainly principles of reinforcement) with the power of reasoning and with the human ability to imagine the consequences of behavior in an effort to bring about behavior change.

cognitive domain Bloom's expression for the area of educational activity and educational objectives relating to acquiring information, understanding, analyzing, synthesizing, and so on. See also *affective domain*.

cognitive learning Learning concerned primarily with acquiring information, developing strategies for processing information, decision-making processes, and logical thought processes.

cognitive strategies The processes involved in learning and remembering. Cognitive strategies include identifying problems, selecting approaches to their solution, monitoring progress in solving problems, and using feedback. Cognitive strategies are closely related to metacognition and metamemory. See also *knowledge acquisition components, learning/thinking strategy, metacognition, metacomponents, metamemory, performance components*.

cognitive structure The organized totality of an individual's knowledge. Also termed *mental structure*. See also *knowledge*.

cognitivism Theories of learning concerned primarily with such topics as perception, problem solving, information processing, and understanding.

cohort A group of individuals born within the same specified period of time. For example, the cohort of the 1950s includes those born between January 1, 1950, and December 31, 1959, inclusive.

collaborative learning See *cooperative learning*.

combined schedule A combination of various types of schedules of reinforcement.

communication The transmission of a message from one organism to another. Communication does not necessarily involve language because some nonhuman animals can communicate, usually through reflexive behaviors. See also *language*.

comparative organizer A concept or idea that serves to facilitate the learning of new material by making use of the similarities and differences between the new material and previous learning.

competence motivation R. W. White's phrase for our innate need to achieve competence and to feel competent. According to White, competence motivation has especially important adaptive value in a species that is born with little innate competence.

competitive learning One of the most common instructional approaches in North America. Involves students working against each other to see who is best. In competitive learning, student rewards are inversely related to the performance of others. See also *cooperative learning, individualistic learning*.

componential theory of intelligence Sternberg's view that intelligence can usefully be viewed as consisting of three sets of components, each of which relates to how the individual processes information: metacomponents (metastrategies), performance components, and knowledge acquisition components. See also *knowledge acquisition components, metacomponents, performance components*.

comprehension The lowest level of understanding in Bloom's hierarchy of educational objectives; defined as the ability to apprehend the meaning of communication without necessarily being able to apply, analyze, or evaluate it.

computer literacy The minimal skills required for interaction with computers. Does not require knowing how a computer functions internally or how to program it.

computer simulations Mimicking or modeling certain actions, procedures, or phenomena using computers. For example, computers might be used to simulate (copy the actions of) weather patterns or chemical reactions.

computer-assisted instruction (CAI) The use of computer facilities to help in instruction.

concept A collection of perceptual experiences or ideas that are related by virtue of their possessing common properties.

concept map See *conceptual model*.

conceptual change movement Literally, cognitive changes such as might be evident in greater understanding, knowledge, and awareness. More specifically, the expression refers to instructional approaches designed to foster mental reorganization rather than simply to increase the number of facts learned.

conceptual model A verbal or graphic representation of concepts and important relationships that exist among them. Designed to assist the learner in developing a clear and useful mental representation. Also termed a *concept map*.

concrete operations The third of Piaget's four major stages, lasting from age 7 or 8 to approximately age 11 or 12, and characterized largely by the child's ability to deal with concrete problems and objects or objects and problems easily imagined.

concurrent validity See *criterion-related validity*.

conditioned response (CR) A response elicited by a conditioned stimulus. In some obvious ways, a conditioned response resembles, but is not identical to, its corresponding unconditioned response. See also *neutral stimulus*.

conditioned stimulus (CS) A stimulus that initially does not elicit any response or that elicits a global, orienting response but that, as a function of being paired with an unconditioned stimulus and its response, acquires the capability of eliciting that same response. For example, a stimulus that is always present at the time of a fear reaction may become a conditioned stimulus for fear.

conditioning A type of learning describable in terms of changing relationships between stimuli, between responses, or between both stimuli and responses. See also *classical conditioning, operant conditioning*.

conditions of learning Robert Gagné's expression for the internal and external circumstances that affect behavior as well as information processing and retrieval. External conditions of learning might include factors such as repetition, reinforcement, stimulus intensity, and so on; internal conditions include motivation, goals, and previously learned capabilities.

conflict management Label given to a program designed to teach individuals acceptable ways of resolving conflicts. Common conflict management techniques include negotiating, compromising, taking turns, explaining, listening, apologizing, mediation, using humor, and invoking chance.

confluence model Zajonc's term for the hypothesis that the intellectual climate of the home, determined principally in terms of the numbers and ages of family members, contributes in important ways to the development of children's intelligence. According to this model, children born into a relatively adult environment (firstborn and only children, for example) should, on average, have an intellectual advantage over those born in a less adult environment (later-born children, children in large families, children in single-parent homes).

connectionism A theory that explains learning as the formation of bonds (connections) between stimuli and responses. The term is attributed to E. L. Thorndike.

conservation A Piagetian term for the realization that certain quantitative attributes of objects remain unchanged unless something is added to or taken away from them. Such characteristics of objects as mass, number, area, and volume are capable of being conserved.

construct validity An estimate of test validity based on the extent to which test results agree with and reflect the theories that underlie the test. See also *content validity, criterion-related validity, face validity, reliability, validity.*

constructivist approach A general term for discovery-oriented approaches to teaching, so-called because of their assumption that learners should build (construct) knowledge for themselves.

content A term used by Guilford to describe the content of a person's intellect. Intellectual activity (operations) involves content and results in products. See also *convergent thinking, creativity, divergent thinking, operation, product.*

content validity Test validity determined by a careful analysis of the content of test items and a comparison of this content with course objectives. See also *construct validity, criterion-related validity, face validity, reliability, validity.*

context Refers to all of the developmentally important characteristics of the environment in which development occurs—for example, culture, cohort influences, the family, historical events, educational experiences, and so on.

contextual theory of intelligence Robert Sternberg's view that intelligence involves adaptation in the real world—that is, adaptation in the individual's context. See also *componential theory of intelligence.*

contiguity The occurrence of things both simultaneously and in the same space. Contiguity is frequently used to explain the occurrence of classical conditioning. It is assumed that the simultaneity of the unconditioned and the conditioned stimulus is sufficient to explain the formation of the link between the two.

continuous reinforcement A reinforcement schedule in which every correct response is followed by a reinforcer. See also *fixed schedule, intermittent reinforcement, interval schedule, random schedule, ratio schedule, schedule of reinforcement.*

convergent thinking A term used by Guilford to describe the type of thinking that results in a single, correct solution for a problem. Most conventional tests of intelligence measure convergent rather than divergent thinking. See also *content, creativity, divergent thinking, operation, product.*

cooperative learning An instructional method in which students work together in small groups so that each member of the group can participate in a clearly assigned, collective task. Also termed *collaborative learning.* See also *competitive learning, individualistic learning.*

corporal punishment Punishment that uses physical force to inflict pain.

corrective strategies Strategies designed to correct discipline problems. Often involve the systematic use of rewards and punishments.

correlation A statistical relationship between variables. See also *variable.*

correlative subsumption The type of learning that takes place when new information requires an extension of what was previously known and could not, therefore, have been derived directly from it. See also *derivative subsumption, subsumption.*

counseling The act of giving advice. See also *client-centered therapy, directive therapy.*

craft knowledge Knowledge of the specifics of teaching. The science of teaching, as well as a sort of practical wisdom that includes general information about teaching as well as specific information about teaching particular subjects and lessons to students with identifiable characteristics.

creativity Generally refers to the capacity of individuals to produce novel or original answers or products. The term *creative* is an adjective that may be used to describe people, products, or processes. See also *convergent thinking, divergent thinking*.

criterion-referenced testing Test in which the student is judged relative to a criterion rather than relative to the performance of other students. The teacher decides beforehand the specific performance expected and tests to see whether the student has reached this criterion. See also *norm-referenced testing*.

criterion-related validity A measure of the extent to which predictions based on test results are accurate (predictive validity) and the extent to which the test agrees with other related measures (concurrent validity). Also termed *predictive validity*. See also *construct validity, content validity, face validity, reliability, validity*.

critical period A period in development during which exposure to appropriate experiences or stimuli will bring about specific learning much more easily than is the case at other times. See also *imprinting*.

crystallized abilities Cattell's term for intellectual abilities that are highly dependent on experience (verbal and numerical abilities, for example). These abilities do not appear to decline significantly with advancing age. See also *fluid abilities*.

culture The pattern of socially acceptable behaviors that characterizes a people or a social group. It includes all the attitudes and beliefs that the group has about the things it considers important.

databases Sources of information accessible by computers. Common databases include library cataloguing systems or abstracts of current journal articles. Databases are often organized by topics. For example, PSYCHINFO is a vast database that contains summaries of an enormous number of articles published in journals relevant to psychology.

declarative knowledge All the facts, information, and experiences that are part of what we know. Also termed *declarative memory*. See also *procedural knowledge*.

declarative memory Explicit, conscious long-term memory, in contrast with implicit (or nondeclarative) memory. Declarative memory may be either semantic or episodic. Also termed *explicit memory*. See also *episodic memory, semantic memory*.

deferred imitation The ability to imitate people or events in their absence. Deferred imitation is assumed to be crucial in the development of language abilities.

deficiency needs Maslow's expression for basic needs, so called because they motivate the person to act when a related deficiency is sensed—for example, a deficiency of food leads to eating, a deficiency of self-esteem leads to behaviors intended to increase esteem. See also *basic needs, growth needs, metaneeds*.

derivative subsumption The type of subsumption (or learning) that takes place when new material can be derived directly from what is already known. See also *correlative subsumption, subsumption*.

desist To stop, to refrain from. In education, desists are teacher behaviors intended to make a student stop (desist from) some ongoing or impending misbehavior. Desists may take the form of threats, simple requests, orders, pleas, and so on. See also *with-it-ness*.

development The growth, maturational, and learning processes from birth to maturity. See also *growth, maturation*.

developmental arithmetic disorder A learning disability evident in specific problems in developing arithmetic skills in the absence of other problems such as mental retardation.

developmental assessments A performance-based assessment that looks at the student's performance in relation to developmental or course-based expectations rather than in relation to the performance of other students. Often uses checklists of expected (desired) behaviors.

developmental reading disorder A learning disability manifested in reading problems of varying severity—sometimes evident in spelling difficulties. Also termed *dyslexia* or *specific reading disability*.

dialectical thinking Thinking that recognizes, accepts, and attempts to resolve conflicts. Dialectical thinking is thought to be more characteristic of adults than of children or adolescents.

differential reinforcement of successive approximations The procedure of reinforcing only some responses and not others. Differential reinforcement is used in the shaping of complex behaviors. See also *shaping*.

direct reinforcement The type of reinforcement that affects the individual in question directly rather than vicariously. See also *vicarious reinforcement*.

direct teaching style A relatively authoritarian approach to teaching in which teachers are the primary source of information. See also *indirect teaching style*.

directive therapy Type of counselor–client relationship in which the counselor takes the major responsibility for directing the client's behavior. See also *counseling*.

discipline The control aspects of teaching.

discovery learning The acquisition of new information or knowledge largely as a result of the learner's own efforts. Discovery learning is contrasted with expository or reception learning and is generally associated with Bruner, among others. See also *reception learning*.

discriminated stimulus(S^D) A stimulus that is perceived by the organism. In operant conditioning, the discriminated stimulus elicits the response.

discrimination Processes involved in learning that certain responses are appropriate in specific situations but inappropriate in other similar situations. Generalization is an opposite process. See also *generalization*.

disinhibition The appearance of a suppressed behavior. See also *inhibitory-disinhibitory effect*.

disposition An inclination or a tendency to do (or not to do) something; an aspect of motivation. See also *motives*.

dissociability A term used by Ausubel to indicate the ease with which material that is to be recalled can be separated (dissociated) from other related material that is also in memory.

distance education An educational delivery system that involves little or no face-to-face contact, but wherein instructional material is presented at a distance, often using one or more of a combination of computers, electronic networking facilities, telephone conferencing, facsimile transmitters, radio, television, film, videocassette recordings, or other communication media.

distance receptors The senses that receive stimulation from a distance (for example, hearing and vision).

divergent thinking An expression used by Guilford to describe the type of thinking that results in the production of several different solutions for one problem. Divergent thinking is assumed to be closely related to creative behavior, and the term is used interchangeably with the term *creativity*. See also *convergent thinking, creativity*.

diversity of training Bruner's expression relating to his belief that exposure to information under a wide range of circumstances is conducive to discovering relationships among concepts.

dizygotic Resulting from two separate eggs and forming fraternal (nonidentical) twins. See also *monozygotic*.

drive The tendency to behave that is brought about by an unsatisfied need—for example, the hunger drive is related to the need for food. See also *needs, need–drive theory*.

echoic memory Neisser's term for sensory memory involving auditory stimulation—the fleeting availability for processing of auditory stimuli to which the individual is not paying attention.

educable mentally retarded (EMR) A label for those who are mildly retarded—approximately between IQ 50 and 70. See *mild retardation*.

educational goals The intended or desired outcomes of the educational process. Often expressed in terms of instructional objectives that can range from highly general to very specific. See also *instructional objectives*.

educational psychology A science concerned primarily with the study of human behavior in educational settings. Applies existing psychological knowledge to instructional problems and develops new knowledge and procedures.

egocentric speech Vygotsky's intermediate stage of language development, common between ages 3 and 7, during which children often talk to themselves in an apparent effort to control their own behavior. See also *inner speech, social speech*.

egocentrism A way of functioning characterized by an inability to assume the point of view of others. A child's early thinking is largely egocentric.

eidetic imagery A particularly vivid type of visual image in memory. In many ways, it is almost as though the individual were actually able to look at what is being remembered—hence the synonym *photographic memory*.

elaboration A long-term memory process involving changing or adding to material, or making associations to make remembering easier. See also *organization, rehearsal*.

electroencephalograph (EEG) A graphlike representation of changes in electrical potential that occur in the brain.

elicited response A response brought about by a stimulus. The expression is synonymous with the term *respondent*. See also *operant, respondent, unconditioned response*.

eliciting effect Imitative behavior in which the observer does not copy the model's responses but simply behaves in a related manner. See also *imitation, inhibitory-disinhibitory effect, modeling effect*.

emitted response A response not elicited by a stimulus but simply emitted by the organism. An emitted response is, in fact, an operant.

empower To enable; to give power to. One of the most important goals of education is to empower students by providing them with both specific information and learning/thinking strategies and by developing within them the feelings of personal power that come with the realization that one is competent and worthwhile.

enactive A term used by Bruner to describe young children's representation of their world. It refers specifically to the belief that children represent the world in terms of their personal actions. See also *iconic, symbolic*.

encoding A process whereby we derive meaning from the environment. To encode is to represent in another form. At a mental level, encoding involves the process of abstracting—representing as a concept or a meaning.

encounter groups See *growth groups*.

enrichment An approach in the education of gifted children. Enrichment involves providing students with additional and different school experiences rather than simply moving them more rapidly through the conventional curriculum. Also termed the *revolving door* model. See also *acceleration*.

entity theory Dweck's label for the belief that ability is a fixed, unchanging entity. Associated with performance goals—that is, with doing well so as to be judged positively by others. See also *incremental theory, mastery goals, performance goals*.

environmentalism The belief that whatever a child becomes is determined by experience (the environment) rather than by genetic makeup.

epilepsy A seizure disorder, sometimes genetic in origin, varying in severity; it is often treatable or controllable with drugs.

episodic memory A type of declarative, autobiographical (conscious, long-term) memory consisting of knowlege about personal experiences, tied to specific times and places. See also *semantic memory*.

equilibration A Piagetian term for the process by which we maintain a balance between assimilation (using old learning) and accommodation (changing behavior, learning new things). Equilibration is essential for adaptation and cognitive growth.

escape learning A conditioning phenomenon whereby the organism learns means of escaping from a situation, usually following the presentation of aversive (unpleasant) stimulation. See also *avoidance learning*.

essay tests Tests that require testees to construct responses of varying length in sentence, paragraph, or essay form. See also *objective tests*.

evaluation In contrast to measurement, involves making a value judgment—deciding on the goodness or badness of performance. Also denotes the highest-level intellectual skill in Bloom's taxonomy of educational objectives, in which it is defined as the ability to render judgments about the value of methods or materials for specific purposes, making use of external or internal criteria. See also *assessment, measurement*.

exceptionality Term used to describe significant deviation from the average in terms of physical, intellectual, or emotional behaviors, abilities, or skills. A two-dimensional concept in that it can indicate significant superiority or significant handicaps. See also *special education teachers, special needs*.

exclusion A time-out punishment procedure whereby a child is not removed from the situation but is excluded from ongoing activities, often by being made to sit behind a screen, in a corner, or facing away from the class. See also *isolation, nonexclusion, time-out*.

executive model A view of the teacher as a master teacher (executive) responsible for arranging the teaching/learning situation, delivering lessons, and teaching learners prescribed skills and information. See also *liberationist model, therapist model.*

exemplary model A good example. A teacher, for example.

exhibitions A performance-based assessment procedure that requires the public display of competence. Exhibitions are most common in the visual or performing arts, as well as in oral examinations for graduate degrees. They underline the social nature of thinking.

expert teachers Teachers who, by virtue of experience, training, and other intangible skills, share a number of characteristics that make them better, more effective teachers than novices. In Sternberg's prototypical model of teaching expertise, these characteristics relate to knowledge, efficiency of problem solving, and insight with respect to solving educational problems.

exploration A cognitive apprenticeship procedure that requires that learners apply or generalize what they have learned in order to investigate and test the potential applications of their learning.

expository organizer An idea or concept that serves as a description (exposition) of concepts that are relevant to new learning.

expository teaching An instructional technique, strongly advocated by Ausubel, wherein the teacher bears the responsibility of organizing and presenting information in relatively final form. This is associated with reception learning rather than with discovery-oriented approaches. See also *reception learning.*

expressive objectives Instructional objectives that are concerned with the affective (emotional) components of learning rather than simply with content or performance.

external orientation A tendency to attribute the outcomes of behavior to factors outside the individual (such as luck or the difficulty of a task). See also *attribution theory, internal orientation, locus of control.*

extinction rate Time lapse between the cessation of a response and the withdrawal of reinforcement.

extinction The cessation of a response as a function of the withdrawal of reinforcement. See also *forgetting.*

extrinsic motives Motives associated with external sources of reinforcement—like food, money, sex. See also *extrinsic reinforcement.*

extrinsic reinforcement Reinforcement that comes from outside rather than from within—for example, high grades, praise, or money. See also *intrinsic reinforcement.*

face validity The extent to which a test appears to be measuring what it is intended to measure. See also *construct validity, content validity, criterion-related validity, reliability, validity.*

fact Something that observation leads us to believe is true or real. Ideally, the observations that determine our facts are sufficiently objective and repeatable that they provide us with some assurance that they accurately reflect the way things actually are.

fading A technique used in cognitive apprenticeship programs. Involves the gradual withdrawal of supports (scaffolds) for the learner as these become progressively less necessary. See also *scaffolding.*

fading theory The belief that inability to recall in long-term memory increases with the passage of time as memory traces fade. Also termed *decay theory.*

Feuerstein's Instrumental Enrichment (FIE) A detailed and comprehensive program designed to teach cognitive strategies and to make learners more aware of their own strategies.

fixed schedule A type of intermittent schedule of reinforcement in which the reinforcement occurs at fixed intervals of time (an interval schedule) or after a specified number of trials (a ratio schedule). See also *continuous reinforcement, intermittent reinforcement, interval schedule, random schedule, ratio schedule, schedule of reinforcement.*

flexibility A factor tapped by production measures of divergent thinking (of creativity). Evident in the ability or propensity to switch from one class of responses or solutions to another. See also *fluency, originality.*

fluency A factor thought to be involved in creativity, evident in the production of a large number of responses or solutions in a problem situation. See also *flexibility, originality.*

fluid abilities Cattell's term for intellectual abilities that seem to underlie much of our intelligent behavior and that are not highly affected by experience (for example, general reasoning, attention span, and memory for numbers). Fluid abilities are more likely to decline in old age. See also *crystallized abilities*.

forgetting The cessation of a response as a function of the passage of time, not to be confused with extinction. See also *extinction*.

formal operations The last of Piaget's four major stages. It begins around age 11 or 12 and lasts until age 14 or 15. It is characterized by the child's increasing ability to use logical thought processes.

formal teaching style An approach to teaching that emphasizes competition, individual work, discipline, order, achievement, and external motivators. See also *informal teaching style*.

formative evaluation Evaluation undertaken before and during instruction, designed primarily to assist the learner in identifying strengths and weaknesses. Formative evaluation is a fundamental part of the process of instruction. See also *summative evaluation*.

frames Units of information presented in programmed instruction. A frame not only presents information but also usually requires the student to make a response.

fraternal twins Twins whose genetic origins are two different eggs. Such twins are as genetically dissimilar as nontwin siblings. See also *identical twins*.

full inclusion The inclusion of all special needs children in regular classrooms regardless of the nature and severity of their handicaps.

g Abbreviation for general intelligence—a basic intellectual capability sometimes assumed to underlie all manifestations of intelligence.

gender roles Attitudes, personality characteristics, behavior, and other qualities associated with being male or female. Gender roles define masculinity and femininity. Also termed *sex roles*. See also *sex typing*.

gender schemas Notions about the characteristics associated with being male or female.

generalization The transference of a response from one stimulus to a similar stimulus (stimulus generalization) or the transference of a similar response for another response in the face of a single stimulus (response generalization). A child who responds with fear in a new situation that resembles an old, fear-producing situation is showing evidence of stimulus generalization. Also termed *transfer*. See also *discrimination*.

generalized reinforcer A stimulus that is not reinforcing before being paired with a primary reinforcer. Generalized reinforcers are stimuli that are present so often at the time of reinforcement that they come to be reinforcing for a wide variety of unrelated activities. Stimuli such as social prestige, praise, and money are generalized reinforcers for human behavior. See also *primary reinforcer*.

global before local A phrase used to describe a sequencing principle in cognitive apprenticeship. Refers to the recommendation that learners should be given some notion of what the final performance, the final task, the final global rendition will be before being asked to work on the individual subtasks that make up the whole.

Gordon technique A creativity-enhancing technique very similar to brainstorming except that an abstraction of a problem rather than a specific problem is presented. See also *brainstorming*.

grade-equivalent scores Standardized test norms that allow users to convert raw scores to grade equivalents—that is, that allow the user to conclude that the testee has performed at a level comparable to that of average children at a specified grade level. See also *age-equivalent scores*, *standardized tests*.

grammar Rules of word classes and functions; characteristic system of word forms and syntax of a language. See also *syntax*.

group investigation A collaborative instructional technique in which students identify topics and related sources of information, form themselves into groups on the basis of shared interests, assign responsibility for collecting material, gather and study relevant material alone and in groups, prepare group reports, and present these to the class.

group tests A type of test, usually used to measure intelligence, that may be given to large groups of subjects at one time. It is typically of the pencil-and-paper variety. See also *individual tests*.

growth The quantitative, physical aspects of development. See also *development, maturation*.

growth groups A general label for group process approaches to therapy and sometimes to instruction. These typically involve the use of techniques designed to foster communication, openness, self-discovery, sharing, conflict resolution, and so on, usually in small group settings. Also termed *sensitivity groups* or *encounter groups*.

growth needs Another expression for Maslow's metaneeds. So called because they motivate behaviors not as a result of deficiencies but because of an intrinsic need to grow, to become, to actualize. Include cognitive, aesthetic, and self-actualization needs.

guided discovery A reflective teaching technique in which students are given much of the responsibility for finding relationships and organizing knowledge, but in which teachers are careful to provide necessary guidance to ensure that discovery and learning occur.

hardware The physical components of a computer, including monitors, controllers, keyboards, chips, cards, circuits, drives, printers, and so on. See also *software*.

heteronomy Piaget's label for the first stage of moral development, marked by reliance on outside authority. See also *autonomy*.

hierarchy of classes An arrangement of concepts or classes in terms of their inclusiveness. At the top of the hierarchy is the concept (class) that is most inclusive (for example, writing instruments); below this highly inclusive concept are those that are included in it (for example, pens, typewriters, pencils, and so on). See also *coding system*.

holistic education A comprehensive term for educational approaches that attempt to remedy what is seen as traditional education's failure to educate the whole brain. Advocates of holistic education believe that the right hemisphere, which speculation links with art, music, and emotion, is neglected by curricula that stress reason, logic, language, science, and mathematics.

holophrase A sentencelike word uttered by young children early in the course of learning a language. A holophrase is a single word by which the child conveys as much meaning as an adult would convey with a much longer phrase.

humanism A philosophical and psychological orientation that is primarily concerned with our humanity—that is, with our worth as individuals and with those processes that are considered to make us more human.

hyperactivity A common term for attention deficit hyperactivity disorder. See also *attention deficit hyperactivity disorder (ADHD)*.

hypertext A basic organizational mode for computer-based information that allows the user to jump from topic to topic and back again.

iconic A term that refers to a developmental stage in children's representation of their world. The term is used by Bruner to describe an intermediate stage of development characterized by a representation of the world in terms of relatively concrete mental images. See also *enactive, symbolic*.

iconic memory Neisser's term for sensory memory involving visual stimulation—the fleeting availability for processing of visual stimuli to which the individual is not attending.

identical twins Twins whose genetic origin is one egg. Such twins are genetically identical. See also *fraternal twins*.

identification A general term referring to the process of assuming the goals, ambitions, mannerisms, and so on of another person—of identifying with that person. An important process in the theories of Freud and Erikson.

identity In Erikson's theory, a term closely related to *self*. Identity refers to the individual's self-definition, a sort of personal sense of who and what one is. To achieve identity is to arrive at a clear notion of who one is. One of the important tasks of adolescence is to select and develop a strong sense of identity.

identity A logical rule that specifies that certain activities leave objects or situations unchanged. See also *reversibility*.

identity diffusion An expression for a stage in early adolescence during which the adolescent has a vague and changing sense of identity with no firm vocational commitment and ambiguous belief systems.

imitation Copying behavior. To imitate a person's behavior is simply to use that person's behavior as a pattern. Piaget also terms this *internal representation*. Bandura and Walters describe three different effects of imitation. See also *eliciting effect, inhibitory-disinhibitory effect, modeling effect, observational learning*.

implicit memory See *nondeclarative memory*.

imprinting Unlearned, instinctlike behaviors that are not present at birth but that become part of an animal's repertoire after exposure to a suitable stimulus during a critical period. The "following" behavior of young ducks, geese, and chickens is an example. See also *critical period*.

in loco parentis A Latin expression meaning, literally, in the place of parents. Teachers are said to have rights and responsibilities *in loco parentis* to the extent that society charges them with the care and education of children.

inclusive education See *mainstreaming*.

inclusive classrooms Classrooms that contain one or more children with special needs in addition to a number of more average children.

incremental theory Dweck's label for the belief that ability is malleable through work and effort. Associated with mastery goals—that is, with increasing personal competence. See also *entity theory, mastery goals, performance goals*.

indirect teaching style A relatively humanistic approach to teaching that favors student-initiated activities and that views the teacher's role as questioning and facilitating learning rather than directing it. See also *direct teaching style*.

individualized educational plans (IEPs) Individualized instructional programs tailored to a child's specific pattern of needs and abilities. IEPs may be used for gifted, learning-disabled, retarded, or average children. Also termed *individualized program plans* or *IPPs*.

individual tests Tests, usually used to measure intelligence, that can be given to only one individual at a time. See also *group tests*.

individualistic learning A common instructional approach in which students work independently and at their own pace, and in which student rewards are independent of the performance of other students. See also *competitive learning, cooperative learning*.

individualized program plans (IPPs) See *individualized educational plans (IEPs)*.

individually guided education (IGE) An individual approach to instruction based on the principle of ungraded schools. It makes use of teams of teachers, extensive inservice teacher training, individual programming for each student, home involvement, and the continual development of new curriculum material. Like IPI, it is also based on mastery learning. See also *individualized educational plans (IEPs), individually prescribed instruction (IPI)*.

individually prescribed instruction (IPI) A complex instructional system that involves reorganizing the entire curriculum for each subject (and over a wide range of grades) into a series of sequential units with clearly defined objectives and tests for each unit. Students progress at their own rate as they master each unit. See also *individualized educational plans (IEPs), individually guided education (IGE)*.

Individuals with Disabilities Education Act (IDEA) See *Public Law 94-142*.

informal teaching style A teaching approach that grants students a relatively high degree of freedom and autonomy and that emphasizes individual growth and fulfillment rather than academic achievement and external rewards. See also *formal teaching style*.

information processing (IP) Relates to how information is modified (or processed), resulting in knowledge, perception, or behavior. A dominant model of the cognitive approaches, it makes extensive use of computer metaphors.

inhibition In imitative learning, the suppression of a previously acquired behavior. This sometimes occurs when a learner observes a model being punished for the behavior. See also *inhibitory-disinhibitory effect*.

inhibitory-disinhibitory effect The type of imitative behavior that results either in the suppression (inhibition) or appearance (disinhibition) of previously acquired deviant behavior. See also *eliciting effect, imitation, modeling effect, observational learning*.

inner speech Vygotsky's final stage in the development of speech, attained at around age 7, and characterized by silent "self-talk," the stream-of-consciousness flow of verbalizations that give direction and substance to our thinking and behavior. Inner speech is involved in all higher mental functioning. See also *egocentric speech, social speech*.

instincts A complex, species-specific, relatively unmodifiable pattern of behaviors such as migration or nesting in some birds and animals. Less complex inherited behaviors are usually referred to as reflexes.

instruction The arrangement of external events in a learning situation in order to facilitate learning, retention, and transfer.

instructional objectives The goal or intended result of instruction. Objectives may be short-range or long-range. Also termed *behavioral objectives*.

integrated learning system (ILS) A computer-based learning/instructional system that includes both hardware and software, often with links to external databases, and that is designed to guide students through part or all of a curriculum. See also *intelligent tutor system (ITS)*.

intellectual skills Robert Gagné's term for the outcomes of the learning process. He describes seven such skills ranging from simple conditioned responses to abstract problem solving.

intelligence A property measured by intelligence tests; seems to refer primarily to the capacity of individuals to adjust to their environments.

intelligence quotient (IQ) A simple way to describe intelligence by assigning it a number that represents the ratio of mental to chronological age, multiplied by 100. Average IQ is therefore 100 and is based on a comparison between an individual's performance and that of comparable others.

intelligent tutor system (ITS) A computer-based learning system that takes into account the individual learner's strengths and weaknesses, and that modifies its presentations accordingly. See also *integrated learning system (ILS)*.

intermittent reinforcement A schedule of reinforcement that does not present a reinforcer for all correct responses. Also termed partial reinforcement. See also *continuous reinforcement, fixed schedule, interval schedule, random schedule, ratio schedule, schedule of reinforcement*.

internal orientation A tendency to attribute the outcomes of behavior to factors within the individual (such as effort or ability). See also *attribution theory, external orientation, locus of control*.

Internet Label for a worldwide, amorphous, changing web of computer linkages, mainly via telephone lines and satellites. The Internet uses the computing resources of many universities and industries and can be accessed by virtually anyone with a computer and a telephone link (modem). The Internet makes inexpensive electronic communication possible worldwide.

interval schedule An intermittent schedule of reinforcement that is based on the passage of time. See also *continuous reinforcement, fixed schedule, intermittent reinforcement, random schedule, ratio schedule, schedule of reinforcement*.

intrinsic motives Motives associated with internal sources of reinforcement—like satisfaction. See also *intrinsic reinforcement*.

intrinsic reinforcement Reinforcement that comes from within the individual rather than from outside (satisfaction, for example). Also termed *internal reinforcement*. See also *extrinsic reinforcement*.

introjected values Rogers' phrase for values that result not from direct experience but that are, in a sense, borrowed—sometimes from the reactions of others to the individual, sometimes from observations of how others appear to be, sometimes from the individual's unrealistic fantasies about the self.

intuitive thinking One of the substages of Piaget's preoperational thought, beginning around age 4 and lasting until age 7 or 8, marked by the child's ability to solve many problems intuitively and by the inability to respond correctly in the face of misleading perceptual features of problems. See also *preconceptual thinking, preoperational thinking*.

isolation A time-out procedure in which a child is removed from an area of reinforcement (typically the classroom, although sometimes the playground or other areas) and isolated in a different place. See also *exclusion, nonexclusion, time-out*.

jargon shock My tongue was in my cheek in Chapter 3, but I'm glad you checked here. See *jargon*.

jargon The unique, technical vocabulary of a discipline—sometimes useful but not always essential.

jerky transitions Kounin's expression for disruptive and abrupt changes in learning activities in the classroom.

jigsaw A cooperative instructional technique in which individual members of groups are given the responsiblity for mastering different aspects of specific tasks and teaching them to other members of their group. The key feature of jigsaw is that successful performance depends on the different contributions of each member.

Jonah complex A phrase used by Abraham Maslow to describe those who avoid and deny their personal capacity for growth and self-actualization.

knowledge A generic term for the information, the ways of dealing with information, the ways of acquiring information, and so on that an individual possesses; also the lowest level objective in Bloom's taxonomy of educational objectives. See also *cognitive structure*.

knowledge base The storehouse of concepts, information, associations, and procedures that we accumulate over time.

knowledge of results Knowledge about the correctness or incorrectness of a response. Knowledge of results is usually immediate in programmed instruction.

knowledge acquisition components One of Sternberg's three facets of human intelligence, related to procedures used for learning new information (separating the important from the unimportant, associating items of information, comparing the new with the old). See also *cognitive strategy, learning/thinking strategy, metacognition, metacomponents, metamemory, performance components*.

language The use of arbitrary sounds in the transmission of messages from one individual or organism to another. Language should not be confused with communication. See also *communication*.

language immersion An approach to teaching a second language that involves placing the learner in an environment in which only the second language is used.

lateral thinking De Bono's term for a way of thinking that leads to creative solutions. See also *vertical thinking*.

lateralization A term that refers to the division of functions and capabilities between the two hemispheres of the brain.

law A statement that is accurate beyond reasonable doubt. See also *belief, model, principle, theory*.

law of effect A Thorndikean law of learning that states that it is the effect of a response that leads to its being learned (stamped in) or not learned (stamped out).

law of exercise Thorndikean law of learning that states that bonds (connections) become strengthened the more often they are repeated (exercised). Thorndike rejected this law later in his career.

law of multiple responses One of Thorndike's laws based on his observation that learning involves the emission of a variety of responses (multiple responses) until one (presumably an appropriate one) is reinforced. It is because of this law that Thorndike's theory is often referred to as a theory of trial-and-error learning.

law of prepotency of elements A Thorndikean law of learning that states that people tend to respond to the most striking (prepotent) of the various elements that make up a stimulus situation.

law of readiness A Thorndikean law of learning that takes into account the fact that certain types of learning are impossible or difficult unless the learner is ready. In this context, readiness refers to maturational level, previous learning, motivational factors, and other characteristics of the individual that relate to learning.

law of response by analogy A Thorndikean law to explain transfer. An analogy is typically an explanation, comparison, or illustration based on similarity. In Thorndike's system, response by analogy refers to responses that occur because of similarities between two situations.

law of set or attitude A Thorndikean law of learning that recognizes the fact that we are often predisposed to respond in certain ways as a result of our experiences and previously learned attitudes. This subsidiary law acknowledges the influence of culture and experience in determining our attitudes and, therefore, our most likely responses in a given situation.

learning Changes in behavior due to experience; does not include changes due to motivation, fatigue, or drugs.

Learning Aptitude Potential Device (LAPD) A measure of aptitude devised by Feuerstein in which the tester is encouraged to actually teach the child, to offer hints and clues, to direct and help, in order to arrive at a more accurate measure of actual potential for further learning rather than simply at a measure of how much the child has profited from past experience.

learning disability A depression in the ability to learn specific things (for example, reading or arithmetic), in which the learning difficulties are not related to mental retardation or emotional disturbance.

Learning Potential Assessment Device (LPAD)
Feuerstein's measure of intelligence, developed
to provide a dynamic rather than passive measure of intelligence—a measure of how the child
can profit from experience rather than simply a
measure of the effects of past experiences.
Assessment procedures allow the examiner to
coach, to provide hints and clues, to direct, and
to help.

learning style A unique and important learner
variable manifested in differences in biological
rhythms (morning versus evening people), perceptual strengths (visual versus auditory learners), sociological preference (whole-group versus
small-group instruction), attention span (long
or short), and a wealth of personality variables
(dependence or independence, for example).

learning styles approach An individualized
instructional system that is designed specifically
to cater to the learning style of each student. See
also *learning style*.

learning together A cooperative instructional
technique in which groups of four to six students work together on a jointly assigned task
using small-group interaction skills, and in
which each member of the group is individually
responsible for mastering the material.

learning/thinking strategy Processes involved in
learning and thinking; another expression for
"cognitive strategy," introduced to emphasize
that the strategies involved in cognition (knowing) are also involved in learning and thinking.
See also *cognitive strategy, knowledge-acquisition
components, metacomponents, metamemory, performance components*.

levels of processing An information-processing
theory, attributed to Craik and Lockhart, maintaining that memory is a function of the level to
which information is processed. At the lowest
level, a stimulus is simply recognized as a physical event (and is available momentarily in short-
term sensory memory); at a much deeper level, a
stimulus is interpreted in terms of its meaning
(and is available in long-term memory).

liberationist model Views the teacher's role as one
of freeing students' minds by providing them
with the tools and the attitudes necessary for
learning. See also *therapist model, executive model*.

linear program The presentation of programmed
material in such a manner that all learners
progress through the same material in the same

order. Linear programs typically make no provision for individual differences in learning; the
material, however, is broken up into very small
steps (frames). See also *branching program, frame*.

link system A mnemonic system wherein items to
be remembered are linked to one another using
visual images. See also *loci system, phonetic system*.

loci system A mnemonic system wherein items to
be remembered are associated with visual images
of specific places. See also *link system, phonetic
system*.

locus of control An aspect of personality evident in
the individual's consistent tendency to attribute
behavioral outcomes to a specific class of
causes—causes over which the individual does,
or does not, have control. See also *attribution
theory, external orientation, internal orientation*.

logical consequences Dreikurs' phrase for a disciplinary tactic that involves contriving or inventing consequences for children's misbehavior in
an attempt to modify that behavior. Unlike
natural consequences, which follow naturally
from a misbehavior, logical consequences are
arranged, explained, discussed, and agreed upon
by teachers and students. See also *natural
consequences*.

Logo Seymour Papert's computer language,
designed for young children to allow them to
learn programming skills easily and painlessly as
they might learn an exciting new game. The
program uses a "turtle"—a small creature that
can be instructed (that is, programmed) to move
in different ways, tracing various geometric
designs as it moves.

long-term memory A type of memory whereby,
with continued rehearsal and recoding of sensory information (processing in terms of meaning, for example), material will be available for
recall over a long period of time.

mainstreaming The practice of placing students in
need of special services in regular classrooms
rather than segregating them. Also termed
inclusive education.

mastery goals Goals directed toward increasing
one's personal competence. See also *entity theory,
incremental theory, performance goals*.

mastery learning model An instructional
approach described by Bloom in which a learning sequence is analyzed into specific objectives,

and progress requires that each learner master sequential objectives.

mastery of specifics A Brunerian term for the learning of details. Mastery of relevant specifics is necessary for acquiring concepts and discovering relationships among them.

maturation The process of normal physical and psychological development. Maturation is defined as occurring independently of particular experiences. See also *development, growth.*

mean The arithmetic average of a set of scores. In distributions that are skewed (top- and bottom-heavy), the mean is not the best index of central tendency; that is, it is not necessarily at the middle of the distribution. See also *central tendency, median, mode.*

measurement The application of an instrument to gauge the quantity of something, as opposed to its quality. Assessing quality involves evaluation, not measurement. See also *assessment, evaluation.*

measurement-driven instruction A general approach to instruction wherein the overriding objective is to increase student performance on specific achievement measures.

median The midpoint or fiftieth percentile of a distribution; the point at or below which 50 percent of all scores fall. See also *central tendency, mean, mode.*

mediator Student who is specially trained to intervene between two or more other students who are in conflict.

memory The effects that experiences are assumed to have on the human mind. Refers to the storage of these effects. See also *retrieval.*

mental retardation A significant general depression in the ability to learn, usually accompanied by deficits in adaptive behavior.

mental structure See *cognitive structure.*

mentor Individual engaged in a one-to-one teaching/learning relationship in which the teacher (mentor) serves as a fundamentally important model with respect to values, beliefs, philosophies, and attitudes, as well as a source of more specific information. See also *tutor.*

merit pay Monetary incentive used to reward teacher competence. See also *teacher competence.*

metacognition Knowledge about knowing. As we grow and learn, we develop notions of ourselves as learners. Accordingly, we develop strategies that recognize our limitations and that allow us to monitor our progress and to take advantage of our efforts. See also *cognitive strategy, learning/thinking strategy, metamemory.*

metacomponents One of Sternberg's three components of human intelligence. Metacomponents include the skills involved in planning, monitoring, and evaluating cognitive performance—in other words, the skills of metacognition. See also *knowledge-acquisition components, metacognition, metamemory, performance components.*

metamemory The knowledge we develop about our own memory processes—our knowledge about how to remember, rather than simply our memories. See also *cognitive strategy, metacognition.*

metaneeds Maslow's term for higher needs. Concerned with psychological, self-related, functions rather than with biology. Include the need to know truth, beauty, justice, and to self-actualize. Also termed *growth needs.*

méthode clinique Piaget's experimental method. It involves an interview technique in which questions are determined largely by the subject's responses. Its flexibility distinguishes it from ordinary interview techniques.

mild retardation A classification of mental retardation identified by degree and usually defined in terms of an IQ range between 50 and about 70. Also termed *educable,* children with mild retardation are capable of achievement at about the sixth-grade level, and of adequate social adaptation.

minimum competency testing A global term for the administration of batteries of tests designed to determine whether students, or teachers, have reached some minimum level of competency in basic areas such as language and mathematics.

mnemonic devices Systematic aids to remembering, like rhymes, acrostics, or visual imagery systems. See also *link system, loci system, phonetic system.*

mode The most frequently occurring score(s) in a distribution.

model A representation, usually abstract, of some phenomenon or system. Alternatively, a pattern for behavior that can be copied by someone. See also *belief, law, principle, theory.*

modeling effect The type of imitative behavior that involves learning a novel response. See also *eliciting effect, imitation, inhibitory-disinhibitory effect, observational learning.*

moderate retardation A degree of mental retardation defined in terms of an IQ range between 35 or 40 and 50 or 55. Can achieve at about the second-grade level, and can profit from training in social and occupational skills.

monozygotic Twins resulting from the division of a single fertilized egg. The process results in identical twins. See also *dizygotic*.

morality The ethical aspect of human behavior. Morality is intimately bound to the development of an awareness of acceptable and unacceptable behaviors. It is therefore linked to what is often called conscience.

morphological analysis A creativity-enhancing technique, advanced by Arnold, involving the analysis of problems into their component parts and subsequent attempts to brainstorm each of these component parts.

motives The causes of behavior. Our motives are the reasons why we engage in some behaviors and not in others. They are what initiate behavior and what direct it. See also *disposition*.

motor learning Learning that involves muscular coordination and physical skills. Such common activities as walking and driving a car involve motor learning.

multicultural education Educational procedures and curricula that are responsive to the different cultures and languages of students, with the goal of assuring that all children experience high-quality education.

naive theory Expression used to describe psychological theories based on intuition and folk-belief rather than on science. Also termed *implicit theory*.

natural consequences Dreikurs' phrase for the ordinary consequences of behavior—or, more specifically, of misbehavior. Natural consequences are the effects and outcomes of behavior that are not arranged or contrived. See also *logical consequences*.

needs Ordinarily refers to a lack or deficit in the human organism. Needs may be either unlearned (for example, the need for food or water) or learned (the need for money). See also *drive, need–drive theory*.

need–drive theory A motivation theory that attempts to explain human behavior on the basis of the motivating properties of needs. Such theories typically assume that humans have certain learned and unlearned needs, which give rise to drives, which in turn are responsible for the occurrence of behavior. See also *drive, needs*.

need state Bruner's expression describing the arousal level of an organism.

negative correlation The type of relationship that exists between two variables when high values in one are associated with correspondingly low values in the other.

negative reinforcer A stimulus that has the effect of increasing the probability of occurrence of the response that precedes it. Negative reinforcement ordinarily takes the form of an unpleasant or noxious stimulus that is removed as a result of a specific response. See also *positive reinforcer, reinforcement, reinforcer, reward*.

neonate A newborn infant. The neonatal period terminates when the infant regains birth weight (about two weeks after birth).

neurofeedback Refers to information subjects are given about the functioning of their nervous systems. Unlike biofeedback, which refers to feedback relating to all biological systems, neurofeedback relates specifically to information about brain functioning (EEG feedback). See also *biofeedback*.

neuron (nerve cell) An elongated cell that forms part of the nervous system. The main part of the neuron is the cell body; the elongated part is the axon.

neutral stimulus A stimulus that does not initially lead reliably to a predictable response. For example, neutral stimuli are not associated with emotional responses until learning has occurred, at which point they are referred to as conditioned (rather than neutral) stimuli. See also *conditioned response*.

nondeclarative memory Refers to unconscious, nonverbalizable effects of experience such as might be manifested in acquired motor skills or in classical conditioning. Also termed *implicit* or *procedural memory*. See also *declarative memory, episodic memory, semantic memory*.

nonexclusion The mildest form of time-out procedure; the child is not allowed to participate in ongoing activity but is required to observe. See also *exclusion, isolation, time-out*.

norm-referenced testing A test in which the student is competing against the performance of other students rather than in relation to some preestablished criterion of acceptable performance. See also *criterion-referenced testing*.

normal curve A mathematical function that can be represented in the form of a bell-shaped curve. A large number of naturally occurring events are normally distributed (the vast majority of the events, or scores, cluster around the middle of the distribution, around the mean or median, with progressively fewer scores being farther and farther away from the average).

object concept Piaget's expression for the child's understanding that the world is composed of objects that continue to exist apart from his or her perception of them.

objective tests Label used for tests in which the scoring procedure is simple, clear, and objective. Includes multiple-choice, completion, matching, and true-false formats. See also *essay tests*.

obliterative subsumption Ausubel's term for forgetting. The incorporation of new material into preexisting cognitive structure so that the new material eventually becomes indistinguishable—in other words, becomes obliterated (reaches zero dissociability, in Ausubel's terms). See also *correlative subsumption, derivative subsumption, subsumption*.

observational learning A term used synonymously with the expression "learning through imitation." See also *imitation*.

open education A student-centered alternative to traditional education that emphasizes personal growth, independence, and cooperation, and that is not committed to the curriculum-bound, pass–fail, age-locked, grade-locked system of the traditional school. Also termed *open classroom*.

operant Skinner's term for a response not elicited by any known or obvious stimulus. Most significant human behaviors appear to be operants (for example, writing a letter or going for a walk). See also *respondent, unconditioned response*.

operant conditioning A type of learning that involves an increase in the probability that a response will occur as a function of reinforcement. Most of Skinner's experimental work investigates the principles of operant conditioning. See also *classical conditioning, conditioning*.

operation A Piagetian term that remains relatively nebulous but refers essentially to a thought process. An operation is an action that has been internalized in the sense that it can be "thought" and is reversible in the sense that it can be "unthought."

operation A term used by Guilford to describe major kinds of intellectual activity, such as remembering, evaluating, and divergent and convergent thinking. See also *content, convergent thinking, creativity, divergent thinking, product*.

organization A memory strategy involving grouping and relating material to maintain it in long-term memory. See also *elaboration, rehearsal*.

originality A measure of creativity evident in the production of novel (unexpected or statistically rare) responses or solutions in a problem situation. See also *flexibility, fluency*.

outcome-based education (OBE) An outgrowth of mastery learning. An individualized instructional program designed to bring about important learning outcomes defined in terms of the skills and knowledge the learner will need upon completion of a course of studies.

overlapping Kounin's term for the simultaneous occurrence of two or more events in the classroom, each requiring the teacher's attention. Good class managers can handle overlapping events without disrupting the flow of classroom activities.

pain/pleasure principle A common expression for psychological hedonism—the belief that we are motivated to seek pleasure and avoid pain. See also *psychological hedonism*.

paradoxical effect Literally, a surprising or contradictory effect. Phrase used to describe the apparently sedating effect that some stimulants (such as Ritalin) have on children who suffer from excessive activity (hyperactivity).

parallel-forms reliability A measure of test consistency (reliability) obtained by looking at the correlation between scores obtained by the same individual on two different but equivalent (parallel) forms of one test. See also *equivalence reliability, repeated-forms reliability, split-half reliability*.

PASS The Das model of intellectual functioning, based on a three-unit model of information processing: attending (involving arousal and paying attention); processing (successive or simultaneous processing); and planning (metacognitive components, that is, involved in monitoring and controlling cognitive activity). See also *planning, simultaneous processing; successive processing*.

pedology A Soviet discipline of child development, very popular in the Soviet Union in the 1930s, that used Western tests for psychoassessment. Vygotsky and Luria were pedologists. In the mid-1930s, the Soviet government decreed that pedology was a "bourgeois pseudoscience" and ordered that it no longer be written about, researched, or even discussed, wiping out all pedology centers and putting all pedologists out of work.

penalty The type of punishment that involves losing or giving up something pleasant.

percentile The point at or below which a specified percentage of scores fall. For example, the fiftieth percentile is the point at or below which 50 percent of all scores fall. A score of 50 percent is not necessarily at the fiftieth percentile.

perception The translation of physical energies into neurological impulses—that is, stimuli into sensations—that can be interpreted by the individual.

performance Actual behavior. The inference that learning has occurred is typically based on observed changes in performance.

performance assessment Assessment that looks at the actual performance of students in situations as close to real life as possible. See also *authentic assessment*.

performance components One of Sternberg's three components of human intelligence. Performance components are the skills and processes actually used in carrying out intellectual tasks (reasoning, encoding, analyzing, remembering, and so on). See also *knowledge-acquisition components, metacomponents*.

performance goals Goals directed toward performing well rather than toward mastering a subject and increasing one's competence. See also *entity theory, incremental theory, mastery goals*.

performance-based assessment Global expression for assessment procedures that try to determine what students know and are capable of on the basis of what they do. Performance-based assessment looks at samples of actual behavior in real-life situations. Also termed *authentic assessment*. See also *authentic assessment*.

person-centered therapy See *client-centered therapy*.

personality The set of characteristics that we typically manifest in our interactions with others. It includes all the abilities, predispositions, habits, and other qualities that make each of us different.

personalized system of instruction (PSI) An instructional approach developed by Keller, based in part on Bloom's mastery learning, in which course material is broken down into small units, study is largely individual, a variety of study material is available, and progress depends on performance on unit tests. Sometimes termed *the Keller plan*. See also *individualized educational plans (IEPs), individually guided education (IGE), individually prescribed instruction (IPI)*.

phenomenal field The feelings, perceptions, and awareness that an individual has at any given moment. See also *phenomenology*.

phenomenology An approach concerned primarily with how individuals view their own world. Its basic assumption is that each individual perceives and reacts to the world in a unique manner and that it is this phenomenological world view that is important in understanding the individual's behavior. See also *phenomenal field*.

phonetic system A particularly powerful mnemonic system that makes use of associations between numbers and letters combined to form words; visual images associated with these words are then linked with items to be remembered. Professional memorizers often use some variation of a phonetic system. See also *link system, loci system*.

phonology The structure of speech sounds of a language.

physiological needs Basic biological needs, such as the need for food and water.

planning In the Das model of intelligence, this is the intentional or conscious aspect; in other terms, metacognitive strategies. See also *PASS, simultaneous processing, successive processing*.

Po A word invented by de Bono, meant to stimulate lateral (creative) thinking. Even as *no* is central to vertical (critical or logical) thinking, *po* is intended to be central to creating. Its meaning is neither to affirm nor to deny but rather to invite creativity, challenge, change, resistance. See also *lateral thinking, vertical thinking*.

portfolio In educational assessment, a collection of actual samples of students' performances and achievements.

positive control The control of human behavior, usually through the presentation of pleasant stimuli. This is in contrast to techniques of aversive control, which generally use negative reinforcement.

positive correlation The type of relationship that exists between two variables so that high or low scores on one are associated with correspondingly high or low scores on the other.

positive reinforcer A stimulus that increases the probability that a response will recur as a result of being added to a situation after the response has occurred once. Usually takes the form of a pleasant stimulus (reward) that results from a specific response. See also *negative reinforcer, reinforcement, reinforcer, reward*.

pragmatics The implicit language rules that govern practical things such as when to speak and how to take turns in conversation.

praise Positive verbal comments or other signs of approval. For example, most of what my grandmother said to or about me (heh! heh!).

preconceptual thinking The first substage in the period of preoperational thought, beginning around age 2 and lasting until age 4. It is so called because the child has not yet developed the ability to classify. See also *intuitive thinking, preoperational thinking*.

predictive validity See *criterion-related validity*.

Premack principle The recognition that behaviors that are chosen frequently by an individual (and that are therefore favored) may be used to reinforce other, less frequently chosen behaviors. (For example, "You can watch television when you have finished your homework.")

preoperational thinking The second of Piaget's four major stages, lasting from around age 2 to age 7 or 8. It consists of two substages: intuitive thinking and preconceptual thinking. See also *intuitive thinking, preconceptual thinking*.

PREP program A cognitive strategies training program based on the PASS model of intellectual functioning. It seeks to identify specific deficiencies and problems in cognitive processing and to remedy them by providing learners with tasks designed to develop processing skills. See also *PASS, planning, simultaneous processing, successive processing*.

preventive strategies Instructional strategies designed to prevent the occurrence of discipline problems. Preventive strategies are an intrinsic part of good classroom management.

primary reinforcer A stimulus that is reinforcing in the absence of any learning. Such stimuli as food and drink are primary reinforcers because, presumably, an organism does not have to learn that they are pleasant. See also *generalized reinforcer*.

principle A statement relating to some uniformity or predictability. Principles are far more open to doubt than are laws but are more reliable than beliefs. See also *belief, law, model, theory*.

principle of opposite control Describes the tendency for sensations and movements on either side of the body to be controlled by the opposite cerebral hemisphere.

proactive inhibition The interference of earlier learning with the retention of subsequent learning. See also *retroactive inhibition*.

procedural knowledge Knowing how to do something; knowing procedures as well as facts (declarative knowledge). Also termed procedural memory. See also *declarative knowledge*.

process disorders A type of learning disability that involves a deficit in a basic psychological process such as perceiving, remembering, or paying attention. In practice, process disorders are difficult to separate from other specific learning disabilities such as developmental reading or arithmetic disorder. See also *developmental arithmetic disorder; developmental reading disorder*.

processing The intellectual or cognitive activities that occur as stimulus information is reacted to, analyzed, sorted, organized, and stored in memory or forgotten.

prodigies A distinct form of giftedness characterized by a highly focused talent or ability, such as in music or art, for example.

product A term used by Guilford to describe the result of applying an operation to content. A product may take the form of a response. See also *content, convergent thinking, creativity, divergent thinking, operation*.

profile A description of individual patterns of strengths, weaknesses, or abilities.

profound retardation A degree of mental retardation defined in terms of a measured IQ below 20 or 25 and marked by limited motor development and a need for nursing care.

programmed instruction An instructional procedure that makes use of the systematic presentation of information in small steps (frames), in the form of a workbook or some other device. Programs typically require learners to make responses and provide immediate knowledge of results.

prompts Devices used in programmed instruction to ensure that the student will probably answer correctly. They may take a variety of forms.

psychological hedonism The belief that humans act primarily to avoid pain and to obtain pleasure.

psychological needs Human needs other than those dealing with basic physical requirements such as food, sex, water, and temperature regulation (physiological needs). Psychological needs described by Maslow include the need to belong, to feel safe, to love and to be loved, to maintain a high opinion of oneself, and to self-actualize. See also *self-actualization*.

psychology The science that examines human behavior (and that of other animals as well).

psychometrics Refers to the measurement of psychological functions and characteristics.

psychosexual A term used to describe psychological phenomena based on sexuality. Freud's theories are psychosexual in that they attribute development to sexually based forces and motives.

psychosocial Pertaining to events or behaviors that relate to the social aspects of development. Erikson's theory is psychosocial in that it deals with the resolution of social crises and the development of social competencies (independence or identity, for example).

puberty Sexual maturity.

pubescence Changes of adolescence leading to sexual maturity.

Public Law 94-142 A 1975 U.S. education act that guarantees for special students: a free and appropriate education, nondiscriminatory evaluation, due process, an individualized educational plan (IEP), and education in the least restrictive environment. Amended in 1990 by the Individuals with Disabilities Education Act (IDEA). See also *individualized educational plan*.

punishment Involves either the presentation of an unpleasant stimulus or the withdrawal of a pleasant stimulus as a consequence of behavior. Punishment should not be confused with negative reinforcement.

radical acceleration model Stanley's acceleration program for gifted children, designed specifi-

cally for very high achievers in mathematics. Also termed a *compression* or *compaction program*, it attempts to compress the mathematics curriculum so that it can be covered in a fraction of the time that would ordinarily be required.

random schedule A type of intermittent schedule of reinforcement. It may be of either the interval or the ratio variety and is characterized by the presentation of rewards at random intervals or on random trials. Although both fixed and random schedules may be based on the same intervals or on the same ratios, one can predict when reward will occur under a fixed schedule, whereas it is impossible to do so under a random schedule. Also termed *variable schedule*. See also *continuous reinforcement, fixed schedule, intermittent reinforcement, interval schedule, ratio schedule, schedule of reinforcement*.

rate of learning A measure of the amount of time required to learn a correct response, or, alternatively, a measure of the number of trials required before the correct response occurs.

ratio schedule An intermittent schedule of reinforcement that is based on a proportion of correct responses. See also *continuous reinforcement, fixed schedule, intermittent reinforcement, interval schedule, random schedule, schedule of reinforcement*.

raw score The actual numerical score a testee obtains on a test. The testee's score before it is converted to a grade- or age-equivalent score, an IQ, or some other norm.

reasoning As a disciplinary strategy, the process of providing a rationale for doing or not doing certain things. May be used as both a corrective and a preventive classroom management tactic. Forms an important part of humanistic and democratic approaches to classroom management.

reasons Explanations for or defenses of an action. In psychology, reasons are often treated as motives. See also *causes*.

reception learning The type of learning that involves primarily instruction or tuition rather than the learner's own efforts. Teaching for reception learning, often associated with Ausubel, usually takes the form of expository or didactic methods; that is, the teacher structures the material and presents it to learners in relatively final form rather than asking them to discover that form. See also *discovery learning*.

reciprocal determinism Bandura's label for the recognition that even though environments affect individuals in important ways, individuals also affect environments by selecting and shaping them. Thus, the influence (determinism) is two-way (reciprocal).

reciprocal teaching Instructional technique that involves teaching four cognitive strategies for increasing reading comprehension: generating questions, summarizing, clarifying word meanings and confusing text, predicting what will happen next.

red light–green light system A behavior management system that makes use of clear, unambiguous signals, such as green or red lights, to indicate to students whether or not specific behaviors are permissible.

reflection In cognitive apprenticeship, a procedure in which learners are asked to think about their cognitive activities and to compare them with that of others or with abstract models.

reflective teaching strategies A loosely defined collection of teaching strategies that involve teachers and students actively and deliberately thinking (reflecting) about events in the teaching/learning process.

reflexes Simple, unlearned stimulus–response links such as salivating in response to food in one's mouth or blinking in response to air blowing in one's eye. For Piaget, behavioral reflexes such as looking, reaching, grasping, and sucking are especially important for early intellectual development.

rehearsal A memory process involving repetition, important in maintaining information in short-term memory and in transferring it to long-term memory. See also *elaboration, organization.*

reinforcement menu A list of activities, objects, or other consequences from which students can select reinforcers.

reinforcement The effect of a reinforcer; specifically, to increase the probability that a response will occur. See also *negative reinforcer, positive reinforcer, reinforcer, reward.*

reinforcer A stimulus that causes reinforcement. See also *negative reinforcer, positive reinforcer, reinforcement, reward.*

reliability The consistency with which a test measures whatever it measures. A perfectly reliable test should yield the same scores on different occasions (for the same individual), providing what it measures has not changed. Most educational and psychological tests are severely limited in terms of reliability. See also *construct validity, content validity, criterion-related validity, face validity, validity.*

relief A common expression for negative reinforcement—the type of reinforcement that results when an unpleasant stimulus is removed as a consequence of behavior. See also *negative reinforcement.*

remedial frame A frame in a branching program to which students are referred when they make an incorrect response. The purpose of the remedial frame is to provide information required for a subsequent correct response.

repeated-measures reliability An estimate of the consistency (reliability) of a test based on the degree of agreement among scores obtained from different presentations of the same test. See also *parallel-forms reliability.*

reprimand A common form of mild punishment that takes the form of an expression of disapproval. Reprimands are often verbal ("You shouldn't do that") but can also be nonverbal (a head shake). See also *response cost, time-out.*

respondent A term used by Skinner in contrast to the term *operant.* A respondent is a response that is elicited by a known, specific stimulus. Unconditioned responses are examples of respondents. See also *operant, unconditioned response.*

response Any organic, muscular, glandular, or psychic process that results from stimulation.

response cost A mild form of punishment whereby tangible reinforcers that have been given for good behavior are taken away for misbehaviors. Response-cost systems are often used in systematic behavior management programs. See also *reprimand, time-out.*

response rate The number of responses emitted by an organism in a given period of time. Response rates for operant behaviors appear to be largely a function of the schedules of reinforcement used.

retention A term often used as a synonym for *memory.* See also *memory.*

retrieval cue failure Inability to remember due to the unavailability of appropriate cues—as opposed to forgetting due to changes in memory traces.

retroactive inhibition The interference of subsequently learned material with the retention of previously learned material. See also *proactive inhibition*.

reversibility A logical property manifested in the ability to reverse or undo activity in either an empirical or a conceptual sense. An idea is said to be reversible when a child realizes the logical consequences of an opposite action. See also *identity*.

revolving door model An enrichment program for gifted children advocated by Renzulli, available to the top 25 percent of students in a program (high ability, high creativity, high motivation) on an optional basis, so that students can opt in and out of the program (hence, the revolving door).

reward An object, stimulus, event, or outcome that is perceived as being pleasant and that may therefore be reinforcing. See also *negative reinforcer, positive reinforcer, reinforcement, reinforcer*.

ripple effect Kounin's term for the tendency of the effects of teacher desists to spread to students other than those to whom they were directed. See also *desists*.

sampling thinking performances An approach to performance-based assessment in which students are given an opportunity to perform real-life activities that require and illustrate the use of specific cognitive processes.

scaffolding A Vygotskian concept to describe the various types of support that teachers/upbringers need to provide for children if they are to learn. Scaffolding often takes the form of directions, suggestions, and other forms of verbal assistance and is most effective if it involves tasks within the child's zone of proximal growth. See also *zone of proximal growth*.

schedule of reinforcement The time and frequency of presentation of reinforcement to organisms. See also *continuous reinforcement, fixed schedule, intermittent reinforcement, interval schedule, random schedule, ratio schedule*.

schemata (singular: *schema*) The label used by Piaget to describe a unit in cognitive structure. A schema is, in one sense, an activity together with whatever structural connotations that activity has. In another sense, a schema may be thought of as an idea or a concept.

schizophrenia A serious mental disorder that may take a variety of forms, sometimes characterized by bizarre behaviors, obsessions, distorted views of reality, and so on. Schizophrenia in infants and children is sometimes confused with autism, although it does not ordinarily begin as early.

science An approach and an attitude toward knowledge that emphasize objectivity, precision, and replicability.

script Term describing our knowledge of what goes with what and in what sequence. Scripts are a part of cognitive structure that deals with the routine and the predictable.

selective perception Gagné's term for the process of paying attention to sensory stimulation so that it becomes available in sensory (working) memory for immediate use (like a phone number) or for further processing and long-term storage.

self-actualization The process or act of becoming oneself, of developing one's potentialities, of achieving an awareness of one's identity, of self-fulfillment. The term is central in humanistic psychology. See also *psychological needs*.

self-concept The concept that an individual has of him- or herself. Notions of the self are often closely allied with individuals' beliefs about how others perceive them.

self-efficacy A term that refers to judgments we make about how efficacious (effective) we are in given situations. Judgments of self-efficacy are important in determining our choices of activities and in influencing the amount of interest and effort we expend.

self-fulfilling prophecies Expectations that are realized because they are expected to be. Teachers' expectations for students are sometimes self-fulfilling prophecies.

self-referent thought Thought that pertains to the self. Self-referent thought is thought that concerns our own mental processes (for example, thoughts that evaluate our abilities or that monitor our progress in solving problems).

semantic encoding The process of assigning or discovering meaningfulness. A largely verbal process involved in transferring information from short-term to long-term memory.

semantic memory A type of declarative (conscious, long-term) memory consisting of stable knowledge about the world, principles, rules, and procedures, and other verbalizable aspects of knowledge, including language. See also *episodic memory*.

semantics The meanings of the words of a language.

sensitive period A period during which specific experiences have their most pronounced effects—for example, the first six months of life during which the infant forms strong attachment bonds to the mother or caregiver.

sensitivity groups See *growth groups*.

sensorimotor intelligence The first stage of development in Piaget's classification. It lasts from birth to approximately age 2 and is so called because children understand their world during that period primarily in terms of their activities in it and sensations of it.

sensory memory See *short-term sensory storage*.

seriation The ordering of objects in terms of one or more properties. To seriate is to place in order.

set A predisposition to react to stimulation in a given manner.

severe retardation A level of mental retardation defined in terms of an IQ range between 20 or 25 and 35 or 40. Can learn to communicate and, with systematic training, to take care of simple hygiene.

sex typing The learning of behaviors according to the gender of an individual in a given society; the acquisition of masculine and feminine gender roles. See also *gender roles*.

shaping A technique whereby animals and people are taught to perform complex behaviors that were not previously in their repertoires. The technique involves reinforcing responses that become increasingly closer approximations of the desired behavior. Also termed *the method of successive approximations* or *the method of differential reinforcement of successive approximations*. See also *differential reinforcement of successive approximations*.

short-term memory A type of memory in which material is available for recall for a matter of seconds. Short-term memory involves primarily rehearsal rather than more in-depth processing. It defines our immediate consciousness. Also termed *primary memory* or *working memory*.

short-term sensory storage The phrase refers to the simple sensory recognition of such stimuli as a sound, a taste, or a sight. Also termed *sensory memory*.

siblings Offspring whose parents are the same. In other words, brothers and sisters.

simultaneous processing One of four major components of the PASS model of intelligence. Involves cognitive processing wherein important elements of the stimulus situation are reacted to simultaneously—as in perceptual recognition, for example. See also *PASS*, *planning*, *successive processing*.

Skinner box Various experimental environments used by Skinner in his investigations of operant conditioning. The typical Skinner box is a cage-like structure equipped with a lever and a food tray attached to a food mechanism. It allows the investigator to study operants (for example, bar pressing) and the relationship between an operant and reinforcement.

social cognitive theory Label for Bandura's theory that attempts to explain human social learning through imitation using principles of operant conditioning while recognizing the importance of intellectual activities, such as imagining and anticipating. Hence, the theory serves as a transition between purely behavioristic and more cognitive approaches.

social learning The acquisition of patterns of behavior that conform to social expectations—learning what is acceptable and what is not acceptable in a given culture.

social speech In Vygotsky's theorizing, the most primitive stage of language development, evident before age 3, during which the child expresses simple thoughts and emotions out loud. The function of social speech is to control the behavior of others. See also *egocentric speech*, *inner speech*.

socialization The complex process of learning both those behaviors that are appropriate within a given culture and those that are less appropriate. The primary agents of socialization are home, school, and peer groups.

software Computer instructions; programs. Also termed *courseware*. See also *hardware*.

SOMPA Mercer's procedure for assessing the learning potential of culturally different children, the system of multicultural pluralistic assessment. It combines assessments in three areas: medical, social, and pluralistic. Pluralistic assessment involves the use of measures of intelligence standardized on culturally different groups.

special education teachers Teachers whose training and/or functions have to do specifically with the education of exceptional children. See also *exceptionality*.

special needs Phrase used to describe individuals whose social, physical, or emotional exceptionalities require special treatment and services if they are to develop their potential. See also *exceptionality*.

spiral curriculum Bruner's term for a curriculum that revisits the same topics repeatedly, often at different grade levels, but at different levels of abstraction and generality depending on the interests and background knowledge of learners.

split-half reliability An index of test reliability (consistency) derived by arbitrarily dividing a test into parallel halves (odd- and even-numbered items, for example) and looking at the agreement between scores obtained by each individual on the two halves. See also *equivalence reliability, parallel-forms reliability*.

stand-alone computer A computer system that is complete by itself in that it includes a processing unit, a monitor, and an input device (keyboard) —in contrast with computer terminals linked to a central computing system.

standard deviation A mathematical measure of the distribution of scores around their mean. In a normal distribution, approximately two-thirds of all scores fall within 1 standard deviation on either side of the mean, and almost 95 percent fall within 2 standard deviations of the mean.

standard language The socially prestigious form of a society's dominant language; the form that is taught in schools and against which other dialects are judged for correctness.

standardized achievement tests Professionally developed and normed tests that are designed to measure achievement and provide some basis for judging the relative quality of that achievement given the student's age and grade placement. See also *standardized test*.

standardized test A professionally developed— rather than teacher-made—test that provides the user with norms (standards) and that typically indicates the average or expected performance of groups of subjects of certain grades and/or ages. See also *age-equivalent scores, grade-equivalent scores*.

stanines Standard scores that make use of a 9-point scale with a mean of 5 and a standard deviation of 2.

stereotype A strong, relatively unexamined belief typically generalized to a class of superficially similar situations or individuals.

stimulus (stimuli) Any change in the physical environment capable of exciting a sense organ.

stimulus–response (S–R) theories Learning theories with primary emphasis on stimuli and responses and the relationships between them. These theories are also termed *behavioristic theories*.

student-centered teaching Rogers's expression for an approach to teaching based on a philosophy of self-discovered learning. The approach requires that the teacher genuinely care for students as individuals and that students be allowed to determine for themselves what is important in their lives.

student teams–achievement divisions (STAD) A cooperative instructional technique in which students are assigned to heterogeneous groups of four to six (including high- and low-ability students and different ethnic groups) to work on certain tasks, after which they are given quizzes (to be answered individually, without cooperation) and rewarded *by team* on the basis of the group's performance on the quizzes. See also *teams–games–tournaments (TGT)*.

subsumer The term used by Ausubel to describe a concept, an idea, or a combination of concepts or ideas that can serve to organize new information. Cognitive structure is therefore composed of subsumers.

subsumption Ausubel's term for the integration of new material or information with existing information. The term implies a process in which a new stimulus becomes part of what is already in cognitive structure. See also *correlative subsumption, derivative subsumption, obliterative subsumption*.

subtractive bilingualism Phrase used to describe a situation in which learning a second language has a generally negative effect often evident in lower proficiency in both languages. See also *additive bilingualism*.

successive processing Cognitive processing where elements of a stimulus situation need to be responded to sequentially—as in solving some logical problems or executing motor tasks. An important element in the PASS model of intelligence. See also *PASS, planning, simultaneous processing.*

summative evaluation The type of evaluation that occurs at the end of an instructional sequence and that is designed primarily to provide a grade. See also *formative evaluation.*

superstitious schedule A fixed-interval schedule of reinforcement in which the reward is not given after every correct response but rather after the passage of a specified period of time. It is so called because it leads to the learning of behaviors that are only accidentally related to the reinforcement.

symbolic The final stage in the development of children's representations of their world. The term is used by Bruner and describes the representation of the world in terms of arbitrary symbols. Symbolic representation includes representation in terms of language as well as in terms of theoretical or hypothetical systems. See also *enactive, iconic.*

symbolic model A model other than a real-life person. Any pattern for behavior may be termed a symbolic model if it is not a person. For example, books, television, and written instructions can provide symbolic models.

sympathetic nervous system Part of the nervous system that instigates the physiological responses associated with emotion.

syntax The arrangement of words to form sentences. See also *grammar.*

synthesis Putting together of parts in order to form a whole; complementary to analysis; a high-level intellectual ability in Bloom's taxonomy of educational objectives.

system of multicultural pluralistic assessment (SOMPA) Mercer's battery of ten separate individual measures of medical status (hearing, vision, health), social functioning (school achievement), and ability, taking into account social and ethnic background. The SOMPA is designed to overcome the limitations of more conventional approaches to assessing ability among cultural and social minorities. See also *SOMPA.*

task analysis The process of analyzing what is to be learned in terms of a sequential series of related tasks. Task analysis provides the teacher with information of important skills and knowledge that might be prerequisite for what is to be taught.

taxonomy of educational objectives An exhaustive list of possible educational outcomes that can serve as a guide in compiling instructional objectives. The best-known taxonomy of educational objectives is Bloom's, which provides objectives in both the cognitive and the affective domain.

teacher competence Phrase used to describe the measurable performance of teachers—often assessed through the achievement of students. See also *merit pay.*

Teacher Effectiveness Training (TET) Gordon's humanistic training program for teachers. It emphasizes good teacher–learner relationships, honest interpersonal communication, and conflict resolution.

teacher-made test Any of the wide variety of tests written, developed, or organized by teachers, usually for the purpose of evaluating students or assessing the effectiveness of instruction. See also *standardized test.*

teaching style An identifiable way of teaching. Teaching activities and routines marked by common features and often characteristic of specific teachers (formal or informal teaching styles, for example).

teams–games–tournaments (TGT) A cooperative instructional technique identical to student teams–achievement divisions (STAD) except that instead of being given quizzes at the end, students play tournaments of competitive games that center around content-relevant questions. See also *student teams–achievement divisions.*

technology of teaching A Skinnerian phrase for the systematic application of the principles of behaviorism (especially of operant conditioning) to classroom practice.

test anxiety A characteristic evident in a fear of taking tests and an expectation of poor performance. Evidence suggests that test anxiety can impair performance on tests.

test blueprint A table of specifications for a teacher-made test. A good test blueprint provides information about the topics to be tested, the nature of the questions to be used, and the objectives (outcomes) to be assessed.

tests of divergent thinking Creativity tests. Usually open-ended, production tests designed to measure factors such as fluency, flexibility, and originality.

theory A body of information pertaining to a specific topic, a method of acquiring and/or dealing with information, or a set of explanations for related phenomena. See also *belief, law, model, principle*.

theory of multiple intelligence Howard Gardner's belief that human intelligence consists of seven distinct and largely unrelated areas of talent or capability: logical-mathematical, linguistic, musical, spatial, bodily kinesthetic, interpersonal, and intrapersonal.

theory of trial-and-error learning See *law of multiple responses*.

therapist model A primarily humanistic view of the teacher's role—namely that of facilitating healthy growth and self-actualization. See also *liberationist model, executive model*.

third-force psychology A general expression for humanistic approaches to psychology such as those exemplified by the work of Carl Rogers and Abraham Maslow. The first two forces are psychoanalysis and behaviorism (S–R psychology).

third wave Toffler's expression for the computer revolution (the first two waves of monumental change being the agricultural and the industrial revolutions).

time-out A procedure in which students are removed from situations in which they might ordinarily be rewarded. Time-out procedures are widely used in classroom management. See also *exclusion, isolation, nonexclusion, reprimand, response cost*.

token system A behavior modification system in which tokens are given as rewards for desirable behaviors. These can be accumulated and later exchanged for other rewards.

tracking An instructional procedure that involves dividing the members of a class into groups according to their ability.

transductive reasoning The type of reasoning that proceeds from particular to particular rather than from particular to general or from general to particular. One example of transductive reasoning is the following:

> *Cows give milk.*
>
> *Goats give milk.*
>
> *Therefore goats are cows.*

transfer See *generalization*.

transitional bilingualism Describes a situation in which a minority language is gradually replaced by the dominant language, essentially disappearing within a few generations.

trial-and-error learning Thorndikean explanation for learning based on the idea that when placed in a problem situation, an individual will emit a number of responses but will eventually learn the correct one as a result of reinforcement. Trial-and-error explanations for learning are sometimes contrasted with insight explanations.

T-score A standardized score with a preset mean of 50 and a standard deviation of 10. A T-score of 70 is therefore quite high because 70 is 2 standard deviations above the mean and only approximately 2.5 percent of all scores ordinarily fall beyond that point.

tutor Teacher involved in a one-on-one teaching situation. Tutors are frequently other students, or may be other teachers or experts. See also *mentor*.

ulterior motives Hidden motives. Reasons for behavior that are not what they seem. Ulterior motives often involve an element of deception (as when my grandmother accused me of having ulterior motives when I said I wanted to help Clarisse with her French verbs).

unconditioned response (UR) A response that is elicited by an unconditioned stimulus. See also *operant, respondent*.

unconditioned stimulus (US) A stimulus that elicits a response before learning. All stimuli that are capable of eliciting reflexive behaviors are examples of unconditioned stimuli. For example, food is an unconditioned stimulus for the response of salivation.

validity The extent to which a test measures what it says it measures. For example, an intelligence test is valid to the extent that it measures intelligence and nothing else. Educational and psychological tests are limited by their frequently low validity. See also *construct validity, content validity, criterion-related validity, face validity, reliability*.

variable A property, measurement, or characteristic that is susceptible to variation. In psychological experimentation, qualities of human beings such as intelligence and creativity are considered variables. See also *correlation*.

variable schedule See *random schedule*.

vertical thinking De Bono's term for thought processes that lead to correct, appropriate, and accepted solutions. This term is in contrast to *lateral thinking*, which leads to creative solutions. See also *lateral thinking*.

vicarious reinforcement Reinforcement that results from observing someone else being reinforced. In imitative behavior, observers frequently act as though they are being reinforced when in fact they are not being reinforced; rather, they are aware, or simply assume, that the model is being reinforced. See also *direct reinforcement*.

virtual reality (VR) A computer simulation that is so realistic it appears almost real. Virtual reality simulations typically involve more than one of the senses and are often designed so that the participant's movements are reflected in realistic changes in visual, auditory, or kinesthetic stimulation.

wild cow (almost literal) A bovine creature found in both forested and nonforested regions of the world. Wild cows are particularly unrestrained creatures, given to a great variety of social and solitary diversions, including playing cards, smoking cigars, and drinking whiskey. They also like to dance and to ice skate, and some are quite wonderful surfers. Sadly, they do not fly nearly as well as pigs. See also *bear, wild cow (metaphoric)*.

wild cow (metaphoric) Wild cows are a lot of the things that are wrong with this planet: starvation, pollution, illiteracy, preventable infant mortality, famine, terrorism, resource depletion, AIDS, murder, puny teacher salaries, and on and on. See also *bear, wild cow (almost literal)*.

with-it-ness Kounin's expression for a quality of teacher behavior manifested in the teacher's awareness of all the important things happening in a classroom. Teachers who are high in with-it-ness make more effective use of desists. See also *desists*.

working memory See *short-term memory*.

Yerkes-Dodson law Law that states that the effectiveness of performance is an inverted U-shaped function of arousal, such that very low and very high levels of arousal are associated with least effective behavior.

Z-score A standardized score with a mean of 0 and a standard deviation of 1. Hence, a Z-score of +3 is very high; a score of –3 is very low.

zero dissociability See *obliterative subsumption*.

zone of proximal growth Vygotsky's phrase for the individual's current potential for further intellectual development. Conventional measures of intelligence assess current intellectual development rather than potential for future development. Vygotsky believed that the zone of proximal growth (future potential) might be assessed by further questioning and the use of hints and prompts while administering a conventional intelligence test.

NAME INDEX

SUBJECT INDEX

Epilepsy, 306
Episodic memory, 166
Equilibration, 75–76
Error of measurement, 248
Escape learning, 130
Essay tests, 477
    objective tests vs., 480–481
    reliability of, 480–481
    suggestions for, 482
Estimated learning potential (ELP) score, 247
Ethics
    of assessments, 493–494
    gifted students and, 270
Ethnicity, 382
    multicultural education and, 51–52
    System of Multicultural Pluralistic
        Assessment (SOMPA), 245–246
Eugenics, 253
Evaluations, 456–457. See also Tests
    formative evaluation, 445
    of individualized instruction, 448–449
    measurement-driven instruction, 459–460
    motivation and, 372–373
    self-evaluation, 373
    summative evaluation, 445
    in taxonomy of educational objectives, 466
    of teacher competence, 461–462
    teacher-made tests, 467–470
Events of instruction, 192–193
Exceptional students. See Gifted students;
    Special needs students
Exclusion time-outs, 410
Executive models, 10–11
Executive skills, 239
Exemplary models, 145–146
Exercise, law of, 119
Exhibitions, 489
Expectations of teachers, 285–287
    research on effects, 286–287
Experience
    beliefs and, 5
    self and, 321
Experimental psychology, 8
Expert module of ITS, 441
Expert teachers
    art of teaching, 21
    belief systems of, 6–7
    characteristics shared by, 20
    classroom management by, 383
    vs. nonexpert teachers, 19–20
Explicit memory, 166
Exploration and apprenticeship control, 220
Expository organizers, 211
Expository teaching, 210–213
    advance organizers, 211–212
    discriminability in, 213
    meaningful learning in, 213
Expressive objectives, 463
Expulsion, 405
External conditions, 196
External orientation, 367
Extinction, 405
    rate, 132
    response, 139
    schedules of reinforcement affecting, 133
Extrinsic motives, 356
Extrinsic reinforcement, 401–402
    categories of, 401
    effects of, 402–403

Face validity of test, 470
Facts, 9

Fading theory, 170–171
    apprenticeship control, 220
    educational implications of, 172
Familiar social behaviors, 79
Family size
    intelligence and, 254
    spacing of children, 254–255
Feedback. See also Biofeedback
    after multiple choice test, 483
    corrective feedback process, 448
Fetal development, 38
Feuerstein's Instrumental Enrichment (FIE),
    181
FIE program, 181
Fixed schedule, 131
Flanagan Tests of General Ability, 285
Flexibility factors, 259
Fluency factors, 259
Fluid abilities, 234–235
    performance components compared, 239
Focus of activity, 394–395
Forgetting, 170–171
    educational implications of, 171–172
    theories of, 173
Formal operations, 88–89
    limits of, 92
Formal schools, 281
Formal teaching style, 283–284
Formative evaluation, 445
Fragmentation of activity, 394
Frames, 431
Fraternal twins, 35
Freedom, reinforcement and, 139–140
Free schools, 324
Frustration control, 219
Full inclusion, 289

Gagné's theory, 190–202
Game of cognition, 176
Gardner's theory of intelligence, 239–240
Gender
    development and, 43–44
    morality and, 57, 58
    punishment and, 406
    teachers and, 23, 68–69
Gender roles, 64–69
    development of, 65
    general knowledge and, 68
    inequity, example of, 66–67
    preference, 66
    reality of differences, 67–68
    stereotypes, 66
    teachers, implications for, 23, 68–69
General and specific objectives, 463–465
General intelligence (g), 235
Generalization, 121–122
    application of concept, 138
    discrimination and, 135–136
    forgetting and, 172
Generalized reinforcers, 127
General models, 10
Generative memories, 15
Generativity vs. self-absorption stage, 71
Genes, 34
G (general intelligence), 235
Gifted students, 269
    acceleration of, 272–273
    classroom climate for, 281
    conceptual model and, 279–280
    creativity, 285–287
    cultural background and, 270, 271–272
    definition of giftedness, 269
    eminence, development of, 282

enrichment of, 272–273
family context and, 280–281
identifying, 270–272
identifying giftedness, 257–258
individualized education plans (IEPs) for,
    274–275
mentoring of, 273–274
overlooking, 272
prevalence of, 271
programs for, 272–275
promoting giftedness, 275–287
Public Law 91-230, 269–270
Strategies Program for Effective Learning/
    Thinking (SPELT), 182–183
techniques for teachers, 275–280
tutoring of, 273–274
Gilligan's phases of moral development, 58
Global before local sequence, 220–221
Global disparity, 23–24
Goals, 16. See also Instructional objectives
    achievement goals, changing, 371–373
    Adler's theory, 396
    educational goals, 460
    long-term/short-term goals, 12
    performance goals, 368–369
    self-efficacy and, 366
Goals 2000, 460
Goodness, morality of, 58
Gordon Technique, 277
Grade-equivalent scores, 475
Grades, 137
Grammar, 46
Grand mal seizures, 306
Group-alerting cues, 395
Group intelligence tests, 244, 247–248
Group investigation, 334
Groups, 325
Growth
    defined, 34
    needs, 361
    rates, 37–39
Guided discovery, 208
Guilford's model of intellect, 261–263
Guilt, initiative vs., 70
Guns to school, 382

Handicapped children, defined, 294
Hardware, computer, 441
Head Start, 40–41
Hearing problems, 306
Helplessness, 369
Hemisphere asymmetry, 38
Hemisphericity, 38–39
Herd behaviors, 149
Heredity, 34
Heteronomy, 55
Hierarchies
    of classes, 85–87
    coding system, 202–203
    intellectual skills and, 195–196
    of needs, 360
Higher mental functions, 97
Higher-order rules, 195
Hispanics
    demographic projections, 48
    punishment and, 406
    System of Multicultural Pluralistic
        Assessment (SOMPA), 245–246
    Wechsler Intelligence Scale for Children
        (WISC-III), 247
Holistic education, 39
Holophrases, 46
Home-based reinforcement, 403